ORACLE® Oracle Press™

Oracle8 DBA Handbook

Kevin Loney

D1532529

Osborne **McGraw-Hill**

Berkeley New York St. Louis San Francisco
Auckland Bogotá Hamburg London Madrid
Mexico City Milan Montreal New Delhi Panama City
Paris São Paulo Singapore Sydney Tokyo Toronto

Osborne/**McGraw-Hill**
2600 Tenth Street
Berkeley, California 94710
U.S.A.

For information on translations or book distributors outside the U.S.A., or to arrange bulk purchase discounts for sales promotions, premiums, or fund-raisers, please contact Osborne/**McGraw-Hill** at the above address.

Oracle8 DBA Handbook

4567890 DOC DOC 901987654321098

ISBN 0-07-8822406-0

Publisher	**Proofreader**
Brandon A. Nordin	Jeff Barash
Editor-in-Chief	**Indexer**
Scott Rogers	David Heiret
Acquisitions Editor	**Computer Designer**
Scott Rogers	Mickey Galicia
Project Editor	**Illustrator**
Mark Karmendy	Roberta Steele
Editorial Assistant	**Series Design**
Ann Sellers	Jani Beckwith
Copy Editor	
Dennis Weaver	

About the Author...

Kevin Loney, a veteran Oracle developer and DBA, is the coauthor of the best-selling *ORACLE8: The Complete Reference* and *Advanced ORACLE Tuning and Administration.* He frequently makes presentations at local and international conferences.

Contents At A Glance

Contents

PART II
Database Management

Acknowledgments

Thanks to Sue and Emily and the rest of the home team. As always, this has been a joint effort.

Other key contributors included:

My colleagues and friends at Astra Merck, including Rob Cohen, Clint Gilliam, David Grube, Joe Waldron, Tod Kehrli, and the rest of the DBSC.

The folks at Osborne/McGraw-Hill who guided this product through its stages: Scott Rogers, Mark Karmendy, Jani Beckwith, Ann Sellers, Dennis Weaver, and the others at Osborne with whom I never directly worked. Thanks also to the "Oracle" component of Oracle Press, including Julie Gibbs and Marsha Bazley.

Eyal Aronoff, Noorali Sonawalla, Rachel Carmichael, and Marlene Theriault for their advice, comments, corrections, and friendship.

Everyone who suggested topics or changes that showed up in this edition.

The writers and friends along the way: Jerry Gross; Jan Riess; Robert Meissner; Marie Paretti; Br. Declan Kane, CFX; Br. William Griffin, CFX; Karen Reynolds; Jeff Pepper; Chris O'Neill; Cheryl Bittner; and the DeVOUG team. This effort would not have been possible without the help of many.

Kevin Loney

xix

Introduction

hether you're an experienced DBA, a new DBA, or an application developer, you need to know how the internal structures of the ORACLE8 database work and interact. Properly managing the database's internals will allow your database to meet two goals: it will work, and it will work *well*.

In this book, you'll find the information you need to achieve both of these goals. The emphasis throughout is on managing the database's capabilities in an effective, efficient manner to deliver a quality product. The end result will be a database that is dependable, robust, secure, extensible, and designed to meet the objectives of the applications it supports.

Several components are integral to these goals, and you'll see all of them are covered here in depth. A well-designed logical and physical database architecture will improve performance and ease administration by properly distributing database objects. Determining the correct number and size of rollback segments will allow your database to support all of its transactions. You'll also see appropriate monitoring, security, and tuning strategies for stand-alone and networked databases. Optimal backup and recovery procedures are also provided to help ensure the database's recoverability. The focus in all of these sections is on the proper planning and management techniques for each area.

You'll also find information on how to manage the support of specific packages, such as Designer/2000, ORACLE Financials, ConText, and the ORACLE utilities.

Because the size of a databases may change the management options available to you, a chapter is devoted to the administration of very large databases. You'll see how to implement partitions in ORACLE8 and how to support the transaction and table types found in very large databases.

Networking issues and the management of *distributed* and *client-server* databases are thoroughly covered. SQL*Net (now known as Net8), networking configurations, snapshots, location transparency, and everything else you need to successfully implement a distributed or client-server database are described in detail in Part III of this book. You'll also find real-world examples for every major configuration.

By following the techniques in this book, you'll no longer have to worry about disasters striking your databases. And your systems be designed and implemented so well that tuning efforts will be minimal. So administering the database will become easier as the users get a better product, while the database works—and works well.

The scripts from this book are available online, under the Oracle Press scripts section at **http://www.osborne.com**.

PART I

Database Architecture

CHAPTER

1

The ORACLE
Architecture

 ith every release, ORACLE adds new features or changes existing features. With the release of ORACLE8, many new features and functionality changes have been added. For example, object-relational features such as abstract datatypes and object views have been added, while existing structures such as tables and VARCHAR2 datatypes have changed.

In this part of this book, you will see an overview of the ORACLE architecture and its implementation. In the second part of this book, you will see specific guidelines for managing aspects of an ORACLE database—such as managing rollback segments and establishing passwords. The third section of the book deals with using ORACLE in a networked environment. The final section of the book provides information for migrating from ORACLE7 to ORACLE8, an overview of ORACLE Enterprise Manager, and a listing of the command syntax for the most-used SQL commands.

This chapter provides the big picture of the ORACLE architecture. You'll also see examples of the components of an ORACLE database and the basic implementation concepts that guide their usage. Administering an ORACLE database requires knowing how these different components interact, where they fit in the big picture, and how to best customize the system to meet your needs. In many ways, this chapter is a road map to the detailed discussions of database administration in the rest of the book.

An Overview of Databases and Instances

Two basic concepts have to be understood in order to make any sense out of the ORACLE architecture: databases and instances. In the following two major sections, you will see descriptions of both of these concepts and their implementation in ORACLE.

Databases

A *database* is a set of data. ORACLE provides the ability to store and access data in a manner consistent with a defined model known as the Relational Model. Because of this, ORACLE is referred to as a relational database management system (RDBMS). Most references to a "database" refer not only to the physical data but also to the combination of physical, memory, and process objects described in this chapter.

Data in a database is stored in tables. Relational tables are defined by their *columns*, and are given a name. Data is then stored as *rows* in the table. Tables can be related to each other, and the database can be used to enforce these relationships. A sample table structure is shown in Figure 1-1.

In addition to storing data in relational format, ORACLE (as of ORACLE8) supports object-oriented (OO) structures such as abstract datatypes and methods. Objects can be related to other objects, and objects can contain other objects. As described in Appendix A, you can use object views to enable OO interfaces to your data without making any modifications to your tables.

Whether you use relational structures or OO structures, an ORACLE database stores its data in files. Internally, there are database structures that provide a logical mapping of data to files, allowing different types of data to be stored separately. These logical divisions are called tablespaces. The next subsections describe tablespaces and files.

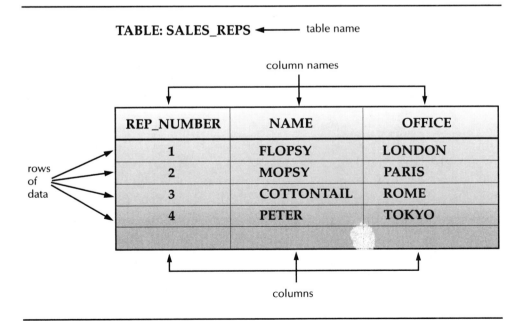

FIGURE 1-1.   *Sample table structure*

Tablespaces

A *tablespace* is a logical division of a database. Each database has at least one tablespace (called the *SYSTEM* tablespace). Other tablespaces may be used to group users or applications together for ease of maintenance and for performance benefits. Examples of such tablespaces would be USERS for general use and RBS for rollback segments (which will be described later in this section). A tablespace can belong to only one database.

Files

Each tablespace is constituted of one or more files, called *datafiles,* on a disk. A datafile can belong to one and only one tablespace. As of ORACLE7.2, datafiles can be resized after their creation. Creating new tablespaces requires creating new datafiles.

Once a datafile has been added to a tablespace, the datafile cannot be removed from the tablespace, and it cannot be associated with any other tablespace.

If you store database objects in multiple tablespaces, then you can physically separate them at the physical level by placing their respective datafiles on separate disks. This separation of data is an important tool in planning and tuning the way in which the database handles the I/O requests made against it. The relationship among databases, tablespaces, and datafiles is illustrated in Figure 1-2.

Instances

In order to access the data in the database, ORACLE uses a set of background processes that are shared by all users. In addition, there are memory structures that are used to store the most recently queried data from the database. These memory areas help to improve database performance by decreasing the amount of I/O performed against the datafiles.

A database *instance* (also known as a *server*) is a set of memory structures and background processes that access a set of database files. It is possible for a single database to be accessed by multiple instances (this is the ORACLE Parallel Server option). The relationship between instances and databases is illustrated in Figure 1-3.

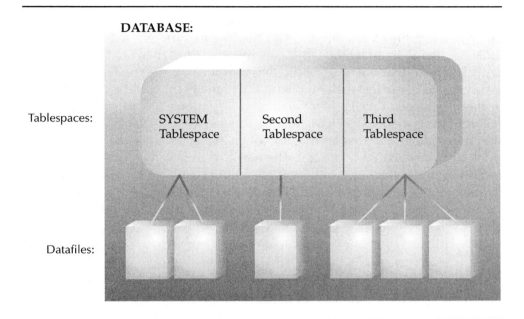

FIGURE 1-2.   *Relationship among databases, tablespaces, and datafiles*

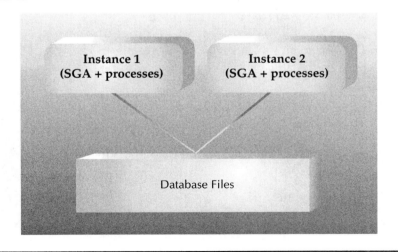

FIGURE 1-3.   *Instances and databases in ORACLE*

The parameters that determine the size and composition of an instance are stored in a file called init.ora. This file is read during instance startup and may be modified by the DBA. Any modifications made to this file will not take effect until the next startup that uses this file. The name of an instance's init.ora file usually includes the name of the instance; if the instance is named ORCL, then the init.ora file will usually be named initorcl.ora. A second configuration file, config.ora, is typically used to store the settings of variables that do not change after database creation (such as the database block size). The name of an instance's config.ora file usually includes the name of the instance; if the instance is named ORCL, then the config.ora file will usually be named configorcl.ora. In order for the config.ora settings to be used, the file must be listed as an included file via the IFILE parameter in the instance's init.ora file.

Internal Database Structures

Given the preceding overview of databases and instances, ORACLE's database structures can be divided among three categories:

■ Those that are internal to the database (such as tables)

■ Those that are internal to memory areas (including shared memory areas and processes)

■ Those that are external to the database

In the following sections, you will find descriptions of each of the elements within each category. The categories will be presented in the order listed above.

First, those elements that are internal to the database will be described. These include

■ Tables, columns, constraints, and datatypes (including abstract datatypes)

■ Users and schemas

■ Indexes, clusters, and hash clusters

■ Views

- Sequences

- Procedures, functions, packages, and triggers

- Synonyms

- Privileges and roles

- Database links

- Segments, extents, and blocks

- Rollback segments

In the following sections, you will see descriptions of each of these elements.

Tables, Columns, and Datatypes

Tables are the storage mechanism for data within an ORACLE database. As shown in Figure 1-1, they contain a fixed set of columns. The columns of a table describe the attributes of the entity being tracked by the table. Each column has a name and specific characteristics.

The characteristics of a column are made up of two parts: its *datatype* and its *length*. For columns using the NUMBER datatype, the additional characteristics of precision and scale can be specified. *Precision* determines the number of significant digits in a numeric value. *Scale* determines the placement of the decimal point. A specification of NUMBER (9,2) for a column has a total of nine digits, two of which are to the right of the decimal point. The default precision is 38 digits, which is also the maximum precision.

The available datatypes are listed in Table 1-1.

In addition to the datatypes listed in Table 1-1, you can create your own abstract datatypes as of ORACLE8. You can also use special REF datatypes that reference row objects elsewhere in the database.

The tables owned by the user SYS are called the *data dictionary tables*. They provide a system catalog that the database uses to manage itself.

Tables are related to each other via the columns they have in common. The database can be used to enforce these relationships via *referential integrity*. If you use ORACLE's object-oriented features, rows may be related to each other via internal references called object IDs (OIDs). Referential integrity is enforced at the database level via constraints.

Datatype	Description
CHAR	A *fixed-length* field, up to 2,000 characters in length.
VARCHAR	Presently synonymous with VARCHAR2, but its functionality may change in future releases. Therefore, use the VARCHAR2 datatype to store variable-length character strings.
VARCHAR2	A *variable-length* field, up to 4,000 characters in length.
DATE	A fixed-length, 7-byte field used to store all dates. The time is stored as part of the date. When queried, the date will be in the format DD-MON-YY, as in 13-APR-99 for April 13, 1999.
NUMBER	A variable-length number column. Allowed values are zero, and positive and negative numbers with magnitude 1.0E-130 to 9.99..E125.
LONG	A variable-length field, up to 2Gb in length.
RAW	A variable-length field used for binary data up to 4,000 characters in length.
LONG RAW	A variable-length field used for binary data up to 2Gb in length.
MLSLABEL	For Trusted ORACLE only. This datatype uses between 2 and 5 bytes per row.
BLOB	Binary large object, up to 4Gb in length.
CLOB	Character large object, up to 4Gb in length.
NCLOB	CLOB datatype for multibyte character sets, up to 4Gb in length.
BFILE	External binary file; size is limited by the operating system.

TABLE 1-1.   *ORACLE Datatypes*

Constraints

A table can have *constraints* placed upon it; when a constraint is applied to a table, every row in the table must satisfy the conditions specified in the constraint definition. In the following **create table** command, an EMPLOYEE table is created with several constraints:

```
create table EMPLOYEE
  (EmpNo          NUMBER(10)    PRIMARY KEY,
```

```
Name              VARCHAR2(40)   NOT NULL,
DeptNo            NUMBER(2)      DEFAULT 10,
Salary            NUMBER(7,2)    CHECK salary<1000000,
Birth_Date        DATE,
Soc_Sec_Num       CHAR(9)        UNIQUE,
foreign key (DeptNo) references DEPT.DeptNo)
tablespace USERS;
```

First, note that the table is given a name (EMPLOYEE). Each of its columns is named (EmpNo, Name, etc.). Each column has a specified datatype and length. The EmpNo column is specified as a NUMBER datatype, with no scale—this is the equivalent of an integer. The Name column is specified as a VARCHAR2(40); this will be a variable-length column up to 40 characters in length.

The *primary key* of the table is the column or set of columns that makes every row in that table unique. A primary key column will be defined within the database as being *NOT NULL*—this means that every row that is stored in that table must have a value for that column; it cannot be left NULL. The NOT NULL constraint can be applied to the columns in the table, as used for the Name column in the above example.

A column can have a *DEFAULT* constraint. This type of constraint will be used to generate a value for a column when a row is **insert**ed in a table, but no value is specified for a column. The *CHECK* constraint is used to ensure that values in a specified column meet a certain criterion (in this case, that the Salary column's value is less than 1,000,000).

Another constraint, *UNIQUE*, is used to specify uniqueness for columns that should be unique but are not part of the primary key. In this example, the Soc_Sec_Num column has a UNIQUE constraint, so every record in this table must have a unique value for this column.

A *foreign key* constraint is used to specify the nature of the relationship between tables. A foreign key from one table references a primary key that has been previously defined elsewhere in the database.

For example, if another table, called DEPT, had a primary key of DeptNo, then the records in that table would list all of the valid DeptNo values. The DeptNo column in the EMPLOYEE table shown above *references* that DEPT.DeptNo column. By specifying EMPLOYEE.DeptNo as a foreign key to DEPT.DeptNo, you guarantee that no DeptNo values can be entered into the EMPLOYEE table unless those values already exist in the DEPT table.

The constraints in the database help to ensure the *referential integrity* of the data. This provides assurance that all of the references within the database are valid and all constraints have been met.

Abstract Datatypes

As of ORACLE8, you can define your own datatypes. For example, you may create a datatype that contains the multiple parts of a person's name—first name, last name, middle initial, suffix, etc.— as a single datatype. In the following listing, the NAME_TY datatype is created:

```
create type NAME_TY as object
(First_Name      VARCHAR2(25),
Middle_Initial  CHAR(1),
Last_Name       VARCHAR2(30),
Suffix          VARCHAR2(5));
```

The **create type** command in the preceding listing is available as of ORACLE8. You can use your user-defined datatypes to standardize the usage of data within your applications. For example, you can use the NAME_TY anywhere you would use any other datatype. In the following example, the EMPLOYEE table is created again; this time, the NAME_TY datatype is used as the datatype for the EMPLOYEE.Name column:

```
create table EMPLOYEE
(EmpNo           NUMBER(10)      PRIMARY KEY,
 Name            NAME_TY,
 DeptNo          NUMBER(2)       DEFAULT 10,
 Salary          NUMBER(7,2)     CHECK salary<1000000,
 Birth_Date      DATE,
 Soc_Sec_Num     CHAR(9)         UNIQUE,
 foreign key (DeptNo) references DEPT.DeptNo)
tablespace USERS;
```

The Name column of the EMPLOYEE table contains four attributes, as shown in the NAME_TY creation statement. If you define methods— programs that act on the attributes of datatypes— on the NAME_TY datatype, then you can apply those methods to the values of the Name column in the EMPLOYEE table. See Appendix A for examples of the use and management of abstract datatypes and other object-oriented structures.

Constructor Methods

When you create an abstract datatype, ORACLE automatically creates a constructor method to support **insert**s into the column that uses the datatype. For the NAME_TY datatype, the constructor method is named NAME_TY, and the parameters for the method are the attributes of the datatype. See Appendix A for examples of the use of constructor methods.

Object Tables

An object table is a table whose rows are all objects— they all have object ID (OID) values. You can create an object table via the **create table** command. For example, you can use the **create table** command in the following listing to create a NAME table based on the NAME_TY datatype:

```
create table NAME of NAME_TY;
```

You will then be able to create references from other tables to the row objects in the NAME object table. If you create references to the NAME row objects, you will be able to select NAME rows via the references— without directly querying the NAME table. See Appendix A for examples of the use of row objects and the simulation of row objects via object views.

Nested Tables and Varying Arrays

A nested table is a column (or columns) within a table that contains multiple values for a single row in the table. For example, if you have multiple addresses for a person, then you may create a row in a table that contains multiple values for an Address column, but only one value for the rest of the columns. Nested tables can contain multiple columns and an unlimited number of rows. A second type of collector, called a varying array, is limited in the number of rows it can contain.

An in-depth discussion of the use of nested tables and varying arrays is beyond the scope of this book; see *ORACLE8: The Complete Reference* for detailed examples of these structures and their related syntax. In general, nested tables give you more flexibility in data management than varying arrays do (particularly in ORACLE8.0, since varying array values can only be selected via PL/SQL). Both nested tables and varying arrays require you to modify the SQL syntax you use to access your data. In general, you can simulate the data relationships of nested tables via related relational tables.

Partitions

As of ORACLE8, you can specify ranges for the database to use when splitting a larger table into smaller tables. These smaller tables, called *partitions*, are generally simpler to manage than larger tables. For example, you can **truncate** the data in a single partition without truncating the data in any other partition.

Partitions may also improve the performance of an application. Since the optimizer will know the range values used as the basis for the partitions, the optimizer may be able to direct queries to only use specific partitions during table accesses. Since less data may be read during the query processing, the performance of the query should improve.

You can partition indexes as well as tables. The ranges of values for the partitions of a partitioned index may match the ranges used for the indexed table—in which case the index is called a *local index*. If the index partitions do not match the value ranges used for the table partitions, then the index is called a *global index*. See Chapter 12 for a description of the management issues for partitions, local indexes, and global indexes.

Users

A *user* account is not a physical structure in the database, but it does have important relationships to the objects in the database: users own the database's objects. The user SYS owns the *data dictionary tables*; these store information about the rest of the structures in the database. The user SYSTEM owns views that access these data dictionary tables, for use by the rest of the users in the database.

When objects are created in the database in support of applications, they are created under user accounts. Each such account can be customized to use a specific tablespace as its default tablespace.

Database accounts can be connected to an operating system account; this allows users to access the database from the operating system without having to enter passwords for both the operating system and the database. They can then access the objects they own or to which they have been granted access.

Schemas

The set of objects owned by a user account is called the user's *schema*. You can create users who do not have the ability to log in to the database. Such user accounts provide a schema that can be used to hold a set of database objects separate from other users' schemas.

Indexes

In a relational database, the physical location of a row is irrelevant—unless, of course, the database needs to find it. In order to make it possible to find data, each row in each table is labeled with a *RowID*. This RowID tells the database exactly where the row is located (by file, block within that file, and row within that block).

NOTE
The structure of RowID values changed between ORACLE7 and ORACLE8. See Appendix A for details on the ORACLE8 RowID structure.

An index is a database structure used by the server to quickly find a row in a table. There are three types of indexes: cluster indexes, table indexes, and bitmap indexes.

Indexes contain a list of entries; each entry consists of a key value and a RowID. The key value is the value of a column in a row or the combination of values of columns in a row. Entries in table and cluster indexes in an ORACLE database are stored using a B*-tree mechanism guaranteeing a short access path to the key value. The I/O required to find a key value is minimal, and once found, the RowID is used to directly access a row.

Indexes are used both to improve performance and to ensure uniqueness of a column. ORACLE automatically creates an index when a UNIQUE or PRIMARY KEY constraint clause is specified in a **create table** command. You can manually create your own indexes via the **create index** command. See Appendix C for the full syntax and options of the **create index** command.

Indexes can be created on one or multiple columns of a table. In the example of the EMPLOYEE table given earlier, ORACLE will automatically create unique indexes on the EmpNo and Soc_Sec_Num columns since they have been specified as PRIMARY KEY and UNIQUE, respectively. Dropping an index will not affect the data within the previously indexed table.

As of ORACLE7.3, you can create *bitmap indexes*. As described in Chapter 12, bitmap indexes are useful when the data is not very selective— there are very few distinct values in the column. Bitmap indexes speed searches in which such nonselective columns are used as the basis for eliminating rows from the rows returned. Bitmap indexes are most effective for very static data.

As of ORACLE8, you can create indexes that *reverse* the order of the data prior to storing it. That is, an entry whose data value is '1002' will be indexed as '2001'. The reversing of the data order prior to indexing helps keep the data sorted better within the index. Because they reverse the data values, reverse order indexes are only useful if you will be performing equivalence operations in your queries, such as

```
where key_col_value = 1002
```

If you are performing range searches, such as

```
where key_col_value > 1000
```

then reverse order indexes will not effectively meet your needs.

As of ORACLE8, you can create an index-only table. In an index-only table (specified via the **organization index** clause of the **create table** command), the entire table is stored within an index structure, with its data sorted by the table's primary key. To create an index-only table, you must specify a primary key constraint for the table. The index-only table will not have RowIDs for its rows, so you cannot create any additional indexes on the table.

Clusters

Tables that are frequently accessed together may be physically stored together. To store them together, a *cluster* is created to hold the tables. The data in the tables is then stored together to minimize the number of I/Os that must be performed and thus improve performance.

The related columns of the tables are called the *cluster key.* The cluster key is indexed using a cluster index, and its value is only stored once for the multiple tables in the cluster. You must create a cluster index prior to **insert**ing any rows into the tables in the cluster.

Hash Clusters

A second type of cluster, *hash clusters*, uses *hashing functions* on the row's cluster key to determine the physical location where the row should be stored. This will yield the greatest performance benefit for equivalence queries, such as the one shown in the following listing:

```
select Name
   from EMPLOYEE
 where EmpNo = 123;
```

In this example, the EMPLOYEE table is queried for an exact match of the EmpNo column. If EMPLOYEE is part of a hash cluster, and EmpNo is part of the cluster key, then the database can use the hashing function to quickly determine where the data is physically located. The same performance gains would not be expected if the **where** clause had specified a range of values, as in the following listing:

```
select Name
   from EMPLOYEE
 where EmpNo > 123;
```

Views

A *view* appears to be a table containing columns and is queried in the same manner that a table is queried. Conceptually, a view can be thought of as a mask overlaying one or more tables, such that the columns in the view are found in one or more underlying tables. Thus, views do not use physical storage to store data. The definition of a view (which includes the query it is based on, its column layout, and privileges granted) is stored in the data dictionary.

When a view is queried, it then queries the tables that it is based on and returns the values in the format and order specified by the view definition. Since there is no physical data directly associated with them, views cannot be indexed.

Views are frequently used to enforce row-level security on data. For example, you could grant a user access to a view that shows only that user's rows from a table, while not granting the user access to all of the rows in the table. Similarly, you could limit the columns the user can see via the view. As of ORACLE8, you can use *object views* to create an object-oriented layer above your tables. You can use object views to simulate abstract datatypes, object IDS, and references. See Appendix A for examples of object views.

Sequences

Sequence definitions are also stored in the data dictionary. Sequences are used to simplify programming efforts by providing a sequential list of unique numbers.

The first time a sequence is called by a query, it returns a predetermined value. Each subsequent query against the sequence will yield a value that is increased by its specified increment. Sequences can cycle, or may continue increasing until a specified maximum value is reached.

Procedures

A *procedure* is a block of PL/SQL statements that is stored in the data dictionary and is called by applications. Procedures allow you to store frequently used application logic within the database. When the procedure is executed, its statements are executed as a unit. Procedures do not return any value to the calling program.

Stored procedures can help enforce data security. To accomplish this, do not grant users access directly to the tables within an application. Instead, grant them the ability to execute a procedure that accesses the tables. When the procedure is executed, it will execute with the privileges of the procedure's owner. The users will be unable to access the tables except via the procedure.

Functions

Functions, like procedures, are blocks of code that are stored in the database. Unlike procedures, though, functions are capable of returning values to the calling program. As of ORACLE7.1, you can create your own functions and call them within SQL statements just as you execute the functions that ORACLE provides.

For example, ORACLE provides a function called **SUBSTR** that performs "substring" functions on strings. If you create a function called **MY_SUBSTR** that performs custom substring operations, you could call it within a SQL command.

```
select MY_SUBSTR('text') from DUAL;
```

If you do not own the **MY_SUBSTR** function, then you must have been granted EXECUTE permission on the function. You can only use a user-defined function within a SQL statement if the function does not modify any database rows.

Packages

Packages are used to arrange procedures and functions into logical groupings; their definitions are stored in the data dictionary. Packages are very useful in the administrative tasks required for the management of procedures and functions. Their usefulness stems from the ability to organize related procedures.

Different elements within the package can be defined as being "public" or "private." Public elements are accessible to the user of the package, while private elements are hidden from the user. Private elements may include procedures that are called by other procedures within the package.

The source code for functions, packages, and procedures is stored in the data dictionary tables. If your applications use packages heavily, then you may need to greatly increase the size of your SYSTEM tablespace to accommodate the increase in data dictionary size. In ORACLE Financials implementations, for example, you may need a SYSTEM tablespace that is greater than 250MB in size.

Triggers

Triggers are procedures that are executed when a specified database event takes place against a specified table. You may use them to augment referential integrity, enforce additional security, or enhance the available auditing options.

There are two types of triggers:

Statement triggers	Fire once for each triggering statement
Row triggers	Fire once for each row in a table affected by the statements

For each of these types, a BEFORE trigger and AFTER trigger can be created for each type of triggering event. Triggering events include **insert**s, **update**s, and **delete**s.

Statement triggers are useful if the code in the trigger action does not rely on the data affected. For example, you may create a BEFORE INSERT statement trigger on a table to prevent **insert**s into a table except during specific time periods.

Row triggers are useful if the trigger action relies on the data being affected by the transaction. For example, you may create an AFTER INSERT row trigger to **insert** new rows into an audit table as well as the trigger's base table.

As of ORACLE8, you can create INSTEAD OF triggers. An INSTEAD OF trigger executes instead of the action that caused it to start. That is, if you create an INSTEAD OF INSERT trigger on a table, then the trigger's code executes and the **insert** that caused the trigger to be executed never occurs. INSTEAD OF triggers can be applied to views. If your view joins multiple tables in its query, then an INSTEAD OF trigger can direct ORACLE's actions if a user attempts to **update** rows via the view.

Synonyms

To completely identify a database object (such as a table or view) in a distributed database, you must specify the host machine name, the server (instance) name, the object's owner, and the object's name. Depending on the location of the object, between one and four of these parameters will be needed. To screen this process from the user, developers can create synonyms that point to the proper object; thus, the user only needs to know the synonym name. Public synonyms are shared by all users of a given database. Private synonyms are owned by individual database account owners.

For example, the EMPLOYEE table that was previously described must be owned by an account—let's say that the owner is HR. From a different user account in the same database, that table could be referenced as HR.EMPLOYEE. However, this requires that the second account knows that the HR account is the owner of the EMPLOYEE table. To avoid this, a public synonym called EMPLOYEE can be created to point to HR.EMPLOYEE. Any time this synonym is referenced, it will point to the proper table. The following SQL statement creates such a synonym:

```
create public synonym EMPLOYEE for HR.EMPLOYEE;
```

Synonyms can be used to provide pointers for tables, views, procedures, functions, packages, and sequences. They can point to objects within the local database or in remote databases. Pointing to remote databases is accomplished via the use of database links, as described later in this section.

You cannot create synonyms for abstract datatypes.

Privileges and Roles

In order to access an object owned by another account, the *privilege* to access that object must first have been granted. Typically, nonowners are granted the privilege to **insert**, **select**, **update**, or **delete** rows from a table or view. Privileges to **select** values from sequences and **execute** procedures and functions may also be granted. No privileges are granted on indexes or triggers, since they are accessed by the database during table activity. You can also grant **select** on snapshots, **read** on directories (for BFILE datatypes) and **execute** on libraries (for external programs called by your application code). Privileges may be granted to individual users or to PUBLIC, which gives the privilege to all users in the database.

Roles, which are groups of privileges, can be used to simplify this process. Privileges can be granted to a role, and the role in turn can be granted to multiple users. Adding new users to applications then becomes a much easier process to manage since it is simply a matter of granting or revoking roles for the user.

The relationship between privileges and roles is shown in Figure 1-4. In Figure 1-4a, the privileges required to grant **select** access on two tables to four users are shown as lines. In Figure 1-4b, the role capability is used to simplify the privileges administration. The privileges are granted to a single role, and that role is granted to the four users.

You can also use roles to grant system-level privileges, such as **create table**. System-level roles will be discussed in detail in Chapter 5 and Chapter 9.

Database Links

ORACLE databases have the ability to reference data that is stored outside of the local database. When referencing such data, the fully qualified name of the remote object must be specified. In the synonym example given

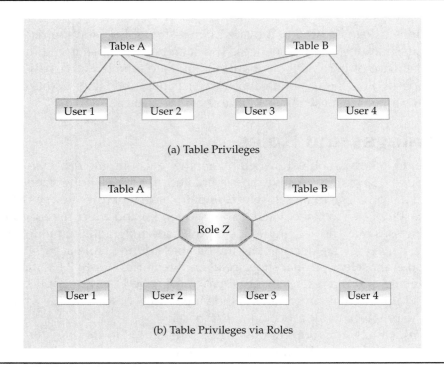

(a) Table Privileges

(b) Table Privileges via Roles

FIGURE 1-4. *Relationship between privileges and roles*

earlier, only two parts of the fully qualified name—the owner and the table name—were specified. What if the table is in a remote database?

To specify an access path to an object in a remote database, you will need to create a *database link*. Database links can either be public (available to all accounts in that database) or private (created by a user for only that account's use). When you create a database link, you specify the name of the account to connect to, the password for the account, and the service name associated with the remote database. If you do not specify an account name to connect to, then ORACLE will attempt to use your local account name and password for the connection to the remote database. In the following listing, a link named MY_LINK is created:

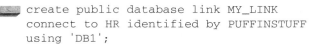

```
create public database link MY_LINK
connect to HR identified by PUFFINSTUFF
using 'DB1';
```

In this example, the link specifies that when it is used, it will open up a session in the database identified by the service named DB1. When it opens the session in the DB1 instance, it will log in as the user account HR, with the password "puffinstuff." The service names for instances are stored in configuration files used by SQL*Net (the most recent version of SQL*Net is called Net8). The configuration file for service names is called tnsnames.ora, and it specifies the host, port, and instance associated with each service name.

To use this link for a table, it must be specified in the **from** clause, as in the following example:

```
select * from EMPLOYEE@MY_LINK;
```

This will access the EMPLOYEE table via the MY_LINK database link. You can create a synonym for this table, as shown in the following SQL command:

```
create synonym EMPLOYEE for EMPLOYEE@MYLINK;
```

Note that the fully qualified designation for the database object has been defined—its host and instance via its service name, its owner (HR), and its name (EMPLOYEE).

The location of the EMPLOYEE table is thus completely transparent to the end user.

Segments, Extents, and Blocks

Segments are the physical counterparts to logical database objects. Segments store data. Index segments, for example, store the data associated with indexes. The effective management of segments requires that the DBA know the objects that an application will use, how data will be entered into those objects, and the ways in which it will be retrieved.

Because a segment is a physical entity, it must be assigned to a tablespace in the database (and will thus be placed in one of the datafiles of that tablespace). A segment is made up of sections called *extents*—contiguous sets of ORACLE blocks. Once the existing extents in a segment can no longer hold new data, the segment will obtain another extent. The extension process will continue as needed until no more free space is available in the tablespace's datafiles or until an internal maximum number of extents per segment is reached. If a segment has multiple extents, there is no guarantee that those extents will be contiguous.

Information about the management of specific types of segments is provided in Chapter 4 and Chapter 7.

Rollback Segments

In order to maintain read consistency among multiple users in the database and to be able to roll back transactions, ORACLE must have a mechanism for reconstructing a "before image" of data for uncommitted transactions. ORACLE uses *rollback segments* within the database to accomplish this.

Rollback segments will grow to be as large as the transactions they support. The effective management of rollback segments is described in Chapter 7.

Internal Memory Structures

There are two different types of memory structures used by the ORACLE database: global areas and background processes. Background processes will be described in the next section; this section will focus on the global memory areas used by all ORACLE database users.

Depending on the database server option used, the implementation of the memory options available may vary widely. The most common implementations will be described here and in Chapter 2.

The elements described in this section include

- System Global Area (SGA)
- Data block buffer cache
- Dictionary cache
- Redo log buffer
- Shared SQL pool
- Context areas
- Program Global Area (PGA)

System Global Area (SGA)

If you were to read a chapter of this book (say, Chapter 4 on planning physical database layouts), what would be the quickest way of passing that information on to someone else? You could have the other person read that chapter as well, but it would be quickest if you could hold all of the information in memory and then pass that information from your memory to the second person.

The *System Global Area (SGA)* in an ORACLE database serves the same purpose—it facilitates the transfer of information between users. It also holds the most commonly requested structural information about the database.

The composition of the SGA is shown in Figure 1-5. The memory elements shown in Figure 1-5 are described in the following sections.

Data Block Buffer Cache

The *data block buffer cache* is a cache in the SGA used to hold the data blocks that are read from the data segments in the database, such as tables, indexes, and clusters. The size of the data block buffer cache is determined by the DB_BLOCK_BUFFERS parameter (expressed in terms of number of

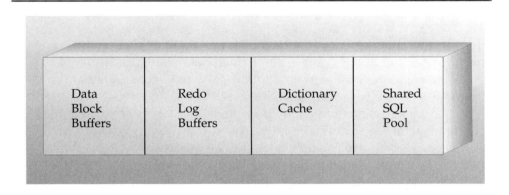

FIGURE 1-5. *SGA structures*

database blocks) in the init.ora file for that database server. Managing the size of the data block buffer cache plays an important part in managing and tuning the database.

Since the data block buffer cache is fixed in size, and is usually smaller than the space used by database segments, it cannot hold all of the database's segments in memory at once. Typically, the data block buffer cache is about 1 to 2 per cent of the size of the database. ORACLE will manage the space available by using a *least recently used (LRU)* algorithm. When free space is needed in the cache, the least recently used blocks will be written out to disk. New data blocks will take their place in memory. In this manner, the most frequently used data is kept in memory.

However, if the SGA is not large enough to hold the most frequently used data, then different objects will contend for space within the data block buffer cache. This is particularly likely when multiple applications share the same SGA. In that case, the most recently used segments from each application constantly contend for space in the SGA with the most recently used segments from other applications. As a result, requests for data from the data block buffer cache will result in a lower ratio of "hits" to "misses." Data block buffer cache "misses" result in physical I/Os for data reads, resulting in performance degradation. For information on monitoring the usage of the data block buffer cache, see the "Interpreting the Statistics Reports" section of Chapter 6.

Dictionary Cache

Information about database objects is stored in the data dictionary tables. This information includes user account data, datafile names, segment names, extent locations, table descriptions, and privileges. When this information is needed by the database (for example, to check a user's authorization to query a table), the data dictionary tables are read and the data that is returned is stored in the SGA in the *dictionary cache.*

This cache is also managed via an LRU algorithm. The size of the dictionary cache is managed internally by the database; it is part of the shared SQL pool whose size is set via the SHARED_POOL_SIZE parameter in the database's init.ora file.

If the dictionary cache is too small, then the database will have to repeatedly query the data dictionary tables for information needed by the database. These queries are called *recursive calls*, and are slower to resolve than are queries that can be handled solely by the dictionary cache in memory. For information on monitoring the usage of the dictionary cache, see the "Interpreting the Statistics Reports" section of Chapter 6.

Redo Log Buffer

Redo log files are described in the section, "Redo Logs," later in this chapter. Redo entries describe the changes that are made to the database. They are written to the online redo log files so that they can be used in roll-forward operations during database recoveries. Before being written to the online redo log files, however, transactions are first recorded in the SGA in an area called the *redo log buffer*. The database then periodically writes batches of redo entries to the online redo log files, thus optimizing this operation.

The size (in bytes) of the redo log buffers is set via the LOG_BUFFER parameter in the init.ora file.

Shared SQL Pool

The *shared SQL pool* stores the data dictionary cache and the *library cache* —information about statements that are run against the database. Thus, while the data block buffer and dictionary cache enable sharing of structural and data information between users in the database, the library cache allows the sharing of commonly used SQL statements.

The shared SQL pool contains the execution plan and parse tree for SQL statements run against the database. The second time that an identical SQL statement is run (by any user), it is able to take advantage of the parse information available in the shared SQL pool to expedite its execution. For information on monitoring the usage of the shared SQL pool, see the "Interpreting the Statistics Reports" section of Chapter 6.

Context Areas

Within the shared SQL area, there are both public and private areas. Every SQL statement issued by a user requires a private SQL area, which continues to exist until the cursor corresponding to that statement is closed. As of ORACLE8, a private object cache is also used when object-relational features are used.

Program Global Area (PGA)

The *Program Global Area* (*PGA*) is an area in memory that is used by a single ORACLE user process. The memory in the PGA is not shareable.

If you are using the *multithreaded server* (MTS), then part of the PGA may be stored in the SGA. The multithreaded server architecture allows multiple user processes to use the same server process, thus reducing the database's memory requirements. If MTS is used, then the user session information is stored in the SGA rather than in the PGA.

Background Processes

The relationships between the database's physical and memory structures are maintained and enforced by *background processes*. These are the database's own background processes, which may vary in number depending on your database's configuration. These processes are managed by the database and require little administrative work.

The relationships between the physical structures and the memory structures in the database, along with the major background processes, are shown in Figure 1-6. The following sections describe each background process and the role it plays in managing the database.

SMON

When the database is started, the *SMON* (System Monitor) process performs instance recovery as needed (using the online redo log files). It also cleans up the database, eliminating transactional objects that are no longer needed by the system.

SMON serves an additional purpose: it coalesces contiguous free extents into larger free extents. The free space fragmentation process is conceptually described in Chapter 4. For some tablespaces, DBAs must manually perform the free space coalescence; instructions for performing this task are given in Chapter 8. SMON only coalesces free space in tablespaces whose default **pctincrease** storage value is nonzero.

PMON

The *PMON* background process cleans up behind failed user processes. PMON frees up the resources that the user was using. Its effects can be seen when a process holding a lock is killed; PMON is responsible for

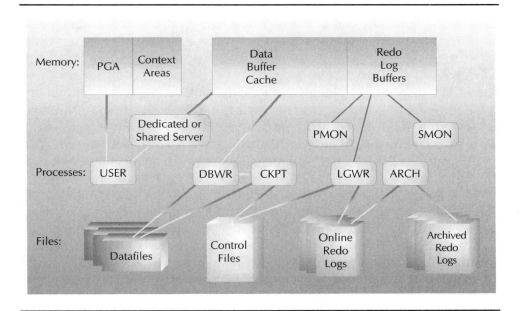

FIGURE I-6.   *Physical, memory, and process structures in ORACLE*

releasing the lock and making it available to other users. Like SMON, PMON wakes up periodically to check if it is needed.

DBWR

The *DBWR* (Database Writer) background process is responsible for managing the contents of the data block buffer cache and the dictionary cache. It reads the blocks from the datafiles and stores them in the SGA (if MTS is used, then a separate server process performs the reads). DBWR performs batch writes of changed blocks back to the datafiles. Tuning the activities of the DBWR process (efficiency of reads from datafiles, efficiency of reads from memory) constitutes much of the tuning effort that DBAs perform.

Although there is only one SMON and one PMON process running per database instance, it is possible to have multiple DBWR processes running at the same time, depending on the platform and operating system. Using multiple DBWR processes helps to minimize contention within DBWR during large queries that span datafiles. The number of DBWR I/O slaves running is set via the DBWR_IO_SLAVES parameter in the database's init.ora file.

LGWR

The *LGWR* (Log Writer) background process manages the writing of the contents of the redo log buffer to the online redo log files. LGWR writes log entries to the online redo log files in batches. The redo log buffer entries always contain the most up-to-date status of the database, since the DBWR process may wait before writing changed blocks from the data block buffers to the datafiles.

Note that LGWR is the only process that writes to the online redo log files and the only one that directly reads the redo log buffers during normal database operation. The online redo log files are written to in sequential fashion, as opposed to the fairly random accesses that DBWR performs against the datafiles. If the online redo log files are mirrored, LGWR writes to the mirrored sets of logs simultaneously. See Chapter 2 for details on this mirroring capability.

As of ORACLE8, you can create multiple LGWR I/O slaves to improve the performance of writes to the online redo log files. The number of LGWR I/O slaves is set via the LGWR_IO_SLAVES parameter in the database's init.ora file.

CKPT

Checkpoints help to reduce the amount of time needed to perform instance recovery. Checkpoints cause DBWR to write all of the blocks that have been modified since the last checkpoint to the datafiles and update the datafile headers and control files to record the checkpoint. Checkpoints occur automatically when an online redo log file fills; the LOG_CHECKPOINT_INTERVAL parameter in the database instance's init.ora file may be used to set a more frequent checkpoint.

An optional background process, *CKPT*, may be created to separate the two functions of LGWR (signaling checkpoints and copying redo entries) between two background processes. The CKPT background process is enabled by setting the CHECKPOINT_PROCESS parameter in the database instance's init.ora file to TRUE. The CKPT background process is not necessary unless the database experiences a high transaction volume, which in turn causes delays at log switches.

ARCH

The LGWR background process writes to the online redo log files in a cyclical fashion; after filling the first log file, it begins writing the second, until that one fills, and then begins writing to the third. Once the last online redo log file is filled, LGWR begins to overwrite the contents of the first redo log file.

When ORACLE is run in ARCHIVELOG mode, the database makes a copy of each redo log file before overwriting it. These archived redo log files are usually written to a disk device. They may also be written directly to a tape device, but this tends to be very operator-intensive.

The archiving function is performed by the *ARCH* background process. Databases using this option will encounter contention problems on their redo log disk during heavy data transaction times, since LGWR will be trying to write to one redo log file while ARCH is trying to read another. They may also encounter database lockups if the archive log destination disk fills. At that point, ARCH freezes, which prevents LGWR from writing, which in turn prevents any further transactions from occurring in the database until space is cleared for the archived redo log files.

As of ORACLE8, you can create multiple ARCH I/O slaves to improve the performance of writes to the archived redo log files. The number of ARCH I/O slaves is set via the ARCH_IO_SLAVES parameter in the database's init.ora file.

For details on the management of the archiving and database backup processes, see Chapter 10.

RECO

The *RECO* background process is used to resolve failures in distributed databases. RECO attempts to access databases involved in in-doubt distributed transactions and resolve the transactions. This process is only created if the Distributed Option is supported on the platform and the DISTRIBUTED_TRANSACTIONS parameter in the init.ora file is set to a value greater than zero.

SNPn

ORACLE's snapshot refreshes and internal job queue scheduling rely on background processes for their execution. The background processes' names start with the letters SNP and end with a number or letter.

The number of SNP processes created for an instance is set via the JOB_QUEUE_PROCESSES parameter in the database's init.ora file (in ORACLE7, the parameter was named SNAPSHOT_REFRESH_PROCESSES).

LCKn
Multiple *LCK* processes, named LCK0 through LCK9, are used for interinstance locking when the ORACLE Parallel Server option is used. The number of LCK processes is set via the GC_LCK_PROCS parameter.

Dnnn
Dispatcher processes are part of the MTS architecture; they help to minimize resource needs by handling multiple connections. At least one dispatcher process must be created for each protocol that is being supported on the database server. Dispatcher processes are created at database startup, based on the SQL*Net (or Net8) configuration, and can be created or removed while the database is open.

Server: Snnn
Server processes are created to manage connections to the database that require a dedicated server. Server processes may perform I/O against the datafiles.

External Structures

The database's datafiles, as described earlier in the "Files" portion of the overview section of this chapter, provide the physical storage for the database's data. Thus, they are both "internal" structures, since they are tied directly to tablespaces, and "external," since they are physical files. The planning process for their distribution across devices is described in Chapter 4.

The following types of files, although related to the database, are separate from the datafiles. These files include

- Redo logs
- Control files
- Trace files and the alert log

Redo Logs

ORACLE maintains logs of all transactions against the database. These transactions are recorded in files called *online redo log files*. These logs are used to recover the database's transactions in their proper order in the event of a database crash. The redo log information is stored external to the database's datafiles.

Redo log files also let ORACLE streamline the manner in which it writes data to disk. When a transaction occurs in the database, it is entered in the redo log buffers, while the data blocks affected by the transaction are not immediately written to disk. This allows the database to perform batch writes to disk, thus optimizing the performance of this function.

Each ORACLE database will have two or more online redo log files. ORACLE writes to online redo log files in a cyclical fashion: after the first log file is filled, it writes to the second log file, until that one is filled. When all of the online redo log files have been filled, it returns to the first log file and begins overwriting its contents with new transaction data. If the database is running in ARCHIVELOG mode, then the database will make a copy of the online redo log files before overwriting them. These archived redo log files can then be used to recover any part of the database to any point in time (see Chapter 10).

Redo log files may be mirrored (replicated) by the database. Mirroring the online redo log files allows you to mirror the redo log files without relying on the operating system or hardware capabilities of the operating environment. See Chapter 2 for details on this mirroring capability.

Control Files

A database's overall physical architecture is maintained by its *control files*. Control files record control information about all of the files within the database. They are used to maintain internal consistency and guide recovery operations.

Since the control files are critical to the database, multiple copies are stored online. These files are typically stored on separate disks to minimize the potential damage due to disk failures. The database will create and maintain the control files specified at database creation.

Trace Files and the Alert Log

Each of the background processes running in an instance has a trace file associated with it. The trace file will contain information about significant events encountered by the background process. In addition to the trace files, ORACLE maintains a file called the *alert log*. The alert log records the commands and command results of major events in the life of the database. For example, tablespace creations, redo log switches, recovery operations, and database startups are recorded in the alert log. The alert log is a vital source of information for day-to-day management of a database; trace files are most useful when attempting to discover the cause of a major failure.

Basic Database Implementation

In its simplest form, an ORACLE database consists of

- One or more datafiles
- One or more control files
- Two or more online redo logs

Internally, that database contains

- Multiple users/schemas
- One or more rollback segments
- One or more tablespaces
- Data dictionary tables
- User objects (tables, indexes, views, etc.)

The server that accesses that database consists of (at a minimum)

- An SGA (includes the data block buffer cache, redo log buffer cache, and the shared SQL pool)
- The SMON background process
- The PMON background process

- The DBWR background process
- The LGWR background process
- User processes with associated PGAs

This is the base configuration; everything else is optional or dependent on the ORACLE version and options you are using.

The remainder of this section will provide an overview of the recovery and security capabilities of the database, as well as sample logical and physical layouts for ORACLE databases.

Backup/Recovery Capabilities

The ORACLE database features a number of backup and recovery options. Each of these will be described in detail in Chapter 10. The available options are described in the following sections.

Export/Import

The *Export* utility queries the database and stores its output in a binary file. The portions of the database that it reads may be customized. You may direct it to read the entire database, a user's or a set of users' schema(s), or a specific set of tables. It also has options that allow it to only export the tables that have changed since the last export (called an *incremental* export) or since the last full system export (called a *cumulative* export).

Full system exports read the full data dictionary tables as well. A full export can thus be used to completely re-create a database, since the data dictionary tracks users, datafiles, and database objects. Full system exports are commonly used during efforts to eliminate fragmentation in the database (see Chapter 8).

The Export utility performs a logical read of the database. To read information out of the binary dump file created by the export, the *Import* utility must be used. Import can selectively choose objects or users from the dump file to import. The Import utility will then attempt to insert that data into the database (rather than overwriting existing records).

Offline Backups

In addition to logical (export) backups of the database, physical backups of its files can also be made. To make a physical backup of the database, there are two options available: *online backups* and *offline backups.* Offline backups are performed by first shutting down the database; the files that constitute the database can then be backed up to a storage device (via disk-to-disk copies or tape writes). Once the backup is complete, the database can be reopened.

Even if offline backups are not the main backup and recovery option being implemented, it is still a good idea to make an offline backup of the database periodically (such as when the host it resides on undergoes routine maintenance).

Online Backups

Online backups are available for those databases that are being run in ARCHIVELOG mode (described in the ARCH process section). Online backups allow you to make physical database backups while the database is open. During an online backup, you place tablespaces temporarily into a backup state, then restore them to their normal state when their files have been backed up. See Chapter 10 for details on implementing the online and offline backup options.

Security Capabilities

The full security-related capabilities within ORACLE will be described in detail in Chapter 9. In this section, you will see an overview of these capabilities within ORACLE.

Account Security

Database accounts may be password protected. This protection is separate from the operating-system password protection. Accounts may also be created using an autologin capability; this allows users who have accessed a host account to access a related database account without entering a database password. Having an account or privileges in one database does not give a user an account or privileges in any other database.

System-Level Privileges

System-level roles can be created from the full set of system-level privileges (such as CREATE TABLE, CREATE INDEX, SELECT ANY TABLE) to extend

the basic set of system-level roles. CONNECT, RESOURCE, and DBA
are provided as standard roles for application users, developers, and
DBAs, respectively.

Object Security
Users who have created objects may grant privileges on those objects to
other users via the **grant** command. They may also **grant** to other users the
ability to make further grants on their objects. For example, you can **grant** a
user **select** access to your tables **with grant option**, in which case that user
can **grant** access to your tables to additional users.

Auditing
User activities that involve database objects may be audited via the **audit**
command. **Audit**ed actions may include table accesses, login attempts, and
DBA-privileged activities. The results of these **audit**s are stored in an audit
table within the database. In addition to the provided **audit**ing capabilities,
you can create database triggers to record changes in data values.

Sample Logical Database Layout
The logical layout of an ORACLE database has a great impact on the
administrative options the DBA has. The tablespace layout shown in
Table 1-2 is based on the design considerations given in Chapter 3. The
objective of this layout is to isolate database segments based on their usage
and characteristics.

Sample Physical Database Layout
The proper physical layout for the database files is database-specific;
however, certain general rules can be applied to correctly separate
database files whose I/O requests will conflict with each other. A detailed
discussion of this topic is given in Chapter 4. The configuration shown in
Figure 1-7 is given as a sample configuration for a 12-disk production
system. The procedures given in Chapter 4 should be followed to determine
the proper distribution of files that will meet your needs.

Tablespace	Use
SYSTEM	Data dictionary
DATA	Standard-operation tables
DATA_2	Static tables used during standard operation
INDEXES	Indexes for the standard-operation tables
INDEXES_2	Indexes for the static tables
RBS	Standard-operation rollback segments
RBS_2	Specialty rollback segments used for data loads
TEMP	Standard-operation temporary segments
TEMP_*USER*	Temporary segments created by a particular user
TOOLS	RDBMS tools tables
TOOLS_I	Indexes for RDBMS tools tables
USERS	User objects, in development databases

TABLE 1-2. *Logical Distribution of Segments in an Optimal Database*

Disk	Contents
1	Oracle software
2	SYSTEM tablespace, Control file 1
3	RBS tablespace, RBS_2 tablespace, Control file 2
4	DATA tablespace, Control file 3
5	INDEX tablespace
6	TEMP tablespace, TEMP_*USER* tablespace
7	TOOLS tablespace, INDEX_2 tablespace
8	Online Redo logs 1, 2, and 3
9	Application software
10	DATA_2
11	Archived redo log destination disk
12	Export dump file destination disk

FIGURE 1-7. *Sample 12-disk configuration for physical database files*

Understanding Logical Modeling Conventions

In the previous section on table constraints, several data-modeling terms were illustrated. In this section, you will see how the relationships implied by those terms are graphically depicted. The information in this section will assist DBAs in interpreting application data models (some of which are used in this book).

A *primary key (PK)* is the column or set of columns that makes each record in a table unique. A *foreign key (FK)* is a set of columns that refers back to an existing primary key.

Tables can be related to each other via three types of relationships: *one to one*, *one to many*, and *many to many*. In a one-to-one (*1:1*) relationship, the tables share a common primary key. In a one-to-many (*1:M*) relationship, a single record in one table is related to many records in another table. In a many-to-many (*M:M*) relationship, many records in one table are related to many records in another table. The following sections provide examples of each type of relationship.

These graphical standards for depicting various types of relationships will be used throughout this book.

One-to-One Relationships

It is rare to have two tables that share the same primary key. This is usually done for performance or security reasons. For example, ORACLE recommends that when a LONG datatype is used in a table, it should be stored in a separate table for performance reasons, with the two tables related to each other in a 1:1 fashion.

Consider the SALES_REPS table from Figure 1-1. What if an additional column, RESUME, with a datatype of LONG, were to be added to the data being stored? Since there is one resume for each sales rep, the RESUME column should be stored in the SALES_REPS table. However, this will force the database to read through the LONG value every time the table is queried, even if only the NAME field is being sought.

To improve performance, create a second table, called SALES_REPS_RESUME. This table will have the same primary key (REP_NUMBER), and one additional column (RESUME). The two tables thus have a 1:1 relationship. This is shown graphically in Figure 1-8.

FIGURE 1-8. *Entity relationship diagram for a 1:1 relationship*

The solid line between the two entities indicates that the relationship is mandatory. Had the relationship been optional, the line would have been partially dashed.

One-to-Many Relationships

One-to-one relationships are rare. It is far more common for a relationship to be of the one-to-many (1:M) variety. In this type of relationship, one record in one table is related to many records in another table.

Consider the SALES_REPS table again. For the records given in Figure 1-1, there is only one sales rep per office. However, it is possible that the data analysis may reveal that multiple sales reps can report to the same office. In this case, a new entity, OFFICE, would be created. The OFFICE column of the SALES_REPS table would then be a foreign key to this new table.

Since many sales reps (records in the SALES_REPS table) can report to a single office (record in the OFFICE table), there is a 1:M relationship between these tables. This is shown graphically in Figure 1-9. Note two differences in the connecting line: the addition of a crow's foot on the "many" side of the relationship, and the use of a dashed line on the "one" side. The dashed line is used to signify that the relation is not mandatory on that side—in other words, that it is possible to have an office with no sales reps assigned to it.

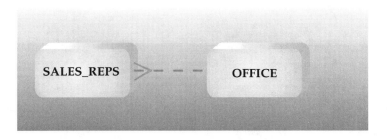

FIGURE 1-9.   *Entity relationship diagram for a 1:M relationship*

Many-to-Many Relationships

It may also be possible that many rows of a table are related to many rows of another table. Consider the SALES_REPS table (Figure 1-1) again. For this example, assume that the data analysis reveals that sales reps contact multiple companies. Furthermore, a single company can be called upon by multiple sales reps. Thus, there is a many-to-many relationship between the SALES_REPS entity and the COMPANIES entity. To understand this relationship, note that a single sales rep (record in the SALES_REPS table) can correspond to multiple companies (records in the COMPANIES table), and that the reverse is also true. This relationship is shown graphically in Figure 1-10.

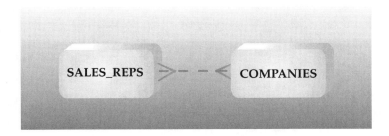

FIGURE 1-10.   *Entity relationship diagram for a M:M relationship*

CHAPTER

2

Hardware Configurations and Considerations

lthough each ORACLE database will be built from the same basic pieces, the options available to you depend on your hardware platform and operating system. For most platforms, you will have a number of options to choose from. This chapter describes the standard architectures available—the ways that the pieces are usually put together. Since ORACLE supports many hardware platforms, it will not be possible to cover all of the options in this chapter. Rather, the focus will be on the most common implementations.

Architecture Overview

An ORACLE database consists of physical files, memory areas, and processes. The distribution of these components varies depending on the database architecture chosen.

The data in the database is stored in physical files (called *datafiles*) on a disk. As it is used, that data is stored in memory. ORACLE uses memory areas to improve performance and to manage the sharing of data between users. The main memory area in a database is called the *System Global Area* (*SGA*). To read and write data between the SGA and the datafiles, ORACLE uses a set of background processes that are shared by all users.

A database *server* (also known as an *instance*) is a set of memory structures and background processes that accesses a set of database files. The relationship between servers and databases is illustrated in Figure 2-1.

The characteristics of the database server—such as the size of the SGA and the number of background processes—are specified during startup. These parameters are stored in a file called init.ora. This file is only read during startup; modifications to it will not take effect until the next startup that uses this file.

Stand-Alone Hosts

The simplest conceptual configuration for a database is a single server accessing a single database on a stand-alone, single-disk host. In this configuration, shown in Figure 2-2, all of the files are stored on the server's sole device, and there is only one SGA and one set of ORACLE background processes on the server.

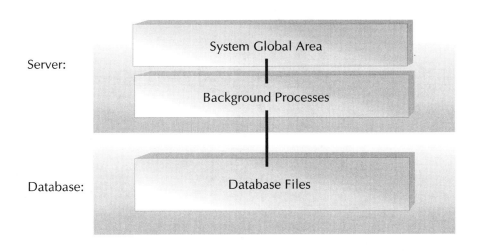

FIGURE 2-1. *Servers and databases in Oracle*

The architecture shown in Figure 2-2 represents the minimum configuration. All of the other database configurations are modifications to this base structure.

The files stored on the disk include the database datafiles and the host's init.ora file. As shown in Figure 2-2, there are two main interface points in the database:

- Between the database files and the background processes
- Between the background processes and the SGA

Tuning efforts mostly consist of improving the performance of these interface points. If the memory area dedicated to the database is large enough, then fewer repetitive reads will be performed against the database files. Since the files are all stored on the sole available disk device in this configuration, you should try to minimize the number of datafile accesses performed. File tuning topics are covered in detail in Chapter 4 and in Chapter 8.

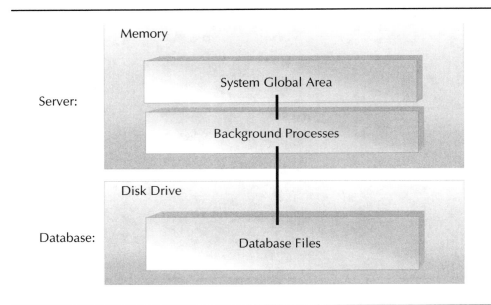

Server:

Memory

System Global Area

Background Processes

Disk Drive

Database:

Database Files

FIGURE 2-2. *Single-server on a stand-alone host*

Stand-Alone Hosts with Disk Arrays

If multiple disks are available, then the database files can be separated onto separate devices. Separating files is done to improve database performance by reducing the amount of contention between the database files. During database operation, it is common for information from multiple files to be needed to handle a transaction or query. If the files are not distributed across multiple disks, then the system will need to read from multiple files on the same disk concurrently. The separation of files across multiple disks is shown in Figure 2-3.

The database uses several types of files. These file types, and guidelines for their optimal distribution across multiple disks, are described in Chapter 4.

Control File Mirroring

The init.ora file for the server that accesses the database is stored in the ORACLE software directories, usually in a directory under the ORACLE software base directory. In the default directory configuration, the init.ora file is stored in a directory named /orasw/app/oracle/admin/

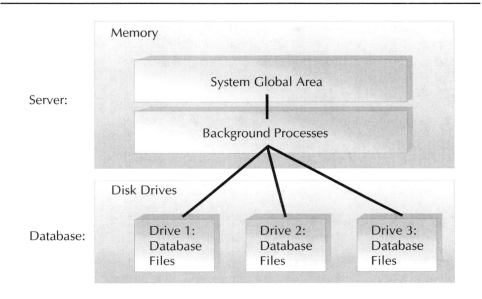

FIGURE 2-3.   *Single server on a stand-alone host with multiple disks*

instance_name/pfile. For example, if the instance name is ORA1, then the init.ora file will be named initora1.ora and it will be stored in /orasw/app/oracle/admin/ORA1/pfile. The init.ora file does not list the names of the datafiles or online redo log files for the database; these are stored within the data dictionary. However, the init.ora file does list the names of the control files for the database. On a multiple disk host, the control files should be stored on separate disks. The database will keep them in sync. By storing mirrored control files on multiple disks, you greatly reduce the risk of database problems caused by media failures.

A second server configuration file, config.ora, is called by init.ora. The config.ora file is used to set values for those parameters that typically do not change within the database; the control files' names are among those parameters. The following listing shows the entry for the CONTROL_FILES parameter in the config.ora file:

```
control_files          = (/db01/oracle/ORA1/ctrl1ora1.ctl,
                           /db02/oracle/ORA1/ctrl2ora1.ctl,
                           /db03/oracle/ORA1/ctrl3ora1.ctl)
```

This entry names the three control files. If it is used during the database creation, then the database will automatically create the three control files listed here. If you want to add additional control files to an existing database, follow this procedure:

1. Shut down the database.

2. Copy one of the current control files to the new location.

3. Edit the config.ora file, adding the new control file's name to the CONTROL_FILES entry.

4. Restart the database.

The new control file will then be activated.

Redo Log File Mirroring

As noted in the previous section, the database will automatically mirror control files. The database can also mirror online redo log files. To mirror online redo log files, use *redo log groups*. If redo log groups are used, then the operating system does not need to perform the mirroring of the online redo log files; it is done automatically by the database.

When using this functionality, the LGWR (Log Writer) background process simultaneously writes to all of the members of the current online redo log group. Thus, rather than cycling through the redo log files, it instead cycles through *groups* of redo log files. Since the members of a group are usually placed on separate disk drives, there is no disk contention between the files, and LGWR thus experiences little change in performance. See Chapter 4 for further information on the placement of redo log files.

Redo log groups can be created via the **create database** command. They can also be added to the database after it has been created, via the **alter database** command. The following listing shows an example of the addition of a redo log group to an existing database. The group is referred to in this example as "GROUP 4." Using group numbers eases their administration; number them sequentially, starting with 1. The **alter database** command in this example is executed from within Server Manager.

```
> svrmgrl
SVRMGR> connect internal
```

```
SVRMGR> alter database
    2> add logfile group 4
    3> ('/db01/oracle/CC1/log_1c.dbf',
    4>  '/db02/oracle/CC1/log_2c.dbf') size 5M;
```

To add a new redo log file to an existing group, use the **alter database** command shown in the following listing. As in the previous example, this command is executed from within Server Manager. It adds a third member to the "GROUP 4" redo log group.

```
> svrmgrl
SVRMGR> connect internal
SVRMGR> alter database
    2> add logfile member '/db03/oracle/CC1/log_3c.dbf'
    3> to group 4;
```

When the **add logfile member** option of the **alter database** command is used, no file sizing information is specified. This is because all members of the group must have the same size. Since the group already exists, the database already knows how large to make the new file.

Stand-Alone Hosts with Disk Shadowing

Many operating systems give you the ability to maintain duplicate, synchronized copies of files via a process known as *disk shadowing* or *volume shadowing*. (This practice is also known as *mirroring*.)

There are two benefits to shadowing your disks. First, the shadow set of disks serves as a backup in the event of a disk failure. In most operating systems, a disk failure will cause the corresponding disk from the shadow set to automatically step into the place of the failed disk. The second benefit is that of improved performance. Most operating systems that support volume shadowing can direct file I/O requests to use the shadow set of files instead of the main set of files. This reduces the I/O load on the main set of disks and results in better performance for file I/Os. The use of disk shadowing is shown in Figure 2-4.

The type of shadowing shown in Figure 2-4 is called RAID-1 (Redundant Array of Independent Disks) shadowing. In this type of shadowing, each disk in the main set of disks is paired up, one-to-one, with a disk in the shadow set. Depending on your operating system, other

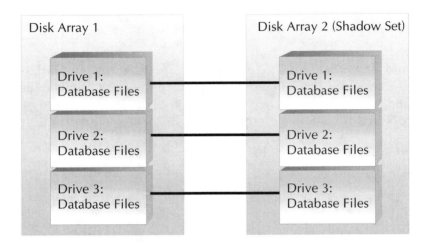

FIGURE 2-4. *Disk shadowing*

shadowing options may be available. In RAID-3 and RAID-5 shadowing, for example, a set of disks is treated as a single logical unit, and each file is automatically "striped" across each disk. A parity check system is then used to provide a means of recovering a damaged or failed member of the set of disks.

The method of shadowing that is used will affect how the files are distributed across devices. For example, datafiles that store tables are usually stored on a different disk than the datafiles that store those tables' indexes. However, if RAID-3 or RAID-5 is used, then the distinction between disks is blurred. Accessing a datafile when using those options will almost always require that all of the disks in the set be accessed. Therefore, contention between the disks is more likely.

Despite this, the contention should not be severe. In RAID-5, for example, the first block of data is stored on the first disk of a set, and the second block is stored on the next disk. Thus, the database only has to read a single block off a disk before moving on to the next disk. In this example, any contention that results from multiple accesses of the same disk should therefore last only as long as it takes to perform a single block read.

Stand-Alone Hosts with Multiple Databases

You may create multiple databases on a single host. Each database will have a separate set of files and will be accessed by a different server. Guidelines for appropriate directory structures are provided in Chapter 4.

Figure 2-5 shows a single host that is supporting two databases. Since each server requires an SGA and background processes, the host must be able to support the memory and process requirements that this configuration will place upon it.

As noted earlier, these configurations are modifications to the base database architecture. In this case, you simply create a second database that mimics the structure of the first. Note that although the two databases are on the same host, they do not (in this case) communicate with each other. The server from the first database cannot access the database files from the second database.

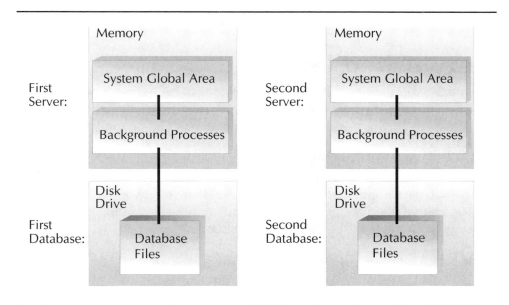

FIGURE 2-5. *Stand-alone host with multiple databases*

Multiple databases on the same server typically share the same ORACLE source code directories. The init.ora files for the two databases in Figure 2-5 are stored in separate directories, since the instance name is part of the directory structure. For example, if the two server names were ORA1 and ORA2, then the associated init.ora files would be named initora1.ora and initora2.ora, respectively. The first would be stored in /orasw/app/oracle/admin/ORA1/pfile, and the second would be stored in /orasw/app/oracle/admin/ORA2/pfile. Their server parameters, like their datafiles, are completely independent of each other. Their CONFIG.ORA files should also include the server name in the filename (for example, configora1.ora and configora2.ora) and be stored in the same directories as their respective init.ora files.

Although the databases will share the same source code directories, their datafiles should be stored in separate directories—and, if available, on separate disks. Directory structures for datafiles are provided in Chapter 4. If multiple databases have datafiles stored on the same device, then neither database's I/O statistics will accurately reflect the I/O load on that device. Instead, you will need to sum the I/O attributed to each disk by each database.

Networked Hosts

When hosts supporting ORACLE databases are connected via a network, those databases can communicate via Oracle Net8 (formerly called SQL*Net). As shown in Figure 2-6, the Net8 drivers rely on the local networking protocol to achieve connectivity between two servers. The Net8 portion then supports communications between the application layers on the two servers. Net8 is described in Part III.

The database configuration options available in a networked environment depend on the network's configurations and options. The following sections describe the main architectures:

- Networks of databases, used for remote queries

- Distributed databases, used for remote transactions

- Parallel server databases, on which multiple servers access the same database

- Client-server databases

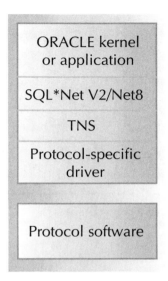

FIGURE 2-6.   *Oracle Net8 architecture*

Networks of Databases

Net8 allows ORACLE databases to communicate with other databases that are accessible via a network. Each of the servers involved must be running Net8. This configuration is illustrated in Figure 2-7.

In Figure 2-7, two hosts are shown. Each host can operate a database in stand-alone fashion, as was previously shown in Figure 2-2 and Figure 2-3. Each host in this example maintains a copy of the ORACLE software and one or more ORACLE databases.

For the databases to be able to communicate, their respective servers must be able to communicate with each other. As shown in Figure 2-6, the database layers of communication rely on the networking software and hardware to establish the communications link between the servers. Once that communications link is created, the database software can use it to transport data packets between remote databases.

The ORACLE software used to transfer data between databases is called Oracle Net8. In its simplest configuration, it consists of a host process that waits for connections via a specific connection path. When those

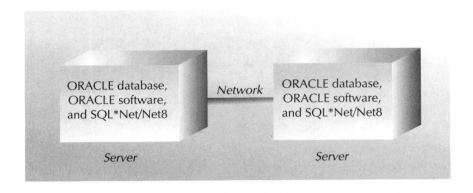

FIGURE 2-7. *Networked hosts with databases*

connections are detected, it follows the instructions passed via the connection and returns the requested data. A full description of Oracle Net8 is found in Part III.

For Net8 to receive and process communications, the host must run a process called the *listener*. The listener process must be running on each host that will be involved in the database communications. Each server must be configured to assign this process to a specific communications port (see Chapter 14 for an example of this).

Examples of the use of database connections are shown in the following sections. They include queries against remote databases and transactions against remote databases.

Remote Queries

Queries against remote ORACLE databases use *database links* to identify the path that the query should take to find the data. A database link specifies, either directly or indirectly, the host, database, and account that should be used to access a specified object. It does this by referring to the *service name* that is to be used. When a database link is referenced by a SQL statement, it opens a session in the specified database and executes the SQL statement there. The data is then returned, and the remote session may stay open in case it is needed again. Database links can be created as public links (by DBAs, making the link available to all users in the local database) or as private links.

The following example creates a public database link called HR_LINK:

```
create public database link HR_LINK
connect to HR identified by PUFFINSTUFF
using 'hq';
```

The **create database link** command, as shown in this example, has several parameters:

- The optional keyword **public**, which allows DBAs to create links for all users in a database

- The name of the link (HR_LINK, in this example)

- The account to connect to (if none is specified, then the local username and password will be used in the remote database)

- The service name ("hq")

To use this link, simply add it as a suffix to table names in commands. The following example queries a remote table by using the HR_LINK database link:

```
select * from EMPLOYEE@HR_LINK
where  Office='ANNAPOLIS';
```

NOTE
*Database links cannot be used to return values
from fields with LONG datatypes.*

Database links allow for queries to access remote databases. They also allow for the information regarding the physical location of the data—its host, database, and schema—to be made transparent to the user. For example, if a user in the local database created a view based on a database link, then any access of the local view would automatically query the remote database. The user performing the query would not have to know where the data resides.

The following listing illustrates this. In this example, a view is created using the HR_LINK database link defined earlier in this section. Access to this view can then be granted to users in the local database, as shown here:

```
create view LOCAL_EMP
as select * from EMPLOYEE@HR_LINK
where Office='ANNAPOLIS';

grant select on LOCAL_EMP to PUBLIC;
```

When a user queries the LOCAL_EMP view, ORACLE will use the HR_LINK database link to open a session using the connection information specified for the HR_LINK database link. The query will be executed against the remote data and will be returned to the local user. The local user of LOCAL_EMP will not be informed that the data came from a remote database.

Remote Updates: The Advanced Replication Option

In addition to querying data from remote databases, databases using the Advanced Replication Option can update databases that are located on remote hosts. The updates against these remote databases can be combined with updates against the local database into a single logical unit of work: either they all get committed or they all get rolled back.

A sample set of transactions is shown in Figure 2-8. One of the transactions goes against a database on a remote host and one against the local host. In this example, a local table named EMPLOYEE is **update**d; a remote table named EMPLOYEE, in a database defined by the HR_LINK database link, is also **update**d as part of the same transaction. If either **update** fails, then both of the transactions will be rolled back. This is accomplished via ORACLE's implementation of Two-Phase Commit, which is described in greater detail in Part III.

The databases involved in this remote update are functionally separate. They each have their own sets of datafiles and memory areas. They each must be running the Advanced Replication Option. The hosts involved must be running Net8 and must be configured to allow host-host communications.

After Net8 is set up for each host, any files associated with it must be properly configured. These configuration files allow the database to interpret the service names shown in the **create database link** command earlier in this chapter.

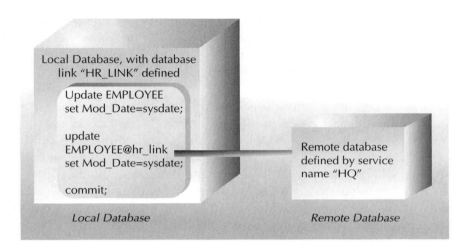

FIGURE 2-8. *Sample distributed transaction*

Each host that runs Net8 must maintain a file called tnsnames.ora. This file defines the connect descriptors for the service names that are accessible from that host. For example, the following listing shows the tnsnames.ora file entry for the "HQ" service name used in the HR_LINK example:

```
HQ =(DESCRIPTION=
     (ADDRESS=
          (PROTOCOL=TCP)
          (HOST=HQ)
          (PORT=1521))
     (CONNECT DATA=
          (SID=loc)))
```

This example shows a number of different aspects of the connection process (its parameters are specific to TCP/IP, but the underlying connection needs are the same for all platforms). First, there is the hardware addressing information—the protocol, the host name, and the communications port to use. The second section defines the instance name—in this case, "loc." Since the tnsnames.ora file tells the database all it needs to know to connect to remote databases, it is important to keep the contents of this file consistent across hosts. See Chapter 15 for information on this and other aspects affecting the management of location transparency.

The logical unit of work for distributed transactions is processed via ORACLE's implementation of Two-Phase Commit (2PC). If there is a network or server failure that prevents the unit of work from successfully completing, then it is possible that the data in the databases affected by the transactions will be out of sync. A background process automatically checks for incomplete transactions and resolves them as soon as all of the resources it needs become available.

The maximum number of concurrent distributed transactions for a database is set via the DISTRIBUTED_TRANSACTIONS parameter of its init.ora file. If it is set to 0, then no distributed transactions will be allowed and the recovery background process will not be started when the instance starts.

Clustered Servers: The ORACLE Parallel Server

Up to this point, all of the configurations discussed have featured databases that are accessed by a single server. However, depending on your hardware configurations, it may be possible to use multiple servers to access a single database. This configuration, called the *ORACLE Parallel Server* (OPS), is illustrated in Figure 2-9.

As shown in Figure 2-9, two separate servers share the same set of datafiles. Usually, these servers are located on separate hosts of a hardware cluster (such as a VAX cluster). Using this configuration provides the following benefits:

■ More memory resources are available, since two machines are being used.

■ If one of the hosts goes down, the other can still access the datafiles, thus providing a means of recovering from disasters.

■ Users can be separated by the type of processing they perform, and high-CPU users will be kept on a separate host from regular online processing transactions.

Despite these advantages, there is a significant potential problem with this configuration—what if both servers try to **update** the same records? Following a transaction, ORACLE does not immediately write modified blocks from the SGA back to the datafiles. While those blocks are in the SGA, another instance may request them. To support that request, ORACLE will write the blocks out to disk, and *then* read them into the second SGA. The result is a database request that becomes very I/O-intensive.

The best way around this potential problem is to plan the distribution of users *not* by their CPU usage, but rather by their data usage. That is, users who update the same table should use the same instance to access the database.

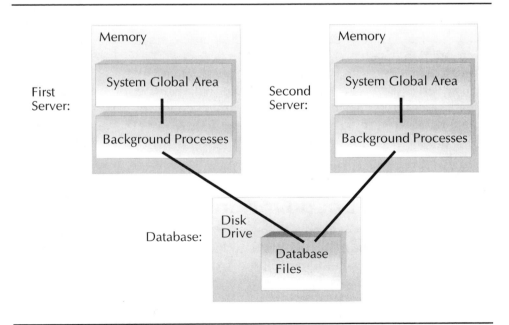

FIGURE 2-9. *The ORACLE Parallel Server*

When setting up a set of servers to use OPS, a number of database structures and parameters specific to OPS must be specified.

First, the central database must be configured to handle separate servers. Its primary requirement is a set of rollback segments that each server can use. To best manage these, create a separate rollback segment tablespace for each server, using the server name as part of the tablespace name. For example, if the server names were ORA1 and ORA2, then the rollback segment tablespace names should be RBS_ORA1 and RBS_ORA2.

To specify which rollback segments to use, each server must name them in its init.ora file. This method for activating rollback segments is described in Chapter 7. There are several other database initialization parameters that must be set for the parallel servers. Since many of these must be the same for each server, the init.ora IFILE parameter should be used. This specifies an "*include file*," which lists values for additional parameters. If both instances refer to the same IFILE, then you will not need to worry about the common values.

In an OPS environment, some of the init.ora parameters (such as INSTANCE_NAME and ROLLBACK_SEGMENTS) must be unique for all instances, while other parameters (such as DB_BLOCK_SIZE) must be the same for all instances. See the *Oracle Parallel Server Administrator's Guide* for a complete listing of all relevant init.ora parameters and OPS-specific administration details.

Further details on all of these parameters are found in the *Oracle Parallel Server Administrator's Guide.* Note that a number of them are tied to the number of servers used. Because of that relationship, the common init.ora parameters must be reevaluated every time a new server is added to the set of servers for a database.

Multiple Processors: The Parallel Query and Parallel Load Options

You can take advantage of multiple processors to perform transactions and queries. The work performed to resolve a single database request can be performed by multiple, coordinated processors. Distributing the workload across multiple processors should improve the performance of transactions and queries.

The Parallel Query Option (PQO) architecture of ORACLE allows almost all database operations to be parallelized. Operations that can take advantage of the PQO include **create table as select**, **create index**, full table scans, index scans, sorts, **insert**s, **update**s, **delete**s, and most queries.

The extent to which parallelism is employed by the database depends on the **degree** and **instances** parameters of the **parallel** keyword used with these commands (see Appendix C). The **degree** parameter specifies the degree of parallelism—the number of query servers used—for the given operation. The **instances** parameter specifies how the table is to be split among the instances of an OPS installation. You can specify your instance's parallelism rules—such as the size of a table at which parallel operations start or the minimum number of query servers—in the instance's init.ora file. The maximum number of concurrently available parallel query server processes is set by the PARALLEL_MAX_SERVERS parameter in init.ora; the minimum number is set by the PARALLEL_MN_SERVERS parameter. The number of disks on which a table's data is stored and the number of processors available on the server are used to generate the default parallelism for a query.

Client-Server Database Applications

In a host-host configuration, as described earlier in this chapter, an ORACLE database exists on each host, and the databases communicate via Net8. However, it is possible for a host without a database to access a remote database. This is typically done by having application programs on one host access a database on a second host. In that configuration, the host running the application is called a *client* and the other is called the *server*. This configuration is illustrated in Figure 2-10.

As shown in Figure 2-10, the client must have the ability to communicate across the network to the server. The application programs are run on the client side; therefore, the database is used mainly for I/O. The CPU costs for running the application programs are thus charged to the client PC rather than to the server.

For this configuration to work, the client must be running Net8 or SQL*Net V2. When the client's application program prompts the user for database connection information, the service name should be specified. The application will then open a session in the remote database.

Using a client-server configuration helps to reduce the amount of work that is being done by the server. However, shifting an application to a client-server configuration will not automatically improve the system's performance, for two main reasons:

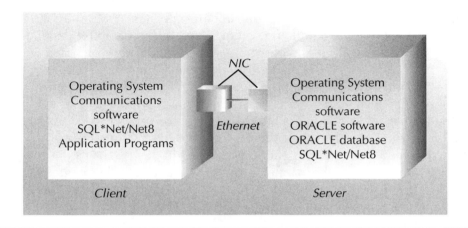

FIGURE 2-10. *Client-server configuration*

■ CPU resources may not have been a problem before. Usually, CPU resources are used often during the day and infrequently during off-hours. You may wish to alter the schedule of CPU usage by running batch processes or large programs at off-hours.

■ The application may not have been redesigned. Designing for a client-server environment requires you to take into account the data volumes that are sent across the network for every database access. In server-based applications, this is not a problem. In client-server applications, the network traffic must be considered during planning and tuning.

There are many different ways to implement the client-server configuration, depending on the hardware that is available. The implementation shown in Figure 2-10 is fairly common; it would be used by an ad hoc query tool running on a PC to access an ORACLE database running on a server.

If you have file servers available in your environment, or if your clients are workstations instead of PCs, then you have a great deal of flexibility with your system architecture. See Chapter 16 for examples. These include using the file server to prevent users from directly accessing the database server and using the file server to store the ORACLE software.

The examples in Chapter 16 also use as examples the most common types of client machines, including IBM-compatible PCs running Microsoft Windows and Network Computers (NCs). Installation guidelines specific to that environment are provided in Chapter 16. In that environment, the PC will also have configuration files that specify how Net8 should perform connections.

CHAPTER
3

Logical Database Layouts

he logical configuration of a database has a dramatic effect on its performance and its ease of administration. This chapter provides guidelines for choosing the proper tablespace layout for any ORACLE database.

The effective distribution of the database's logical objects was first formalized by Cary Millsap of ORACLE, who named the resulting architecture the *Optimal Flexible Architecture* (OFA). The logical database design described here will define and extend OFA as it relates to logical database design. Planning the layout using this architecture will greatly ease database administration while allowing the DBA greater options when planning and tuning the physical layout. The standard OFA tablespace layout is automatically created when you use the ORACLE installation software; in this chapter you will see explanations of that layout and useful alternatives to the standard layout.

The End Product

The objective of the database design described here is to configure the database so that its objects are separated by object type and activity type. This configuration will greatly reduce the amount of administrative work that must be done on the database, while decreasing the monitoring needs as well. Problems in one area thus will not affect the rest of the database.

Distributing the database objects in the manner described here will also allow the DBA greater flexibility when planning the database's physical layout. That exercise, described in Chapter 4, is easiest to do when the logical design is as distributive as possible.

In order to distribute the objects, a system of classification must first be established. The logical objects within the database must be classified based on how they are to be used and how their physical structures impact the database. This includes separating tables from their indexes and high-activity tables from low-activity tables. Although the volume of activity against objects can only be determined during production usage, a core set of highly used tables can usually be isolated.

The Optimal Flexible Architecture (OFA)

In the following sections you will see the object categories as defined by OFA. Thereafter, you will be introduced to suggested OFA extensions.

The Starting Point: The SYSTEM Tablespace

SYSTEM

It is possible, though not advisable, to store all of the database's objects in a single tablespace; this is analogous to storing all your files in your root directory. The SYSTEM tablespace, which is the ORACLE equivalent of a root directory, is where the data dictionary tables (owned by SYS) are stored. It is also the location of the SYSTEM rollback segment, and during database creation the SYSTEM tablespace is temporarily used to store a second rollback segment (which is then deactivated or dropped).

There is no reason for anything other than the data dictionary tables and the SYSTEM rollback segment to be stored in the SYSTEM tablespace. Storing other segment types in SYSTEM increases the likelihood of space management problems there, which may require the tablespace to be rebuilt. Since the only way to rebuild the SYSTEM tablespace is to re-create the database, anything that can be moved out of SYSTEM should be moved.

The *data dictionary segments* store all of the information about all of the objects in the database. Data dictionary segments are stored in the SYSTEM tablespace and are fairly static unless large structural changes are made to the applications within the database. They are created during the database creation process and are fairly small. The more procedural objects (such as triggers and procedures) you create and the more abstract datatypes and object-oriented features you use, the larger the data dictionary segments will be. These objects store PL/SQL code in the database, and their definitions are stored in the data dictionary tables.

To prevent users from creating objects in the SYSTEM tablespace, any quotas on SYSTEM (which gives them the ability to create objects there) must be revoked:

```
alter user USER quota 0 on SYSTEM;
```

When you create a user (via the **create user** command) you can specify
a default tablespace:

```
create user USERNAME identified by PASSWORD
default tablespace TABLESPACE_NAME;
```

Once a user has been created, the

```
alter user USERNAME default tablespace TABLESPACE_NAME;
```

command can be used to reassign the default tablespace for a user.
Specifying a default tablespace for users and developers will direct objects
created without a **tablespace** clause to be stored outside of the SYSTEM
tablespace.

The following sections describe each type of database object, its usage,
and why it should be stored apart from the rest of the database. The end result
will be a standard database configuration with up to 15 standard tablespace
types, depending on the manner in which the database is to be used.

Separating Application Data Segments: DATA

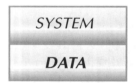

Data segments are the physical areas in which the
data associated with tables and clusters is stored.
These segments tend to be very actively accessed
by the database, experiencing a high number
of data manipulation transactions. Managing
the access requests against the data segments is the main goal of a
production database.

A typical DATA tablespace contains all of the tables associated with an
application. The high traffic volumes against these tables make them ideal
candidates for isolation in their own tablespace. If you isolate the
application tables to a DATA tablespace, you can separate that tablespace's
datafiles from the other datafiles in the database. This separation of
datafiles across disk drives may improve performance (through reduced
contention for I/O resources) and simplify file management.

Segments in a DATA tablespace are likely to be fragmented. This means
that the segments were not properly sized when created; the database then
acquires more space by allocating additional space in the tablespace. This
problem, which is described in greater detail in Chapter 4, and is resolved

in Chapter 8, also drives the need to separate DATA from SYSTEM. Separating data segments from data dictionary segments makes it much easier to resolve fragmentation problems.

Separating Application Index Segments: INDEXES

The indexes associated with tables are subject to the same I/O and growth/fragmentation considerations that encouraged the movement of data segments out of the SYSTEM tablespace. Index segments should not be stored in the same tablespace as their associated tables, since they have a great deal of concurrent I/O during both data manipulation and queries.

Index segments are also subject to fragmentation due to improper sizing or unpredicted table growth. Isolating the application indexes to a separate tablespace greatly reduces the administrative efforts involved in defragmenting either the DATA or the INDEXES tablespace.

Separating existing indexes from their tables may be accomplished by using the **rebuild** option of the **alter index** command. If an index has been created in the same tablespace as the table it indexes, you can move it with a single command. In the following example, the EMPLOYEE$DEPT_NO index is moved to the INDEXES tablespace, and new **storage** values are assigned for it:

```
alter index EMPLOYEE$DEPT_NO rebuild
tablespace INDEXES
storage (initial 2M next 2M pctincrease 0);
```

Separating Tools Segments: TOOLS

Despite the previous sections' admonitions about not storing data segments in the SYSTEM tablespace, many tools do exactly that. They do this not because they specifically call for their objects to be stored in the SYSTEM tablespace, but rather because they store them under the SYSTEM database account, which normally has the SYSTEM tablespace as its default area for storing objects. To avoid this, change the

SYSTEM account's default tablespace to the TOOLS tablespace and revoke its quota on the SYSTEM tablespace.

Many ORACLE and third-party tools create tables owned by SYSTEM. If the tables have already been created in the database, their objects can be moved by exporting the database, dropping the old tools tables, revoking quota from the SYSTEM tablespace account, granting the SYSTEM user quota only on the TOOLS tablespace, and importing the tables.

The following listing shows this process. In the first step, the quota is revoked from the SYSTEM user. The second step grants quota on the TOOLS tablespace to the SYSTEM user.

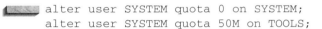

```
alter user SYSTEM quota 0 on SYSTEM;
alter user SYSTEM quota 50M on TOOLS;
```

Separating Rollback Segments: RBS

Rollback segments maintain the data concurrency within the database. In order to create non-SYSTEM tablespaces, you must first create a second rollback segment within the SYSTEM tablespace. To isolate rollback segments (which incur I/O for transactions in the database) from the data dictionary, create a rollback segment tablespace that contains nothing but rollback segments. Splitting them out in this fashion also greatly simplifies their management (see Chapter 7).

Once the RBS tablespace has been created, and a rollback segment has been activated within it, the second rollback segment in the SYSTEM tablespace can be dropped. You may find it useful to keep this rollback segment in SYSTEM inactive but still available in the event of a problem with the RBS tablespace.

Rollback segments dynamically expand to the size of the largest transaction and shrink to a specified optimal size. I/O against rollback segments is usually concurrent with I/O against the DATA and INDEXES tablespaces. Separating them thus helps avoid I/O contention while making them easier to administer.

Separating Temporary Segments: TEMP

SYSTEM
DATA
INDEXES
TOOLS
RBS
TEMP

Temporary segments are dynamically created objects within the database that store data during large sorting operations (such as **select distinct**, **union**, and **create index**). Due to their dynamic nature, temporary segments should not be stored with any other types of segments. The proper structure of temporary segments is described in Chapter 4. When a TEMP tablespace is "at rest," there are no segments stored within it. Separating temporary segments from SYSTEM thus removes a problem child from the data dictionary area and creates a tablespace that is simple to administer.

You can use the **create user** command to specify a non-SYSTEM temporary tablespace, as shown in the following listing:

```
create user USERNAME identified by PASSWORD
default tablespace SOME_TABLESPACE
temporary tablespace TEMP;
```

After the account has been created, the

```
alter user USERNAME temporary tablespace TEMP;
```

command can be used to reassign the temporary tablespace. This will cause all future temporary segments created for that user's account to be created in TEMP.

As of ORACLE7.3, you can create tablespaces that can *only* contain temporary segments. Users cannot create permanent segments such as tables and indexes in those tablespaces. See the syntax for the **create tablespace** command in Appendix C.

Separating Users: USERS

Although they typically do not have object creation privileges in production databases, users may have such privileges in development databases. User objects are usually transient in nature. Their sizing efforts are usually not thorough. As a result, these objects should be separated from the rest of the database. This will help to minimize the impact of user experimentation on the functioning of the database.

To do this, revoke users' quotas on other tablespaces and change their default tablespace settings to the USERS tablespace. You can use the **create user** command to specify an alternate default tablespace, as shown here:

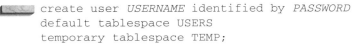

```
create user USERNAME identified by PASSWORD
default tablespace USERS
temporary tablespace TEMP;
```

After a user's account has been created, the

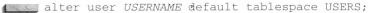

```
alter user USERNAME default tablespace USERS;
```

command can be used to reassign the default tablespace. Reassigning the default tablespace this way will direct objects created without a **tablespace** clause to be stored in USERS.

Beyond OFA

The USERS tablespace is the last major section called for by traditional OFA. However, there are several extensions that may be appropriate for your database. These extensions, described in the following sections, help to further isolate objects with differing usage requirements while handling exceptions without impacting the production setup.

Separating Low-Usage Data Segments: DATA_2

SYSTEM	
DATA	DATA_2
INDEXES	
TOOLS	
RBS	
TEMP	
USERS	

When reviewing your list of data tables, it is likely that they can very easily be combined into two or more groups based on their characteristics: some will contain very dynamic data, others very static data; the latter type of table may contain a list of states, for example. The static data tables tend to experience less I/O than the active data tables; when queried, the access against a static data table is usually concurrent with an access against a dynamic data table.

This concurrent I/O can be split among multiple files (and thus among multiple disks, to improve performance) by placing all static data tables in a dedicated tablespace. Administrative functions performed against the DATA tablespace, such as defragmentation, now only occur against those tables most likely to require assistance. Meanwhile, the tablespace for static data tables, DATA_2, should remain static and simple to maintain.

Separating Low-Usage Index Segments: INDEXES_2

SYSTEM	
DATA	DATA_2
INDEXES	INDEXES_2
TOOLS	
RBS	
TEMP	
USERS	

The indexes for low-usage, static data tables also tend to be low usage and static. To simplify the administrative actions for the INDEXES tablespace, move the static tables' indexes to a separate INDEXES_2 tablespace. This also helps to improve performance tuning options, since concurrent I/O among indexes can now be split across disk drives.

If the low-usage indexes have already been created in the INDEXES tablespace, then they must be dropped and re-created in INDEXES_2. This is usually done concurrent with the moving of low-usage tables to

DATA_2. If the index was created via a PRIMARY KEY or UNIQUE constraint definition, then that constraint may need to be modified.

The following listing shows a sample tablespace specification for an automatically created index. This example creates a unique constraint on the Description column in a static table called EMPLOYEE_TYPE. The unique index that the database will create for this constraint is directed to be stored in the INDEXES_2 tablespaces.

```
alter table EMPLOYEE_TYPE
   add constraint UNIQ_DESCR  unique(DESCRIPTION)
using index tablespace INDEXES_2;
```

If the index already exists, you can use the **rebuild** clause of the **alter index** command to move the index from its current tablespace to a new tablespace. See the "INDEXES" section earlier in this chapter.

Separating Tools Indexes: TOOLS_I

SYSTEM	
DATA	DATA_2
INDEXES	INDEXES_2
TOOLS	**TOOLS_I**
RBS	
TEMP	
USERS	

If your database shows a lot of activity against the TOOLS tablespace, then the indexes for those tools tables may be moved to a separate tablespace. This is most applicable to those environments in which the TOOLS tablespace is treated as a DATA tablespace; that is, its tables are the subject of much of the I/O in the database.

You can use the **rebuild** clause of the **alter index** command to move an existing index to a different tablespace while rebuilding it. See the "INDEXES" section earlier in this chapter for an example, and see Appendix C for the syntax for the **alter index** command.

Separating Specialty Rollback Segments: RBS_2

SYSTEM	
DATA	DATA_2
INDEXES	INDEXES_2
TOOLS	TOOLS_1
RBS	**RBS_2**
TEMP	
USERS	

The rollback segments in the RBS tablespace should be of the proper size and number to support production usage of the application (see Chapter 7). There will almost always be a transaction whose size is unsupported by the production rollback segment configuration. When it is executed, it will take over one of the production rollback segments and extend it greatly, using up as much free space as it can before the transaction succeeds or fails.

It doesn't have to be that way. The production rollback segments should be used by production users. Special transactional requirements should be handled by a separate rollback segment. To specify this rollback segment, the user must use the

```
set transaction use rollback segment SEGMENT_NAME
```

command prior to executing the transaction. However, this solves only part of the problem since the chosen rollback segment is still using space in the production rollback segment tablespace.

Create a separate rollback segment tablespace that will exist solely to support this type of transaction (such as large data loads). When the transaction completes, the rollback segment may be either deactivated or dropped (as well as its tablespace, thus saving disk space). Once again, separating logical objects based on their functional requirements serves to greatly simplify their administration.

Separating User-Specific Temporary Segments: TEMP_*USER*

SYSTEM	
DATA	DATA_2
INDEXES	INDEXES_2
TOOLS	TOOLS_I
RBS	RBS_2
TEMP	**TEMP_USER**
USERS	

The final major tablespace is, like RBS_2, a specialty tablespace designed to address specific needs of the application users. Certain users, such as GL (the General Ledger schema) in an ORACLE Financials application, may require much larger temporary segments than the rest of the application's users. In such a case, it makes sense to separate those temporary segments from the standard TEMP tablespace. This eases administration, since you can now design for the common usage of the system, while handling the exceptions via TEMP_*USER*. In practice, name this tablespace after the name of the user, as in TEMP_GL or TEMP_SCOTT.

You can use the **create user** command to specify a temporary tablespace for a user:

```
create user USERNAME identified by PASSWORD
default tablespace TABLESPACE_NAME
temporary tablespace temp_USER;
```

If the user has already been created, the following command can be used to change the temporary tablespace setting:

```
alter user USERNAME temporary tablespace TEMP_USER;
```

This command will cause all future temporary segments created for that user's account to be created in the user's custom TEMP_*USER* tablespace.

Additional Application-Specific OFA Extensions

Depending on your application, you may have additional types of objects in your database. Each distinct type of object should be stored in its own tablespace to minimize the impact objects have on each other. The types are

SNAPS	For snapshots (see Chapter 15). Snapshot tables and indexes are managed differently than most other tables in the database.
PARTITIONS	For partitions (see Chapter 12). You can use partitions to distribute the I/O load and improve the ease of management for large tables. You should identify the most commonly used partitions and manage them as if they were separate tables.
TEMP_WORK	For use during large data loads (see Chapter 12). Temporary work segments are characterized by large batch loads of data followed by deletion of the data or truncation of the table.

If you do not use replication, partitions, or temporary work tables for data loads, then you will not need any of these tablespaces. If you use partitions, you can move the partitions to different tablespaces once they exist (see Chapter 12 and the **alter table** command in Appendix C). If you use local partition indexes (see Chapter 12), you should separate the local indexes from their respective table partitions.

Common-Sense Logical Layouts

The resulting logical design of the database should meet the following criteria:

- Segment types that are used in the same way should be stored together.

- The system should be designed for standard usage.

- Separate areas should exist for exceptions.

- Contention among tablespaces should be minimized.

- The data dictionary should be isolated.

Note that meeting these criteria requires the DBA to know the application being implemented: which tools it will use, which tables will be most active, when data loads will occur, which users will have exceptional resource requirements, and how standard transactions behave. Gaining this knowledge requires a very high level of involvement of the DBA in the application development process (see Chapter 5).

Meeting these criteria results in a system whose varied segment types do not interfere with each other's needs. This makes it much simpler to manage the database, and to isolate and resolve performance problems. When fragmentation of segments or free space does occur (see Chapter 4 and Chapter 8), it is much simpler to resolve when the database is laid out in this manner.

The only potential tablespace in which multiple types of segments may exist is the USERS tablespace. If the development environment is also used as a testing environment, then it may be a good idea to separate users' indexes into a USERS_I tablespace.

The combination of a sensible logical database layout with a well-designed physical database layout (see Chapter 4) results in systems that require very little tuning after the first postproduction check. The up-front planning efforts pay off immediately in both the flexibility and the performance of the database. The cost of implementing this design from the start is minimal; it can be built into all of your database creation scripts automatically, and is now a part of the database creation scripts automatically generated by the ORACLE software installation process. The final overall design of the system should be an appropriate combination of the logical divisions shown in Table 3-1.

Tablespace	Use
SYSTEM	Data dictionary
DATA	Standard-operation tables
DATA_2	Static tables used during standard operations
INDEXES	Indexes for the standard-operation tables
INDEXES_2	Indexes for the static tables
RBS	Standard-operation rollback segments
RBS_2	Specialty rollback segments used for data loads
TEMP	Standard-operation temporary segments
TEMP_*USER*	Temporary segments created by a specific user
TOOLS	RDBMS tools tables
TOOLS_I	Indexes for heavily used RDBMS tools tables
USERS	User objects, in development databases
USERS_I	User indexes, in testing databases
SNAPS	Snapshots (a SNAPS_I can be created for their indexes)
PARTITIONS	Partitions of table or index segments; create multiple tablespaces for them
TEMP_WORK	Temporary tables used during data load processing

TABLE 3-1.   *Logical Distribution of Segments in an Optimal Database*

CHAPTER
4

Physical Database
Layouts

icture a crowded lecture hall, in which every seat is taken. Now, eliminate half of the seats by combining groups of attendees onto seats. For the combinations to work, characteristics of the people must be estimated: their relative weights, their space needs, etc. Now eliminate half of the remaining seats. The cycle of planning the appropriate distribution of attendees must be repeated.

This same repetitive reallocation of resources happens to DBAs every day. In the DBA's case, it occurs when the number of database-related files exceeds the number of disks available. The characteristics of those files must then be considered in order to arrive at the optimal combinations.

In this chapter, you will see the manner in which ORACLE manages physical data storage, along with the optimal physical database layouts for any number of disks. These layouts will be the result of understanding the ways in which various database files operate and interact.

Too often, the physical layout of the database is not planned; it is only considered when the database is experiencing performance problems. Just as the logical layout of the database should be planned (see Chapter 3), the physical layout of the database's files must be designed and implemented to meet the database's goals. Failure to plan the layouts before creating the database will result in a recurring cycle of layout-related problems and performance tuning efforts.

In this chapter, you will see where to place database-related files relative to each other to ensure optimal recoverability and performance. A method for verifying the planned layout will be provided. The directory structure for the system's disks will also be covered, and an overview on database space usage will be presented. These four sections, taken together, provide an understanding of the impact of system-level file layout decisions on each level of an ORACLE database.

Database File Layout

By establishing the clear goals of the file distribution design, and by understanding the nature of the database (e.g., transaction-oriented versus read-intensive), the proper design can be determined for distributing the files across any number of devices. This chapter will provide designs for the most common configurations as well as guidelines for applying them to any situations not directly covered.

This process will be accomplished via the following steps:

1. Identifying I/O contention among datafiles

2. Identifying I/O bottlenecks among all database files

3. Identifying concurrent I/O among background processes

4. Defining the security and performance goals for the database

5. Defining the system hardware and mirroring architecture

6. Identifying disks that can be dedicated to the database

In most cases, only the datafile contention, hardware mirroring, and disk acquisition tasks are performed before creating databases, thus designing contention into the system. By accomplishing all of the steps listed here, the end product will be a physical database layout that has your needs designed into it.

I/O Contention Among Datafiles

When designing a database that will hold an application, follow the design procedures given in Chapter 3. Doing so should result in a database that contains some combination of the tablespaces shown in Table 4-1.

Each of these tablespaces requires a separate datafile. You can monitor database I/O among datafiles *after* the database has been created; this capability is only useful during the planning stages if an analogous database is available for reference. If no such database is available, then the DBA must estimate the I/O load for each datafile.

Start the physical layout planning process by estimating the relative I/O of the datafiles. Assign the most active tablespace an I/O "weight" of 100. Then estimate the I/O against the other data tablespaces relative to that tablespace. Assign the SYSTEM tablespace files a weight of 35, and the index tablespaces a value equal to one-third of the weighting for their associated data tablespaces.

What about the TOOLS, RBS, and TEMP tablespaces? The I/O against these tablespaces varies widely, depending on the nature of the database. TOOLS will experience very little I/O in a production environment. If the database will be very transaction-oriented, RBS's weight may go as high as 75 (in most cases, it should be between 10 and 40). TEMP, in production,

Tablespace	Use
SYSTEM	Data dictionary
DATA	Standard-operation tables
DATA_2	Static tables used during standard operation
INDEXES	Indexes for the standard-operation tables
INDEXES_2	Indexes for the static tables
RBS	Standard-operation rollback segments
RBS_2	Specialty rollback segments used for data loads
TEMP	Standard-operation temporary segments
TEMP_USER	Temporary segments created by a particular user
TOOLS	RDBMS tools tables
TOOLS_I	Indexes for RDBMS tools tables
USERS	User objects, in development databases

TABLE 4-1.   *Logical Distribution of Segments in an Optimal Database*

will only be used by large sorts; its weight will therefore vary widely during usage, ranging from 0 to 75. Choose a value that is reflective of the database you are implementing.

The message in this weighting procedure is twofold: first, the file I/O weight has to be estimated before the files are created; and second, this procedure has to be done for each database. Table 4-2 shows the I/O weights for a sample transaction-oriented production database.

In this example, the DATA tablespace has been given a weight of 100. Its associated index tablespace, INDEXES, has a weight of one-third of that, 33. The SYSTEM tablespace has been given a weight of 35, and RBS (the rollback segments tablespace) has been given an estimated I/O weight of 40. TEMP and TOOLS have been estimated to have weights of 5 and 1, respectively. The DATA_2 and INDEXES_2 tablespaces have been estimated to be very lightly used, with weights of 4 and 2, respectively.

Note that 94 percent of the I/O is concentrated in the top four tablespaces. In order to properly distribute the datafile I/O, you would therefore need at least five disks: one for each of the top four tablespaces (by I/O weight) and one for the lower I/O tablespaces. The DBA of this

Tablespace	Weight	Percent of Total
DATA	100	45
RBS	40	18
SYSTEM	35	16
INDEXES	33	15
TEMP	5	2
DATA_2	4	2
INDEXES_2	2	1
TOOLS	1	1
Total	220	

TABLE 4-2.   *Estimated I/O Weights for Sample Tablespaces*

database should also avoid putting additional database files on the disks holding the top four tablespaces.

These weightings serve to reinforce several cardinal rules about database file placement on disks: the DATA tablespaces should be stored separate from their INDEXES tablespaces, the RBS tablespaces separate from the DATA tablespaces, and the SYSTEM tablespace separate from the other tablespaces in the database. The weightings and characteristics of the lower I/O tablespaces will be used to determine which of them should be stored on the same devices when that becomes necessary.

Scripts that will monitor the database (and thus verify the I/O weighting estimates) are given in the "Verification of I/O Weighting Estimates" section of this chapter.

Only One DATA Tablespace?

In Table 4-2, only one DATA tablespace is shown. For the sake of keeping this example simple to understand, only one DATA tablespace will be used throughout this chapter. In production databases, you will likely have multiple DATA tablespaces (particularly if you use partitions). When estimating I/O weights, you will then have to estimate the I/O weight of each of your DATA tablespaces.

I/O Bottlenecks Among All Database Files

Once the I/O weightings of the datafiles have been estimated, the location of the datafiles relative to each other can be designed. However, this is only part of the picture. Other database file types must be considered as well.

Online Redo Log Files

The most confusing aspect of database file placement concerns *online redo log files*. These are the files that store the records of each transaction in the database. Each database must have at least two online redo log files available to it. The database will write to one log file in a sequential fashion until it is filled, then it will start writing to the second redo log file. When the last online redo log file is filled, the database will begin overwriting the contents of the first redo log file with new transactions.

Online redo log files are the database's Achilles' heel. Since they maintain information about the current transactions in the database, they cannot be recovered from a backup. They are the only type of file in the database that cannot be recovered via the database backup utilities.

Because of this, DBAs need to make sure that the online redo log files are mirrored by some means. Within ORACLE, *redo log groups* can be set up to allow the database to dynamically maintain multiple sets of the online redo log files. This uses the database to mirror the online redo log files, thus minimizing the recovery problems caused by a single disk failure. You can also rely on the operating system to mirror the redo log files.

In general, you should place online redo log files apart from datafiles because of potential performance implications. Understanding the performance implications requires knowing how the two types of files (datafiles and online redo log files) are used.

Every transaction that is not executed with the **nologging** parameter in effect is recorded in the redo log files. Transaction entries are written to the online redo log files by the *LGWR (Log Writer)* background process. The data in the transactions is concurrently written to several tablespaces (such as the RBS rollback segments tablespace and the DATA tablespace). The writes to the tablespaces are done via the *DBWR (Database Writer)* background process. Thus, even though the datafile I/O may be properly distributed, contention between the DBWR and LGWR background processes will occur if a datafile is stored on the same disk as a redo log file.

Redo log files are written sequentially. Thus, if there is no concurrent activity on the disk, then the disk hardware will already be properly positioned for the next log write. By contrast, datafiles are read and written to in a comparatively random fashion. Since the log files are written sequentially, they will process I/O the fastest if they do not have to contend with other activity on the same disk.

If you must store a datafile on the same disk as redo log files, then it should not belong to the SYSTEM tablespace, the RBS tablespace, or a very active DATA or INDEX tablespace. All of these will have direct conflicts with the redo log files and will increase the likelihood of the log writes being affected by the database reads.

Control Files

Control files can be internally mirrored by ORACLE. The number and name of the control files should be specified via the CONTROL_FILES parameter in the database's init.ora or config.ora file. If the control filenames are specified via this parameter during database creation, then they will be automatically created during the database creation process. The database will thereafter maintain the control files as identical copies of each other.

Each database should have a minimum of three copies of its control files, located across three drives. Very little I/O occurs in these files relative to that of the other database files.

Archived Redo Log Files

The LGWR background process writes to the online redo log files in a cyclical fashion; after filling the first log file, it begins writing the second until that one fills, and then begins writing to the third. Once the last online redo log file is filled, LGWR begins to overwrite the contents of the first online redo log file.

When ORACLE is run in ARCHIVELOG mode, the database makes a copy of each online redo log file before overwriting it. These archived redo log files are usually written to a disk device. They may also be written directly to a tape device, but this tends to be operator-intensive.

The archiving function is performed by the ARCH background process. Databases using this option will encounter contention problems on their online redo log disk during heavy data transaction times, since LGWR will be trying to write to one redo log file while ARCH is trying to read another. The only way to avoid this contention is to distribute the online redo log files across multiple disks. Therefore, if you are running in ARCHIVELOG mode on a very transaction-oriented database, avoid LGWR-ARCH contention by splitting up your online redo log files across devices.

You should also be careful with the placement of the archived redo log files. Remember that this device, by its nature, will have the same amount of I/O as the online redo logs device. Therefore, the rules regarding placement of online redo log files apply also to the archived redo log files. They should not be stored on the same device as the SYSTEM, RBS, DATA, or INDEXES tablespace, and they should not be stored on the same device as any of the online redo log files. Since running out of space on the archived redo log device will freeze the database, archived redo log files should only be stored with small, static files.

ORACLE Software

The specific ORACLE software files that are accessed during normal database operation vary according to the packages that are licensed for the host on which the server resides. The I/O against these files is not recorded within the database. Since the location of the files is also variable (particularly in a distributed or client-server architecture), a system or network monitor should be used to determine the I/O against these files. The actual I/O against these files can then be compared with the actual I/O measurements for the database files to determine if the files need to be redistributed.

To minimize contention between the database files and the database code, avoid placing database files on the same disk device as the code files. If datafiles must be placed on that disk device, then the least frequently used datafiles should be placed there.

Concurrent I/O Among Background Processes

When evaluating contention among various processes, it is important to identify the type of I/O being performed and its timing. Files contend with each other if I/O from one file interferes with I/O for the second file, so two random-accessed files that are never accessed at the same time can be placed on the same device.

Based on the discussion in the previous section, two types of I/O contention can be defined: *concurrent I/O* and *interference*. Concurrent I/O contention occurs when multiple accesses are performed against the same device at the same instant. This is the kind of contention that is eliminated by isolating tables from their associated indexes. Interference contention occurs when writes to a sequentially written file are interrupted by reads or writes to other files on the same disk, even if those reads or writes occur at a different time than the sequential reads and writes.

There are three database background processes that actively access the database files on disk: the Database Writer (DBWR), the Log Writer (LGWR), and the Archiver (ARCH). DBWR reads and writes to files in a fairly random manner, LGWR writes sequentially, and ARCH reads and writes sequentially. Eliminating the contention possibilities between these three background processes will effectively eliminate all contention at the database level.

Note that LGWR and ARCH are always writing to one file at a time. DBWR, on the other hand, may be attempting to read or write to multiple files at once. There is thus the potential for DBWR to cause contention with itself! To combat this problem, certain operating systems (including UNIX) can create multiple DBWR processes for each instance. The number of DBWRs is set via the init.ora parameter DBWR_IO_SLAVES; ORACLE recommends setting DBWR_IO_SLAVES to a value between n and $2n$, where n is the number of disks. You can also start multiple LGWR I/O slaves (via the LGWR_IO_SLAVES parameter) and multiple ARCH I/O slaves (via ARCH_IO_SLAVES). If this option is not available on your system, then you may be able to use asynchronous I/O to reduce internal DBWR contention. With asynchronous I/O, only one DBWR process is needed since the I/O processing is performed asynchronously.

The nature of the contention that will occur between the background processes is thus a function of the backup scheme used (ARCH), the transaction load on the system (LGWR), and the host operating system (DBWR). Designing a scheme that will eliminate contention between files and processes requires a clear understanding of the ways in which those files and processes will interact in the production system.

Defining the Recoverability and Performance Goals for the System

Before designing the database's disk layout, the goals for the layout must be clearly defined. Otherwise, you'll end up with contradictory designs.

The database goals that relate directly to disks are (1) *recoverability* and (2) *performance*. The recoverability goals must take into account all processes that impact disks. These should include, at a minimum, the storage area for archived redo log files (if used) and the storage area for Export dump files.

The performance tuning goals must take into account the projected database file I/O distribution and the relative access speeds of the disks available (since heterogeneous systems may feature some disks that are faster than others).

In order to avoid conflicting advice on disk layouts, the goal of the layout must be clearly defined: Are you trying to optimize performance or recoverability? If recoverability is the primary goal of the layout, then all critical database files should be placed on mirrored drives, and the database should be run in ARCHIVELOG mode. In such a scenario, performance is a secondary consideration.

Recoverability of a database should always be a primary concern. But once the database has been secured, the performance goals of the system should be taken into consideration. For example, the server on which the database resides may have fully mirrored disks, in which case performance is the only real issue.

To ensure database recoverability, you must mirror your online redo log files. This can be done via the operating system or via mirrored redo log groups, but it must be done. The architecture put in place for recoverability should complement the performance tuning architecture; the two goals may yield two different file layouts. If the performance tuning design conflicts with the recoverability design, then the recoverability design must prevail. Recoverability issues should only involve a few disks; once the database recovery options have been chosen (see Chapter 10), the performance issues can be addressed.

Defining the System Hardware and Mirroring Architecture

Since the Systems Management group allocates and manages the server's disk farm, DBAs must work with that team to manage the system's hardware and mirroring architecture. This involves specifying

■ The number of disks required

■   The models of disks required (for performance or size)

■   The appropriate mirroring strategy

The number of disks required will be driven by the size of the database and the database I/O weights. Wherever possible, those disks should be dedicated to ORACLE files to avoid concurrent I/O and interference contention with non-ORACLE files. If the disk farm is heterogeneous, then the size and speed of the drives available should be taken into consideration when determining which are to be dedicated to ORACLE files.

Disk mirroring is used to provide fault tolerance with regard to media failures. Mirroring is performed either by maintaining a duplicate of each disk online (known as *RAID-1* or *volume shadowing*) or by using a *parity-check* system among a group of disks (usually *RAID-3* or *RAID-5*). The parity-check systems implicitly perform file striping across disks. In RAID-5, for example, each file is striped on a block-by-block basis across the disks in the mirroring group. A parity check is then written on another disk in the set so that if one disk is removed, its contents can be regenerated based on knowing the parity check and the contents of the rest of the mirrored set.

The system mirroring architecture thus impacts the distribution of database files across those disks. Disks that are mirrored on a one-to-one basis (RAID-1) can be treated as stand-alone disks. Disks that are part of a parity-check system (such as RAID-3 or RAID-5) must be considered as a set, and can take advantage of the implicit striping.

Identifying Disks That Can Be Dedicated to the Database

Whatever mirroring architecture is used, it is important that the disks chosen be dedicated to the database. Otherwise, the nondatabase load on those disks will impact the database, and that impact is usually impossible to forecast correctly. User directory areas, for example, may experience sudden increases in size—and wipe out the space that was intended for the archived redo log files, bringing the database to a halt. Other files may have severe I/O requirements that were not factored into the database I/O weights estimated earlier.

Choosing the Right Layout

The basis for deciding the appropriate disk layout can now be deduced:

- The database must be recoverable.

- The online redo log files must be mirrored via the system or the database.

- The database file I/O weights must be estimated.

- Contention between DBWR, LGWR, and ARCH must be minimized.

- Contention between disks for DBWR must be minimized.

- The performance goals of the system must be defined.

- The disk hardware options must be known.

- The disk mirroring architecture must be known.

- Disks must be dedicated to the database.

The Dream Database Physical Layout: The 22-Disk Solution

The layouts presented in this section assume that the disks involved are dedicated to the database and that the online redo log files are being mirrored via the operating system. It is also assumed that the disks have identical size and performance characteristics.

The configuration shown in Figure 4-1 is not likely to be available, but it's important to start with goals that aim high. This configuration eliminates contention between datafiles completely by giving each a separate disk to occupy. It also eliminates LGWR-ARCH contention by giving each redo log a separate disk. It also assigns a disk (number 14) to the software for the application that will access the database.

This configuration is unlikely because of the capital resources that are required; on the control file disks, an entire disk (usually up to 2Gb) is used to maintain a single, low-access file that seldom exceeds 200K. To reach a more realistic configuration, the disk layout should be iteratively revised until the available number of disks is reached.

Disk	Contents
1	Oracle software
2	SYSTEM tablespace
3	RBS tablespace
4	DATA tablespace
5	INDEXES tablespace
6	TEMP tablespace
7	TOOLS tablespace
8	Online Redo log 1
9	Online Redo log 2
10	Online Redo log 3
11	Control file 1
12	Control file 2
13	Control file 3
14	Application software
15	RBS_2
16	DATA_2
17	INDEXES_2
18	TEMP_*USER*
19	TOOLS_I
20	USERS
21	Archived redo log destination disk
22	Export dump file destination disk

FIGURE 4-1.   *The 22-disk solution*

The First Iteration: The 17-Disk Solution

Each successive iteration of the disk layout will involve placing the contents of multiple disks on a single disk. The first iteration (in Figure 4-2) moves the three control files onto the three redo log disks. Control files will cause interference contention with the online redo logs, but only at log switch points and during database recovery. During normal operation of the database, very little interference will occur.

Assuming that this will be a production database, the TOOLS_I tablespace's contents will be merged with the TOOLS tablespace (they are usually only separated in intense development environments). For

```
Disk       Contents
1          Oracle software
2          SYSTEM tablespace
3          RBS tablespace
4          DATA tablespace
5          INDEXES tablespace
6          TEMP tablespace
7          TOOLS tablespace
8          Online Redo log 1, Control file 1
9          Online Redo log 2, Control file 2
10         Online Redo log 3, Control file 3
11         Application software
12         RBS_2
13         DATA_2
14         INDEXES_2
15         TEMP_USER
16         Archived redo log destination disk
17         Export dump file destination disk
```

FIGURE 4-2. *The 17-disk solution*

production environments, users will not have resource privileges, so the
USERS tablespace will not be considered in these configurations.

The Second Iteration: The 15-Disk Solution

The second iteration of file combinations (in Figure 4-3) begins the process
of placing multiple tablespaces on the same disk. In this case, the RBS and
RBS_2 tablespaces are placed together because they are seldom used
concurrently; as previously defined, RBS_2 contains specialty rollback
segments that are used during large data loads. Since data loads should not
be occurring during production usage (which RBS is used for), there should
be no contention between RBS and RBS_2, so they can be placed together.

The TEMP and TEMP_*USER* tablespaces can also be placed on the same
disk. The TEMP_*USER* tablespace is dedicated to a specific user (such as GL
in ORACLE Financials) who has temporary segment needs that are far
greater than the rest of the system's users. The TEMP tablespace's
weighting, as previously noted, can vary widely; however, it should be
possible to store it on the same device as TEMP_*USER* without overly
impacting its I/O.

Disk	Contents
1	Oracle software
2	SYSTEM tablespace
3	RBS tablespace, *RBS_2 tablespace*
4	DATA tablespace
5	INDEXES tablespace
6	TEMP tablespace, *TEMP_USER tablespace*
7	TOOLS tablespace
8	Online Redo log 1, Control file 1
9	Online Redo log 2, Control file 2
10	Online Redo log 3, Control file 3
11	Application software
12	DATA_2
13	INDEXES_2
14	Archived redo log destination disk
15	Export dump file destination disk

FIGURE 4-3. *The 15-disk solution*

The Third Iteration: The 12-Disk Solution

Before putting any more combinations of tablespaces on multiple disks, the online redo logs should be placed together on the same disk (see Figure 4-4). In databases that use ARCHIVELOG backups, this will cause concurrent I/O and interference contention between LGWR and ARCH on that disk. Thus, this combination is not appropriate for very high-transaction systems running in ARCHIVELOG mode.

Because the online redo log file disks have been combined into one, the control files must be moved. In this example, they coexist with the three most critical tablespaces (SYSTEM, RBS, and DATA). As previously stated, the control files are not I/O intensive and should cause little contention. The only other change for this configuration is the combination of the TOOLS tablespace with the INDEX_2 tablespace.

The Fourth Iteration: The 9-Disk Solution

As you may have noted, most of the changes have consisted of moving items from the highest-numbered disks onto the lower-numbered disks. This is because the first disks were assigned to those files that were judged to be most critical to the database. The later disks were assigned to files that

Disk	Contents
1	Oracle software
2	SYSTEM tablespace, *Control file 1*
3	RBS tablespace, RBS_2 tablespace, *Control file 2*
4	DATA tablespace, *Control file 3*
5	INDEXES tablespace
6	TEMP tablespace, TEMP_*USER* tablespace
7	TOOLS tablespace, *INDEXES_2 tablespace*
8	Online Redo logs 1, *2, and 3*
9	Application software
10	DATA_2
11	Archived redo log destination disk
12	Export dump file destination disk

FIGURE 4-4. *The 12-disk solution*

would be helpful to have on separate devices, but whose isolation was not a necessity.

This iteration (shown in Figure 4-5) combines the three highest-numbered disks (disks 10, 11, and 12) with good matches for their characteristics. First, the DATA_2 tablespace (weighted as 2 percent of the total datafile I/O) is combined with the TEMP tablespaces, creating a disk that now handles 4 percent of the datafile I/O. This should be a good match because the static tables are less likely to have large group operations performed on them than are the tables in the DATA tablespace. Second, the Export dump files have been moved to the online redo log file disk. This may seem an odd combination at first, but they are well suited to each other, since the online redo log files never increase in size (and usually take less than 15MB), while the process of exporting a database causes very little transaction activity (and therefore little contention between the redo log file and the Export dump file). The third combination in this iteration is that of the application software with the archived redo log file destination area. The application software is assumed to be both static and small, using less than 10 percent of the available disk space. This leaves the ARCH background process ample space to write log files to while avoiding conflicts with DBWR.

Disk	Contents
1	Oracle software
2	SYSTEM tablespace, Control file 1
3	RBS tablespace, RBS_2 tablespace, Control file 2
4	DATA tablespace, Control file 3
5	INDEXES tablespace
6	TEMP tablespace, TEMP_*USER* tablespace, *DATA_2 tablespace*
7	TOOLS tablespace, INDEXES_2 tablespace
8	Online Redo logs 1, 2, and 3, *Export dump file destination disk*
9	Application software, *Archived redo log destination disk*

FIGURE 4-5.   *The 9-disk solution*

The Fifth Iteration: The 7-Disk Compromise

From this point onward, the tablespace combinations should be driven by the weights assigned during the I/O estimation process. For the weightings given earlier in this chapter, the distribution of I/O among the disks after the fourth iteration is shown in Table 4-3.

The weighting for disk 1 is not shown because it is installation-specific, since applications may be of widely varying size and different ORACLE software is licensed for different sites.

The weightings for disks 8 and 9 are based on the weighting for the rollback segments tablespaces, since transactions written to RBS will also be written to the online redo log files. If the database is running in ARCHIVELOG mode, then disk 9's archived redo log files will have the same I/O as disk 8's online redo log files. Because other files are on these disks (the Export dump files and the application software), their weight is indicated as being some value greater than the RBS disk's I/O weight.

From the weightings shown in Table 4-3, there are no good solutions going forward. In order to compress the disk farm further, you must either store data on the same disk as its associated index (by combining disks 6 and 7, which feature DATA_2 and INDEXES_2, respectively), or you must store extra tablespaces on one of the top four weighted disks (disks 2, 3, 4, and 5). The last two disks, which are being used to support the online redo

Disk	Weight	Contents
1		ORACLE software
2	35	SYSTEM tablespace, Control file 1
3	40	RBS tablespace, RBS_2 tablespace, Control file 2
4	100	DATA tablespace, Control file 3
5	33	INDEXES tablespace
6	9	TEMP tablespace, TEMP_USER tablespace, DATA_2 tablespace
7	3	TOOLS tablespace, INDEXES_2 tablespace
8	40+	Online Redo logs 1, 2, and 3, Export dump file destination disk
9	40+	Application software, Archived redo log destination disk

TABLE 4-3. *Estimated I/O Weightings of the 9-Disk Solution*

log files, exports, application software, and archived redo log files, which are key to the database's recoverability, should not be further burdened.

The I/O weighting for the fifth iteration results in the compromise distribution of files shown in Figure 4-6.

For this iteration, the TOOLS and INDEXES_2 tablespaces are moved from old disk 7 to the disk that contains the SYSTEM tablespace. The TEMP, TEMP_USER, and DATA_2 tablespaces are moved from old disk 6 to the disk that features the INDEXES tablespace (since temporary segments dynamically extend, they should be kept separate from the SYSTEM tablespace).

The database's tablespace files are shown in bold in Figure 4-6. They are now spread over just four disks (disks 2, 3, 4, and 5). Each of these four disks features one of the top four I/O weighted files for the database; their relative weightings will be the same for most databases. If systems have a very high transaction volume, then this design will not change since the rollback segment tablespaces (RBS and RBS_2) are already isolated.

Going beyond this level of file combinations forces the DBA to compromise even further. Since the database's recoverability should not be compromised, disks 6 and 7 should remain as they are. Additional combinations of tablespace files will compromise performance. Therefore,

Disk	Weight	Contents
1		Oracle software
2	38	**SYSTEM,** *TOOLS, INDEXES_2 tablespaces,* Control file 1
3	40	**RBS, RBS_2 tablespaces,** Control file 2
4	100	**DATA tablespace,** Control file 3
5	42	**INDEXES,** *TEMP, TEMP_USER, DATA_2 tablespaces*
6	40+	Online Redo logs 1, 2, and 3, Export dump file destination disk
7	40+	Application software, Archived redo log destination disk

FIGURE 4-6. *The 7-disk compromise*

any further combinations of datafiles must be based on actual measurements of database I/O against these datafiles.

Verification of I/O Weighting Estimates

"I often say that when you can measure what you are talking about and express it in numbers, you know something about it; but when you cannot measure it, when you cannot express it in numbers, your knowledge is of a meagre and unsatisfactory kind."

—Lord Kelvin

The statistics tables within the data dictionary record the amount of I/O for each datafile. You can query the internal statistics tables to verify the weightings assigned in the estimation process. The following listings provide queries for generating the actual I/O weights.

Note that this script is not run for a specific time interval, but instead records all I/O against the database since it started up; the I/O against the SYSTEM tablespace will therefore be slightly higher than its value during everyday usage. Also note that the weightings are relative to the largest single file's I/O, not to the total I/O in the database.

The query uses a SQL feature available as of ORACLE7.2: the ability to have subquery as part of the **from** clause. In this case, the subquery selects the maximum file I/O from the V$FILESTAT view. The file with this I/O value will be assigned an I/O weight of 100. The script queries V$FILESTAT for the file I/O of each file and compares the file I/O with the maximum total I/O to determine the file's I/O weighting. The output from the query is written to a file called io_weights.lst via the **spool** command.

```
set pagesize 60 linesize 80 newpage 0 feedback off
ttitle skip center "Database File IO Weights" skip center -
"ordered by Drive" skip 2
column Total_IO format 999999999
column Weight format 999.99
column file_name format A40
break on Drive skip 2
compute sum of Weight on Drive

select
substr(DF.Name, 1,5) Drive,
DF.Name File_Name,
FS.Phyblkrd+FS.Phyblkwrt Total_IO,
100*(FS.Phyblkrd+FS.Phyblkwrt)/MaxIO Weight
from V$FILESTAT FS, V$DATAFILE DF,
   (select MAX(Phyblkrd+Phyblkwrt) MaxIO
     from V$FILESTAT)
where DF.File# = FS.File#
order by Weight desc

spool io_weights
/
spool off
```

The following listing shows sample output from this query:

```
               Database File I/O Weights
                    Ordered by Drive

DRIVE    FILE_NAME                         TOTAL_IO     WEIGHT
-----    ----------------------------      --------     -------
/db01    /db01/oracle/DEMO/sys01.dbf          31279       40.65
         /db01/oracle/DEMO/tools.dbf           2112        2.74
*****                                                     -------
sum                                                        43.39
```

/db02	/db02/oracle/DEMO/rbs01.dbf	3799	5.94
	/db02/oracle/DEMO/rbs02.dbf	2465	3.20
	/db02/oracle/DEMO/rbs03.dbf	1960	2.55
	/db02/oracle/DEMO/rbs04.dbf	1675	2.18
*****			-------
sum			13.87
/db03	/db03/oracle/DEMO/ddata.dbf	76950	100.00
*****			-------
sum			100.00
/db04	/db04/oracle/DEMO/demondx.dbf	36310	47.19
	/db04/oracle/DEMO/temp.dbf	4012	5.21
*****			-------
sum			52.40

In this example, the main data tablespace (DDATA, using the *ddata.dbf* datafile on /db03) is rated at a weight of 100. The index tablespace associated with that data (DEMONDX, using the *demondx.dbf* datafile on /db04) is rated at 47.19, and the SYSTEM tablespace (using the *sys01.dbf* datafile on /db01) has a weight of 40.65. The biggest difference between these actual values and the estimates made earlier is in the rollback segments' RBS tablespace, which has a weight of only 13.87, rather than its estimated weight of 40. This information should be used to reorganize the database file layout to take advantage of the lighter-than-forecast transaction load in the database.

The Sixth Iteration: Back to the Planning Stage

Given these actual I/O weights for this database, the disk layout should be reevaluated. The disk layout for this example, with the estimated and actual I/O weights, is shown in Figure 4-7. Note that this example, for a small demo database, did not use the RBS_2, DATA_2, INDEXES_2, USER, or TEMP_*USER* tablespaces.

Clearly, the INDEXES tablespace is being much more actively used than had been forecast (by about 25 percent). Also, the rollback segment usage is much lower than the estimates (13.87 instead of 40). As a result, two moves can be made for this system to better distribute the I/O weight; first, move TEMP from the INDEXES disk to the RBS disk, then move TOOLS

Disk	Est Weight	Actual Weight	Contents
1			Oracle software
2	38	43.39	SYSTEM, TOOLS tablespaces, Control file 1
3	40	13.87	RBS tablespace, Control file 2
4	100	100	DATA tablespace, Control file 3
5	42	53.40	INDEXES, TEMP tablespaces
6	40+	13.87+	Online Redo logs 1, 2, and 3, Export dump files
7	40+	13.87+	Application software, Archived redo logs

FIGURE 4-7. *Estimated and actual I/O weights for the 7-disk compromise*

from the SYSTEM to the RBS disk as well. This will result in a more leveled distribution of the I/O weight, as shown in Figure 4-8.

It is worth noting that the final example configuration process consisted of five iterations during the planning stage and only one iteration during the tuning stage. The single tuning iteration's cost, in terms of database downtime, CPU usage, and time for completion, was greater than that of all of the planning stage's costs combined. Planning must not be an afterthought.

Disk	Actual Weight	Contents
1		Oracle software
2	40.65	SYSTEM tablespace, Control file 1
3	21.82	RBS, TEMP, and TOOLS tablespaces, Control file 2
4	100	DATA tablespace, Control file 3
5	47.19	INDEX tablespace
6	13.87+	Online Redo logs 1, 2, and 3, Export dump files
7	13.87+	Application software, Archived redo logs

FIGURE 4-8. *The 7-disk compromise, revised for the example's actual weights*

File Location

In order to simplify database management, the files associated with a database should be stored in directories created specifically for that database. Database files from different databases should not be stored together.

Furthermore, the database's datafiles should be separated from the software used to access the database (despite the fact that this is the default for some of the installation programs). The disk layouts shown in the previous sections all featured "ORACLE software" as their disk #1. This disk (Figure 4-9) includes all active versions of all ORACLE software, and should not be allowed to cause contention with the datafiles.

The file layout shown in Figure 4-9 uses the most recent version of OFA (optimal flexible architecture) for the software directories. In previous versions of ORACLE, the configuration files such as init.ora were stored in the /dbs subdirectory under the software version directory (such as 8.0.3). The problem with that configuration is that each time the database software version is upgraded, the configuration files must be moved. The modified version shown in Figure 4-9 resolves this problem and stores dump files in directories that are specific to the instance name ("CC1") instead of the database version.

```
        Disk 1        (/orasw)
/orasw
   /app
      /oracle
         /product
                  /8.0.3
                        /bin
                        /rdbms (and other directories)
         /admin
                  /CC1
                        /pfile
                            initCC1.ora
                            configCC1.ora
                        /bdump
                        /udump
```

FIGURE 4-9. *Disk layout for ORACLE software*

Storing the datafiles at the same level in a directory hierarchy will simplify the management procedures. It also allows you to avoid putting the instance identifier in the filename, using it instead as part of the directory path, as in the sample directory structure listing shown in Figure 4-10.

The layout shown in Figure 4-10 allows the same filenames to be used across instances. In this configuration, the files are logically separated from each other in a consistent fashion. This separation allows wildcards or search lists to be used when referencing them (if the disks are named in a consistent fashion). For example, in UNIX environments, all of the files belonging to a specific instance could be copied to a tape device with a single command, as in the following:

```
> tar /dev/rmt/1hc /db0[1-8]/oracle/CASE
```

In this example, the system will write out to the tape device (/dev/rmt/1hc) the contents of the /oracle/CASE subdirectory on the devices named /db01 through /db08.

```
        Disk 2        (/db01)
/db01
    /oracle
        /CASE
                control1.dbf
                sys01.dbf
                tools.dbf
        /CC1
                control1.dbf
                sys01.dbf
                tools.dbf
        /DEMO
                control1.dbf
                sys01.dbf
```

FIGURE 4-10.   *Disk hierarchy for a sample data disk*

Database Space Usage Overview

In order to understand how space should be allocated within the database, you first have to know how the space is used within the database. This section will provide an overview of the ORACLE database space usage functions.

When a database is created, it is divided into multiple logical sections called tablespaces. The SYSTEM tablespace is the first tablespace created. Additional tablespaces are then created to hold different types of data, as described in Chapter 3.

When a tablespace is created, datafiles are created to hold its data. These files immediately allocate the space specified during their creation. There is thus a one-to-many relationship between databases and tablespaces, and a one-to-many relationship between tablespaces and datafiles.

A database can have multiple users, each of whom has a *schema*. Each user's schema is a collection of logical database objects such as tables and indexes. These objects refer to physical data structures that are stored in tablespaces. Objects from a user's schema may be stored in multiple tablespaces, and a single tablespace can contain objects from multiple schemas.

When a database object (such as a table or index) is created, it is assigned to a tablespace via user defaults or specific instructions. A *segment* is created in that tablespace to hold the data associated with that object. The space that is allocated to the segment is never released until the segment is dropped, shrunk, or **truncate**d. As of ORACLE7.3, you can deallocate some space from tables, indexes, and clusters. See the "How to Deallocate Space in Oracle7.3" section later in this chapter for details.

A segment is made up of sections called *extents*—contiguous sets of ORACLE blocks. Once the existing extents can no longer hold new data, the segment will obtain another extent. The extension process will continue until no more free space is available in the tablespace's datafiles or until an internal maximum number of extents per segment is reached. If a segment is composed of multiple extents, there is no guarantee that those extents will be contiguous.

The logical interrelationships between these database objects are shown in Figure 4-11.

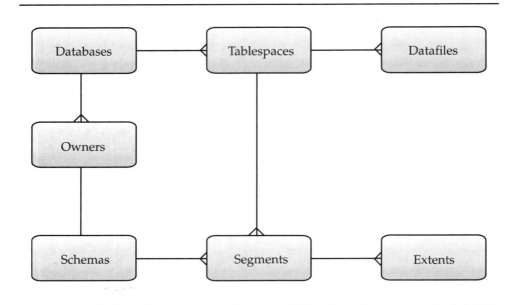

FIGURE 4-11.   *Logical relationships between database structures*

As shown in Figure 4-11, a tablespace may contain multiple segments. The segment types available in ORACLE include

TABLE
INDEX
ROLLBACK
TEMPORARY
PARTITION
CLUSTER

Managing the space used by each is one of the basic functions of the DBA. Chapters 6, 7, 8, and 12 contain detailed information on the monitoring and tuning of these segments. The intent of this overview is to aid in the planning of their physical storage.

Implications of the storage Clause

The amount of space used by a segment is determined by its storage parameters. These parameters are determined by the database at segment creation time; if no specific **storage** parameters are given in the **create table**, **create index**, **create cluster**, or **create rollback segment** command, then it will use the default storage parameters for the tablespace in which it is to be stored. The storage parameters specify the **initial** extent size, the **next** extent size, the **pctincrease** (a factor by which each successive extent will geometrically grow), the **maxextents** (maximum number of extents), and **minextents** (minimum number of extents). After the segment has been created, the **initial** and **minextents** values cannot be altered. The default values for the storage parameters for each tablespace are contained in the DBA_TABLESPACES and USER_TABLESPACES views.

When a segment is created, it will acquire at least one extent (other values can be set via **minextents**). This extent will be used to store data until it no longer has any free space available (the **pctfree** clause can be used to reserve, within each block in each extent, a percentage of space that will remain available for updates of existing rows). When additional data is added to the segment, the segment will extend by obtaining a second extent of the size specified by the **next** parameter. There is no guarantee that the second extent will be physically contiguous to the first extent.

The **pctincrease** parameter is designed to minimize the number of extents in growing tables. A nonzero value for this parameter can be dangerous—it causes the size of each successive extent to increase geometrically by the **pctincrease** factor specified. For example, consider the case of a data segment with an **initial** extent size of 20 ORACLE blocks, a **next** extent size of 20 blocks, and a **pctincrease** of 50. Table 4-4 shows the sizes of the first 10 extents in this segment.

In just 10 extents, the segment's size has increased by 7,700 percent! Besides being an indicator of inappropriate space planning by the developer, this is also an administrative problem for the DBA. The table is badly fragmented, the extents are most likely not contiguous, and the next time this table extends (for even one row of data), it will need over 750 ORACLE blocks (for a 2K block size, that's 1.5MB). A preferable situation would be to have a single extent of the right size, with a small value for **next** and a **pctincrease** of 0. This would obviate the need for segment defragmentation efforts (as described in Chapter 8).

Never change **pctincrease** without also changing **next**. The size of each successive extent is calculated by going back to the storage parameters for the table; the size of the last extent added is not considered. If, for example, you were to now change the **pctincrease** value to 0 for the segment in

Extent Number	Size (in Oracle Blocks)	Total	Comments on Extent Size
1	20	20	INITIAL
2	20	40	NEXT
3	30	70	NEXT*1.5
4	45	115	NEXT*1.5*1.5
5	70	185	NEXT*1.5*1.5*1.5
6	105	290	etc.
7	155	445	
8	230	675	
9	345	1020	
10	520	1540	

TABLE 4-4. *The Effect of Using a Nonzero **pctincrease***

Table 4-4, then extent number 11 would have a size of 20 ORACLE blocks (**next***1.0*1.0 etc.), *not* 520 blocks.

Table Segments

Table segments, also called *data segments*, store the rows of data associated with tables or clusters. Each data segment contains a header block that serves as a space directory for the segment.

Unless it is very large, a properly sized table will have one extent. The more extents a data segment has, the more work is involved in retrieving data from it. In some cases, it is not possible to have single-extent data segments; since extents cannot span datafiles, a segment that is larger than the largest datafile available will have multiple extents. Multiple extents can also be used to stripe a segment across disks; this operation, though, is better handled outside of the database (for example, by using RAID-3 or RAID-5 disk mirroring, as described earlier in this chapter).

Once a data segment acquires an extent, it keeps that extent until the segment is either dropped or **truncate**d. Deleting rows from a table has no impact on the amount of space that has been allocated to that table. The number of extents will increase until either (1) the **maxextents** value is reached, (2) the user's quota in the tablespace is reached, or (3) the tablespace runs out of space.

To minimize the amount of wasted space in a data segment, tune the **pctfree** parameter. This parameter specifies the amount of space that will be kept free within each data block. The free space can then be used when **NULL**-valued columns are updated to have values, or when updates to other values in the row force the row to lengthen. The proper setting of **pctfree** is database-specific since it is dependent on the nature of the updates that are being performed. For information on setting this and other storage parameters for tables and indexes, see Chapter 5.

Index Segments

Like table segments, *index segments* hold the space that has been allocated to them until they are dropped; however, they can also be indirectly dropped if the table or cluster they index is dropped. To minimize contention, indexes should be stored in a tablespace that is separated from their associated tables.

Indexes are subject to the same space problems that tables experience. Their segments have **storage** clauses that specify their **initial**, **next**, **minextents**, **maxextents**, and **pctincrease** values, and they are as likely to be fragmented as their tables are. They must be sized properly before they are created; otherwise, their fragmentation will drag down the database performance—exactly the opposite of their purpose.

Rollback Segments

Rollback segment functionality will be discussed in detail in Chapter 7. The principles of sound design for tables apply also to rollback segments. However, while optimal tables have one extent that is suited to their size requirements, optimal rollback segments will have multiple evenly sized extents that add up to their optimal total size (they will have a minimum of two extents when created). Each extent should be large enough to handle all of the data from a single transaction. If it is not, or if too many users request the same rollback segment, then the rollback segment may extend.

Rollback segments can dynamically shrink to a specified size, or they can be manually shrunk to a size of your choosing. The **optimal** clause, which allows rollback segments to shrink to an **optimal** size after extending, helps to provide interim support to systems that have not been properly implemented for the way they are being used. Frequent shrinks (see the "Interpreting the Statistics Reports" section of Chapter 6, and Chapter 7) indicate the need for the rollback segments to be redesigned. Since ORACLE gives DBAs great flexibility in the management of rollback segments, they can be maintained easily.

This does not address the most commonly asked question: How many rollback segments should you have? The answer to that is database-dependent; it's like asking how large your DATA tablespace should be. For guidance in choosing the right number and size of rollback segments, see the "Choosing the Number and Size" section of Chapter 7.

Temporary Segments

Temporary segments are used to store temporary data during sorting operations (such as large queries, index creations, and unions). Each user has a temporary tablespace specified when the account is created via **create user** or altered via **alter user**. The user's temporary tablespace should be pointed to some place other than SYSTEM (the default).

When a temporary segment is created, it uses the default storage parameters for that tablespace. While it is in existence, its storage parameters cannot be altered by changing the default storage parameters for the tablespace. It extends itself as necessary, and drops itself when the operation completes or encounters an error. Since the temporary segment itself can lead to errors (by exceeding the maximum number of extents or running out of space in the tablespace), the size of large sorting queries and operations should be taken into consideration when sizing the temporary tablespace.

The temporary tablespace, usually named TEMP, is fragmented by its nature. Temporary segments are constantly created, extended, and then dropped. It is therefore necessary to maximize the reusability of dropped extents. To accomplish this, choose an **initial** and **next** extent size of 1/20th to 1/50th of the size of the tablespace. The default settings for **initial** and **next** should be equal for this tablespace. Choose a **pctincrease** of 0; the result will be segments made up of identically sized extents. When these segments are dropped, the next temporary segment to be formed will be able to reuse the dropped extents.

You can specify a tablespace as a "temporary" tablespace. A "temporary" tablespace cannot be used to hold any permanent segments, only temporary segments created during queries. The first sort to use the temporary tablespace allocates a temporary segment within the temporary tablespace; when the query completes, the space used by the temporary segment is not dropped. Instead, the space used by the temporary segment is available for use by other queries; this allows the sorting operation to avoid the costs of allocating and releasing space for temporary segments. If your application frequently uses temporary segments for sorting operations, the sorting process should perform better if a dedicated temporary tablespace is used.

To dedicate a tablespace for temporary segments, specify the **temporary** clause of the **create tablespace** or **alter tablespace** command, as shown in the following listing:

```
alter tablespace TEMP temporary;
```

If there are any permanent segments (tables or indexes, for example) stored in TEMP, then the command shown in the preceding listing will fail.

To enable the TEMP tablespace to store permanent (i.e., nontemporary) objects, use the **permanent** clause of the **create tablespace** or **alter tablespace** command, as shown in the following listing:

```
alter tablespace TEMP permanent;
```

The Content column in the DBA_TABLESPACES data dictionary view displays the status of the tablespace as either 'TEMPORARY' or 'PERMANENT'.

Free Space

A *free extent* in a tablespace is a collection of contiguous free blocks in the tablespace. A tablespace may contain multiple data extents and one or more free extents (see Figure 4-12a). When a segment is dropped, its extents are deallocated and marked as free. However, these free extents are not always recombined with neighboring free extents; the barriers between these free extents may be maintained (see Figure 4-12b). The SMON background process periodically coalesces neighboring free extents (see Figure 4-12c)—provided the default **pctincrease** for the tablespace is nonzero.

When servicing a space request, the database will not merge contiguous free extents unless there is no alternative; thus the large free extent at the

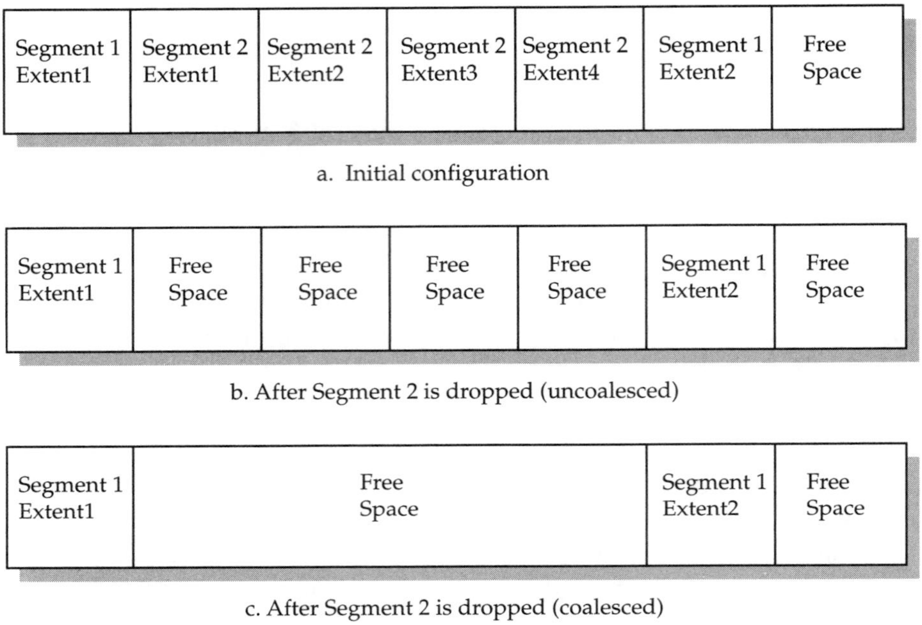

Segment 1 Extent1	Segment 2 Extent1	Segment 2 Extent2	Segment 2 Extent3	Segment 2 Extent4	Segment 1 Extent2	Free Space

a. Initial configuration

Segment 1 Extent1	Free Space	Free Space	Free Space	Free Space	Segment 1 Extent2	Free Space

b. After Segment 2 is dropped (uncoalesced)

Segment 1 Extent1	Free Space	Segment 1 Extent2	Free Space

c. After Segment 2 is dropped (coalesced)

FIGURE 4-12. *Free extent management in ORACLE*

rear of the tablespace tends to be used while the smaller free extents toward the front of the tablespace are relatively unused, becoming "speed bumps" in the tablespace because they are not, by themselves, of adequate size to be of use. As this usage pattern progresses, the database thus drifts further and further from its ideal space allocation.

If your tablespace has a default **pctincrease** value of 0, then the space coalesce will not happen automatically. However, you can force the database to recombine the contiguous free extents, thus emulating the SMON functionality. This will increase the likelihood of the free extents near the front of the file being reused, thus preserving the free space near the rear of the tablespace file. As a result, new requests for extents are more likely to meet with success.

To force the tablespace to coalesce its free space, use the **coalesce** clause of the **alter tablespace** clause, as shown in the following listing.

```
alter tablespace DATA coalesce;
```

The preceding command will force the neighboring free extents in the DATA tablespace to be coalesced into larger free extents. The **alter tablespace** command will not coalesce free extents that are separated by data extents.

In an ideal database, all objects are created at their appropriate size (in one extent if possible), and all free space is always stored together, a resource pool waiting to be used. In reality, the image shown in the bottom half of Figure 4-12 is often encountered: fragmented tables, fragmented free space, and free space that is separated from other free space by data extents. Resolutions to these fragmentation issues are described in Chapter 8. Monitoring scripts to determine the severity of these conditions are given in Chapter 6.

Resizing Datafiles in ORACLE7.2 and Above

As of ORACLE7.2, existing datafiles can be resized via the **alter database** and **alter tablespace** commands. You can specify values for storage extension parameters for each datafile in a database; ORACLE will use those values when automatically extending the datafile. Datafiles can also be extended manually, and can be resized down (to a smaller size) manually as well.

To manually extend a datafile, use the **alter database** command, as shown in the following example:

```
alter database
datafile '/db05/oracle/CC1/data01.dbf' resize 200M;
```

After the **alter database** command shown in the last example is executed, the specified file will be resized to 200MB in size. If the file was already more than 200MB in size, it will decrease in size to 200MB.

The **alter tablespace** command can also be used to manually resize datafiles. When using the **alter tablespace** command to resize datafiles, you must specify the name of the tablespace to which the datafile belongs. An example of this functionality is shown in the following example:

```
alter tablespace DATA
datafile '/db05/oracle/CC1/data01.dbf' resize 200M;
```

After the **alter tablespace** command shown in the last example is executed, the datafile listed will be resized to 200MB.

Automating Datafile Extensions

When creating datafiles, you can specify parameters that will allow ORACLE to automatically extend your datafiles. The datafiles could then be automatically extended whenever their current allocated length is exceeded. You can specify three sizing parameters for each datafile:

autoextend	A flag, set to ON or OFF to indicate if the file should be allowed to automatically extend. If set to OFF, the other sizing parameters will be set to zero.
next *size*	The size, in bytes, of the area of disk space to allocate to the datafile when more space is required. You can qualify the *size* value with 'K' and 'M' for kilobytes and megabytes, respectively.
maxsize *size*	The maximum size, in bytes, to which the datafile should be allowed to extend. You can qualify the *size* value with 'K' and 'M' for kilobytes and megabytes, respectively.

If no **maxsize** value is specified, then the maximum size of the datafile will be limited only by the available space on the file's disk.

The **autoextend**, **next**, and **maxsize** parameters can be specified for a datafile via the **create database**, **create tablespace**, and **alter tablespace** commands. In the following example, the **create tablespace** command is used to create a datafile that will automatically extend as needed:

```
create tablespace DATA
datafile '/db05/oracle/CC1/data01.dbf' size 200M
autoextend ON
next 10M
maxsize 250M;
```

The tablespace created in this example will have a single datafile with an initial size of 200MB. When that datafile fills, and the objects within it require additional space, the datafile will extend itself by 10MB. The extension process will continue as needed until the file has reached 250MB in size, at which point the file will have reached its maximum size.

You cannot modify an existing datafile in a tablespace. You can add a new datafile, via the **alter tablespace** command, to enable **autoextend** capabilities for the tablespace. The command in the following listing adds a new datafile to the DATA tablespace, specifying **autoextend on** and **maxsize unlimited**:

```
alter tablespace DATA
add datafile '/db05/oracle/CC1/data02.dbf'
size 50M
autoextend ON
maxsize unlimited;
```

Another way of making the same change is shown in the following example. The **alter database** command can be used to modify the storage values for datafiles, as shown here:

```
alter database
datafile '/db05/oracle/CC1/data01.dbf'
autoextend ON
maxsize unlimited;
```

How to Move Database Files

Once a file has been created in a database, it may be necessary to move it in order to better manage its size or I/O requirements. In the following sections you'll see the procedures for moving datafiles, online redo log files, and control files. In all of the procedures, operating system commands are used to move the files; the ORACLE commands serve primarily to reset the pointers to those files.

Moving Datafiles

There are two methods for moving datafiles: via the **alter database** command and via the **alter tablespace** command. The **alter tablespace** method only applies to datafiles whose tablespaces do not include SYSTEM, rollback segments, or temporary segments. The **alter database** method will work for all datafiles.

The alter database Method

When using the **alter database** method to move datafiles, the datafile is moved after the instance has been shut down. The steps involved, detailed in the following sections, are as follows:

1. Shut down the instance, using Server Manager.

2. Use operating system commands to move the datafile.

3. Mount the database and use **alter database** to rename the file within the database.

4. Start the instance, using Server Manager.

Step 1. Shut down the instance, using Server Manager.

```
> svrmgrl
SVRMGR> connect internal;
SVRMGR> shutdown;
SVRMGR> exit;
```

Step 2. Use operating system commands to move the datafile.

Use an operating system command to move the datafile. In UNIX, the **mv** command moves files to new locations. The following example shows the 'data01.dbf' file being moved from the device named '/db01' to one named '/db02':

```
> mv /db01/oracle/CC1/data01.dbf /db02/oracle/CC1
```

The filename must fully specify a filename using the conventions of your operating system.

Step 3. Mount the database and use alter database to rename the file within the database.

In the following example, the CC1 instance is started and the 'data01.dbf' datafile moved in Step 2 is renamed within the database. The database will then be able to find that file during instance startup. The **alter database** command shown here does not rename the file; the file must have already been renamed or moved.

```
> svrmgrl
SVRMGR> connect internal;
SVRMGR> startup mount CC1;
SVRMGR> alter database rename file
    2> '/db01/oracle/CC1/data01.dbf' to
    3> '/db02/oracle/CC1/data01.dbf';
```

Do not disconnect after this step is complete; stay logged in to the database and proceed to Step 4.

When the **alter database** command is executed, ORACLE will check to see if the name you are naming the file 'to' exists. If this step fails, check the accuracy of the destination filename.

Step 4. Start the instance.

Now that the database knows how to find the moved file, the instance can start.

```
SVRMGR> alter database open;
```

The instance will now be opened, using the new location for the datafile that was moved.

The alter tablespace Method

When using the **alter tablespace** method to move datafiles, the datafile is moved while the instance is still running. The steps involved, detailed in the following sections, are as follows:

1. Take the tablespace offline.

2. Use operating system commands to move the file.

3. Use the **alter tablespace** command to rename the file within the database.

4. Bring the tablespace back online.

NOTE
This method can only be used for non-SYSTEM tablespaces. It cannot be used for tablespaces that contain active rollback segments or temporary segments.

Step 1. Take the tablespace offline.

Use the **alter tablespace** command within Server Manager to put the tablespace into **offline** state, as shown in the following example. This command is executed while the instance is running. It cannot be used for the SYSTEM tablespace or for tablespaces containing active rollback segments or temporary segments.

```
> svrmgrl
SVRMGR> connect internal;
SVRMGR> alter tablespace DATA offline;
SVRMGR> exit;
```

Step 2. Use operating system commands to move the file.

Use an operating system command to move the datafile. In UNIX, the **mv** command moves files to new locations. The following example shows the 'data01.dbf' file being moved from the device named '/db01' to one named '/db02':

```
> mv /db01/oracle/CC1/data01.dbf /db02/oracle/CC1
```

The filename must fully specify a filename using the conventions of your operating system.

Step 3. Use the alter tablespace command to rename the file within the database.

In the following example, the 'data01.dbf' datafile moved in Step 2 is renamed within the database. The database will then be able to access that file. The **alter tablespace** command shown here does not rename the file; the file must have already been renamed or moved.

```
> svrmgrl
SVRMGR> connect internal;
SVRMGR> alter tablespace DATA rename datafile
     2> '/db01/oracle/CC1/data01.dbf' to
     3> '/db02/oracle/CC1/data01.dbf';
```

Do not disconnect after this step is complete; stay logged in to the database and proceed to Step 4.

When the **alter tablespace** command is executed, ORACLE will check to see if the name you are naming the file 'to' exists. If this step fails, check the accuracy of the destination filename.

Step 4. Bring the tablespace back online.

Use the **alter tablespace** command to bring the tablespace back online from within Server Manager.

```
SVRMGR> alter tablespace DATA online;
```

The DATA tablespace will then be brought back online, using the new location for the datafile.

Moving Online Redo Log Files

Online redo log files can be moved while the database is shut down, and renamed within the database via the **alter database** command. The procedures for moving online redo log files are very similar to those used to move datafiles via the **alter database** command.

First, the database is shut down and the online redo log file is moved. The database is then mounted and the **alter database** command is used to tell the database the new location of the online redo log file. The instance can then be opened, using the online redo log file in its new location.

Step 1. Shut down the instance.

```
> svrmgrl
SVRMGR> connect internal;
SVRMGR> shutdown;
SVRMGR> exit;
```

Step 2. Move the online redo log file.

Use an operating system command to move the file. In UNIX, the **mv** command moves files to new locations. The following example shows the 'redo01CC1.dbf' file being moved from the device named '/db05' to one named '/db02':

```
> mv /db05/oracle/CC1/redo01CC1.dbf /db02/oracle/CC1
```

The filename must fully specify a filename using the conventions of your operating system.

Step 3. Mount the database and use the alter database to rename the file within the database.

In the following example, the CC1 instance is started and the 'redo01CC1.dbf' file moved in Step 2 is renamed within the database. The database will then be able to find that file during instance startup. The **alter database** command shown here does not rename the file; the file must have already been renamed or moved.

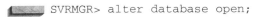

```
> svrmgrl
SVRMGR> connect internal;
SVRMGR> startup mount CC1;
SVRMGR> alter database rename file
    2> '/db05/oracle/CC1/redo01CC1.dbf' to
    3> '/db02/oracle/CC1/redo01CC1.dbf';
```

Do not disconnect after this step is complete; stay logged in to the database and proceed to Step 4.

When the **alter database** command is executed, ORACLE will check to see if the name you are naming the file 'to' exists. If this step fails, check the accuracy of the destination filename.

Step 4. Start the instance.

Now that the database knows how to find the moved file, the instance can start.

```
SVRMGR> alter database open;
```

The instance will now be opened, using the new location for the online redo log file that was moved.

Moving Control Files

The location of control files is specified in the init.ora or config.ora file for the instance; the config.ora file usually maintains this information. To move a control file, you must shut down the instance, move the file, edit the config.ora file, and then restart the instance.

Step 1. Shut down the instance.

```
> svrmgrl
SVRMGR> connect internal;
SVRMGR> shutdown;
SVRMGR> exit;
```

Step 2. Move the control file.

Use an operating system command to move the file. In UNIX, the **mv** command moves files to new locations. The following example shows the 'ctrl1CC1.ctl' file being moved from the device named '/db05' to one named '/db02':

```
> mv /db05/oracle/CC1/ctrl1CC1.ctl /db02/oracle/CC1
```

The filename must fully specify a filename using the conventions of your operating system.

Step 3. Edit the config.ora file.

The config.ora file for an instance is usually located in the /pfile subdirectory under the instance directory (see Figure 4-9). In previous versions of ORACLE, the instance configuration files were found in the /dbs subdirectory under the ORACLE software home directory. The name of the configuration file typically includes the name of the instance—for the CC1 instance, the config.ora file may be named configCC1.ora. The exact name and location of the config.ora file is specified in the init.ora file for the instance (usually located in the same directory as the config.ora file, with the same naming convention applied).

Within the config.ora file, there will be an entry for the "control_files" parameter; an example is shown in the following listing:

```
control_files     = (/db01/oracle/CC1/ctrl1CC1.ctl,
                      /db03/oracle/CC1/ctrl1CC1.ctl,
                      /db05/oracle/CC1/ctrl1CC1.ctl)
```

Edit this entry to reflect the change to the file you moved in Step 2:

```
control_files     = (/db01/oracle/CC1/ctrl1CC1.ctl,
                      /db03/oracle/CC1/ctrl1CC1.ctl,
                      /db02/oracle/CC1/ctrl1CC1.ctl)
```

Step 4. Start the instance.

```
> svrmgrl
SVRMGR> connect internal;
SVRMGR> startup;
SVRMGR> exit;
```

The instance will then be started, using the control file in its new location.

How to Deallocate Space in Oracle7.2 and Oracle7.3

As of ORACLE7.2, you can reclaim unused space from existing datafiles. As of ORACLE7.3, you can reclaim space from tables, indexes, and clusters. In the following sections, you'll see examples of datafiles, tables, and indexes that are "shrunk" to reclaim previously allocated space.

Shrinking Datafiles

You can use the **alter database** command to reclaim unused space datafiles. You cannot resize a datafile if the space you are trying to reclaim is currently allocated to a database object.

For example, if the datafile is 100MB in size, and 70MB of the datafile is currently in use, then you will need to leave at least 70MB in the datafile. The **resize** clause of the **alter database** command is used to reclaim the space, as shown in the following example:

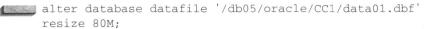
```
alter database datafile '/db05/oracle/CC1/data01.dbf'
resize 80M;
```

As shown in the listing, you specify the name of the file to be shrunk and its new size. If there are no database objects beyond the first 80MB of the specified datafile, the datafile will be shrunk to 80MB.

If space is used within the datafile beyond the first 80MB, then an error will be returned. As shown in the following listing, the error will show the amount of space that is used within the datafile beyond the specified **resize** value:

```
alter database datafile '/db05/oracle/CC1/data01.dbf'
resize 80M;
*
ERROR at line 1:
ORA-03297: file contains 507 blocks of data beyond
requested RESIZE value
```

If the database block size is 4K, then 507 database blocks is equivalent to 1.98MB. If you increase the **resize** value specified to 82MB, then the datafile can be resized.

To minimize the chances of encountering an error during free space reclamation from datafiles, you can "map" the free space within a datafile. See the "Measuring Fragmentation" section of Chapter 8 for a script that maps the free and used space within a tablespace and datafile. If your free space is fragmented, ORACLE may not be able to reclaim it all during a datafile resize operation.

Shrinking Tables, Clusters, and Indexes

When ORACLE writes data to a segment, it updates the *high-water mark* for the segment. The high-water mark is the highest block number in which data has been stored in the segment. If you **insert** thousands of rows in the table, the high-water mark will be incremented; if you **delete** the records, the high-water mark will *not* decrease. The high-water mark for a segment is only reset when you issue a **truncate** command or the segment is dropped and recreated.

As of ORACLE7.3, unused space above the high-water mark in a segment can be reclaimed. If you have overestimated the storage requirements for an object, or have used a nonzero **pctincrease** setting (see Table 4-4), then you may wish to reclaim space that was allocated unnecessarily. You can reclaim the space from the segment without dropping and recreating it—with the limitation that you can only reclaim the space above the high-water mark for the table.

Before you can reclaim space from a table, you should therefore determine the high-water mark for the table. ORACLE provides a package named DBMS_SPACE that you can use to determine how much, if any, space can be reclaimed from a segment. In the following listing, the UNUSED_SPACE procedure within the DBMS_SPACE package is used to determine the space usage of the table named SPACES owned by the user OPS$CC1:

```
declare
        VAR1 number;
        VAR2 number;
        VAR3 number;
        VAR4 number;
        VAR5 number;
        VAR6 number;
        VAR7 number;
begin
dbms_space.unused_space('OPS$CC1','SPACES','TABLE',
                        VAR1,VAR2,VAR3,VAR4,VAR5,VAR6,VAR7);
    dbms_output.put_line('OBJECT_NAME        = SPACES');
    dbms_output.put_line('--------------------------');
    dbms_output.put_line('TOTAL_BLOCKS       = '||VAR1);
    dbms_output.put_line('TOTAL_BYTES        = '||VAR2);
    dbms_output.put_line('UNUSED_BLOCKS      = '||VAR3);
    dbms_output.put_line('UNUSED_BYTES       = '||VAR4);
    dbms_output.put_line('LAST_USED_EXTENT_FILE_ID  = '||VAR5);
    dbms_output.put_line('LAST_USED_EXTENT_BLOCK_ID = '||VAR6);
    dbms_output.put_line('LAST_USED_BLOCK    = '||VAR7);
end;
/
```

The high-water mark of the table (in bytes) is the difference between the TOTAL_BYTES value and the UNUSED_BYTES value returned by this procedure call. The UNUSED_BLOCKS value represents the number of blocks above the high-water mark; the TOTAL_BLOCKS value reflects the total number of blocks allocated to the table.

If you want to reclaim space from the table, and its UNUSED_BLOCKS value is nonzero, then you can use the **alter table** command to reclaim the space above the high-water mark. For example, assume that the TOTAL_BLOCKS value is 200 and the UNUSED_BLOCKS value is 100, with a database block size of 4K. Then, 100 blocks—400K—could be reclaimed.

If you want to leave 20 blocks within the table as unused space above the high-water mark, you can alter the table, specifying that the database keep 20 blocks—80K.

To reclaim space from a table, use the **alter table** command, as shown in the following listing. The **keep** parameter specifies the amount of free space to keep.

```
alter table SPACES deallocate unused keep 80K;
```

If you had not specified the **keep** clause, the **minextents** and **initial** storage values for the table would have been preserved. If **keep** is used, you can eliminate free space from any extent—even from the initial extent if there is no data in any other extent!

You can deallocate space from clusters via the **deallocate unused** clause of the **alter cluster** command. After deallocating space from a segment, you should execute the DBMS_SPACE procedure again to see the new values for the total and unused blocks allocated to the segment.

You can deallocate space from indexes via the **deallocate unused** clause of the **alter index** command. However, there is another option for indexes that allows you even greater flexibility when manipulating index space usage—**alter index rebuild**, as described in the next section.

How to Rebuild Indexes

Prior to ORACLE7.3, the only way to rebuild an index was to drop the index and recreate it completely. As of ORACLE7.3, you can use the **alter index rebuild** command to rapidly change the **storage** and **tablespace** parameters for an existing index—without having to drop the original index.

When you use the **alter index rebuild** command, the existing index is used as the data source for the new index (instead of using the table as the data source), improving performance of index creation). During the index re-creation, you can change the index's **storage** and **tablespace** parameters.

In the following example, the IU_SPACES$DB_TS_CD index is rebuilt via the **alter index rebuild** command. Its **storage** parameters are changed to use an initial extent size of 10MB and a next extent size of 5MB in the INDX_1 tablespace.

```
alter index IU_SPACES$DB_TS_CD rebuild
storage (initial 10M next 5M pctincrease 0)
tablespace INDX_1;
```

While the new IU_SPACES$DB_TS_CD index is being built, it will exist simultaneously with the old index in the database. Therefore, there must be enough space available to store both the old index and the new index in the database in order to use **alter index rebuild**. After the command has completed and the new index is available, the old index will be dropped automatically and the space will be reclaimed—but the space has to be available during the command execution or the new index creation will fail.

You can use the **alter index rebuild** command to quickly move indexes to different tablespaces. Index rebuilds allow you to set up a simple maintenance schedule for the most used indexes in your database. If the records in a table are frequently **delete**d and **insert**ed, the space used by the indexes on the table will continue to grow, even if the overall number of records remains unchanged. As records are **delete**d from the index, the space used by the records' index entries is not available for reuse. Therefore, if the table is volatile, then your indexes may grow even if there is no growth in the number of records—simply due to the increase in unavailable space within the index.

To reclaim the space previously used by since-**delete**d records, you can use the **alter index rebuild** command. Schedule a batch job to run periodically to rebuild the indexes on your most active tables. Run the batch job at off-hours, to avoid scheduling conflicts with users. If you adhere to a maintenance schedule for your indexes, you will be able to reclaim the unusable space quickly. During each **alter index rebuild** command, specify both the **tablespace** and **storage** parameters for your index.

For information on rebuilding index partitions, see Chapter 12.

Physically Fit

In your databases, the file allocation must be planned (using I/O weightings) and the weightings must be verified once the system goes into production. The file layout can then be modified to better balance the I/O requirements of the files. The result will be a database that achieves its performance goals without sacrificing recoverability, and its recoverability goals without sacrificing performance.

Each facet of the database—tables, indexes, rollback segments, and temporary segments—must be sized correctly as well. Correct sizing requires knowing the way in which the data is to be entered, how it is to be stored, and the processes that will be performed on it once it gets there. The costs of planning the storage parameters are minimal when compared to the costs of manipulating the system once it has been released to production. Postproduction tuning should be a final, minor step in the database physical design planning process.

PART
II

Database
Management

CHAPTER
5

Managing the
Development Process

ontrolling application developers is like herding cats; it's not a simple process. Since developers can't be controlled, the best way to manage the development process is for DBAs to become an integral part of it. In this chapter, you will see the activities involved in migrating applications into databases and the technical details needed for implementation. These details will include system role specifications and sizing formulas for database objects.

This chapter focuses on controlling the activities that create objects in the database at various stages. These activities should follow the database planning activities that were described in Chapter 3 and Chapter 4. Chapter 6 and Chapter 8 address the monitoring and tuning activities that follow the database creation.

Implementing an application in a database by merely running a series of **create table** commands fails to integrate the creation process with the other major areas (planning, monitoring, and tuning). The DBA must be involved in the application development process in order to correctly structure the database that will support the end product. The methods described in this chapter will also provide important information for structuring the database monitoring and tuning efforts.

The Three Critical Elements of Success

The life cycle of a database is defined by the four actions referred to previously: planning, creating, monitoring, and tuning. The elements of a successful implementation of this cycle can be identified as belonging to three key categories: *cultural processes, management processes,* and *technology*.

Managing the implementation efforts of database developers requires action on all three points:

1. Cultural: The corporate culture and the development team must support the DBA's involvement in this level of activity.

2. Management: The developers' adherence to a life cycle methodology must be enforceable.

3. Technology: The developers and DBAs must define mechanisms for making sure the appropriate level of involvement and attention to detail is taking place.

Attempting to implement a development life cycle methodology without corporate buy-in or without technology that allows for the tracking of deliverables will yield no long-term benefit.

Cultural Processes

In order to break down the traditional barrier between DBAs and developers, the relationship between them must be formalized. The revised nature of the relationship must be accepted by all of the parties involved. This can only be accomplished if the groups being brought together feel that the new team's structure adds value to the development process. There must be a corporate commitment to the team structure to overcome the initial turf wars that may otherwise disrupt the process from the start.

A joint DBA/developer team adds value by

- Building applications that are easier to maintain

- Building applications that are properly sized and organized, and thus require no downtime for reorganizations

- Creating appropriate indexes to maximize performance

- Building into each application an understanding of the interface needs of outside applications

- Identifying technical problems earlier in the development process

- Allowing the DBA, who will eventually provide much of the application's support, to accept partial ownership of the application during its development

Difficult to maintain, fragmented, slow, and isolated database applications cost the organization in terms of downtime, tuning time, and user frustration. These costs can be avoided by entering into true team relationships between developers and DBAs. The methodology must clearly define the roles and responsibilities within these relationships. It must be accepted by all levels within the personnel groups responsible for applications development. This will greatly ease the need for third-party enforcement of the methodology.

Management Processes

In order to properly manage development efforts, the methodology must not only spell out the relationships between the different functional areas, but must also clearly define the deliverables required in each phase of application development. For example, when does an application move out of Development and into Test, or from Test to Production? Who decides?

The answer is, the methodology decides. If the deliverables for the Development section are complete, reviewed, and approved, then the application can be moved into the Test environment, under whose constraints the developers must then work.

Defining the Environment

Most application environments are divided into two to five areas. They are *Development*, *System Test*, *Acceptance Test*, *Stress Test*, and *Production*. For the purposes of this discussion, the three Test areas will be combined. The exact number of areas maintained is methodology-specific.

Consider each of the areas. The methodology needs to specify what the finished product will be from each area, and what completing that section will provide to subsequent areas. Once this has been defined, the database needs for the different areas can be deduced.

In Development, for instance, users may have free reign to make table changes, test new ideas, and create new objects. An integrated CASE (computer-aided systems engineering) tool such as Designer/2000 should be used to maintain a constantly synchronized logical model. The CASE repository should be used to generate the first set of database objects in each environment; the developers should be responsible for maintaining the CASE dictionary thereafter.

Once the system enters the Test phase, its final configuration should be within sight. At this point, the table volumes, user accounts, and performance needs should be identified. These will allow the DBA to create a proper database for the application on the first try, and to monitor for performance problems that are outside of the defined acceptable bounds.

In Production, developers are locked out. From the database's perspective, they are just another set of users. All changes to database objects in the Production database should have first passed through the Test environment. Any modifications to the system's needs should have been clearly defined in Test.

In order to maintain the proper level of user system-level privileges, developer accounts must be configured differently for each area. The next section will describe the proper system role definitions for developers given the Development/Test/Production areas previously described.

Role Definitions

Of the system-level roles provided by ORACLE, three roles (CONNECT, RESOURCE, and DBA) apply to the development environment (the others are related to the administration of the database, and are described in Chapter 9). You can create your own system-level roles to define system privileges beyond CONNECT, RESOURCE, and DBA, but these may be more difficult to use and maintain than the system-provided roles. You can grant roles to the users and developers depending on the system privileges they need in their environment.

CONNECT

The CONNECT role gives users privileges beyond just creating sessions in the database. In addition to the CREATE SESSION system privilege, the CONNECT role gives users the following system privileges: ALTER SESSION, CREATE CLUSTER, CREATE DATABASE LINK, CREATE SEQUENCE, CREATE SYNONYM, CREATE TABLE, and CREATE VIEW. That's far more than just connecting to the database. However, the users do not have the ability to create tables or clusters (objects that use space in the database) unless you grant them a quota on a tablespace. See Chapter 9 for details on the granting of space quotas.

In general, the CONNECT role will be sufficient for your end users in all environments. Depending on the needs of your developers, it may be sufficient for them as well. For example, if your developers do not need to create objects such as procedures, packages, triggers, and abstract datatypes, then the CONNECT role serves their needs.

If you wish to limit the system privileges of your application users, you can create your own role—APPLICATION_USER—which has just the CREATE SESSION privilege:

```
create role APPLICATION_USER;
grant CREATE SESSION to APPLICATION_USER;
grant APPLICATION_USER to username;
```

RESOURCE

The RESOURCE role has the following system privileges: CREATE CLUSTER, CREATE INDEX, CREATE PROCEDURE, CREATE SEQUENCE, CREATE TABLE, CREATE TRIGGER, and CREATE TYPE. As with the CONNECT role, users who have the RESOURCE role do not have the ability to create tables, indexes, and clusters unless you first grant them a space quota in a tablespace. You should grant the RESOURCE role to developers who will be creating PL/SQL objects such as procedures and triggers.

If you wish to restrict developers' privileges, then you can create your own role and grant system level privileges to it. For example, you may want to restrict developers' ability to create abstract datatypes. If that is the case, then you could create a system-level role and grant it all of the system privileges that constitute RESOURCE except for the CREATE TYPE privilege. In general, you should only grant developers the RESOURCE role in Development; in Test and Production, the CONNECT role should be sufficient.

DBA

The DBA role has all system privileges **with admin option**, which means that the DBA can grant the system privileges to any other user. You should not grant the DBA role to application developers or users in any Development, Test, or Production database. If you grant developers the DBA role in Development, they may code their application with the assumption that they will have the same system privileges when the application is released into the Production environment. If you cannot restrict access to DBA-privileged accounts, then you cannot guarantee the security of the data in your database—and that is one of the key job functions of the DBA.

In Test and Production

The appropriate role designations for the Test environment depend on how that environment is to be used. If it is to be used as a true Acceptance Test region, mirroring the eventual production database, then its roles should be assigned to mirror the Production roles. If, however, developers will be allowed to make modifications to the Test database, then they will require access to an account that has the RESOURCE role.

The tables and other database objects used by the application are typically owned by a single account in Test and Production. If the change must be performed within the account that owns the application schema (for example, the creation of a database link), then the DBA can temporarily log in to that account and perform the change. In general, developers should not have the RESOURCE role in a Test environment. If a change is to be made to the system, then the change should be made first in Development and then migrated to Test.

Deliverables

How do you know if the methodology is being followed? Doing so requires establishing a list of items called *deliverables* that must be completed during the application development. The methodology must clearly define, both in format and in level of detail, the required deliverables for each stage of the life cycle. These should include specifications for each of the following items:

- Entity Relationship diagram
- Physical Database diagram
- Space requirements
- Tuning goals
- Data requirements
- Execution plans
- Acceptance test procedures

In the following sections, you will see descriptions of each of these items.

Entity Relationship Diagram

The *Entity Relationship (E-R) diagram* illustrates the relationships that have been identified among the entities that make up the application. E-R diagrams are critical for providing an understanding of the goals of the system. They also help to identify interface points with other applications, and to ensure consistency in definitions across the enterprise. Modeling conventions for E-R diagrams are described in Chapter 1.

Physical Database Diagram

A *Physical Database diagram* shows the physical tables generated from the entities and the columns generated from the defined attributes in the logical model. A physical database diagramming tool is usually capable of generating the DDL necessary to create the application's objects. Modeling conventions for physical database diagrams are described in Chapter 1.

Space Requirements

The space requirements deliverable should show the initial space requirements for each database table and index. The calculations necessary to determine the proper size for tables, clusters, and indexes are shown in the "Sizing Database Objects" section later in this chapter.

Tuning Goals

You must identify the performance goals of a system *before* it goes into production. The role of expectation in perception cannot be overemphasized. If the users have an expectation that the system will be at least as fast as an existing system, then anything less will be unacceptable. The estimated response time for each of the most-used components of the application must be defined and approved.

It is important during this process to establish two sets of goals: reasonable goals and "stretch" goals. *Stretch goals* represent the results of concentrated efforts to go beyond the hardware and software constraints that limit the system's performance. Maintaining two sets of performance goals helps to focus efforts on those goals that are truly mission-critical versus those that are beyond the scope of the core system deliverables.

Security Requirements

The development team must specify the account structure that the application will use. This should include the ownership of all objects in the application and the manner in which privileges will be granted. All roles and privileges must be clearly defined. The deliverables from this section will be used to generate the account and privilege structure of the production application.

Depending on the application, it may be necessary to specify the account usage for batch accounts separately from that of online accounts. This may occur in situations in which the batch accounts will use the database's autologin features, while the online users have to manually sign in.

Like the space requirements deliverable, this is an area in which the DBA's involvement is critical. The DBA should be able to design an implementation that meets the application's needs while fitting in with the enterprise database security plan.

Data Requirements

The methods for data entry and retrieval must be clearly defined. They will need to be tested and verified while the application is in the Test environment. Any special data archiving requirements of the application must also be documented, since they will be application-specific.

You must also describe the backup and recovery requirements for the application. These requirements can then be compared to the site database backup plans (see Chapter 10 for guidelines). Any database recovery requirements that go beyond the site's standard will require modifying the site's backup standard or adding a module to accommodate the application's needs.

Execution Plans

Execution plans are the steps that the database will go through while executing queries. They are generated via the **explain plan** statement, which is described in Chapter 8. Recording the execution plans for the most important queries against the database will aid in planning the index usage and tuning goals for the application. Generating them prior to production implementation will simplify tuning efforts and identify potential performance problems before the application is released. This will also facilitate the process of performing code reviews of the application.

Acceptance Test Procedures

The developers and users should very clearly define what functionality and performance goals must be achieved before the application can be migrated to Production. These goals will form the foundation of the test procedures that will be executed against the application while it is in the Test environment.

The procedures should also describe how to deal with unmet goals. They should very clearly list the functional goals that must be met before the system can move forward. A second list of noncritical functional goals should also be provided. This separation of functional capabilities will aid in both resolving scheduling conflicts and structuring appropriate tests.

Sizing Database Objects

Choosing the proper space allocation for database objects is critical. Developers should begin estimating space requirements before the first database objects are created. Afterwards, the space requirements can be refined based on the actual usage statistics. In the following sections, you will see the space requirement calculations for tables, indexes, and clusters. The proper setting of **pctfree** is also discussed.

A Note About Approximations

In the formulas provided by ORACLE, there are a number of extremely detailed calculations you must perform in order to size your tables and indexes. The level of detail required in those calculations is unnecessary, since the calculations conclude with the advice to add 10 to 20 percent to the calculated space requirements.

Why make a detailed calculation if you know ahead of time that it will wrong by at least 10 percent?

The error in the space estimation is caused by the way ORACLE manages space after the objects have been created. As you **insert**, **update**, and **delete** rows, ORACLE manages the space inside the database blocks. Because of the manner in which ORACLE manages the space, your space usage will frequently be less than optimal. As a result, your space needs will increase—in some cases they may double.

Given the dynamic nature of the space management in ORACLE, the precise space calculations provided are only valid if you are loading static data into static tables. Since that represents a small percentage of the tables whose space usage is of a great concern, the calculations in this chapter approximate the space usage rather than carry out extremely detailed calculations. In all cases, the difference between the exact calculation and the approximation should be less than 5 percent—well within the bounds set by ORACLE.

Sizing Nonclustered Tables

In addition to showing the initial space requirements for a table, the space requirements deliverable should show the estimated yearly percentage increase in number of records for each table. If applicable, a maximum number of records should also be defined.

Once the table's column definitions and data volumes are known, its storage requirements can be determined. This is a process of educated guessing, since the true data volumes and row lengths will not be known until after the table is created. It is important that sample data be available at this point in order to make the results of these calculations as accurate as possible.

First, estimate the amount of space used by the block header; this is space that ORACLE will use to manage the data within the block. The size of the block header is approximately 90 bytes. If you use a 2K database block size, this leaves 1,958 bytes free; for a 4K block size, this leaves 4,006 bytes free.

```
2048 - 90 = 1958 bytes available.
```

Next, factor in the table's **pctfree** setting, and multiply that by the free space to determine how much space will be kept free for row updates.

If you use a **pctfree** value of 10, then multiply the available free space by 0.10, as shown in the following listing:

```
1958*(pctfree/100) = 1958*0.1 = 196 (rounded up)
```

Of the available free space, 196 bytes will be kept for row extensions. The available free space is the block free space minus the space kept by **pctfree**:

```
1958 - 196 = 1762 bytes available.
```

Of the 2,048 bytes in the block, 1,762 bytes are available to store rows (see Figure 5-1).

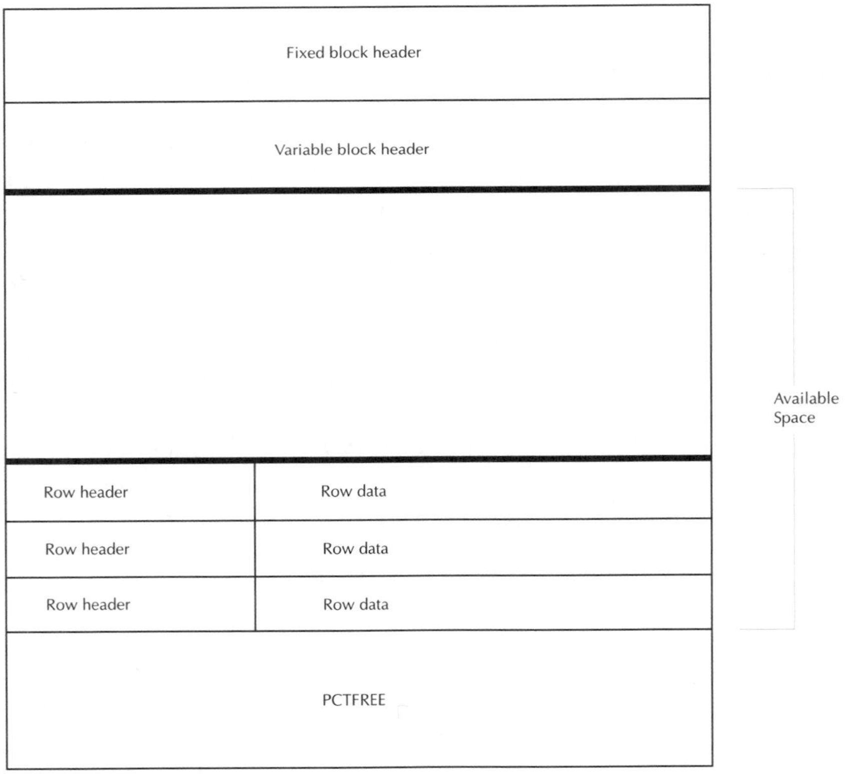

FIGURE 5-1. *Space allocation within blocks*

The next step is to calculate the space used per row. To estimate the space used per row, you need to estimate the *average row length*. The average row length is the total of the average length of each value in a row. If no data is available, then estimate the actual length of the values in a column. Do not use the full length of a column as its actual length unless the data will always completely fill the column.

For example, consider a table containing three columns, all of which are VARCHAR2(10). The average row length cannot exceed 30; its actual length depends on the data that will be stored there.

If the sample data is available, then the **VSIZE** function can be used to determine the actual space used by the data. Again, assume a table has three columns. To determine its average row length, perform the following query:

```
select AVG(NVL(VSIZE(Column1),0))+
       AVG(NVL(VSIZE(Column2),0))+
       AVG(NVL(VSIZE(Column3),0))    Avg_Row_Length
from TABLENAME;
```

In this example, the average length of each column is determined, and the averages are totaled to determine the average row length.

For example, in the sample three-column table, assume that the average row length is 24 bytes. To that total, add 1 byte for each column in the table, for a total of 27 bytes per row. If the table has columns that contain data that is more than 250 characters long, add an extra byte for each such column. Finally, add 3 bytes for the row header.

```
Space used per row = Avg_Row_Length
                   + 3
                   + Number of columns
                   + Number of long columns
```

For the example table, the space per row is

```
Space used per row = 24
                   +3
                   +3
                   +0
                 = 30 bytes per row.
```

Given 1,762 bytes available and 30 bytes per row, you can fit 58 rows in a block:

```
rows per block = TRUNC(1762 free bytes/30 bytes per row)
              = 58 rows per block
```

Since you can fit 58 rows per block, you can estimate the number of blocks needed as soon as you can estimate the number of rows you expect. As noted in the previous section, this is an approximation of the storage requirements of the table. As records in the table are manipulated, their space requirements will increase. The greater the number of **delete**s and **update**s that occur, the greater the amount of space required.

Determining the Proper pctfree

The proper **pctfree** value must be determined for each table. This value represents the percentage of *each data block* that is reserved as free space. This space is used when a row that has already been stored in that data block grows in length, either by updates of previously **NULL** fields or by updates of existing values to longer values.

There is no single value for **pctfree** that will be adequate for all tables in all databases. But since **pctfree** is tied to the way in which updates occur in an application, determining the adequacy of its setting is a straightforward process. The **pctfree** setting controls the number of records that are stored in a block in a table. To see if **pctfree** has been set correctly, first determine the number of rows in a block. You can use the **analyze** command to determine the number of rows per block in an existing table. In the following listing, the **compute statistics** clause of the **analyze** command is used to generate statistics for the table; you can then select those statistics from the data dictionary views:

```
analyze table TABLENAME compute statistics;
```

Once the table has been analyzed, query its record in the USER_TABLES view and record its Num_Rows and Blocks values. Dividing Num_Rows by Blocks yields the number of rows stored per block, as shown in the following query:

```
select Num_Rows,              /*number of rows*/
       Blocks,                /*number of blocks used*/
       Num_Rows/Blocks        /*number of rows per block*/
  from USER_TABLES
 where Table_Name='TABLENAME';
```

Once the number of rows per block is known, **update** records in the table in a manner that mimics its production usage. Once the **update**s are complete, check the number of rows per block by analyzing the table and rerunning these queries. If **pctfree** was not set high enough, then some of the rows may have been moved to new data blocks to accommodate their new lengths. If the value has not changed, then the **pctfree** value is adequate.

This **pctfree** value, though, may be too high, resulting in wasted space. The **analyze** command shown earlier also generates values for the Avg_Space column of the USER_TABLES view. This column shows the average number of bytes that are free in each data block. If this value is high after the **update** test, then the **pctfree** value can be decreased.

Determining the Proper pctused

The **pctused** parameter determines when a used block is readded to the list of blocks into which rows can be inserted. For example, consider a table that has a **pctfree** value of 20 and a **pctused** value of 50. When rows are inserted into the table, ORACLE will keep 20 percent of each block free (for use by later updates of the **insert**ed records). If you now begin to **delete** records from the block, ORACLE will not automatically reuse the freed space inside the blocks. New rows will not be **insert**ed into the block until the block's used space falls below its **pctused** percentage—50 percent.

The **pctused** parameter, by default, is set to 40. If your application features frequent deletions, and you use the default value for **pctused**, then you may have many blocks in your table that are only 40 percent used.

For best results, set **pctused** to be (95-**pctfree**). If your **pctfree** setting is 20 percent, then set your **pctused** parameter for 75 percent. That way, at least 75 percent of each block will always be used, while saving 20 percent of the block for **update**s and row extensions.

Sizing Indexes

The process of sizing indexes is very similar to the table sizing process described previously. There are several differences in the object sizing, since tables and indexes have differing structures. As with the table space estimates, the sizing calculations provided here are approximations.

Once an index's column definitions and data volumes are known, its space requirements can be determined. This is a process of educated guessing, since the true data volumes and row lengths will not be known until after the table is created. It is important that sample data be available at this point in order to make the results of these calculations as accurate as possible.

First, estimate the amount of space used by the block header; this is space that ORACLE will use to manage the data within the block. The size of the block header is approximately 161 bytes. If you use a 2K database block size, this leaves 1,887 bytes free; for a 4K block size, this leaves 3,935 bytes free.

```
2048 - 161 = 1887 bytes available.
```

Next, factor in the table's **pctfree** setting, and multiply that by the free space to determine how much space will be kept free for row updates.

If you use a **pctfree** value of 10, then multiply the available free space by 0.10, as shown in the following listing:

```
1887*(pctfree/100) = 1887*0.1 = 189 (rounded up)
```

Of the available free space, 189 bytes will be kept for row extensions. The available free space is the block free space minus the space kept by **pctfree**.

```
1887 - 189 = 1698 bytes available.
```

Of the 2,048 bytes in the block, 1,698 bytes are available to store index entries.

The next step is to calculate the space used per row. To estimate the space used per row, you need to estimate the *average row length of the columns in the index*. For tables, you calculate the average row length of all columns; for indexes, you only need to be concerned about the indexed columns. The average row length is the total of the average length of each value in the indexed columns. If no data is available, then estimate the actual length of the values. Do not use the full length of a column as its actual length unless the data will always completely fill the column.

For example, consider an index containing two columns, both of which are VARCHAR2(10). The average indexed row length cannot exceed 20; its actual length depends on the data that will be stored there.

If the sample data is available, then the **VSIZE** function can be used to determine the actual space used by the data. Again, assume an index has two columns. To determine its average row length, perform the following query:

```
select AVG(NVL(VSIZE(Column1),0))+
       AVG(NVL(VSIZE(Column2),0))    Avg_Row_Length
from TABLENAME;
```

In this example, the average length of each column is determined and the averages are totaled to determine the average row length.

For example, in the sample two-column index, assume that the average row length for the indexed columns is 16 bytes. To that total, add 1 byte for each column in the index for a total of 18 bytes per row. If the index has columns that contain data that is more than 127 characters long, add an extra byte for each such column. Finally, add 8 bytes for the index entry header.

```
Space used per row = Avg_Row_Length
                     + Number of columns
                     + Number of long columns
                     + 8 header bytes
```

For the example index, the space per row is

```
Space used per row = 16
                     +2
                     +0
                     +8
                   = 26 bytes per index entry.
```

If the index is a unique index, add 1 to this total.

```
26 + 1 = 27 bytes per row
```

Given 1,698 bytes available and 27 bytes per row, you can fit 62 index entries in a block.

```
entries per block = TRUNC(1698 free bytes/27
                    bytes per entry)
                  = 62 entries per block
```

Since you can fit 62 index entries per block, you can estimate the number of blocks needed as soon as you can estimate the number of rows you expect. As noted previously, this is an approximation of the storage requirements of the table. As records in the table are manipulated, their space requirements will increase. The greater the number of **delete**s and **update**s that occur, the greater the amount of space required.

Deleted space within indexes is seldom reused, so indexes may grow even if the table does not. For example, if you **delete** 100 rows from the table and then **insert** 100 new rows, the table may use the freed space from the **delete**d records for the **insert**ed records, and its space usage will remain constant. The table's index, however, will most likely not be able to reuse the space freed by the **delete**d records, so its space usage will increase.

Sizing Clustered Tables

Clusters are used to store data from different tables in the same physical data blocks. They are appropriate to use if the records from those tables are frequently queried together. By storing them in the same data blocks, the number of database block reads needed to fulfill such queries decreases, thereby improving performance. They may have a negative performance impact on data manipulation transactions and on queries that only reference one of the tables in the cluster.

Because of their unique structure, clustered tables have different storage requirements than nonclustered tables. Each cluster stores the tables' data, as well as maintaining a *cluster index* that it uses to sort the data.

The columns within the cluster index are called the *cluster key*—the set of columns that the tables in the cluster have in common. Since the cluster key columns determine the physical placement of rows within the cluster, they should not be subject to frequent updates. The cluster key is usually the foreign key of one table that references the primary key of another table in the cluster.

After the cluster has been created, the cluster index is created on the cluster key columns. After the cluster key index has been created, data can then be entered into the tables stored in the cluster. As rows are **insert**ed, the database will store a cluster key and its associated rows in each of the cluster's blocks.

NOTE
Because of their complex structure, the sizing of clusters is more complex than that of either indexes or tables, even when using this simplified method.

Sizing a cluster thus involves elements of table sizing and index sizing. For this example, consider the table used in the previous sections: a three-column table, each column of which has a datatype and length of VARCHAR2(10). If this table is very frequently joined to another table, then it may be appropriate to cluster the two tables together. For the purposes of this example, assume that the second table has two columns: a VARCHAR2(10) column and a VARCHAR2(5) column, the former of which is used to join the tables together.

Since the two tables are joined using the VARCHAR2(10) column that they have in common, that column will be the cluster key.

First, estimate the amount of space used by the block header; this is space that ORACLE will use to manage the data within the block. The size of the cluster block header is approximately 110 bytes. If you use a 2K database block size, this leaves 1,938 bytes free; for a 4K block size, this leaves 3,986 bytes free.

```
2048 - 110 = 1938 bytes available.
```

Next, factor in the cluster's **pctfree** setting and multiply that by the free space to determine how much space will be kept free for row **update**s.

If you use a **pctfree** value of 10, then multiply the available free space by 0.10, as shown in the following listing:

```
1938*(pctfree/100) = 1938*0.1 = 194 (rounded up)
```

Of the available free space, 194 bytes will be kept for row extensions. The available free space is the block free space minus the space kept by **pctfree**.

```
1938 - 194 = 1744 bytes available.
```

Next, subtract the header space needed for table header entries. The buffer space is four times the number of tables, plus 4 bytes. For a two-table cluster, the available free space will now be

```
bytes available = 1744 bytes available
                  - 4 bytes
                  - 4*number of tables

                = 1744
                  - 4
                  - 8

                = 1732 bytes available
```

Of the 2,048 bytes in the block, 1,732 bytes are available to store cluster entries.

Next, calculate the space required for a single row in each of the tables, excluding the length due to the column(s) in the cluster key.

If the sample data is available, then the **VSIZE** function can be used to determine the actual space used by the data. Again, assume a table has three columns and a second table has two columns. To determine the average row length, perform the following query:

```
select AVG(NVL(VSIZE(Column1),0))+
       AVG(NVL(VSIZE(Column2),0))    Avg_Row_Length_1
from TABLE1;

select AVG(NVL(VSIZE(Column1),0))    Avg_Row_Length_2
from TABLE2;
```

In this example, the average length of each column that is not in the cluster key is determined, and the averages are totaled to determine the average row length. This example assumes that the cluster key is "Column3" in TABLE1, and "Column2" in TABLE2.

For this example, assume the average row length for TABLE1's nonclustered columns will be 20, and the average row length for TABLE2's nonclustered column is 3.

```
Average row length = 23 bytes
```

Each row in the cluster has *row header* information stored with it. The total row space requirements, including the header space requirements, are calculated via the following formula. In the formula, a "long" column is one in which the data value is more than 250 characters long. This distinction is necessary because of the number of length bytes that the database must store for the values.

```
Row header space = 4 bytes
                 + number of columns
                 + number of long columns
```

Combining the average row length with the row header space yields

```
Space used per row = average row length + row header space
        = 23 + 4 + number of columns + number of long columns
        = 23 + 4 + 3 + 0
        = 30 bytes
```

Thus, each cluster entry will require 30 bytes. This space does not take into account the space requirements of the cluster index.

The next step in the cluster sizing process is to determine the value of the **size** parameter, which is unique to clusters. The **size** parameter is the estimated number of bytes required by a cluster key and its associated rows.

The **size** parameter is dependent on the distribution of the data. That is, how many rows are there in a table for each distinct value in the cluster key? To determine these values, query the clustered tables and divide the number of records in the table by the number of distinct cluster key values.

```
select
    COUNT(DISTINCT(column name))/    /* Num of records in table*/
    COUNT(*)   rows_per_key          /* Num of cluster key values*/
from tablename;
```

For this example, assume that in TABLE1, there are 30 rows per cluster key value. In TABLE2, there is one row per cluster key value for this example.

The **size** parameter also needs to know the average length of the cluster key value. Query the clustered tables using the **VSIZE** query shown previously. Since it should be the same in both tables (via referential integrity), only one table has to be queried.

```
select
    AVG(NVL(VSIZE(cluster key column),0)) Avg_Key_Length
from TABLE1;
```

For this example, assume that the average key column value is 5 bytes.
The value for **size** can now be calculated.

```
SIZE=
    (Rows per cluster key in Table1*Average row size for Table1)+
    (Rows per cluster key in Table2*Average row size for Table2)+
    cluster key header+
    column length of the cluster key+
    average length of cluster key+
    2*(Rows per cluster key in Table1+Rows per cluster key in
    Table2+ Rows per cluster key for any other tables in the cluster)
```

The "cluster key header" is 19 bytes in length. Thus, for the
example data,

```
SIZE    = (30 rows per key in Table1*20 bytes per row)+
      (1 row per key in Table2*3 bytes per row)+
      19  bytes for the cluster key header+
      10  bytes for the column length of the cluster key+
      5   bytes for the average length of the cluster key+
      2*(30 rows+1 row)
    = (30*20)+(1*3)+19+10+5+(2*31)
    = 600+3+19+10+5+62
    = 699 bytes
```

Thus, each cluster key will require 699 bytes, rounded up to 700 bytes.
This will be placed in the available space in the block. The available space
was earlier calculated to be 1,732 bytes. The number of cluster keys per
block is

```
cluster keys per block = free space /(SIZE + 42)
                       = 1732/(700+42)
                       = 1732/742
                       = 2 (rounded down)
```

Each database block can store the values for two cluster keys.
Since each block can store values for two cluster keys, the number of
blocks required for the cluster is one-half the number of cluster key values.

That is, if there are 40 distinct values of the cluster key, then you will need to allocate 20 blocks for the cluster.

Sizing Tables Based on Abstract Datatypes

As of ORACLE8, you can create tables that use abstract datatypes for their column definitions. For example, you could create an abstract datatype for addresses.

```
create type ADDRESS_TY as object
(Street     VARCHAR2(50),
City        VARCHAR2(25),
State       CHAR(2),
Zip         NUMBER);
```

Once the ADDRESS_TY datatype has been created, you can use it as a datatype when creating your tables.

```
create table CUSTOMER
(Name       VARCHAR2(25),
Address     ADDRESS_TY);
```

When you create an abstract datatype, ORACLE creates a *constructor method* for use during **insert**s. The constructor method has the same name as the datatype, and its parameters are the attributes of the datatype. When you **insert** records into the CUSTOMER table, you need to use the ADDRESS_TY datatype's constructor method to **insert** Address values.

```
insert into CUSTOMER values
(1,ADDRESS_TY('My Street', 'Some City', 'ST', 10001));
```

The use of abstract datatypes increases the space requirements of your tables by 8 bytes for each datatype used. If a datatype contains another datatype, then you should add 8 bytes for both of the datatypes.

> **NOTE**
> The **VSIZE** function does not appear to work
> properly for columns based on abstract
> datatypes in ORACLE8.0.3.

See Appendix A for information on object views. You can use object
views to overlay abstract datatypes on existing tables without changing
their space usage.

Sizing Bitmap Indexes

If you create a bitmap index, then ORACLE will dynamically compress the
bitmaps generated. The compression of the bitmap may result in substantial
storage savings. To estimate the size of a bitmap index, estimate the size of
a normal (B*tree) index on the same columns using the formulas provided
in the preceding sections of this chapter. After calculating the space
requirements for the B*tree index, divide that size by 10 to determine the
size of a bitmap index for those columns. In general, bitmap indexes will
be between 5 and 10 percent of the size of a comparable B*tree index.

Sizing Object Tables and REFs

When you create an object table, ORACLE generates an OID value for each
of the rows in the table. An OID (Object ID) value adds 16 bytes to the
average row length. When you create a table that has a reference to an
object table, that table will contain a column with a REF datatype. When
estimating the space requirements for a table, estimate the length of the REF
datatype column to be 16 bytes.

Sizing Index-Only Tables

An index-only table is stored sorted by its primary key. The space
requirements of an index-only table closely mirror those of an index on
all of the table's columns. The difference in space estimation comes in
calculating the space used per row, since an index-only table does not
have RowIDs.

For an index-only table, the space used per row calculation reflects the
reduction of the header bytes from 8 bytes to 2.

```
Space used per row = Avg_Row_Length
                   + Number of columns
                   + Number of long columns
                   + 2 header bytes
```

Sizing Tables that Contain Large Objects (LOBs)

LOB data (in BLOB or CLOB datatypes) is usually stored apart from the main table. You can use the **lob** clause of the **create table** command to specify the storage for the LOB data. In the main table, ORACLE stores a *LOB locator* value that points to the LOB data. Estimate a length of 24 bytes for the **lob** locator value.

ORACLE does not always store the LOB data apart from the main table. In general, the LOB data is not stored apart from the main table until the LOB data exceeds 4K in length. Therefore, if you will be storing short LOB values, you need to consider its impact on the storage of your main table. If your LOB values are less than 4,000 characters, you may be able to use VARCHAR2 datatypes instead of LOB datatypes for the data storage.

Iterative Development

Iterative development methodologies typically consist of a series of rapidly developed prototypes. These prototypes are used to define the system requirements as the system is being developed. These methodologies are attractive because of their ability to show the customers something tangible as development is taking place. However, there are a few common pitfalls that occur during iterative development that undermine its effectiveness.

First, effective *versioning* is not always used. Creating multiple versions of an application allows certain features to be "frozen" while others are changed. It also allows different sections of the application to be in Development while others are in Test. Too often, one version of the application is used for every iteration of every feature, resulting in an end product that is not adequately flexible to handle changing needs (which was the alleged purpose of the iterative development!).

Second, the prototypes are not thrown away. Prototypes are developed to give the customer an idea of what the final product will look like; they should not be intended as the foundation of a finished product. Using them as a foundation will not yield the most stable and flexible system possible. When performing iterative development, treat the prototypes as temporary legacy systems. You wouldn't want to base a brand new system on a legacy system; think of the prototypes in the same light.

Third, the Development/Test/Production divisions are clouded. The methodology for iterative development must very clearly define the conditions that have to be met before an application version can be moved to the next stage. It may be best to keep the prototype development completely separate from the development of the full application.

Lastly, unrealistic time lines are often set. The same deliverables that applied to the structured methodology apply to the iterative methodology. The fact that the application is being developed at an accelerated pace does not necessarily mean that the deliverables will be any quicker to generate.

Technology

Following the methodology is not enough if it is done in isolation. The in-process deliverables must be made available while development is underway. Since most development teams include multiple developers (and now, at least one DBA), a means of communication must be established. The communication channels will help maintain consistency in planning and execution.

Four technological solutions are needed in order to make the methodology work. At present, this will require four separate technologies, since no integrated product development package is available. They are CASE tools, shared directories, project management databases, and discussion databases.

CASE Tools

A CASE tool can be used to generate the Entity Relationship diagram and the Physical Database diagram. ORACLE's Designer/2000 is a multiuser CASE tool that can create the Entity Relationship diagram and has an integrated data dictionary. It allows for entities to be shared across applications and can store information about table volumes and row sizes. This functionality will help to resolve several of the deliverables that have been defined here. Its multiuser capability helps to ensure consistency between developers. It also allows for different versions of a data model to be maintained or frozen.

The SQL commands that create the database objects for the application should be generated directly from the CASE tool. The CASE tool may also be used to create generic versions of applications based on the defined database objects.

Shared Directories

Several of the deliverables, such as the backup requirements, have no specific tool in which they must be created. These deliverables should be created in whatever tools are most appropriate and available at your site. The resulting files should be stored in shared project directories so that all involved team members can access them. The formats and naming conventions for these files must be specified early in the development process.

Project Management Databases

In order to communicate the status of the application and its deliverables to people outside the development team, a project management database should be maintained. It should provide an outsider with a view of the project and its current milestones. This will allow those people who are not directly involved in the project (such as systems management personnel) to anticipate future requirements. It also allows for the impact of scheduling changes or delays on the critical-path milestones to be analyzed. This analysis may result in modifications to the resource levels assigned to the tasks in the project.

Discussion Databases

Most of the information in these three shared areas—the CASE tools, the shared deliverables directories, and the project management databases—represents a consensus of opinion. For example, several team members may have opinions about the backup strategy, and the system management and DBA staffs must have input as well. To facilitate this communication, a set of discussion databases (usually using a groupware product on a local area network) can be created. Drafts can be posted to these areas before the final resolution is placed in the shared deliverables directory.

Managing Package Development

Imagine a development environment with the following characteristics: none of your standards are enforced; objects are created under the SYS or SYSTEM accounts; proper distribution and sizing of tables and indexes is only lightly considered; and every application is designed as if it were the only application you intend to run in your database.

Welcome to the management of packages.

Properly managing the implementation of packages involves many of the same issues that were described for the application development processes in the previous sections. This section will provide an overview of how packages should be treated so they will best fit with your development environment.

Generating Diagrams

Most CASE tools have the ability to *reverse engineer* packages into a Physical Database diagram. This consists of analyzing the table structures and generating a Physical Database diagram that is consistent with those structures, usually by analyzing column names and indexes to identify key columns. However, normally there is no one-to-one correlation between the Physical Database Diagram and the Entity Relationship diagram. Entity Relationship diagrams for packages can usually be obtained from the package vendor; they are helpful in planning interfaces to the package database.

Space Requirements

Most packages provide fairly accurate estimates of their database resource usage during production usage. However, they usually fail to take into account their usage requirements during data loads and software upgrades. For this reason, it is wise to create a special rollback segment tablespace (RBS_2) to be used to handle large data loads. A spare data tablespace may be needed as well if the package creates copies of all of its tables during upgrade operations.

Tuning Goals

Just as custom applications have tuning goals, packages must be held to tuning goals as well. Establishing and tracking these control values will help to identify areas of the package in need of tuning (see Chapter 8).

Security Requirements

Unfortunately, most packages that use ORACLE databases fall into one of two categories: either they were migrated to ORACLE from another database system, or they assume they will have full DBA privileges for their object owner accounts.

If the packages were first created on a different database system, then their ORACLE port very likely does not take full advantage of ORACLE's functional capabilities. These capabilities include row-level locking, the use of sequence objects, triggers, and methods. Tuning such a package to meet your needs may require modifying the source code.

If the package assumes that it has full DBA authority, then it must not be stored in the same database as any other critical database application. Most packages that require DBA authority do so in order to add new users to the database. You should determine exactly which system-level privileges the package administrator account actually requires (usually just CREATE SESSION and CREATE USER). A specialized system-level role can then be created to provide this limited set of system privileges to the package administrator.

Packages that were first developed on non-ORACLE databases may require the use of the same account as another ORACLE-ported package. For example, ownership of a database account called SYSADM may be required by multiple applications. The only way to resolve this conflict with any confidence is to create the two packages in separate databases.

Data Requirements

Any processing requirements that the packages have, particularly on the data entry side, must be clearly defined. These are usually well documented in package documentation.

Execution Plans

Generating execution plans requires accessing the SQL statements that are run against the database. The shared SQL area in the SGA (see Chapter 1 and Chapter 6) maintains the SQL statements that are executed against the database. Matching the SQL statements against specific parts of the application is a time-consuming process. It is best to identify specific areas whose functionality and performance are critical to the application's success, and work with the package's support team to resolve performance issues.

Acceptance Test Procedures

The acceptance test procedures for a package are typically created after the application has been installed. However, packages should be held to the same functional requirements that custom applications must meet. The acceptance test procedures should therefore be developed before the package has been selected; they can be generated from the package selection criteria. By testing in this manner, you will be testing for the functionality that you need, rather than what the package developers thought you wanted.

Be sure to specify what your options are in the event the package fails its acceptance test for functional or performance reasons. Critical success factors for the application should not be overlooked just because it is a purchased application.

The Managed Environment

The result of implementing the three critical elements—cultural processes, management processes, and technology—will be a development environment that has quality control built into it. This will allow for improvements to be made in the development process. The production applications will benefit from this in the form of improved performance, better integration with other enterprise applications, and simpler maintenance.

CHAPTER

6

Monitoring Multiple
Databases

t the risk of tipping off future interview candidates, here are two questions that I always ask when interviewing to fill DBA positions:

1. "What are the critical success factors for your database?"

2. "How do you monitor them?"

These seem like fairly straightforward questions, but many candidates suddenly realize that they don't know their database's critical success factors—"Something with space, right?" And without knowing those factors, their monitoring systems are either insufficient or overkill. The database must be monitored in a fashion that takes its specific structure and usage into account. Monitoring should focus on revealing problems with the system implementation, rather than tracking the problems' symptoms.

Putting out a fire in a hotel results in an extinguished fire, but it does not make the hotel any less likely to catch fire in the future. Reacting to problems requires understanding the underlying system faults that led to them; otherwise, only the symptom is being treated while the cause remains.

To avoid falling into permanent DBA fire-fighting mode, four things are necessary:

1. A well-defined understanding of how the database will be used by its applications

2. A well-structured database

3. A set of metrics that gauge the database's health

4. A systematic method for making those measurements and determining trends

The first two points, on database design, have been covered in Chapters 3–5. This chapter addresses the third and fourth points, providing measurement guides and a method for monitoring them. The first part of this chapter will concentrate on measuring physical elements of the database via a "Command Center" database; the second section will focus on monitoring memory objects via the ORACLE statistics scripts.

Common Problem Areas

There are several potential problem areas in all ORACLE databases. These include

- Running out of free space in a tablespace

- Insufficient space for temporary segments

- Rollback segments that have reached their maximum extension

- Fragmentation of data segments and free space

- Improperly sized SGA areas

An effective database monitoring system, such as the one whose details are provided in this chapter, should be able to detect unacceptable values for each of these areas.

In the following sections you will see a brief synopsis of the problem areas to be tracked, followed by details for creating a system tailored for their monitoring.

Running Out of Free Space in a Tablespace

Each tablespace in the database has datafiles assigned to it. The total space in all of the datafiles in a tablespace serves as the upper limit of the space that can be allocated in the tablespace.

When a segment is created in a tablespace, space is allocated for the initial extent of the segment from the available free space in the tablespace. When the initial extent fills with data, the segment acquires another extent. This process of extension continues either until the segment reaches a maximum number of extents or until the free space in the tablespace is less than the space needed by the next extent.

The free space in a tablespace therefore provides a cushion of unallocated space that can be used either by new segments or by the extensions of existing segments. If the available free space falls to a value that does not allow new segments or extents to be created, then additional space will have to be added to the tablespace (by adding new datafiles or resizing existing datafiles).

Therefore, you should monitor not only the current available free space in tablespaces, but also the trend in the available free space—is there more or less available today than there was a week ago? You must be able to determine the effectiveness of the current space allocation and predict what it will look like in the near future.

Insufficient Space for Temporary Segments

Temporary segments are used to store temporary data during sorting operations (such as large queries, index creations, and unions). Each user has a temporary tablespace specified when the account is created via the **create user** or **alter user** command. The temporary tablespace should be pointed to some place other than the SYSTEM tablespace (the default).

When a temporary segment is created, it uses the default storage parameters for that tablespace. While it is in existence, its storage parameters cannot be altered by changing the default storage parameters for the tablespace. It extends itself as necessary, and drops itself when the operation completes or encounters an error. Since the temporary segment itself can lead to errors (by exceeding the maximum number of extents or running out of space in the tablespace), the size of large sorting queries and operations should be taken into consideration when sizing the temporary tablespace.

If the temporary tablespace runs out of free space during the execution of a sorting operation, then the operation will fail. Since it is difficult to accurately size such segments, it is important to monitor whether the temporary tablespace created to hold them is large enough. As with data tablespaces, both the current value and the trend will be monitored via the scripts provided in this chapter.

Rollback Segments That Have Reached Their Maximum Extension

Rollback segments are involved in every transaction that occurs within the database. They allow the database to maintain read consistency between multiple transactions. The number and size of rollback segments available is specified by the DBA during database creation.

Since rollback segments are created within the database, they must be created within a tablespace. The first rollback segment, called *SYSTEM*, is stored in the SYSTEM tablespace. Further rollback segments are usually created in at least one other separate tablespace. Because they are created in tablespaces, their maximum size is limited to the amount of space in the tablespaces' datafiles.

Since they allocate space in the same manner as data segments, rollback segments are subject to two potential problems: running out of available free space in the tablespace and reaching the maximum allowable number of extents. When either situation is encountered, the transaction that is forcing the rollback segment to extend will fail. A single transaction cannot span multiple rollback segments.

Thus, in addition to tracking the free space (current and trends) for tablespaces that contain rollback segments, the number of extents in each segment must also be monitored.

The **optimal** storage parameter is available only for rollback segments. This parameter is used to set the optimal size of a rollback segment; when it extends beyond this size, it dynamically eliminates its unused extents to shrink itself. This capability makes it difficult to determine whether the rollback segments are extending just by looking at the segment's space usage. Instead, the dynamic performance tables, which track the number of times each rollback segment extends and shrinks, must be used. The monitoring system provided here monitors both rollback segment space usage and the number of times they extend and shrink.

Fragmentation of Data Segments

As noted earlier in this chapter, ORACLE manages space in segments by allowing a segment to acquire multiple extents. While this allows for flexibility when sizing tables, it can also cause performance degradation. Ideally, a segment's data will be stored in a single extent. That way, all of the data is stored near the rest of the data in the segment and there are fewer pointers needed to find the data.

If a segment has multiple extents, there is no guarantee that those extents are stored near each other. A query against a single table in the database may thus require data that is stored in several different physical locations; this may have a negative impact on performance.

Each segment in the database has a maximum allowable number of extents. As of ORACLE7.3, you can specify that a segment's maximum number of extents is **unlimited**. If a segment's maximum number of extents is not set to **unlimited**, then the maximum number of extents is determined by the database block size. For a 2,048-byte block size, no segment can exceed 121 extents; for a 4,096-byte block size, the maximum number of extents is 249.

Any transaction that causes a segment to attempt to exceed its maximum number of extents will fail. Any segment that continually extends has been improperly sized and may contribute to poor performance. Compressing segments into single extents is described in Chapter 8. The monitoring utility provided in this chapter will track the current extension and extension trends for segments in the database.

Fragmented Free Space

Just as data segments can become fragmented, the available free space in a tablespace can become fragmented. This problem is most prevalent in tablespaces whose default **pctincrease** storage value is set to 0.

When a segment is dropped, its extents are deallocated and are marked as being "free." However, these free extents are not always recombined with neighboring free extents; the barriers between these free extents may be maintained. The free space available to a new data extent can be affected by this.

If the default **pctincrease** for a tablespace is nonzero, ORACLE automatically combines neighboring free extents into single, large extents. However, it is possible that free extents may be physically separated from each other by data extents, blocking their combination with other free extents.

To detect these potential problems, the utility provided in this chapter tracks the number and size of the available free extents in each tablespace.

Improperly Sized SGA Areas

The size of the System Global Area (SGA) used to store shared memory objects for a database is usually set once, and rarely monitored or tuned after that. However, the proper sizing of the SGA is critical to the performance of the database. Thus, the scripts in the second half of this chapter focus on ways in which the usage of the SGA can be tracked.

Target Selection

Based on the common problem areas described, the following statistics are important:

■ Free space in all tablespaces

■ Rate of changes in free space for all tablespaces

■ Total space usage by temporary segments at any one time

■ Sizes and number of extents for rollback segments

■ Number of extents for all segments

This list is a minimum acceptable starting point that should be customized for each database in a system. It should be expanded to include those statistics that, combined, determine the success or failure of the system. For each statistic, upper and lower control limits must be defined. Once the acceptable ranges have been defined, the monitoring system can be designed. Note that the ranges may be related to either the physical measurements (such as free space in a tablespace) or to the rate at which they change.

The End Product

Before describing the configuration and implementation of the monitoring system, decide what the output should provide. Here are sample listings from the system that will be described in this chapter. If further detail or different information is needed, the system can be easily modified.

The first report, shown in Figure 6-1, is a trend report of free space by tablespace for all databases. This report shows the current percentage of unallocated ("free") space in each tablespace (the TS column) of each database (the DB_NM column). This value is shown in the "Today" column of the sample report. The other columns show the free space percentage for each tablespace for the last four weeks. The change between today's free space percentage and its value as of four weeks ago is shown in the Change column. The tablespaces experiencing the greatest negative changes in free space percentage are listed first.

The report shown in Figure 6-1 shows the current values, the previous values, and the trend for the percentage of free space in each tablespace. This report is part of the output from the monitoring scripts you will see in this chapter.

The SQL scripts used to generate this report include a variable that can be set to restrict the output to only those tablespaces whose free space

```
                    Percent Free•Trends for Tablespaces

                          4Wks   3Wks   2Wks   1Wk
     DB_NM      TS        Ago    Ago    Ago    Ago   Today  Change
     ---------- --------- ----   ----   ----   ----  -----  ------
     CASE       CASE       56     56     55     40     40    -16
                USERS      86     64     75     77     76    -10
                SYSTEM     22     22     22     21     21     -1
                TOOLS      25     25     25     25     25
                RBS        32     32     32     32     32
                TEMP      100    100    100    100    100

     CC1        CC         94     94     93     92     92     -2
                TESTS      71     70     70     70     70     -1
                SYSTEM     24     24     24     24     24
                RBS        32     32     32     32     32
                CCINDX     51     51     51     51     51
                TEMP      100    100    100    100    100
```

FIGURE 6-1. *Free space trends for Tablespaces sample report*

percentages have changed more than a given threshold value. It may also be restricted to only show specific databases or tablespaces. Note that these threshold limits, which are used to define whether the system is "in control" or "out of control," can also be hardcoded into the reports. That allows this report to function as an exception report for the databases.

Extent allocation among segments may be seen in the report shown in Figure 6-2. This report, also generated from the monitoring scripts shown in this chapter, shows the trends in extent allocation for all segments that presently have more than ten extents. It shows all rollback segments regardless of their extent procurement.

This report shows the current number of extents (the Today column) for each of the segments listed. The segment's database (DB_NM), tablespace (TS), owner (Owner), name (Name), and type (Type) are listed to fully identify it. Its current size in ORACLE blocks (the Blocks column) is also shown. The current and previous number of extents are shown, as well as the change in the number of extents during the past four weeks (the Change column).

The report shown in Figure 6-2 shows the current values, the previous values, and the trend for the number of extents for badly fragmented

```
              Extent Trends for Segments with 10 or more Extents

                                     4Wks 3Wks 2Wks 1Wk
    DB_NM TS    Owner    Name      Type      Blocks Ago  Ago  Ago  Ago  Today Change
    ----- ----- -------- --------- -------- ------ ---- ---- ---- ---- ----- ------
    CASE  CASE  CASEMGR  TEMP_TBL  TABLE       100                      20   20    20
                         TEMP_IDX  INDEX        80                      16   16    16

          RBS   SYSTEM   ROLL1     ROLLBACK   3800  19   19   19   19   19
                         ROLL2     ROLLBACK   3800  19   19   19   19   19

          USERS AL1      TEST1     TABLE       120       12   12   12   12    12
                         TEST2     TABLE       140       14   14   14   14    14

    CC1   RBS   SYSTEM   ROLL1     ROLLBACK   3800  19   19   19   19   19
                         ROLL2     ROLLBACK   3800  19   19   19   19   19
```

FIGURE 6-2. *Extent trends for Segments sample report*

segments. It also shows these statistics for all rollback segments. This report is part of the output from the monitoring application provided in this chapter.

This report can also be customized to show only those values that have changed. However, it is more informative when all of the alert (>9 extents) records are shown. It can then be compared with the free space trends report to reach conclusions about the database. Given these two example reports, one could conclude that

■ All rollback segments appear to be appropriately sized. None of them have increased in size despite the creation of new tables in the databases. (Note: This assumes that the **optimal** sizes of the rollback segment have not yet been reached.)

■ The AL1 user in the CASE database has created several tables in the USERS tablespace. Although they have contributed to the decline in the free space in that tablespace, they cannot by themselves account for the dip down to 64% three weeks ago. That dip appears to have been caused by transient tables (since the space has since been reclaimed).

■ The CASE_MGR account has impacted a production tablespace by creating a temporary table and index in the CASE tablespace. These segments should be moved unless they are part of the production application.

These two reports, which are generated from the application described in the rest of this chapter, are sufficient to measure all of the variables listed as targets earlier in this section—free space, rollback segments status, extent allocation, and trends for these. More importantly, they provide information about the appropriateness of the database design, given the application's behavior. The sample reports show that the rollback segments were sized correctly, but that the CASE_MGR account has created developmental tables in a production database. This reveals a lack of control in the production system that may eventually cause a production failure.

Since it may be helpful to see a summary of each database, the final sample report summarizes the CC1 database. It lists all files and tablespaces, and the space details for each. The CC1 database is the Command Center database, which will be defined in the next section of this chapter.

The sample output shown in Figure 6-3 is divided into two sections. In the first section, each of the datafiles in the databases is listed (the "File nm" column), along with the tablespace it is assigned to (the Tablespace column). The number of ORACLE blocks (Orablocks) and disk blocks (DiskBlocks) in each datafile is also displayed in this section.

In the second half of the report, the free space statistics for the tablespaces are displayed. For each tablespace, the number of free extents is displayed (NumFrExts). This column shows how many fragments the available free space in a tablespace is broken into. The largest single free extent, in ORACLE blocks, is shown in the MaxFrExt column, as well as the sum of all free space in the tablespace (SumFrBl). The percentage of the tablespace that is unallocated is shown in the PercentFr column.

The MaxFrPct column displays the ratio of the largest single free extent to the total free space available. A high value for this column indicates that most of the free space available is located in a single extent. The last two columns display the free space available, in disk blocks (DiskFrBl), out of the total available disk blocks (DiskBlocks) for each tablespace.

This listing is for a database that uses a 2KB database block size, with a 512-byte operating system block size (as found in most VMS and UNIX environments).

The report shown in Figure 6-3 provides an overview of the space usage in the database. The first section shows where the free space is coming from—the datafiles assigned to the tablespaces—and the second section shows how that free space is currently being used. This report is part of the output of the monitoring application provided in this chapter.

The combination of the reports shown in Figures 6-1, 6-2, and 6-3 is sufficient to measure all of the targets listed earlier. They were all generated based on queries against a single "Command Center" database. The database design is given in the next section, followed by instructions for data acquisition and a set of standard queries to provide a baseline for your reporting needs.

```
                    Oracle Tablespaces in CC1
                     Check Date = 07-NOV-97


    Tablespace    File nm                       Orablocks    DiskBlocks
    ------------  --------------------------    ---------    ----------
    CC            /db03/oracle/CC1/cc.dbf          30,720       122,880
    CCINDX        /db04/oracle/CC1/ccindx.dbf      20,480        81,920
    RBS           /db02/oracle/CC1/rbs01.dbf        5,120        20,480
                  /db02/oracle/CC1/rbs02.dbf        5,120        20,480
                  /db02/oracle/CC1/rbs03.dbf        5,120        20,480
    SYSTEM        /db01/oracle/CC1/sys01.dbf       10,240        40,960
    TEMP          /db01/oracle/CC1/temp01.dbf      15,360        61,440
    TESTS         /db04/oracle/CC1/tests01.dbf     15,360        61,440


                 Oracle Free Space Statistics for CC1
                    (Extent Sizes in Oracle blocks)
                     Check Date = 07-NOV-97


    Tablespace   NumFrExts MaxFrExt  SumFrBl PERCENTFR MaxFrPct DiskFrBl DiskBlocks
    -----------  --------- --------  ------- --------- -------- -------- ----------
    CC                   1    21504    21504     70.00      100    86016     122880
    CCINDX               1    15360    15360     75.00      100    61440      81920
    RBS                  3     2019     2057     13.39       98     8228      61440
    SYSTEM               1     6758     6758     66.00      100    27032      40960
    TEMP                 6    12800    15360    100.00       83    15360      15360
    TESTS                1    21504    21504     70.00      100    86016     122880
```

FIGURE 6-3. *Sample space summary report*

Creating the Command Center Database

Establishing a separate database that is used solely for monitoring other systems resolves three problems with traditional ORACLE database monitoring capabilities:

■ Monitoring activities can be coordinated across multiple databases.

■ The monitoring activities will not affect the space usage in the system they are monitoring.

■ Trends can be detected for the parameters being monitored.

This section will describe the creation, structure, and implementation of a stand-alone monitoring database.

The system described here is a *reactive monitor*. It is not designed to perform proactive, real-time monitoring of systems, since our well-designed, well-implemented, and well-monitored systems are fundamentally sound. It should ideally be called from a system or network monitor, since focusing solely on the database will fail to address the factors that affect the performance of client-server or distributed databases (and this entire function can then be given to the systems management team).

The monitoring database in this example is given the instance name "CC1" to designate it as the first command center database in the system. Based on your system architecture, you may wish to have multiple databases to perform this function. The database architecture is

SYSTEM tablespace	20MB
RBS tablespace	30MB
	Two 10MB rollback segments, 10MB free
CC tablespace	30MB
CCINDX tablespace	20MB
TESTS tablespace	30MB
TEMP tablespace	15MB
Redo Logs	Three 2MB redo logs

The design of the application that will store the monitoring results is fairly simple. For each instance, we will store descriptive information about its location and usage. Information about each file in each database will also be stored (this is very useful information to have during recoveries when the database being recovered is not open). Each tablespace's free space statistics will also be stored, and every segment will be checked for excessive extents. Figure 6-4 shows the physical database diagram for the monitoring tables.

A view of the FILES table, called FILES_TS_VIEW, is created by grouping the FILES table by instance ID, tablespace (TS), and check date (Check_Date). This view is needed when comparing data in the FILES table (allocated space) with data in the SPACES table (used and free space). The

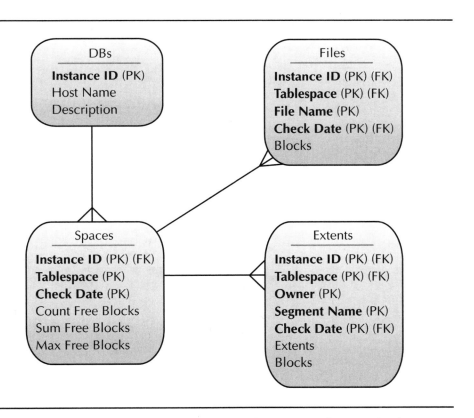

FIGURE 6-4. *Physical database diagram for the command center database*

DDL for creating these objects is given in the following listings. The objects are described in Table 6-1.

```
drop table dbs;

rem * This table will store information about instances*/

create table DBS
(Db_Nm        VARCHAR2(8),      /*instance name*/
 Host_Nm      VARCHAR2(8),      /*host (server) name*/
 Description  VARCHAR2(80))     /*instance description*/
tablespace CC;

drop table FILES;

rem /*This table will store information about datafiles*/

create table FILES
(Db_Nm        VARCHAR2(8),      /*instance name*/
 TS           VARCHAR2(30),     /*tablespace name*/
 Check_Date   DATE,             /*date entry was made */
 File_Nm      VARCHAR2(80),     /*file name*/
 Blocks       NUMBER,           /*size of the file*/
 primary key(Db_Nm, TS, Check_Date,File_Nm))
tablespace CC;

drop view FILES_TS_VIEW;

rem /*This view groups the file sizes by tablespace*/

create view FILES_TS_VIEW as
select
    Db_Nm,                          /*instance name*/
    TS,                             /*tablespace name*/
    Check_Date,                     /*date entry was made */
    SUM(Blocks) Sum_File_Blocks /*blocks allocated for ts*/
from FILES
group by
    Db_Nm,
    TS,
    Check_Date;

drop table SPACES;

rem /*This table will store information about free space*/
```

```
create table SPACES
(Db_Nm          VARCHAR2(8),     /*instance name*/
TS              VARCHAR2(30),    /*tablespace name*/
Check_Date      DATE,            /*date entry was made */
Count_Free_Blocks NUMBER,        /*number of free extents*/
Sum_Free_Blocks NUMBER,          /*free space, in Ora blocks*/
Max_Free_Blocks NUMBER,          /*largest free extent */
primary key (Db_Nm, Ts, Check_Date))
tablespace CC;

drop table EXTENTS;

rem /*This table will store information about extents */

create table EXTENTS
(Db_Nm   VARCHAR2(8),        /*instance name*/
TS       VARCHAR2(30),       /*tablespace name*/
Seg_Owner    VARCHAR2(30),   /*segment owner*/
Seg_Name VARCHAR2(32),       /*segment name*/
Seg_Type VARCHAR2(17),       /*segment type*/
Extents  NUMBER,             /*number of extents allocated*/
Blocks   NUMBER,             /*number of blocks allocated*/
Check_Date      DATE,        /*date entry was made */
primary key (Db_Nm, TS, Seg_Owner, Seg_Name, Check_Date))
tablespace CC;
```

These database structures will allow the DBA to track all of the "targets" listed previously, across all databases. Note that there is no table for rollback segments. These segments will be tracked via the EXTENTS table.

Object	Description
DBS	Table for storing descriptive information about instances
FILES	Table for storing information about files
FILES_TS_VIEW	View of the FILES table, grouped by tablespace
SPACES	Table for storing information about free space
EXTENTS	Table for storing information about used extents

TABLE 6-1. *Tables Used in the Command Center Database*

Getting the Data

The first object listed in Table 6-1, DBS, is provided as a reference for sites where there are multiple DBAs. It allows the entry of descriptive information about instances and is the only component of this application that requires manual entry of the data. All other data will be automatically loaded into the tables. All of the standard data reports will also be automated, with ad hoc capabilities available as well.

The data that is needed to populate these tables is accessible via the SYSTEM account of each database. (A secondary DBA account may also be used for this purpose; this account requires access to DBA-privileged tables, so a specialized system role or the SELECT_CATALOG_ROLE may be created for this purpose.)

Within the CC1 database, you can create an account that will own the monitoring application. This account does not require the DBA role. Within that account, create private database links to a DBA-privileged account in each remote database. The database link's name should be the same as the name of the instance that it links to. For example:

```
create database link CASE
connect to system identified by manager
using 'case';
```

This link accesses the "system" account in the database identified by the service name "case." When used, it will log into that database as the user "system," with a password of "manager."

Note that the **connect to** line is not necessary if the username and password will be the same on the remote system as they are on the local system.

The outline of the data acquisition process is shown in Figure 6-5.

A batch scheduler will be used to call a command script that will start the process. The job should be scheduled to run daily, at off-peak hours.

As shown in Figure 6-5, the monitoring application will perform the following steps:

1. The command script (called ins_cc1) calls a SQL*Plus script (named inserts.sql) that lists all of the databases to monitor.

2. Each of those databases is checked via a SQL*Plus script (named ins_all.sql).

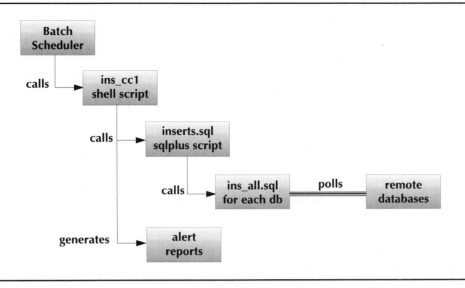

FIGURE 6-5. *Process flow for database monitoring*

3. The results of those queries are stored in tables in the Command Center database by ins_all.sql.

4. The command script then generates alert reports based on the latest values in the Command Center database.

To start the system, construct a command file that is run using the operating system's batch scheduler. A sample shell file for UNIX (to be called via **cron**) is shown below. This file first sets up its environment variables to point to the CC1 database. It then goes into Server Manager and opens the CC1 database. Once the database is open, a command is executed to start the inserts.sql script. After it completes, the CC1 database is again shut down.

```
# file:  ins_cc1
#
# This script is run once daily to insert records into the
# CC1 database recording the space usage of the databases
# listed in inserts.sql file called by this file.  New
# databases need to have new links created in CC1 and have
```

```
# to have entries in the # inserts.sql script.
#
ORACLE_SID=cc1; export ORACLE_SID
ORAENV_ASK=NO; export ORAENV_ASK
. oraenv
cd /orasw/dba/CC1
svrmgrl <<EOF
connect internal
startup;
!sqlplus / @inserts
shutdown
EOF
```

Note that this file assumes that the database is closed when this monitoring is not taking place. This allows the memory normally used by CC1's SGA and background processes to be freed during regular working hours. Monitoring is assumed to be taking place once a day, at a fixed time when the system is lightly loaded.

The shell script shown in the previous listing calls a file named inserts.sql, located in the /orasw/dba/CC1 directory. A sample inserts.sql file is shown below. This script calls the ins_all.sql script for each database that is to be monitored. Once that is complete, two alert reports, named space_watcher.sql and extent_watcher.sql, are executed.

```
rem
rem  file:  inserts.sql
rem  location:  /orasw/dba/CC1
rem  Called from ins_cc1 shell script.
rem  New entries must be made here every time a new database
rem  is added to the system.
rem
set verify off
@ins_all CASE
@ins_all CC1
analyze table FILES compute statistics;
analyze table SPACES compute statistics;
analyze table EXTENTS compute statistics;
analyze table RSEGS compute statistics;
@space_watcher
@extent_watcher
```

This file lists all of the databases for which monitoring statistics will be gathered. When new databases are added to the system, an additional line should be added for each. This file thus provides a layer of process management that allows easy changes without altering the submitted batch program or the SQL statements that access the remote databases.

After executing the ins_all.sql script for two databases (CASE and CC1), the tables that store the monitoring data are analyzed. The analysis of the tables is necessary to improve the performance of the reports against the monitoring tables. Since the data in the monitoring tables changes frequently, these tables should be frequently analyzed.

The last two lines in this script call a pair of SQL scripts named space_watcher.sql and extent_watcher.sql. These scripts will generate versions of the "Percent Free by Tablespace" and "Segments with over 10 Extents" reports shown earlier in Figures 6-1 and 6-2, respectively. Since they will be used for alerting purposes, only rows with changes exceeding defined limits will be shown in the next listing.

So far, we've seen the first two layers of the data acquisition system. Continuing down the process path depicted in Figure 6-5, the next step is to run a script (ins_all. sql) that inserts records into all applicable monitoring tables based on queries against remote databases. These queries use the database links created earlier to search each instance in turn and record the statistics returned. A sample ins_all.sql SQL*Plus script, for **insert**s into the FILES, SPACES, and EXTENTS tables, is shown in the next listing.

The first part of the ins_all.sql script **insert**s records into the FILES table. It queries each database for information about all of its datafiles, the tablespaces to which they are assigned, and their sizes.

The second part of the script queries the free space statistics of each database. It stores the output in the SPACES table, recording the number of free extents in each tablespace, the total free space available, and the size of the largest single free extent.

The third part of the script checks the space usage by segments and stores its results in the EXTENTS table. It records the information needed to identify the segment (such as its owner and name), as well as its current size and number of extents. To limit the number of records returned by this query, only rollback segments and segments with greater than nine extents are selected.

```
rem
rem   file:  ins_all.sql
rem   location:  /orasw/dba/CC1
rem   Used to perform all inserts into CC1 monitoring
```

```
rem   tables.  This script is called from inserts.sql for
rem   each instance.
rem   For best results, name the database links after the
rem   instances they access.
rem
insert into FILES
    (Db_Nm,
    TS,
    Check_Date,
    File_Nm,
    Blocks)
select
    UPPER('&&1'),      /*insert database link,instance name*/
    Tablespace_Name,   /*tablespace name*/
    TRUNC(SysDate),    /*date query is being performed*/
    File_Name,         /*full name of database file*/
    Blocks             /*number of database blocks in file*/
from sys.DBA_DATA_FILES@&&1
/
commit;
rem
insert into SPACES
    (Db_Nm,
    Check_Date,
    TS,
    Count_Free_Blocks,
    Sum_Free_Blocks,
    Max_Free_Blocks)
select
    UPPER('&&1'),      /*insert database link,instance name*/
    TRUNC(SysDate),    /*date query is being performed*/
    Tablespace_Name,   /*tablespace name*/
    COUNT(Blocks),     /*num. of free space entries */
    SUM(Blocks),       /*total free space in the tablespace*/
    MAX(Blocks)        /*largest free extent in the ts*/
from sys.DBA_FREE_SPACE@&&1
group by Tablespace_Name
/
commit;
rem
insert into EXTENTS
    (Db_Nm,
    TS,
    Seg_Owner,
    Seg_Name,
```

```
    Seg_Type,
    Extents,
    Blocks,
    Check_Date)
select
    UPPER('&&1'),      /*insert database link,instance name*/
    Tablespace_Name,  /*tablespace name*/
    Owner,             /*owner of the segment*/
    Segment_Name,      /*name of the segment*/
    Segment_Type,      /*type of segment (ex. TABLE, INDEX)*/
    Extents,           /*number of extents in the segment*/
    Blocks,           /*number of database blocks in segment*/
    TRUNC(SysDate)    /*date the query is being performed*/
from sys.DBA_SEGMENTS@&&1
where Extents>9         /*only record extended segments*/
or Segment_Type = 'ROLLBACK'   /*or rollback segments*/
/
commit;
rem
undefine 1
```

Note that the inserts into the EXTENTS table only take place for rollback segments and those segments that have exceeded nine extents. This is therefore an incomplete listing of the segments in the database. Since these two **where** clauses establish the threshold for the extent alert report, change the extent limit to best suit your needs.

This series of scripts will perform all of the data acquisition functions necessary to generate the reports shown earlier. It is assumed throughout that they will be run on a daily basis. If more frequent monitoring is needed, then the primary keys of the tables will need to be modified to include both Check_Date and Check_Hour (for hourly reporting).

Now that the data has been inserted into the CC1 monitoring tables, ORACLE can automatically generate alert reports. This will be accomplished via the space_watcher.sql and extent_watcher.sql files that are called from the inserts.sql file shown earlier.

Generating Alert Reports

The composition of the alert scripts, described in the previous section, depends entirely on the nature of the databases being monitored. They are simply modifications to the generic free space and extent trends reports shown in Figures 6-1 and 6-2. They feature **where** and **group by** clauses to eliminate those entries that have not exceeded some threshold value. The setting of these values should be customized for each site—they are based on the control limits defined during the target variable selection process.

Since these reports are called automatically following the insertion of records into the Command Center database, the DBA may wish to have them automatically mailed or printed so they are seen each morning before the production users begin to access the databases.

The following script generates the space trend report for tablespaces whose percentage of free space has changed by at least 5 per cent in the last four weeks:

```
rem
rem   file:  space_watcher.sql
rem   location:  /orasw/dba/CC1
rem   Called from inserts.sql
rem
rem   ...like some watcher of the skies
rem   when a new planet swims into his ken (Keats)
rem
column Db_Nm format A8
column TS format A20
column Week4 format 999 heading "1Wk|Ago"
column Week3 format 999 heading "2Wks|Ago"
column Week2 format 999 heading "3Wks|Ago"
column Week1 format 999 heading "4Wks|Ago"
column Today format 999
column Change format 999

set pagesize 60
break on Db_Nm skip 2
ttitle center 'Tablespaces whose PercentFree values have -
decreased 5 pct this month' skip 2

select
   SPACES.Db_Nm,
   SPACES.TS,
   MAX(DECODE(SPACES.Check_Date, TRUNC(SysDate-28),
      ROUND(100*Sum_Free_Blocks/Sum_File_Blocks),0)) Week1,
   MAX(DECODE(SPACES.Check_Date, TRUNC(SysDate-21),
      ROUND(100*Sum_Free_Blocks/Sum_File_Blocks),0)) Week2,
   MAX(DECODE(SPACES.Check_Date, TRUNC(SysDate-14),
      ROUND(100*Sum_Free_Blocks/Sum_File_Blocks),0)) Week3,
```

```
      MAX(DECODE(SPACES.Check_Date, TRUNC(SysDate-7),
         ROUND(100*Sum_Free_Blocks/Sum_File_Blocks),0)) Week4,
      MAX(DECODE(SPACES.Check_Date, TRUNC(SysDate),
         ROUND(100*Sum_Free_Blocks/Sum_File_Blocks),0)) Today,
      MAX(DECODE(SPACES.Check_Date, TRUNC(SysDate),
         ROUND(100*Sum_Free_Blocks/Sum_File_Blocks),0)) -
      MAX(DECODE(SPACES.Check_Date, TRUNC(SysDate-28),
         ROUND(100*Sum_Free_Blocks/Sum_File_Blocks),0)) Change
from SPACES, FILES_TS_VIEW FTV
where SPACES.Db_Nm = FTV.Db_Nm            /*same DB name*/
and SPACES.TS = FTV.TS                     /*same TS name*/
and SPACES.Check_Date = ftv.Check_Date    /*same check date*/
and exists                                /*does ts exist?*/
   (select 'x' from spaces x
   where x.db_nm = SPACES.db_nm
   and x.ts = SPACES.ts
   and x.Check_Date = TRUNC(SysDate))
group by
   SPACES.Db_Nm,
   SPACES.Ts
having                /*has percentfree dropped 5 pct?*/
(  MAX(DECODE(SPACES.Check_Date, TRUNC(SysDate),
         ROUND(100*Sum_Free_Blocks/Sum_File_Blocks),0)) -
   MAX(DECODE(SPACES.Check_Date, TRUNC(SysDate-28),
         ROUND(100*Sum_Free_Blocks/Sum_File_Blocks),0))
>5    )
or                    /*is percentfree less than 10?*/
( MAX(DECODE(SPACES.Check_Date, TRUNC(SysDate),
      ROUND(100*Sum_Free_Blocks/Sum_File_Blocks),0)) <10)
order by SPACES.Db_Nm,
   DECODE(MAX(DECODE(SPACES.Check_Date,TRUNC(SysDate),
     ROUND(100*Sum_Free_Blocks/Sum_File_Blocks),0)) -
   MAX(DECODE(SPACES.Check_Date, TRUNC(SysDate-28),
     ROUND(100*Sum_Free_Blocks/Sum_File_Blocks),0)),0,9999,
   MAX(DECODE(SPACES.Check_Date,TRUNC(SysDate),
     ROUND(100*Sum_Free_Blocks/Sum_File_Blocks),0)) -
   MAX(DECODE(SPACES.Check_Date, TRUNC(SysDate-28),
     ROUND(100*Sum_Free_Blocks/Sum_File_Blocks),0))),
   MAX(DECODE(SPACES.Check_Date,TRUNC(SysDate),
     ROUND(100*Sum_Free_Blocks/Sum_File_Blocks),0))

spool space_watcher.lst
/
spool off
```

```
              Tablespaces whose Percent Free values have
                    decreased 5 pct this month


                          4Wks    3Wks    2Wks    1Wk
   DB_NM        TS        Ago-    Ago     Ago     Ago    Today   Change
   ----------   ----------  ----    ----    ----    ----   -----   ------
   CASE         CASE         56      56      55      40      40     -16
                USERS        86      64      75      77      76     -10
```

FIGURE 6-6. *Sample alert report for tablespace percent free trends*

If the **exists** section is left out of the above query, then all tablespaces will be shown, even after they have been dropped from the database. The two limiting conditions within the **having** clauses define the threshold for the alert report. In this example, only those tablespaces whose percentfree values have decreased by more than 5 percent in the past 28 days will pass the first **having** condition. The second **having** condition identifies those tablespaces whose current percent free value is less than 10 percent, regardless of its trends.

If incremental changes in specific databases are critical to their success, then you may wish to add a **having** clause to this report that lists those specific databases regardless of their trends.

Sample output (based on the percent free trend report in Figure 6-1) is shown in Figure 6-6.

Note that this alert report does not show fluctuations that have since been resolved (for example, a 4-week percent free trend of 70-70-20-70-70 would not be shown). It is expected that this alert will be run and viewed on a daily basis; thus, if a tablespace's space problems have been resolved, then it is no longer shown on the alert reports.

The second report is the extent watcher (extent_watcher.sql). Like the space watcher report, this SQL*Plus query uses the **group by** clause to transpose multiple rows into multiple columns for a single row. It will provide a subset of the data listed in the generic extent trends report that was shown in Figure 6-2.

```
rem
rem  file:  ext_watcher.sql
rem  location:  /orasw/dba/CC1
```

```
rem   Called from inserts.sql
rem
rem   ...like some watcher of the skies
rem   when a new planet swims into his ken (Keats)
rem
column Db_Nm format A8
column TS format A18
column Seg_Owner format a14
column Seg_Name format a32
column Seg_Type format a8
column Blocks format 99999999
column Week4 format 999 heading "1Wk|Ago"
column Week3 format 999 heading "2Wks|Ago"
column Week2 format 999 heading "3Wks|Ago"
column Week1 format 999 heading "4Wks|Ago"
column Today format 999
column Change format 999

set pagesize 60 linesize 132
break on Db_Nm skip 2 on TS skip 1 on Seg_Owner
ttitle center 'Segments whose extent count is over 10' -
skip 2

select
   EXTENTS.Db_Nm,
   EXTENTS.TS,
   EXTENTS.Seg_Owner,
   EXTENTS.Seg_Name,
   EXTENTS.Seg_Type,
   MAX(DECODE(EXTENTS.Check_Date, TRUNC(SysDate),
         Blocks,0)) Blocks,
   MAX(DECODE(EXTENTS.Check_Date, TRUNC(SysDate-28),
         Extents,0)) Week1,
   MAX(DECODE(EXTENTS.Check_Date, TRUNC(SysDate-21),
         Extents,0)) Week2,
   MAX(DECODE(EXTENTS.Check_Date, TRUNC(SysDate-14),
         Extents,0)) Week3,
   MAX(DECODE(EXTENTS.Check_Date, TRUNC(SysDate-7),
         Extents,0)) Week4,
   MAX(DECODE(EXTENTS.Check_Date, TRUNC(SysDate),
         Extents,0)) Today,
   MAX(DECODE(EXTENTS.Check_Date, TRUNC(SysDate),
         Extents,0)) -
   MAX(DECODE(EXTENTS.Check_Date, TRUNC(SysDate-28),
         Extents,0)) Change
```

```
from EXTENTS
where exists  /*did this segment show up today?*/
   (select 'x' from EXTENTS x
   where x.Db_Nm = EXTENTS.Db_Nm
   and x.TX = EXTENTS.TX
   and x.Seg_Owner = EXTENTS.Seg_Owner
   and x.Seg_Name = EXTENTS.Seg_Name
   and x.Seg_Type = EXTENTS.Seg_Type
   and x.Check_Date = TRUNC(SysDate))
group by
   EXTENTS.Db_Nm,
   EXTENTS.TX,
   EXTENTS.Seg_Owner,
   EXTENTS.Seg_Name,
   EXTENTS.Seg_Type
order by EXTENTS.Db_Nm, EXTENTS.TS,
   DECODE(MAX(DECODE(EXTENTS.Check_Date,TRUNC(SysDate),
         Extents,0)) -
   MAX(DECODE(EXTENTS.Check_Date, TRUNC(SysDate-28),
         Extents,0)),0,-9999,
   MAX(DECODE(EXTENTS.Check_Date,TRUNC(SysDate),
         Extents,0)) -
   MAX(DECODE(EXTENTS.Check_Date, TRUNC(SysDate-28),
         Extents,0))) desc,
   MAX(DECODE(EXTENTS.Check_Date,TRUNC(SysDate),
         Extents,0)) desc

spool extent_watcher.lst
/
spool off
```

Note that the only portion of this query that limits the records to be shown is the **exists** clause that queries to see if the segment was returned from the current day's query. It is assumed that the threshold values for the "number of extents" variable was enforced during the **insert** into the EXTENTS table (see ins_all.sql, shown in the "Getting the Data" section of this chapter). The EXTENTS table is the only one that has the threshold enforced during **insert**s rather than during querying, since there may be thousands of segments in a database.

If incremental changes in specific segments are critical to their success, then you may wish to add a **where** clause to the portion of the ins_all.sql script that inserts the rows for those segments into the EXTENTS table. The report will then list those specific segments regardless of their trends.

Sample output from the extent_watcher.sql report is shown in Figure 6-7, which is identical to Figure 6-2. This is because the queries used for the **insert**s into the EXTENTS table only selected those segments that were already fragmented. No additional restrictions were needed to produce an alert report.

The Space Summary Report

Since every day's statistics are being stored in the CC1 Command Center database, a summary report can be generated for any database, for any specified date. This report should be generated on a weekly basis via the batch scheduler. It does not have to be printed out at that time. It should, however, be available online to the DBA. This will shorten the time delay in getting the report, since the CC1 database is usually kept closed after its daily batch run is completed (as specified in the ins_cc1 shell script).

```
              Extent Trends for Segments with 10 or more Extents


                                                  4Wks 3Wks 2Wks  1Wk
    DB_NM  TS     Owner   Name     Type    Blocks  Ago  Ago  Ago  Ago Today Change
    -----  ------ ------- -------- -------- ------ ---- ---- ---- ---- ----- ------
    CASE   CASE   CASEMGR TEMP_TBL TABLE      100                   20   20     20
                          TEMP_IDX INDEX       80                   16   16     16

           RBS    SYSTEM  ROLL1    ROLLBACK  3800   19   19   19   19   19
                          ROLL2    ROLLBACK  3800   19   19   19   19   19

           USERS AL1      TEST1    TABLE      120        12   12   12   12     12
                          TEST2    TABLE      140        14   14   14   14     14

    CC1    RBS    SYSTEM  ROLL1    ROLLBACK  3800   19   19   19   19   19
                          ROLL2    ROLLBACK  3800   19   19   19   19   19
```

FIGURE 6-7. *Sample alert report for extent usage trends*

This SQL*Plus report should be run once for each database. It generates an output file whose name includes the name of the database link that was used in the query. It takes three parameters. They are, in order:

1. The database link name (since this will be stored in the output file name, it should have the same name as the instance it accesses).

2. The check date (since this report can be run for any date).

3. The ratio of the ORACLE block size (such as 2K) to the host operating block size (such as 512 bytes). For these block sizes, the ratio is $2,048/512 = 4$.

The report is divided into two sections. The first part queries the FILES table to determine the current filenames and sizes for the database. The second part of the query compares the values in the SPACES table (free space sizes) to those in the FILES table (via the FILES_TS_VIEW view). Since these tables contain information about the space allocated to a tablespace, and the amount of it that has yet to be allocated, the percentage of free space remaining in each tablespace can be measured.

```
rem
rem space_summary.sql
rem   parameter 1: database link name
rem   parameter 2: check date
rem   parameter 3: ratio of Oracle to OS block size
rem
rem   to call this report from within sqlplus:
rem   @space_summary link_name Check_Date block_ratio
rem
rem   Example:
rem   @space_summary CASE 07-NOV-98 4
rem
rem   Should be called weekly for each database.
rem
set pagesize 60 linesize 132 verify off feedback off
set newpage 0
column TS heading 'Tablespace' format A18
column File_Nm heading 'File nm' format A40
column Blocks heading 'Orablocks'
column Percentfree format 999.99
column Diskblocks format 99999999
column Cfb format 9999999 heading 'NumFrExts'
column Mfb format 9999999 heading 'MaxFrExt'
```

```
column Sfb format 9999999 heading 'SumFrBl'
column Dfrb format 9999999 heading 'DiskFrBl'
column Sum_File_Blocks heading 'DiskBlocks'
column Maxfrpct heading 'MaxFrPct' format 9999999

break on TS
ttitle center 'Oracle Tablespaces in ' &&1 skip center -
'Check Date = ' &&2 skip 2 center
spool &&1._space_summary.lst

select
   Ts,                        /*tablespace name*/
   File_Nm,                   /*file name*/
   Blocks,                    /*Oracle blocks in the file*/
   Blocks*&&3 Diskblocks      /*OS blocks in the file*/
from FILES
where Check_Date = '&&2'
and Db_Nm = UPPER('&&1')
order by TS, File_Nm
/

ttitle center 'Oracle Free Space Statistics for ' &&1 -
skip center '(Extent Sizes in Oracle blocks)' skip center -
  'Check Date = ' &&2 skip 2

select
   SPACES.TS,                        /*tablespace name*/
   SPACES.Count_Free_Blocks Cfb,    /*number of free extents*/
   SPACES.Max_Free_Blocks Mfb,      /*lgst free extent*/
   SPACES.Sum_Free_Blocks Sfb,      /*sum of free space*/
   ROUND(100*Sum_Free_Blocks/Sum_File_Blocks,2)
       Percentfree,                  /*percent free in TS*/
   ROUND(100*Max_Free_Blocks/Sum_Free_Blocks,2)
    Maxfrpct,                        /*ratio of largest extent to sum*/
   SPACES.Sum_Free_Blocks*&&3 Dfrb, /*disk blocks free*/
   Sum_File_Blocks*&&3 Sum_File_Blocks /*disk blocks allocated*/
from SPACES, FILES_TS_VIEW FTV
where SPACES.Db_Nm = FTV.Db_Nm
and SPACES.TS = FTV.TS
and SPACES.Check_Date = FTV.Check_Date
and SPACES.Db_Nm = UPPER('&&1')
and SPACES.Check_Date = '&&2'
/
spool off
undefine 1
undefine 2
undefine 3
```

A sample output report is shown in Figure 6-8. Based on the **spool** command listed in the query, the output file will be called CC1_space_summary.lst. This is based on using the period (.) as the concatenation character in SQL*Plus.

Figure 6-8 is identical to Figure 6-3 earlier in this chapter. The sample output shown in Figure 6-8 is divided into two sections. In the first section, each of the datafiles in the databases is listed (the "File nm" column), along with the tablespace it is assigned to (the Tablespace column). The number of ORACLE blocks (Orablocks) and disk blocks (DiskBlocks) in each datafile is also displayed in this section.

In the second half of the report, the free space statistics for the tablespaces are displayed. For each tablespace, the number of free extents

```
                        Oracle Tablespaces in CC1
                         Check Date = 07-NOV-97


     Tablespace     File nm                          Orablocks      DiskBlocks
     -------------  ----------------------------     ---------      -------------

     CC             /db03/oracle/CC1/cc.dbf            30,720         122,880
     CCINDX         /db04/oracle/CC1/ccindx.dbf        20,480          81,920
     RBS            /db02/oracle/CC1/rbs01.dbf          5,120          20,480
                    /db02/oracle/CC1/rbs02.dbf          5,120          20,480
                    /db02/oracle/CC1/rbs03.dbf          5,120          20,480
     SYSTEM         /db01/oracle/CC1/sys01.dbf         10,240          40,960
     TEMP           /db01/oracle/CC1/temp01.dbf        15,360          61,440
     TESTS          /db04/oracle/CC1/tests01.dbf       15,360          61,440


                 Oracle Free Space Statistics for CC1
                    (Extent Sizes in Oracle blocks)
                        Check Date = 07-NOV-97


     Tablespace  NumFrExts MaxFrExt  SumFrBl PERCENTFR MaxFrPct DiskFrBl DiskBlocks
     ----------- --------- --------  ------- --------- -------- -------- ----------

     CC               1      21504    21504    70.00     100     86016     122880
     CCINDX           1      15360    15360    75.00     100     61440      81920
     RBS              3       2019     2057    13.39      98      8228      61440
     SYSTEM           1       6758     6758    66.00     100     27032      40960
     TEMP             6      12800    15360   100.00      83     15360      15360
     TESTS            1      21504    21504    70.00     100     86016     122880
```

FIGURE 6-8. *Sample space summary report*

is displayed (NumFrExts). This column shows how many fragments the available free space in a tablespace is broken into. The largest single free extent, in Oracle blocks, is shown in the MaxFrExt column, as well as the sum of all free space in the tablespace (SumFrBl). The percentage of the tablespace that is unallocated is shown in the PercentFr column.

The MaxFrPct column displays the ratio of the largest single free extent to the total free space available. A high value for this column indicates that most of the free space available is located in a single extent. The last two columns display the free space available, in disk blocks (DiskFrBl), out of the total available disk blocks (DiskBlocks) for each tablespace.

This listing is for a database that uses a 2KB database block size, with a 512-byte operating system block size (as found in most VMS and UNIX environments).

Purging Data

Left unchecked, the tables described in the previous sections will grow until they use all of the free space in the available tablespaces. To prevent data volume-related problems, you should periodically **delete** records from the EXTENTS, SPACES and FILES tables.

The amount of data to retain depends on your needs. If you never will need data more than 60 days old from these tables, then you can automate the data purges as part of the data **insert** process. For example, at the end of the ins_all.sql script that performs the **insert**s, you could add the following commands:

```
delete from FILES
  where Check_Date < SysDate-60;

commit;

delete from SPACES
  where Check_Date < SysDate-60;

commit;

delete from EXTENTS
  where Check_Date < SysDate-60;

commit;
```

If you execute this command each day, then the size of the **delete** transactions should be small enough to be supported by the rollback segments.

If the tables become large, then you can improve the performance of the **delete**s by creating indexes on the Check_Date columns of the FILES, SPACES, and EXTENTS tables.

Monitoring Memory Objects

ORACLE's memory objects, such as the System Global Area (SGA) and the background processes, can also be monitored. Since most of the monitoring of the background processes is done at the operating system level (and is operating system specific), this section will focus on tuning the SGA.

ORACLE continuously updates a set of internal statistics. These statistics should only be stored in tracking tables (such as the tables used in the space monitoring section of this chapter) when you can be sure that the database will not be shut down between monitoring checks. This is necessary because these internal statistics are reset each time the database is shut down and restarted.

In order to facilitate monitoring of these statistics, ORACLE provides two scripts that should be modified, called UTLBSTAT.SQL and UTLESTAT.SQL. They are located in the /rdbms/admin subdirectory under the ORACLE software home directory. The first file, UTLBSTAT (Begin Statistics) creates a set of tables and populates them with the statistics in the database at that time. The second file, UTLESTAT, runs at a later time, creates a set of tables based on the statistics in the database at that time, and then generates a report (called REPORT.TXT) that lists the changes in the statistics during the interval between the run times for the beginning and ending scripts.

Necessary Modifications to **UTLBSTAT** and **UTLESTAT**

Before running the statistics scripts provided by ORACLE, change them. First, modify the scripts to include database links as part of the **from** clause—this will allow them to be run from a Command Center database. Second, add a **tablespace** clause to allow the segments to be stored in a data or scratch area tablespace.

Why make these modifications? Failing to do so causes two problems: First, since these scripts insert records into tables, storing the tables in a database that is being monitored automatically skews the file I/O statistics for the database (since the monitoring activity is being factored into the I/O activity). Second, the scripts are written to be run from within Server Manager, connected INTERNAL. If no alternate tablespace is named, then the SYSTEM tablespace will be fragmented by the create-and-drop table operations of these scripts.

Both the beginning and ending statistics tables are created by UTLBSTAT.SQL. UTLESTAT.SQL then creates a series of tables to store the differences between the beginning and ending statistics before generating REPORT.TXT. The script must be run under a DBA account due to a reference to the SYS.FILE$ table. All other tables referenced by these scripts are accessible to users who have been granted access to the monitoring tables.

To reference a remote database from within the statistics scripts, add a database link that points to the target database. In order to access all of the tables needed by these scripts, you will need to either create a link to the target SYS account or grant the remote SYSTEM account privileges on the SYS tables used by the scripts. To minimize your risk, create a link to SYS specifying a temporary password.

```
create database link CASE_STAT
connect to sys identified by only_for_a_minute
using 'case';
```

Once the link is established, log in to the CASE database, change the SYS password to "only_for_a_minute" (or whatever you choose), go back to CC1, and run the statistics script. When it completes, reset the SYS password.

To tell the query to use this link, append the database link name to the table name being queried. The following listing shows the table creation portion of UTLBSTAT.SQL after it has been modified to use this link. If you are managing multiple databases, then use a variable in place of the database link name.

For this example, the tables will be stored in the "CC" data tablespace of the CC1 Command Center database. Each **create table** command will have the **tablespace CC** clause appended to it, and each query of a remote table will have the **@case_stat** clause added to it so the database link named CASE_STAT will be used.

After this script has been run, all of the statistics from the remote database's dynamic performance tables will be stored in the CC tablespace of the local database.

```
rem
rem  Modified version of $ORACLE_HOME/rdbms/admin/utlbstat.sql
rem  Note the addition of tablespace clauses and database links
rem
rem  ****************************************************************
rem                  First create all the tables
rem  ****************************************************************

drop table stats$begin_stats;
create table stats$begin_stats
TABLESPACE CC
as select * from v$sysstat@CASE_STAT where 0 = 1;
drop table stats$end_stats;
create table stats$end_stats
TABLESPACE CC
as select * from stats$begin_stats;

drop table stats$begin_latch;
create table stats$begin_latch
TABLESPACE CC
as select * from v$latch@CASE_STAT where 0 = 1;

drop table stats$end_latch;
create table stats$end_latch
TABLESPACE CC
as select * from stats$begin_latch;

drop table stats$begin_roll;
create table stats$begin_roll
TABLESPACE CC
as select * from v$rollstat@CASE_STAT where 0 = 1;

drop table stats$end_roll;
create table stats$end_roll
TABLESPACE CC
as select * from stats$begin_roll;

drop table stats$begin_lib;
```

```
create table stats$begin_lib
TABLESPACE CC
as select * from v$librarycache@CASE_STAT where 0 = 1;

drop table stats$end_lib;
create table stats$end_lib
TABLESPACE CC
as select * from stats$begin_lib;

drop table stats$begin_dc;
create table stats$begin_dc
TABLESPACE CC
as select * from v$rowcache@CASE_STAT where 0 = 1;

drop table stats$end_dc;
create table stats$end_dc
TABLESPACE CC
as select * from stats$begin_dc;

drop table stats$begin_event;
create table stats$begin_event
TABLESPACE CC
as select * from v$system_event@CASE_STAT where 0 = 1;

drop table stats$end_event;
create table stats$end_event
TABLESPACE CC
as select * from stats$begin_event;

drop table stats$begin_bck_event;
create table stats$begin_bck_event
  (event varchar2(200),
   total_waits number,
   time_waited number)
TABLESPACE CC;
drop table stats$end_bck_event;
create table stats$end_bck_event
as select * from stats$begin_bck_event;

drop table stats$dates;
create table stats$dates (stats_gather_times varchar2(100))
TABLESPACE CC;

drop view stats$file_view;
create view stats$file_view
```

```
as                    /*NOTE:  Have to change the FROM clause here*/
   select ts.name     ts,
          i.name      name,
          x.phyrds pyr,
          x.phywrts pyw,
          x.readtim prt,
          x.writetim pwt,
          x.phyblkrd pbr,
          x.phyblkwrt pbw,
          ROUND(i.bytes/1000000) megabytes_size
   from   v$filestat@CASE_STAT x,
          ts$@CASE_STAT ts,
          v$datafile@CASE_STAT i,
          file$@CASE_STAT f
 where i.file#=f.file#
   and ts.ts#=f.ts#
   and x.file#=f.file#;

drop table stats$begin_file;
create table stats$begin_file   /*No link needed here*/
TABLESPACE CC
as select * from stats$file_view where 0 = 1;

drop table stats$end_file;
create table stats$end_file
TABLESPACE CC
as select * from stats$begin_file;

drop table stats$begin_waitstat;
create table stats$begin_waitstat
TABLESPACE CC
as select * from v$waitstat@CASE_STAT where 1=0;
drop table stats$end_waitstat;
create table stats$end_waitstat
TABLESPACE CC
as select * from stats$begin_waitstat;
```

A modification that was added for the ORACLE8 version of UTLBSTAT introduced a math error. In the STATS$FILE_VIEW view creation script, the following column was added for ORACLE8:

```
ROUND(i.bytes/1000000) megabytes_size
```

However, there are not 1,000,000 bytes in a megabyte. There are 1,048,576 bytes in a megabyte (1,024*1,024). You should correct this entry to read:

```
ROUND(i.bytes/1048576) megabytes_size
```

The UTLESTAT.SQL script also needs to be changed, since it creates tables and inserts data based on queries of remote tables. In the following listing, the statistics gathering portion of UTLESTAT.SQL is shown with the appropriate database links:

```
insert into stats$end_latch select * from v$latch@CASE_STAT;
insert into stats$end_stats select * from v$sysstat@CASE_STAT;
insert into stats$end_lib select * from v$librarycache@CASE_STAT;
update stats$dates set end_time = SysDate;
insert into stats$end_event select * from v$system_event@CASE_STAT;
insert into stats$end_bck_event
  select event, sum(total_waits), sum(time_waited)
    from v$session@CASE_STAT s, v$session_event@CASE_STAT e
    where type = 'BACKGROUND' and s.sid = e.sid
    group by event;
insert into stats$end_waitstat select * from v$waitstat@CASE_STAT;
insert into stats$end_roll select * from v$rollstat@CASE_STAT;
insert into stats$end_file select * from stats$file_view; /*no link*/
insert into stats$end_dc select * from v$rowcache@CASE_STAT;
```

The following listing shows the table creation portion of UTLESTAT.SQL, assuming that the original tables have been created in the CC tablespace of the CC1 Command Center database.

For this example, the tables will once again be stored in the "CC" data tablespace of the CC1 Command Center database. Each **create table** command will have the **tablespace CC** clause appended to it, and each query of a remote table will have the **@case_stat** clause added to it so the database link named CASE_STAT will be used.

```
create table stats$stats
TABLESPACE CC
as select  e.value-b.value change , n.name
    from v$statname n ,  stats$begin_stats b , stats$end_stats e
    where n.statistic# = b.statistic# and n.statistic# =
e.statistic#;
```

```
create table stats$latches
TABLESPACE CC
as select e.gets-b.gets gets,
    e.misses-b.misses misses,
    e.sleeps-b.sleeps sleeps,
    e.immediate_gets-b.immediate_gets immed_gets,
    e.immediate_misses-b.immediate_misses immed_miss,
    n.name
    from v$latchname n ,  stats$begin_latch b , stats$end_latch e
    where n.latch# = b.latch# and n.latch# = e.latch#;

create table stats$event
TABLESPACE CC
as select  e.total_waits-b.total_waits event_count,
        e.time_waited-b.time_waited time_waited,
        e.event
    from  stats$begin_event b , stats$end_event e
    where b.event = e.event
  union
  select  e.total_waits event_count,
        e.time_waited time_waited,
        e.event
    from  stats$end_event e
    where e.event not in (select b.event from stats$begin_event b);

create table stats$bck_event tablespace CC_ as
  select  e.total_waits-b.total_waits event_count,
        e.time_waited-b.time_waited time_waited,
        e.event
    from  stats$begin_bck_event b , stats$end_bck_event e
    where b.event = e.event
  union all
  select  e.total_waits event_count,
        e.time_waited time_waited,
        e.event
    from  stats$end_bck_event e
    where e.event not in (select b.event from stats$begin_bck_event b);

update stats$event e
  set (event_count, time_waited) =
    (select e.event_count - b.event_count,
          e.time_waited - b.time_waited
      from stats$bck_event b
        where e.event = b.event)
    where e.event in (select b.event from stats$bck_event b);
```

```
create table stats$waitstat as
select  e.class,
        e.count - b.count count,
        e.time - b.time time
   from stats$begin_waitstat b, stats$end_waitstat e
   where e.class = b.class;

create table stats$roll
TABLESPACE CC
as select  e.usn undo_segment,
        e.gets-b.gets trans_tbl_gets,
     e.waits-b.waits trans_tbl_waits,
     e.writes-b.writes undo_bytes_written,
     e.rssize segment_size_bytes,
        e.xacts-b.xacts xacts,
     e.shrinks-b.shrinks shrinks,
        e.wraps-b.wraps wraps
     from stats$begin_roll b, stats$end_roll e
        where e.usn = b.usn;

create table stats$files
TABLESPACE CC
as select b.ts table_space,
        b.name file_name,
        e.pyr-b.pyr phys_reads,
        e.pbr-b.pbr phys_blks_rd,
        e.prt-b.prt phys_rd_time,
        e.pyw-b.pyw phys_writes,
        e.pbw-b.pbw phys_blks_wr,
        e.pwt-b.pwt phys_wrt_tim,
        e.megabytes_size
   from stats$begin_file b, stats$end_file e
        where b.name=e.name;

create table stats$dc
TABLESPACE CC
as select b.parameter name,
        e.gets-b.gets get_reqs,
        e.getmisses-b.getmisses get_miss,
        e.scans-b.scans scan_reqs,
        e.scanmisses-b.scanmisses scan_miss,
        e.modifications-b.modifications mod_reqs,
        e.count count,
        e.usage cur_usage
   from stats$begin_dc b, stats$end_dc e
```

```
        where b.cache#=e.cache#
         and  nvl(b.subordinate#,-1) = nvl(e.subordinate#,-1);

create table stats$lib
TABLESPACE CC
as select e.namespace,
       e.gets-b.gets gets,
       e.gethits-b.gethits gethits,
       e.pins-b.pins pins,
       e.pinhits-b.pinhits pinhits,
       e.reloads - b.reloads reloads,
       e.invalidations - b.invalidations invalidations
  from stats$begin_lib b, stats$end_lib e
       where b.namespace = e.namespace;
```

The before and after "snapshots" of these statistics tables will provide information about all of the relevant memory objects that can be monitored in ORACLE. These include the dictionary cache, the Hit Ratio ((db block gets + consistent gets)/physical reads) and the I/O statistics on a file-by-file basis. Information about rollback segment usage and latch usage is also reported.

Interpreting the Statistics Reports

The UTLBSTAT/UTLESTAT scripts create a report called REPORT.TXT that lists information about all sections of the database. The ORACLE8 REPORT.TXT contains the 13 sections listed in Table 6-2.

The following discussion describes the sections of the report, in the order in which they appear in the report.

Library Cache Statistics

The Library Cache (LC) contains shared SQL and PL/SQL areas. The statistics in this section of the report help determine if shared SQL statements are being reparsed due to insufficient memory being allocated to the LC. The listing shown in Figure 6-9 shows sample data that will be used for this discussion.

The Pins column shows the number of times that an item was executed, while Reloads shows the number of misses. The ratio of reloads to pins indicates the percentage of executions that resulted in reparsing. For this sample data, that ratio is 6/378, or 1.6 percent. That means that 1.6 percent

---

Report Sections

Library Cache statistics

Overall statistics

Average length of dirty buffer write queue

Systemwide wait events

Systemwide wait events for background processes

Latch statistics

No-wait gets of latches

Buffer busy wait statistics

Rollback segments

init.ora values

Dictionary cache

File I/O, summed by tablespace

File I/O

TABLE 6-2. *REPORT.TXT Sections*

of the time, a statement had to be reparsed prior to execution. An ideal value for this ratio is 0; ORACLE recommends adding memory to the shared SQL pool if the value is greater than 1 percent (as in this example). Memory is added to this pool via the init.ora SHARED_POOL_SIZE parameter.

LIBRARY	GETS	GETHITRATI	PINS	PINHITRATI	RELOADS	INVALIDATI
BODY	0	1	0	1	0	0
SQL AREA	89	.843	282	.879	5	0
TABLE/PROCED	106	.83	96	.802	1	0
TRIGGER	0	1	0	1	0	0

Note: Sum of Pins column = 378. Sum of Reloads column = 6.

FIGURE 6-9. *Sample Library Cache statistics*

Overall Statistics

The Overall Statistics section of the report shows the total changes for many system statistics, as well as giving *per transaction* and *per logon* values (but since running UTLESTAT requires logging in to the database, the *per logon* numbers will always reflect one more logon than actually took place). Only nonzero changes are shown. This section of the report is useful for determining the overall Hit Ratio and for detecting indications of possible problems in the database setup.

To determine the Hit Ratio, use the formula (Logical Reads-Physical Reads)/Logical Reads. "Logical Reads" is the sum of the "consistent gets" and "db block gets" statistics; "Physical Reads" is shown on the report as "physical reads." For the statistics shown in Figure 6-10, the Hit Ratio is 93.4 percent ((1358 + 214) - 103) / (1358 + 214).

When analyzing the other statistics, note that many of them should be zero or very low for best results. These include recursive calls (which should also show up in the Dictionary Cache section of the report), "Table scans (long tables)," and enqueue time outs. High values for these statistics indicate that the database and the applications that use it should be altered in order to improve performance.

Average Length of Dirty Buffer Write Queue

The query for this portion of the report revisits the statistics tables used by the Overall Statistics section. It compares two of the entries there, calculating the ratio of the change in the "summed dirty queue length" record to the change in the "write requests" record. If the average length (the value returned by the query) is greater than 0.25 times the value of the db_block_buffers init.ora parameter (see "init.ora values" section), then either (1) the database I/O is unevenly distributed among the datafiles, or (2) the db_file_simultaneous_writes parameter is set low. In either case, the database write operations are performing poorly.

Statistic	Total	Per Transact	Per Logon
consistent gets	1358	1358	226.33
db block gets	214	214	35.67
physical reads	103	103	17.17

FIGURE 6-10. *Sample Hit Ratio statistics*

Systemwide Wait Events

This part of the report lists the count, total time, and average time for a number of system events. There is no documentation in the report to establish ranges for the values shown. Since the query for this part of REPORT.TXT calculates the time spent per event, the initiation parameter—TIMED_STATISTICS—should be set to TRUE in init.ora to get nonzero values.

Systemwide Wait Events for Background Processes

This part of the report lists the event, total number of waits, and total time waited for the background processes. Since the query for this part of REPORT.TXT calculates the time spent per event, the initiation parameter—TIMED_STATISTICS—should be set to TRUE in init.ora to get nonzero values. Background processes that experience a high number of waits may use options available as of ORACLE8. The DBWR process can have multiple I/O slave processes; their number is determined by the setting of the DBWR_IO_SLAVES parameter in the init.ora file. The LGWR and ARCH processes can also have I/O slaves.

Latch Statistics

You can use this section of the report to determine the proper number of redo log allocation latches and redo log copy latches that are appropriate for your database.

Redo log copy latches are used on multiple-CPU servers to distribute the processing that is normally done via the redo log allocation latch. In such a setup, the copy latches are used to copy a process's redo information into the redo log buffer area in the SGA. If copy latches are not used, then the allocation latch must both manage the latch allocation and perform the copy, thus slowing down the transaction logging process.

If the Misses value for redo allocation is greater than 10 percent of the Gets column, and if you have multiple processors on your server, then consider adding redo log copy latches. To do this, decrease the init.ora parameter LOG_SMALL_ENTRY_SIZE and increase the LOG_SIMULTANEOUS_COPIES and LOG_ENTRY_PREBUILD_THRESHOLD values. These will determine the number of latches and the maximum size of a redo entry that should be copied using the allocation latch (all others will be passed on to the copy latches). After changing these values, regenerate the statistics reports to see if further latch changes are necessary.

No-wait Gets of Latches

This section of the report calculates the percentage of no-wait latch requests that were satisfied immediately. For the sample data shown in Figure 6-11, all of the no-wait hit ratios are calculated to be 100 percent.

Buffer Busy Waits

This section of the report identifies the type of block for which contention is occurring. If you have too few rollback segments, then you will see a high value (>2,000) for 'undo segment headers'. A high value for 'data block' waits (> 10,000) indicates that you should add DBWR I/O slaves via the DBWR_IO_SLAVES init.ora parameter.

Rollback Segments

This section of the report shows statistics regarding the usage of rollback segments. You should consider making several changes to this section of the report to improve its usefulness:

■ Remove the XACTS column, which is the number of active transactions. Since this statistic is not a cumulative statistic, it is not really helpful to determine the difference between the starting and ending values.

■ Add the Extends column, which is cumulative and can be added to the rollback segment queries of the UTLBSTAT queries. The Extends column lists the number of times the rollback segment was extended.

LATCH_NAME	NOWAIT_GETS	NOWAIT_MISSES	NOWAIT_HIT_RATIO
cache buffers chai	60643	0	1
cache buffers lru	1021	0	1
library cache	96	0	1
library cache pin	14	0	1
row cache objects	11	0	1

FIGURE 6-11. *Sample no-wait latch gets statistics*

The actions that these columns track are described in Chapter 7.

The UNDO_SEGMENT column's value can be used to determine the rollback segment name by querying the V$ROLLNAME table.

```
select Name from V$ROLLNAME
where USN = &UNDO_SEGMENT;
```

Waits for the rollback segment, as indicated in the Trans_Tbl_Waits column of the report, indicate that more rollback segments may be needed in the database. Nonzero values for Shrinks and Wraps indicate that the rollback segments are dynamically expanding and shrinking (back to their **optimal** settings). This activity shows that the rollback segments need to be redesigned in order to reflect the kinds of transactions being performed against the database.

init.ora Values

This section shows the nondefault init.ora parameter settings. You may wish to remove the **where** clause in this query so that all of the parameters and their values will be listed.

Dictionary Cache

The Dictionary Cache (DC) portion of REPORT.TXT reflects the setting (Count) and current usage (Usage) of the dictionary cache in the shared SQL area. The report only shows those parameters that have nonzero values for the time interval being reported. The ratio of Misses to Gets should be low (generally less than 10 percent). Figure 6-12 shows the DC portion of REPORT.TXT.

File I/O, Summed by Tablespace

This section of the report provides the same information as the File I/O section, except that it is summed at the tablespace level instead of the file level. For a description of the most relevant columns in this report, see the "Extensions to the Statistics Reports" section of this chapter.

File I/O

This section records the physical and logical I/O against the datafiles in the database. A description of the most relevant columns is provided in the "Extensions to the Statistics Reports" section of this chapter.

NAME	GET_REQS	GET_MISS	SCAN_REQ	SCAN_MIS	MOD_REQS	COUNT	CUR_USAG
dc_free_extents	246	0	0	0	0	97	82
dc_segments	2	1	0	0	0	128	126
dc_rollback_seg	36	0	0	0	0	17	7
dc_users	46	0	0	0	0	14	13
dc_user_grants	32	0	0	0	0	43	10
dc_objects	60	10	0	0	0	221	218
dc_tables	116	5	0	0	0	195	190
dc_columns	446	27	53	5	0	1880	1871
dc_table_grants	54	24	0	0	0	1626	764
dc_indexes	17	1	37	2	0	261	140
dc_constraint_d	1	0	9	0	0	396	13
dc_synonyms	3	0	0	0	0	18	17
dc_usernames	15	0	0	0	0	20	15
dc_sequences	5	0	0	0	0	7	1

FIGURE 6-12. *Sample Dictionary Cache statistics*

Extensions to the Statistics Reports

By using the queries that generated the REPORT.TXT file, you can generate very useful reports that can be run in an ad hoc manner. These queries will be run against the current values of the statistics in the database, rather than against the tables created by the UTLBSTAT and UTLESTAT scripts. The statistics generated from these queries will thus reflect all of the activities in the database since it was last started.

File I/O

The following SQL*Plus scripts generate a listing of all database files, by disk, and total the I/O activities against each disk. The scripts' output helps to illustrate how well the file I/O is currently being distributed across the available devices.

NOTE
*Both queries assume that the drive names are five characters long (such as /db01). If your drive names are other than five characters long, you will need to modify the **SUBSTR** functions in the queries and the formatting commands for the Drive column.*

```
clear columns
clear breaks
column Drive format A5
column File_Name format A30
column Blocks_Read format 99999999
column Blocks_Written format 99999999
column Total_IOs format 99999999
set linesize 80 pagesize 60 newpage 0 feedback off
ttitle skip center "Database File I/O Information" skip 2
break on report
compute sum of Blocks_Read on report
compute sum of Blocks_Written on report
compute sum of Total_IOs on report

select substr(DF.Name,1,5) Drive,
       SUM(FS.Phyblkrd+FS.Phyblkwrt) Total_IOs,
       SUM(FS.Phyblkrd) Blocks_Read,
       SUM(FS.Phyblkwrt) Blocks_Written
  from V$FILESTAT FS, V$DATAFILE DF
 where DF.File#=FS.File#
 group by substr(DF.Name,1,5)
 order by Total_IOs desc;
```

Sample output is shown in the following listing:

```
DRIVE TOTAL_IOS BLOCKS_READ BLOCKS_WRITTEN
----- --------- ----------- --------------
/db03     57217       56820            397
/db01     39940       27712           6228
/db04     15759       14728           1031
/db02      1898          10           1888
          --------- ----------- --------------
sum      108814       99270           9544
```

The second file I/O query shows the I/O attributed to each datafile, by disk:

```
clear breaks
clear computes
break on Drive skip 1 on report
compute sum of Blocks_Read on Drive
compute sum of Blocks_Written on Drive
compute sum of Total_IOs on Drive
compute sum of Blocks_Read on Report
compute sum of Blocks_Written on Report
compute sum of Total_IOs on Report
ttitle skip center "Database File I/O by Drive" skip 2
```

```
select substr(DF.Name,1,5) Drive,
       DF.Name File_Name,
       FS.Phyblkrd+FS.Phyblkwrt Total_IOs,
       FS.Phyblkrd Blocks_Read,
       FS.Phyblkwrt Blocks_Written
  from V$FILESTAT FS, V$DATAFILE DF
 where DF.File#=FS.File#
 order by Drive, File_Name desc;
```

Sample output for this query is shown in the following listing:

```
DRIVE FILE_NAME                        TOTAL_IOS BLOCKS_READ BLOCKS_WRITTEN
----- ------------------------------- --------- ----------- --------------
/db01 /db01/oracle/CC1/sys.dbf            29551       27708           1843
      /db01/oracle/CC1/temp.dbf            4389           4           4385
*****                                  --------- ----------- --------------
sum                                       33940       27712           6228

/db02 /db02/oracle/CC1/rbs01.dbf           1134           3           1131
      /db02/oracle/CC1/rbs02.dbf            349                        349
      /db02/oracle/CC1/rbs03.dbf            415           7            408
*****                                  --------- ----------- --------------
sum                                        1898          10           1888

/db03 /db03/oracle/CC1/cc.dbf             57217       56820            397
*****                                  --------- ----------- --------------
sum                                       57217       56820            397

/db04 /db04/oracle/CC1/ccindx.dbf         15759       14728           1031
      /db04/oracle/CC1/tests01.dbf
*****                                  --------- ----------- --------------
sum                                       15759       14728           1031

*****                                  --------- ----------- --------------
sum                                      108814       99270           9544
```

The data in the preceding listing shows the format of the queries' output. The first part of the report shows a drive-by-drive comparison of the database I/O against datafiles. It shows that the device called "/db03" is the most heavily used device during database usage. The second report shows that the I/O on device "/db03" is due to one file, since no other database files exist on that drive for the CC1 database. It also shows that accesses against the file on "/db03" are read-intensive by an overwhelming margin.

The second most active device is "/db01," which has two database files on it. Most of the activity on that disk is against the SYSTEM tablespace file, with the TEMP tablespace demanding much less I/O. The SYSTEM tablespace's readings will be high during these queries because you are not looking at I/O for a specific interval, but for the entire time that the database has been opened. Since this is the case, all of the I/O involved in database startup and initial SGA population show up here.

This report is excellent for detecting possible conflicts among file I/O loads. Given this report and the I/O capacity of your devices, you can correctly distribute your database files to minimize I/O contention and maximize throughput. See Chapter 4 for further information on minimizing I/O contention.

Segments at Maximum Extension

The alert reports in this chapter use control limit criteria that are established at the system level (for example, ten extents per segment). However, it is useful to compare the current extent usage of segments against the limits defined specifically for that segment, via the **maxextents** storage parameter.

The following SQL*Plus report queries remote databases to detect any segment that is within a specified factor of its maximum extension. It is written to access those databases via a database link, and the link name is used as part of the output file name. The multiplier value should always be greater than 1—it is the value by which the actual extent count will be multiplied when it is compared with the maximum extent count. To determine which segments are within 20 percent of their maximum extension, set the multiplier value to 1.2.

This query checks four different types of segments: clusters, tables, indexes, and rollback segments. For each one, it determines whether the current number of extents is approaching the maximum number of extents that segment can have (as set via the **maxextents** storage parameter). The "multiplier" variable is used to determine how close to its maximum extension a segment must be before it is returned via this query. If the segment is approaching its maximum extension, then its owner, name, and current space usage information will be returned.

NOTE
As of ORACLE7.3, you can specify a **maxextents**
value of **unlimited**. *When you specify a*
maxextents *value of* **unlimited** *for a segment,*
ORACLE assigns the segment a **maxextents**
value of 2,147,483,645. Therefore, a segment
with a **maxextents** *value of* **unlimited** *could*
theoretically reach its maximum extension,
although that is highly unlikely.

```
rem
rem    file:  over_extended.sql
rem    parameters:  database link name (instance name), multiplier
rem
rem    The "multiplier" value should always be greater than 1.
rem    Example:  To see segments that are within 20 per cent of
rem    their maximum extension, set the multiplier to 1.2.
rem
rem    Example call:
rem    @over_extended CASE 1.2
rem

select
   Owner,                  /*owner of segment*/
   Segment_Name,           /*name of segment*/
   Segment_Type,           /*type of segment*/
   Extents,                /*number of extents already acquired*/
   Blocks                  /*number of blocks already acquired*/
from DBA_SEGMENTS@&&1 s
where                      /*for cluster segments*/
(S.Segment_Type = 'CLUSTER' and exists
(select 'x' from DBA_CLUSTERS@&&1 c
where C.Owner = S.Owner
and C.Cluster_Name = S.Segment_Name
and C.Max_Extents <= S.Extents*&&2))
or                         /*for table segments*/
(s.segment_type = 'TABLE' and exists
(select 'x' from DBA_TABLES@&&1 t
where T.Owner = S.Owner
and T.Table_Name = S.Segment_Name
and T.Max_Extents <= S.Extents*&&2))
or                         /*for index segments*/
(S.Segment_Type = 'INDEX' and exists
(select 'x' from DBA_INDEXES@&&1 i
where I.Owner = S.Owner
```

```
and I.Index_Name = S.Segment_Name
and I.Max_Extents <= S.Extents*&&2))
or                          /*for rollback segments*/
(S.Segment_Type = 'ROLLBACK' and exists
(select 'x' from DBA_ROLLBACK_SEGS@&&1 r
where R.Owner = S.Owner
and R.Segment_Name = S.Segment_Name
and R.Max_Extents <= S.Extents*&&2))
order by 1,2

spool &&1._over_extended.lst
/
spool off
undefine 1
undefine 2
```

The output file for this report will contain the database link name in its title. The output file name uses the period (.) as the concatenation character in SQL*Plus.

The Well-Managed Database

The effective management of any system requires strategic planning, quality control, and action to resolve out-of-control parts of the system. The database management systems described in this chapter provide a broad foundation for the monitoring of all of your databases. Individual databases may require additional monitoring to be performed, or may have specific thresholds. These can be easily added to the samples shown here.

Establishing a Command Center database allows the other databases in the system to be monitored without impacting the measures being checked. It also allows for easy addition of new databases to the monitoring system and trend analysis of all statistics. It should be tied in to your existing operating system monitoring programs in order to coordinate the distribution and resolution of alert messages.

Like any system, the Command Center database must be planned. The examples in this chapter were designed to handle the most commonly monitored objects in the database, and threshold values were established for each. Do not create the CC1 database until you have fully defined what you are going to monitor and what the threshold values are. Once that has been done, create the database—and in a great example of recursion, use the monitoring database to monitor itself.

CHAPTER
7

Managing Rollback Segments

ollback segments are ORACLE's version of time machines. They capture the "before image" of data as it existed prior to the start of a transaction. Queries by other users against the data that is being changed will return the data as it existed *before* the change began.

Rollback segments are the problem children of an ORACLE database. No matter how well-behaved the rest of the database is, they will almost always require special attention. And since they control the database's ability to handle transactions, they play a key role in the database's success.

This chapter will cover the key managerial tasks that DBAs need to perform for rollback segments. You will see

- The basic functional aspects of rollback segments

- The unique way in which they use available space

- How to monitor their usage

- How to select the correct number and size of rollback segments for your database

Rollback Segments Overview

The SQL command **rollback** allows users to undo transactions that have been made against a database. This functionality is available for any **update**, **insert**, or **delete** transaction; it is not available for changes to database objects (such as **alter table** commands). When you select data that another user is changing, ORACLE uses the rollback segments to show you the data as it existed before the changes began.

How the Database Uses Rollback Segments

Rollback segments are involved in every transaction that occurs within the database. They allow the database to maintain read consistency between multiple transactions. The number and size of rollback segments available are specified by the DBA during database creation.

Since rollback segments are created within the database, they must be created within a tablespace. The first rollback segment, called *SYSTEM*, is stored in the SYSTEM tablespace. Further rollback segments are usually created in at least one other separate tablespace. Because they are created in tablespaces, their maximum size is limited to the amount of space in the tablespaces' datafiles. Appropriate sizing of rollback segments is therefore a critical task. Figure 7-1 depicts the storage of rollback segments in tablespaces.

A *rollback segment entry* is the set of before-image data blocks that contain rows that are modified by a transaction. Each rollback segment entry must be completely contained within one rollback segment. A single rollback segment can support multiple rollback segment entries. This makes the number of rollback segments available a critical factor for the database's performance. Figure 7-2 illustrates the relationship between rollback segments and rollback segment entries.

The database assigns transactions to rollback segments in a round-robin fashion. This results in a fairly even distribution of the number of transactions in each rollback segment. Although it is possible to specify which rollback segment a transaction should use (see "Specifying a

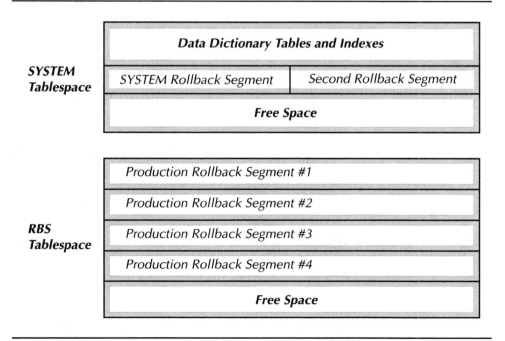

FIGURE 7-1. *Storage of rollback segments in tablespaces*

RBS Tablespace

Production Rollback Segment #1:	Entry for transaction 1	Entry for transaction 5
Production Rollback Segment #2:	Entry for transaction 2	Free Space
Production Rollback Segment #3:	Entry for transaction 3	Free Space
Production Rollback Segment #4:	Entry for transaction 4	Free Space
	Free Space

FIGURE 7-2. *Storage of rollback segment entries in rollback segments*

Rollback Segment for a Transaction," later in this chapter), this is usually not done. It is therefore not advantageous to have rollback segments of varied sizes.

It is possible to create rollback segments that are designated as *private* or *public*. These designations refer to whether the rollback segment is available to a single instance or to multiple instances that access that database. Private rollback segments are explicitly acquired when an instance opens a database (as shown in the "Activating Rollback Segments" section of this chapter). If a second instance accesses the same database, then it may not use the same private rollback segment that the first instance has already acquired. Instead, it can either use its own private rollback segments or it can draw from a pool of public rollback segments. The administrative discussions in this chapter will focus on private rollback segments.

The SYSTEM Rollback Segment

The SYSTEM rollback segment is created automatically during database creation. Its name and storage parameters are not specified in the **create database** command. Rather, it is implicitly created in the SYSTEM tablespace.

The usage of the SYSTEM rollback segment varies depending on your configuration. If your database has multiple tablespaces (as almost all databases do), then you will have to create a second rollback segment to support them. If other rollback segments are available, then the SYSTEM rollback segment is used only to manage database-level transactions (such as modifications to the data dictionary tables that record user privileges).

The Second Rollback Segment

If your database will have multiple tablespaces, then you will have to create a second rollback segment. During database creation, this must be created in the SYSTEM tablespace. However, it should not be made available for production transactions; doing so would put the SYSTEM tablespace's free space in jeopardy during large transactions.

Therefore, the second rollback segment should be used only during database creation. As soon as a tablespace for rollback segments has been created, create rollback segments in it and deactivate or drop the second rollback segment in the SYSTEM tablespace.

With regard to rollback segments, your database creation procedures should do the following:

1. Create a database, which implicitly creates a SYSTEM rollback segment in the SYSTEM tablespace.

2. Create a second rollback segment, named r0, in the SYSTEM tablespace.

3. Make the new rollback segment available. Other tablespaces can then be created.

4. Create a tablespace called RBS for further rollback segments.

5. Create additional rollback segments in the RBS tablespace.

6. Deactivate the second rollback segment (r0) in the SYSTEM tablespace and activate the new rollback segments in RBS.

Although it is no longer needed after database creation, you may wish to keep the second rollback segment available but inactive. To do this, deactivate the rollback segment (see "Activating Rollback Segments" later in this chapter) but do not drop it. This rollback segment can then be quickly reactivated during emergency situations that affect the RBS tablespace.

The Production Rollback Segments

Non-SYSTEM *production rollback segments* support the rollback segment entries generated by production usage of the database. They support the use of the **rollback** command to restore the previous image of the modified records. They also roll back transactions that are aborted prior to completion, either because of a problem with the rollback segment or because of user cancellation of the transaction. During queries, rollback segments are used to construct a consistent "before image" of the data that was changed—but not committed—prior to the execution of the query.

The database assigns rollback segment entries to the production rollback segments in a round-robin fashion. This method is designed to distribute the transaction load being carried by the rollback segments (as seen in Figure 7-2). Since a single rollback segment can support multiple transactions, it is possible to create a single, large rollback segment to handle all transactions in a database. However, such a design would result in performance problems due to contention for the rollback segment.

Conversely, the DBA may choose to create many small rollback segments, so that each transaction will be guaranteed its own rollback segment. This implementation will also run into performance problems if the rollback segments are created so small that they must dynamically extend in order to service their transactions. Planning a database's rollback segment design involves finding the proper balance between the two extremes. The "Choosing the Number and Size" section of this chapter addresses this critical design issue.

Activating Rollback Segments

Activating a rollback segment makes it available to the database users. A rollback segment may be deactivated without being dropped. It will maintain the space already allocated to it, and can be reactivated at a later date. The following examples provide the full set of rollback segment activation commands.

An active rollback segment can be deactivated via the command:

```
alter rollback segment SEGMENT_NAME offline;
```

Dropping the rollback segment requires a separate command:

```
drop rollback segment SEGMENT_NAME;
```

Creating a rollback segment requires the following command:

```
create rollback segment SEGMENT_NAME
tablespace RBS;
```

Note that this command creates a private rollback segment (since the **public** keyword was not used) and that it creates it in a non-SYSTEM tablespace called RBS. Since no storage parameters are specified, it will use the default storage parameters for that tablespace.

Although the rollback segment has been created, it is not yet in use by the database. To activate it, bring it online using the following command:

```
alter rollback segment SEGMENT_NAME online;
```

Once it has been created, you should list a rollback segment in the database's init.ora file. This file is only read during database startups. A sample init.ora entry for rollback segments is shown in the following listing:

```
rollback_segments    = (r0,r1,r2)
```

NOTE
The SYSTEM rollback segment should never be listed here. The SYSTEM rollback segment can never be dropped; it is always acquired along with any other rollback segments the instance may acquire.

For this database, the rollback segments named r0, r1, and r2 are online. If you take a rollback segment offline, remove its entry from the init.ora file.

Specifying a Rollback Segment for a Transaction

You can use the **set transaction** command to specify which rollback segment a transaction should use. This should be used before large transactions to ensure that they use rollback segments that are created specifically for them.

The settings that are specified via this command will be used only for the current transaction. The following example shows a series of transactions. The first transaction is directed to use the ROLL_BATCH rollback segment. The second transaction (following the second **commit**) will be randomly assigned to a production rollback segment.

```
commit;

set transaction use rollback segment ROLL_BATCH
insert into TABLE_NAME
select * from DATA_LOAD_TABLE;

commit;

REM*   The commit command clears the rollback segment assignment.
REM*   Implicit commits, like those caused by DDL commands, will
REM*   also clear the rollback segment designation.

insert into TABLE_NAME select * from SOME_OTHER_TABLE;
```

Space Usage Within Rollback Segments

When a transaction begins, ORACLE starts writing a rollback segment entry in a rollback segment. The entry cannot expand into any other rollback segments, nor can it dynamically switch to use a different rollback segment. The entry begins writing sequentially to an extent within the rollback segment. Each block within that extent must contain information for only one transaction. Blocks from different transactions can be stored in the same extent. This is shown in Figure 7-3.

In Figure 7-3, the first five blocks of an extent of a rollback segment are shown. Two separate transactions are storing active rollback information in that rollback extent.

In an ideal database, each transaction will fit within a single extent. However, this is rarely the case. When a transaction can no longer acquire space within an extent, the rollback segment looks for another extent to which it can continue writing the rollback segment entry.

The database will first try to extend the entry into the next extent within the rollback segment. If the current extent is the last extent within the rollback segment, then the database will attempt to extend the entry into the first extent.

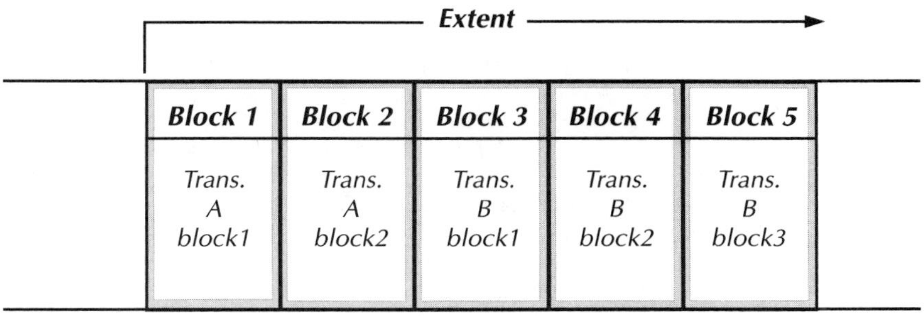

FIGURE 7-3. *Two transactions in a single rollback segment extent*

However, that extent may already be in use. If it is, then the rollback segment will be forced to acquire a new extent. The entry will then be continued in this new extent. This process of selective extension is illustrated in Figure 7-4.

As shown in Figure 7-4a, a transaction (referred to here as "transaction A") presently has its entry data stored in four extents of rollback segment r1. Since it started in extent #3 of this rollback segment, the first two extents must have been unavailable when the transaction started. At this point, it has acquired four extents and is in search of a fifth.

Since it already occupies the last extent (extent #6) of the rollback segment, the database checks to see if the first extent of that rollback segment contains any active transaction data. If it does not, then that extent is used as the fifth extent of transaction A's entry (see Figure 7-4b). If, however, that extent is actively being used by a transaction, then the rollback segment will dynamically extend itself. Extent #7 will then be used as the fifth extent of transaction A (see Figure 7-4c).

Note that once a transaction is complete, its data is not deleted from the rollback segment. It remains there to service the queries and transactions that began executing before it was committed. This may cause a problem with long queries; namely, they may get the error message:

ORA-1555: snapshot too old (rollback segment too small)

Rollback Segment r1

Extent 1	Extent 2	Extent 3	Extent 4	Extent 5	Extent 6
		Transaction A, extent 1	Transaction A, extent 2	Transaction A, extent 3	Transaction A, extent 4

(a) Transaction A started in Extent 3 and has filled Extent 6.

Extent 1	Extent 2	Extent 3	Extent 4	Extent 5	Extent 6
Transaction A, extent 5		Transaction A, extent 1	Transaction A, extent 2	Transaction A, extent 3	Transaction A, extent 4

(b) If Extent 1 is now available, Transaction A uses it.

Extent 1	Extent 2	Extent 3	Extent 4	Extent 5	Extent 6	Extent 7
(in use)		Transaction A, extent 1	Transaction A, extent 2	Transaction A, extent 3	Transaction A, extent 4	Transaction A, extent 5

(c) If Extent 1 is in use, the rollback segment will extend.

FIGURE 7-4.   *Selective extension of rollback segments*

This problem arises from the definition of "active" data. Consider the large transaction referred to as "Transaction A" in Figure 7-4. If a long-running query accesses the same table as Transaction A, then it will need to use the data blocks stored by Transaction A's rollback segment entry. However, once Transaction A has completed, those blocks are marked as being "*inactive.*" Those blocks may then be overwritten by other transactions, even though the separate long-running query against those blocks has not completed. The query, upon attempting to read the blocks that have been overwritten, will fail. This situation is depicted in Figure 7-5.

As shown in Figure 7-5, a transaction can span multiple extents. In Figure 7-5a, transaction A uses five extents of a rollback segment and then completes. Other users may be using that data even after the transaction completes. For example, if other users were querying the data before transaction A completed, they would need the rollback segment entry in

Extent 1	Extent 2	Extent 3	Extent 4	Extent 5	Extent 6	Extent 7
		Transaction A, extent 1	Transaction A, extent 2	Transaction A, extent 3	Transaction A, extent 4	Transaction A, extent 5

(a) Transaction A is in progress; its data is used by a large query.

Extent 1	Extent 2	Extent 3	Extent 4	Extent 5	Extent 6	Extent 7
Transaction B, extent 1		OLD Trans. A, extent 1	OLD Trans. A, extent 2	OLD Trans. A, extent 3	OLD Trans. A, extent 4	OLD Trans. A, extent 5

(b) Transaction A completes. Its entry data stays and is used by the long-running query. Transaction B starts.

Extent 1	Extent 2	Extent 3	Extent 4	Extent 5	Extent 6	Extent 7
Transaction B, extent 1	**Transaction B, extent 2**	**Transaction B, extent 3**	OLD Trans. A, extent 2	OLD Trans. A, extent 3	OLD Trans. A, extent 4	OLD Trans. A, extent 5

(c) Transaction B overwrites blocks used by the large query. Query fails.

FIGURE 7-5. *Query failure due to "snapshot too old" error*

order to reconstruct the table's data for their queries. The rollback entry data for transaction A is inactive, but it is in use. When transaction B begins (Figure 7-5b), it starts in the first available extent of the rollback segment. When it extends beyond the second extent, the rollback segment entry data from transaction A is overwritten (since it is inactive) and any process using that rollback segment entry data will fail (since it is in use).

There are two problems that are the true cause of the query's failure. First, a long-running query is being executed at the same time as data manipulation transactions. In other words, batch processing and online transaction processing are being performed simultaneously in the database. From the earlier discussions of rollback segment functionality, the problems with this strategy should be clear: the long-running query must not only access all of the tables and indexes it needs to complete, but must also access data stored in the rollback segments to return a consistent version of the data.

Since it must continue to access the rollback segments until it completes, the long-running query requires that the rollback segment entries it is using not be overwritten. But once those entries have completed, there is no guarantee that this will be the case. The advice given in the error message ("rollback segment too small") solves the problem by resolving the second, related problem: to avoid overwriting existing entries in the rollback segment, add more space to it so it will take longer to wrap around back to the first extent.

This is not a true solution. It is only a delaying tactic, since the rollback segment may eventually overwrite all of its data blocks. The proper solution is to schedule long-running queries at times when online transaction processing is at a minimum.

The OPTIMAL Storage Clause

As shown previously in Figure 7-4, rollback segments dynamically extend to handle large transaction entry loads. Once the transaction that forced the extension completes, the rollback segment *keeps* the space that it acquired during the extension. This can be a major cause of rollback segment space management problems. A single large transaction may wipe out all of the available free space in the rollback segment tablespace. This prevents the other rollback segments in that tablespace from being able to extend.

This problem is solved via two changes in the **storage** clause used for rollback segments. First, the **pctincrease** parameter is no longer available. This is important because it forces rollback segments to grow at an even pace, rather than at a geometrically increasing rate (see Chapter 4, the "Implications of the **storage** Clause" section, for an illustration of this problem).

The second change in the **storage** clause for rollback segments is the addition of a parameter called **optimal**. This parameter allows DBAs to specify an optimal length of the rollback segment (in bytes). When the rollback segment extends beyond this length, it later dynamically *shrinks* itself by eliminating its oldest extent.

At first glance, this seems like a terrific option. It prevents a single rollback segment from using all of the free space in a tablespace. However, note that the database is

1. Dynamically extending the rollback segment, causing a performance hit

2. Dynamically choosing and eliminating old extents, causing a performance hit

3. Eliminating inactive data earlier than it would have under the old method

The last point causes databases with **optimal** sizes set too low to experience a greater incidence of the "snapshot too old" scenario depicted in Figure 7-5. This is because old transaction data may now be eliminated in two ways: by being overwritten and by being discarded during shrinks.

The process of extending and shrinking a rollback segment via the **optimal** parameter is shown in Figure 7-6. Note that this parameter is very useful for handling situations in which the transaction size is completely unknown and the available free space in the rollback segment tablespace is limited. However, it is not a substitute for the correct sizing of the rollback segments. This topic will be covered in the "Choosing the Number and Size" section later in this chapter.

As shown in Figure 7-6, when a rollback segment must extend itself, it checks its **optimal** size value. If it is already beyond its **optimal** size, it will

Extent 1	Extent 2	Extent 3	Extent 4	Extent 5	Extent 6
OLD Trans. C, extent 1	OLD Trans. C, extent 2	Transaction D, extent 1	Transaction D, extent 2	Transaction E, extent 1	Transaction E, extent 2

(a) Transaction A has completed. Transaction D occupies Extents 3 and 4, while transaction E uses Extents 5 and 6. The OPTIMAL setting is set to the equivalent of 6 extents.

Extent 2	Extent 3	Extent 4	Extent 5	Extent 6	Extent 7
OLD Trans. C, extent 2	Transaction D, extent 1	Transaction D, extent 2	Transaction E, extent 1	Transaction E, extent 2	Transaction D, extent 3

(b) Transaction D extends into Extent 7. To maintain its OPTIMAL size, the rollback segment eliminates its oldest inactive extent (Extent 1).

FIGURE 7-6. *Dynamic shrinking of rollback segments to an optimal size*

acquire a new extent (Extent #7 in Figure 7-6b). After the transaction completes, the rollback segment will eliminate its oldest extent (Extent #1). This keeps the rollback segment to a prespecified size while servicing queries. It has the side effect of reducing the amount of inactive rollback data available to current transactions.

What would have happened if there had been no inactive extents in the rollback segment when it exceeded its **optimal** size? The rollback segment would have continued to extend to support the transaction. Each time the transaction forced the rollback segment to extend again, it would check to see if it could reclaim any inactive extents. If the rollback segment is forced (for instance, by a single, large transaction) to extend beyond its **optimal** size, then the space it acquired would remain part of that rollback segment temporarily. The next transaction that wrapped into a second extent would force the database to reclaim any space that forced it to exceed its **optimal** setting.

Monitoring Rollback Segment Usage

The monitoring requirements for rollback segments are similar to those for data segments. Monitoring the space and memory usage of segments was described in Chapter 6. Since rollback segments are dynamic objects that are accessed during transactions, they have additional features that should be monitored.

Monitoring Current Space Allocation

The current space allocation for a database's rollback segments can be determined by querying the DBA_SEGMENTS dictionary view, where the Segment_Type column equals 'ROLLBACK':

```
select * from DBA_SEGMENTS
where Segment_Type = 'ROLLBACK';
```

Table 7-1 lists the columns of interest that will be returned from this query.

Column Name	Description
SEGMENT_NAME	Name of the rollback segment
TABLESPACE_NAME	Tablespace in which the rollback segment is stored
HEADER_FILE	File in which the first extent of the rollback segment is stored
BYTES	Actual allocated size of the rollback segment, in bytes
BLOCKS	Actual allocated size of the rollback segment, in ORACLE blocks
EXTENTS	Number of extents in the rollback segment
INITIAL_EXTENT	Size, in ORACLE blocks, of the initial extent
NEXT_EXTENT	Size, in ORACLE blocks, of the next extent
MIN_EXTENTS	Minimum number of extents for the rollback segment
MAX_EXTENTS	Maximum number of extents for the rollback segment

TABLE 7-1. *Rollback Segment-Related Columns in DBA_SEGMENTS*

There's one column missing. The value for the **optimal** parameter is not stored in DBA_SEGMENTS. Rather, it is stored in the OptSize column of the dynamic performance table named V$ROLLSTAT. To retrieve this value, query V$ROLLSTAT, joining it to V$ROLLNAME to get the rollback segment's name.

```
select
    N.Name,              /* rollback segment name */
    S.OptSize            /* rollback segment OPTIMAL size */
from V$ROLLNAME N, V$ROLLSTAT S
where N.USN=S.USN;
```

If no **optimal** size was specified for the rollback segment, then the OptSize value returned by this query will be **NULL**.

Since rollback segments are physical segments in the database, they are included in the space monitoring scripts given in Chapter 6. The tablespace space monitoring programs will report any change in the free space available in the RBS or SYSTEM tablespace. The extent monitoring scripts store records for all of the rollback segments regardless of their number of extents. By doing this, all changes in the rollback segment space allocations can be detected immediately.

The queries for the Command Center space monitoring scripts in Chapter 6 query the DBA_SEGMENTS view, the main columns of which are listed in Table 7-1.

Shrinking Rollback Segments

You can force rollback segments to shrink. You can use the **shrink** clause of the **alter rollback segment** command to shrink rollback segments to any size you want. If you do not specify a size the rollback segment should **shrink** to, then it will **shrink** to its **optimal** size. You cannot **shrink** a rollback segment to fewer than two extents.

In the following listing, the R1 rollback segment is altered twice. The first command **shrink**s R1 to 15MB. The second command **shrink**s the R1 rollback segment to its **optimal** size.

```
alter rollback segment R1 shrink to 15M;

alter rollback segment R1 shrink;
```

Monitoring Current Status

Information about the rollback segments' status is accessible via the DBA_ROLLBACK_SEGS view. This view contains the storage parameters (Tablespace_Name, Initial_Extent, Next_Extent, Min_Extents, Max_Extents) provided in DBA_SEGMENTS. It includes two additional columns, which are listed in Table 7-2.

The status of a rollback segment will be one of the values listed in Table 7-3.

Column Name	Description
STATUS	Status of the rollback segment.
INSTANCE_NUM	Instance the rollback segment belongs to. For a single-instance system, this value is **NULL**.

TABLE 7-2. *Additional Columns in DBA_ROLLBACK_SEGS*

Status	Description
IN USE	The rollback segment is online.
AVAILABLE	The rollback segment has been created, but has not been brought online.
OFFLINE	The rollback segment is offline.
INVALID	The rollback segment has been dropped. Dropped rollback segments remain listed in the data dictionary with this status.
NEEDS RECOVERY	The rollback segment contains data that cannot be rolled back, or is corrupted.
PARTLY AVAILABLE	The rollback segment contains data from an unresolved transaction involving a distributed database.

TABLE 7-3.   *Rollback Segment Status Values in DBA_ROLLBACK_SEGS*

Monitoring Dynamic Extensions

Rollback segments can extend and shrink. In addition, rollback segment entries "*wrap*" from one extent to another within a rollback segment each time they grow beyond their present extent. All three of these actions require the database to perform additional work to handle transactions. This extra work affects performance.

Consider the case of a large transaction that extends beyond its **optimal** value when an entry wraps and causes the rollback segment to expand into another extent. The sequence of events to handle this looks like:

1. The transaction begins.

2. An entry is made in the rollback segment header for the new transaction entry.

3. The transaction entry acquires blocks in an extent of the rollback segment.

4. The entry attempts to wrap into a second extent. None is available, so the rollback segment must extend.

5. The rollback segment extends.

6. The data dictionary tables for space management are updated.

7. The transaction completes.

8. The rollback segment checks to see if it is past its **optimal** value. It is.

9. The rollback segment chooses its oldest inactive extent.

10. The oldest inactive extent is eliminated.

If the rollback segment had been sized so that the entry fit in one extent, the sequence of events would instead look like:

1. The transaction begins.

2. An entry is made in the rollback segment header for the new transaction entry.

3. The transaction entry acquires blocks in an extent of the rollback segment.

4. The transaction completes.

The savings in the amount of overhead needed for space management are clear.

The incidence of shrinks, wraps, and extensions can be monitored via the V$ROLLSTAT dynamic performance table. The records from this view may be retrieved for a specified time interval or via ad hoc queries, as described in the next two sections.

Dynamic Extensions During a Time Interval

To determine the changes in the values of the V$ROLLSTAT columns during a specific time interval, the system statistics scripts can be used. These scripts, located in the /rdbms/admin subdirectory under the ORACLE software home directory, are UTLBSTAT.SQL and UTLESTAT.SQL. Running these scripts is described in Chapter 6.

The UTLBSTAT script creates a table that stores the current values in the V$ROLLSTAT table. When UTLESTAT is run at a later date, V$ROLLSTAT's values at that time will be compared to those that were stored. The difference will be reported. It is important that the database not be shut down between the running of the UTLBSTAT script and the UTLESTAT script. This is because the database resets the statistics in the V$ROLLSTAT table during system startup; therefore, the baseline values generated by UTLBSTAT would be of no use following a database restart.

In the UTLBSTAT script, the following commands are used to create the tables at the beginning of the time interval. The first two **create table** commands create tables called STATS$BEGIN_ROLL and STATS$END_ROLL, both with no records in them. The **insert** command then stores the current values from the V$ROLLSTAT table into STATS$BEGIN_ROLL.

```
DROP TABLE stats$begin_roll;
CREATE TABLE stats$begin_roll
AS SELECT * FROM v$rollstat WHERE 0 = 1;

DROP TABLE stats$end_roll;
CREATE TABLE stats$end_roll
AS SELECT * FROM stats$begin_roll;

INSERT INTO stats$begin_roll SELECT * FROM v$rollstat;
```

When UTLESTAT is run, it populates the STATS$END_ROLL table by querying the V$ROLLSTAT table for the then-current values. A table called STATS$ROLL is then created. Its sole purpose is to hold the results of a query that determines the difference between the records in STATS$BEGIN_ROLL and STATS$END_ROLL. This is the table that is queried to generate the output report from UTLESTAT.

```
INSERT INTO stats$end_roll SELECT * FROM v$rollstat;

CREATE TABLE stats$roll
AS SELECT   e.usn undo_segment,
        e.gets-b.gets trans_tbl_gets,
    e.waits-b.waits trans_tbl_waits,
    e.writes-b.writes undo_bytes_written,
    e.rssize segment_size_bytes,
        e.xacts-b.xacts xacts,
    e.shrinks-b.shrinks shrinks,
        e.wraps-b.wraps wraps
    FROM stats$begin_roll b, stats$end_roll e
        WHERE e.usn = b.usn;
```

The data in the STATS$ROLL table lists each rollback segment and the statistics that accumulated during the time between the running of UTLBSTAT and UTLESTAT.

Querying the STATS$ROLL table will return the columns listed in Table 7-4 for the interval.

You should make two modifications to the rollback segment portion of UTLESTAT.SQL. First, the Xacts reference in the UTLESTAT query should be changed. This column reflects the *current* number of active transactions, not the *cumulative* number of transactions. As such, the difference between the beginning and ending values for Xacts has no significance. Change that line from

```
e.xacts-b.xacts xacts,
```

to

```
e.xacts        xacts,
```

if you care about this value. Otherwise, remove it entirely.

Second, you may wish to include the Extends column (which *is* cumulative) in the report. This column shows the number of times the

Column Name	Description
TRANS_TBL_GETS	The number of rollback segment header requests.
TRANS_TBL_WAITS	The number of rollback segment header requests that resulted in waits.
UNDO_BYTES_WRITTEN	The number of bytes written to the rollback segment.
SEGMENT_SIZE_BYTES	The size of the rollback segment, in bytes. Note that this column only considers the ending value.
XACTS	The number of active transactions.
SHRINKS	The number of **shrink**s that the rollback segment had to perform in order to stay at the **optimal** size.
WRAPS	The number of times a rollback segment entry wrapped from one extent into another.

TABLE 7-4. *Columns Available in STATS$ROLL*

rollback segment was extended. It is most appropriate for those rollback segments whose **optimal** size has not yet been reached.

The monitoring of dynamic extension, wrapping, and shrinking of the rollback segments is thus fairly simple. The rollback segment portions of the UTLBSTAT/UTLESTAT reports can be used to determine the nature of all dynamic extension within the rollback segments.

A final note of caution: these scripts **insert** records into tables. In other words, they perform transactions, which in turn generate rollback segment entries, skewing the results. The number of bytes generated via these queries is less than 100. This skew can be avoided by performing the queries from a remote database (see Chapter 6 for information on this topic).

Ad Hoc Querying

The V$ROLLSTAT table can be queried in an ad hoc fashion by anyone who has been granted access to it. This access is usually granted via PLUSTRACE role.

The columns available in V$ROLLSTAT are shown in Table 7-5. When querying V$ROLLSTAT, you will also want to query V$ROLLNAME. This table maps the rollback segment number to its name (for example, 'SYSTEM','R0').

There is a one-to-one relationship between the two tables. They both have a primary key called USN ("Undo Segment Number"). When querying the tables in an ad hoc fashion, join them on this key as shown in the following example:

```
select
    N.Name,                          /* rollback segment name */
    S.RsSize                         /* rollback segment size */
from V$ROLLNAME N, V$ROLLSTAT S
where N.USN=S.USN;
```

Transactions Per Rollback Segment

Determining the users who own active entries in each rollback segment effectively answers two questions: how are the rollback segments currently distributed, and who is where?

Understanding this query requires knowing that transactions acquire locks within the rollback segment header. The V$LOCK table can thus be

Column Name	Description
USN	Rollback segment number.
EXTENTS	Number of extents in the rollback segment.
RSSIZE	The size of the rollback segment, in bytes.
WRITES	The number of bytes of entries written to the rollback segment.
XACTS	The number of active transactions.
GETS	The number of rollback segment header requests.
WAITS	The number of rollback segment header requests that resulted in waits.
OPTSIZE	The value of the **optimal** parameter for the rollback segment.
HWMSIZE	The highest value (high-water mark), in bytes, of RsSize reached during usage.
SHRINKS	The number of shrinks that the rollback segment has had to perform in order to stay at the **optimal** size.
WRAPS	The number of times a rollback segment entry has wrapped from one extent into another.
EXTENDS	The number of times that the rollback segment had to acquire a new extent.
AVESHRINK	The average number of bytes freed during a shrink.
AVEACTIVE	The average size of active extents.
STATUS	Status of the rollback segment; similar to the status values listed earlier. Values are ONLINE (same as 'IN USE') and PENDING OFFLINE (same as 'PARTLY AVAILABLE').

TABLE 7-5. *Columns Available in V$ROLLSTAT*

joined to V$ROLLNAME. Since locks are owned by processes, the V$LOCK table can be joined to V$PROCESS. The result is a mapping of user processes in V$PROCESS to rollback segment names in V$ROLLNAME.

```
REM   Users in rollback segments
REM
column rr heading 'RB Segment' format a18
column us heading 'Username' format a15
column os heading 'OS User' format a10
column te heading 'Terminal' format a10
```

```
select R.Name rr,
       nvl(S.Username,'no transaction') us,
       S.Osuser os,
       S.Terminal te
  from V$LOCK L, V$SESSION S, V$ROLLNAME R
 where L.Sid = S.Sid(+)
   and trunc(L.Id1/65536) = R.USN
   and L.Type = 'TX'
   and L.Lmode = 6
order by R.Name
/
```

Sample output for the preceding query is shown in the following listing:

```
RB Segment            Username           OS User     Terminal
------------------    ----------------   ----------  ----------
R01                   APPL1_BAT          georgehj    ttypc
R02                   APPL1_BAT          detmerst    ttypb
```

This shows that only two users are actively writing to the rollback segments (two different sessions of the APPL1_BAT ORACLE user, by two different operating system users). Each user is writing to a rollback segment that no one else is using. Rollback segments R01 and R02 are the only rollback segments presently used by active transactions. If there were more than one user using a rollback segment, there would be multiple records for that rollback segment.

Data Volumes in Rollback Segments

The number of bytes written to a rollback segment can be determined via the dynamic performance table V$ROLLSTAT. This table contains a column called Writes, which records the number of bytes that have been written to each rollback segment since the database was last started.

To determine the amount of activity in a rollback segment for a specific time interval, select the Writes value at the start of the test period. When the testing completes, query that value for the then-current value. The difference will be the number of bytes written to the rollback segment during that time interval. Since shutting down the database resets the statistics in the V$ROLLSTAT table, it is important that the database remain open during the testing interval.

Select the Writes value from the V$ROLLSTAT table using the following query:

```
select
    N.Name,                          /* rollback segment name */
    S.Writes                         /* bytes written to date */
from V$ROLLNAME N, V$ROLLSTAT S
where N.USN=S.USN;
```

Detecting the size of the rollback segment entry created by a single transaction requires combining these queries with a command given earlier in this chapter. First, isolate the transaction by executing it in a database in which it is the only process. Direct the transaction to a specific rollback segment via the

```
set transaction use rollback segment SEGMENT_NAME
```

command. Then, query the Writes column of the V$ROLLSTAT table for that rollback segment. When the transaction completes, requery V$ROLLSTAT. The exact size of the transaction's rollback segment entry will be the difference between the two Writes values.

Choosing the Number and Size

You can use the descriptions of rollback segment entries given in this chapter to properly design the appropriate rollback segment layout for your database. Note that the final design will be different for each database—unless your databases are functionally identical with respect to their transactions.

The design process involves determining the transaction volume and estimating the number and type of transactions. In the following sections you will see this process illustrated for a sample application.

From this transaction data, the proper number, size, and structure of the rollback segments can be derived.

Transaction Entry Volume

The first step in the design process is to determine the total amount of rollback segment entry data that will be active or in use at any instant. Note that there are two distinct types of entries being considered here:

■ *Active* entries, which have not yet been committed or rolled back

■ *Inactive, in-use* (IIU) entries, which have been committed or rolled back, but whose data is in use by separate processes (such as long-running queries)

Rollback segment entries that are inactive, and are not in use by separate processes, are unimportant in these calculations.

The key to managing rollback segments effectively is to minimize the amount of "Inactive, in-use" (IIU) entry data. As a DBA, you have no way of detecting the amount of rollback segment space being used by inactive, in-use entries. Their existence only becomes evident when users begin reporting the ORA-1555 "snapshot too old" error described previously in this chapter (see Figure 7-5).

Minimizing the amount of IIU data in rollback segments involves knowing when long-running queries are being executed. If they are occurring concurrently with multiple transactions, there will be a steady accumulation of IIU rollback segment entries. No matter how large the rollback segments are, this poor transaction distribution will ultimately cause queries to fail.

To solve this problem, isolate all large queries so that they run at times when very little transaction activity is occurring. This minimizes the amount of IIU rollback segment entry data while also helping to prevent potential concurrent I/O contention between the queries and the transactions.

To determine the amount of rollback segment entry data being written to the rollback segments, use the queries given in the "Data Volumes in Rollback Segments" section shown previously. Each large transaction should be sized via the methods described there (in a test environment). Sizing of transactions should be a standard part of the database sizing process during application development.

Care should also be taken to minimize the amount of inactive, in-use rollback data that is shared between transactions. Large amounts of IIU data would result from concurrent transactions in which one transaction referenced a table that the other was manipulating. If this is minimized, the result will be a system whose rollback segment data needs are distributed and measurable.

There is overhead associated with each transaction. However, this header information is counted in the statistics queries given in the previous sections of this chapter. Thus, those queries give a very accurate report of the amount of rollback segment space that is needed.

Number of Transactions

Once the total amount of rollback segment entry data is known, the number of transactions must be considered. Segregate the transactions into types by their relative volume. For each group, determine the maximum and average transaction size. For this part of the rollback segment sizing process, only consider the transactions that occur during normal production usage of the system, excluding all data loads.

Create a spreadsheet of the structure shown in Table 7-6. Sample data is shown for reference. The "Transaction Types" for this table are for a data entry application at a zoo safari exhibit. The "Number" column refers to the number of *concurrent* transactions of each type. The "Total Entry Size" column refers to the total entry size, in bytes, of all the *concurrent* entries of this type.

Note that the "Number" column refers to the number of separate transactions. If multiple records are being updated in a single transaction, then that still counts as only one transaction.

The transactions listed in Table 7-6 reflect that, for this application, users commit after every 10 to 100 records. For example, the average "Visitor Log" transaction is 40K in size—which may be 10 4K records or 100 400-byte records, depending on the record length and the frequency of **commit**s.

Transaction Type	Number	Total Entry Size	Average Entry Size	Largest Entry
FEEDING_LOG	3	210K	70K	70K
NEW_BIRTH	1	500K	500K	500K
VISITOR_LOG	20	800K	40K	40K
VISITOR_EATEN	1	700K	700K	700K
TIME_SHEETS	10	500K	50K	50K
Total	**35**	**2,710K**		

TABLE 7-6. *Sample Transaction Distribution*

According to the data in Table 7-6, there are, on average, 35 concurrent transactions in the database. They take, on average, 2,710K of data at any one time.

The largest single transaction in the database is 700K long. Use this as the starting point for the rollback segment sizing. That transaction must fit in a single rollback segment. That rollback segment will contain rollback segment header space as well, and may also contain inactive data. To calculate the minimum possible size for a rollback segment that can support this single transaction, use the following formula. This formula makes the following assumptions:

■ Twenty percent of the rollback segment will remain as free space.

■ Fifteen percent of the rollback segment will be used for inactive, in-use data.

■ Five percent of the rollback segment will be used by the rollback segment header area.

```
Minimum Possible Size (MPS) = Largest Transaction Size *100 /
                                 (100 - (Free Pct + In Use Pct + Header Pct))
                            = Largest Transaction Size *100 /
                               (100-(20+15+5))
                            = Largest Transaction Size *100/60
                            = Largest Transaction Size * 1.67
                            = 700K bytes * 1.67
                            = 1170K bytes
```

Since the database chooses a rollback segment to use in a round-robin fashion, each rollback segment that may have to handle this transaction must be at least this size.

The total rollback segment space needed at any one time can also be calculated. The same space assumptions will be used.

```
Minimum Total Size (MTS)  = Sum(Total Entry Size) *100 /
                               (100 - (Free Pct + In Use Pct + Header Pct))
                          = Sum(Total Entry Size) *100 /
                             (100 - (20 + 15 + 5))
                          = Sum(Total Entry Size) * 100/60
                          = Sum(Total Entry Size) * 1.67
                          = 2710K bytes * 1.67
                          = 4525K bytes
```

So, the minimum total rollback space available in all of the rollback segments combined at any one time must be at least 4,525K for this example.

How many rollback segments should this space be divided among? Since the rollback segments should all be of the same size, the minimum value is easy to estimate. You have already seen that the minimum size of each rollback segment is 1,170K. The total minimum size of all rollback segments is 4,525K. The following equation compares these two values to determine the minimum number of rollback segments needed:

```
Minimum Num of Rollback Segs (MNRS) = Minimum Total Size /
                                      Minimum Possible Size
                                    = 4525K / 1170K
                                    = 3.87 (round up to 4)
```

This will be our starting point for the number of rollback segments needed. Note that it only considers the space requirements at this point.

To refine this calculation, consider the number of concurrent transactions. The fewer transactions there are in a rollback segment, the less work the database will have to do to manage its space needs. The maximum number of rollback segments is the number of concurrent transactions (assuming one transaction per rollback segment). For the example data shown in Table 7-6, this number is 35.

```
Maximum Number of Rollback Segs = Number of Concurrent Transactions
                                = 35
```

So, the production database requires somewhere between 4 and 35 rollback segments. To restrict this range further, you must determine the number of transactions per rollback segment. Each transaction will now be fit into its own extent, rather than into its own rollback segment. To do this, you must evaluate the distribution of transaction sizes.

As shown in Table 7-7, there are two distinct groupings of the safari transactions. The first group features entries whose average entry sizes are between 40K and 70K. The second grouping contains entries whose average sizes are between 500K and 700K. Since there is an order of magnitude of difference between average entry size for these two groups, it will not be possible to resolve their space needs without wasting space or forcing wraps to occur.

Transaction Type	Number	Total Entry Size	Average Entry Size	Largest Entry
VISITOR_LOG	20	800K	40K	40K
TIME_SHEETS	10	500K	50K	50K
FEEDING_LOG	3	210K	70K	70K
Subtotal	33	1,510K		
NEW_BIRTH	1	500K	500K	500K
VISITOR_EATEN	1	700K	700K	700K
Subtotal	2	1,200K		
Total	35	2,710K		

TABLE 7-7. *Sample Transaction Distribution, Grouped by Average Entry Size*

The transactions in the large entry size group are very few in number. Of the 35 concurrent transactions, they constitute just 2. Therefore, you can design to handle the small entry group, while leaving space to handle the exceptions in the large entry group. The sizing for the small entry group size will thus form the lower bound for the design requirements.

For the small entry size group, the sum of the total entry sizes is 1,510K bytes. So, the minimum total size of the rollback segments needed just for that group is

```
MTS = 1510K * 1.67  = 2522 K
```

The minimum extent size for that group is the size of the largest transaction in that group.

```
Minimum Extent Size (MES) = 70K bytes
```

A 70K extent size will handle each of the small entry transactions. For the large entry transactions, it will require a minimum of seven wraps (eight 70K extents for the 500K entry). To minimize the number of wraps for the large entry transactions, consider a larger extent size. An extent size of 125K would require fewer wraps, at the cost of increased storage space. An extent size of 250K bytes would require even fewer wraps for all transactions. However, it would require a great deal of additional physical space, as shown in Table 7-8.

In Table 7-8, three different extent sizes are compared. The first, 70K, was based on the calculated minimum average extent size. The second, 125K, was proposed to reduce the number of wraps needed to support the larger transactions. The third, 250K, was proposed to reduce even further the number of wraps needed to support the larger transactions.

The "Space Req" column in Table 7-8 shows that with a 70K extent, and one transaction per extent, 3,570K of rollback segment space would be needed while incurring 16 wraps. Increasing the extent size to 125K increases the space requirements by a third, to 5,350K, while decreasing the number of wraps to 7. Doubling that extent size, to 250K, increases the space requirement to 9,500K while only reducing the number of wraps to 3.

Extent Size	Transaction Entry Type	Number	Space Req	Number of Wraps
70K	small (<70K)	33	2,310K	0
	large (500K)	1	560K	7
	large (700K)	1	700K	9
	Totals		3,570K	16
125K	small (<70K)	33	4125K	0
	large (500K)	1	500K	3
	large (700K)	1	750K	5
	Totals		5,350K	8
250K	small (<70K)	33	8,250K	0
	large (500K)	1	500K	1
	large (700K)	1	750K	2
	Totals		9,500K	3

TABLE 7-8. *Extent Sizing Trade-offs*

The space calculations all assume one transaction per extent. That assumption may result in overestimating the space requirements, but it is usually accurate.

Based on Table 7-8, it is possible to cut this example's number of wraps in half by increasing the extent size by only two-thirds. Extending it much beyond that will not reduce the number of wraps appreciably. Note that these calculations still assume one transaction per extent, even for the larger extent sizes.

You have to be able to estimate your transaction volume in order to reach this point. Since this calculation assumes that only 15 percent of the rollback segment is being used to support IIU entries, such entries must be minimized via scheduling. You have to be able to estimate the type, quantity, and nature of the system's transactions in order to be able to reach this decision point.

Given the trade-off between the two options in Table 7-8, a small extent size will almost always be the proper choice since it is usually the most common type of transaction. The deciding factor will be the distribution of the number of transactions. Since 33 of 35 concurrent transactions are small in this example, the largest extent size can be discarded. The choice is then between the two smaller extent sizes (70K and 125K). Since the number of wraps falls so rapidly with the small increase in extent size, choose the 125K size. Note that the choice of an extent size, falling between the minimum extent size (MES) and the minimum extent size necessary to eliminate all wraps, should always be the best compromise. This compromise assumes that (1) the additional disk space needed is available and (2) the performance penalties due to the wraps are acceptable.

The Minimum Total Size of all rollback segments for the database was previously calculated as 4,525K. The Minimum Possible Size for a rollback segment was calculated as 1,170K, yielding a minimum of four rollback segments.

In that configuration, each of the four rollback segments would support nine transactions at a time (35 transactions divided by 4 rollback segments, rounded). ORACLE recommends a number closer to four transactions per rollback segments. For this implementation, split the difference and start with six transactions per rollback segment, yielding six rollback segments (35/6, rounded). The actual space requirements for them can now be determined.

Each of the six rollback segments will contain an extent that is used for the rollback segment header. Its extent distribution is listed in Table 7-9.

Extent Number	Description
1	Rollback segment header
2	Transaction #1
3	Transaction #2
4	Transaction #3
5	Transaction #4
6	Transaction #5
7	Transaction #6
8	Inactive, in-use data
9	Inactive, in-use data
10	Expansion space for large transactions
11	Expansion space for large transactions
12	Expansion space for large transactions
13	Expansion space for large transactions
14	Expansion space for large transactions
15	Expansion space for large transactions
16	Free space
17	Free space
18	Free space

TABLE 7-9. *Extent Distribution Within the Sample Rollback Segments*

The resulting rollback segment consists of a total of 2,250K, in 18 evenly sized extents. It can handle the high transaction load of the small entry transactions. It can support the large transactions. And it contains free space in the event that the transaction volume or the transaction load is greater than has been predicted.

For details on monitoring the adequacy of this design, see Chapter 6. The next section describes the calculations used to reach this final layout.

Determining the optimal Size

The **optimal** size of a rollback segment must accommodate the transaction volume and the overhead needed to manage the transactions. The design should allow most of the transactions to be handled within a single extent.

The amount of transaction data in a rollback segment should therefore be measured in extents. The number of extents required for each rollback segment is

```
Min Num of Extents/Segment = Number of Single-Extent Transactions
    +((Number of Wraps in Long Transactions +1)*
                    Average Number of Long Transactions)
```

Applying this to our sample data,

```
Min Num of Extents/Segment      = (33 small-entry transactions
                                  /6 rollback segments) +
                                  (5 wraps +1 )*1
                                = 5.6 + 6
                                = 11.6, rounded up to 12
```

The longest transaction is 700K, which will require six 125K extents. This requires five wraps. Since only one such transaction is active at a time, a rollback segment needs to have an extent for each transaction, plus an additional extent for each wrap.

Using this many extents will allow the rollback segment to handle its share of the small entry transaction load while also having room to support an average large transaction load. This distribution of extents was shown graphically in Table 7-9. In that table, extents 2 through 7 support the first extents of six different transactions. Extents 10 through 15 handle the expansion needs of the large transactions.

The transaction data thus requires 12 extents. The overhead needs of the rollback segment must now be estimated. They consist of three parts.

```
Rollback Segment Overhead = Rollback segment header space +
                            Inactive, In-Use space +
                            Free Space
```

The rollback segment header should always be estimated to take an extent (shown as Extent #1 in Table 7-9).

The IIU space is determined by the transaction scheduling for the application. If long-running queries are executing concurrently with online transactions that use the same data, then this value will have to be set high. It is possible that the amount of IIU data may exceed the currently used transaction volume.

If the transactions have been distributed correctly, then no long-running queries will be run concurrently with data manipulation transactions. Even so, there may be some overlap between the transactions. This overlap results in IIU space, and usually requires at least 10 percent of the rollback segment's transaction volume.

For the safari example, the overlap between transactions is estimated to be 15 percent.

```
IIU Space        = (Per cent Inactive, In-Use) *
                       Number of Data Extents
                 = .15*12
                 = 1.80, rounded up to 2 extents.
```

These two extents are shown as extents 8 and 9 in Table 7-9.

The final overhead factor is the free space. The free space must accommodate the worst-case scenario of transaction allocations. In this case, that would be for both of the large entry transactions to be assigned to the same rollback segment.

The space needed for a single large transaction has already been factored into the Minimum Number of Extents per Segment calculation. Therefore, you only need to add the number of wraps that would occur for a second large transaction. Since that is listed as 500K (Table 7-7), and the extent size is 125K (Table 7-8), such a transaction would require four extents (three wraps).

```
Free Space Extents  = Maximum Number of Additional Extents Needed
                    = 3
```

These extents are shown as Extents 16, 17, and 18 of Table 7-9.

The **optimal** size of the rollback segment, and the value for the **optimal** storage parameter, is thus

```
OPTIMAL  = (Minimum Number of Data Extents per Segment
               + Rollback Segment Header extents
               + Inactive, In Use extents
               + Free Space extents)
           * Extent Size

         = (12+1+2+3) * 125K/extent
         = 18 * 125K/extent
         = 2250K bytes
```

To minimize the dynamic extension of the rollback segment in reaching this size, set **minextents** to 18. The **optimal** size of the rollback segment will then be preallocated.

Creating the Rollback Segments

The rollback segments can now be created. They should all be created with the same storage parameters. The storage parameters for the safari application are listed in Table 7-10.

All of the production rollback segments will be created in the RBS tablespace. Therefore, the default storage settings for that tablespace can be used to enforce the desired storage values for the rollback segments. Use the following command to set these parameters:

```
alter tablespace RBS
default storage
(initial 125K next 125K minextents 18 maxextents 249)
```

When creating rollback segments in that tablespace, you now only have to specify the tablespace and the **optimal** value, as shown in the following set of commands:

```
create rollback segment R4 tablespace RBS
    storage (optimal 2250K);
alter rollback segment R4 online;
```

The RBS tablespace will have to contain at least enough space to hold six 2,250K rollback segments (13,500K). When planning its space requirements, it

Parameter	Value
INITIAL	125K
NEXT	125K
MINEXTENTS	18
MAXEXTENTS	249
OPTIMAL	2,250K

TABLE 7-10. *Storage Parameters for the Sample Rollback Segments*

is helpful to think of it graphically. Figure 7-7, which should call to mind Figures 7-1 and 7-2, shows a potential layout for the RBS tablespace.

In the layout shown in Figure 7-7, six equally sized rollback segments are shown. An additional area of free space of the same size is added at the bottom. That space will be available for adding a seventh segment (if rollback segment header contention is a problem) or for temporary extensions of the six rollback segments.

Figure 7-7 also shows that these rollback segments may be separated into their own files. In such files, a small amount of space will be reserved for overhead. Figure 7-7 shows seven 2,300K files; you could also have stored all of the rollback segments in a single datafile. Using multiple files may improve your options during database tuning efforts, since these files could be placed on different disks to distribute the transaction I/O load.

Production Versus Data Load Rollback Segments

All of the calculations performed here assumed that the application had no way of assigning transactions to specific rollback segments. The rollback

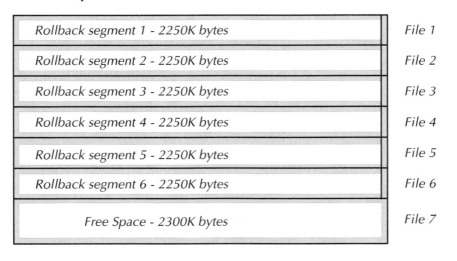

RBS Tablespace

Rollback segment 1 - 2250K bytes	File 1
Rollback segment 2 - 2250K bytes	File 2
Rollback segment 3 - 2250K bytes	File 3
Rollback segment 4 - 2250K bytes	File 4
Rollback segment 5 - 2250K bytes	File 5
Rollback segment 6 - 2250K bytes	File 6
Free Space - 2300K bytes	File 7

FIGURE 7-7. *Potential layout for the sample RBS tablespace*

segments thus had to support both large and small entry sizes. This is acceptable for most production usage, but it is not acceptable for handling data load transactions.

Data load transactions are used to manipulate large volumes of data in an application. These may include initial data loads or the creation of large summary tables from detail tables. Either way, they involve transaction volumes that are orders of magnitude greater than those designed for here.

Data loads not only deal with large volumes of data, but the transactions within those loads are larger. For example, when using the ORACLE *Import* utility, its default functionality is to perform one **commit** for each table's data. To support that, a rollback segment the size of the table would be needed. See Chapter 10 for alternatives to Import's default transaction size.

Data load transactions must be assigned to specific rollback segments. This can be done via the

```
set transaction use rollback segment SEGMENT_NAME
```

command, or it may be done by deactivating all but one production rollback segment (during off-peak hours). The size of the data load transactions should be measured using the V$ROLLSTAT queries shown previously in this chapter.

Once the data load transactions have been isolated to specific rollback segments, those rollback segments should be isolated in the RBS_2 tablespace. This tablespace, as described in Chapter 3, is used solely for rollback segments that have extraordinary space requirements. Placing them in RBS_2 allows their extensions into the RBS_2 free space to be performed without impacting the free space available to the production rollback segments (in the RBS tablespace). See Chapter 12 for a discussion of the support of large batch transactions.

The result will be production rollback segments that are properly sized and preallocated. Their extents are designed to be large enough to handle an entire transaction. Space is allocated to handle those transactions that are not properly distributed. The worst-case scenario is covered, and the best-case scenario is achieved: the time machine works.

CHAPTER
8

Database Tuning

uning is a part of the life of every database application. As noted in previous chapters, most performance problems are not isolated symptoms, but rather are the result of the system design. Tuning efforts should therefore focus on identifying and fixing the underlying flaws that yield the unacceptable performance.

Tuning is the final step in a four-step process: Planning (Chapters 3 and 4), Doing (Chapter 5), and Monitoring (Chapter 6) must precede it. If you tune only for the sake of tuning, then you are failing to address the full cycle of activity, and will likely never resolve the underlying flaws that caused the performance problem.

Most of the database objects that can be tuned are discussed elsewhere in this book—for example, rollback segments are covered thoroughly in Chapter 7. This chapter will only discuss the tuning-related activities for such objects, while their own chapters cover planning and monitoring activities.

Tuning activities will be described for the following areas:

- Application design
- SQL
- Memory usage
- Data storage
- Data manipulation
- Physical storage
- Logical storage
- Network traffic

Tuning Application Design

Why should a DBA tuning guide include a section on application design? And why should this section come first? Because *nothing* you can do as a DBA will have as great an impact on the system performance as the design of the application. The requirements for making the DBA's involvement in application development a reality are described in Chapter 5. In designing an application, several steps can be taken to make effective and proper use of the available technology, as described in the following sections.

Effective Table Design

"No major application will run in Third Normal Form."
George Koch—*ORACLE8: The Complete Reference*

No matter how well designed your database is, poor table design will lead to poor performance. Not only that, but overly rigid adherence to relational table designs will lead to poor performance. That is due to the fact that while fully relational table designs (said to be in the *Third Normal Form*) are logically desirable, they are physically undesirable.

The problem with such designs is that although they accurately reflect the ways in which an application's data is related to other data, they do not reflect the normal access paths that users will employ to access that data. Once the user's access requirements are evaluated, the fully relational table design will become unworkable for many large queries. Typically, the first problems will occur with queries that return a large number of columns. These columns are usually scattered among several tables, forcing the tables to be joined together during the query. If one of the joined tables is large, then the performance of the whole query may suffer.

In designing the tables for an application, developers should therefore consider denormalizing data—for example, creating small summary tables from large, static tables. Can that data be dynamically derived from the large, static tables on demand? Of course. But if the users frequently request it, and the data is largely unchanging, then it makes sense to periodically store that data *in the format in which the users will ask for it.*

User-centered table design, rather than theory-centered table design, will yield a system that better meets the users' requirements. Design options include separating a single table into multiple tables, and the reverse—combining multiple tables into one. The emphasis should be on providing the users the most direct path possible to the data they want in the format they want.

Distribution of CPU Requirements

When effectively designed, and given adequate hardware, an ORACLE database application will be *CPU-bound*. That is, the limiting factor to its performance will be the availability of CPU resources. Short of purchasing additional CPU power for the available servers, there are several options that should be used.

First, the CPU load should be scheduled. This topic was mentioned in Chapter 7 with regard to reducing rollback segment overhead. However, it applies in general as well: schedule long-running batch query or update programs to run at off-peak hours. Rather than run them at lower operating system priority while online users are performing transactions, run them at normal operating system priority *at an appropriate time*. This will minimize potential locking, rollback, and CPU conflicts.

Second, as distributed computing becomes more widespread, take advantage of the opportunity to physically shift CPU requirements from one server to another. Wherever possible, isolate the database server from the application's CPU requirements. The data distribution techniques described in Part III of this book will result in data being stored in its most appropriate place, and the CPU requirements of the application may be separated from the I/O requirements against the database.

Third, you can use the Parallel Query Option (PQO) to distribute the processing requirements of SQL statements among multiple CPUs. Parallelism can be used by almost every SQL command, including the **select**, **create table as select**, **create index**, **recover**, and SQL*Loader Direct Path loading options.

The degree to which a transaction is parallelized depends on the defined degree of parallelism for the transaction. Each table has a defined degree of parallelism (see the **create table** and **alter table** commands in Appendix C), and a query can override the default degree of parallelism by using the PARALLEL hint. As of ORACLE7.3, the database evaluates the number of CPUs available on the server and the number of disks on which the table's data is stored in order to determine the default degree of parallelism.

The maximum available parallelism is set at the instance level. The PARALLEL_MAX_SERVERS init.ora sets the maximum number of parallel query server processes that can be used at any one time by all the processes in the database. For example, if you set PARALLEL_MAX_SERVERS to 32 for your instance, and you run a query that uses 30 parallel query server processes for its query and sorting operations, then only two parallel query server processes are available for all of the rest of the users in the database. Therefore, you need to carefully manage the parallelism you allow for your queries and batch operations.

For each table, you can set a default degree of parallelism via the **parallel** clause of the **create table** and **alter table** commands. The *degree of parallelism* tells ORACLE how many parallel query server processes to attempt to use for each part of the operation. For example, if a query that performed both table scanning and data sorting operations had a degree of parallelism of 5, then there could be ten parallel query server processes used—five for scanning, five for sorting. You can also specify a degree of parallelism for an index when it is created, via the **parallel** clause of the **create index** command.

The minimum number of parallel query server processes started is set via the PARALLEL_MIN_SERVERS init.ora parameter. In general, you should set this parameter to a very low number (less than 5). Setting this parameter to a low value will force ORACLE to repeatedly start new query server processes, but it will greatly decrease the amount of memory held by idle parallel query server processes. If you set a high value for PARALLEL_MIN_SERVERS, then you may frequently have idle parallel query server processes on your server, holding onto the memory they had previously acquired but not performing any functions. You can set an idle time parameter that tells ORACLE how many minutes a parallel query server process can be idle before it is terminated by the database.

Parallelizing operations distributes their processing requirements across multiple CPUs; however, you should use these features carefully. If you use a degree of parallelism of 5 for a large query, then you will have five separate processes accessing the data. If you have that many processes accessing the data, then you may create contention for the disks on which the data is stored, hurting performance! When using the PQO, you should selectively apply it to those tables whose data is well distributed over many physical devices. Also, you should avoid using it for all tables; as noted earlier, a single query may use all of the available parallel query server processes, eliminating the parallelism for all of the rest of the transactions in your database.

Effective Application Design

In addition to the application design topics described later in this chapter, there are several general guidelines for ORACLE applications.

First, they should minimize the number of times they request data from the database. Options for doing this include the use of sequences and using PL/SQL blocks. The denormalization of tables discussed earlier in this chapter also applies here. Distributed database objects such as snapshots may also be used to help reduce the number of times a database is queried.

Second, different users of the same application should query the database in a very similar fashion. This will increase the likelihood that their requests may be resolved by information that is already available in the SGA. This sharing of data includes not only the tables and rows retrieved, but also the actual queries that are used. If the queries are identical, then the parsed version of a query may already exist in the Shared SQL Pool, reducing the amount of time needed to process the query.

Stored procedures are available for use in application development. When they are used, it is very likely that the same code will be executed multiple times, thus taking advantage of the Shared SQL Pool. You can also manually compile procedures, functions, and packages to avoid run-time compilation. For example, to create a procedure, use a **create procedure** command, as shown in the following listing:

```
create procedure MY_RAISE (My_Emp_No IN NUMBER, Raise IN NUMBER)
as begin
      update EMPLOYEE
         set Salary = Salary+Raise
       where Empno = My_Emp_No;
end;
/
```

When you create a procedure, ORACLE automatically compiles it. If the procedure later becomes invalid, the database must recompile it before executing it. To avoid incurring this compilation cost at run time, use the **alter procedure** command shown in the following listing:

```
alter procedure MY_RAISE compile;
```

The SQL text for all procedures in a database can be viewed via the Text column in the DBA_SOURCE view. The USER_SOURCE view will display the procedures owned by the user performing the query. Text for packages, functions, and package bodies is also accessible via these views. These views reference a table named SYS.SOURCE$. Since this table is part of the data dictionary, the procedural code is stored in the SYSTEM tablespace. Therefore, if you use these objects, you must be sure to allocate more space to the SYSTEM tablespace—usually doubling its size.

The two design guidelines discussed—limiting the number of user accesses and coordinating their requests—require that the application developer know as much as possible about how the data is to be used and the access paths involved. For this reason, it is critical that users be as involved in the application design as they are in the table design. If the users spend long hours drawing pictures of tables with the data modelers, and little time with the application developers discussing the access paths, then the application will most likely not meet the users' needs.

Tuning SQL

As with application design, the tuning of SQL statements seems far removed from a DBA's duties. However, DBAs should be involved in reviewing the SQL that is written as part of the application. A well-designed application may still experience performance problems if the SQL it uses is poorly constructed. Application design and SQL problems cause most of the performance problems in properly designed databases.

In a relational database, the physical location of data is not as important as its logical place within the application design. However, the database has to find the data in order to return it to a user performing a query. The key to tuning SQL is to minimize the search path that the database uses to find the data.

In most ORACLE tables, each row has a RowID associated with it. The RowID contains information about the physical location of the row—its file, the block within that file, and the row within the database block. The RowID format changed significantly between ORACLE7 and ORACLE8. See Appendix A for details on the ORACLE8 RowID format and the functions provided by ORACLE for retrieving data location information from the RowID values.

When a query with no **where** clause is executed, the database will usually perform a *full table scan*, reading every block from the table. To do this, the database locates the first extent of the table and then reads sequentially through all other extents in the table. For large tables, this can be a very time-consuming process.

When specific rows are queried, the database may use an index to help speed the retrieval of the desired rows. An index maps logical values in a table to their RowIDs—which in turn map them to a specific physical location. Indexes may either be unique—in which case there is no more than one occurrence for each value—or nonunique. They only store RowIDs for **NOT NULL** values in the indexed columns.

You may index several columns together. This is called a *concatenated* index, and it will be used if its leading column is used in the query's **where** clause. Simply throwing an index at a query will not necessarily make it run faster—the index must be tailored to the access path needed.

Consider the case of a three-column, concatenated index. As shown in the following listing, it is created on the City, State, and Zip columns of the EMPLOYEE table:

```
create index CITY_ST_ZIP_NDX
on EMPLOYEE(City, State, Zip)
tablespace INDEXES;
```

If a query of the form

```
select * from EMPLOYEE
  where State='NJ';
```

is executed, then the index will *not* be used, because its *leading* column (City) is not used in the **where** clause. If users will frequently run this type of query, then the index's columns should be reordered with State first in order to reflect the actual usage pattern.

It is also important that the table's data be as ordered as possible. Again, this is unimportant in relational theory, but plays a critical role in retrieving data for queries. If users are frequently executing *range* queries—selecting those values that are within a specified range—then having the data ordered may require fewer data blocks to be read while resolving the query, thus improving performance. The ordered entries in the index will point to a set of neighboring blocks in the table rather than blocks that are scattered throughout the datafile(s).

For example, a range query of the type shown in this listing:

```
select * from EMPLOYEE
where Empno between 1 AND 100;
```

will require fewer data blocks to be read if the physical records in the EMPLOYEE table are ordered by the Empno column. This should improve the performance of the query. To guarantee that the rows are properly ordered in the table, extract the records to a flat file, sort the records in the file, and then delete the old records and reload them from the sorted file.

If the data is not very selective, then you may consider using *bitmap indexes*. As described in Chapter 12, bitmap indexes are most effective for queries against large, static data sets with few distinct values. You can create both bitmap indexes and normal (B*-tree indexes) on the same table, and ORACLE will perform any necessary index conversions dynamically during query processing. See Chapter 12 for details on using bitmap indexes.

If two tables are frequently queried together, then *clusters* may be effective in improving performance. Clusters store rows from multiple tables in the same physical data blocks, based on their logical values (the cluster key). See Chapter 5 for more information on clusters.

Queries in which a column's value is compared to an exact value are called *equivalence* queries. A *hash cluster* stores a row in a specific location based on its value in the cluster key column. Every time a row is inserted, its cluster key value is used to determine which block it should be stored in; this same logic can be used during queries to quickly find data blocks that are needed for retrieval. These are designed to improve the performance of equivalence queries; they will not be as helpful in improving the performance of the range queries discussed earlier.

How can you determine which access path the database will use to perform a query? This information can be viewed via the **explain plan** command. This command will evaluate the execution path for a query and will place its output into a table (named PLAN_TABLE) in the database. A sample **explain plan** command is shown in the following listing:

```
explain plan
set Statement_Id = 'TEST'
for
select * from EMPLOYEE
where City > 'Y%';
```

The first line of this command tells the database that it is to explain its execution plan for the query without actually executing the query. The second line labels this query's records in the PLAN_TABLE with a Statement_Id equal to "TEST". Following the keyword **for**, the query to be analyzed is listed.

The account that is running this command must have a PLAN_TABLE in its schema. ORACLE provides the **create table** commands needed for this table. The file, named UTLXPLAN.SQL, is usually located in the /rdbms/admin subdirectory under the ORACLE software home directory. Users may run this script to create the table in their schemas.

Query the plan table using the query in the following listing. Records in that table are related to each other, so the **connect by** clause of the **select** statement can be used to evaluate the hierarchy.

```
select
  LPAD(' ',2*Level)||Operation||' '||Options||' '||Object_Name
  Q_Plan
  from PLAN_TABLE
 where Statement_Id = 'TEST'
connect by prior ID = Parent_ID and Statement_ID = 'TEST'
 start with ID=0;
```

This query will report on the types of operations the database must perform to resolve the query. Sample output is shown in the following listing:

```
Q_PLAN
-----------------------------------------------------------
SELECT STATEMENT
  TABLE ACCESS BY ROWID EMPLOYEE
    INDEX RANGE SCAN CITY_ST_ZIP_NDX
```

To read the explain plan, read the order of operations from inside out of the hierarchy until you come to a set of operations at the same level of indentation; then read from top to bottom. In this example, there are no operations at the same level of indentation; therefore, you read the order of operations from inside out. The first operation is the index range scan, followed by the table access; the "SELECT STATEMENT" operation displays the output to the user.

This plan shows that the data that is returned to the user comes via a "Table Access by ROWID." The RowIDs are supplied by an index range scan, using the CITY_ST_ZIP_NDX index described earlier in this section.

As of ORACLE7.3, you can use the **set autotrace on** command in SQL*Plus to automatically generate the **explain plan** output and trace information for every query you run. The autotrace-generated output will not be displayed until after the query has completed (while the **explain plan** output is generated without running the command).

When evaluating the output of the **explain plan** command, you should make sure that the most selective indexes (that is, the most nearly unique indexes) are used by the query. If a nonselective index is used, you may be forcing the database to perform unnecessary reads to resolve the query. A full discussion of SQL tuning is beyond the scope of this book, but you should focus your tuning efforts on making sure that the most resource-intensive SQL statements are using the most selective indexes possible.

When using the **explain plan** command, you need to make sure you are using the latest version of PLAN_TABLE. Each time you upgrade your database to a new kernel version, drop and re-create your PLAN_TABLE table (using the current version of UTLXPLAN.SQL to create the table). As of ORACLE8, new columns were added to the PLAN_TABLE table. If you do not drop and re-create your PLAN_TABLE, you will never see the new columns or the data they contain.

The **set autotrace on** command described earlier will automatically display all of the new PLAN_TABLE columns as part of its output.

The **set autotrace on** command will help you to measure the "cost" of each step within an **explain plan**. In general, transaction-oriented applications (such as multiuser systems used for data entry) evaluate performance based on the time it takes to return the first row of a query. For transaction-oriented applications, you should focus your tuning efforts on using indexes to reduce the database's response time to the query.

If the application is batch-oriented (with large transactions and reports), then you should focus on improving the time it takes to complete the overall transaction instead of the time it takes to return the first row from the transaction. Improving the overall throughput of the transaction may require using full table scans in place of index accesses—and may improve the overall performance of the application. Since full table scans can take advantage of the Parallel Query Option, you may be able to involve more computing resources in the execution of the scan, thereby improving its performance.

If the application is distributed across multiple instances, focus on reducing the number of times database links are used in queries. If a remote database is frequently accessed during a query, then the cost of accessing that remote database is paid each time the remote data is accessed. Even if the cost of accessing the remote data is low, accessing it thousands of times will eventually place a performance burden on your application. See the "Reducing Network Traffic" section later in this chapter for additional tuning suggestions for distributed databases.

See *Advanced Oracle Tuning and Administration* (Osborne/McGraw-Hill/Oracle Press) for further details on tuning SQL.

Tuning Memory Usage

Monitoring the usage of ORACLE's memory areas is discussed in Chapter 6. Specifically, that chapter describes the proper use of the ORACLE statistics scripts and the interpretation of their output. These scripts, called UTLBSTAT.SQL and UTLESTAT.SQL, summarize the changes in system statistics for a given period. They help point out areas to which not enough resources have been given.

The data block buffer cache and the Shared SQL Pool are managed via a *least recently used (LRU)* algorithm. A preset area is set aside to hold values; when it fills, the least recently used data is eliminated from memory and written back to disk. An adequately sized memory area keeps the most frequently accessed data in memory; accessing less frequently used data requires physical reads.

Sizing of both the dictionary cache and the Shared SQL Pool is described in Chapter 6. The Hit Ratio calculation in that chapter also helps to alert you to an improperly sized data buffer cache.

The Hit Ratio is a measure of how well the data buffer cache is handling requests for data. It is calculated as

```
Hit Ratio = (Logical Reads - Physical Reads)/Logical Reads
```

Thus, a perfect Hit Ratio would have a value of 1.00. In that instance, all requests for database blocks (logical reads) would be fulfilled without requesting any data from datafiles (physical reads); all requests would be handled by the data that is already in memory.

In general, the online transaction portion of applications should have Hit Ratios in excess of 0.97. In a batch-oriented system, the Hit Ratio should not fall below 0.89. The overall Hit Ratio for an application will be lowered by its batch activity. The method for measuring the Hit Ratio is described in Chapter 6.

You can manipulate the actions of the LRU algorithm in the data block buffer cache via the **cache** option. The option automatically loads an entire table into the SGA the first time that table is accessed, and will mark it as *most* recently used. That table's data will still be subject to the LRU algorithms that manage the SGA caches, but it will stay in the SGA longer than if it had been treated normally. The **cache** option can be specified at a table level via the **create table** and **alter table** commands, and can also be specified via query hints. The **cache** option is most useful for frequently accessed tables that change infrequently. You can then run queries that will reload the most-used tables into the SGA caches each time the database is restarted.

With all of the areas of the SGA—the data block buffers, the dictionary cache, and the Shared SQL Pool—the emphasis should be on sharing data among users. Each of these areas should be large enough to hold the most commonly requested data from the database. In the case of the Shared SQL Pool, it should be large enough to hold the parsed versions of the most commonly used queries. When they are adequately sized, the memory areas in the SGA can dramatically improve the performance of individual queries and of the database as a whole. Instructions for proper sizing of tables, indexes, and clusters are provided in Chapter 5.

Using the Cost-Based Optimizer

With each release of its software, ORACLE has added new features to its optimizer, and has improved its existing features. As a result, performance when using the cost-based optimizer (CBO) should be consistently predictable. Although the RULE hint and rule-based optimization is available in ORACLE8, the role of rule-based optimization will probably diminish over time, and you should begin converting to cost-based optimization if you have not already done so.

Effective use of the cost-based optimizer requires that the tables and indexes in your application be analyzed regularly. The frequency with which you analyze the objects depends on the rate of change within the objects. For batch transaction applications, you should reanalyze the objects after each large set of batch transactions. For OLTP applications, you should reanalyze the objects on a time-based schedule (such as via a weekly or nightly process).

Statistics on objects are gathered via the **analyze** command. If you analyze a table, then its associated indexes are automatically analyzed as well. You can specify that only the table be reanalyzed, but this should only be done if the only changes to the table were in nonindexed columns. You can analyze only the indexed columns, speeding the analysis process. In general, you should analyze a table's indexes each time you analyze the table. In the following listing, the COMPANY table and all of its indexes are completely scanned and their statistics are gathered by the first **analyze** command. The second command analyzes just the table and its indexed columns.

```
analyze table COMPANY compute statistics;

analyze table COMPANY compute statistics for table
    for all indexed columns;
```

The statistics on the COMPANY table and its indexes can be viewed via DBA_TABLES, DBA_TAB_COL_STATISTICS, and DBA_INDEXES. Some column-level statistics are still provided in DBA_TAB_COLUMNS, but they are provided there strictly for backward compatibility. The statistics for the columns of partitioned tables are found in DBA_PART_COL_STATISTICS.

As of ORACLE7.3, you can use the **analyze** command to generate histograms. A histogram reflects the distribution of data values within a table. For example, there may be many distinct values for a column, in which case the column may seem ideal as a limiting value for a query. However, 90 percent of those values may all be clustered together, with the remaining 10 percent of the values outside the cluster. If your query performs a range scan with a limiting value inside the cluster, the index may not help the performance of your query. The use of an index for values outside the cluster would have a greater performance impact.

How does the optimizer know where data value clusters are? When you run the **analyze** command, you can tell ORACLE to generate a histogram for the cluster. By default, ORACLE will create a histogram that divides the data values into 75 *buckets*. Each bucket reflects the values of the same number of records as every other bucket. The more buckets you create, the better the distribution of database values will be reflected via the histogram. You can specify the number of buckets to use via the **size** parameter of the **analyze** command. The maximum number of buckets per table is 254.

To **analyze** all objects in a schema, you can use the ANALYZE_SCHEMA procedure within the DBMS_UTILITY package. As shown in the following listing, it has two parameters: the name of the schema and the **analyze** option used ("COMPUTE" or "ESTIMATE"):

```
execute DBMS_UTILITY.ANALYZE_SCHEMA('APPOWNER','COMPUTE');
```

When the command in the preceding listing is executed, all of the objects belonging to the APPOWNER schema will be analyzed, using the **compute statistics** option of the **analyze** command. If you are using rule-based optimization, then the statistics, although not used during the optimization process, will provide useful information to the developers during the query tuning process. See the **analyze** command entry in Appendix C for the full syntax of the command.

Implications of compute statistics

In the examples in the preceding section, the **compute statistics** option of the **analyze** command was used to gather statistics about objects. ORACLE also provides an **estimate statistics** option which, by default, scans only the first 1064 rows of a table during its analysis. The **estimate statistics** option, therefore, may not be appropriate if your tables will be growing—since new records added to the table might not be considered during subsequent analyses of the table. If you choose to use **estimate statistics**, analyze as much of the table as possible (you can specify a percentage of the rows to analyze)—analyze at least 20 percent of the table. If you do not analyze enough of the table, then your statistics will not accurately reflect the data in the table.

To generate the most accurate statistics, you should use the **compute statistics** option wherever possible. There are, however, management issues associated with the **compute statistics** option of the **analyze** command. Specifically, **compute statistics** can require large amounts of temporary segment space (up to four times the size of the table). You need to make sure that the user performing the analysis has the proper temporary tablespace settings and that the temporary tablespace can handle the space requirements. As the table grows over time, the temporary segment space requirements of **compute statistics** will grow. Although **compute statistics** places an additional management burden on the system, the benefits gained from the use of accurate statistics should outweigh the management burdens.

Tuning Data Storage

How the database actually *stores* data also has an effect on the performance of queries. If the data is fragmented into multiple extents, then resolving a query may cause the database to look in several physical locations for related rows.

Fragmentation may slow performance when storing new records. If the free space in a tablespace is fragmented, then the database may have to dynamically combine neighboring free extents to create a single extent that is large enough to handle the new space requirements. Tuning data storage thus involves tuning both used space and free space, as described in the next sections.

Defragmentation of Segments

Space: The **initial** Frontier.

As described in Chapter 4, when a database object (such as a table or index) is created, it is assigned to a tablespace via user defaults or specific instructions. A *segment* is created in that tablespace to hold the data associated with that object. The space that is allocated to the segment is never released until the segment is dropped, shrunk, or truncated.

A segment is made up of sections called *extents*. The extents themselves are contiguous sets of ORACLE blocks. Once the existing extents can no longer hold new data, the segment will obtain another extent. This extension process will continue until no more free space is available in the tablespace's datafiles, or until an internal maximum number of extents per segment is reached. If a segment consists of multiple extents, there is no guarantee that those extents will be contiguous.

Thus, a fragmented data segment not only may cause performance problems, but it may also lead to space management problems within the tablespace. It is therefore beneficial to have each data segment have only one extent; its **initial** storage parameter, which specifies the size of its initial extent, should be set large enough to handle all of the segment's data. The monitoring system provided in Chapter 6 checks for fragmented data segments via its EXTENTS table.

That monitoring system checks the DBA_SEGMENTS data dictionary view to determine which segments have ten or more extents. A general query of the DBA_SEGMENTS view is shown in the following listing. This query will retrieve the tablespace name, owner, segment name, and segment type for each segment in the database. The number of extents and blocks used by the segment will be displayed.

```
select
        Tablespace_Name,    /*Tablespace name*/
        Owner,              /*Owner of the segment*/
        Segment_Name,       /*Name of the segment*/
        Segment_Type,       /*Type of segment (ex. TABLE, INDEX)*/
        Extents,            /*Number of extents in the segment*/
```

```
        Blocks,             /*Number of db blocks in the segment*/
        Bytes               /*Number of bytes in the segment*/
from DBA_SEGMENTS
/
```

Segment types include TABLE, INDEX, CLUSTER, ROLLBACK, TEMPORARY, DEFERRED ROLLBACK, and CACHE. The DBA_SEGMENTS view does not list the size of the individual extents in a segment. To see that, query the DBA_EXTENTS view, as shown in the following listing:

```
select
        Tablespace_Name,    /*Tablespace name*/
        Owner,              /*Owner of the segment*/
        Segment_Name,       /*Name of the segment*/
        Segment_Type,       /*Type of segment (ex. TABLE, INDEX)*/
        Extent_ID,          /*Extent number in the segment*/
        Block_ID,           /*Starting block number for the extent*/
        Bytes,              /*Size of the extent, in bytes*/
        Blocks              /*Size of the extent, in Oracle blocks*/
  from DBA_EXTENTS
where Segment_Name = 'segment_name'
order by Extent_ID;
```

This query selects the extent information for a single segment (identified via the **where** clause). It returns the storage information associated with the segment's extents, including the size and location of each data extent. A similar query shown later in this chapter is used when mapping the distribution of free extents and used extents in a tablespace.

If a segment is fragmented, the easiest way to compress its data into a single extent is to rebuild it with the proper storage parameters. Since the **initial** storage parameter cannot be changed after a table has been created, a new table must be created with the correct storage parameters. The old data can then be **insert**ed into the new table, and the old table can be dropped.

This process can be automated via the Export/Import utilities. As noted in Chapter 10 the Export command has a COMPRESS flag. This flag will cause Export, when reading a table, to determine the total amount of space allocated to that table. It will then write to the export dump file a new **initial** storage parameter—equivalent to the total of the allocated space—for the table. If the table is then dropped, and Import is used to re-create it, then its data should all fit in the new, larger initial extent.

Note that it is the *allocated,* not the *used,* space that is compressed. An empty table with 300MB allocated to it in three 100MB extents will be compressed into a single, empty 300MB extent. No space will be reclaimed. Also, the database will not check to see if the new **initial** extent size is greater than the size of the largest datafile for the tablespace. Since extents cannot span datafiles, this would result in an error during Import.

The data segment compression procedure is shown in the following example. First, export the tables.

```
exp system/manager file=exp.dmp compress=Y grants=Y indexes=Y
    tables=(HR.T1,HR.T2)
```

Next, if the Export succeeded, then go into SQL*Plus and drop the exported tables. Then, import the tables from the export dump file.

```
imp system/manager file=exp.dmp commit=Y buffer=64000 full=Y
```

In this example, the DBA exported two tables, named T1 and T2, owned by the user HR. The tables were exported with the COMPRESS=Y flag, which modified their storage parameters during the Export. The tables were then dropped. When they were then imported, the Import utility created the tables with the new, compressed storage parameters.

This method may also be used on the entire database. Export the database with the COMPRESS=Y flag, re-create the database, and then perform a full Import. With some restrictions, it may also be applied to the defragmentation of tablespaces. See Chapter 10 for further details on tablespace rebuilds.

Defragmentation of Free Extents

As noted in Chapter 4 a *free extent* in a tablespace is a collection of contiguous free blocks in the tablespace. When a segment is dropped, its extents are deallocated and are marked as free. However, these free extents are not always recombined with neighboring free extents; the barriers between these free extents may be maintained. The SMON background process periodically coalesces neighboring free extents if the default **pctincrease** setting for the tablespace is nonzero. If the default **pctincrease** setting for a tablespace is zero, then the free space in the tablespace will not be coalesced automatically by the database. You can use the **coalesce** option of the **alter tablespace** command to force neighboring free extents to be coalesced, regardless of the default **pctincrease** setting for the tablespace.

> **NOTE**
> *The SMON background process only coalesces tablespaces whose default* **pctincrease** *value is nonzero.*

Not forcing the coalescing of free extents affects the allocation of space within the tablespace during the next space request (such as by the creation or expansion of a table). In its quest for a large enough free extent, the database will not merge contiguous free extents unless there is no other alternative; thus the large free extent at the rear of the tablespace tends to be used while the smaller free extents toward the front of the tablespace are relatively unused, becoming "speed bumps" in the tablespace because they are not, by themselves, of adequate size to be of use. As this usage pattern progresses, the database thus drifts further and further from its ideal space allocation. Free space fragmentation is particularly prevalent in environments in which database tables and indexes are frequently dropped and re-created, especially if their storage parameters are changed in the process.

However, you can force the database to recombine the contiguous free extents, thus emulating the SMON functionality. Coalescing the free extents will increase the likelihood of the free extents near the front of the file being reused, thus preserving the free space near the rear of the tablespace file. As a result, new requests for extents are more likely to meet with success.

In the ideal ORACLE tablespace, each database object is stored in a single extent and all of the available free space is in one large contiguous extent. This will minimize recursive calls during retrievals while maximizing the likelihood of acquiring a large enough free extent when an object needs additional storage space. The commands presented here will provide a means of accomplishing the second goal, that of automated free space defragmentation, as well as mapping database space allocations and providing a means of evaluating the severity of the free space fragmentation problems you may experience.

Measuring Fragmentation

To judge whether a tablespace could benefit from a free space rebuild, it is necessary to establish a baseline on an arbitrary scoring system. Since free space fragmentation is made up of several components (number of extents, size of largest extent), create a scoring index that considers both. The weightings presented here are arbitrary, and were chosen to reflect the potential for the database to acquire a large extent. Thus, the number of extents is given little importance. The critical factor is the size of the largest extent as a percentage of the total free space (that is, how close is the tablespace to the ideal?). The score for each tablespace is referred to as the *Free Space Fragmentation Index* (FSFI). You may wish to tailor your index to give greater importance to other criteria. Note that it does not consider how much free space is available, only its structure.

$$FSFI = 100 * \sqrt{\frac{\text{largest extent}}{\text{sum all extents}}} * \frac{1}{(\text{number of extents})^{1/4}}$$

The largest possible FSFI (for an ideal single-file tablespace) is 100. As the number of extents increases, the FSFI rating drops slowly. As the size of the largest extent drops, however, the FSFI rating drops rapidly. The following script calculates the FSFI values for all tablespaces in a database:

```
rem
rem  file: fsfi.sql
rem  location: /orasw/dba/contig
rem
rem  This script measures the fragmentation of free space
rem  in all of the tablespaces in a database and scores them
rem  according to an arbitrary index for comparison.
rem
set newpage 0 pagesize 60
column fsfi format 999.99
```

```
select
      Tablespace_Name,
      SQRT(MAX(Blocks)/SUM(Blocks))*
      (100/SQRT(SQRT(COUNT(Blocks)))) Fsfi
from DBA_FREE_SPACE
group by
      Tablespace_Name
order by 1

spool fsfi.lis
/
spool off
```

Output from this query, showing the FSFI values for a sample database, is shown in Figure 8-1.

Given your database's FSFI ratings, you must then establish a baseline. You should rarely encounter free space availability problems in tablespaces that have adequate free space available and FSFI ratings over 30. If a tablespace appears to be approaching that borderline, you may wish to generate a mapping of space usage in the tablespace. The following script

Tablespace_Name	FSFI
DEMODATA	87.91
DEMONDX	30.39
RBS	68.24
SYSTEM	73.78
TEMP	100.00
TOOLS	100.00

FIGURE 8-1. *Sample Free Space Fragmentation Index values*

will show all space marked as free or used by database objects. This is useful (1) to show the distribution and size of the free extents and (2) to determine which database objects are barriers between free extents.

```
rem
rem    file: mapper.sql
rem    location: /orasw/dba/contig
rem    Parameters: the tablespace name being mapped
rem
rem    Sample invocation:
rem    @mapper DEMODATA
rem
rem    This script generates a mapping of the space usage
rem    (free space vs used) in a tablespace. It graphically
rem    shows segment and free space fragmentation.
rem
set pagesize 60 linesize 132 verify off
column file_id heading "File|Id"

select
      'free space' Owner,    /*"owner" of free space*/
      '  ' Object,           /*blank object name*/
      File_ID,               /*file ID for the extent header*/
      Block_ID,              /*block ID for the extent header*/
      Blocks                 /*length of the extent, in blocks*/
 from DBA_FREE_SPACE
where Tablespace_Name = UPPER('&&1')
union
select
      SUBSTR(Owner,1,20),          /*owner name (first 20 chars)*/
      SUBSTR(Segment_Name,1,32),   /*segment name*/
      File_ID,                     /*file ID for extent header*/
      Block_ID,                    /*block ID for block header*/
      Blocks                       /*length of the extent in blocks*/
 from DBA_EXTENTS
where Tablespace_Name = UPPER('&&1')
order by 3,4

spool &&1._map.lst
/
spool off
undefine 1
```

Sample output from this mapping query is shown in Figure 8-2. The query output displays the owner and segment name for each extent in the

Owner	OBJECT	File Id	BLOCK_ID	Blocks
OPS$CC1	FILES	6	2	20
OPS$CC1	SPACES	6	22	20
OPS$CC1	EXTENTS	6	42	20
OPS$CC1	FILES	6	62	20
free space		6	82	5
free space		6	87	5
free space		6	92	5
OPS$CC1	SPACES	6	97	20
OPS$CC1	EXTENTS	6	117	20
free space		6	137	10
OPS$CC1	FILES	6	147	20
free space		6	167	14,833

FIGURE 8-2. *Sample extent map of used and free space*

tablespace. If their extent is a free extent, then the owner is listed as "free space," and the segment name (the "OBJECT" column) is left blank.

The output in Figure 8-2 shows 12 rows. Five of them are of free space extents, and seven are from data segments. Note that the first three free space extents are contiguous. Following two more data extents, there is another free space extent. Because it is separated from the other free extents in the tablespace, the fourth free extent cannot be combined with any of the other free extents unless the tablespace is defragmented.

Combining the Free Extents
If a tablespace would benefit from having its free extents coalesce (as shown in its FSFI value and free extent map), then you should either manually coalesce the extents or enable the SMON process to coalesce the extents.

To enable the SMON process to coalesce the extents, you should set the default **pctincrease** value for the tablespace to a nonzero value. In the following listing, the default storage for the DEMONDX tablespace is altered to use a **pctincrease** of 1:

```
alter tablespace DEMONDX
default storage (pctincrease 1);
```

If an object is created in the DEMONDX without a specified **pctincrease** value, then the object will use the default **pctincrease** value for the tablespace. In general, low **pctincrease** values accurately reflect the normal linear growth in the number of rows in the database. Therefore, the lowest allowable nonzero value (1) was used for the **pctincrease** value. You can override the default via the **storage** clause of the object you create.

To manually coalesce the free extents of the tablespace, use the **coalesce** option of the **alter tablespace** command.

```
alter tablespace DEMONDX coalesce;
```

The neighboring free extents will then be coalesced. You can reexecute the mapper.sql script shown earlier in this chapter to see the new structure of used and free extents in the tablespace. If there are many free extents located between data extents, then you will need to re-create the tablespace (for example, by export and importing its data) in order to be able to coalesce the free extents.

Identifying Chained Rows

When a data segment is created, a **pctfree** value is specified. This parameter tells the database how much space should be kept free *in each data block*. This space is then used when rows that are already stored in the data block extend in length via **update**s.

If an **update** to a row causes that row to no longer completely fit in a single data block, then that row may be moved to another data block, or the row may be *chained* to another block. If you are storing rows whose length is greater than the ORACLE block size, then you will automatically have chaining.

Chaining affects performance because of the need to look in multiple physical locations for data from the same logical row. By eliminating unnecessary chaining, you reduce the number of physical reads needed to return data from a datafile.

Chaining can be avoided by setting the proper value for **pctfree** during creation of data segments. For instructions for setting this value, see the "Determining the Proper **pctfree**" section of Chapter 5.

You can use the **analyze** command to collect statistics about database objects. The cost-based optimizer can use these statistics to determine the best execution path to use. The **analyze** command has an option that detects and records chained rows in tables. Its syntax is

```
analyze table TABLE_NAME list chained rows into CHAINED_ROWS;
```

This command will put the output from this operation into a table called CHAINED_ROWS in your local schema. The SQL to create the CHAINED_ROWS table is in a file named UTLCHAIN.SQL, in the /rdbms/admin subdirectory under your ORACLE software directory. The following query will select the most significant columns from the CHAINED_ROWS table:

```
select
        Owner_Name,      /*Owner of the data segment*/
        Table_Name,      /*Name of the table with the chained rows*/
        Cluster_Name,    /*Name of the cluster, if it is clustered*/
        Head_RowID       /*Rowid of the first part of the row*/
from CHAINED_ROWS;
```

The output will show the RowIDs for all chained rows. This will allow you to quickly see how much of a problem chaining is in each table. If chaining is prevalent in a table, then that table should be rebuilt with a higher value for **pctfree**.

Increasing the ORACLE Block Size

The effect of increasing the database block size is stunning. In most environments, at least two block sizes are supported—for example, 2K and 4K. Most of the installation routines are set to use the lower of the two. However, using the next higher value for the block size may improve the performance of query-intensive operations by up to 50 percent.

This gain comes relatively free of charge. To increase the database block size, the entire database must be rebuilt, and all of the old database files have to be deleted. The new files can be created in the same location as the old files, with the same size, but will be managed more efficiently by the database. The performance savings comes from the way that ORACLE manages the block header information. Doubling the size of the ORACLE blocks has little effect on the block header; thus, a smaller percentage of space is used to store block header information.

To change the block size, modify the init.ora parameter called DB_BLOCK_SIZE. The DB_BLOCK_SIZE parameter may be specified in the config.ora file that your database's init.ora file calls.

Be careful when doing this, since several of the database's init.ora parameters are set in terms of the number of ORACLE blocks. For example, the DB_BLOCK_BUFFERS parameter, which sets the size of the data buffer cache, is set in this manner. If you double the block size, you should cut the DB_BLOCK_BUFFERS parameter in half. Failing to modify the DB_BLOCK_BUFFERS parameter when doubling the database block size will double the size of the data buffer cache, possibly causing problems with the memory management on your server.

Tuning Data Manipulation

There are several data manipulation tasks that may involve the DBA. These tend to involve manipulation of large quantities of data. You have several options when loading and deleting large volumes of data, as described in the following sections.

You can improve the performance of database reads and writes by creating multiple DBWR (Database Writer) I/O slaves. Creating multiple DBWR slaves will prevent access requests against multiple disks from causing performance bottlenecks. ORACLE recommends creating at least as many DBWR slaves as you have disks. The number of DBWR slaves that should be created for an instance is set via the DBWR_IO_SLAVES parameter in the database's init.ora file.

In addition to creating I/O slaves for DBWR, you can create I/O slaves for the LGWR and ARCH processes. To create multiple LGWR processes, set a value for the LGWR_IO_SLAVES init.ora parameter. The number of ARCH I/O slaves is set via the ARCH_IO_SLAVES init.ora parameter.

Bulk Inserts: Using the SQL*Loader Direct Path Option

When used in the Conventional Path mode, SQL*Loader reads a set of records from a file, generates **insert** commands, and passes them to the ORACLE kernel. ORACLE then finds places for those records in free blocks in the table and updates any associated indexes.

In Direct Path mode, SQL*Loader creates formatted data blocks and writes directly to the datafiles. This requires occasional checks with the database to get new locations for data blocks, but no other I/O with the database kernel is required. The result is a data load process that is dramatically faster than Conventional Path mode.

If the table is indexed, then the indexes will be placed in "DIRECT PATH" state during the load. After the load is complete, the new keys (index column values) will be sorted and merged with the existing keys in the index. To maintain this temporary set of keys, the load will create a temporary index segment that is at least as large as the largest index on the table. The space requirements for this can be minimized by presorting the index and using the SORTED INDEXES clause in the SQL*Loader control file.

To use the Direct Path option, a series of views must be created in the database. These views are created during database creation via the script CATLDR.SQL, located in $ORACLE_HOME/rdbms/admin.

To get the best performance from the load, the data segment that you are loading into should already be created, with all of the space it will need already allocated. This will minimize the amount of dynamic space allocation necessary. You should also presort the data on the columns of the largest index in the table. Sorting the data and leaving the indexes on the table during a Direct Path load will yield better performance than if you were to drop the indexes before the load and then re-create them after it completed.

To take advantage of this option, the table cannot be clustered, and there can be no other active transactions against it. During the load, only NOT NULL, UNIQUE, and PRIMARY KEY constraints will be enforced; after the load has completed, the CHECK and FOREIGN KEY constraints can be automatically reenabled. To force this to occur, use the

```
REENABLE DISABLED_CONSTRAINTS
```

clause in the SQL*Loader control file.

The only exception to this reenabling process is that table Insert triggers, when reenabled, are not executed for each of the new rows in the table. A separate process must manually perform whatever commands were to have been performed by this type of trigger.

The SQL*Loader Direct Path loading option provides significant performance improvements over the SQL*Loader Conventional Path loader in loading data into ORACLE tables by bypassing SQL processing, buffer cache management, and unnecessary reads for the data blocks. The Parallel Data Loading option of SQL*Loader allows multiple loading processes to work on loading the same table, utilizing spare resources on the system and thereby reducing the overall elapsed times for loading. Given enough CPU and I/O resources, this can significantly reduce the overall loading times.

To use Parallel Data Loading, start multiple SQL*Loader sessions using the PARALLEL keyword (otherwise, SQL*Loader puts an exclusive lock on the table). Each session is an independent session requiring its own control file. The following listing shows three separate Direct Path loads, all using the PARALLEL=TRUE parameter on the command line:

```
sqlload USERID=ME/PASS CONTROL=PART1.CTL DIRECT=TRUE PARALLEL=TRUE
sqlload USERID=ME/PASS CONTROL=PART2.CTL DIRECT=TRUE PARALLEL=TRUE
sqlload USERID=ME/PASS CONTROL=PART3.CTL DIRECT=TRUE PARALLEL=TRUE
```

Each session creates its own log, bad, and discard files (part1.log, part2.log, part3.log, part1.bad, part2.bad, etc.) by default. Since you have multiple sessions loading data into the same table, only the APPEND option is allowed for Parallel Data Loading. The SQL*Loader REPLACE, TRUNCATE and INSERT options are not allowed for Parallel Data Loading. If you need to delete the table's data before starting the load, you must manually delete the data (via **delete** or **truncate** commands). You cannot use SQL*Loader to delete the records automatically if you are using Parallel Data Loading.

NOTE
*If you use Parallel Data Loading, indexes are not maintained by the SQL*Loader session. Before starting the loading process, you must drop all indexes on the table and disable all of its PRIMARY KEY and UNIQUE constraints. After the loads complete, you can re-create the table's indexes.*

In serial Direct Path loading (PARALLEL=FALSE), SQL*Loader loads data into extents in the table. If the load process fails before the load completes, some data could be committed to the table prior to the process failure. In Parallel Data Loading, each load process creates temporary segments for loading the data. The temporary segments are later merged with the table. If a Parallel Data Load process fails before the load completes, the temporary segments will not have been merged with the table. If the temporary segments have not been merged with the table being loaded, then no data from the load will have been committed to the table.

You can use the SQL*Loader FILE parameter to direct each data loading session to a different datafile. By directing each loading session to its own datafile, you can balance the I/O load of the loading processes. Data loading is very I/O-intensive and must be distributed across multiple disks for parallel loading to achieve significant performance improvements over serial loading.

After a Parallel Data Load, each session may attempt to reenable the table's constraints. As long as at least one load session is still underway, attempting to reenable the constraints will fail. The final loading session to complete should attempt to reenable the constraints, and should succeed. You should check the status of your constraints after the load completes. If the table being loaded has PRIMARY KEY and UNIQUE constraints, you can create the associated indexes in parallel prior to enabling the constraints.

Bulk Deletes: The truncate Command

Occasionally, users attempt to delete all of the records from a table at once. When they encounter errors during this process, they complain that the rollback segments are too small, when in fact their transaction is too large.

A second problem occurs once the records have all been deleted. Even though the segment no longer has any records in it, it still maintains all of the space that was allocated to it. Thus, deleting all those records saved you not a single byte of space.

The **truncate** command resolves both of these problems. It is a DDL command, not a DML command, *so it cannot be rolled back*. Once you have used the **truncate** command on a table, its records are gone, and none of its Delete triggers are executed in the process. However, the table retains all of its dependent objects—such as grants, indexes, and constraints.

The **truncate** command is the fastest way to delete large volumes of data. Since it will delete all of the records in a table, this may force you to alter your application design so that no protected records are stored in the same table as the records to be deleted. If you use partitions, you can

truncate one partition of a table without affecting the rest of the table's partitions (see Chapter 12).

A sample **truncate** command for a table is shown in the following listing:

```
truncate table EMPLOYEE drop storage;
```

This example, in which the EMPLOYEE table's records are deleted, shows a powerful feature of **truncate**. The **drop storage** clause is used to deallocate the non**initial** space from the table (this is the default option). Thus, it is now possible to delete all of a table's rows, and to reclaim all but its initial extent's allocated space, without dropping the table.

This command also works for clusters. In this example, the **reuse storage** option is used to leave all allocated space empty within the segment that acquired it.

```
truncate cluster EMP_DEPT reuse storage;
```

When this command is executed, all of the records in the EMP_DEPT cluster will be instantly deleted.

To **truncate** partitions, you need to know the name of the partition. In the following example, the partition named PART3 of the EMPLOYEE table is **truncate**d via the **alter table** command:

```
alter table EMPLOYEE
truncate partition PART3
drop storage;
```

The rest of the partitions of the EMPLOYEE table will be unaffected by the truncation of the PART3 partition. See Chapter 12 for details on creating and managing partitions.

Tuning Physical Storage

Although the database should be CPU-bound, this can only happen if its physical I/O is evenly distributed and handled correctly. Chapter 4 describes a process for planning file distribution across disks. Planning file distribution involves understanding the interactions of the DBWR, LGWR, and ARCH background processes. A means of verifying the adequacy of the final layouts is also provided there.

In addition to that level of physical storage tuning, several other factors should be considered. The following sections address factors that are external to the database, but may have a profound impact on its ability to access data quickly.

Tuning File Fragmentation

Back in ORACLE Version 5, there was a command called CCF—Create Contiguous File. This command created datafiles that were contiguous on the physical disk. In the current version of ORACLE, however, there is no way to guarantee that any of the database's files are created in contiguous areas on their disks.

Why is this significant? Consider the case of a perfectly sized and compressed table. All of its data is in a single extent. However, that extent is located in a datafile—and that datafile may not be contiguous on the disk. Thus, the disk hardware has to keep moving to find the data, even though the database considers the table to be contiguous.

The method for determining whether a file is contiguous or not is operating-system dependent. In most cases, you will have to dump the header of the file and analyze the output to determine how many fragments the file is physically broken into. This process should be done in coordination with the systems management personnel.

Their participation is important because they hold the key to resolving the situation. To have the best chance at creating a contiguous file, create a new file on an unused disk and then check its fragmentation. To minimize file fragmentation, keep nondatabase files off of database disks, and avoid dropping and re-creating files. This problem highlights the need for disks that are dedicated to your database files.

Using Raw Devices

Raw devices are available with some UNIX operating systems. When they are used, the DBWR process bypasses the UNIX buffer cache and eliminates the file system overhead. For I/O-intensive applications, they may result in a performance improvement of around 20 percent.

Raw devices cannot be managed with the same commands as file systems. For example, the **tar** command cannot be used to back up individual files; instead, the **dd** command must be used. This is a much less flexible command to use and limits your recovery capabilities.

Tuning Logical Storage

From a logical standpoint, like objects should be stored together. As discussed in Chapter 3 objects should be grouped based on their space usage and user interaction characteristics. Based on these groupings, tablespaces should be created that cater to specific types of objects.

A suggested tablespace layout is presented in Table 8-1, along with details about the characteristics of the types of objects stored in each tablespace.

Tablespace	Use
SYSTEM	Data dictionary tables and indexes. Created during the database creation. No other objects should be stored here.
DATA	Standard-operation tables for an application. They tend to be actively used and to be the most likely to grow.
DATA_2	Static tables used during standard operation of an application. They tend to be fixed in size and infrequently accessed other than as reference tables.
INDEXES	Indexes for the standard operation tables. They tend to be actively used and to be likely to grow.
INDEXES_2	Indexes for the static tables. They tend to be fixed in size.
RBS	Standard operation rollback segments.
RBS_2	Specialty rollback segments used for data loads. When no data loads are taking place, they may be taken offline.
TEMP	Standard operation temporary segments for all regular users of an application.
TEMP_USER	Temporary segments created by a particular user. This is intended to isolate exceptional space requirements from the main application.
TOOLS	RDBMS tools tables for tools.
TOOLS_I	Indexes for RDBMS tools tables.
USERS	User objects, in development databases. In production databases, this tablespace typically does not exist.

TABLE 8-1. *Logical Distribution of Segments in an Optimal Database*

For further information on this distribution of segment types and extensions to the Optimal Flexible Architecture (OFA), see Chapter 3. For information on detecting and managing contention for rollback segments, see Chapter 7.

Reducing Network Traffic

As databases and the applications that use them become more distributed, the network that supports the servers may become a bottleneck in the process of delivering data to the user. Since DBAs typically have little control over the network management, it is important to use the database's capabilities to reduce the number of network packets that are required for the data to be delivered. Reducing network traffic will reduce your reliance on the network, and thus eliminate a potential cause of performance problems.

Replication of Data

As described in Chapter 1 and Part III of this book, you can manipulate and query data from remote databases. However, it is not desirable to have large volumes of data constantly sent from one database to another. To reduce the amount of data being sent across the network, different data replication options should be considered.

In a purely distributed environment, each data element exists in one place, as shown in Figure 8-3. When data is required, it is accessed from remote databases via database links. In the example shown in Figure 8-3, the EMPLOYEE data is queried from the MASTER1 database, and the DEPT data is queried from the REMOTE1 database. Both databases are accessible via database links created within the REMOTE2 database.

This purist approach (having data stored in only one place) is similar to implementing an application in Third Normal Form—and as stated earlier in this chapter, that approach will not support any major production application. Modifying the application's tables to improve data retrieval performance involves denormalizing data. This process deliberately stores redundant data in order to shorten users' access paths to the data.

In a distributed environment, replicating data accomplishes this goal. Rather than force queries to cross the network to resolve user requests, selected data from remote servers is replicated to the local server.

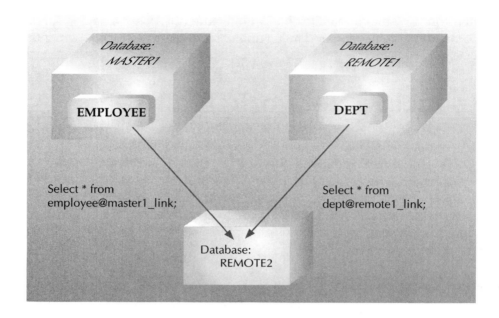

FIGURE 8-3. *Sample distributed environment*

This can be accomplished via a number of means, as described in the following sections.

Using the copy Command to Replicate Data

In the first option, the data can be periodically copied to the local server. This is best accomplished via the SQL*Plus **copy** command, as described in Part III. The **copy** command allows selected columns and rows to be replicated to each server. This option is illustrated in Figure 8-4.

For example, the remote server may have a table called EMPLOYEE. The local server would be able to replicate the data that it needs by using the **copy** command to select records from the remote EMPLOYEE table. The **copy** command can be used to store those selected records in a table in the local database. This command includes a query clause; thus, it is possible to return only those rows that meet the specified criteria.

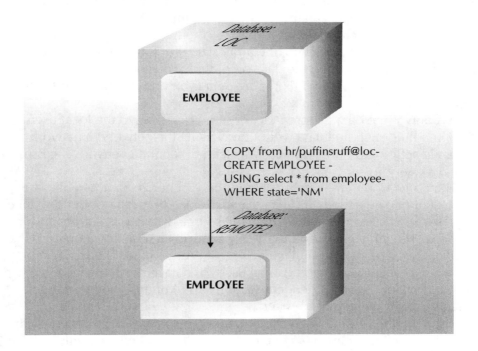

FIGURE 8-4.   *Data replication using the* ***copy*** *command*

In this example, a portion of the EMPLOYEE table is copied down from the headquarters database to a local database. A **where** clause is used to restrict which records are selected.

```
set copycommit 1
set arraysize 1000
copy from HR/PUFFINSTUFF@loc -
create EMPLOYEE -
using -
select * from EMPLOYEE -
where State = 'NM'
```

The **copy from** clause in this example specifies the name of the remote database. In this case, the query is told to use the database identified by the service name "loc". During the connection, a session should be started by using the "hr" account, with the password "puffinstuff".

The **set copycommit** and **set arraysize** commands are used to specify the size of array of data. Setting the array size allows the DBA to force the database to commit during the data copy, thus reducing the size of the transactions to be supported. For more details on this capability and other **copy** options, see Part III.

As soon as the data is stored locally, it is accessible to the local users. They can thus query the data without traversing the network; a network access is performed during the **copy** instead of separate network accesses for each query.

The down side to replicating data in this manner is that the replicated data is out of date as soon as it is created. Replicating data for performance purposes is thus most effective when the source data is very infrequently changed. The **copy** command must be performed frequently enough so that the local tables contain useful, sufficiently accurate data. The **replace** option of the **copy** command can be used to replace the contents of the local tables during subsequent **copy**s. See Part III of this book for further usage notes for the **copy** command.

Although the local table may be updatable, none of the changes made to it will be reflected in the source table. Thus, this scenario is only effective for improving the performance of query operations. If you need to be able to update the local data and have those changes sent back to the master database, then you will need to use some of the advanced replication options available within ORACLE. ORACLE supports multimaster configurations as well as read-only snapshots and updatable snapshots. The following section provides a brief overview of the use of snapshots from a performance standpoint; for a more detailed explanation of snapshots, see Part III of this book.

Using Snapshots to Replicate Data

The ORACLE Distributed Option offers a means of managing the data replication within a database. This option uses *snapshots* to replicate data from a master source to multiple targets. It also takes care of refreshing the data, updating the targets at specified time intervals. This option is illustrated in Figure 8-5.

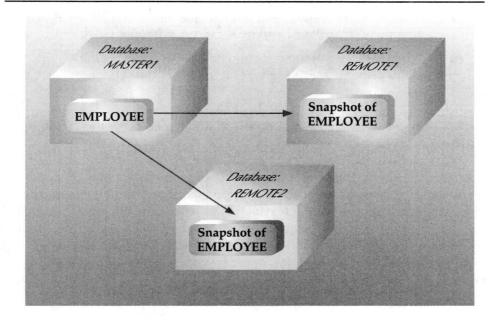

FIGURE 8-5. *Data replication using snapshots*

Snapshots may be read-only or updatable. This section will focus on performance tuning aspects of snapshots. Managing snapshots is covered in Chapter 15.

Before creating a snapshot, a database link to the source database should first be created. The following example creates a private database link called HR_LINK, using the "loc" service name:

```
create database link HR_LINK
connect to HR identified by PUFFINSTUFF
using 'loc';
```

The **create database link** command, as shown in this example, has several parameters:

■ The name of the link ("hr_link," in this example).

- The account to connect to (if none is specified, then the local username and password will be used in the remote database).

- The service name of the remote database (as found in the tnsnames.ora file for the server). In this case, the service name is "loc".

For more information on this command, see the entry for the **create database link** command in Appendix C.

There are two styles of snapshots available: simple snapshots and complex snapshots. The proper type to use for your environment depends on the amount of replicated data and the manner in which it is queried. The type of snapshot used affects which data refresh options are available.

The type of snapshot is determined by the query that defines it. A *simple* snapshot is one that is based on a query that does not contain **group by** clauses, **connect by** clauses, joins, or set operations. A *complex* snapshot contains at least one of these options. For example, a snapshot based on the query

```
select * from EMPLOYEE@HR_LINK;
```

would be a simple snapshot, while a snapshot based on the query

```
select DEPT, MAX(Salary)
   from EMPLOYEE@HR_LINK
 group by DEPT;
```

would be a complex snapshot because it uses grouping functions.

The syntax used to create the snapshot on the local server is shown in the following listing. In this example, the snapshot is given a name ("local_emp"), and its storage parameters are specified. Its base query is given, as well as its refresh interval. In this case, the snapshot is told to immediately retrieve the master data, then to perform the snapshot operation again in seven days ("SysDate+7").

```
create snapshot LOCAL_EMP
pctfree 5
tablespace data_2
storage (initial 100K next 100K pctincrease 0)
refresh fast
     start with SysDate
```

```
       next SysDate+7
as select * from EMPLOYEE@HR_LINK;
```

The **refresh fast** clause tells the database to use a *snapshot log* to refresh the local snapshot. This capability is only available with simple snapshots. When a snapshot log is used, only the changes to the master table are sent to the targets. If a complex snapshot is used, then the **refresh complete** clause must be used instead; in that scenario, the refresh completely replaces the existing data in the snapshot table.

Snapshot logs must be created in the master database, via the **create snapshot log** command. An example of this command is shown in the following listing:

```
create snapshot log on EMPLOYEE
tablespace DATA
storage (initial 10K next 10K pctincrease 0);
```

The snapshot log is always created in the same schema as the master table.

Using simple snapshots with snapshot logs allows you to reduce the amount of network traffic involved in maintaining the replicated data. Since only the changes to the data will be sent via a snapshot log, the maintenance of simple snapshots should use fewer network resources than complex snapshots require. This is particularly true if the master tables for the snapshots are large, fairly static tables. If this is not the case, then the volume of transactions sent via the snapshot log may not be any less than would be sent to perform a complete refresh.

This plays a part in your application design as well. If your data access paths require joining information from multiple remote tables, then you have two choices, as shown in Figure 8-6. The first option—see Figure 8-6a—is to create multiple simple snapshots and then perform the join query on the local server. The second option—see Figure 8-6b—is to create a single complex snapshot on the local server based on multiple remote tables.

Which option will retrieve data faster? The answer to that depends on several factors:

■ The size of the master tables. How long does a complete refresh take?

■ The volume of transactions against the master tables. How large are the snapshot logs?

■ The frequency of the refreshes. How often will the data be replicated?

If the data is rarely refreshed, and there are few transactions against the master tables, then it should be quicker to use a complex snapshot—see Figure 8-6b. If the data is frequently updated and refreshed, then the time savings from using fast refreshes should outweigh the cost of performing the join when the query is executed (rather than ahead of time via the snapshot). In that case, using a set of simple snapshots would result in a faster response time.

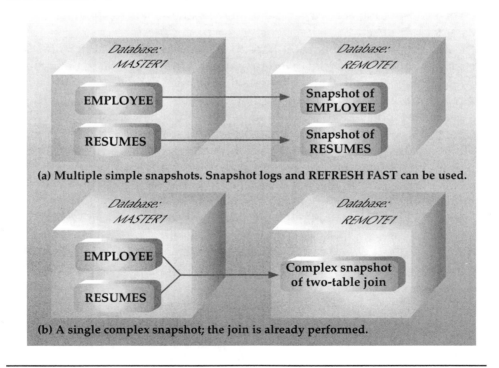

(a) Multiple simple snapshots. Snapshot logs and REFRESH FAST can be used.

(b) A single complex snapshot; the join is already performed.

FIGURE 8-6. *Data replication options for joins*

NOTE
In general, a fast refresh will outperform a complete refresh if fewer than 25 percent of the rows have changed. If more than 25 percent of the rows have changed, then you should consider using a complete refresh instead. Although a complete refresh may complete faster in that case, it will generate a greater volume of network traffic than a fast refresh will.

The goal is to minimize the time it takes to satisfy the user's data request. The decision on the proper type of snapshot configuration to use can only be made if you know most common joins ahead of time. For further information on the management of snapshots, see Chapter 15.

Using Remote Procedure Calls

When using procedures in a distributed database environment, there are two options: to create a local procedure that references remote tables or to create a remote procedure that is called by a local application. These two options are illustrated in Figure 8-7.

The proper location for the procedure depends on the distribution of the data and the way it is to be used. The emphasis should be on minimizing the amount of data that must be sent through the network in order to resolve the data request. The procedure should reside within the database that contains most of the data that is used during the procedure's operations.

For example, consider this procedure:

```
create procedure MY_RAISE (My_Emp_No IN NUMBER, Raise IN NUMBER)
as begin
      update EMPLOYEE@HR_LINK
      set Salary = Salary+Raise
      where Empno = My_Emp_No;
end;
/
```

In this case, the procedure only accesses a single table (EMPLOYEE) on a remote node (as indicated by the database link "hr_link"). To reduce the amount of data sent across the network, move this procedure to the remote

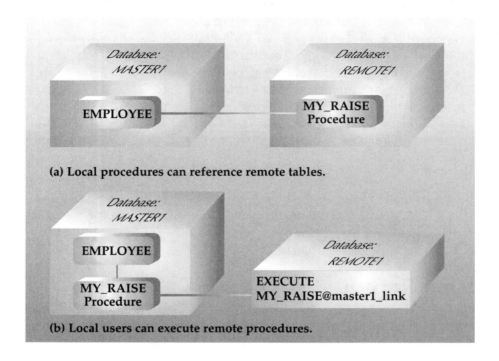

(a) Local procedures can reference remote tables.

(b) Local users can execute remote procedures.

FIGURE 8-7. *Options for procedure location*

database identified by the database link "hr_link" and remove the reference to that database link from the **from** clause in the procedure. Then, call the procedure from the local database by using the database link, as shown in the following listing:

```
execute MY_RAISE@HR_LINK(1234,2000);
```

In this case, two parameters are passed to the procedure—My_Emp_No is set to '1234' and Raise is set to '2000'. The procedure is invoked using a database link to tell the database where to find the procedure.

The benefit of this is that all of the procedure's processing is performed in the database where the data resides. This minimizes the amount of network traffic necessary to complete the procedure's processing.

To maintain location transparency, you may create a local synonym that points to the remote procedure. The database link name will be specified in the synonym so that user requests will automatically use the remote database.

```
create synonym MY_RAISE for MY_RAISE@HR_LINK;
```

A user could then enter the command:

```
execute MY_RAISE(1234,2000);
```

and it would execute the remote procedure defined by the synonym MY_RAISE.

CHAPTER
9

Database Security
and Auditing

eadbolt locks, secret passwords, iron bars, gated driveways, access cards, security patrols—layers of physical security in the real world are found in the database world as well.

Creating and enforcing security procedures helps to protect what is rapidly becoming the most important corporate asset: data. And while storing that data in a database makes it more useful and available companywide, it also makes it susceptible to unauthorized access. Such access attempts must be prevented and detected.

The ORACLE database has several layers of security, and the ability to audit each level. In this chapter, you will see descriptions for each layer in the auditing process. You will also see methods for setting impossible passwords and forcing passwords to expire.

Security Capabilities

ORACLE makes several levels of security available to the DBA:

- Account security for validation of users
- Access security for database objects
- System-level security for managing global privileges

Each of these capabilities is described in the following sections; the "Implementing Security" section of this chapter provides details for effectively using the available options.

Account Security

In order to access data in an ORACLE database, you must have access to an account in that database. This access can be direct—via user connections into a database—or indirect. Indirect connections include access via preset authorizations within database links. Each account must have a password associated with it. A database account can also be tied to an operating system account.

Passwords are set for a user when the user's account is created. They may then be altered by either the DBA or the user. The database stores an encrypted version of the password in a data dictionary table. If the account is directly related to an operating system account, then it is possible to bypass the password check.

As of ORACLE8, passwords can expire, and the DBA can establish the conditions under which a password can be reused. Also, you can use profiles to enforce standards for the passwords (such as minimum length) and you can automatically lock accounts if there are multiple consecutive failures to connect to the account.

Object Privileges

Access to objects within a database is accomplished via *privileges*. These allow specific database commands to be used against specific database objects via the **grant** command. For example, if the user THUMPER owns a table called EMPLOYEE, and executes the command

```
grant select on EMPLOYEE to PUBLIC;
```

then all users (PUBLIC) will be able to select records from THUMPER's EMPLOYEE table. *Roles*—named groups of privileges—can be used to simplify the administration of privileges. For applications with large numbers of users, roles greatly reduce the number of **grant** commands needed. Since roles can be password-protected and can be dynamically enabled or disabled, they add an additional layer of security to the database.

System-Level Roles and Privileges

You can use roles to manage the system-level commands available to users. These commands include **create table** and **alter index**. Actions against each type of database object are authorized via separate privileges. For example, a user may be granted the CREATE TABLE privilege, but not the CREATE TYPE privilege. You can create customized system-level roles that grant users the exact privileges they need without granting them excessive authority within the database. As noted in Chapter 5, the CONNECT and RESOURCE roles are useful for the basic system privileges required by end users and developers, respectively.

Implementing Security

The security capabilities in ORACLE include roles, profiles, and direct grants of privileges. In the following sections you will see the usage of all of these features, including several undocumented capabilities.

The Starting Point: Operating System Security

You cannot access a database unless you can first access, either directly or indirectly, the server on which the database is running, The first step in securing your database is to secure the platform and network on which it resides. Once that has been accomplished, the operating system security must be considered.

ORACLE uses a number of files that its users do not require direct access to. For example, the datafiles and the online redo log files are written and read only via ORACLE's background processes. Thus, only DBAs who will be creating and dropping these files require direct access to them at the operating system level. Export dump files and other backup files must also be secured.

Creating Users

When creating a user, the goal is to establish a secure, useful account that has adequate privileges and proper default settings. You can use the **create user** command to create a new database account. When the account is created, it will not have any capabilities—and will not even be able to log in until that privilege is granted.

All of the necessary settings for a user account can be specified within a single **create user** command. These settings include values for all of the parameters listed in Table 9-1.

The following listing shows a sample **create user** command. In this example, the user THUMPER is created, with a password of RABBIT, a default tablespace of USERS, a temporary tablespace of TEMP, no quotas, and the default profile.

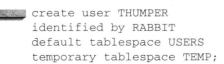

```
create user THUMPER
identified by RABBIT
default tablespace USERS
temporary tablespace TEMP;
```

Parameter	Usage
Username	Name of the schema.
Password	Password for the account; may also be tied directly to the operating system host account name.
Default tablespace	The default tablespace in which objects created in this schema will be stored. This setting does not give the user rights to create objects; it only sets a default value.
Temporary tablespace	The tablespace in which temporary segments used during sorting transactions will be stored.
Quota [on tablespace]	Allows the user to store objects in the specified tablespace, up to the total size specified as the quota.
Profile	Assigns a profile to the user. If none is specified, then the default profile is used. Profiles are used to restrict the usage of system resources and to enforce password management rules.

TABLE 9-1. *Parameters for the* **create user** *Command*

Since no profile was specified, the default profile for the database will be used. This is an actual profile named DEFAULT; its initial settings are for all resource consumption limits to be set to UNLIMITED. See the "User Profiles" section of this chapter for further details on profiles.

Since no quotas were specified, the user cannot create objects in the database.

When granting resource quotas, the **quota** parameter of the **create user** or **alter user** command is used, as shown in the following listing. In this example, THUMPER is granted a quota of 100MB in the USERS tablespace.

```
alter user THUMPER
quota 100M on USERS;
```

The THUMPER user can now create up to 100MB worth of segments in the USERS tablespace. Users do not need space quotas on the TEMP tablespace in order for their queries to create temporary segments there.

Except for the username, all of the parameters in the **create user** command may be altered via the **alter user** command.

Dropping Users

A user can be completely dropped from the database via the **drop user** command. This command has one parameter, **cascade**, which drops all objects in the user's schema before dropping the user. If the user owns objects, then you must specify **cascade** in order to drop the user. A sample **drop user** command is shown in the following listing:

```
drop user THUMPER cascade;
```

Any views, synonyms, procedures, functions, or packages that referenced objects in the schema of the dropped user will be marked as INVALID. If another user with the same name is created at a later date, there will be nothing for the new user to inherit from the previous user with that name.

System-Level Privileges

You can use system-level roles to distribute the availability of system-level commands used to manage the database. You can either create customized system-level roles or use the ones that come with the database. The available privileges that can be granted via system-level roles are listed in Table 9-2. The "ANY" keyword in a privilege signifies that the user has the privilege for all schemas in the database. If the keyword "ANY" is enclosed in brackets ("[ANY]"), then it is optional when granting that privilege.

NOTE
"ANY" and "PUBLIC" are not synonymous. A "public" object is accessible to all users in a database; all other objects are privately owned. The "ANY" option allows you to create private objects in other users' schemas.

The **with grant option** clause of the **grant** command is used to pass along to the grantee the ability to grant the privilege to other users.

SQL reference information for these options may be found in Appendix C.

There are eight system-level roles provided with ORACLE. They are CONNECT, RESOURCE, DBA, IMP_FULL_DATABASE, EXP_FULL_DATABASE, SELECT_CATALOG_ROLE, EXECUTE_CATALOG_ROLE, and

Privilege	Capabilities Granted
Object Management:	
CREATE [ANY] CLUSTER	Create clusters.
CREATE [ANY] DIRECTORY	Create directories (for BFILE LOBs).
CREATE [ANY] INDEX	Create index.
CREATE ANY LIBRARY	Create library for external function calls.
CREATE [ANY] PROCEDURE	Create procedures, functions, or packages.
CREATE [ANY] SEQUENCE	Create sequences.
CREATE [ANY] SNAPSHOT	Create snapshots; must also have CREATE TABLE.
CREATE ANY SYNONYM	Create synonyms in other users' schemas.
CREATE [PUBLIC] SYNONYM	Create [public] synonyms.
CREATE [ANY] TABLE	Create tables. The user must have a quota for a tablespace or have been granted UNLIMITED TABLESPACE.
CREATE [ANY] TRIGGER	Create triggers.
CREATE [ANY] TYPE	Create abstract datatypes.
CREATE [ANY] VIEW	Create views.
ALTER ANY CLUSTER	Alter any cluster.
ALTER ANY INDEX	Alter any index.
ALTER ANY PROCEDURE	Alter any procedure, function, or package.
ALTER ANY SEQUENCE	Alter any sequence.
ALTER ANY SNAPSHOT	Alter any snapshot.
ALTER ANY TABLE	Alter any table. Also gives the user the ability to compile any view in any schema.
ALTER ANY TRIGGER	Enable, disable, or compile any trigger.
ALTER ANY TYPE	Alter any abstract datatype.
DROP ANY CLUSTER	Drop any cluster.
DROP ANY DIRECTORY	Drop any directory (used for BFILE LOBs).
DROP ANY INDEX	Drop any index.
DROP ANY LIBRARY	Drop any library.
DROP ANY PROCEDURE	Drop any procedure, function, or package.
DROP ANY SEQUENCE	Drop any sequence.

TABLE 9-2. *System-Level Privileges*

Privilege	Capabilities Granted
DROP ANY SNAPSHOT	Drop any snapshot.
DROP ANY SYNONYM	Drop any private synonym.
DROP PUBLIC SYNONYM	Drop public synonyms.
DROP ANY TRIGGER	Drop any trigger.
DROP ANY TYPE	Drop any abstract datatype.
DROP ANY VIEW	Drop any view.
BACKUP ANY TABLE	Perform an incremental export. See Chapter 10 for more details.
COMMENT ANY TABLE	Create comments for any table, view, or column.
DROP ANY TABLE	Drop any table.
LOCK ANY TABLE	Lock any table.
SELECT ANY TABLE	Select records from any table, view, or snapshot.
INSERT ANY TABLE	Insert records into any table or view.
UPDATE ANY TABLE	Update records in any table or view.
DELETE ANY TABLE	Delete rows from any table or view, and **truncate** any table or cluster.
ALTER SESSION	Alter session parameters.
CREATE SESSION	Connect to the database.
EXECUTE ANY PROCEDURE	Execute any procedure or function, and reference any public package variable.
EXECUTE ANY TYPE	Use any abstract datatype or methods of abstract datatypes.
SELECT ANY SEQUENCE	Select a value from any sequence.

Database Management:

Privilege	Capabilities Granted
CREATE [PUBLIC] DATABASE LINK	Create links to other databases.
CREATE PROFILE	Create profiles for database users.
CREATE ROLE	Create roles.
CREATE ROLLBACK SEGMENT	Create rollback segments.
CREATE TABLESPACE	Create tablespaces.

TABLE 9-2. *System-Level Privileges (continued)*

Privilege	Capabilities Granted
CREATE USER	Create new users (see Table 9-1 for options).
ALTER PROFILE	Modify existing profiles.
ALTER RESOURCE COST	Change the costs of resources specified in the profiles.
ALTER ANY ROLE	Alter any role.
ALTER ROLLBACK SEGMENT	Alter rollback segments.
ALTER TABLESPACE	Alter tablespaces.
ALTER USER	Alter user.
DROP PROFILE	Drop an existing profile.
DROP PUBLIC DATABASE LINK	Drop a public database link.
DROP ANY ROLE	Drop any role.
DROP ROLLBACK SEGMENT	Drop an existing rollback segment.
DROP TABLESPACE	Drop a tablespace.
DROP USER	Drop a user. Append the **cascade** keyword if the user owns objects.
ALTER DATABASE	Issue **alter database** statements.
ALTER SYSTEM	Issue **alter system** statements.
ANALYZE ANY	Analyze any table, cluster, or index.
AUDIT ANY	Audit any schema object.
AUDIT SYSTEM	Audit system-level operations.
BECOME USER	Become another user; used by Import.
FORCE [ANY] TRANSACTION	Force the commit or rollback of [any] in-doubt distributed transactions in the local database.
GRANT ANY PRIVILEGE	Grant any of these system-level privileges.
GRANT ANY ROLE	Grant any role to a user.
MANAGE TABLESPACE	Manage the status of tablespaces (online/offline and begin backup/end backup states).
RESTRICTED SESSION	Can connect when the database has been started using **startup restrict**.
UNLIMITED TABLESPACE	Can use an unlimited amount of storage space in any tablespace. This overrides any resource quotas, and cannot be granted to roles.

TABLE 9-2. *System-Level Privileges (continued)*

Privilege	Capabilities Granted
SYSDBA	Can perform system management functions (recover, startup, shutdown) as well as create databases.
SYSOPER	Can perform system management functions related to backups and startup/shutdowns (mount, recovery, open, and close a database).

TABLE 9-2. *System-Level Privileges (continued)*

DELETE_CATALOG_ROLE. Using these roles allows you to limit the system-level privileges granted to database management roles.

The CONNECT role is typically granted to end users. Although it does have some object creation abilities (including the CREATE TABLE privilege), it does not give the user any quota on any tablespace. Since the users will not have tablespace quotas unless you grant them to them, the users will not be able to create tables.

The RESOURCE role is granted to developers. As described in Chapter 5, the RESOURCE role gives developers the most-used application development privileges.

The DBA role includes all of the system-level privileges.

The IMP_FULL_DATABASE and EXP_FULL_DATABASE roles are used during Import and Export, respectively, when you perform a full database Import or Export (see Chapter 10). These roles are part of the DBA role; you can use these roles to grant users limited database management privileges.

The SELECT_CATALOG_ROLE, EXECUTE_CATALOG_ROLE, and DELETE_CATALOG_ROLE roles are new roles as of ORACLE8.

The simplest of these three roles is DELETE_CATALOG_ROLE. If you grant a user DELETE_CATALOG_ROLE, then the user can delete records from the table SYS.AUD$. The SYS.AUD$ table is the table into which audit records are written. By granting this role to a user, you are giving the user the ability to delete records from the audit trail table without giving the user any other DBA-level commands. The use of this role may simplify your audit trail management process.

The SELECT_CATALOG_ROLE and EXECUTE_CATALOG_ROLE roles grant users privileges to select or execute exportable data dictionary objects. That is, not every database object is exported during a full system export (see Chapter 10). For example, the dynamic performance views (see Chapter 6) are not exported. Thus, SELECT_CATALOG_ROLE does not give the user the ability to select from the dynamic performance tables; it does, however, give the user the ability to query from most of the data dictionary. Similarly, EXECUTE_CATALOG_ROLE grants users the ability to execute procedures and functions that are part of the data dictionary.

The account creation process may be reexamined. Like the database backup process, DBA-level privileges are required to perform account creation. However, as seen from the privileges listed in Table 9-2, you can select out a subset of privileges that are needed to create new users.

For example, a new system-level role called ACCOUNT_CREATOR can be created. It will only be able to create users; it will not be able to perform any other DBA-level commands. The commands that create this role are shown in the following listing:

```
create role ACCOUNT_CREATOR;
grant CREATE SESSION, CREATE USER, ALTER USER
    to ACCOUNT_CREATOR;
```

The first command in this listing creates a role called ACCOUNT_CREATOR. The second command grants that role the ability to log in (CREATE SESSION) and create and alter accounts (CREATE USER and ALTER USER). The ACCOUNT_CREATOR role can then be granted to a centralized help desk, which will then be able to coordinate the creation of all new accounts.

Centralizing account creation helps to ensure that proper authorization procedures are followed when accounts are requested. The flexibility of system-level privileges and roles allows this capability to be given to a user—in this case, a help desk—without also giving that user the ability to query data from the database.

The ability to create an ACCOUNT_CREATOR role is particularly useful when you are implementing packaged software. Many third-party packaged applications assume they will have full DBA authority in your database, when in fact they only need the ability to execute **create user** and **alter user** commands. By creating an ACCOUNT_CREATOR role, you can limit the package schema owner's privileges in the rest of your database.

You can alter the default role for a user via the **default role** clause of the **alter user** command. For example, you can alter a user to have no roles enabled by default.

```
alter user THUMPER default role NONE;
```

You can specify the roles to enable.

```
alter user THUMPER default role CONNECT;
```

And you can specify the roles that should not be enabled when the session starts.

```
alter user THUMPER default role all except ACCOUNT_CREATOR;
```

If you use the **default role all** clause, then all of a user's roles will be enabled when the user's session begins. If you plan to dynamically enable and disable roles at different parts of an application (via **set role** commands), then you should control which of the roles are enabled by default.

User Profiles

You can use profiles to place limits on the amount of system and database resources available to a user and to manage password restrictions. If no profiles are created in a database, then the default profile, which specifies unlimited resources for all users, will be used.

The resources that can be limited via profiles are listed in Table 9-3.

NOTE
PASSWORD_REUSE_MAX and PASSWORD_REUSE_TIME are mutually exclusive. If one of these resources is set to a value, the other must be set to UNLIMITED.

As shown in Table 9-3, a number of resources may be limited. However, all of these restrictions are *reactive*; no action takes place until the user has exceeded the resource limit. Thus, profiles will not be of much assistance in preventing runaway queries from using large amounts of

Resource	Description
SESSIONS_PER_USER	The number of concurrent sessions a user can have in an instance.
CPU_PER_SESSION	The CPU time, in hundredths of seconds, that a session can use.
CPU_PER_CALL	The CPU time, in hundredths of seconds, that a parse, execute, or fetch can use.
CONNECT_TIME	The number of minutes a session can be connected to a database.
IDLE_TIME	The number of minutes a session can be connected to the database without being actively used.
LOGICAL_READS_PER_SESSION	The number of database blocks that can be read in a session.
LOGICAL_READS_PER_CALL	The number of database blocks that can be read during a parse, execute, or fetch.
PRIVATE_SGA	The amount of private space a session can allocate in the SGA's Shared SQL Pool (for MTS).
COMPOSITE_LIMIT	A compound limit, based on the preceding limits.
FAILED_LOGIN_ATTEMPTS	The number of consecutive failed login attempts that will cause an account to be locked.
PASSWORD_LIFE_TIME	The number of days a password can be used before it expires.
PASSWORD_REUSE_TIME	The number of days that must pass before a password can be reused.
PASSWORD_REUSE_MAX	The number of times a password must be changed before a password can be reused.
PASSWORD_LOCK_TIME	The number of days an account will be locked if the FAILED_LOGIN_ATTEMPTS setting is exceeded.

TABLE 9-3.   *Resources Limited by Profiles*

Resource	Description
PASSWORD_GRACE_TIME	The length, in days, of the "grace period" during which a password can still be changed when it has reached its PASSWORD_LIFE_TIME setting.
PASSWORD_VERIFY_FUNCTION	The name of a function used to evaluate the complexity of a password; ORACLE provides one you can edit.

TABLE 9-3. *Resources Limited by Profiles (continued)*

system resources before they reach their defined limit. Once the limit is reached, the query will be stopped.

Profiles are created via the **create profile** command. The **alter profile** command, shown in the following example, is used to modify existing profiles. In this example, the DEFAULT profile for the database is altered to allow a maximum idle time of one hour:

```
alter profile DEFAULT
idle_time 60;
```

The primary use for profiles is the management of password lifetimes, as described in the next section.

Password Management

As of ORACLE8, you can use profiles to manage the expiration, reuse, and complexity of passwords. For example, you can limit the lifetime of a password, and lock an account whose password is too old. You can also force a password to be at least moderately complex, and lock any account that has repeated failed login attempts.

For example, if you set the FAILED_LOGIN_ATTEMPTS resource of the user's profile to 5, then five consecutive failed login attempts will be allowed for the account; the sixth will cause the account to be locked. In the following listing, the LIMITED_PROFILE profile is created, for use by the JANE user:

```
create profile LIMITED_PROFILE limit
FAILED_LOGIN_ATTEMPTS 5;

create user JANE identified by EYRE
profile LIMITED_PROFILE;

grant CREATE SESSION to JANE;
```

If there are six consecutive failed connects to the JANE account, then the account will be automatically locked by ORACLE. When you then use the correct password for the JANE account, you will receive an error:

```
connect jane/eyre
ERROR: ORA-28000: the account is locked
```

To unlock the account, use the **account unlock** clause of the **alter user** command (from a DBA account), as shown in the following listing:

```
alter user JANE account unlock;
```

Following the unlocking of the account, connections to the JANE account will once again be allowed. You can manually lock an account via the **account lock** clause of the **alter user** command.

```
alter user JANE account lock;
```

If an account becomes locked due to repeated connection failures, it will automatically become unlocked when its profile's PASSWORD_LOCK_TIME value is exceeded. For example, if PASSWORD_LOCK_TIME is set to 1, then the JANE account in the previous example would be locked for one day, at which point the account would be unlocked.

You can establish a maximum lifetime for a password via the PASSWORD_LIFE_TIME resource within profiles. For example, you could force users of the LIMITED_PROFILE profile to change their passwords every 30 days.

```
alter profile LIMITED_PROFILE limit
PASSWORD_LIFE_TIME 30;
```

In this example, the **alter profile** command is used to modify the LIMITED_PROFILE profile. The PASSWORD_LIFE_TIME value is set to 30, so each account that uses that profile will have its password expire after 30 days. If your password has expired, you must change it the next time you log in unless the profile has a specified grace period for expired passwords. The grace period parameter is called PASSWORD_GRACE_TIME. If the password is not changed within the grace period, then the account expires.

An "expired" account is different from a "locked" account. A locked account, as shown earlier in this section, may be automatically unlocked by the passage of time. An expired account, however, requires manual intervention by the DBA to be reenabled. To reenable an expired account, you will need to execute the **alter user** command, as shown in the following example. In this example, the user JANE first has her password expired manually by the DBA:

```
alter user jane password expire;

User altered.
```

Next, Jane attempts to connect to her account. When she provides her password, she is immediately prompted for a new password for the account.

```
connect jane/eyre
ERROR: ORA-28001: the account has expired

Changing password for jane
Old password:
New password:
Retype new password:
Password changed
Connected.
SQL>
```

You can also force users to change their passwords when they first access their accounts, via the **password expire** clause of the **create user** command. The **create user** command does not, however, allow you to set an expiration date for the new password set by the user; to do that, you must use the PASSWORD_LIFE_TIME profile parameters shown in the previous examples.

To see the password expiration date of any account, query the Expiry_Date column of the DBA_USERS data dictionary view. Users who wish to see the password expiration date for their accounts can query the Expiry_Date column of the USER_USERS data dictionary view.

Preventing Password Reuse

To prevent a password from being reused, you can use one of two profile parameters: PASSWORD_REUSE_MAX and PASSWORD_REUSE_TIME. These two parameters are mutually exclusive; if you set a value for one of them, then the other must be set to UNLIMITED.

The PASSWORD_REUSE_TIME parameter specifies the number of days that must pass before a password can be reused. For example, if you set PASSWORD_REUSE_TIME to 60, then you cannot reuse the same password within 60 days.

The PASSWORD_REUSE_MAX parameter specifies the number of password changes that must occur before a password can be reused. If you attempt to reuse the password before the limit is reached, ORACLE will reject your password change.

For example, you can set PASSWORD_REUSE_MAX for the LIMITED_PROFILE profile created earlier in this chapter.

```
alter profile LIMITED_PROFILE limit
PASSWORD_REUSE_MAX 3
PASSWORD_REUSE_TIME UNLIMITED;
```

If the user Jane now attempts to reuse a recent password, the password change attempt will fail. For example, suppose she changes her password.

```
alter user JANE identified by austen;
```

And then changes it again.

```
alter user JANE identified by eyre;
```

During her next password change, she attempts to reuse a recent password, and the attempt fails.

```
alter user jane identified by austen;
alter user jane identified by austen
*
ERROR at line 1:
ORA-28007: the password cannot be reused
```

She cannot reuse any of her recent passwords; she will need to come up with a new password.

Password histories are stored in the table named USER_HISTORY$ under the SYS schema. In this table, ORACLE stores the userid, encrypted password value, and the date/timestamp for the creation of the password. When the PASSWORD_REUSE_TIME value is exceeded or the number of changes exceeds PASSWORD_REUSE_MAX, the old password records are deleted from the SYS.USER_HISTORY$ table. If a new encryption matches an existing encryption, the new password is rejected.

Because the old passwords are stored in a table owned by SYS, the data is stored in the SYSTEM tablespace. Therefore, if you will maintain a very large password history for a very large number of users who are forced to change passwords frequently, the space requirements of the password history table (SYS.USER_HISTORY$) may impact the space requirements of your SYSTEM tablespace.

Setting Password Complexity

You can force users' passwords to meet standards for complexity. For example, you can require that they be of at least a minimum length, that they not be simple words, and that they contain at least one number or punctuation mark. The PASSWORD_VERIFY_FUNCTION parameter of the **create profile** and **alter profile** commands specifies the name of the function that will evaluate the passwords. If a user's proposed password does not meet the criteria, it is not accepted. For example, you could have rejected 'austen' and 'eyre' as passwords since they do not contain any numeric values.

To simplify the process of enforcing password complexity, ORACLE provides a function called VERIFY_FUNCTION. By default, this function is *not* created. The VERIFY_FUNCTION function is only created if you run the utlpwdmg.sql script located in the /rdbms/admin subdirectory under the ORACLE software home directory. In the following listing, an abridged version of this file is shown. The sections shown in bold will be referenced in the description following the listing.

```
Rem utlpwdmg.sql
Rem
Rem  Copyright (c) Oracle Corporation 1996. All Rights Reserved.
Rem
Rem    NAME
```

```
Rem       utlpwdmg.sql - script for Default Password Resource Limits
Rem
Rem      DESCRIPTION
Rem        This is a script for enabling the password management features
Rem        by setting the default password resource limits.
Rem
Rem      NOTES
Rem        This file contains a function for minimum checking of password
Rem        complexity. This is more of a sample function that the customer
Rem        can use to develop the function for actual complexity checks
Rem        that the customer wants to make on the new password.
Rem
Rem      asurpur     12/12/96 - Changing the name of
Rem      password_verify_function
-- This script sets the default password resource parameters
-- This script needs to be run to enable the password features.
-- However the default resource parameters can be changed based
-- on the need.
-- A default password complexity function is also provided.
-- This function makes the minimum complexity checks like
-- the minimum length of the password, password not same as the
-- username, etc. The user may enhance this function according to
-- the need.
-- This function must be created in SYS schema.
-- connect sys/<password> as sysdba before running the script

CREATE OR REPLACE FUNCTION verify_function
(username varchar2,
  password varchar2,
  old_password varchar2)
  RETURN boolean IS
   n boolean;
   m integer;
   differ integer;
   isdigit boolean;
   ischar  boolean;
   ispunct boolean;
   digitarray varchar2(20);
   punctarray varchar2(25);
   chararray varchar2(52);

BEGIN
   digitarray:= '0123456789';
   chararray:= 'abcdefghijklmnopqrstuvwxyzABCDEFGHIJKLMNOPQRSTUVWXYZ';
```

```
punctarray:='!"#$%&()''*+,-/:;<=>?_';

-- Check if the password is same as the username
IF password = username THEN
  raise_application_error(-20001, 'Password same as user');
END IF;


-- Check for the minimum length of the password
IF length(password) < 4 THEN
    raise_application_error(-20002, 'Password length less than 4');
END IF;


-- Check if the password is too simple. A dictionary of words may be
-- maintained and a check may be made so as not to allow the words
-- that are too simple for the password.
IF password IN ('welcome', 'password', 'oracle', 'computer', 'abcd') THEN
    raise_application_error(-20002, 'Password too simple');
END IF;


-- Check if the password contains at least one letter, one digit and one
-- punctuation mark.
-- 1. Check for the digit
isdigit:=FALSE;
m := length(password);
FOR i IN 1..10 LOOP
    FOR j IN 1..m LOOP
       IF substr(password,j,1) = substr(digitarray,i,1) THEN
          isdigit:=TRUE;
           GOTO findchar;
       END IF;
    END LOOP;
END LOOP;
IF isdigit = FALSE THEN
    raise_application_error(-20003, 'Password should contain at least one digit,
one character and one punctuation');
   END IF;
   -- 2. Check for the character
   <<findchar>>
   ischar:=FALSE;
   FOR i IN 1..length(chararray) LOOP
      FOR j IN 1..m LOOP
         IF substr(password,j,1) = substr(chararray,i,1) THEN
            ischar:=TRUE;
```

```
            GOTO findpunct;
        END IF;
    END LOOP;
END LOOP;
IF ischar = FALSE THEN
    raise_application_error(-20003, 'Password should contain at least one \
            digit, one character and one punctuation');
END IF;
-- 3. Check for the punctuation
<<findpunct>>
ispunct:=FALSE;
FOR i IN 1..length(punctarray) LOOP
    FOR j IN 1..m LOOP
        IF substr(password,j,1) = substr(punctarray,i,1) THEN
            ispunct:=TRUE;
            GOTO endsearch;
        END IF;
    END LOOP;
END LOOP;
IF ispunct = FALSE THEN
    raise_application_error(-20003, 'Password should contain at least one \
            digit, one character and one punctuation');
END IF;


<<endsearch>>
-- Check if the password differs from the previous password by at least
-- 3 letters
IF old_password = '' THEN
    raise_application_error(-20004, 'Old password is null');
END IF;
-- Everything is fine; return TRUE ;
RETURN(TRUE);
differ := length(old_password) - length(password);

IF abs(differ) < 3 THEN
    IF length(password) < length(old_password) THEN
        m := length(password);
    ELSE
        m := length(old_password);
    END IF;
    differ := abs(differ);
    FOR i IN 1..m LOOP
        IF substr(password,i,1) != substr(old_password,i,1) THEN
            differ := differ + 1;
        END IF;
```

```
        END LOOP;
        IF differ < 3 THEN
            raise_application_error(-20004, 'Password should differ by at \
            least 3 characters');
        END IF;
    END IF;
    -- Everything is fine; return TRUE ;
    RETURN(TRUE);
END;
/
-- This script alters the default parameters for Password Management
-- This means that all the users on the system have Password Management
-- enabled and set to the following values unless another profile is
-- created with parameter values set to different value or UNLIMITED
-- is created and assigned to the user.

ALTER PROFILE DEFAULT LIMIT
PASSWORD_LIFE_TIME 60
PASSWORD_GRACE_TIME 10
PASSWORD_REUSE_TIME 1800
PASSWORD_REUSE_MAX UNLIMITED
FAILED_LOGIN_ATTEMPTS 3
PASSWORD_LOCK_TIME 1/1440
PASSWORD_VERIFY_FUNCTION verify_function;
```

NOTE
This function should be created under the SYS schema.

The first three **if** clauses in the function check if the password is the same as the username, if the password is fewer than four characters, and if the password is in a set of specific words. You can modify any of these checks or add your own. For example, your corporate security guideline may call for passwords to have a minimum of six characters; simply update that portion of the utlpwdmg.sql file prior to running it.

The next major section of the function is a three-part check of the contents of the password string. In order to pass these checks, the password must contain at least one character, number, and punctuation mark. As with the earlier checks, these can be edited. For example, you may not require your users to use punctuation marks in their passwords; simply bypass that part of the password check.

The next section of the function compares the old password to the new password on a character-by-character basis. If there are not at least three differences, the new password is rejected.

The last command in the script is not part of the function; it is an **alter profile** command that changes the DEFAULT profile. If you change the DEFAULT profile, then every user in your database who uses the DEFAULT profile will be affected. The command shown in the listing creates the following limits: password lifetimes of 60 days, with a 10 day grace period; no password reuse for 1,800 days; and account locks after three failed attempts with automatic unlocking of the account after one minute (1/1,440 of a day). These parameters may not reflect the settings you want. The most important setting is the last one— it specifies that the PASSWORD_VERIFY_FUNCTION to use is the VERIFY_FUNCTION function created by the utlpwdmg.sql script.

NOTE
This function will only apply to the users of the specified profile.

Notice that the VERIFY_FUNCTION function does not make any database accesses and does not update any database values. If you modify the function, you should make sure that your modifications do not require database accesses or modifications.

You can alter the default profile to use the VERIFY_FUNCTION without altering the password expiration parameters.

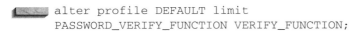

```
alter profile DEFAULT limit
PASSWORD_VERIFY_FUNCTION VERIFY_FUNCTION;
```

If you alter the DEFAULT profile, you need to make sure that all users of the profile can successfully use it. For example, the SYS and SYSTEM users use DEFAULT; can you manage their passwords according to the settings specified here? You may wish to create a new profile and assign the new profile to non-DBA users and nonapplication owners to simplify profile management. The problem with that approach is that you will need to remember to assign the new profile to all new users. The more you standardize your user administration activities, the better your chances of implementing this process.

The name of the password verification function does not have to be "VERIFY_FUNCTION". As shown in the last listing, you pass the name of the function as a parameter in the **alter profile** command. Since the name "VERIFY_FUNCTION" could apply to almost any function, you should change it to a name that makes sense for your database. For example, you could change it to "VERIFY_ORACLE_PASSWORD". You should give it a name that is descriptive and easy to remember; doing so will improve the likelihood of other DBAs understanding what functions the program performs.

Additional management options for passwords are described in the "Password Encryption and Trickery" section later in this chapter.

Tying Database Accounts to Host Accounts

Users are allowed to access a database once they have entered a valid username and password for that database. However, it is possible to take advantage of the operating system to provide an additional level of user authentication.

A database account may be paired with an operating system account on the same server. The two account names will differ only in the prefix of the database account name. The prefix defaults to "OPS$" but can be set to another value via the OS_AUTHENT_PREFIX parameter of the database's init.ora file. This prefix can even be set to a null string, so that no prefix will be used.

NOTE
If you change the OS_AUTHENT_PREFIX to anything other than "OPS$", then the database accounts can either be used as autologin accounts or accessed via username/password, but not both ways. If you use "OPS$" as the authentication prefix, then you can access the account both as an autologin account and via a username/password combination. Most installations use "OPS$".

For example, consider an operating system account named FARMER. The matching database account name for this user is OPS$FARMER. When the FARMER user is logged in to his or her operating system account, he or she can access the OPS$FARMER account without specifying a password, as shown in the following listing:

```
> sqlplus /
```

The "/" takes the place of the username/password combination that would normally be required for access.

Accounts may be created with passwords. Considering the OPS$FARMER account again, its creation command may be in the following format:

```
create user OPS$FARMER
identified by SOME_PASSWORD
default tablespace USERS
temporary tablespace TEMP;
```

Even though the password will not be used, it still may be specified. Because the account has a password, it is possible to access the OPS$FARMER database account from a different operating system account if you know the password for the database account. The following listing shows a sample connection to the OPS$FARMER account from a different operating system account:

```
> sqlplus ops$farmer/some_password
```

There are two ways around this potential problem. First, you can create the account without a specific password, using the **identified externally** clause, as shown in the following listing. This clause bypasses the need for an explicit password for the account while keeping the connection between the host account name and the database account name.

```
create user OPS$FARMER
identified externally
default tablespace USERS
temporary tablespace TEMP;
```

When the **identified externally** clause is used, it forces the database to validate the operating system account being used to access the database.

The operating system account name and the database account name must be identical (except for the database account name prefix).

The second option is to create the account with an impossible password. This method, described in the "Setting Impossible Passwords" section of this chapter, prevents the user from logging in to any database account other than through the operating system account associated with it.

Password Protection

Both accounts and roles can be protected via passwords. Passwords for both are set when they are created, and may be modified via the **alter user** and **alter role** commands.

The initial password for an account is set via the **create user** command, as shown in the following listing. In this example, the THUMPER account is created with an initial password of RABBIT:

```
create user THUMPER
identified by RABBIT;
```

Passwords for accounts should be changed via the **alter user** command. A sample **alter user** command is shown in the following listing:

```
alter user THUMPER identified by NEWPASSWORD;
```

As of ORACLE8, you can use the SQL*Plus **password** command to change a user's password. The **password** command will prompt you for the old password, a new password, and a verification of the new password. The password values entered are not echoed to the screen.

To change your own password within SQL*Plus, type the **password** command, as shown in the following listing:

```
password
```

To change another user's password, use the **password** command followed by the username.

```
password JANE
```

You will be prompted for JANE's old password, new password, and a verification. The **password** command is very useful for your end users, since it greatly simplifies the commands they need to use when changing passwords. If they do not use the **password** command, then they will need to use the command

```
alter user USERNAME identified by NEWPASSWORD;
```

The **password** command simplifies the password changing process, which is important in ORACLE8 since you can force the users to change their passwords.

Passwords for roles are set at the time the role is created, via the **create role** command. You do not need to set a password for a role; if one is specified, then the password must be entered when the role is enabled by the user.

```
create role ACCOUNT_CREATOR identified by HELPDESK_ONLY;
```

The **alter role** command is used to change the password associated with roles. Like user passwords, roles can also be **identified externally**, thereby enforcing a link between the host account name and the role name. Unlike user accounts, it is possible to have roles with no passwords (the default). It is also possible to remove a password from a role via the **not identified** clause, as shown in the following example:

```
alter role ACCOUNT_CREATOR not identified;
```

After this command has been executed, the ACCOUNT_CREATOR role will not be password-protected.

Roles can be tied to operating system privileges. If this capability is available on your operating system, then you invoke it by using the **identified externally** clause of the **alter role** command. When the role is enabled, ORACLE will check the operating system to verify your access. Altering a role to use this security feature is shown in the following example:

```
alter role MANAGER identified externally;
```

In VMS, the verification process uses operating system rights identifiers. In most UNIX systems, the verification process uses the /etc/group file. In order to use this for any operating system, the OS_ROLES database startup parameter in the **init.ora** file must be set to TRUE.

The following example of this verification process is for a database instance called "Local" on a UNIX system. The server's /etc/group file may contain the following entry:

```
ora_local_manager_d:NONE:1:dora
```

This entry grants the MANAGER role to the account named Dora. The "_d" suffix indicates that this role is to be granted by default when Dora logs in. An "_a" suffix would indicate that this role is to be enabled **with admin option**. If this role were also the user's default role, then the suffix would be "_ad". If more than one user were granted this role, then the additional usernames would be appended to the /etc/group entry, as shown in the following listing:

```
ora_local_manager_d:NONE:1:dora,judy
```

If you use this option, then all roles in the database will be enabled via the operating system.

Object-Level Privileges

Object-level privileges give users access to data that they do not own. You can use roles to ease the administration of privileges. Explicit privileges are also available, and are in fact necessary in some circumstances.

Privileges are created via the **grant** command, and are recorded in the data dictionary. Access to tables, views, sequences—as well as synonyms for these—plus the ability to execute procedures, functions, packages, and types can be granted to users. The privileges that may be granted on objects are listed in Table 9-4.

You can use the **with grant option** clause to pass along to the grantee the ability to make further grants on the base table. The following listing from SQL*Plus shows an example of this. In this example, the user named THUMPER grants the user named MCGREGOR both SELECT and partial UPDATE access on a table called EMPLOYEE, **with grant option**. This user then grants one of these privileges to another user (named JFISHER).

```
grant select, update (Employee_Name, Address)
on EMPLOYEE to MCGREGOR
with grant option;

connect MCGREGOR/FARMER
grant select on THUMPER.EMPLOYEE to JFISHER;
```

Privilege	Capabilities Granted
SELECT	Can query the object.
INSERT	Can insert rows into the object. This privilege may be granted for specific columns of the object.
UPDATE	Can update rows in the object. This privilege may be granted for specific columns of the object.
DELETE	Can delete rows from the object.
ALTER	Can alter the object.
INDEX	Can create indexes on the table.
REFERENCES	Can create foreign keys that reference the table.
EXECUTE	Can execute the function, package, procedure, library, or type.
READ	Can access the directory.

TABLE 9-4. *Available Object Privileges*

NOTE
Granting the privileges to PUBLIC makes them available to all users in the database.

The management of privileges can quickly become a time-consuming task. Each user must be granted the appropriate privileges for each object in a database application. Consider a small application that has 20 tables and 30 users; 600 privileges (20 tables times 30 users) must be managed.

With the advent of roles, the management of such privileges became much easier. Roles are groups of privileges; the roles are then granted to users, greatly simplifying the privilege management process.

The following listing shows an example of the usage of roles. In this example, two roles are created. The first, APPLICATION_USER, is given the system-level privilege CREATE SESSION; a user who has been granted this role will be able to log in to the database. The second role, DATA_ENTRY_CLERK, is granted privileges on tables.

```
create role APPLICATION_USER;
grant CREATE SESSION to APPLICATION_USER;
```

```
create role DATA_ENTRY_CLERK;
grant select, insert on THUMPER.EMPLOYEE to DATA_ENTRY_CLERK;
grant select, insert on THUMPER.TIME_CARDS to DATA_ENTRY_CLERK;
grant select, insert on THUMPER.DEPARTMENT to DATA_ENTRY_CLERK;
```

Roles can be granted to other roles. For example, the APPLICATION_USER role can be granted to the DATA_ENTRY_CLERK role, as shown in this example:

```
grant APPLICATION_USER to DATA_ENTRY_CLERK;
```

The role can then be granted to a user. This role can be dynamically enabled and disabled during the user's session via the **set role** command.

```
grant DATA_ENTRY_CLERK to MCGREGOR;
```

Roles and system privileges (such as CREATE TABLE) may be granted to users with the privilege to pass them on to other users. For roles, the **with admin option** clause is used. In the following listing, the DATA_ENTRY_CLERK role created earlier is granted to a user (BPOTTER), along with the privilege to administer the role:

```
grant DATA_ENTRY_CLERK to BPOTTER with admin option;
```

Given this privilege, the user BPOTTER can now **grant** and **revoke** the role to and from other users, and can drop the role as well.

NOTE
Users who have table privileges via roles cannot create views or procedures based on those tables. This restriction is needed because the grants made via a role are only valid while the user is logged in and the role is enabled. The creation of views by nonowners requires explicit privileges on the tables.

The dynamic nature of roles is very useful for restricting users' privileges. If a role is enabled when a user starts an application (via the **set role** command), and then disabled upon leaving the application, then the user cannot take advantage of the role's privileges except when using the application.

For example, when MCGREGOR logs into an application, the command

```
set role DATA_ENTRY_CLERK;
```

may be executed. When this user leaves the application, the command

```
set role NONE;
```

will disable any privileges that had been granted via roles.

You can use the **revoke** command to revoke privileges and roles from users. You may either revoke some of a user's privileges (by explicitly listing them) or all of the user's privileges (via the **all** keyword). In the following example, a specific privilege is revoked for the EMPLOYEE table from one user, while another user's privileges are completely revoked:

```
revoke delete on EMPLOYEE from PETER;
revoke all on EMPLOYEE from MCGREGOR;
```

In the following example, the role ACCOUNT_CREATOR is revoked from the user account named HELPDESK:

```
revoke ACCOUNT_CREATOR from HELPDESK;
```

Because user accounts can be completely deleted via the

```
drop user USERNAME cascade;
```

command, privilege cleanup of deleted accounts is not required. The **revoke** command is thus used mostly when users change status, or when applications move from one environment (such as Acceptance Test) to another (such as Production).

Listing Privileges

Information about privileges that have been granted is stored in the data dictionary. This data is accessible via the data dictionary views.

You can use the data dictionary views listed in Table 9-5 to list the privileges that have been granted within the database. User-level views are also available.

Data dictionary view	Contents
DBA_ROLES	Names of roles and their password status
DBA_ROLE_PRIVS	Users who have been granted roles
DBA_SYS_PRIVS	Users who have been granted system privileges
DBA_TAB_PRIVS	Users who have been granted privileges on tables
DBA_COL_PRIVS	Users who have been granted privileges on columns
ROLE_ROLE_PRIVS	Roles that have been granted to other roles
ROLE_SYS_PRIVS	System privileges that have been granted to roles
ROLE_TAB_PRIVS	Table privileges that have been granted to roles

TABLE 9-5. *Privilege-Related Data Dictionary Views*

For example, you may wish to display which system privileges have been granted to which roles. In that case, the following query would display that information:

```
select
      Role,            /*Name of the role*/
      Privilege,       /*System privilege*/
      Admin_Option     /*Was admin option granted?*/
 from ROLE_SYS_PRIVS;
```

To retrieve table grants for users, you now have to look for two types of grants: explicit grants of privileges to users and those that are granted via roles. To view the grants made via explicit grants, query the DBA_TAB_PRIVS view, as shown in the following listing:

```
select
      Grantee,         /*Recipient of the grant*/
      Owner,           /*Owner of the object*/
      Table_Name,      /*Name of the object*/
      Grantor,         /*User who made the grant*/
      Privilege,       /*Privilege granted*/
      Grantable        /*Was admin option granted?*/
 from DBA_TAB_PRIVS;
```

To view the table privileges granted via a role, find the user's records in DBA_ROLE_PRIVS and compare those to the role's table privileges (which are listed in ROLE_TAB_PRIVS).

```
select
      DBA_ROLE_PRIVS.Grantee,        /*Recipient of the grant*/
      ROLE_TAB_PRIVS.Owner,          /*Owner of the object*/
      ROLE_TAB_PRIVS.Table_Name,     /*Name of the object*/
      ROLE_TAB_PRIVS.Privilege,      /*Privilege granted*/
      ROLE_TAB_PRIVS.Grantable       /*Was admin option granted?*/
  from DBA_ROLE_PRIVS, ROLE_TAB_PRIVS
where DBA_ROLE_PRIVS.Granted_Role = ROLE_TAB_PRIVS.Role
  and DBA_ROLE_PRIVS.Grantee = 'some username';
```

This query will retrieve the role-granted table privileges for a particular user.

To view the profile limits that are in place for your current session, you can query USER_RESOURCE_LIMITS. Its columns are

Resource_Name	The name of the resource (e.g., SESSIONS_PER_USER)
Limit	The limit placed upon this resource

USER_PASSWORD_LIMITS describes the password profile parameters for the user. It has the same columns as USER_RESOURCE_LIMITS.

There is no "DBA" version of the USER_PASSWORD_LIMITS view; it is strictly limited to the user's current session. To see the cost associated with each available resource, you can query the RESOURCE_COST view. DBAs can access the DBA_PROFILES view to see the resource limits for all profiles. The Resource_Type column of DBA_PROFILES indicates whether the resource profile is a 'PASSWORD' or 'KERNEL' profile.

In addition to these views, there are two views, each with a single column, that list the privileges and roles currently enabled for the current session. They are

SESSION_PRIVS	The Privilege column lists all system privileges available to the session, whether granted directly or via roles.
SESSION_ROLES	The Role column lists all roles that are currently enabled for the session.

SESSION_PRIVS and SESSION_ROLES are available to all users.

Limiting Available Commands: Product User Profiles

Within SQL*Plus, an additional level of security is provided—individual commands may be disabled for specific users. That way, users with the UPDATE privilege on a table can be prevented from using the SQL*Plus command-line interface to update the table in an uncontrolled fashion.

This capability allows DBAs to prevent users from accessing the operating system from within SQL*Plus (via the **host** command). This prevention is useful when an application includes an option to access SQL*Plus and you do not want the users to have access to the operating system.

In addition to revoking users' ability to use the **host** command from within SQL*Plus, you may also revoke their use of the **connect** command. Eliminating the access to those commands will force users to stay within their own accounts. The following listing shows the results of these commands when this level of security is in place:

```
SQL> host
invalid command: host
SQL> connect system/manager
invalid command: connect
```

In each case, the "invalid command" message is returned. The user must remain in his or her own account.

To create this level of security, the *Product User Profile* tables must be created. The script for creating them is called pupbld.sql, and it is found in the /sqlplus/admin subdirectory under the ORACLE software home directory. This script creates several tables and views, and should be run from within the SYSTEM account.

For SQL*Plus, the most important table is accessed via a synonym named PRODUCT_USER_PROFILE. The key columns for security purposes are listed in Table 9-6. Insert records into this table to create the desired level of security.

Roles can also be disabled via this table. To disable a role, set the Attribute column to "ROLES", and place the role name in the Char_Value column. Disabling of roles is usually done in coordination with the disabling of the **set** command (see Table 9-6).

Column Name	Description
PRODUCT	Set to "SQL*Plus". The name must be in mixed case, as shown here.
USERID	Username, in uppercase, for users whose commands are being disabled. The "%" wildcard may be used to specify multiple users. An entry for "%" used by itself will apply to all users.
ATTRIBUTE	The name, in uppercase, of the command being disabled. Disabling the "SET" command in SQL*Plus also disables **set role** and **set transaction**.
CHAR_VALUE	Set to "DISABLED", in uppercase.

TABLE 9-6.   *Columns in PRODUCT_USER_PROFILE*

Password Security During Logins

When you connect to a database server from a client machine, or from one database to another via a database link, ORACLE transmits the password you enter in an unencrypted format unless you specify otherwise. As of ORACLE8, you can set parameters that force ORACLE to encrypt the password values prior to transmitting them. To enable password encryption, set the following parameters:

For your client machines, set the ORA_ENCRYPT_LOGIN parameter in your sqlnet.ora file to TRUE.

For your server machines, set the DBLINK_ENCRYPT_LOGIN parameter in your init.ora file to TRUE.

Once these parameters are set (and the database is shut down and restarted), your passwords will be sent from client to server and server to server in an encrypted form.

Password Encryption and Trickery

Knowing how the database encrypts and sets passwords enables DBAs to perform a number of otherwise impossible tasks. These tasks include the setting of impossible passwords and the ability to become other users, as described in the following sections.

How Passwords Are Stored

When a password is specified for a user account or a role, the database stores the *encrypted* version of that password in the data dictionary. Setting the same password for two different accounts will result in different encryptions. For all passwords, the encrypted value is 16 characters long and contains numbers and capital letters.

How are passwords validated? When a password is entered during a user validation, that password is encrypted, and the encryption that is generated is compared to the one in the data dictionary for that account. If they match, then the password is correct and the authorization succeeds.

Setting Impossible Passwords

Knowing how the database stores passwords is important because it adds new options to account security. What would happen if you could specify the *encryption* of a password, rather than the password itself? And what if the encryption you generated did not follow the format rules for encrypted passwords? The result would be an account that could never be logged in to, since no password could generate the invalid encryption.

Consider the accounts and encrypted passwords selected by the following query. The query selects the Username and Password fields from the DBA_USERS view.

```
select
        Username,          /*Username*/
        Password           /*Encrypted password*/
from DBA_USERS
where Username in ('MCGREGOR','THUMPER','OPS$FARMER');

USERNAME          PASSWORD
----------------  ----------------
MCGREGOR          1A2DD3CCEE354DFA
THUMPER           F3DE41CBB3AB4452
OPS$FARMER        4FF2FF1CBDE11332
```

Note that each of the encrypted passwords in the output is 16 characters in length.

Since the password is not stored in the data dictionary—but its encryption is—how does Import know what the passwords are? After all, when a Full Import is done from an export dump file, the passwords are imported as well.

Import executes SQL commands. During a Full Import, Import executes an undocumented version of the **create user** command. Importing the MCGREGOR user from the database shown in the last listing would generate the following **create user** command:

```
create user MCGREGOR identified by VALUES '1A2DD3CCEE354DFA';
```

In other words, Import uses the undocumented **values** clause within the **identified by** clause to specify the *encrypted* password for the user it is creating.

Import shouldn't get to have all the fun. You can use this same command to set an encryption for any account. As long as the encryption you set violates the encryption rules (16 characters, all capitals), it will be impossible to match during user authentication. The result will be an account that is only accessible from the correct operating system account on the server. In the following listing, the encryption is set to the phrase "no way". The DBA_USERS view is then queried.

```
alter user OPS$FARMER identified by VALUES 'no way';

select
     Username,           /*Username*/
     Password            /*Encrypted password*/
from DBA_USERS
where Username in ('MCGREGOR','THUMPER','OPS$FARMER');

USERNAME              PASSWORD
----------------      ----------------
MCGREGOR              1A2DD3CCEE354DFA
THUMPER               F3DE41CBB3AB4452
OPS$FARMER            no way
```

It is now impossible to access the OPS$FARMER account except via the FARMER account on the server, and even then it is only accessible via the "/" autologin. Impossible passwords are also useful for locking non-OPS$ accounts that should never be logged into directly, such as SYS.

Becoming Another User

Since the encrypted passwords can be set, you can temporarily take over any account and then set it back to its original password without ever knowing the account's password. This capability allows you to become another user (which is very useful when testing applications or troubleshooting problems in Production).

Temporarily becoming another user requires going through the following steps:

1. Query DBA_USERS to determine the current encrypted password for the account.

2. Generate the **alter user** command that will be needed to reset the encrypted password to its current value after you are done.

3. Spool the **alter user** command to a file.

4. Change the user's password.

5. Access the user's account and perform your testing.

6. When the testing is complete, run the file containing the **alter user** command to reset the user's encrypted password to its original value.

This process is automated via the following SQL*Plus script. This script automatically generates the command necessary to reset the user's account once your testing is complete.

```
REM*   become_another_user.sql
REM*
REM*   This script generates the commands necessary to allow
REM*   you to temporarily become another user.
REM*
REM*   It MUST be run from a DBA account.
REM*
REM*   Input variable: The username of the account to be taken
REM*   over.
REM*
REM*   Steps 1, 2, and 3: Query DBA_USERS. Generate the ALTER USER
REM*   command that will be necessary to reset the password to its
REM*   present value.
REM*
```

```
set pagesize 0 feedback off verify off echo off termout off
REM*
REM*   Create a file called reset.sql to hold the commands
REM*   generated
REM*
spool reset.sql
REM*
REM*   Select the encrypted password from DBA_USERS.
REM*
SELECT 'alter user &&1 identified by values '||''''||
password||''''||';'
FROM dba_users WHERE username = upper('&&1');

prompt 'host rm -f reset.sql'
prompt 'exit'
spool off
exit
```

NOTE
In the **select** *statement, there are two sets of four single quotes.*

This script generates as its output a script called reset.sql. This file will have three lines in it. The first line will contain the **alter user** command, with the **values** clause followed by the encrypted password. The second line will contain a **host** command that deletes the reset.sql file (since it will not be needed after it is used in step 6). The third line contains an **exit** command to leave SQL*Plus. A sample reset.sql file is shown in the following listing:

```
alter user MCGREGOR identified by values '1A2DD3CCEE354DFA';
host rm -f reset.sql
exit
```

The "rm -f" command in the second line should be replaced by the appropriate file deletion command for your operating system.

You may now proceed with steps 4 and 5, which involve changing the user's password (via the **alter user** command) and accessing the account. These actions are shown in the following listing:

```
alter user MCGREGOR identified by MY_TURN;
connect MCGREGOR/MY_TURN
```

You will now be logged into the MCGREGOR account. When you have completed your testing, log in to SQL*Plus and run the reset.sql script shown above. The execution of the reset.sql script is shown in the following listing:

```
sqlplus system/manager @reset
```

If you are testing multiple accounts simultaneously, you may wish to embed the username in the "reset.sql" filename; otherwise, the first "reset.sql" file may be overwritten by later versions. If you are doing this for OPS$ accounts, be careful, since "$" is a special character in some operating systems (such as UNIX).

The account will now be reset to its original encrypted password—and thus its original password. The testing of the account took place without your needing to know what its password was and without its password being destroyed.

Auditing

The database has the ability to audit all actions that take place within it. Audit records may be written to either the SYS.AUD$ or the operating system's audit trail. The ability to use the operating system's audit trail is operating system-dependent.

Three different types of actions may be audited: login attempts, object accesses, and database actions. Each of these action types will be described in the following sections. When performing audits, the database's default functionality is to record both successful and unsuccessful commands; this may be modified when each audit type is set up.

To enable auditing in a database, the init.ora file for the database must contain an entry for the AUDIT_TRAIL parameter. The AUDIT_TRAIL values are

NONE	Disables auditing
DB	Enables auditing, writing to the SYS.AUD$ table
OS	Enables auditing, writing to the operating system's audit trail (operating system-dependent)

AUDIT_TRAIL values of TRUE and FALSE are supported for backward compatibility with prior versions of ORACLE. TRUE is equivalent to DB and FALSE is equivalent to NONE.

The **audit** commands described in the following sections can be issued regardless of the setting of the AUDIT_TRAIL parameter. They will not be activated unless the database is started using an init.ora AUDIT_TRAIL value that enables auditing.

If you elect to store the audit records in the SYS.AUD$ table, then that table's records should be periodically archived, and the table should then be **truncate**d. Since it is in the data dictionary, this table is in the SYSTEM tablespace and may cause space problems if its records are not periodically cleaned out. You can grant DELETE_CATALOG_ROLE to a user to give the user the ability to delete from the SYS.AUD$ table.

Login Audits

Every attempt to connect to the database can be audited. The command to begin auditing of login attempts is

```
audit session;
```

To audit only those connection attempts that result in successes or failures, use one of the commands shown in the following listing:

```
audit session whenever successful;
audit session whenever not successful;
```

If the audit records are stored in the SYS.AUD$ table, then they may be viewed via the DBA_AUDIT_SESSION data dictionary view of that table.

The query shown in the following listing retrieves login audit records from the DBA_AUDIT_SESSION view. It lists the operating system account that was used (OS_Username), the ORACLE account name (Username), and the terminal ID that was used (Terminal). The Returncode column is evaluated: if it is 0, then the connection attempt succeeded; otherwise, two common error numbers are checked to determine the cause of the failure. The login and logoff times are also displayed.

```
select
    OS_Username,        /*Operating system username used.*/
    Username,           /*Oracle username of the account used.*/
    Terminal,           /*Terminal ID used.*/
```

```
DECODE(Returncode,'0','Connected',
                '1005','FailedNull',
                '1017','Failed',Returncode),        /*Failure check*/
    TO_CHAR(Timestamp,'DD-MON-YY HH24:MI:SS'),      /*Login time*/
    TO_CHAR(Logoff_Time,'DD-MON-YY HH24:MI:SS')     /*Logoff time*/
from DBA_AUDIT_SESSION;
```

The error numbers that are checked are ORA-1005 and ORA-1017. These two error codes cover most of the login errors that occur. ORA-1005 is returned when a user enters a username but no password. ORA-1017 is returned when a user enters an invalid password.

To disable session auditing, use the **noaudit** command, as shown in this example:

```
noaudit session;
```

Action Audits

Any action affecting a database object—such as a table, database link, tablespace, synonym, rollback segment, user, or index—can be audited. The possible actions—such as **create**, **alter**, and **drop**—that can affect those objects can be grouped together during auditing. This grouping of commands reduces the amount of administrative effort necessary to establish and maintain the audit settings.

All of the system-level commands can be audited, and groups of commands are provided. For example, to audit all commands that affect roles, enter the command

```
audit role;
```

To disable this setting, enter the command

```
noaudit role;
```

The SQL command groupings for auditing are listed in Table 9-7. Each group can be used to audit all of the SQL commands that affect it (see Table 9-2 for a detailed listing of the related privileges). For example, the **audit role** command shown earlier will audit **create role**, **alter role**, **drop role**, and **set role** commands.

Option	Audits
CLUSTER	Create, alter, drop, or truncate cluster
DATABASE LINK	Create or drop database link
DIRECTORY	Create or drop directory
EXISTS	SQL statements that fail because an object already exists (Trusted Oracle)
INDEX	Create, alter, or drop index
NOT EXISTS	SQL statements that fail because an object does not exist
PROCEDURE	Create, alter, or drop procedure, function, or package, and create package body
PROFILE	Create, alter, or drop profile
PUBLIC DATABASE LINK	Create or drop public database link
PUBLIC SYNONYM	Create or drop public synonym
ROLE	Create, alter, drop, or set role
ROLLBACK SEGMENT	Create, alter, or drop rollback segment
SEQUENCE	Create, alter, or drop sequence
SESSION	Logon attempts
SYNONYM	Create or drop synonym
SYSTEM AUDIT	Audit or noaudit of SQL statements
SYSTEM GRANT	Audit or noaudit of system privileges and roles
TABLE	Create, alter, drop, or truncate table
TABLESPACE	Create, alter, or drop tablespace
TRIGGER	Create, alter, or drop trigger, alter table with enableIdisable all triggers
TYPE	Create, alter, or drop type or type body
USER	Create, alter, or drop user
VIEW	Create or drop view

TABLE 9-7. *Object Audit Options*

In addition to the audit options shown in Table 9-7, you may audit each individual command covered by the statement option. ORACLE also provides the following groups of statement options:

CONNECT	Audits ORACLE logons and logoffs
DBA	Audits commands that require DBA authority, such as **grant, revoke, audit, noaudit, create**, or **alter tablespace**, and **create** or **drop public synonym**
RESOURCE	Audits **create** and **drop** for tables, clusters, views, indexes, tablespaces, types, and synonyms
ALL	Audits all of these commands

Each action that can be audited is assigned a numeric code within the database. These codes are accessible via the AUDIT_ACTIONS view. The following query will display the available action codes for your database:

```
select
      Action,        /*Action code.*/
      Name           /*Name of the action, such as ALTER USER.*/
from AUDIT_ACTIONS;
```

Once the action code is known, the DBA_AUDIT_OBJECT view can be used to determine how an object was affected by the action. The query shown in the following listing retrieves login audit records from the DBA_AUDIT_OBJECT view. It lists the operating system account that was used (OS_Username), the ORACLE account name (Username), and the terminal ID that was used (Terminal). The object owner (Owner) and name (Obj_Name) are selected, along with the action code (Action_Name) for the action performed. The Returncode column is evaluated: if it is 0, then the connection attempt succeeded; otherwise, the error number is reported. The login and logoff times are also displayed.

```
select
   OS_Username,            /*Operating system username used.*/
   Username,               /*Oracle username of the account used.*/
   Terminal,               /*Terminal ID used.*/
   Owner,                  /*Owner of the affected object.*/
   Obj_Name,               /*Name of the affected object.*/
   Action_Name,            /*Numeric code for the action.*/
   DECODE(Returncode,'0','Success',Returncode),   /*Failure check*/
```

```
    TO_CHAR(Timestamp,'DD-MON-YY HH24:MI:SS')        /*Timestamp*/
from DBA_AUDIT_OBJECT;
```

You can also specify particular users to audit, using the **by *username***
clause of the **audit** command, as shown in the following listing. In this
example, all **update** actions by the user MCGREGOR will be audited:

```
audit update table by MCGREGOR;
```

Object Audits

In addition to system-level actions on objects, data manipulation actions
to objects can be audited. These may include auditing **select**, **insert**,
update, and **delete** operations against tables. Actions of this type are
audited in a manner that is very similar to the action audits described in the
previous section. The only difference is the addition of a new clause in the
audit command.

The additional clause for object audits is the **by session** or **by access**
clause. This clause specifies whether an audit record should be written
once for each session (**by session**) or once for each time an object is
accessed (**by access**). For example, if a user executed four different **update**
statements against the same table, then auditing **by access** would result in
four audit records being written—one for each table access. On the other
hand, auditing the same situation **by session** would result in only one audit
record being written.

Auditing **by access** can therefore dramatically increase the rate at
which audit records are written. It is generally used on a limited basis to
gauge the number of separate actions taking place during a specific time
interval; when that testing is done, the auditing should be reverted to **by
session** status.

Examples of these options are shown in the following listing. In the first
command, all **insert** commands against the EMPLOYEE table are audited. In
the second command, every command that affects the TIME_CARDS table
is audited. In the third command, all **delete** operations against the
DEPARTMENT table are audited, on a per session basis.

```
audit insert on THUMPER.EMPLOYEE;
audit all on THUMPER.TIME_CARDS;
audit delete on THUMPER.DEPARTMENT by session;
```

The resulting audit records can be viewed via the query against the DBA_AUDIT_OBJECT view shown in the previous section.

Protecting the Audit Trail

Since the database audit trail table, SYS.AUD$, is stored within the database, any audit records that are written there must be protected. Otherwise, a user may attempt to delete his or her audit trail records after attempting unauthorized actions within the database.

The ability to write audit records to the operating system audit trail helps to get around this problem by storing the records external to the database. However, this option is not available for all operating systems.

If you must store the audit trail information in SYS.AUD$, then you *must* protect that table. First, audit actions against the table via the following command:

```
audit all on SYS.AUD$ by access;
```

If any actions are made against the SYS.AUD$ table (**insert**s generated via audits of other tables don't count), then those actions will be recorded in the audit trail. Not only that, but actions against SYS.AUD$ can only be deleted by users who have the ability to CONNECT INTERNAL (i.e., are in the DBA group). Any actions made while connected as INTERNAL are automatically written to the audit trail.

Wherever possible, coordinate your database auditing and your operating system auditing. This will make it easier to track problems and coordinate security policies across the two environments. Since the system managers will most likely not want to see reams of audit trail entries, it also forces the DBA to analyze exactly which actions are the most critical to audit. Your aim should be to have an audit trail in which every record is significant. If it is not, then use the commands given in this chapter to modify the auditing options to reflect the true actions of interest.

Security in a Distributed Environment

Opening up a database to access from other servers also opens it up to potential security threats from those servers. Since such access comes via

Net8 (and SQL*Net), modifications to Net8 parameters can provide most of the protection against unauthorized remote access. For details on the security aspects of Net8, see Part III of this book. As a guiding principle, all access to data should be on a "need-to-know" basis. Extending this principle, all access to your server and operating system and network should be on a "need-to-know" basis. You should periodically review the current access privilege within the database and at the operating system level, and work with the systems management team to evaluate current network access privileges.

CHAPTER
10

Optimal Backup and Recovery Procedures

y in-depth introduction to ORACLE's backup and recovery techniques occurred at 3 A.M. on a Friday morning as I attempted to perform a difficult recovery. The recovery process operations themselves were not difficult; rather, their implementation in the system I supported limited my options and made applying them difficult. ORACLE provides a variety of backup procedures and options that help protect an ORACLE database. If they are properly implemented, these options will allow you to effectively back up your database—and recover them easily and efficiently.

ORACLE's backup capabilities include both logical and physical backups, both of which have a number of options available. This chapter will not detail every possible option and recovery scenario; ORACLE's documentation has already accomplished that. Rather, the focus will be on using the best options in the most effective manner possible. You will see how to best integrate the available backup procedures with each other and with the operating system backups. Backup capabilities introduced as of ORACLE8 will also be highlighted.

Capabilities

There are three standard methods of backing up an ORACLE database: *Exports*, *offline backups*, and *online (ARCHIVELOG) backups.* An export is a *logical* backup of the database; the other two backup methods are *physical* file backups. In the following sections, you will see each of these options fully described.

Logical Backups

A *logical backup* of the database involves reading a set of database records and writing them to a file. These records are read independent of their physical location. In ORACLE, the *Export* utility is used to perform this type of database backup. To recover using the file generated from an export, ORACLE's *Import* utility is used.

Export

ORACLE's Export utility reads the database, including the data dictionary, and writes the output to a binary file called an *export dump file.* You can export the full database, specific users, or specific tables. During exports, you may choose whether or not to export the data dictionary information associated with tables, such as the grants, indexes, and constraints associated with them. The file written by Export will contain the commands necessary to completely re-create all of the chosen objects.

Full database exports may be performed for all tables (called *Complete* exports), or for only those tables that have changed since the last export. There are two different types of incremental exports: *Incremental* and *Cumulative*. *Incremental* exports will export all tables that have changed since the last export, while *Cumulative* exports will export all tables that have changed since the last full export.

You can use the Export utility to compress the extents of fragmented data segments (see Chapter 8).

Import

Once data has been exported, it may be imported via ORACLE's Import utility. The Import utility reads the binary export dump file created by Export and executes the commands found there. For example, these commands may include a **create table** command, followed by an **insert** command to load data into the table.

The data that has been exported does not have to be imported into the same database, or the same schema, as was used to generate the export dump file. The export dump file may be used to create a duplicate set of the exported objects under a different schema or in a separate database.

You can import either all or part of the exported data. If you import the entire export dump file from a Full export, then all of the database objects—including tablespaces, datafiles, and users—will be created during the import. However, it is often useful to precreate tablespaces and users in order to specify the physical distribution of objects in the database.

If you are only going to import part of the data from the export dump file, then the tablespaces, datafiles, and users that will own and store that data must be set up prior to the import.

The data may also be imported into an ORACLE database created under a higher version of the ORACLE kernel. This is used between consecutive major releases of ORACLE (such as from ORACLE7 to ORACLE8). The reverse capability—importing from an export file created by a more recent major release—is not supported. When going between nonconsecutive major releases (for example, from ORACLE6 to ORACLE8), you should first import the data into the intermediate release (in this example, ORACLE7), then from that database into the later major release (ORACLE8).

Physical Backups

Physical backups involve copying the files that constitute the database without regard to their logical content. These backups are also referred to as *file system backups* since they involve using operating system file backup commands.

ORACLE supports two different types of physical file backups: the *offline* backup and the *online* backup (also known as the "hot" or "ARCHIVELOG" backup).

Offline Backups

Offline backups occur when the database has been shut down normally (that is, not due to instance failure). While the database is "offline," the following files are backed up:

- All datafiles

- All control files

- All online redo logs

- The init.ora file (optional)

It is easiest to back up the datafiles if the database file architecture uses a consistent directory structure. A sample of such an architecture is shown in the "Database File Layout" section of Chapter 4.

Having all of these files backed up *while the database is closed* provides a complete image of the database as it existed at the time it was closed. The full set of these files could be retrieved from the backups at a later date and the database would be able to function. It is *not* valid to perform a file system backup of the database while it is open unless a hot backup is being performed.

Online (ARCHIVELOG) Backups

You can use online backups for any database that is running in ARCHIVELOG mode. In this mode, the online redo logs are archived, creating a full log of all transactions within the database.

ORACLE writes to the online redo log files in a cyclical fashion; after filling the first log file, it begins writing to the second until that one fills, and then begins writing to the third. Once the last online redo log file is filled, the LGWR (Log Writer) background process begins to overwrite the contents of the first redo log file.

When ORACLE is run in ARCHIVELOG mode, the ARCH (Archiver) background process makes a copy of each redo log file before overwriting it. These archived redo log files are usually written to a disk device. They may also be written directly to a tape device, but this tends to be very operator intensive.

You can perform file system backups of a database while that database is open, provided it is running in ARCHIVELOG mode. An online backup involves setting each tablespace into a backup state, then backing up its datafiles, then restoring the tablespace to its normal state. The database can be fully recovered from such a backup, and can, via the archived redo logs, be rolled forward to any point in time. When the database is then opened, any committed transactions that were in the database at that time will have been restored.

While the database is open, the following files are backed up:

- All datafiles
- All archived redo log files
- One control file, via the **alter database** command

Online backup procedures are very powerful for two reasons. First, they provide full point-in-time recovery. Second, they allow the database to remain open during the file system backup. Thus, even databases that cannot be shut down due to user requirements can still have file system backups. Keeping the database open also keeps the SGA (System Global

Area) of the database instance from being reset, as occurs during database startups. Keeping the memory from being reset will improve the database's performance since it will reduce the number of physical I/Os required by the database.

Implementations

In this section, you will find the commands necessary to use each of the backup methods available in ORACLE, as well as sample command files for performing them.

Export

The Export utility has three levels of functionality: *Full* mode, *User* mode, and *Table* mode. You can Export partitions via a modified version of Table mode exports.

In Full mode, the full database is exported. The entire data dictionary is read, and the DDL needed to re-create the full database is written to the export dump file. This file includes definitions for all tablespaces, all users, and all of the objects, data, and privileges in their schemas.

In User mode, a user's objects are exported, as well as the data within them. All grants and indexes created by the user on the user's objects are also exported. Grants and indexes created by users other than the owner are not exported via this option.

In Table mode, a specified table is exported. The table's structure, index, and grants are exported along with its data. Table mode can also export the full set of tables owned by a user (by specifying the schema owner, but no table names). You can also specify partitions of a table to Export.

Export can be run either interactively or via command files. The run-time options that can be specified for Export are listed in Table 10-1.

A number of the parameters conflict with each other or may result in inconsistent instructions for Export. For example, setting FULL=Y and OWNER=HR would fail, since the FULL parameter calls for a Full export, while the OWNER parameter specifies a User export.

The default values for these keywords for ORACLE8 are shown in Table 10-2.

Keyword	Description
USERID	Username/password of the account running the export. If this is the first parameter after the "exp" command, then the "USERID" keyword does not have to be specified.
BUFFER	Size of the buffer used to fetch data rows. The default is system dependent; this value is usually set to a high value (>64,000).
FILE	Name of the export dump file.
COMPRESS	A Y/N flag to indicate whether export should compress fragmented segments into single extents. This affects the **storage** clauses that will be stored in the export file for those objects.
GRANTS	A Y/N flag to indicate whether grants on database objects will be exported.
INDEXES	A Y/N flag to indicate whether indexes on tables will be exported.
ROWS	A Y/N flag to indicate whether rows should be exported. If this is set to "N", then only the DDL for the database objects will be created in the export file.
CONSTRAINTS	A Y/N flag to indicate whether constraints on tables are exported.
FULL	If set to "Y", then a Full database export is performed.
OWNER	A list of database accounts to be exported; User exports of those accounts may then be performed.
TABLES	A list of tables to be exported; Table exports of those tables may then be performed.
RECORDLENGTH	The length, in bytes, of the dump export file record. Usually left at the default value unless you are going to transfer the export file between different operating systems.
INCTYPE	The type of export being performed (valid values are "COMPLETE" (default), "CUMULATIVE", and "INCREMENTAL"). The export types are described in the following sections.

TABLE 10-1.   *Export Options*

Keyword	Description
DIRECT	A Y/N flag to indicate if a Direct Export should be performed. A "direct" export bypasses the buffer cache during the export, generating significant performance gains for the export process.
RECORD	For Incremental exports, this Y/N flag indicates whether a record will be stored in data dictionary tables recording the export.
PARFILE	The name of a parameter file to be passed to Export. This file may contain entries for all of the parameters listed here.
STATISTICS	A parameter to indicate whether **analyze** commands for the exported objects should be written to the export dump file. Valid values are "COMPUTE", "ESTIMATE," (the default) and "N". In earlier versions of ORACLE, this parameter was called "ANALYZE".
CONSISTENT	A Y/N flag to indicate whether a read-consistent version of all exported objects should be maintained. This is needed when tables that are related to each other are being modified by users during the Export process.
LOG	The name of a file to which the log of the export will be written.
FEEDBACK	The number of rows after which to display progress during table exports. The default value is 0, so no feedback is displayed until a table is completely exported.
POINT_IN_TIME_RECOVER	A Y/N flag used to signal ORACLE if you are exporting metadata for use in a tablespace point-in-time recovery. This is an advanced recovery technique; see the "Recovery Scenarios" section of this chapter.
RECOVERY_TABLESPACES	The tablespaces whose metadata should be exported during a tablespace point-in-time recovery; see the "Recovery Scenarios" section of this chapter.

TABLE 10-1. *Export Options (continued)*

Keyword	Oracle8 Default Value
USERID	Undefined
BUFFER	System dependent
FILE	EXPDAT.DMP
COMPRESS	Y
GRANTS	Y
INDEXES	Y
ROWS	Y
CONSTRAINTS	Y
FULL	N
OWNER	Current user
TABLES	Undefined
RECORDLENGTH	System dependent
INCTYPE	COMPLETE
RECORD	Y
PARFILE	Undefined
STATISTICS	ESTIMATE
CONSISTENT	N
LOG	Undefined
DIRECT	N
FEEDBACK	0
POINT_IN_TIME_RECOVER	N
RECOVERY_TABLESPACES	Undefined

TABLE 10-2. *Default Values for Export Parameters*

These parameters may be displayed online via the following command:

```
exp help=Y
```

The COMPRESS=Y option alters the **initial** parameter of the **storage** clause for segments that have multiple extents. The total allocated space for that segment is thus compressed into a single extent. There are two important points to note concerning this functionality:

- First, it is the *allocated,* not the *used,* space that is compressed. An empty table with 300MB allocated to it in three 100MB extents will be compressed into a single empty 300MB extent. No space will be reclaimed.

- Second, if the tablespace has multiple datafiles, a segment may allocate space that is greater than the size of the largest datafile. In that case, using COMPRESS=Y would change the **storage** clause to have an **initial** extent size that is greater than any datafile size. Since extents cannot span datafiles, this will fail during Import.

In the following example, the COMPRESS=Y option is used, as the HR and THUMPER owners are exported:

```
exp system/manager file=expdat.dmp compress=Y owner=(HR,THUMPER)
```

Complete Versus Incremental/Cumulative Exports

The INCTYPE Export parameter, when used with the FULL parameter, allows the DBA to export only those tables that have changed since the last Export. If *any* row in a table has changed, then *every* row of that table will be exported via an Incremental or Cumulative export. The available INCTYPE options are described in Table 10-3.

Complete exports form the basis for an export backup strategy. Incremental and Cumulative exports may be useful if very few of the database's tables change, and if those tables are very small. For example, in a decision support database that featured large, static tables, Incremental exports would be helpful since only the smaller, changed tables would be Exported. For databases using Incremental exports, Cumulative exports should be run periodically. The Incremental exports run prior to the last Cumulative export can then be discarded. During a recovery in such a database, you will need

- The last Complete export
- The last Cumulative export
- Every Incremental export since the last Cumulative or Complete export, whichever was run later

Option	Description
COMPLETE	The default value. All tables specified will be exported.
CUMULATIVE	If FULL=Y, then this can be specified. Only those tables that contain rows that have changed since the last Full export of any type will be exported.
INCREMENTAL	If FULL=Y, then this can be specified. This option exports all tables whose rows have changed since the last Cumulative or Complete export.

TABLE 10-3. *INCTYPE Options for Export*

You should investigate using Complete exports in place of Incremental exports. For example, in the decision support database example, you could create a parameter file (specified via the PARFILE parameter) that lists the tables to be exported. If you can use Complete exports, then you can reduce the number of files required during a recovery and thereby simplify the recovery process.

Consistent Exports

During the process of writing the database's data to the export dump file, Export reads one table at a time. Thus, although the Export started at a specific point in time, each table is read at a different time. The data as it exists in each table at the moment Export starts to read *that table* is what will be exported. Since most tables are related to other tables, this may result in inconsistent data being exported if users are modifying data during the Export.

Consider the following scenario:

1. The Export begins.

2. Sometime during the Export, table A is exported.

3. After table A is exported, table B, which has a foreign key to table A, is exported.

What if transactions are occurring at the same time? Consider a transaction that involves both table A and table B, but does not **commit** until after table A has been exported.

1. The Export begins.

2. A transaction against table A and table B begins.

3. Later, table A is exported.

4. The transaction is **commit**ted.

5. Later, table B is exported.

The transaction's data will be exported with table B, but not with table A (since the **commit** had not yet occurred). The export dump file thus contains inconsistent data—in this case, foreign key records from table B without matching primary key records from table A.

To avoid this problem, there are two options. First, you should schedule Exports to occur when no one is making modifications to tables. Second, you can use the CONSISTENT parameter. This parameter is only available for Complete exports; Incremental and Cumulative exports cannot use it.

When CONSISTENT=Y, the database will maintain a rollback segment to track any modifications made since the Export began. The rollback segment entries can then be used to re-create the data as it existed when the Export began. The result is a consistent set of exported data, with two major costs: the need for a very large rollback segment and the reduced performance of the Export as it searches the rollback segment for changes.

Whenever possible, guarantee the consistency of exported data by running Exports while the database is mounted in **restricted session** mode. If you are unable to do this, then perform a CONSISTENT=Y export of the tables being modified, and a CONSISTENT=N export of the full database. This will minimize the performance penalties you incur while ensuring the consistency of the most frequently used tables.

Tablespace Exports

In order to defragment a tablespace, or to create a copy of its objects elsewhere, you will need to do a tablespace-level export. As you may have noted, there is not a "TABLESPACE=" parameter for Export. However, if your users are properly distributed among tablespaces, it is possible to use a series of User exports that, taken together, produce the desired result.

User exports record those database objects that are created by a user. However, there are certain types of user objects that are not recorded by

User exports. Specifically, indexes and grants on tables owned by other accounts are not recorded via User exports.

Consider the case of two accounts, THUMPER and FLOWER. If THUMPER creates an index on one of FLOWER's tables, then a User export of THUMPER will not record the index (since THUMPER does not own the underlying table). A User export of FLOWER will also not record the index (since the index is owned by THUMPER). The same thing happens with grants: when a second account is capable of creating indexes and grants on objects, the usefulness of User exports rapidly diminishes.

Assuming that such *third-party objects* do not exist, or can be easily re-created via scripts, the next issue involves determining which users own objects in which tablespaces. This information is available via the data dictionary views. The following query maps users to tablespaces to determine their distribution of their objects. It does this by looking at the DBA_TABLES and DBA_INDEXES data dictionary views, and spools the output to a file called user_locs.lst.

```
rem
rem    user_tablespace_maps.sql
rem
rem  This script maps user objects to tablespaces.
rem
set pagesize 60
break on Owner on Tablespace
column Objects format A20
select
       Owner,
       Tablespace_Name,
       COUNT(*)||' tables' Objects
  from DBA_TABLES
group by
       Owner,
       Tablespace_Name
union
select
       Owner,
       Tablespace_Name,
       COUNT(*)||' indexes' Objects
from DBA_INDEXES
group by
       Owner,
```

```
        Tablespace_Name

spool user_locs.lst
/
spool off
```

Sample output from this query is shown in the following listing:

```
OWNER           TABLESPACE_NAME     OBJECTS
-------------   -----------------   ---------------
FLOWER          USERS               3 tables
                                    2 indexes
HR              HR_TABLES           27 tables
                HR_INDEXES          35 indexes
THUMPER         USERS               5 tables
```

The sample output shown in the preceding listing shows that the user account FLOWER owns tables and indexes in the USERS tablespace, and that THUMPER owns several tables in that tablespace as well. The user HR owns objects in both the HR_TABLES and the HR_INDEXES tablespaces.

Before determining the proper combinations of users to export for a tablespace, the inverse mapping—of tablespaces to users—should be done. The following query accomplishes this task. It queries the DBA_TABLES and DBA_INDEXES data dictionary views, and stores the output in a file called TS_LOCS.LST.

```
rem
rem     user_tablespace_maps.sql
rem
rem  This script maps user objects to tablespaces.
rem
set pagesize 60
break on Tablespace on Owner
column Objects format A20
select
        Tablespace_Name,
        Owner,
        COUNT(*)||' tables' Objects
from DBA_TABLES
group by
        Tablespace_Name,
        Owner
union
select
```

```
      Tablespace_Name,
      Owner,
      COUNT(*)||' indexes' Objects
from DBA_INDEXES
group by
      Tablespace_Name,
      Owner

spool ts_locs.lst
/
spool off
```

Sample output from this query is shown in the following listing:

```
TABLESPACE_NAME    OWNER        OBJECTS
---------------    -----------  -------------
HR_INDEXES         HR           35 indexes
HR_TABLES          HR           27 tables
USERS              FLOWER       3 tables
                                2 indexes
                   THUMPER      5 tables
```

The sample output shown in the preceding listing shows that the HR_TABLES tablespace contains objects from just one user (the HR account). The HR_INDEXES tablespace is similarly isolated. The USERS tablespace, on the other hand, contains both tables and indexes from several accounts.

The importance of properly distributing users' objects among tablespaces can be seen in the results of the preceding queries. Since the HR_TABLES tablespace only contains tables owned by the HR account (from the second query), exporting the HR tables will export all of the objects in the HR_TABLES tablespace. As seen from the first query, HR does not own any tables anywhere else in the database. Because HR's tables are isolated to the HR_TABLES tablespace, and because that tablespace is only used by the HR account, a User export of HR will export all of the tables in HR_TABLES. Since the indexes on those tables are stored in HR_INDEXES, that tablespace can be defragmented at the same time from the same export dump file.

```
exp system/manager file=hr.dmp owner=HR indexes=Y compress=Y
```

The tablespaces can then be dropped and re-created, and the full export file can be imported. They will contain all of HR's tables and indexes. The following listing shows this process, using Server Manager to manipulate the tablespaces. The full **create tablespace** commands are not shown since those details are not relevant to this example.

```
svrmgrl
SVRMGR> connect internal
SVRMGR> drop tablespace HR_INDEXES including contents;
SVRMGR> drop tablespace HR_TABLES including contents;
SVRMGR> create tablespace HR_TABLES...
SVRMGR> create tablespace HR_INDEXES...
SVRMGR> exit

imp system/manager file=hr.dmp full=Y buffer=64000 commit=Y
```

Note that before reaching this point, you had to first analyze the distribution of users' objects in the database. If users are isolated to tablespaces, and if tablespaces are dedicated to users, then this process becomes simple.

What if HR had also owned objects in the USERS tablespace in this example? In that case, there would have been two alternatives. First, you could have queried the data dictionary views to determine the table names involved and then specified the rest of HR's tables in the Export command via the TABLES parameter. Second, you could have exported HR's objects via a User export, dropped the HR_TABLES and HR_INDEXES tablespaces, dropped any HR objects located elsewhere in the database, re-created the HR_TABLES and HR_INDEXES tablespaces, and then performed the Import.

For the sample data given in the earlier listings, re-creating the USERS tablespace requires performing User exports of both the THUMPER and the FLOWER accounts. Neither of these accounts owns objects in tablespaces other than USERS.

Note that this procedure *cannot* be used for tablespaces that contain temporary segments or rollback segments. The **drop tablespace** command will result in errors in those cases.

As noted previously, User exports do not export third-party grants and indexes. To determine if third-party grants or indexes exist, query the data dictionary views, as shown in the following queries.

The first set of queries searches for third-party grants.

```
Rem
rem   third_party_grants.sql
rem
rem   This query searches for grants made by users
rem   other than the table owners.  These grants cannot
rem   be exported via User exports.
rem
break on Grantor skip 1 on Owner on Table_Name
select
        Grantor,            /*Account that made the grant*/
        Owner,              /*Account that owns the table*/
        Table_Name,         /*Name of the table*/
        Grantee,            /*Account granted access*/
        Privilege,          /*Privilege granted*/
        Grantable           /*Granted with admin option?*/
from DBA_TAB_PRIVS
where Grantor ! = Owner
order by Grantor, Owner, Table_Name, Grantee, Privilege

spool third_parts_privs.lst
/
spool off
```

As shown in the following listing, the search for third-party indexes queries the DBA_INDEXES data dictionary view to retrieve those records in which the index owner and the table owner columns do not have the same value.

```
rem
rem   third_party_indexes.sql
rem
rem   This query searches for indexes created by
rem   anyone other than the table owner.
rem
select
        Owner,                  /*Owner of the index*/
        Index_Name,             /*Name of the index*/
        Table_Owner,            /*Owner of the table*/
```

```
        Table_Name                /*Name of the indexed table*/
from DBA_INDEXES
where Owner != Table_Owner

spool third_party_indexes.lst
/
spool off
```

If these queries show that third-party indexes or grants exist, and you plan to rely on User exports, then you must supplement those exports with scripts that generate the third-party grants and indexes. Those supplemental scripts are necessary because those grants and indexes will not be recorded during User exports.

Exporting Partitions

You can reference partitions within tables when you perform Table exports. For example, if the SALES table in the THUMPER schema is partitioned into PART1, PART2, and PART3, then you can export the entire table or its partitions.

To export the entire table, use the TABLES parameter of Export.

```
exp system/manager FILE=expdat.dmp TABLES=(Thumper.SALES)
```

To export a specific partition, list the partition following the table name. The table name and the partition name should be separated by a colon (:). In the following listing, the PART1 partition is exported:

```
exp system/manager FILE=expdat.dmp TABLES=(Thumper.SALES:Part1)
```

As shown in this example, you can list specific partitions to export. This capability is frequently used during reorganizations of partitioned tables (see Chapter 12 for full details on partitioned tables). For example, you can export a full table, drop and re-create the table with different partition ranges, and then Import the table, effectively altering the partition ranges for the partitions. In the next section, you will see how to use the Import utility to recover data.

Import

The *Import* utility reads the export dump file and runs the commands stored there. Import may be used to selectively bring back objects or users from the export dump file.

When importing data from an Incremental or Cumulative export, you must first import from the most recent Incremental export, followed by the most recent Complete export. After that Import is complete, the most recent Cumulative export must be imported, followed by all Incremental exports since that export.

Import can be run either interactively or via command files. The run-time options that can be specified for Import are listed in Table 10-4.

Keyword	Description
USERID	Username/password of the account running the import. If this is the first parameter after the "imp" command, then the "USERID" keyword does not have to be specified.
BUFFER	Size of the buffer used to fetch data rows. The default is system dependent; this value is usually set to a high value (>100,000).
FILE	Name of the export dump file to be imported.
SHOW	A Y/N flag to specify whether the file contents should be displayed rather than executed.
IGNORE	A Y/N flag to indicate whether the Import should ignore errors encountered when issuing **create** commands. This is used if the objects being imported already exist.
GRANTS	A Y/N flag to indicate whether grants on database objects will be imported.
INDEXES	A Y/N flag to indicate whether indexes on tables will be imported.

TABLE 10-4. *Import Keywords*

Keyword	Description
ROWS	A Y/N flag to indicate whether rows should be imported. If this is set to "N", then only the DDL for the database objects will be executed.
FULL	A Y/N flag; if set to "Y", then the full export dump file is imported.
FROMUSER	A list of database accounts whose objects should be read from the export dump file (when FULL="N").
TOUSER	A list of database accounts into which objects in the export dump file will be imported. FROMUSER and TOUSER do not have to be set to the same value.
TABLES	A list of tables to be imported.
RECORDLENGTH	The length, in bytes, of the export dump file record. Usually left at the default value unless you are going to transfer the export file between different operating systems.
INCTYPE	The type of import being performed (valid values are "COMPLETE" (default), "CUMULATIVE", and "INCREMENTAL").
COMMIT	A Y/N flag to indicate whether Import should **commit** after each array (whose size is set by BUFFER). If this is set to "N", then Import will **commit** after every table is imported. For large tables, COMMIT=N requires equally large rollback segments.
PARFILE	The name of a parameter file to be passed to Import. This file may contain entries for all of the parameters listed here.
INDEXFILE	This very powerful option writes all of the **create table**, **create cluster**, and **create index** commands to a file, rather than running them. All but the **create index** commands will be commented out. This file can then be run (with slight modifications) after importing with INDEXES=N. It is very useful for separating tables and indexes into separate tablespaces.
DESTROY	A Y/N flag to indicate whether the **create tablespace** commands found in dump files from Full exports will be executed (thereby destroying the datafiles in the database being imported into).

TABLE 10-4. *Import Keywords (continued)*

Keyword	Description
LOG	The name of a file to which the log of the Import will be written.
CHARSET	Character set to use during the Import.
POINT_IN_TIME_ RECOVER	A Y/N flag to indicate if the Import is part of a tablespace point-in-time recovery. This is an advanced recovery technique; see the "Recovery Scenarios" section of this chapter.
SKIP_UNUSABLE_ INDEXES	A Y/N flag that indicates if Import should skip partition indexes marked as "unusable". You may wish to skip the indexes during Import and manually create them later to improve index creation performance.
ANALYZE	A Y/N flag to indicate whether Import should execute the **analyze** commands found in the Export dump file.
FEEDBACK	The number of rows after which to display progress during table imports. The default value is 0, so no feedback is displayed until a table is completely imported.

TABLE 10-4. *Import Keywords (continued)*

Note that a number of the parameters conflict with each other or may result in inconsistent instructions for Import. For example, setting FULL=Y and OWNER=HR would fail, since the FULL parameter calls for a Full import, while the OWNER parameter specifies a User import.

The default values for these options are shown in Table 10-5.

The DESTROY parameter is very useful for DBAs who run multiple databases on a single server. Since Full database Exports record the entire data dictionary, the tablespace and datafile definitions are written to the export dump file. The datafile definitions will include the full path name for the files. If this export dump file is used to migrate to a separate database on the same server, a problem may arise.

The problem is that when importing into the second database from the Full export of the first database, Import will execute the **create tablespace** commands found in the export dump file. These will instruct the database to create files in exactly the same directory, with the same name, as the

Keyword	Oracle8 Default Value
USERID	Undefined
BUFFER	System dependent
FILE	EXPDAT.DMP
SHOW	N
IGNORE	N
GRANTS	Y
INDEXES	Y
ROWS	Y
FULL	N
FROMUSER	Undefined
TOUSER	Undefined
TABLES	Undefined
RECORDLENGTH	System dependent
INCTYPE	Undefined
COMMIT	N
PARFILE	Undefined
INDEXFILE	Undefined
DESTROY	N
LOG	Undefined
CHARSET	NLS_LANG for the instance
POINT_IN_TIME_RECOVER	N
SKIP_UNUSABLE_INDEXES	N
ANALYZE	Y
FEEDBACK	0

TABLE 10-5.   *Default Values for Import Parameters*

files from the first database. Without using DESTROY=N (the default option), the first database's datafiles may be overwritten. The only alternative when doing such an Import is to precreate all of the tablespaces, forcing the **create tablespace** commands to return errors (and thus not attempt to create any datafiles during the Import).

Rollback Segment Requirements

By default, the database will issue a **commit** after every table is completely imported. Thus, if you have a table with 300MB of data in it, then your rollback segments must accommodate a rollback segment entry that is at least that large. This is an unnecessary burden for the rollback segments. To shorten the sizes of the rollback segment entries, specify COMMIT=Y along with a value for BUFFER. A **commit** will then be executed after every BUFFER worth of data, as shown in the following example. In the first Import command shown, a commit is executed after every table is loaded. In the second command shown, a commit is executed after every 64,000 bytes of data are inserted.

```
imp system/manager file=expdat.dmp
imp system/manager file=expdat.dmp buffer=64000 commit=Y
```

How large should BUFFER be? BUFFER should be large enough to handle the largest single row to be imported. In tables with LONG or LOB datatypes, this may be greater than 64K. If you do not know the longest row length that was exported, start with a reasonable value (e.g., 50,000) and run the Import. If an IMP-00020 error is returned, then the BUFFER size is not large enough. Increase it and try the Import again.

When using COMMIT=Y, remember that a **commit** is being performed for each BUFFER array. This implies that if the Import of a table fails, it is possible that some of the rows in that table may have already been Imported and **commit**ted. The partial load may then be either used or **delete**d prior to running the Import again.

Importing into Different Accounts

To move objects from one user to another user via Export/Import, export the owner of the objects. During the Import, specify the owner as the FROMUSER and the account that is to own the objects as the TOUSER. For example, to export THUMPER's objects into the FLOWER account, execute the following commands. The first command exports the THUMPER owner and the second command imports the THUMPER objects into the FLOWER account.

```
exp system/manager file=thumper.dat owner=thumper grants=N
   indexes=Y compress=Y rows=Y
```

```
imp system/manager file=thumper.dat FROMUSER=thumper TOUSER=flower
     rows=Y indexes=Y
```

Importing Structures that Failed to Import

The ROWS parameter is very useful for two reasons. First, it can be used to re-create just the database structure, without the tables' data, even if that data was exported. Second, it is often needed during successive Imports to recover objects that were not created during the first Import attempt. This is necessary because of the order in which objects are exported and imported.

When the Export program is run, it exports users in the order in which they were created in the database. A user's tables are then exported alphabetically. While this does not cause a problem during Exports, it may cause problems when those same objects are imported. The problems arise from the dependencies that may exist between objects in the database. If Import attempts to create an object (such as a view) before it creates the objects on which it depends, then an error may result. In such cases, the Import can be rerun, with ROWS=N and IGNORE=N, which will only import the structures that did not get imported during the first Import.

The following example shows this usage. The first Import attempts to bring in the entire export dump file. If there are failures during this Import, then a second pass is made to attempt to bring in those structures that failed the first time.

```
imp system/manager file=expdat.dmp full=Y commit=Y buffer=64000
```

During the import, several views fail with an ORA-00942 (table or view does not exist) error. Now run the Import a second time, with IGNORE=N and ROWS=N.

```
imp system/manager file=expdat.dmp ignore=N rows=N commit=Y buffer=64000
```

The IGNORE=N parameter in the second command tells Import to ignore any objects that were created during the first pass. It will only import those objects that failed. These are usually views that reference tables owned by multiple users.

Note that if a table referenced by a view is dropped, the view definition stays in the data dictionary. This definition can be exported, and the view creation will fail during an Import. In that case, since the view was invalid to begin with, a second Import will fail as well.

Using Import to Separate Tables and Indexes

You can use two Import options—INDEXFILE and INDEXES—to reorganize the tablespace assignments of tables and indexes.

Using the INDEXFILE option during an Import will result in the export dump file being read and, instead of being imported, its table and index creation scripts will be written to an output file. This file can be edited to alter the **tablespace** and **storage** parameters of the tables and indexes listed there. It may then be run via SQL*Plus to either precreate all objects prior to importing their data or to create only specified objects (such as indexes).

When the indexfile is created, the **create index** scripts are the only ones that are not commented out via the **rem** command. This default functionality allows DBAs to separate a user's tables and indexes into separate tablespaces during Import. To do so, create the indexfile and alter the **tablespace** clauses for the indexes. Then, import the user, with INDEXES=N, so that the user's indexes will not be imported. Then run the altered indexfile to create the indexes in their new tablespace.

Note that the indexfile may contain entries for multiple users (if multiple users were exported). In practice, it is useful to separate the indexfile into multiple files, one for each user. This will make it easier to keep the tablespace assignments consistent. The following listing shows the steps involved in this process. In this example, THUMPER's objects are being copied into the FLOWER account, and the indexes are being separated from the tables in the process.

NOTE
The INDEXFILE parameter requires that either FULL=Y or a FROMUSER value is specified.

1. Export the user.

```
exp system/manager file=expdat.dmp owner=thumper
```

2. Create the indexfile from this export dump file.

```
imp system/manager file=expdat.dmp indexfile=indexes.sql full=Y
```

3. Edit the indexfile to change the **tablespace** settings of the indexes.

4. Import the user, without its indexes.

```
imp system/manager file=expdat.dmp fromuser=thumper touser=flower
indexes=N commit=Y buffer=64000
```

5. Log in to SQL*Plus as the user and run the altered indexfile to create the indexes.

```
sqlplus flower/password
SQL> @indexes
```

Offline Backups

A cold backup is a physical backup of the database files, made after the database has been shut down normally. While it is shut down, each of the files that are actively used by the database is backed up. These files thus capture a complete image of the database as it existed at the moment it was shut down.

The following files should be backed up during cold backups:

- All datafiles
- All control files
- All online redo logs
- The init.ora file (optional)

It is easiest to back up the datafiles if the database file architecture uses a consistent directory structure. A sample of such an architecture is shown in the "Database File Layout" section of Chapter 4.

In that architecture, all of the datafiles are located in directories at the same level on each device. The following listing shows a sample directory tree for a data disk named /db01:

```
/db01
        /oracle
                /CASE
                        control1.dbf
                        sys01.dbf
                        tools.dbf
                /CC1
                        control1.dbf
                        sys01.dbf
                        tools.dbf
                /DEMO
                        control1.dbf
                        sys01.dbf
```

In the sample directory tree, all database files are stored in an instance-specific subdirectory under an /oracle directory for the device. Directories such as these should contain all of the datafiles, redo log files, and control files for a database. The only file you may optionally add to the cold backup that will not be in this location is the production init.ora file, which should be in /orasw/app/oracle/admin/*INSTANCE_NAME*/pfile.

If this directory structure is used, the backup commands are greatly simplified. The following listing shows a sample UNIX **tar** command, which is used here to back up files to a tape drive called "/dev/rmt/0hc". Because the directory structure is consistent and the drives are named "/db01" through "/db09", the following command will back up all of the CC1 database's datafiles, redo log files, and control files:

```
> tar -cvf /dev/rmt/0hc /db0[1-9]/oracle/CC1
```

The **-cvf** flag is used to create a new **tar** saveset. To append the init.ora file to this saveset, use the **-rvf** flag. This option, which appends files to the tape, is not available on all UNIX systems. If your installation does not support this, then the best alternative is to copy the files directly to a staging area on another disk (see "Database and Operating System Backups Integration" later in this chapter).

```
> tar -rvf /dev/rmt/0hc /orasw/app/oracle/CC1/pfile/initcc1.ora
```

These two commands, taken together, will back up all of the database's files to one tape device.

Since cold backups involve changes to the database's availability, they are usually scheduled to occur at night. A command file to automate these backups would resemble the following listing. In this example, the ORACLE_SID and ORACLE_HOME environment variables are set to point to the CC1 database. This database is then shut down and the backup commands are executed. The database is then restarted.

```
ORACLE_SID=cc1; export ORACLE_SID
ORAENV_ASK=NO; export ORAENV_ASK
. oraenv
svrmgrl
SVRMGR> connect internal
SVRMGR> shutdown immediate;
SVRMGR> exit
insert backup commands like the "tar" commands here
```

```
svrmgrl
SVRMGR> connect internal
SVRMGR> startup
```

These examples are generic so that non-UNIX operating systems can use them with little modification. In VMS, for example, environment variables are set via instance-specific command files. For example, if the ORACLE software home directory was DB01:[ORASW], then to set the environment variables, you would first go to the instance directory (via the **set def** command). Once there, you would run the instance-specific ORAUSER file there. This is shown in the following example:

```
set def DB01:[ORASW.DB_instance_name]
@ORAUSER_DB_instance_name
```

The Server Manager commands are the same across operating systems. The backup commands are operating system-specific. For VMS systems, the backup commands are of the form shown in the following example.

In this example, the VMS **Backup** command is used. The command is told to back up the files even if they have been marked as "NOBACKUP", and even if they are interlocked (the "interl" parameter in this example). The "/log" clause logs the results of the backup command.

```
$Backup/ignore=(nobackup,interl)/log file tape1:oracle_backup.bck/sav
```

The file in this example is backed up to a tape device called "tape1". It is written to a saveset (as indicated by the "/sav" clause) called oracle_backup.bck. As with the UNIX **tar** command, you can back up multiple files at once via this command. The same backup command can be used to back up different files to savesets on the same tape. Those savesets will be appended to the tape.

Online (ARCHIVELOG) Backups

Offline backups can only be performed while the database is shut down. However, you can perform physical file backups of a database while the database is open—provided the database is running in ARCHIVELOG mode and the backup is performed correctly. These backups are variously referred to as "hot" backups, "online" backups, or "ARCHIVELOG" backups.

ORACLE writes to the online redo log files in a cyclical fashion; after filling the first log file, it begins writing the second until that one fills, and it then begins writing to the third. Once the last online redo log file is filled, the LGWR (Log Writer) background process begins to overwrite the contents of the first redo log file.

When ORACLE is run in ARCHIVELOG mode, the ARCH background process makes a copy of each redo log file before overwriting it. These archived redo log files are usually written to a disk device. They may also be written directly to a tape device, but this tends to be very operator intensive.

Getting Started

To make use of the ARCHIVELOG capability, the database must first be placed in ARCHIVELOG mode. The following listing shows the steps needed to place a database in ARCHIVELOG mode:

```
svrmgrl
SVRMGR>connect internal
SVRMGR>startup mount cc1;
SVRMGR>alter database archivelog;
SVRMGR>archive log start;
SVRMGR>alter database open;
```

The following command will display the current ARCHIVELOG status of the database from within Server Manager:

```
archive log list
```

To change a database back to NOARCHIVELOG mode, use the following sets of commands:

```
svrmgrl
SVRMGR>connect internal
SVRMGR>startup mount cc1;
SVRMGR>alter database noarchivelog;
SVRMGR>alter database open;
```

A database that has been placed in ARCHIVELOG mode will remain in that mode until it is placed in NOARCHIVELOG mode.

The location of the archived redo log files is determined by the settings in the database's init.ora file. The archive log destination parameter may also be set via the config.ora file that is referenced as a parameter file in the init.ora. The two parameters to note are as follows (with sample values):

```
log_archive_dest        = /db01/oracle/arch/CC1/arch
log_archive_start       = TRUE
```

In this example, the archived redo log files are being written to the directory "/db01/oracle/arch/CC1". The archived redo log files will all begin with the letters "arch", followed by a sequence number. For example, the archived redo log file directory may contain the following files:

```
arch_170.dbf
arch_171.dbf
arch_172.dbf
```

Each of these files contains the data from a single online redo log. They are numbered sequentially, in the order in which they were created. The size of the archived redo log files varies, but does not exceed their size of the online redo log files.

If the destination directory of the archived redo log files runs out of space, then ARCH will stop processing the online redo log data and the database will stop itself. This situation can be resolved by adding more space to the archived redo log file destination disk or by backing up the archived redo log files and then removing them from this directory.

NOTE
Never delete archived redo log files until you have backed them up. There is no way to skip a missing archived redo log file during a recovery.

In a database that is currently running, you can show the current ARCHIVELOG settings (including the destination directory) via the **archive log list** command within Server Manager, as shown earlier in this section. You can also query the parameter settings from the V$PARAMETER dynamic performance view.

```
select Name,
       Value
  from V$PARAMETER
 where Name like 'log_archive%';
```

Although the LOG_ARCHIVE_START parameter may be set to TRUE, the database will *not* be in ARCHIVELOG mode unless you have executed the **alter database archivelog** command shown earlier in this section. Once the database is in ARCHIVELOG mode, it will remain in that mode through subsequent database shutdowns and startups until you explicitly place it in NOARCHIVELOG mode via the **alter database noarchivelog** command.

Performing Online Database Backups

Once a database is running in ARCHIVELOG mode, it may be backed up while it is open and available to users. This capability allows round-the-clock database availability to be achieved while still guaranteeing the recoverability of the database.

Although hot backups can be performed during normal working hours, they should be scheduled for the times of the least user activity for several reasons. First, the hot backups will use operating system commands to back up the physical files, and these commands will use most of the available I/O resources in the system (thus slowing down the interactive users). Second, while the tablespaces are being backed up, the manner in which transactions are written to the archived redo log files changes. If the physical block size of the operating system is less than the ORACLE block size, then changing one record in a block will cause the record's entire block, not just the transaction data, to be written to the archived redo log file. This will use a great deal more space in the archived redo log file destination directory.

The command file for a hot backup has three parts:

1. A tablespace-by-tablespace backup of the datafiles, which in turn consists of

   a) Setting the tablespace into backup state

   b) Backing up the tablespace's datafiles

   c) Restoring the tablespace to its normal state

2. Backing up the archived redo log files, which consists of

   a) Temporarily stopping the archiving process

   b) Recording which files are in the archived redo log destination directory

c) Restarting the archiving process

d) Backing up the archived redo log files, then deleting them

3. Backing up the control file via the **alter database backup controlfile** command.

NOTE
During step 2, the archiver is stopped briefly to prevent new archived redo log files from being written while the names of the existing archived redo log files are recorded. If you don't stop the archiver during this operation, you may delete (in step 2-d) files not recorded (in step 2-b). There is no way to re-create the contents of a deleted archived redo log file, and no way to skip past it during a recovery if you cannot recover the file. Be careful when deleting archived redo log files.

A command file to perform a hot backup of a database will resemble the following listing. It is structured the same as the description just given. This example is for a UNIX database. In the first section, the environment variables ORACLE_SID and ORACLE_HOME are set for the database. Server Manager is then used to put each tablespace in **begin backup** state. The datafiles associated with each tablespace are then backed up.

When the datafiles are being backed up, there are two choices available: they may be backed up directly to tape or they may be backed up to disk. If you have enough disk space available, choose the latter option since it will greatly reduce the time necessary for the backup procedures to complete. For this example, the datafiles will be written directly to tape.

```
#
# Sample Hot Backup Script for a UNIX File System database
#
# Set up environment variables:
ORACLE_SID=cc1; export ORACLE_SID
ORAENV_ASK=NO; export ORAENV_ASK
. oraenv
#
```

```
#   Step 1.  Perform a tablespace-by-tablespace backup
#   of the datafiles.  Set each tablespace, one at a time,
#   into begin backup state.  Then back up its datafiles
#   and return the tablespace to its normal state.
#
# Note for UNIX:  Set up an indicator for Server Manager
# (called EOFarch1 here) so that the command file will
#  stay within Server Manager.
#
svrmgrl <<EOFarch1
connect internal
REM
REM    Back up the SYSTEM tablespace
REM
alter tablespace SYSTEM begin backup;
!tar -cvf /dev/rmt/0hc /db01/oracle/CC1/sys01.dbf
alter tablespace SYSTEM end backup;
REM
REM  The SYSTEM tablespace has now been written to a
REM    tar saveset on the tape device /dev/rmt/0hc.  The
REM    rest of the tars must use the "-rvf" clause to append
REM    to that saveset.
REM
REM    Back up the RBS tablespace
REM
alter tablespace RBS begin backup;
!tar -rvf /dev/rmt/0hc /db02/oracle/CC1/rbs01.dbf
alter tablespace RBS end backup;
REM
REM    Back up the DATA tablespace
REM    For the purposes of this example, this tablespace
REM    will contain two files, data01.dbf and data02.dbf.
REM    The * wildcard will be used in the filename.
REM
alter tablespace DATA begin backup;
!tar -rvf /dev/rmt/0hc /db03/oracle/CC1/data0*.dbf
alter tablespace DATA end backup;
REM
REM    Back up the INDEXES tablespace
REM
alter tablespace INDEXES begin backup;
!tar -rvf /dev/rmt/0hc /db04/oracle/CC1/indexes01.dbf
alter tablespace INDEXES end backup;
REM
REM    Back up the TEMP tablespace
```

```
REM
alter tablespace TEMP begin backup;
!tar -rvf /dev/rmt/0hc /db05/oracle/CC1/temp01.dbf
alter tablespace TEMP end backup;
REM
REM    Follow the same pattern to back up the rest
REM    of the tablespaces.
REM
REM
REM           Step 2.   Back up the archived redo log files.
REM
REM   First, stop the archiving process.   This will keep
REM   additional archived redo log files from being written
REM   to the destination directory during this process.
REM
archive log stop
REM
REM    Exit Server Manager, using the indicator set earlier.
exit
EOFarch1
#
#   Record which files are in the destination directory.
#      Do this by setting an environment variable that is
#   equal to the directory listing for the destination
#   directory.
#   For this example, the log_archive_dest is
#   /db01/oracle/arch/CC1.
#
FILES='ls /db01/oracle/arch/CC1/arch*.dbf'; export FILES
#
#   Now go back into Server Manager and restart the
#   archiving process.   Set an indicator (called EOFarch2
#   in this example).
#
svrmgrl <<EOFarch2
connect internal
archive log start;
exit
EOFarch2
#
#   Now back up the archived redo logs to the tape
#   device via the "tar" command, then delete them
#   from the destination device via the "rm" command.
#
tar -rvf /dev/rmt/0hc $FILES
```

```
rm -f $FILES
#
#     Step 3.   Back up the control file to a disk file.
#
svrmgrl <<EOFarch3
connect internal
alter database backup controlfile to
   'db01/oracle/CC1/CC1controlfile.bck';
exit
EOFarch3
#
#   Back up the control file to the tape.
#
tar -rvf /dev/rmt/0hc /db01/oracle/CC1/CC1controlfile.bck
#
#   End of hot backup script.
```

This backup script explicitly lists each datafile within each tablespace. Therefore, this backup procedure must be altered each time a datafile is added to the database.

Note that only one tablespace is in **begin backup** state at a time. Having only one tablespace in **begin backup** state at a time minimizes vulnerability to potential damage caused by database crashes. If the database is closed abnormally while a tablespace is in **begin backup** state, then recovery may be necessary. Using the one-at-a-time method shown here greatly reduces the possible impact of such a crash.

In the "Database and Operating System Backups Integration" section later in this chapter, this script will be modified to take advantage of file system backups performed by systems management personnel.

To back up an ORACLE database in a VMS operating system, make several small changes to the backup script above:

1. Instead of the "#" signs in the UNIX script, use "$!" to signal a remark in the command file.

2. Remove the references to EOFarch1, EOFarch2, and EOFarch3. These aren't needed in VMS.

3. Replace the UNIX "tar" commands with VMS "Backup" commands, as shown earlier in this chapter.

4. Replace the UNIX "rm" command with a VMS "Delete" command.

5. Set up the environment variables that point to the instance via the instance-specific command file referred to earlier in this chapter.

6. When backing up the archived redo logs, set the "FILES" variable equal to the directory listing of the archived redo log destination directory.

Automation of the Backup Scripts

In the preceding section, the backup scripts explicitly list each file to be backed up. Although you should know whenever a file is added or moved in your database, changing the backup scripts may be a process you wish to avoid as the number of databases you support increases. Therefore, you may wish to automate the backup script generation process.

When automating the backup script generation process, you will find it simplest to put all of the tablespaces into **begin backup** state at once. As noted earlier in this chapter, you should only put all of your tablespaces into **begin backup** state simultaneously if both of these conditions are met:

1. There are very few transactions occurring in the database. Tablespaces in **begin backup** state generate very high volumes of redo log information.

2. The hardware used by the database is mirrored. Since having all of the tablespaces in **begin backup** state greatly increases your vulnerability to media failures, you should make sure that the disk drives and other hardware used by the datafiles are well protected.

If both of these conditions are met, then you can consider placing all of your tablespaces in **begin backup** state. In the revised backup script, the order of events will be

1. A backup of all datafiles, which consists of

   a) Setting all tablespaces into backup state

   b) Backing up all datafiles

   c) Restoring all tablespaces to their normal state

2. Backing up the archived redo log files, which consists of

   a) Temporarily stopping the archiving process

b) Recording which files are in the archived redo log destination directory

c) Restarting the archiving process

d) Backing up the archived redo log files, then deleting them

3. Backing up the control file via the **alter database backup controlfile** command.

The differences between this order of commands and the commands given earlier in this chapter are found in step 1. Instead of placing tablespaces into **begin backup** state one at a time, all of the tablespaces are placed into **begin backup** state at the same time. To automatically generate the commands needed to alter the tablespaces, query DBA_TABLESPACES as shown in the following listing:

```
set pagesize 0

select
     'alter tablespace '||Tablespace_Name||' begin backup;'
  from DBA_TABLESPACES
 where Status <> 'INVALID'

spool alter_begin.sql
/
spool off
```

The output of this query will be a command named alter_begin.sql. Its entries will resemble the following:

```
alter tablespace SYSTEM begin backup;
alter tablespace RBS begin backup;
alter tablespace TEMP begin backup;
alter tablespace DATA begin backup;
alter tablespace INDEXES begin backup;
```

When you execute this command file, all of the tablespaces will be placed into **begin backup** state. You can now back up all of the datafiles. Instead of backing up specific datafiles, you can back up all datafiles in the proper directories without regard to their tablespace affiliations. In the following listing, the datafiles from disks /db01 to /db09 are backed up via a single **tar** command:

```
tar -cvf /dev/rmt/0hc /db0[1-9]/oracle/CC1
```

NOTE
You may want to exclude the archived redo log file directory from this backup step since those files will be backed up via step 2 of the backup procedure.

Once the datafiles are backed up, you can change them from **begin backup** state to their normal state. You can automatically generate the script to perform this change, as shown in the following listing:

```
set pagesize 0

select
    'alter tablespace '||Tablespace_Name||' end backup;'
  from DBA_TABLESPACES
 where Status <> 'INVALID'

spool alter_end.sql
/
spool off
```

When you execute the alter_end.sql script generated by this query, your tablespaces will be back in their normal state and you can now proceed to steps 2 (archived redo log file backups) and 3 (control file backup) of the backup process.

The automation of backup scripts generates the greatest benefit when you have many databases that are changing frequently. If you rely on automated backup scripts, you should make sure your server hardware is very reliable. As of ORACLE7.2, you can alter a tablespace to **end backup** state prior to opening the database if the database shut down abnormally while the tablespace was in **begin backup** state. Ideally, you should avoid server activity—and server failures—during your database backup process.

Archived Redo Log File Backups

Since the archived redo log file destination directory may become full before the hot backup procedure is run, it is useful to have a backup procedure that only backs up that directory. The files in that directory can then be deleted, leaving space for new archived redo log files.

This procedure is simply a portion of the full hot backup process. It is a five-step process:

1. Temporarily stop the archiving process
2. Record which files are in the archived redo log destination directory
3. Restart the archiving process
4. Back up the archived redo log files
5. Delete those files from the destination directory

The following command procedure performs this function. It is for UNIX databases using file systems. The **tar** command is used to back up the files to tape.

```
#       Step 1: Stop the archiving process. This will keep
#       additional archived redo log files from being written
#       to the destination directory during this process.
#
svrmgrl <<EOFarch1
connect internal
archive log stop;
REM
REM   Exit Server Manager using the indicator set earlier.
exit
EOFarch1
#
#       Step 2: Record which files are in the destination
# directory.
#       Do this by setting an environment variable that is
#   equal to the directory listing for the destination
#   directory.
#   For this example, the log_archive_dest is
#   /db01/oracle/arch/CC1.
#
FILES='ls /db01/oracle/arch/CC1/arch*.dbf'; export FILES
#
#       Step 3: Go back into Server Manager and restart the
#   archiving process. Set an indicator (called EOFarch2
#   in this example).
#
svrmgrl <<EOFarch2
connect internal
```

```
archive log start;
exit
EOFarch2
#
#       Step 4. Back up the archived redo logs to the tape
#   device via the "tar" command, then delete them
#   from the destination device via the "rm" command.
#
tar -rvf /dev/rmt/0hc $FILES
#
#       Step 5. Delete those files from the destination directory.
#
rm -f $FILES
#
#       End of archived redo log file backup script.
```

The archived redo logs that are backed up via this procedure should be stored with the last previous hot backup.

Standby Databases

You can maintain a *standby database* for quick disaster recovery. A standby database maintains a copy of the production database in a permanent state of recovery. In the event of a disaster in the production database, the standby database can be opened with a minimal amount of recovery necessary. You may, however, lose the contents of your online redo log files in your production database during the switch to the standby database. As of ORACLE7.3, the management of standby databases is greatly simplified.

The standby database must use the same version of the kernel that the production system uses. You can create a standby database from a copy of the current production database (generated via either an offline backup or an online backup). As archived redo log files are generated by the production instance, they should be copied to the standby system and applied to the standby database. Maintaining a standby database requires keeping the file structures and software versions of the production and standby databases continuously synchronized. See the *ORACLE Server Administrator's Guide* for detailed directions for setting up and maintaining standby databases.

Integration of Backup Procedures

Since there are three different methods for backing up the ORACLE database, there is no need to have a single point of failure. Depending on your database's characteristics, one of the three methods should be chosen, and at least one of the two remaining methods should be used to back it up.

In the following sections, you will see how to choose the primary backup method for your database, how to integrate logical and physical backups, and how to integrate database backups with file system backups.

For backup strategies specific to very large databases, see Chapter 12.

Logical and Physical Backups Integration

Which backup method is appropriate for your database? Or rather, which backup method is appropriate to use as the *primary* backup method for your database?

The backup method selection process should take into account the characteristics of each method, as listed in Table 10-6.

As shown in Table 10-6, offline backups are the least flexible method of backing up the database if the database is running in NOARCHIVELOG mode. Offline backups are a point-in-time snapshot of the database; and since they are a physical backup, DBAs cannot selectively recover logical

Method	Type	Recovery Characteristics
Export	Logical	Can recover any database object to its status as of the moment it was exported.
Offline Backups	Physical	Can recover the database to its status as of the moment it was shut down; if the database is run in ARCHIVELOG mode, you can recover the database to its status at any point in time.
Online Backups	Physical	Can recover the database to its status at any point in time.

TABLE 10-6.   *Comparison of Characteristics of Backup Methods*

objects (such as tables) from them. Although there are times when they are appropriate, offline backups should normally be used as a fallback position in the event that the primary backup method fails. If you are running the database in ARCHIVELOG mode, you can use the offline backups as the basis for a media recovery, but an online backup would normally be more appropriate for that situation.

Of the two remaining methods, which one is more appropriate? The answer depends on the nature of your database.

First, consider the recovery requirements. If your database is transaction oriented, you will most likely want to use online backups. Using online backups will minimize the amount of transaction data lost in the event of a database failure. Using an Export-based strategy would limit you to only being able to go back to the data as it existed the last time the data was exported.

Next, consider the size of the database and what objects you will likely be recovering. Given a standard recovery scenario—such as the loss of a disk—how long will it take for the data to be recovered? If a file is lost, the quickest way to recover it is usually via a physical backup, which again favors online backups over Exports.

There are, however, scenarios in which other methods are preferable. If the database is small and transaction volume is very low, then either offline backups or Export will serve your needs. If you are only concerned about one or two tables, then use Export to selectively back them up. However, if the database is large, then the recovery time needed for Export/Import may be prohibitive. For such large, low-transaction environments, offline backups may be appropriate.

Regardless of your choice for primary backup method, the final implementation should include an Export and a physical backup. This is necessary because these methods validate different things about the database: Export validates that it is logically sound, and physical backups that it is physically sound. Three sample integrations of these methods are shown in Table 10-7.

As shown in Table 10-7, a good database backup strategy integrates logical and physical backups, based on the database's usage characteristics.

Other database activities may call for ad hoc backups. These may include offline backups before performing database upgrades and Exports during application migration between databases.

Database Type	Online Backups	Offline Backups	Exports
All sizes, transaction intensive	Nightly	Weekly	Weekly
Small, mostly read only	Not done	Weekly	Nightly
Large, mostly read only	Not done	Weekly	Weekly

TABLE 10-7. *Sample Integration of Database Backup Methods*

Database and Operating System Backups Integration

As described in this chapter, the DBA's backup activities involve a number of tasks normally assigned to a Systems Management group: monitoring disk usage, maintaining tapes, and so on. Rather than duplicate these efforts, it is best to integrate them. The database backup strategy should be modified so that the System Management personnel's file system backups will take care of all tape handling.

How is this to be done? It is usually accomplished by dedicating disk drives as destination locations for physical file backups. Instead of backing up files to tape drives, the backups will instead be written to other disks on the same server. Those disks should be targeted for backups by the Systems Management personnel's regular file system backups.

Consider the datafile backups shown earlier in the online backups section of this chapter. The datafiles were written directly to tape via a **tar** command, as shown in this example:

```
REM
REM    Back up the RBS tablespace - directly to tape
REM
alter tablespace RBS begin backup;
!tar -rvf /dev/rmt/0hc /db02/oracle/CC1/rbs01.dbf
alter tablespace RBS end backup;
REM
```

Instead of backing up the files to tape, copy them to the target device for database file backups. For this example, "/db10" will be used as the device name. As shown in this listing, the RBS tablespace is put into **begin backup** state. Its files are then copied (here, via the UNIX **cp** command) to a new device, and the tablespace is returned to its normal state.

The commands in the following listing are executed from within Server Manager:

```
REM
REM    Back up the RBS tablespace - to another disk (UNIX)
REM
alter tablespace RBS begin backup;
!cp /db02/oracle/CC1/rbs01.dbf /db10/oracle/CC1/backups
alter tablespace RBS end backup;
REM
```

The VMS version is identical except for the operating system command used. In this case, the **Backup** command is used.

The commands in the following listing are executed from within Server Manager:

```
REM
REM    Back up the RBS tablespace - to another disk (VMS)
REM
alter tablespace RBS begin backup;
!backup/ignore=(no backup, interl)DB01:[ORACLE.CC1]RBS01.DBF
DB10:[ORACLE.CC1.BACKUPS]
alter tablespace RBS end backup;
REM
```

To minimize the amount of space required for this task, you may also wish to have the operating system compress the file on the destination device once it has been copied there, if that option is available in your operating system.

Using disk-to-disk backups also changes the way in which archived redo log files are backed up. The new process is shown in the following listing. The UNIX **mv** command is used to move the files to the backup destination device. This does away with the need for the FILES environment variable that was used in the backup-to-tape method. As shown in this listing, the archiving process is temporarily stopped; when the files have all been moved, it is restarted.

```
#
# Procedure for moving archived redo logs to another device
#
```

```
svrmgrl <<EOFarch2
connect internal
archive log stop;
!mv /db01/oracle/arch/CC1 /db10/oracle/arch/CC1
archive log start;
exit
EOFarch2
#
# end of archived redo log directory move.
```

The control file can also be automatically backed up to the backup destination device. The final distribution of files will resemble that shown in Table 10-8. In this example, the destination device is named "/db10".

The "/db10" device can then be backed up by the Systems Management file system backups. The DBA does not have to run a separate tape backup job.

Recovery Scenarios When Using These Procedures

Unless you test and validate your backup procedures, you cannot be certain that you will be able to recover from *any* type of database failure. Recovery thus begins with testing. Create a sample database and use your chosen procedures. Then test your ability to recover from different types of database failures.

On most servers, the mean time between failure (MTBF) for disks is between three and four years. Failures due to disk errors are the most common hardware failures encountered. The *ORACLE Server*

Disk /DB01-/DB09	Disk /DB10
Datafiles	Copies of datafiles
Online redo logs	
Archived redo log file directory	Old archived redo log files
Control files	Backed up control file

TABLE 10-8.   *File Distribution After Online Backups to a Destination Device*

Administrator's Guide and the *ORACLE Backup and Recovery Handbook* (by Rama Velpuri, published by Oracle Press) include an exhaustive description of the recovery procedures needed for each type of possible failure. As of ORACLE8, ORACLE provides an additional file named RECOVER.PIT with the ORACLE software distribution. The RECOVER.PIT file describes an advanced method for performing point-in-time recovery of tablespaces; in this section, you will see a simpler method for performing the same type of recovery. In general, the simpler method is much easier to manage and potentially slower to execute.

In the following sections, you will see how to apply the integrated database backups to the three most common scenarios: instance failure, disk failure, and user failure. "User failure" occurs when users execute DDL commands (such as **drop table**) that they need to undo.

Instance Failure

Recovery from instance failure should be automatic. The database will need access to all of its control files, online redo log files, and datafiles—in their proper locations. Any uncommitted transactions that existed in the database will be rolled back. Following an instance failure, such as one brought on by a server failure, be sure to check the alert log for the database for any error messages when the database attempts to restart itself.

When the database is started following an instance failure, ORACLE checks the datafiles and the online redo log files and synchronizes all the files to the same point in time. ORACLE will perform this synchronization even if the database is not running in ARCHIVELOG mode.

Media (Disk) Failure

Disk failure, also called *media failure*, occurs when a disk on which an active database file resides becomes unreadable by the database. This may occur due to a disk crash or to a compilation of read errors on the disk. Either way, the files on the disk must be replaced.

The disks on which *online redo log files* reside should always be mirrored (either by using redo log groups or by mirroring files at the operating system level). Since these files are mirrored, they should never be lost due to a media failure.

This leaves three types of files to consider: control files, archived redo log files, and datafiles.

If the lost file is a *control file*, it is easy to recover regardless of the backup method chosen. Every database should have multiple copies of its control file (which the database will keep in sync), all stored on different devices. The default database creation scripts generated by the ORACLE Installer create three control files for each database and locate them on three different drives. To recover from the loss of a control file, shut the database down and copy one of the remaining control files to the proper location.

If all control files are lost, you can use the **create controlfile** command. This command allows you to create a new control file for the database, specifying all of the datafiles, online redo logs, and database parameters that are in the database. If you are unsure of the parameters to use here and you are running ARCHIVELOG backups, there is a helpful option available. It is

```
alter database backup controlfile to trace;
```

When you execute this command, the proper **create controlfile** command will be written to a trace file. You can then edit the trace file created by ORACLE as necessary. Do not use the **create controlfile** command unless *all* of the control files have been lost.

If the lost file is an *archived redo log file*, you cannot recover it. For this reason, it is important that the archived redo log file destination device be mirrored as well. Archived redo log files should be regarded as being as important as the online redo log files.

If the lost file is a *datafile*, it can be recovered from the previous night's hot backup. Follow these steps:

1. Restore the lost file from the backup to its original location.

```
cp /db10/oracle/CC1/data01.dbf /db03/oracle/CC1/data01.dbf
```

You will now have the current control files, the current online redo log files, and current versions of all datafiles except for the one you just recovered. ORACLE will realize the old datafile is not current and will not open the database. You can now recover the data in the old file (making it current) by applying all of the archived redo log files since the old datafile was backed up.

2. Mount the database.

```
ORACLE_SID=cc1; export ORACLE_SID
ORAENV_ASK=NO; export ORAENV_ASK
. oraenv
svrmgrl
SVRMGR> connect internal
SVRMGR> startup mount cc1;
```

3. Recover the database. You will be prompted for the name of each archived redo log file that is needed for recovery.

```
SVRMGR> recover database;
```

When prompted, enter the filenames for the requested archived redo log files. Alternatively, you can use the 'AUTO' option when prompted by the database recovery operation. The 'AUTO' option uses the defined archive log destination directory and filename format to generate default values for archived redo log filenames. If you have moved archived redo log files, you will not be able to use the 'AUTO' option.

4. Open the database.

```
SVRMGR> alter database open;
```

When the datafile is restored from the backup, the database will recognize that it is from an earlier point in time than the rest of the database. To bring it forward in time, it will apply the transactions it finds in the archived redo log files.

The datafiles may be recovered from either the hot or the cold backup (if the database was in ARCHIVELOG mode at the time). If there are complications with the recovery, such as corruption in the files, see the recovery documentation referred to earlier in this chapter for a full list of your options.

Usually, a media recovery is performed using the current control file. If no current control file is available, then you can restore an old control file and use it during the recovery. In that scenario, you would have current online redo log files, at least one old datafile, the rest of the current datafile, and old control files. When you recover the database while using old control files, you need to let ORACLE know that you are using a backup control file; otherwise, there would be no way to apply changes from the archived redo logs that occurred at a time after the timestamp in the control file. In this case, use the **recover database using backup controlfile** command to recover the database.

Recovering Accidentally Dropped or Altered Objects

Occasionally, users will make errors that they will not be able to roll back or undo. Such errors may consist of DDL commands, such as **alter table** and **drop table**, or DML commands, such as **update** and **delete**.

In all such cases, the users' desire is to return to a point in time prior to the database event that they wish to retract. This calls for a point-in-time recovery.

The simplest type of point-in-time recovery uses the most recent export dump file. If the user can go back that far in time, then this may be an acceptable alternative. Use the Import commands shown earlier in this chapter to selectively import the objects and users desired.

However, going back to the last Export may not suffice. The users may need a more up-to-date version of the table—for example, as it existed an hour before the offending command was executed.

To perform a point-in-time recovery, you must be running in ARCHIVELOG mode. Follow these steps:

1. There are two options for the first step for this method of recovery:

   a) Back up the current database (via an offline backup, usually) and replace it with a prior version of itself, then roll that version forward in time to the desired time;

   b) Create a database with the same instance name on a different server, leaving the current database intact, while using the prior version of the primary database as the basis for the second database.

   Regardless of the option chosen, the second step is

2. Roll the temporary database forward in time, using the following command from within Server Manager in place of the **recover database** command used for normal recoveries: The date is in the format "YYYY-MM-DD:HH24:MI:SS". The sample date below is for November 28 (11-28), 1998, at 2:40 p.m. (14:40).

```
SVRMGR> connect internal
SVRMGR> startup mount instance_name;
SVRMGR> recover database until time '1998-11-28:14:40:00';
```

3. While still in Server Manager, open the database using the **resetlogs** option of the **alter database open** command. This forces the database to reset the redo log sequence number information in the control files and the online redo log files. This in turn makes sure that any redo log entry data that followed the **recover database until time** specification will not be applied to the database.

```
SVRMGR> alter database open resetlogs;
```

The database will now be opened and available, and will look as it did at the time specified during the **recover database until time** command. The dropped or altered objects can now be backed up via Export.

4. Export the logical objects that were affected.

```
> exp system/manager file=saved.dmp tables=(owner.tablename)
```

The altered or dropped objects are now recorded in the export dump file. The temporary database created in step 1 can now be dropped.

5. Restore the production database to its former state. Then use the Export dump file created in step 4 to Import the altered/dropped objects back into the production database in their former state.

6. After restoring the production database, prepare it for the Import of the old version of the data. These preparations may involve dropping the objects that were altered by the users. Once this is complete, Import the earlier versions of those objects from the export dump file. The production database is thus returned to its state before step 1, and the damaged objects have been replaced by their earlier incarnations.

```
> imp system/manager file=saved.dmp full=Y commit=Y
buffer=64000
```

The purpose of the integration of the available backup methods is to be able to recover easily from the most common types of failures. Since each backup method has different characteristics, the proper combination of backup methods will vary from database to database. Regardless of the backup methods chosen, they should be integrated with the regular file system backups and *tested*. Properly used, they will be able to support the recovery from any type of database crash.

The steps shown in this section allow you to perform a point-in-time recovery of one part of the database. For example, you could create a temporary database, roll it forward to a point in time, and Export just one table from it. You could then Import that data into your primary database, and the Imported data would reflect data from a different point in time than the rest of the database.

Because you are relying on Export and Import, the performance of this recovery option may not meet your timing requirements. As of ORACLE8, ORACLE provides a new mechanism for performing point-in-time recovery for part of the database. ORACLE now supports point-in-time recovery for tablespaces. The method provided by ORACLE may improve the performance of your recoveries since they do not involve using Import to load the data into the primary database, but rather rely on using the temporary database's datafiles during the recovery. The ORACLE tablespace point-in-time recovery option is limited to tablespaces; you cannot recover only one object out of a tablespace. For full details on this advanced recovery option, see the recover.pit file in the /rdbms/doc subdirectory under your ORACLE software home directory. At this time, the procedure is not documented in the standard ORACLE database backup and recovery documentation.

Parallel Recovery

You can use the Parallel Recovery option to use multiple recovery processes. A single Server Manager session can read the archived redo log files during a media recovery, and can pass the recovery information to multiple recovery processes, which apply the changes to the datafiles concurrently. The recovery processes are automatically started and managed by ORACLE. If you have a very long recovery process and your datafiles are distributed among many disks, using Parallel Recovery may improve your recovery performance.

To use Parallel Recovery, set a value for the RECOVERY_PARALLELISM parameter in your instance's init.ora file. RECOVERY_PARALLELISM specifies the number of concurrent processes that will participate in Parallel Recovery during instance or media recovery. A value of 0 indicates that recovery is performed serially by a single process.

For media recovery, the RECOVERY_PARALLELISM setting is the default degree of parallelism unless overridden by the **parallel** clause of the **recover** command. The RECOVERY_PARALLELISM setting cannot be greater than the PARALLEL_MAX_SERVERS setting.

If you have an I/O-intensive recovery process (which is typical), and you cannot spread the I/O across many disks, then you may not see any performance benefit from Parallel Recovery. In fact, the increased I/O bottleneck may degrade your performance. You should therefore be sure that your disk environment is highly distributed before implementing Parallel Recovery.

Recovery Manager

As of ORACLE8, the ORACLE Enterprise Manager product includes a "Recovery Manager". The Recovery Manager keeps track of your backups and adds new backup capabilities. The Recovery Manager product replaces the Enterprise Backup Utility introduced with later versions of ORACLE7.

Recovery Manager does not shield you from the backup steps described in this chapter and it does not simplify your recovery strategy. In fact, since it adds new features, it may complicate your recovery strategy. The most significant new capability provided via Recovery Manager is the ability to perform incremental physical backups of your datafiles. During a full (called a *level 0*) datafile backup, all of the blocks ever used in the datafile are backed up. During a cumulative (*level 1*) datafile backup, all of the blocks used since the last full datafile backup are backed up. An incremental (*level 2*) datafile backup backs up only those blocks that have changed since the most recent cumulative or full backup.

The ability to perform incremental and cumulative backups of datafiles may greatly improve the performance of your backups. The greatest performance improvements will be realized by very large databases in which only a small subset of a large tablespace changes. Using the traditional backup methods, you would need to back up all of the datafiles in the tablespace. Using Recovery Manager, you only back up the blocks that have changed since the last backup.

Using Recovery Manager, however, does not diminish your backup planning issues. For example, what type of datafile backup will you use? What are the implications for your recovery procedures? What tapes and backup media will you need to have available in order to perform a recovery? You should only use backup procedures that fit your specific database backup performance and capability requirements.

During database recovery using Recovery Manager, you will need to know which files are current, which are restored, and the backup method you plan to use. In its present form, Recovery Manager does not shield you from the commands needed to recover the database. Also, Recovery Manager stores its catalog of information in an ORACLE database—and you need to back up *that* database or else you may lose your entire backup and recovery catalog of information.

You can use the scripts and methods provided in this chapter to successfully back up your database. As the Recovery Manager product matures, you may wish to migrate your backup procedures to use that tool. No matter what tool you use, you should ensure that your backups accurately reflect your recovery requirements. Once you have established your backup procedures and scripts, test them and document your recovery procedures and the performance you experienced. You will then be able to implement the available procedures in a way that makes the most sense for your installation. The result should be a well-protected database and quick, efficient recoveries. And that, in turn, should lead to fewer calls to ORACLE Support at 3 A.M.

CHAPTER
11

Managing Oracle
Financials and Other
Packages and Utilities

hen you install a software package that will be used with your ORACLE database, you will normally customize the front-end portion of the application to reflect your business practices. Just as your business requirements lead to customizations of the front end, the back-end portion of the application will likely need to be modified. To get the most out of the package, you will need to modify the default database structures used by the package. In this chapter, you will see guidelines for managing packages. Specific guidelines are provided for ORACLE Financials, Designer/2000 (ORACLE's CASE tool), and the ORACLE utilities such as ConText and Export.

General Guidelines for Managing Packages

Managing packages requires that you know the technical details of the packages and the business processes being served by the packages. In most cases, the default installation of packaged software does not seamlessly meet your business process requirements. As a result, there may be a problem with the space management or performance of the package when it is installed. As the package use increases, the number of problems associated with the package increase.

If you start with a database environment that does not properly support the package, then the burden of production usage will quickly cause a problem. Production problems may include transactions that fail to complete, queries that run excessively long, or segments that cannot allocate enough space. All of these production problems will cause either a production service outage or a severe performance problem for the package. On the other hand, if you start with a production environment that is flexible and supportive of the package, then you will improve your ability to respond to production crises. The better you understand how the package will be used, the better you will be able to tune the environment prior to production release of the package.

To effectively manage packaged software, you need to provide a database environment that is as stable as possible. In this section, you will see guidelines for customizing database structures, managing transactions, monitoring, and other system-level considerations. Following this section of this chapter, you will see application-specific guidelines for ORACLE Financials, Designer/2000, ConText, and other packages.

Customizing Database Structures

If you are installing third-party software that was not written by ORACLE Corporation, you should not assume that the software will take proper advantage of ORACLE-specific features such as sequences, stored procedures, triggers, and the ORACLE optimizer. You should also question the package's data distribution, space allocation assumptions, and indexing schemes. If the package was developed by ORACLE Corporation (such as ORACLE Financials or Designer/2000), then you should focus your database structure customization efforts on supporting the business processes unique to your business. For example, if your business performs many iterations of its budgeting process, you should size the ORACLE Financials tables that store budgeting information differently than if your business performs few budgeting iterations.

Database structures that should be customized include tablespaces, indexes, and rollback segments, as described in the following sections.

Tablespaces

In general, most packages developed by companies other than ORACLE Corporation will use as few tablespaces as possible. For example, a package may expect the following tablespaces to be created within your database (in addition to SYSTEM, TEMP, and ROLLBACK):

APP_TABLES	For all application tables
APP_INDEXES	For all application indexes

When the package is installed, all of its tables are created within the APP_TABLES tablespace, and all of its indexes are created within the APP_INDEXES tablespace (although some packages do not, by default, store their tables and indexes in different tablespaces). Although this may make it simpler to manage tables and indexes, this design fails to take into account the different kinds of tables involved in an application. For example, some of their tables may be small and static, while others are large and highly volatile.

In Chapter 3, you saw recommendations for extensions beyond the typical OFA (Optimal Flexible Architecture) tablespace architecture. The DATA_2 tablespace was identified for low-usage data segments, and INDEXES_2 for those tables' indexes. Consider a modified set of application tablespaces:

APPS_TABLES	For high-use application tables
APPS_STATIC_TABLES	For static application tables
APPS_INDEXES	For high-use application indexes
APPS_STATIC_INDEXES	For static application indexes

By removing the static tables and indexes from the main application tablespaces, you simplify the management of the space within all tablespaces. Under the revised tablespace organization, the APPS_STATIC_TABLES and APPS_STATIC_INDEXES tablespaces should require very little direct management, allowing you to focus your management and tuning efforts on the main data tablespaces. Separating the tables across tablespaces in this manner also separates the active and static tables into separate datafiles, simplifying the management of I/O distribution.

You may wish to further divide the highly used application tables. For example, if your package uses many "interim" tables that are used during data interface processing, you may separate those tables from the rest of the high-use application tables. You can also add tablespaces to support the specific temporary segment requirements and transaction sizes for the package.

NOTE
If you modify the tablespace assignments of the package's tables and indexes, you may need to modify scripts provided by the vendor for subsequent upgrades, since the vendor's scripts may assume that the objects are in their original tablespaces. Also, if the owning schema for the application has APPS_TABLES as its default tablespace, then any upgrade

> *script that performs a* **create table** *or* **create index** *command will create the objects in the APPS_TABLES tablespace unless the command explicitly names a tablespace. This may cause objects you have moved out of APPS_TABLES to be moved back into APPS_TABLES during the upgrade process.*

Indexes

You cannot conceive all of the questions your users may ask of the database; a developer who does not work for your company likely cannot conceive of your users' demands either. As a result, any package in which users can perform ad hoc queries will likely encounter performance problems for a small set of queries. Although those queries may be few in number, they can consume enough of the available system resources to negatively impact every other user of the database.

The most common cause of such resource-intensive queries is a lack of appropriate indexes. Until you understand how your users, in carrying out their business processes, will use the package, you cannot fully understand the data access paths required. As such, you cannot fully identify all of the indexes the users require. If you understand the business processes well, you may identify many of the key indexes; but since you are using package software, you may not be able to see all of the SQL that the package is executing, and thus may be unable to properly index the tables until the problem SQL is identified—via user complaints.

Indexes may become fragmented over time. As records are deleted from a table, the matching entries are deleted from the table's indexes. The space released within the table may be reused, but the space released within the index may not be reused. Thus, an indexed table from which rows are frequently deleted should have its indexes periodically rebuilt in order to avoid space fragmentation within the index. The most common occurrence of this problem is found in tables used temporarily during loading processes. For example, if the package **insert**s received records into an interim table, processes the records, and then **delete**s the records from the interim table, then the table's indexes will continue to grow over time, even though there are no rows in the table. To avoid this problem, you should periodically **truncate** the table when it is empty; the **truncate** command cannot be rolled back, and it deletes all rows from the table. The **truncate** command also eliminates the index fragmentation and reduces the table to a single extent (by default; you can use the **reuse storage** option of the **truncate** command to retain the previously allocated extents).

Rollback Segments

Most packages contain an online user component—for data entry or ad hoc reporting—and a batch processing component—for large data processing operations. The online users need enough rollback segments to support the number of concurrent transactions they generate. The batch processes require rollback segments large enough to support the largest batch transaction. In Chapter 7, you saw how to determine the number of rollback segments needed, and their size. If one of the transactions in the package is significantly larger than any other transaction in the package, then you should create a rollback segment that is specifically designed to support this transaction. The special rollback segment should be stored in its own tablespace (see Chapter 3). Before starting the transaction, issue the **set transaction use rollback segment** command to force the transaction to use that rollback segment. You will need to repeat that command after every **commit** within the transaction.

If you cannot alter the transaction code to include the **set transaction use rollback segment** command, then you should schedule the transaction to occur at a specific time when no online users will be active within the database. Immediately prior to the start of the transaction, take the other rollback segments in the database offline, leaving only the SYSTEM rollback segment and the special rollback segment online. Use the **alter rollback segment** *segment_name* **offline** command to take the rollback segments offline. When the transaction starts, it will be forced to use the special rollback segment. When the transaction completes, bring the rest of the rollback segments back online.

Temporary Segments

Batch transactions may require large temporary segments for their processing. For example, large data loads using the SQL*Loader Direct Path option require temporary segments to hold the data from the table's indexes during the data load. If you make extensive use of the Parallel Query Option (PQO) during index creations, then you may need to support a large number of temporary segments since each parallel query server process may obtain a temporary segment. If you use many concurrent parallel query server processes during the batch processing, your temporary segment space requirements will most likely exceed the resources normally available for users of the package.

Depending on the nature of the application, you may want to segregate users—or application schema owners—into different sets of temporary tablespaces. You could, for example, create four separate temporary tablespaces and split your online user community into four sets. If the users' temporary tablespace requirements are separated in this manner, users will have less impact on each other during processes that require temporary segments. If a single transaction or query requires a much larger temporary segment than any other transaction or query in the package, then you should give the users of that transaction or query a default temporary tablespace that is specifically designed to support the transaction.

Table and Index Sizes

For small, stagnant tables, the default table and index sizes that come with the package are usually accurate—particularly if the package was developed by ORACLE Corporation. You should still validate the default storage parameters against your space estimates (see Chapter 5). For large or very active tables, you should assume that the default storage parameters for the tables are incorrect. There is no way for the application developers to know exactly how you will use the package, so you will need to customize the table and index sizes to support your anticipated data volumes.

Do not rely on periodic table defragmentation via Export/Import to do all of the resizing work that needs to be done. For example, consider a table that was not properly sized when the package was first made available to users. The table has an **initial** extent size of 100K, with a **next** extent size of 100K and a **pctincrease** value of 0. Each extent of the table will be 100K in size. Within the first month of usage, the table reaches ten extents—and it is clear that as more users are added to the system, the rate of space increases in the table will increase. If you use Export/Import to compress the table's extents to a single extent, then the new storage parameters will be **initial** 1MB, **next** 100K. Thus, although the Export/Import process may give you a better size for your **initial** extent, it will do nothing to resolve the problems with your **next** extent size. You will need to manually **alter** the table to reflect a more appropriate **next** extent size.

Managing the Shared SQL Area

NOTE
*In this section only, the term "package" refers
to stored PL/SQL objects created via the* **create
package** *command.*

PL/SQL objects, when used, are stored in the library cache of the shared
SQL area within the SGA (System Global Area). If a package has already
been loaded into memory by a user, then other users will experience
improved performance when executing that package. Keeping a package
"pinned" in memory decreases the response time for the user during
procedure executions.

To improve the ability to keep large PL/SQL objects pinned in the
library cache, you should load them into the SGA as soon as the database is
opened. Pinning packages immediately after startup increases the
likelihood that a contiguous section of memory will be available to store
the package. You can use the DBMS_SHARED_POOL package to pin
PL/SQL objects in the SGA. To use DBMS_SHARED_POOL, you first need
to reference the objects that you want to pin in memory. To load a package
in memory, you can reference a dummy procedure defined in the package
or you can recompile the package.

Once the object has been referenced, you can execute the
DBMS_SHARED_POOL.KEEP procedure to pin the object. The KEEP
procedure of DBMS_SHARED_POOL, as shown in the following listing,
takes as its input parameters the name of the object and the type of object
('P' for packages is the default).

```
alter procedure APPOWNER.ADD_CLIENT compile;
execute DBMS_SHARED_POOL.KEEP('APPOWNER.ADD_CLIENT','P');
```

The example shown in the preceding listing illustrates the two-step
process involved in pinning packages in memory: the package is first
referenced (via the compilation step) and is then marked for keeping.
Pinning your most-used packages in memory immediately after startup
will improve your chances of acquiring contiguous space for them within
the SGA.

Each database will have two sets of packages to pin: the core set used
by each database and the set of packages specific to a particular

application. The core set of packages to pin usually includes the SYS-owned packages STANDARD, DBMS_SQL, DBMS_UTILITY, and DIUTIL. To determine which packages should be pinned for your instance, query DBA_OBJECT_SIZE. You should pin the largest packages first. To determine packages to pin and the order in which to pin them, use the script shown in the following listing. The script uses the DBA_OBJECT_SIZE view to list the order in which the objects will be pinned.

```
select Owner,
       Name,
       Type,
  Source_Size+Code_Size+Parsed_Size+Error_Size   Total_Bytes
   from DBA_OBJECT_SIZE
  where Type in ('PACKAGE BODY','PROCEDURE')
  order by 4 desc;
```

Security and Data Access Control

In addition to the database structures you need to alter, you should examine the way in which the package implements security. The assumptions that the developers of the package made regarding security may not be valid in your environment. Remember, the developers did not have access to your database and your company's security policies when developing the package. As a result, you may find that the application requires that all users have DBA privilege, or that users share accounts, or that user passwords can be easily seen during regular use of the package. You should work with the package vendor to determine whether the package can be implemented along the guidelines specified in your corporate security guidelines.

Within the database, you should determine if the application makes extensive use of roles, and which roles must be the default roles for the user. If there are many roles within the package, or if the database supports multiple applications, then you may reach the limit on the number of roles permitted per user (set via the MAX_ENABLED_ROLES init.ora parameter). Try to reduce the number of system privileges (such as ALTER ANY TABLE) granted to the roles used by the package. Often, packages will by default use a higher level of access than required—such as requiring DBA role access when the users just need the ALTER USER privilege so they can change their passwords. See Chapter 9 for details on user configuration commands.

Transaction Management

Transaction management for a package requires understanding the batch and online portions of the application, and separating their processing to the greatest extent possible. Most of the problems with transactions in an application arise from the concurrent scheduling of long-running batch processes and online transactions. See Chapter 7 for information on the implications of different types of transactions on your rollback segments. As noted earlier in this chapter, you will need to have enough rollback segments to support the online users and special rollback segments to handle the extraordinary requirements of large batch transactions.

In addition to properly sizing your rollback segments, you should determine how the package implements locking. If the package has been ported from another RDBMS to ORACLE, then the package may not take full advantage of the granularity of locking available in ORACLE. You need to discover *when* the records are locked—are they locked **for update** when a user first queries them? If so, then another user attempting to query the same set of records **for update** will be forced to wait for the first user to release the locks for their query to complete. You should be aware of how the package resolves data concurrency issues, particularly if it is a client-server application. For example, if two users separately query and **update** the same row, which **update** is accepted? Different packages answer this question differently, and you need to be aware of the implementation in your package. Once you know the locking scheme used, you can help the application team to implement the package in a manner that makes the best use of the available technology and resources.

File Locations

In your development and test environment, you should monitor the package to determine which files are the most-used files (see Chapter 4). In the production environment, you should move the most-used files so they do not contend with each other for I/O resources on the server. You should be aware of the disk layout on the server so you can distribute the database across disks and across disk controllers. Postproduction, you should monitor the package's usage to determine if the actual usage mirrors the anticipated usage, and alter your file locations accordingly. See Chapter 4 for details on planning physical I/O distribution.

Monitoring

Monitoring the package involves implementing the basic environment monitoring described in Chapter 6, along with any special monitoring required for the package. For example, the package's batch transactions may vary wildly in size, forcing you to closely monitor their scheduling and resource usage. You should automate the monitoring process as much as possible, reducing the amount of time you need to spend actively watching the database activity. The best method for accomplishing this goal is to isolate the nonstandard activities (such as batch loads or a sudden increase in the number of users). During the period of nonstandard activity, monitor the database closely. The rest of the time, the database activity should fall within the normal control boundaries. If the database exceeds the normal control boundaries—for example, if the overall hit ratio for the day is less than the threshold value—then you should be notified, and you should evaluate the causes for the problem.

Versioning Considerations

How will you develop a new version of the package while supporting the current version of the package? Does a second copy of the package require a second instance, or can two copies of the package coexist in the same instance? You need to be able to answer these questions in order to properly plan the support environment required for the implementation of new versions of the package.

For example, suppose a package assumes that its objects will be accessed via public synonyms. Thus, when a user queries EMPLOYEE, the user is really accessing the object defined by the public synonym EMPLOYEE. In that environment, you can create a second set of application tables within the same instance! For example, the main package object owner—call it APP_SYS—will own the first set of tables. The public synonyms will all point to the APP_SYS objects. The second set of tables can be created under a second user—call it APP_SYS_TWO. Users who should be accessing the second set of tables should have private synonyms pointing to the APP_SYS_TWO tables. The users' private synonyms will override the public synonyms when object names are resolved by the database.

If a package requires its tables to be stored under specific usernames, then you may not be able to create a copy of the package within the same database. Instead, you will need to create a separate instance for the second copy of the package. Thus, if you have a Development database, a Test database, and a Production database, then when you upgrade to a new version of the package, you may need a second Development database, a second Test database, and a second Production database. You may not be able to use your first Development database during the upgrade because you will need to have that database available to support the development of modifications for the current Production database. Once you know how the package handles such versioning considerations, you can plan for the resources you'll need to support the required instances.

The DBA's Role

If you are implementing a custom application, the DBA should be involved at each step of the development process (see Chapter 5). The DBA should serve as a technical consultant to the development team, assisting in the planning, testing, and implementation of the application.

If you purchase a package to implement, the DBA's role expands. Instead of just dealing directly with the development team, the DBA must now also deal directly with the technical support staff of the vendor that developed the package. Since the package was not developed by your developers, you may need direct contact with the package vendor in order to understand how the application performs locking, or how you can manage its batch transactions. You will also need to determine which versions of the RDBMS are supported by the package, and how this affects your database software upgrade path for the rest of your applications.

As with all database application implementations, the DBA must work with the application team to develop a plan for creating and monitoring the database. Any special considerations—such as large batch transactions or tables known to be highly used by the package—should be addressed prior to the creation of the database for use by the package. It is simple to change the tablespace designation of a table that has not yet been created; once the table has been created within the database, there are more steps involved in managing it (not the least of which is arranging for a service interruption in your production environment so you can move the table).

In the following sections, you will see specific guidelines for managing ORACLE Financials, Designer/2000, ConText, and other packages and utilities. The general guidelines outlined in the previous sections apply to all packages.

Specific Guidelines for Managing ORACLE Financials

ORACLE's accounting package, ORACLE Financials, is an application developed and sold by ORACLE to manage corporate accounting. It includes modules for the General Ledger (GL), Accounts Payable (AP), Purchase Orders (PO), Fixed Assets (FA), and other major financial categories. It is created using a wide variety of ORACLE tools. This chapter will focus on issues related to the management of Oracle Financials Release 10, although its implementation recommendations will be applicable to earlier versions as well.

From the DBA's perspective, ORACLE Financials is a fairly complex application, even in those installations that do not use all of the modules. The following sections describe the key features of the database that you should be aware of, and the specific package management guidelines for ORACLE Financials.

Database Structures

Because ORACLE Financials relies so heavily on stored objects such as packages and triggers, the size of your SYSTEM tablespace will need to be increased to at least 150MB in order to store the code. The space required by the code is independent of the rest of the database sizing; you will need that space even if there are no records in the ORACLE Financials tables. ORACLE Financials databases commonly have SYSTEM tablespaces up to 300MB in size.

Each module of ORACLE Financials corresponds to an ORACLE account. That account, such as "GL" for the General Ledger module, owns all of the tables and indexes for that module. Another account, "FND," owns the tables that the application uses to generate the front-end forms. The FND tables are queried by the applications during production usage of the forms.

Since each module's objects are created under its own account, create two tablespaces for each account: one for its tables (such as "GL_TABLES") and one for its indexes (such as "GL_INDEXES"). Separating the tables and indexes into different tablespaces may be done by editing the application creation scripts. You may further separate the application tables by moving the most-used tables to separate tablespaces. For example, if you actively use the GL journal entry tables, the GL_JE_LINES table may be moved to a separate tablespace to minimize its impact on other GL tables.

Even if you are not using all of the modules of Financials, each module's tables must be installed. Many of the views in ORACLE Financials will query tables from multiple modules—and thus from multiple owners. Failing to install the unused modules will therefore cause the views to be unusable.

These views may present problems during database rebuilds, particularly if developers create their own views. Since the order in which the structures are imported may cause the view to be imported before its underlying tables are, the view may fail to be created via the Import. In order to resolve this problem, you can run the Import twice: first with only the structures being imported (using the "rows=N" flag), then a second run to bring in the data (using the "rows=Y" and "ignore=Y" flags). The second Import will create any views that experienced errors during the first Import. The two Import commands are

```
imp system/manager file=export.dmp rows=N
imp system/manager file=export.dmp full=y buffer=64000
   commit=Y ignore=Y
```

The first command imports all of the database structures, but none of the rows ("rows=N"). The second Import brings in the structures and the data, with a commit point set for every 64,000 bytes of data imported. The "ignore=Y" flag allows the second Import to succeed even though the objects already exist. The use of Import is described in greater detail in Chapter 10.

Sizing Tables and Indexes

Sizing for the Financials application objects is the responsibility of the Financials systems administrator. The database size required is dependent on a number of factors specific to the implementation of the application.

The calculations needed to determine the proper size are in the Oracle Financials Installation Guide.

Managing Rollback Segments

ORACLE Financials contains both online and batch modules. You should monitor the online usage to determine the number of rollback segments required; see Chapter 7 for details. For the batch modules, you should create rollback segments that are designed to support the specific transactions being run. Use the methods described earlier in this chapter to force the package to use the special rollback segments during large batch transactions.

Managing Temporary Segments

The GL user in the ORACLE Financials package has processing space requirements that exceed those of all the rest of the database users combined. It needs to have a large temporary tablespace available for its processing. Since its requirements are so unique, isolate its temporary tablespace from the rest of the users by creating a tablespace that is used only for GL's temporary segments. Start with a tablespace that is between 50MB and 100MB in size. Create it so that it has 20 to 50 divisions (as shown in the following listing) so that you can measure the actual usage in the tablespace; then assign the GL user to this tablespace using the commands shown in the following listing:

```
create tablespace TEMP_GL
datafile '/db01/oracle/FIN/temp_gl.dbf' size 100m
default storage
(initial 5m next 5m pctincrease 0);

alter user GL temporary tablespace TEMP_GL;
```

In the preceding listing, the tablespace is created with a size of 100MB. Its default storage parameters will use that space in 5MB extents. Therefore, as a large GL transaction is running, you can determine how large a temporary segment is created by querying DBA_SEGMENTS, as shown in the following listing:

```
select
    Extents,  /*how many extents does the segment have?*/
```

```
   Bytes,     /*how large is the temp segment, in bytes? */
   Blocks     /*how large is it, in Oracle blocks? */
from DBA_SEGMENTS
where Segment_Type = 'TEMPORARY'
  and Tablespace_Name = 'TEMP_GL';
```

The query in the preceding listing will provide information about each of the GL user's temporary segments currently in use in the database. The query output will display the number of extents and total size of each such segment.

Pinning Packages

To facilitate the pinning of packages in the shared SQL area, ORACLE Financials provides a script that pins the most commonly used packages. The script, named ADXCKPIN.sql, is usually stored in the /sql subdirectory under the directory identified by the $AD_TOP environment variable. You can edit the script to remove packages from the pinning list if you know they will not be commonly used in your implementation. The script should be run immediately following each database startup.

Managing Interim Tables

ORACLE Financials maintains a set of "interim" tables that are used to process data received via interfaces. For example, budget loads use the GL_BUDGET_INTERIM table. Because these tables are only used for transitional data—data that is loaded and then unloaded—the tables and their indexes expand. As noted in the "Indexes" section earlier in this chapter, indexes may not reuse space freed by deleted entries. Therefore, even if the interim tables remain constant in size, their indexes may increase in size.

To eliminate problems with the space consumption by the interim tables, you should be sure to periodically **truncate** the tables after the records have been removed from them. The **truncate** command will delete any remaining records from the table (and this operation *cannot* be rolled back). The **truncate** command will also truncate the table's indexes, freeing unused space within the index. By default, the **truncate** command will also reduce the table to a single extent.

You should schedule periodic **truncate**s for all of your interim tables. As your ORACLE Financials implementation grows in size and complexity, the number of interfaces to the package will increase, so the number of uses of the interim tables will increase. To avoid persistent space usage problems caused by these tables, you must actively manage them.

Database Access

Access to the Financials application is controlled within the application. Users log into the application as themselves, are validated, and are then logged into the modules they are using as the module owners. This means that all users of GL get logged in as GL.

The use of common database accounts removes the administration of user accounts from the DBA's tasks. The only accounts in a production Financials database will be those that belong to the module owners. The Financials system administrator will be responsible for all user authorizations. From an account management perspective, the DBA will only be involved in setting up the module owner accounts (such as GL and PO) and any accounts created for access to the Financials database from outside databases, typically created to allow query-only access to restricted views of Financials data.

The DBA must also grant **select** access on the V$SESSION and V$PROCESS dynamic performance tables to all Financials users, via the commands shown in the following listing. You should grant direct **select** access on V$PROCESS and V$SESSION to the APPLSYS user using the **with grant option** clause.

```
svrmgrl
SVRMGR> connect internal;
SVRMGR> grant select on V$PROCESS to applsys with grant option;
SVRMGR> grant select on V$SESSION to applsys with grant option;
SVRMGR> grant select on V$PROCESS to public;
SVRMGR> grant select on V$SESSION to public;
```

The APPLSYS user needs explicit grants to the V$PROCESS and V$SESSION views because that user creates views based on those system views. The APPLSYS-owned views are named FND_V$PROCESS and FND_V$SESSION. If you do not grant the privileges shown in the preceding listing, the APPLSYS views cannot be created.

These privileges may cause problems during database re-creations. After you create a new database, create the APPLSYS user prior to importing data from a Financials database. Grant the V$PROCESS and V$SESSION privileges to APPLSYS prior to performing an Import. If you do not, then APPLSYS will not be able to create its views that are based on those system views. The privileges on V$PROCESS and V$SESSION are not maintained during an Export/Import process.

Concurrent Managers

ORACLE Financials features an internal job queue manager called the concurrent manager. A single Financials database can run several concurrent managers (but usually fewer than five). These are set up by the Financials SysAdmin and run as background processes, waking up at specified intervals to check for jobs waiting to be executed.

Jobs in the concurrent manager queue are stored in a table called FND_CONCURRENT_REQUESTS, owned by the FND account. They will have one of the following status values:

Status	Description
Q	The job is waiting in the queue.
R	The job is running.
C	The job has completed.

Once a request has been run and completed, its record remains in the FND_CONCURRENT_REQUESTS table. These old records provide an audit trail of request submissions, but they do so at the expense of database space. Records of completed jobs should be archived to flat files on a regularly scheduled basis and then **delete**d from the table. The Financials systems administrator should be responsible for doing this, since the concurrent manager should be shut down during this process. If the FND_CONCURRENT_REQUESTS table begins extending, the DBA should advise the Financials systems administrator to decrease the time between these data archiving operations.

The regular deletion of records can cause fragmentation in indexes, as described earlier in this chapter. Therefore, you should periodically **truncate** the FND_CONCURRENT_REQUESTS table after archiving its records, or rebuild its indexes (see **alter index** in Appendix C).

The Financials systems administrator can customize the concurrent managers. Concurrent managers can be restricted to run jobs of a particular type or those run by a specific user. Concurrent managers may also be restricted based on the program run. These restrictions allow long-running reports to be executed at off-peak hours. Separating jobs in this manner will greatly reduce the amount of rollback segment space needed by minimizing the inactive, in-use rollback segment data (see Chapter 7).

Although it is possible to configure the concurrent managers so that their processes run at a low operating system priority, this is not an optimal choice. The better solution is to run all jobs at the same priority *at the appropriate times.* The result? Better performance for everyone. The DBA should work with the Financials systems administrator to evaluate system usage cycles and determine how jobs can be more effectively scheduled.

The Demo Database

ORACLE delivers a full copy of a Demo database along with Financials. This is actually an Export dump file, which is intended to be imported into a single user account. This account should point to its own tablespace. It will own all 1,000+ tables that are part of Financials, as well as the associated views and indexes. Since the demo database may be modified during training or demos, DBAs should be prepared to reimport this data periodically.

Versioning

Financials is a modifiable package, so there must be a Development area established. Since the data is critical to corporate finances, a Test area is normally used as well. For further information on the development process, see Chapter 5. You may need six instances—one each for Development, Test, and Production, plus a second set of instances for development, testing, and rollout of a new version of Financials.

Since ORACLE Financials uses ORACLE tools for its data entry and reporting capabilities, developers may create new reports and add them to the application. Because of this capability, the development of add-ons to Financials must be managed via a methodology based on the guidelines in Chapter 5.

Since the tools used to access Financials may actively use the database during execution, all development must take place outside of the Production instance. Since a separate Development database will be needed, the Demo database is unnecessary in the Production instance. The Demo database should be loaded into the Test database for system testing or training purposes.

File Locations

The optimal file locations for the files used by the Financials database depend on your specific implementation of the application. However, there are several generic guidelines that can be used to establish a baseline configuration. The guidelines in Chapter 4, including estimating the relative I/O weight for each file in the database, can then be used to further refine the file placements.

When designing the file layout on the available server hardware, you should follow these guidelines:

- ORACLE software and the application software for Financials should be stored on separate disks to avoid concurrent I/O contention.

- Online redo logs should be fairly large in size—5 to 10MB each. There should be at least six of them for each Financials instance. Since they will typically experience heavy usage, they should be stored on a disk with little other activity.

- The "FND" account should have two tablespaces: one for its tables and one for its indexes. These tables and indexes will store the data used by the applications. These tablespaces will generally have a high I/O weight (see Chapter 4), and they should be stored on separate devices to minimize concurrent I/O contention.

- Each module (such as General Ledger) will need a pair of tablespaces: one for its tables and one for its indexes. These tablespaces should be created on different devices to help minimize concurrent I/O contention. The main modules installed at your site (such as GL, FA, and AP) should be separated across disks as well. That is, you should not store the GL tables on the same disk as the AP tables since entries into one module's tables may impact another module's tables, triggering concurrent I/O contention.

- There should be at least two rollback segment tablespaces. Create one for the production data entry usage, and another (RBS_2) to be used during large data loads and month-end closings. They may be stored on the same device, since they are rarely used at the same time.

■ A small TOOLS tablespace will be needed to support the ORACLE tools that are installed with Financials. It typically experiences very little I/O relative to the rest of the database files.

■ As previously noted, two temporary tablespaces are needed: TEMP for all users but GL and TEMP_GL for the GL account's exclusive use. They may be stored on the same device. Of the two, TEMP_GL will experience far greater I/O. Its relative weight within the database is dependent on the way in which the application is being used. If many periods are open at once, then the processing requirements for postings will increase greatly, which will in turn increase the size of the temporary tables created by GL.

■ In the Development and Test databases, a DEMO tablespace will be needed to hold the objects created for the Demo account. This tablespace should be relatively dormant outside of training times.

init.ora Parameters

There are several database initialization parameters that can be set (via the init.ora initialization parameter file) to improve the performance of ORACLE Financials. The major parameters to set are listed in the following sections.

SGA Size

The System Global Area (SGA) is the memory area that is available to the instance. Data that is read from the database is held in the SGA for quick retrieval by other users. Structural information about the database and the data returned by transactions is stored in the SGA. An additional area, called the Shared SQL Area, stores the parsed version of statements run against the database.

For Financials, make the SGA as large as possible given the memory available on your server. The Oracle Financials Installation Guide gives calculations for the minimum SGA size that should be used. In general, expect the data buffer cache in the Financials Production SGA to take at least 80MB in order to function effectively. The shared SQL area should also be at least 80MB in size in order to support the pinning of packages. The size of the shared SQL area is set, in bytes, by the SHARED_POOL_SIZE init.ora parameter. The size of the data block buffer cache is set, in database blocks, by the DB_BLOCK_BUFFERS init.ora parameter.

Open Cursors

The init.ora "open_cursors" parameter limits the number of open cursors (context areas) that can be simultaneously held by each user process. The maximum value for the parameter is operating system dependent. Set this parameter to its maximum value; although this may be documented as 255, you can exceed this value on most operating systems.

Optimizer Changes

Prior to the release of ORACLE7, the internal ORACLE optimizer was modified to change the manner in which nested subqueries were handled by the optimizer. A side effect of this change was to slow down the performance of Financials reports that had been created with the previous optimizer functionality in mind.

To offset this change, a special init.ora parameter must be used. Its first character is an underscore (_), and its entry is shown in the following listing:

```
_optimizer_undo_changes    = TRUE
```

When this parameter is detected at startup, the changes made to the handling of subqueries will be ignored by the optimizer during query processing.

Block Size

To maximize performance within Financials, increase the ORACLE block size used. Rather than using a 2,048-byte block size, increase it to 4,096 or 8,192. Increasing the database block size will reduce the percentage of each block that is devoted to overhead. As a result, more data will be read with each I/O. This should in turn result in fewer I/Os being necessary to resolve a query, thus improving performance. The init.ora entry for this parameter is

```
db_block_size    = 4096
```

You cannot change the block size of a database after it has been created. You can only change the database block size by completely re-creating the database and all of its datafiles (along with an Export/Import of the current data).

Most Active Tables and Indexes

The tables and indexes that are most likely to extend depend on the specific modules that have been installed and the manner in which they are being used. In general, several tables and their indexes experience growth spurts that cause them to become fragmented quickly. Since Financials is heavily indexed, expect the indexes to encounter problems first. The tables to monitor are listed in Table 11-1. Their indexes will be the ones most likely to extend.

The actual tables that will experience extension problems in your Financials database will vary. Creating and running a Command Center monitoring database (see Chapter 6) will greatly simplify the process of identifying problem areas. Note that most of the FND tables, since they define the application's forms interface, are fairly static and large in size. Other tables, such as GL.GL_CODE_COMBINATIONS, may experience great expansion during initial database load and setup, then become very static.

Owner	Table Name
AR	AR_CUSTOMER_PROFILES
AR	AR_PAYMENT_SCHEDULES
AP	AP_INVOICES
AP	AP_PAYMENT_SCHEDULES
GL	GL_BALANCES
GL	GL_BUDGET_INTERIM
GL	GL_JE_HEADERS
GL	GL_JE_LINES
GL	GL_SUMMARY_INTERIM
PO	PO_VENDOR_SITES
PO	PO_VENDORS

TABLE 11-1.   *Tables Likely to Extend in Oracle Financials Databases*

The Optimizer

ORACLE Financials relies on the rule-based optimizer to resolve the query execution paths to be used. You should not analyze the ORACLE Financials tables.

In order to enhance the performance of ORACLE Financials, a custom cost-based optimizer was developed to serve the application. This optimizer populates the GL.GL_SEGMENT_RATIOS table, which is then used to determine which index should be used for each of the Financial Statement Generator (FSG) reports. When an FSG report is run, the optimizer suppresses all but the most selective index for that report.

Since the FSG reports rely on the GL.GL_SEGMENT_RATIOS table, they will only choose the proper index if the GL.GL_SEGMENT_RATIOS table is up to date. The optimizer should be run to repopulate this table when the account structure of the general ledger changes, when the summary template structure changes, and periodically during regular usage (for example, following month-end closings). To run the GL optimizer, the Financials systems administrator chooses the Optimizer option from the Financials Navigate|Setup|System menu. Although the DBA is not directly involved in this task, the GL optimizer has a direct effect on performance and appropriate scheduling and should thus be coordinated between the DBA and the Financials systems administrator.

Specific Guidelines for Managing Designer/2000

ORACLE's Designer/2000 CASE tool is the successor to its earlier Oracle*CASE product. Designer/2000 is a client-server application, with the data repository stored on the server and the application's presentation on the client (usually a Windows-based PC). The client software usually requires over 300MB for its installation.

On the server, you should set up the database and applications by following the guidelines in Chapter 4. In the following sections, you will see guidelines for setup and administration of the Designer/2000 package. Much of the administration of Designer/2000 database structures can be performed via the Repository Administration Utility provided with Designer/2000.

Database Structures

The Designer/2000 repository should be stored in an isolated instance, apart from any active application development databases. You should create several instances of the Designer/2000 repository—one for Development, one for Test, and one for Production. When it is time to implement a new version of the tool, you may need a second set of instances if you will be providing development support to the current production version while testing the new version.

Because Designer/2000 makes extensive use of stored procedures and packages, the SYSTEM tablespace will need to be large enough to hold the stored code. You should start with a SYSTEM tablespace that is between 100MB and 150MB in size, and monitor its freespace availability.

Within the application, you can use the Repository Management screen of the Repository Administration Utility to manipulate the database objects (such as indexes, views, triggers, and packages) in an ad hoc fashion. This screen can simplify the process of dropping and re-creating your indexes following a large deletion of data. You can use the "Pre-Check" option on this screen to check the SQL that is generated prior to executing it. Since the SQL commands that are executed (such as **create view** and **create trigger**) require DDL (Data Dictionary Language) locks, these commands should only be executed when no other users are using the database.

Sizing Tables and Indexes

The majority of the records in the Designer/2000 repository are stored in two tables: SDD_ELEMENTS and SDD_STRUCTURE_ELEMENTS. You should carefully size these tables and their indexes; the required size is heavily influenced by your *model versioning* strategy and the amount of *model sharing* implemented. The frequency of extracts, described in the next section, also influences the space requirements of the repository.

Model versioning allows developers to maintain different versions of the same model within the Designer/2000 repository. Since the application design's data is stored in the database, this means that two versions of the same application will double that application's storage requirements in the repository. You must work with the Designer/2000 users to make sure a consistent versioning strategy is in place for all application teams. If creating multiple versions of a model is to be the exception to the rule, then the frequency of such exceptions must still be estimated. Those estimates should then be used to calculate the amount of additional space that the repository is likely to need.

Model sharing involves sharing objects between separate models within the repository. For example, if a model contains a CUSTOMER entity, a second model can share the first model's CUSTOMER entity. The ability to share common objects in your repository facilitates the development of enterprise-wide entities and objects, and thus an enterprise model encompassing all of your applications.

When you share an object belonging to a different model and then create a new version of your model, the repository will make copies of *all* models that own objects that have been shared into your model. If you shared the CUSTOMER entity from another model and then created a new version of your model, then the repository would make a new version of your model *and* of the model containing the CUSTOMER entity. Thus, your strategies for model versioning and model sharing have a great impact on the amount of space required within your repository. If you have five models and they each share objects from each other, then creating a new version of one model would require the creation of five new models (for the one that you're copying plus the four that are shared). Although you have only created a new version of one model, you have doubled the space usage within the repository!

Managing Rollback Segments

The Designer/2000 application has an online component and a batch component. The online component is used by the developers during application design and development. The batch component is used during large data manipulation transactions (such as extracts or model versioning) performed by the repository administrator.

You should design your rollback segments to support the online users. Typically, the amount of online activity in a repository will be less than that in a comparable online application since there is not usually a consistent volume of transactions to be entered into the repository.

To support large transactions such as model versioning and extracts, you will need to have at least one large rollback segment that is dedicated to these activities. Extracts do not, as their name might suggest, write data from the repository into a flat file external to the database. Rather, they

create tables that are copies of the repository tables via commands like
those shown in the following listing:

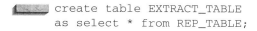
```
create table EXTRACT_TABLE
as select * from REP_TABLE;
```

The command shown in the preceding listing combines a **create table**
command with a single implicit **insert** command. The **insert** command
creates a single transaction that holds all of the data from the REP_TABLE
table for inserting into the extract table. Since a transaction cannot span
rollback segments, there must be a single rollback segment available that is
large enough to handle such a transaction. Therefore, a single large-volume
rollback segment is needed for use during the repository administrator's
extracts. However, this large rollback segment does not reflect the online
requirements of the application. Typically, a Designer/2000 environment
features very low transaction volume. To support this transaction volume,
rollback segments of 10MB in size are usually sufficient. Create one
rollback segment for every four to six active transactions. See Chapter 7 for
information on how to monitor the amount of rollback segment data being
written and the number of active transactions per rollback segment.

The storage requirements for extract tables mirror the storage
requirements for the application design data. Therefore, at least 50 percent
of the space in the repository's tablespace must be unused before the
extract starts. The space used by the extract tables is only temporary; the
application assumes that those tables will be either exported to flat files or
read into another repository. Thus, the additional space in the repository
tablespace is not used by the online users, and is used for very short periods
of time by the repository administrator during extracts. However, the
additional space is critical to the success of the extraction procedure.

Pinning Packages

You can use the Repository Management screen within the Repository
Administration Utility to pin any package in the Designer/2000 repository.
However, you should perform pinning operations in a batch mode, not via
an ad hoc administration utility. You should write a script that queries all of
the repository's packages and procedures from DBA_OBJECTS (where
Object_Type='PACKAGE') and alter your database startup scripts to
automatically include the pinning script. If you include pinning as part of

your database startup, then your database will always have its packages pinned when the application is in use.

init.ora Parameters

There are several database initialization parameters that can be set (via the init.ora initialization parameter file) to improve the performance of Designer/2000. The major parameters to set are listed in the following sections.

SGA Size

The System Global Area (SGA) is the memory area that is available to the instance. Data that is read from the database is held in the SGA for quick retrieval by other users. Structural information about the database and the data returned by transactions is stored in the SGA. An additional area called the Shared SQL Area stores the parsed version of statements run against the database.

For Designer/2000, the data buffer cache in the SGA is usually at least 30MB in size in order to function effectively. The shared SQL area should also be at least 30MB in size in order to support the pinning of packages. The size of the shared SQL area is set, in bytes, by the SHARED_POOL_SIZE init.ora parameter. The size of the data block buffer cache is set, in database blocks, by the DB_BLOCK_BUFFERS init.ora parameter.

Open Cursors

The INIT.ORA "open_cursors" parameter limits the number of open cursors (context areas) that can be simultaneously held by each user process. The maximum value for the parameter is operating system dependent. Set this parameter to its maximum value; although this may be documented as 255, you can exceed this value on most operating systems.

Block Size

To maximize performance within Designer/2000, increase the ORACLE block size used. Rather than using a 2,048-byte block size, increase it to 4,096 or 8,192. Increasing the database block size will reduce the percentage of each block that is devoted to overhead. As a result, more data will be read with each I/O. This should in turn result in fewer I/Os being necessary to resolve a query, thus improving performance. The init.ora entry for this parameter is

```
db_block_size    = 4096
```

You cannot alter the database block size of an existing database.

Most Active Tables and Indexes

As noted previously in this section of this chapter, the SDD_ELEMENTS and SDD_STRUCTURE_ELEMENTS tables are the most frequently accessed tables in the repository. If you **delete** elements from the repository, you are deleting records from these two tables. As records are **delete**d, the indexes on these tables may become fragmented. You should schedule periodic re-creations of the indexes in order to relieve the performance and space management problems caused by the indexes. You should monitor the segment extensions for the tables and indexes in the repository to determine which other tables are being actively used in your Designer/2000 implementation. See Chapter 6 for details on extent allocation trend monitoring.

The Optimizer

Designer/2000 relies on the rule-based optimizer to resolve the query execution paths to be used. You should not analyze the Designer/2000 repository tables.

Managing Other Packages and Utilities

In the following sections, you will see management directions for several common packages: ConText, Export, SQL*Loader, the programmatic interfaces, and SQL*Plus.

ConText

The ConText Cartridge for ORACLE relies on a series of background servers to process text portions of queries. Thus, you can execute queries combining relational and text criteria for limiting conditions, as shown in the following listing. The example assumes that a Resume column has been added to the PROSPECT table; the column can either contain the text data or can point to an external file containing the data.

```
select Name
  from PROSPECT
 where Name like 'B%'
   and contains (Resume, 'digging') > 0;
```

The query shown in the preceding listing has a **contains** clause, so ConText will be invoked to determine which Resume values contain the word "digging." You can also use ConText to perform "fuzzy matches," proximity searches, and wild card searching. When the preceding query is executed, the text portion is processed via ConText, and the relational portion is processed via the RDBMS. The results are merged and returned to the user.

To process the text portion of the query, ConText uses a series of background processes and queues within the database. The DBA should work with the teams developing ConText-based applications to determine the number and categories (Query, DML, DDL, Linguistic, and DBA) of the servers required. The servers must be started each time the database is started.

You can start the ConText servers via command line commands (for starting them in batch mode following scheduled database startups) or interactively. To start the ConText servers interactively, you can use the CTXCTL utility. The command file for the CTXCTL utility is located in the /bin subdirectory under the ORACLE software home directory.

To start the ConText servers from the command line, use the CTXSRV utility. When you start a ConText server, you specify the server's *personality*. The personality of a server defines the categories of commands that the server can process. In the following example, a server is started with a personality that enables it to support four categories of commands: Q for queries, D for DDL, M for DML, and L for Linguistic services. When executing the following command, you should replace *ctxsys_pass* with the password for the CTXSYS account:

```
ctxsrv -user ctxsys/ctxsys_pass -personality QDML
```

You can view the status of ConText servers via the CTS_ALL_SERVERS view, as shown in the following query:

```
column Ser_Name format A32

select Ser_Name,
       Ser_Status,
       Ser_Started_At
from CTX_ALL_SERVERS;
```

Sample output from CTX_ALL_SERVERS is shown in the following listing:

```
SER_NAME                          SER_STAT SER_START
--------------------------------- -------- ---------
DRSRV_42736                       IDLE     03-AUG-97
```

The sample output shows that a single ConText server has been started in the instance. The system-assigned name of the server is DRSRV_42736. To shut down all of the servers in an instance, you can use the SHUTDOWN procedure within the CTX_ADM package, as shown in the following listing:

```
execute CTX_ADM.SHUTDOWN;
```

To shut down a single ConText server, you specify the ConText server name as a parameter when executing the CTX_ADM.SHUTDOWN procedure, as shown in the following listing. The server name is listed in the Ser_Name column of CTX_ALL_SERVERS.

```
execute CTX_ADM.SHUTDOWN('DRSRV_42736');
```

NOTE
The CTXSYS.CTX_SETTINGS table must be populated prior to attempting to start a server with the Linguistics personality. If there are no rows in this table, you can use an ORACLE-supplied file to populate the CTX_SETTINGS table. To populate this table, you can Import the ctxset.dmp file, which is located in the /ctx/admin subdirectory under the ORACLE software home directory. The Import should insert 11 rows into the table. Once the CTX_SETTINGS table has been populated, you will be able to start ConText Linguistics servers.

NOTE
*To enable case-sensitivity for the ConText
Linguistic servers, you need to populate the
CTX_PROPER_NAME table owned by
CTXSYS. To populate this table, Import the
ctxprop.dmp file located in the /ctx/admin
directory under the ORACLE software home
directory. The imported data requires about
150MB of space in the database.*

To enable one-step ConText searches (that is, queries using the **contains**
clause), you should set the following parameter within your database's
init.ora file:

```
text_enable = TRUE
```

NOTE
*The text_enable parameter is only a valid
init.ora parameter as of ORACLE7.3.*

Within the database, the ConText data dictionary is owned by the
CTXSYS user. The CTXSYS user is the only user who should have the
CTXADMIN role. Other ConText-related roles include CTXAPP (application
owner) and CTXUSER (application user). You should grant the CTXAPP role
to all users who will be developing ConText applications. When a user
executes a ConText-related query, records are stored in an interim table.
When the query completes, the database **truncate**s the interim table, thus
eliminating any space management problems that may occur because of
the use of the interim tables.

You can rebuild all of the text indexes via the OPTIMIZE_INDEX
procedure within the CTX_DDL package. The term "text index" refers to the
group of tables and indexes used to facilitate text searches within the
RDBMS. The OPTIMIZE_INDEX procedure compresses fragmented indexes
and tables into fewer extents and removes references and related
information for modified or deleted text entries.

Export

The ORACLE Export utility reads data from the database and writes it to a binary file called an export dump file. This file can then be used by the Import utility to read data into a database. See Chapter 10 for descriptions of the usage of Export and Import.

How does Export know which objects to select, and in what order? To select objects, Export makes use of a set of views created under the SYS user. The creation script for these views is named catexp.sql. The script is located in the /rdbms/admin subdirectory under the ORACLE software home directory.

In certain circumstances, you may need to edit this view script. For example, if there is a single table in your database that is corrupt and you wish to Export the entire rest of the database, how can you do it? The easiest way is to modify the view that lists the tables that will be exported; this view is called EXUTAB.

NOTE
If you make a change to the export views, be sure that the change is well documented and tested beforehand. You should return the views to their normal state as soon as possible afterward.

To remove an object from the list of those that will be exported, edit the export view creation script. In the **where** clause of the EXUTAB view, append the line

```
and O$.Name <> 'table name'
```

In the view's query, "O$" is the alias given to the SYS.OBJ$ table. This is a kernel table that holds information about all database objects. The "O$.Name" column lists the names of the objects to be exported. By adding this additional clause to the view's **where** clause, you eliminate any object with that name from the list of those to be exported.

Once the view has been modified, rerun the export view creation script to drop and re-create the EXUTAB view. All subsequent exports of that database will not export any tables with the name you specified in your addition to the **where** clause.

NOTE
When the special export is complete, you should restore the original base query to the EXUTAB view.

SQL*Loader

SQL*Loader is a utility for loading data into ORACLE tables from external files. As a DBA, you have to be concerned with two aspects of its usage:

1. Are the tables and indexes properly sized for the data load that is expected?

2. Is the Direct Path option being used?

The table and index size calculations (see Chapter 5) should take into account the data that is coming in via flat files. Typically, this data's length and volume are very well defined, so the sizing estimates should be accurate. If it is a one-time load used for initial population of the data, then do not create the indexes until after the data has been loaded and the table's sizing has been verified.

The Direct Path option is a high-speed method for inserting data into tables. It bypasses the normal processing of **insert** statements and instead writes directly to the table's data blocks. When using Direct Path, the data in the flat file should be presorted by the indexed columns of the tables. For large data loads, the performance gains are considerable.

Of course, such performance gains must have a cost. In this case, the cost is borne by the tablespace used for temporary segments. When a Direct Path load is started, the table's indexes are placed in an invalid state for the duration of the load. As data is loaded into the table, the new index key values are written to a temporary segment. When the load completes, the old index values and the new values are merged, and the index once again becomes valid.

The implication of Direct Path loads for temporary segment storage space can be considerable. SQL*Loader requires that enough space be available in the temporary tablespace to hold, at a minimum, the **initial** extent sizes of all the indexes on the table being loaded. Since the Direct Path option is normally used on large data loads, the space requirements for the temporary tablespace are usually large. For unsorted data loads, the temporary tablespace size requirements may be twice the index size requirements.

To determine the status of an index, query the DBA_INDEXES view, as shown in the following listing. Valid Status values are "DIRECT LOAD" and "VALID".

```
select Owner,          /*Owner of the index*/
       Index_Name,     /*Name of the index*/
       Status          /*Either DIRECT LOAD or VALID*/
  from DBA_INDEXES;
```

If an index is left in "DIRECT PATH" state following a data load, then the load did not meet the index's criteria. For example, you may have loaded duplicate records into a table with a unique index. When the load completed, the index could not be reapplied to the table, and the index was left in "DIRECT PATH" state. As a result, you will need to drop the index, correct the data, and then re-create the index.

Programmatic Interfaces

The programmatic interfaces to ORACLE allow application developers to write programs in 3GL programming languages that can access the database. Oracle supports a number of such programming languages, including C, FORTRAN, and COBOL. As a DBA, the most important support note for the programmatic interfaces concerns upgrades to the database or operating system software. Since the users' programs use the ORACLE kernel's software libraries, and since the operating system software libraries are also used, any modification to either library requires that the users' programs be relinked. This should take place any time the database software is upgraded (for example, from version 7.3.3 to 8.0.3) or the operating system software is upgraded.

Using PRODUCT_USER_PROFILE in SQL*Plus

SQL*Plus is the command line interface to the ORACLE database. Following the creation of a new database, you should create the PRODUCT_USER_PROFILE tables in the SYSTEM schema. The PRODUCT_USER_PROFILE tables and views allows DBAs to restrict which SQL*Plus commands are available to users. The usage of these tables is described in Chapter 9.

The PRODUCT_USER_PROFILE tables should always be loaded; otherwise, users will get warning messages during logins. Before creating the tables, make sure that the SYSTEM user's default tablespace is set to TOOLS. Only two tables, SQLPLUS_PRODUCT_PROFILE and USER_PROFILE, will be created, along with several views. The script that creates these tables and views is called pupbld.sql, and it is located in the /sqlplus/admin subdirectory under the ORACLE software home directory. The script must be run from within SQL*Plus, when logged in as the SYSTEM user. See Chapter 9 for information on how to implement command access restrictions via the PRODUCT_USER_PROFILE tables and views.

CHAPTER
12

Managing Large
Databases

he definition of a "large" database keeps changing. In 1995, a large database was considered to be one that was greater than 100GB in size. Just a few years later, multiterabyte databases were going into production. The acronym VLDB, meaning "very large database," quickly loses its meaning unless it is defined by something other than a numerical threshold for size. The technological changes that support faster backups, larger systems, and I/O distribution constantly increase the largest supportable database size.

Instead of defining "large" by a given size, define it by its recovery time: if you can't completely recover the database in a 24-hour period, then it's a large database. This definition allows the size of a "large" database to increase over time as operating systems and hardware improve their performance.

When you are managing a large database, you need to view the database from a slightly different perspective. In this chapter, you will see management advice specific to large databases, including

- Loading data
- Partitioning data
- Logging transactions
- Implementing backup strategies
- Tuning queries

Some of the advice in this chapter will not be applicable for smaller systems. If you are managing a database that can be fully recovered in less than 24 hours, then you should follow the advice found in the other chapters of this book.

Setting Up the Environment

Within a large database, the majority of the data space is used by a small number of tables. For example, in a large database used for decision support purposes, you may have 100 tables, of which 5 tables account for over 90 per cent of the records in the database. The remaining 95 tables are used for codes tables or special reporting functions. To improve the performance of queries against the application, you may choose to create tables that contain aggregations of data from the largest table; each of those aggregation tables will be small relative the largest table. Codes tables will be even smaller.

When you create and manage a large database, the bulk of your effort will likely be devoted to managing the few very large tables that account for the majority of the rows. The database configuration tips provided in this section include methods for transparently splitting the large table into smaller (more easily managed) tables and distributing the I/O requirements of the large table across many devices.

Sizing Large Databases

When creating a large database, categorize each table you will be creating according to the following types:

- *Small codes table* A codes table rarely increases in size.

- *Large business transactions table* This is the type of table that accounts for the majority of the records in the database. It may increase in size over time.

- *Aggregation table* This type of table may increase in size over time or may remain at a constant size, depending on your application design. Ideally, it does not increase in size over time.

- *Temporary work table* A temporary work table is used during data load processing and bulk data manipulation.

In the following sections, you will see sizing and configuration advice for each type of table.

Sizing Codes Tables

A codes table contains a list of codes and descriptions— such as a list of state abbreviations and state names. A codes table should be fairly constant in size.

Since a codes table's data may be very static over time, you should be able to properly size the codes table and not have to worry about it becoming fragmented over time. If the codes tables are small, you should be able to create them with the proper storage parameters so that each table fits in a single extent. If there are multiple codes tables with the same relative size, you can place them in a tablespace whose default storage parameters are correct for the codes tables. For example, if all of your codes tables require between 500K and 1MB, you may store them all in the CODES_TABLES tablespace:

```
create tablespace CODES_TABLES
datafile '/u01/oracle/VLDB/codes_tables.dbf'
default storage
  (initial 1M next 1M pctincrease 0 pctfree 2);
```

If you create a table in the CODES_TABLES tablespace, the table will use the default storage parameters for the tablespace unless you specify values of your own. In this example, each table created in CODES_TABLES that uses the default storage values will have an initial extent 1MB in size, and all subsequent extents will be 1MB in size. Having all of the extents the same size maximizes the likelihood that a dropped extent will be reused. If you must use differently sized extents, then they should be sized to maximize the reuse of dropped extents. A common strategy for extent sizing is to use extent sizes of 1MB, 2MB, 4MB, 8MB, 16MB, etc.

As part of the **default storage** clause for the CODES_TABLES tablespace, the **pctfree** setting is set very low. The low setting for **pctfree** means that very little space will be held free in each database block for subsequent updates. In general, codes table values are rarely updated (for example, state names do not change frequently). If one of your codes tables has values that are frequently updated, then you will need to set **pctfree** to a higher value to support the updates.

Since they have similar storage and usage characteristics, codes tables are frequently stored together. If you have multiple sets of codes tables, you can store them in multiple tablespaces. For example, if some of your codes tables are used more frequently than others, you can move them to their own tablespace so they do not cause contention with the other codes tablespaces.

Sizing Business Transaction Tables

The business transaction tables store the majority of the data in the database. They store the raw data on which the aggregation tables are based. When sizing the business transaction tables, you first need to understand how historical data is handled within the application. Does the application always store the same volume of data in its transaction tables, or are past records kept indefinitely?

If the business transaction tables always store the same volume of data, then sizing the tables is straightforward. You should be able to estimate the number of rows in the table and the size of each row. In large databases, the business transaction tables are typically loaded via batch programs. Thus, you know two things about the data: the size of the input file and the source of data changes.

By analyzing the input file, you should be able to estimate the size of the rows in the business transaction tables. The source of data changes is equally important. If the table is **truncated** and reloaded with each subsequent data load, then there is no need for a high **pctfree** setting for the table. If records are **updated**, however, then you will need to set **pctfree** high enough so that an **updated** row can still fit in its original block. If a row cannot fit in its original block, then ORACLE may migrate the row to a new block or cause the row to span multiple blocks (both conditions are referred to as "chaining").

The **pctincrease** value for a table should support the growth pattern of the table. If the table grows at a constant rate, then you should use a **pctincrease** of 0. If the table's data volume grows geometrically, then you should use a nonzero value for **pctincrease**. For most tables, a **pctincrease** setting of 0 correctly mirrors their growth.

NOTE

In most tables, the number of rows grows at a linear rate—such as 10 rows, then 20, then 30, then 40 for the cumulative number of records. In each case, a constant volume of 10 rows was added. If the number of records increases at a geometric rate, then the number of records added each time could be 10, then 20, then 40, then 80, yielding a cumulative total of 10, then 30, then 70, then 150.

As of ORACLE8, you can easily partition a large business transaction table into multiple smaller tables. When you split a table into partitions, you need to size each of the partitions. Correctly sizing partitions requires that you know the distribution of data values within the table. Since the data is typically loaded in batch, the data distribution information may already be available to you prior to loading the data. The creation of partitions is described in the "Partitions" section later in this chapter.

Sizing Aggregation Tables

An aggregation table stores summaries of the data in the business transaction table. This redundant data storage is usually designed to improve the performance of frequently accessed screens or reports within an application. Most users of an application rarely need to see the detailed business transaction data. By storing the aggregations of the business transaction tables' data in aggregation tables, you can achieve two goals:

- Improving the performance of queries against the application. You don't want your database to have to support users who frequently perform aggregation operations (**SUM**, **MIN**, **MAX**, **AVG**, for example) of the largest table in your database. If you store the aggregated data in its own set of tables, then the users query the smaller, customized aggregation tables instead of the huge transaction data.

- Reducing the number of times the business transaction table is accessed. The aggregation tables are created via a batch process, so the business transaction table is only accessed via the batch programs. This reduction in the number of accesses significantly improves your ability to maintain, load, alter, and manage the business transaction tables. For example, if users only use aggregation tables, then you can **truncate** the main transaction table without affecting the availability of the application.

If the business transaction table grows in size over time, then the aggregation tables may grow in size over time. However, it is more common for the aggregation tables to grow in number, not size, over time. For example, you may create an aggregation table that holds the sales data for a particular time period, such as the first sales period after a product is launched. Where do you store data for the next time period? You can either expand the existing aggregation table or you can create a new table to hold the new data. If the data is placed in a new table (as is often the case), then you should be able to accurately predict the data volume of the new table based on the storage requirements of the existing aggregation tables. If the new data is stored in an existing aggregation table, then you will need to estimate the number of periods' worth of data to be stored in a single aggregation table. If there is no limit to the data volume in the aggregation tables, then those tables will eventually become large and the performance and management of those tables may become problematic.

Sizing Temporary Work Tables

A temporary work table is used during the processing of batch data loads. For example, you may use a loading process that performs no constraint checking of the incoming data. Prior to loading the new data into the business transaction table, you should "clean" the data to make sure it is correct and acceptable. Since batch loads typically use outside data sources as their source of data, it is likely that some of the records to be inserted will fail your system's criteria. You can either apply the logic checks during the data load or, if you use temporary work tables, following the data load.

Applying the data cleaning logic following the data load allows you to tune the data load for very rapid processing of rows. However, it increases the amount of space required within the database since the data must be stored in a separate table prior to being loaded into the production business transaction tables. The temporary work tables should be stored in a tablespace apart from any production tables, and their size should match the space required to hold the records from a data load.

Sizing Other Database Areas

In addition to the space required by the production tables and their associated indexes, you also need to provide adequate space for other core database objects: the data dictionary, rollback segments, and temporary segments.

The data dictionary is stored in the SYSTEM tablespace. The source code for packages, procedures, functions, triggers, and methods is stored in the data dictionary tables. If your application makes extensive use of these objects, you may need to increase the space available to the SYSTEM tablespace. The use of auditing also increases the potential space usage within the SYSTEM tablespace.

Rollback segments support the transactions within the database. In a large database, there are typically three distinct types of transactions:

- ■ *Large batch loads* These should be supported by large, dedicated rollback segments.

■ *Batch aggregations* The data volume and transaction size for the aggregations are typically smaller than those of the large data loads. You will typically need several dedicated rollback segments to support aggregations. Although the individual aggregation rollback segments may be smaller than the rollback segment used to support the initial data loads, their total space allocation may exceed the data load rollback segment space allocation.

■ *Small transactions executed by users* If your users will frequently be making small transactions of the database, you need to provide a number of rollback segments with multiple extents to support the transactions.

See Chapter 7 for information on determining the required number, size, and structure for your rollback segments.

Temporary segments are used during the processing of sorting operations. The initial data load may use temporary segments if you use the SQL*Loader Direct Path option and the loaded table is indexed. In general, most of the temporary segment activity in a large database comes from the aggregation activity and the creation of indexes. When estimating the required size of a temporary segment, first estimate the size of the table or index being created. For instance, suppose the aggregation table being created will be 50MB in size. Next, multiply that size by 4. For the aggregation table being created, you should be able to support a temporary segment that is 200MB in size. The temporary segment will be created in the user's temporary tablespace, using the default storage parameters for the tablespace, so you need to make sure that those storage values are large enough to support the aggregations and sorting operations performed.

Sizing Support Areas

Outside of the database, there are several types of files that may use considerable disk space; you need to plan for this area prior to implementing your system.

First, you may need space for the raw data files to be loaded. Unless you are loading data directly from a tape or CD, you will likely be storing raw data files on the disks of your system. Second, you may need space for file processing that occurs before the data is loaded into the database. For example, it is common to sort the data prior to loading it; you therefore need space for both the original file and the sorted version of that file. Lastly, depending on your backup strategy, you may need disk space available for archived redo log files or export files. You will see details on backup strategies for large databases in the "Backups" section of this chapter.

The sizes for these three areas vary depending on your implementation of your application and your backup strategies. Prior to finalizing your space estimate for the new system, be sure to finalize the size of the non-database areas you will need.

Choosing a Physical Layout

In implementing the physical layout for a large database, you should have two primary objectives:

1. Spread the I/O burden across as many disks as possible.

2. Reduce I/O contention between dissimilar types of objects.

In order to spread the I/O burden across many disks, many large systems use RAID arrays of disks. A RAID array treats a set of disks as a single logical volume; when a file is created within that volume, the operating system spreads the file across the disks. For example, if there are four disks in the RAID array, then the first disk may contain the first block of a file, the second disk may contain the second block, the third disk may contain the third block, and the fourth disk may contain a parity block. If one of the disks is lost due to a media failure, the operating system can use the existing disks to reconstruct the missing data.

The more disks there are in the RAID array, the more the I/O burden is distributed. Because they involve writing and maintaining parity information, RAID arrays are usually most effective for large reads of data. If the data will frequently be updated, then you should consider an alternative storage mechanism (such as mirroring, described presently). During an **update** to a data value, for example, the system would need to read the original data block, read the original parity block, and update and write both blocks back to the disk. Many large RAID systems use a disk cache to improve the performance of such operations, but they still may experience performance degradation.

An alternative architecture uses *mirroring*. In a mirrored system there are multiple copies of each disk, maintained by the operating system. For example, there may be Disk1 and a second disk that is a duplicate of Disk1. During reads and writes, the operating system may read or write to either copy of Disk1. The operating system maintains the read consistency of the files on the mirrored disks. Mirroring is effective (for writes as well as for reads), but you will need to double your disk space availability in order to use it.

To reduce I/O contention between dissimilar types of objects, use the strategies described in Chapter 4 to categorize the types of files you will be storing. Then, categorize the tables within your application based on the categories described earlier in this chapter (codes tables, aggregation tables, etc.). You should separate the temporary work tables from their data source (the external data files). You should store the business transaction tables apart from their data source (either the temporary work tables or the external data files). You should store the aggregation tables apart from their data source (the business transaction tables). All of these should be separated from the rollback segments, data dictionary, and temporary segments.

What if you are using RAID devices? In that case, treat each set of RAID disks as a single disk. Store the business transaction tables on a different RAID set than the aggregation tables are stored on. Store the tables' indexes on a different RAID set than the tables are stored on.

Partitions

In order to make the large tables easier to manage, you can use partitions. Partitions dynamically separate the rows in your table into smaller tables. You can have ORACLE create a view that spans all of the partitions; thus, the data will appear to be together logically although it is separated physically. Splitting a large table into multiple smaller tables may improve the performance of maintenance operations, backups, recoveries, transactions, and queries.

The criteria used to determine which rows are stored in which partitions are specified as part of the **create table** command. Dividing a table's data across multiple tables in this manner is called *partitioning* the table; the table that is partitioned is called a *partitioned table*, and the parts are called *partitions*.

The ORACLE optimizer will know that the table has been partitioned; as shown later in this section, you can also specify the partition to use as part of the **from** clause of your queries.

Creating a Partitioned Table

To create a partitioned table, you must specify the ranges of values to use for the partitions as part of the **create table** command.

Consider the EMPLOYEE table:

```
create table EMPLOYEE (
EmpNo          NUMBER(10) primary key,
Name           VARCHAR2(40),
DeptNo         NUMBER(2),
Salary         NUMBER(7,2),
Birth_Date     DATE,
Soc_Sec_Num    VARCHAR2(9),
State_Code     CHAR(2),
constraint FK_DeptNO foreign key (DeptNo)
   references DEPT(DeptNo),
constraint FK_StateCode foreign key (State_Code)
   references State(State_Code),
);
```

If you will be storing a large number of records in the EMPLOYEE table, then you may wish to separate the EMPLOYEE rows across multiple tables. To partition the table's records, use the **partition by range** clause of the **create table** command. The ranges will determine the values stored in each partition.

The column used as the basis for the partition logic is very rarely the primary key for the table. More often, the basis for partitioning is one of the foreign key columns in the table. In the EMPLOYEE table, the only foreign key column is the DeptNo column. If you frequently query by the DeptNo column, and it makes sense to split the data based on that column, then use it as the partition key. In a system that tracks historical data (such as sales history or salary history), it may be more appropriate to partition the data based on one of the time-based columns (such as sales period or effective date of salary change).

```
create table EMPLOYEE (
EmpNo          NUMBER(10) primary key,
Name           VARCHAR2(40),
```

```
DeptNo            NUMBER(2),
Salary            NUMBER(7,2),
Birth_Date        DATE,
Soc_Sec_Num       VARCHAR2(9),
 constraint FK_DeptNO foreign key (DeptNo)
   references DEPT(DeptNo)
)
partition by range (DeptNo)
 (partition PART1   values less than (11)
   tablespace PART1_TS,
  partition PART2   values less than (21)
   tablespace PART2_TS,
  partition PART3   values less than (31)
   tablespace PART3_TS,
  partition PART4   values less than (MAXVALUE)
   tablespace PART4_TS)
;
```

The EMPLOYEE table will be partitioned based on the values in the DeptNo column:

```
partition by range (DeptNo)
```

For any DeptNo values less than 11, the record will be stored in the partition named PART1. The PART1 partition will be stored in the PART1_TS tablespace. Any DeptNo in the range between 11 and 20 will be stored in the PART2 partition; values between 21 and 30 will be stored in the PART3 partition. Any value greater than 30 will be stored in the PART4 partition. Note that in the PART4 partition definition, the range clause is

```
partition PART4   values less than (MAXVALUE)
```

You do not need to specify a maximum value for the last partition; the **maxvalue** keyword tells ORACLE to use the partition to store any data that could not be stored in the earlier partitions.

For each partition, you only specify the maximum value for the range. The minimum value for the range is implicitly determined by ORACLE.

When partitioning a table, you should store the partitions in separate tablespaces. Separating them by tablespace allows you to control their physical storage location and avoid contention between the partitions. After all, you don't want to design I/O contention into your system.

How many partitions should you have? You should have as many partitions as are required to logically separate your data. The additional maintenance work involved in having many partitions is negligible. Focus on dividing the rows of your table into logical groups. If the partition ranges make sense for your application, then they are the ones you should use. If your largest table is 100GB in size, then using 100 evenly sized partitions generates 100 partitions that are each 1GB in size. Although a 1GB table is not always simple to manage, it is certainly simpler to manage than a 100GB table is. Use enough partitions to reduce the size of the tables to a size that is easily manageable in your operating system and hardware configuration.

NOTE
You cannot partition object tables or tables that use LOB datatypes.

QUERYING DIRECTLY FROM PARTITIONS   If you know the partition from which you will be retrieving your data, then you can specify the name of the partition as part of the **from** clause of your query. For example, what if you wanted to query the records for the employees in Departments 11 through 20? The optimizer should be able to use the partition definitions to determine that only the PART2 partition could contain data that can resolve this query. If you wish, you can tell ORACLE to use PART2 as part of your query.

```
select *
  from EMPLOYEE (PART2)
 where DeptNo between 11 and 20;
```

This example explicitly names the partition in which ORACLE is to search for the matching employee records. If the partition is modified (for example, if its range of values is altered), then PART2 may no longer be the partition that contains the needed records. Thus, you should use great care when using this syntax.

In general, this syntax is not necessary because ORACLE places CHECK constraints on each of the partitions. When you query from the partitioned table, ORACLE uses the CHECK constraints to determine which partitions should be involved in resolving the query. This process may result in a small number of rows being searched for the query, improving query performance. Additionally, the partitions may be stored in different tablespaces (and thus on separate disk devices), helping to reduce the potential for disk I/O contention during the processing of the query.

During an **insert** into the partitioned table, ORACLE uses the partitions' CHECK constraints to determine which partition the record should be inserted into. Thus, you can use a partitioned table as if it were a single table, and rely on ORACLE to manage the internal separation of the data.

Indexing Partitions

When you create a partitioned table, you should create an index on the table. The index may be partitioned according to the same range values that were used to partition the table. In the following listing, the **create index** command for the EMPLOYEE table is shown:

```
create index EMPLOYEE_DEPTNO
   on EMPLOYEE(DeptNo)
    local
    (partition PART1
      tablespace PART1_NDX_TS,
     partition PART2
      tablespace PART2_NDX_TS,
     partition PART3
      tablespace PART3_NDX_TS,
     partition PART4
      tablespace PART4_NDX_TS)
```

Notice the **local** keyword. In this **create index** command, no ranges are specified. Instead, the **local** keyword tells ORACLE to create a separate index for each partition of the EMPLOYEE table. There were four partitions created on EMPLOYEE. This index will create four separate indexes—one for each partition. Since there is one index per partition, the indexes are "local" to the partitions.

Local partitions mimic the way indexes traditionally work in ORACLE; a single index applies to only one table. If you use local partitions, it should be simple to manage the index along with its matching table.

You can also create "global" indexes. A global index may contain values from multiple partitions. That is, the index's values span multiple tables. This type of index is typically used when there are many transactions occurring in the partitions and you need to guarantee the uniqueness of the data values across all partitions. Local indexes will also guarantee uniqueness, but global indexes should perform the uniqueness check faster. The index itself may be partitioned, as shown in this example:

```
create index EMPLOYEE_DEPTNO
on EMPLOYEE(DeptNo)
 global partition by range (DeptNo)
 (partition PART1   values less than (11)
   tablespace PART1_NDX_TS,
  partition PART2   values less than (21)
   tablespace PART2_NDX_TS,
  partition PART3   values less than (31)
   tablespace PART3_NDX_TS,
  partition PART4   values less than (MAXVALUE)
   tablespace PART4_NDX_TS)
;
```

The **global** clause in this **create index** command allows you to specify ranges for the index values that are different from the ranges for the table partitions. In this case, the same partition ranges were used. Even though the same partition ranges are used for both the table and the global index, the index partitions are not directly related to the table partitions. Instead, the index partitions are part of a global index whose values span all of the table partitions. There is a direct relationship between table partitions and index partitions only when the index is a local index.

In most cases, you should use local index partitions. If you use local partitions of your indexes, you will be able to easily relate index partitions to table partitions. Local indexes are simpler to manage than global indexes since they represent only a portion of the data in the partitioned table. In the next section, you will see aspects of partition management.

Managing Partitions

You can use the **alter table** command to **add**, **drop**, **exchange**, **move**, **modify**, **rename**, **split**, and **truncate** partitions. These commands allow you to alter the existing partition structure, as may be required after a partitioned table has been used heavily. For example, the distribution of the DeptNo values within the partitioned table may have changed or the maximum value may have increased.

The following listing shows the syntax of the **alter table** command as it relates to partitions. The syntax for the full **alter table** command is shown in Appendix C under "DBA SQL Commands."

```
alter table [user.]TABLE
    | modify partition PARTITION_NAME
                { storage
                | [logging | nologging] } ...
    | move partition PARTITION_NAME
                { physical_attributes_clause
                | [logging | nologging]
                | tablespace tablespace
                | parallel parallel_clause} ...
    | add partition [NEW_PARTITION_NAME]
          values less than (value_list)
                { physical_attributes_clause
                | [logging | nologging]
                | tablespace tablespace } ...
    | drop partition PARTITION_NAME
    | truncate partition PARTITION_NAME
                [drop storage | reuse storage]
    | split partition PARTITION_NAME_OLD
                at (value_list)
      [into ( partition [SPLIT_PARTITION_1]
                [storage
                | [logging | nologging]
                | tablespace tablespace ] ...
            , partition [SPLIT_PARTITION 2]
                [storage
                | [logging | nologging]
                | tablespace tablespace ] ...) ]
                [ parallel parallel_clause ] ...
    | exchange partition PARTITION_NAME
          with table NON_PARTITIONED_TABLE_NAME
        [{including | excluding} indexes]
        [{with | without} validation ]
    | modify partition unusable local indexes
    | modify partition rebuild unusable local indexes }
```

The **alter table** command allows you to manage the storage parameters
of the partitions. When the EMPLOYEE table was partitioned earlier in this
chapter, no storage parameters were specified for its partitions. For
example, the first partition, PART1, was assigned to the PART1_TS
tablespace, with no **storage** clause.

```
partition by range (DeptNo)
  (partition PART1   values less than (11)
    tablespace PART1_TS,
```

The PART1 partition will use the default storage for the PART1_TS tablespace. If you wish to use different storage parameters, you must either specify them when the table is created (via a **storage** clause) or alter the partition's storage after it has been created.

For example, the following command changes the storage parameters for the PART1 partition of the EMPLOYEE table:

```
alter table EMPLOYEE
    modify partition PART1
    storage (next 1M pctincrease 0);
```

You can also **truncate** partitions. This capability allows you to use the **truncate** command on a partition of a table, while the rest of the table's partitions are unaffected.

```
alter table EMPLOYEE
   truncate partition PART3
   drop storage;
```

You can also use the **alter table** command to move partitions to new tablespaces, split existing partitions into multiple new partitions, exchange partitions, drop partitions, and add new partitions.

For index partitions, the options are more limited. The partition-related syntax for the **alter index** command is shown in the following listing:

```
alter index [user.]INDEX
 | modify partition PARTITION_NAME
             [ storage
             | {logging | nologging}
             | unusable ]
 | rename partition PARTITION_NAME
             to NEW_PARTITION_NAME
 | drop partition PARTITION_NAME
 | split partition PARTITION_NAME_OLD
             at (value_list)
    [ into ( partition [SPLIT_PARTITION_1]
             [ storage
             | tablespace tablespace
             | {logging | nologging} ... ]
           partition [SPLIT_PARTITION_2]
             [ storage
             | tablespace tablespace
             | {logging | nologging} ... ] ) ]
```

```
    [ parallel parallel_clause | noparallel ]
| rebuild partition PARTITION_NAME
            [ storage
            | tablespace tablespace
            | {parallel parallel_clause | noparallel}
            | {logging | nologging} ... ]
| unusable
```

The partition-related extensions to the **alter index** command allow you to manage the index partitions the same way you manage normal indexes. For example, you can rebuild an existing index partition via the **rebuild partition** clause of the **alter index** command.

```
alter index EMPLOYEE_DEPTNO
rebuild partition PART4
storage (initial 2M next 2M pctincrease 0);
```

When you use the **rebuild** option for an index or an index partition, you must have enough storage space available to simultaneously hold both the old index and the new index.

Creating Fully Indexed Tables

You should consider fully indexing tables that have few columns and contain static data. To fully index a table is to create a set of indexes that contains all of the columns of a table, with each column used as the leading column of at least one index. For example, if the STATE table has two columns, State_Code and Description, then you would need to create two indexes in order to fully index the table: one two-column index with State_Code as
the leading column and one two-column index with Description as the leading column. The **create index** commands required are shown in the following listing:

```
create index STATE_CODE_DESCRIPTION
on STATE(State_Code, Description);

create index STATE_DESCRIPTION_CODE
on STATE(Description, State_Code);
```

Whenever you query from the STATE table using a **where** clause, one of these two indexes can be used. Since each index contains all of the data available in the table, there is no need for any subsequent table accesses. The indexes contain all of the data that users could query from the table.

Fully indexing tables is particularly useful for the codes tables, which tend to have few columns and fairly static data. As of ORACLE8, you can create index-only tables, as described in the next section.

Creating and Managing Index-Only Tables

An *index-only table* keeps its data sorted according to the primary key column values for the table. Index-only tables store their data as if the entire table was stored in an index. A normal index only stores the indexed columns in the index; an index-only table stores all of the table's columns in the index.

Because the table's data is stored as an index, the rows of the table do not have RowIDs. Therefore, you cannot select the RowID pseudocolumn values from an index-only table. Also, you cannot create additional indexes on the table; the only valid index is the primary key index.

To create an index-only table, use the **organization index** clause of the **create table** command, as shown in the following example:

```
create table STATE (
State_Code      CHAR(2) primary key,
Description     VARCHAR2(25)
)
organization index;
```

In order to create STATE as an index-only table, you must create a PRIMARY KEY constraint on it, as shown in the example. When you create STATE as an index-only table, its data is stored in sorted order (sorted by the primary key values). You cannot index the Description column of STATE.

Because you cannot index any additional columns in the STATE table, an index-only table is appropriate if you will always be accessing the STATE data only by the State_Code column (in the **where** clauses of your queries). To minimize the amount of active management of the index required, you should use index-only tables only if the table's data is *very* static. If the table's data changes frequently, or if you need to index additional columns of the table, then you should use a regular table, with indexes as appropriate. In most cases, fully indexing tables gives you greater performance benefits, but at higher costs in terms of space allocation.

An index-only table will require less space than if the data were stored in a normal table. Within the index, no RowID values are stored (since the table has none), so it also takes less space than an index would if the index contained all of the columns of the table. The space savings, however, should be weighed against the prohibition against indexing the nonprimary columns.

Creating and Managing Bitmap Indexes

Normally, indexes are created on columns that are very selective; that is, there are very few rows that have the same value for the column. A column whose values are only ever 'Y' or 'N' is a very poor candidate for an index because the index contains only two unique values, so any access via that column will return an average of half of the table. However, if the values in those columns belong to a fairly static group of values, then you should consider using bitmap indexes for them.

For example, if there are very few distinct State_Code values in a very large EMPLOYEE table, then you would not usually create a B-tree index on State_Code, even if it is commonly used in **where** clauses. However, State_Code may be able to take advantage of a bitmap index.

Internally, a bitmap index maps the distinct values for the columns to each record. For this example, assume there are only two State_Code values ('NH' and 'DE') in a very large EMPLOYEE table. Since there are two State_Code values, there are two separate bitmap entries for the State_Code bitmap index. If the first five rows in the table have a State_Code value of 'DE' and the next five have a State_Code value of 'NH', then the State_Code bitmap entries would resemble those shown in the following listing:

```
State_Code bitmaps:
    DE:  < 1 1 1 1 1 0 0 0 0 0 >
    NH:  < 0 0 0 0 0 1 1 1 1 1 >
```

In the preceding listing, each number represents a row in the EMPLOYEE table. Since there are ten rows considered, there are ten bitmap

values shown. Reading the bitmap for State_Code, the first five records
have a value of 'DE' (the '1' values), and the next five do not (the '0'
values). You could have more than two possible values for the column, in
which case there would be a separate bitmap entry for each possible value.

The ORACLE optimizer can dynamically convert bitmap index entries to
RowIDs during query processing. This conversion capability allows the
optimizer to use indexes on columns that have many distinct values (via
B-tree indexes) and those that have few distinct values (via bitmap indexes).

To create a bitmap index, use the **bitmap** clause of the **create index**
command, as shown in the following listing. You should indicate its status
as a bitmap index within the index name so that it will be easy to detect
during tuning operations.

```
create bitmap index EMPLOYEE$STATE_CODE$BMAP
     on EMPLOYEE(State_Code);
```

If you choose to use bitmap indexes, you will need to weigh the
performance benefit during queries against the performance cost during
data manipulation commands. The more bitmap indexes there are on a
table, the greater the cost will be during each transaction. You should not
use bitmap indexes on a column that frequently has new values added to it.
Each addition of a new value to the State_Code column will require that a
new bitmap be created for the new State_Code value.

When creating bitmap indexes, ORACLE compresses the bitmaps that
are stored. As a result, the space required for a bitmap index may be only 5
to 10 percent of the space required for a normal index. Therefore, you
should consider using bitmap indexes for any nonselective column that is
frequently used in **where** clauses, provided the set of values for the column
is limited. If there are new values frequently added to the column's list of
values, then the bitmaps will have to be constantly adjusted.

Within a large database, bitmap indexes will yield the biggest impact
when used on columns in the business transaction and aggregation tables.
Codes tables are usually better served by fully indexing them; larger tables
typically benefit from bitmap indexing strategies. You can create both
bitmap indexes and normal (B-tree indexes) on the same table, and
ORACLE will perform any necessary index conversions dynamically during
query processing.

Managing Transactions

In a large database, batch data loads usually account for the bulk of the transactions. There is a simple logistical reason for this; machines can collect and insert data faster than an individual can process it and type it in. Consider a very effective data processing operator who enters two purchase orders per minute into a database application. At that rate, the operator would insert 120 records per hour into the system, with a total of 960 rows per day; an extra 20 minutes work rounds the total up to 1,000 rows per day.

Contrast that with the work done by a batch-load process. Using SQL*Loader Direct Path loads, you should be able to insert 1,000 rows in less than a second. Thus, you can match a full day's output of a very skilled and consistent operator with less than a second of work. In a way, this is good news for the operators since they can now turn their attention to things more appropriate for their minds— such as analyzing data trends— rather than endlessly typing in values. The entire data collection and data loading process can occur without requiring any person to enter any command; and it can work much faster than any comparable operator-driven system.

There may be small transactions within your large database, but most of the transactions will be generated by batch operations. Therefore, when managing the transactions within a large database, you should pay special attention to the batch transactions involved in loading and aggregating the data.

The timing of your batch transactions is critical. As discussed previously in Chapter 7, executing large batch operations concurrently with small online transactions is a common cause of rollback segment-related problems in the database. Ideally, the batch loads should occur when there is no online processing occurring. The more you can isolate the batch-load transactions, the more likely they will be to succeed.

Configuring the Batch Transaction Environment

In the following sections, you will see management advice for loading and deleting data from the large tables in your database. Prior to performing large batch transactions, you should create an environment that is capable of supporting the transactions.

Create Dedicated Rollback Segments

The rollback segments used by batch transactions have different characteristics than those used by transactions entered by online application users. Instead of having many small transactions, batch systems tend to have few, larger transactions. Therefore, your rollback segments that support the batch transactions will typically be few in number and have larger extent sizes than those that support online users. For example, you may have 10 rollback segments with 20 extents each to support your online users, but only a single large rollback segment with 10 extents to support the batch transaction.

To force a transaction to use a particular rollback segment, use the

```
set transaction use rollback segment SEGMENT_NAME;
```

command within SQL*Plus. This command should immediately follow a **commit**, even if you have not yet entered any transactions in your session. You will need to provide the name of the rollback segment you will be using for the transaction. If you are working with multiple databases, you should standardize the names of your batch transaction rollback segments to simplify your load processing. For example, you could call the batch data load rollback segment ROLL_BATCH in each database. If you use a consistent naming standard, you won't have to alter your data loading programs as you move from one database to another.

Disable Archiving of Redo Logs

Archiving the contents of your online redo log files allows you to recover in the event of a media failure. However, consider the transactions that are being written to the online redo log files during the batch load: they are the **insert**s that are occurring because of the data load. If you can completely re-create those **insert**s by reexecuting your data load, then you do not need to enable archiving of the transactions.

For example, if you are already running in ARCHIVELOG mode, you could shut the database down prior to the data load (which we'll call time T1). Start the database in NOARCHIVELOG mode (point in time T2).

Execute the data load until it completes (time T3). Then, shutdown and restart the database in ARCHIVELOG mode. If a media failure occurs prior to time T1, you can use the archived redo log files to recover your data. If it fails between time T2 and time T3, you can recover from that as well: recover to time T1 and reexecute the data load.

If you turn off the archiving of online redo log files during your data load, you need to make sure that no other transactions are occurring during your data load. If other transactions are occurring at the same time, then their data may be lost during a recovery. As of ORACLE8, you can use the **nologging** parameter to avoid logging transactions against specific tables or parts of tables, as described in the next section.

Disable Logging for the Large Tables

When ORACLE7.2 was released, a new keyword was introduced to the **create table as select** and **create index** commands: **unrecoverable**. The **unrecoverable** keyword eliminated the writing of online redo log file entries during the execution of the command. As of ORACLE8, the keyword **unrecoverable** has been replaced with the more powerful **nologging** keyword.

When you create a table using the **nologging** keyword, the transactions within that table are *never* written to the online redo log files—not during the initial data population and not during any subsequent transaction. Thus, you can target specific tables (such as your large business transaction tables or the aggregation tables) for no logging. Being able to avoid writing these transactions to the online redo log files allows you to keep the full database in ARCHIVELOG state while the largest tables are essentially in NOARCHIVELOG state. You can also specify **nologging** for the LOB portions of tables that use BLOB or CLOB datatypes.

Rebuild Indexes after Data Loads

Efficient indexes are the key to fast data access in a large database. ORACLE does not perfectly manage the data in its indexes, so you must periodically rebuild your indexes. You should rebuild your indexes after every major data load. You can use the **rebuild** clause of the **alter index** command to build a new index that uses the old index as its data source.

Even if you use the SQL*Loader Direct Patch option (while leaving the indexes on during the data load), you should still periodically rebuild your indexes. If you are not using that load option, then you should drop your indexes prior to the data load and then re-create them once the load completes.

The same advice holds true for mass deletions and updates: if many index values have been deleted or updated, you should rebuild the indexes. The better organized an index is, the faster the associated data access will be.

Loading Data

When loading data from files into your business transaction tables, you should try to eliminate factors that can slow down **insert**s. You should disable the constraints on the table and disable any triggers on the table (although batch-loaded tables should typically not have triggers anyway), and you should drop indexes prior to the data load. If you do not drop the indexes and the data is sorted prior to loading, then you can use the SQL*Loader Direct Path option. In addition to managing indexes, this option allows you to insert entire blocks of rows at a time rather than performing one **insert** per row.

During a normal **insert** of a row, ORACLE checks the list of free blocks in the table—those new blocks that have more than **pctfree** space left in them. ORACLE finds the first block that can hold the record and **insert**s it. For the next record, ORACLE performs the search for free space again. The search is repeated for each record. SQL*Loader Direct Path avoids the cost of these searches by inserting entire blocks of data at a time.

To know where to load data, SQL*Loader first determines the *high-water mark* of the table. The high-water mark is the highest-numbered block that has ever held data in the table. For example, if you load 1,000 blocks worth of rows into the table and then **delete** the rows, the high-water mark will point to block number 1,000. During a SQL*Loader Direct Path insert, ORACLE does not search for open space in currently used blocks. Instead, it loads blocks of data at the first block after the high-water mark. If there is space available below the high-water mark, the SQL*Loader Direct Path option will not use it.

There are only two ways to reset the high-water mark for a table: drop and re-create the table or **truncate** the table. Thus, you need to be aware of the methods used to delete records from a table. If you load 1,000 blocks worth of rows into a table and later **delete** them, then the high-water mark is left unchanged. A subsequent SQL*Loader Direct Path load of the same data would use 1,000 blocks—starting at block 1,001. Instead of using 1,000 blocks, the table would now use 2,000 blocks!

In addition to allowing you to use the very efficient Direct Path option, SQL*Loader also has options for parallel operations and unlogged operations. See the "Tuning" section later in this chapter for further details on parallel operations. See the "Disable Logging for the Large Tables" section earlier in this chapter for information on the **nologging** parameter.

Inserting Data

If the data being inserted is from another table (such as an **insert as select** used to populate an aggregation table), you can take advantage of a new hint provided as of ORACLE8. The hint, called APPEND, uses the high-water mark as the basis for **insert**s of blocks of data, the same way SQL*Loader Direct Path does (see the previous section of this chapter for a discussion of high-water marks).

The APPEND hint tells ORACLE to find the last block into which the table's data has been inserted. The new records will be inserted starting in the next block following the high-water mark.

For instance, if a table had previously used 20 blocks within the database, then an **insert** command that used the APPEND hint would start writing its data in the 21st block. Since the data is being written into new blocks of the table, there is much less space management work for the database to do during the **insert**. Therefore, the **insert** may complete faster when the APPEND hint is used. The table's space requirements may increase because of unused space below the high-water mark.

You specify the APPEND hint within the **insert** command. A hint looks like a comment—it starts with /* and ends with */. The only difference in syntax is that the starting set of characters includes a '+' before the name of the hint. The following example shows an **insert** command whose data is appended to the table:

```
insert /*+ APPEND */ into SALES_PERIOD_CUST_AGG
select Period_ID, Customer_ID, SUM(Sales)
  from SALES
 group by Period_ID, Customer_ID;
```

The records from the SALES business transaction table will be inserted into the SALES_PERIOD_CUST_AGG aggregation table. Instead of attempting to reuse previously used space within the

SALES_PERIOD_CUST_AGG table, the new records will be placed at the end of the table's physical storage space.

Since the new records will not attempt to reuse available space that the table has already used, the space requirements for the SALES_PERIOD_CUST_AGG table may increase. In general, you should use the APPEND hint only when inserting large volumes of data into tables with little reusable space.

The APPEND hint is ideal for the creation of aggregate tables, since their data source is a table stored elsewhere in the database. Since they store redundant data, aggregate tables are also good candidates for the **nologging** parameter discussed earlier in this chapter.

Deleting Data

When managing large volumes of data, you should try to set up your tables so you can use the **truncate** command. If the data is all stored in a single large table, you should consider using partitions since you can **truncate** partitions via the **alter table** command shown earlier in this chapter. If you need to delete large volumes at once via the **delete** command, however, you will need to either configure your environment to support a large transaction or you will need to use a procedural method to break the transaction into smaller pieces.

Configuring the Environment

The configuration requirements for large **delete**s are identical to those required for large **insert**s; you need to create and maintain a rollback segment that is large enough to support the transaction. To force the rollback segment to be used by the transaction, use the **set transaction use rollback segment** command immediately following a **commit**. You should schedule the bulk **delete** to occur during a time when there are few other transactions occurring in the database to avoid potential read concurrency problems.

Using a Procedural Method

You can use PL/SQL to break a single deletion into multiple transactions. For example, you can create a PL/SQL block that takes as its input the **delete** command and the number of records to **commit** in each batch. For example, if there are one million records to **delete** and you cannot use the

truncate command, you can force a **commit** after every 1,000 records. To do this, you will need to use dynamic PL/SQL and loops. In the following PL/SQL procedure (developed and distributed by ORACLE Support), the two input parameters are the SQL statement and the number of records to be committed in each batch. For example, suppose the **delete** command is

```
delete from SALES where Customer_ID=12;
```

and you want to commit after each 1,000 rows committed. The procedure, named DELETE_COMMIT, will be called with those two parameters:

```
execute DELETE_COMMIT('delete from SALES where Customer_ID=12',1000);
```

If the values in the **where** clause are character strings, enclose them in double sets of quotes:

```
execute DELETE_COMMIT('delete from SALES where State_Code = ''NH''',500)
```

The code for the DELETE_COMMIT procedure is shown here:

```
create or replace procedure DELETE_COMMIT
( p_statement in varchar2,
  p_commit_batch_size   in number default 10000)
is
        cid                             integer;
        changed_statement               varchar2(2000);
        finished                        boolean;
        nofrows                         integer;
        lrowid                          rowid;
        rowcnt                          integer;
        errpsn                          integer;
        sqlfcd                          integer;
        errc                            integer;
        errm                            varchar2(2000);
begin
        /* If the actual statement contains a WHERE clause, then
           append a rownum < n clause after that using AND, else
           use WHERE rownum < n clause */
        if ( upper(p_statement) like '% WHERE %') then
                changed_statement := p_statement||' AND rownum < '
                ||to_char(p_commit_batch_size + 1);
        else
changed_statement := p_statement||' WHERE rownum < '
||to_char(p_commit_batch_size + 1);
```

```
        end if;
        begin
cid := dbms_sql.open_cursor; -- Open a cursor for the task
            dbms_sql.parse(cid,changed_statement, dbms_sql.native);
                    -- parse the cursor.
rowcnt := dbms_sql.last_row_count;
                    -- store for some future reporting
        exception
            when others then
                    errpsn := dbms_sql.last_error_position;
                    -- gives the error position in the changed sql
                    -- delete statement if anything happens
    sqlfcd := dbms_sql.last_sql_function_code;
                    -- function code can be found in the OCI manual
                    lrowid := dbms_sql.last_row_id;
                    -- store all these values for error reporting.
                    -- However all these are really useful in a
                    -- stand-alone proc execution for dbms_output
                    -- to be successful, not possible when called
                    -- from a form or front-end tool.
                errc := SQLCODE;
                errm := SQLERRM;
                dbms_output.put_line('Error '||to_char(errc)||
                    ' Posn '||to_char(errpsn)||
            ' SQL fCode '||to_char(sqlfcd)||
        ' rowid '||rowidtochar(lrowid));
                    raise_application_error(-20000,errm);
                    -- this will ensure the display of at least
                    -- the error message if something happens,
                    -- even in a front-end tool.
        end;
        finished := FALSE;
        while not (finished)
        loop -- keep on executing the cursor till there is no more
            -- to process.
                begin
nofrows := dbms_sql.execute(cid);
                    rowcnt := dbms_sql.last_row_count;

                exception
                    when others then
                        errpsn := bms_sql.last_error_position;
                    sqlfcd := dbms_sql.last_sql_function_code;
                lrowid := dbms_sql.last_row_id;
    errc := SQLCODE;
```

```
                                errm := SQLERRM;
                      dbms_output.put_line('Error
'||to_char(errc)||
                               ' Posn '||to_char(errpsn)||
                    ' SQL fCode '||to_char(sqlfcd)||
               ' rowid '||rowidtochar(lrowid));
                             raise_application_error(-20000,errm);
             end;
             if nofrows = 0 then
                    finished := TRUE;
             else
              finished := FALSE;
             end if;
             commit;
     end loop;
     begin
             dbms_sql.close_cursor(cid);
                    -- close the cursor for a clean finish
         exception
             when others then
                    errpsn := dbms_sql.last_error_position;
                    sqlfcd := dbms_sql.last_sql_function_code;
                    lrowid := dbms_sql.last_row_id;
    errc := SQLCODE;
                    errm := SQLERRM;
    dbms_output.put_line('Error '||to_char(errc)||
     ' Posn '||to_char(errpsn)||
                            ' SQL fCode '||to_char(sqlfcd)||
                            ' rowid '||rowidtochar(lrowid));
                    raise_application_error(-20000,errm);
         end;
end;
/
```

Much of the code in the DELETE_COMMIT procedure handles any exceptions that may be encountered during statement processing. Conceptually, the executable command section follows this logic:

If the **delete** command contains a **where** clause already, append an **and** clause to the statement; otherwise, append a **where** clause. These clauses are used to limit the number of rows **delete**d at a time. Process and **commit** the **delete** for the specified number of records. The second time the **delete** is executed, a second set of rows will be **delete**d. Reexecute the **delete** until there are no more records that match the **where** clause criteria.

The exceptions that may be raised are documented within the procedure and are rarely encountered. For best performance, be sure that the **delete** command's **where** clause can use indexes. You can use the **explain plan** command prior to executing the command to determine if a **delete** command will use indexes. See Chapter 8 for information on the **explain plan** command.

Backups

Why bother backing up a large database?

That may seem a bit of a heretical question for a DBA to ask, but it is relevant and appropriate. By definition, you cannot recover the large database in less than 24 hours. Often, you can reload the database and re-create the aggregations in less time than it would take to recover the data using the ORACLE backup and recovery utilities. If you can reload the data faster than you can recover it, do you need to back up the data at all? The answer depends on the way in which your data load processing occurs.

Evaluating Backup Needs and Strategies

As described earlier in this chapter, most large databases have four types of tables:

- Large business transaction tables, which contain the majority of the raw data in the database

- Aggregation tables, which store aggregated data from the business transaction tables

- Codes tables

- Temporary work tables

When evaluating your database's backup needs, you should evaluate the backup needs for each type of table.

The backup requirements for business transaction tables are driven by the data load processing methods used. If the business transaction data is completely replaced with each data load, then you can use the data load process to recover the data; you do not need to rely on ORACLE's tools such as Export. If the business transaction data is not completely replaced with each data load, you may be able to use a combination of backup methods to recover the data.

For example, if each data load consists of only one period's worth of data in the SALES table, then you will need to back up the prior periods' data as well as the current period's data. There are two ways to do this:

1. Export the old data and use the data load process to re-create the current period's data.

2. Save the old data files and during a recovery run the data load for each period separately.

In general, the second option will allow your recovery to complete faster. You can still use the Export utility as a backup to your data load recovery method.

If the data in your business transaction tables can be updated after loading, then you will need to be able to re-create those transactions. You can either Export the data following the transactions or you can run the database in ARCHIVELOG mode. If you are relying on the archived redo log files to re-create the transaction data, then you cannot place the business transaction table in **nologging** mode. If the table is in **nologging** mode, then transactions against it are not written to the online redo log files, so they are not archived.

In an ideal scenario, the business transaction table is completely reloaded during each data load and no **update**s occur following the data load. If you need to recover the business transaction table, you can simply reexecute the data load procedure and the table can be kept in **nologging** state. As an additional backup method, you can Export the data following each data load. If your data can be updated following a data load, or if the data load does not account for all of the data in the table, then you need to back up the user transactions or the historical data.

Aggregation tables store redundant data. All of the data in the aggregation tables can be generated by rerunning the commands used to create them. If you lose an aggregation table (for example, if it is accidentally dropped by someone performing application support), you can re-create it by executing the **create table as select** command used to populate it. You should not permit modifications to the aggregation tables following their creation. If data needs to be changed, it should be changed in the business transaction tables that are the data source of the aggregation tables, and the aggregation tables should then be re-created.

Given these characteristics of aggregation tables, there is no need to use ARCHIVELOG backups for them (and as noted earlier in this chapter, they should be in **nologging** state anyway). You may wish to Export the data following the table creation, but you can usually re-create the table faster via SQL than via Import. This performance difference is greatest if you use the APPEND hint of the **insert** command as described earlier in this chapter.

Codes tables store static data. There should be very few transactions occurring in the codes tables. Therefore, Exports are usually sufficient for the codes tables. Since there are so few transactions occurring, there is no need to use archived redo log files to recover them; if you time your Export properly, you should be able to use the Exports during recovery with no data loss.

Temporary work tables are used during data load processing and are typically not accessed as part of the production application. Therefore, the only recovery needs for the temporary work tables arise as part of the data load process. For example, you may wish to back up the temporary work tables at different points in the data load in order to minimize the amount of recovery activity needed if the data load process fails. Since there are no online transactions occurring within the temporary work tables, Exports are usually used to back up these tables.

Developing the Backup Plan

Consider a large database whose business transaction tables are fully reloaded during each load (with no subsequent transactions in them) and whose codes tables are unchanging. What is the appropriate backup strategy? For such a system, there is no need to use ARCHIVELOG mode anywhere; indeed, it may be appropriate to put many of the tables into **nologging** state to eliminate the writing of redo entries to the online redo log files. The backup strategy could be

1. Export the business transaction tables following data loads. Rely primarily on the data load process for recovery.

2. Export the aggregation tables following their creation. Rely primarily on table re-creation for recovery.

3. Export the codes tables after major changes. If the tables are small enough, you can also create copies of the codes tables via **create table as select** commands. Rely primarily on the Exports for recovery.

4. Export the temporary work tables after critical steps in the data load process. Rely primarily on the data load process for recovery.

Although each of the table types relies on Exports, the Exports are performed at different times in the data processing. Only one of the table types (codes tables) relies on Exports as its primary recovery method.

It is very likely that this kind of backup strategy is inconsistent with the backup strategy used on your other, online transactions systems. However, there are a few key similarities:

1. Each table has a primary backup method and a secondary backup method. If, for example, the **create table as select** for an aggregation table fails, you can rely on the Export of that table as a secondary recovery method. Never rely on just one backup method.

2. Each recovery type should be fully tested. If you have not tested a recovery operation, then you cannot rely on it.

If you follow these guidelines, your large database will be recoverable—even if you rely on Exports only for the backup of the codes tables. As you tune your data load process, you should be able to reduce the time required to recover the database, giving you greater flexibility in its management.

Tuning

Tuning a large database is a two-part process: first tune the environment, then tune the specific queries and transactions that place the largest performance burden on the database. The tuning of database environments was discussed in Chapter 8, and some transaction tuning tips were provided earlier in this chapter. For example, your data load processes should use the block insert methods found in the SQL*Loader Direct Path loader and the APPEND hint of the **insert** command.

For a large database, the data block buffer portion of the System Global Area (SGA) should be approximately 2 percent of the database size. For a 100GB database, the SGA may be 2GB. An SGA that large implies that the database is being run on a host and operating system that can support the management of large memory areas.

When creating the database, you should set the database block size to the highest value supported by ORACLE on your operating system. The larger the database block is, the more efficiently data is stored. When you are managing a small database, the improvements in storage efficiency and data access that come from using a larger database block size are noticeable. When you are managing a large database, they are substantial. Doubling the database block size typically results in performance gains of about 40 percent on most batch operations.

You cannot alter the database block size after a database has been created. The database block size is set based on the value of the DB_BLOCK_SIZE parameter in the init.ora file used when the database was created.

You should consider partitioning the main tables of the large database as described in the "Partitions" section of this chapter. By partitioning the table, you can dramatically improve your ability to effectively manage it. For example, you can use partitioning to distribute the I/O burden due to a table's accesses across multiple smaller tables, based on the table values. You can then **truncate** or modify one partition of the table without affecting the rest of the table. Use local indexes for the greatest flexibility in managing index partitions.

Outside of the database, you should take advantage of the available devices and disk storage architectures to properly distribute the system I/O requirements. See the "Choosing a Physical Layout" section earlier in this chapter for information on disk options and architectures such as RAID devices and disk mirroring.

If your host machine has multiple CPUs available, then you may be able to take full advantage of ORACLE's Parallel Query Option (PQO). When you use PQO, multiple processes are created to complete a single task— such as a query or an index creation. Because they involve large transactions and sorts, large databases typically benefit from the use of the PQO. See Chapter 8 for information on the usage of the PQO.

Tuning Queries of Large Tables

In addition to creating fully indexed tables, creating bitmap indexes, partitioning tables and indexes, and using the PQO for queries of large tables, you can further tune queries of large tables to minimize their impact on the rest of the database. Whereas multiple users can benefit from sharing data from small tables in the SGA, that benefit disappears when very large tables are accessed. For very large tables, index accesses can have a negative effect on the rest of the database.

When a table and its indexes are small, there can be a high degree of data sharing within the SGA. Multiple users performing table reads or index range scans can use the same blocks over and over. As a result of the reuse of blocks within the SGA, the *hit ratio*—a measure of the reuse of blocks within the SGA—increases.

As a table grows, the table's indexes grow too. If a table and its indexes grow much larger than the available space in the SGA, it becomes less likely that the next row needed by a range scan will be found within the SGA. The reusability of data within the SGA's data block buffer cache will diminish. The hit ratio for the database will decrease. Eventually, each logical read will require a separate physical read.

The SGA is designed to maximize the reuse (among multiple users) of the blocks read from the datafiles. To do this, the SGA maintains a list of the blocks that have been read; if the blocks were read via index accesses or via table access by RowID, those blocks are kept in the SGA the longest. If a block is read into the SGA via a full table scan, that block is the first to be removed from the SGA when more space is needed in the data block buffer cache.

For applications with small tables, the data block buffer cache management in the SGA maximizes the reuse of blocks and increases the hit ratio. What happens, though, if an index range scan is performed on a very large table? The index's blocks will be kept for a long time in the SGA, even though it is likely that no other users will be able to use the values in the index's blocks. Since the index is large, many of its blocks may be read, consuming a substantial portion of the available space in the SGA's data block buffer cache. A greater amount of space will be consumed by the table blocks accessed by RowID, and those blocks will be even less likely to be reused. The hit ratio will begin to drop—ironically, because index scans are being performed. The tuning methods used for very large tables

therefore focus on special indexing techniques and on alternatives
to indexes.

Manage Data Proximity

If you intend to continue using indexes during accesses of very large tables,
you must be concerned about *data proximity*—the physical relationship
between logically related records. To maximize data proximity, insert
records into the table sequentially, ordered by columns commonly used in
range scans of the table. For example, the primary key of the large SALES
table is the combination of Period_ID, Customer_ID, and Sale_No.
Accesses that use Period_ID as a limiting condition will be able to use the
unique index on the primary key; but if range scans are commonly
performed on the SALES.Customer_ID column, the data should be stored in
order of Customer_ID.

   If the data is stored in an ordered format, then during range searches,
such as

```
where Customer_ID between 123 and 241
```

you will more likely be able to reuse the table and index blocks read into
the SGA because all of the Customer_ID values with a value of 123 will be
stored together. Fewer index and table blocks will be read into the SGA's
data block buffer cache, minimizing the impact of the index range scan on
the SGA. Storing data in an ordered fashion helps range scans regardless of
the size of the table, but it is particularly critical for large tables due to the
negative implications of large range scans.

Avoid Unhelpful Index Scans

If you are going to use index scans against a large table, you cannot assume
that the index scan will perform better than a full table scan. Unique
scans or range scans of indexes that are not followed by table accesses
perform well, but a range scan of an index followed by a table access by
RowID may perform poorly. As the table grows to be significantly larger
than the data block buffer cache, the break-even point between index
scans and full table scans decreases—eventually, if you read more than 1
percent of the rows in a 10,000,000 row table, you are better off
performing a full table scan rather than an index range scan and table
access by RowID combination.

Full table scans may perform better because of the way ORACLE manages the data block buffer cache of the SGA. If a large index scan is performed in a large table, then many index blocks will be stored in the SGA— and they will be kept in the SGA as long as possible. By contrast, blocks read by the full table scan will be flushed out of the SGA as quickly as possible. Therefore, if any other objects have blocks of data in the SGA, they will be unaffected by the full table scan; the index-based access, however, would flush them from the cache.

There are a few blocks from the full table scan that are retained in the SGA. The blocks held in the SGA because of the full table scan are those blocks read in via the last read; the number of blocks read is determined by the setting of the DB_FILE_MULTIBLOCK_READ_COUNT init.ora parameter. The size of the cache area used by the full table scan blocks is the product of the DB_FILE_MULTIBLOCK_READ_COUNT parameter and the DB_BLOCK_SIZE parameter.

If the query is run in batch mode, with no other users in the database, it may be acceptable to completely remove all other data from the SGA. If there are multiple users of the database, the performance cost of keeping the data in the SGA can be significant. The performance cost of the changes to the SGA could be so great for the other users of the database (due to the size of the table and indexes) that you may be better off using the full table scan method even when querying just 1 percent of the table.

Favoring full table scans is not a typical tuning method. However, if a table is so large that its index-based accesses will override the SGA, you should consider using a full table scan for queries of very large tables in multiuser environments. To improve the performance of the full table scan, consider parallelizing the operation.

PART
III

Networked Oracle

CHAPTER
13

SQL*Net V2 and Net8

t's hard to find a computer these days that isn't tied into a network. Distributing computing power across servers and sharing information across networks greatly enhances the value of the computing resources available. Instead of being a stand-alone server, the server becomes an entry point for the information superhighway.

Databases can also be distributed; the ORACLE tool *SQL*Net* functions as the on-ramp to the database information highway. As of ORACLE8, SQL*Net has been modified and is referred to as Net8; Net8 and SQL*Net V2 share many common architectural components, and both can be used to connect to ORACLE databases. SQL*Net V2 and Net8 facilitate the sharing of data between databases, even if those databases are on different types of servers running different operating systems and communications protocols. They also allow for *client-server* applications to be created; the server can then function primarily for database I/O, while the data presentation requirements of an application can be moved to the front-end client machines.

SQL*Net V2 and Net8 support both ORACLE7 and ORACLE8. Thus, you could use SQL*Net V2 to access your ORACLE8 databases while you migrate your applications from ORACLE7 to ORACLE8. The major differences between SQL*Net V2 and Net8 are in their administrative tools and in the area of connection management. In this chapter, you will see how to administer both SQL*Net V2 and Net8.

The installation and configuration instructions for SQL*Net V2 and Net8 depend on the particular hardware, operating system, and communications software you are using. The material provided here will help you get the most out of your database networking, regardless of your configuration.

Overview of SQL*Net V2 and Net8

Using SQL*Net V2 or Net8 distributes the workload associated with database applications. Since many database queries are performed via applications, a server-based application forces the server to support both the CPU requirements of the application and the I/O requirements of the database (see Figure 13-1a). Using a *client-server* configuration allows this load to be distributed between two machines. The first, called the *client,* supports the application that initiates the request from the database. The backend machine on which the database resides is called the *server.* The client bears the burden of presenting the data, while the database server is

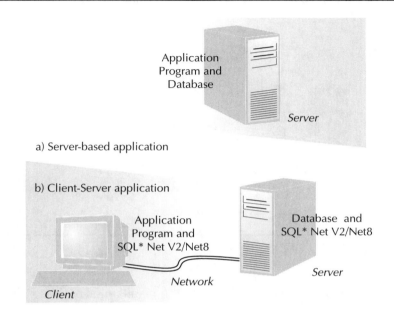

a) Server-based application

b) Client-Server application

FIGURE 13-1. *Client-server architecture*

dedicated to supporting queries, not applications. This distribution of resource requirements is shown in Figure 13-1b.

When the client sends a database request to the server, the server receives and executes the SQL statement that is passed to it. The results of the SQL statement, plus any error conditions that are returned, are then sent back to the client.

In addition to client-server implementations, *server-server* configurations are often needed. In this type of environment, databases on separate servers share data with each other. Each server can then be physically isolated from every other server without being logically isolated from it. A typical implementation of this type involves corporate headquarters servers that communicate with departmental servers in various locations. Each server supports client applications, but it also has the ability to communicate with other servers in the network. This architecture is shown in Figure 13-2.

When one of the servers sends a database request to another server, the sending server acts like a client. The receiving server executes the SQL

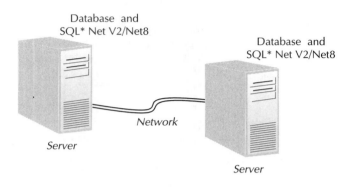

FIGURE 13-2. *Server-server architecture*

statement that is passed to it, and returns the results plus error conditions to the sender.

SQL*Net V2 and Net8 allow both of these architectures to become reality. When run on both the client and the server, they allow database requests made from one database (or application) to be passed to another database on a separate server. In most cases, machines can function both as clients and servers; the only exceptions are operating systems with single-user architectures, such as MS-DOS. In such cases, those machines can only function as clients.

The end result of a SQL*Net V2 or Net8 implementation is the ability to communicate with all databases that are accessible via the network. You can then create synonyms that give applications true network transparency; the user who submits the query will not know the location of the data that is used to resolve it. In this chapter, you will see the main configuration methods and files used to manage the interdatabase communications, along with usage examples. You will see more detailed examples of distributed database management in Chapter 15.

Each object in a database is uniquely identified by its owner and name. For example, there will only be one table named EMPLOYEE owned by the user HR; there cannot be two objects of the same name in the same schema.

Within distributed databases, two additional layers of object identification must be added. First, the name of the instance that accesses the database must be identified. Next, the name of the server on which that instance resides must be identified. Putting together these four parts of the object's name—its server, its instance, its owner, and its name—results in a *Fully Qualified Object Name (FQON)*. In order to access a remote table, that table's FQON must be known. DBAs and application administrators can set up access paths to automate the selection of all four parts of the FQON. In the following sections, you will see how to set up the access paths used by SQL*Net V2 and Net8.

SQL*Net V2 has as its foundation the Transparent Network Substrate (TNS), which resolves all server-level connectivity issues. SQL*Net V2 relies on configuration files on the client and the server to manage the database connectivity. If the client and server use different communications protocols, the MultiProtocol Interchange (described in a later section of this chapter) manages the connections. The combination of the MultiProtocol Interchange and the TNS allows SQL*Net V2 connections to be made independent of the operating system and communications protocol run by each server.

SQL*Net V2 also has the capability to send and receive data requests in an asynchronous manner; this allows it to support the multithreaded server (MTS) architecture. The Net8 Connection Manager replaces the MultiProtocol Interchange and further expands ORACLE's support of the MTS architecture.

Connect Descriptors

The server and instance portions of an object's FQON in SQL*Net V2 are identified by means of a *connect descriptor*. A connect descriptor specifies the communications protocol, server name, and instance name to use when performing the query. Because of the protocol-independence of SQL*Net V2, the descriptor also includes hardware connectivity information. The format for a SQL*Net V2 connect descriptor is shown in the following listing. The example shown here uses the TCP/IP protocol, and specifies a connection to an instance named LOC on a server named HQ. The keywords are protocol-specific.

```
(DESCRIPTION=
     (ADDRESS=
          (PROTOCOL=TCP)
          (HOST=HQ)
          (PORT=1521))
```

```
(CONNECT DATA=
        (SID=loc)))
```

In this connect descriptor, the protocol is set to TCP/IP, the server
("HOST") is set to HQ, and the port on that host that should be used for the
connection is port 1521 (which is the recommended port assignment for
SQL*Net V2 in UNIX installations). The instance name is specified in a
separate part of the descriptor as the "SID" assignment.

The structure for this descriptor is consistent across all protocols. Also,
the descriptors can be automatically generated via the Network Manager
tool provided by ORACLE (this tool has been desupported by ORACLE as of
ORACLE8, and has been replaced by the Net8 Assistant). As previously
noted, the keywords used by the connect descriptors are protocol-specific.
The keywords to use and the values to give them are provided in the
operating-system-specific documentation for SQL*Net V2.

Service Names

Users are not expected to type in a SQL*Net V2 connect descriptor each
time they want to access remote data. Indeed, they would probably mutiny
at such a suggestion. Instead, the DBA can set up *service names* (aliases),
which refer to these connect descriptors. Service names are stored in a file
called tnsnames.ora. This file should be copied to all servers on the
database network. Every client should have a copy of this file.

On the server, the tnsnames.ora file should be located in the directory
specified by the TNS_ADMIN environment variable. The file is usually
stored in a common directory such as the /etc directory on UNIX systems.
On the client, the file should be located in the /network/admin subdirectory
under your ORACLE software home directory.

A sample entry in the tnsnames.ora file is shown in the following listing.
This example assigns a service name of LOC to the connect descriptor
given above.

```
LOC =(DESCRIPTION=
        (ADDRESS=
                (PROTOCOL=TCP)
                (HOST=HQ)
                (PORT=1521))
        (CONNECT DATA=
                (SID=loc)))
```

A user wishing to connect to the LOC instance on the HQ server can now use the LOC service name, as shown in this example:

```
> sqlplus hr/puffinstuff@LOC;
```

The "@" sign tells the database to use the service name that follows it to determine which database to log in to. If the username and password are correct for that database, then a session is opened there and the user can begin using the database.

The creation of aliases for connect descriptors has already been accomplished via the use of service names. The use of synonyms to further enhance location transparency will be described in the "Usage Example: Database Links" section of this chapter.

Additional tnsnames.ora Parameters and Issues

In addition to the parameters shown in the preceding tnsnames.ora example, there are additional configuration options. For example, you can specify the buffer sizes for SQL*Net to use (see the "Tuning SQL*Net and Net8" section later in this chapter for details). In SQL*Net V2, you can specify a COMMUNITY setting, for use by the MultiProtocol Interchange. The MultiProtocol Interchange is obsolete as of Net8, so Net8 simply ignores the COMMUNITY parameter if it exists. See "The MultiProtocol Interchange" later in this chapter for a description of that service.

The MultiProtocol Interchange is replaced by the Connection Manager in Net8. If you set the SOURCE_ROUTE parameter in tnsnames.ora to YES, then Net8 will create a source route of addresses through the connection managers to the destination database. See the "Using Connection Manager" section later in this chapter for further details.

Keep the tnsnames.ora file as short as possible, since it is fully read each time a service name is referenced. If the tnsnames.ora file contains extraneous data (such as instance specifications for instances that no longer exist), then you are adversely impacting the performance of every database connection.

Listeners

Each server on the network must contain a listener.ora file. The listener.ora file lists the names and addresses of all of the listener processes on the

machine and the instances they support. Listener processes receive
connections from SQL*Net V2 and Net8 clients.

A listener.ora file has four parts:

- A header section

- An interprocess calls (IPC) address definition section

- Instance definitions

- Operational parameters

This file is automatically generated by the Network Manager (SQL*Net
V2) or Net8 Assistant tools. You can edit the resulting file, as long as you
follow its syntax rules. The following listing shows sample sections of a
listener.ora file—an address definition and an instance definition:

```
LISTENER =
  (ADDRESS_LIST =
      (ADDRESS=
         (PROTOCOL=IPC)
         (KEY= loc.world)
      )
  )
SID_LIST_LISTENER =
  (SID_LIST =
    (SID_DESC =
      (SID_NAME = loc)
      (ORACLE_HOME = /orasw/app/oracle/product/8.0.3.1)
    )
  )
```

The first portion of this listing contains the address list—one entry per
instance. In this case, the listener is listening for connections to the service
identified as 'loc.world.' The '.world' suffix is the default domain name for
SQL*Net V2 connections. In Net8, the default domain name has been
changed to be a null string.

The second portion of the listing identifies the ORACLE software home
directory for each instance the listener is servicing. If you change the
ORACLE software home directory for an instance, you need to change the
listener.ora file for the server.

Additional listener.ora parameters

The listener.ora file supports a number of additional parameters. The parameters should each be suffixed with the listener name. For example, the default listener name is LISTENER, so the LOG_FILE parameter is named LOG_FILE_LISTENER. The additional listener.ora parameters are listed in Table 13-1.

You can modify the listener parameters after the listener has been started. If you use the SAVE_CONFIG_ON_STOP option (available as of Net8), then any changes you make to a running listener will be written to its listener.ora file. See Chapter 14 for examples of controlling the listener in a UNIX environment.

Parameter	Description
CONNECT_TIMEOUT	Time, in seconds, that the Listener will wait for a valid connection request after the Listener has started. Default is 10.
LOG_DIRECTORY	The directory for the Listener log file.
LOG_FILE	The name of the Listener log file.
LOGGING	A flag to set logging ON or OFF.
PASSWORDS	The password for the Listener. Default is LISTENER.
SAVE_CONFIG_ON_STOP	Available as of Net8. A flag to indicate if changes made to the Listener while it is running should be saved to the listener.ora file.
SERVICE_LIST	The services list supported by the Listener (more general than the SID_LIST shown in the example).
STARTUP_WAIT_TIME	The number of seconds the Listener sleeps before responding to a start-up command.
TRACE_DIRECTORY	The directory for the Listener trace file.
TRACE_FILE	The name of the Listener trace file.
TRACE_LEVEL	The level of tracing (ADMIN, USER, SUPPORT, or OFF).
USE_PLUG_AND_PLAY	A flag (ON or OFF) to instruct the Listener to register with a Names server.

TABLE 13-1. *Additional listener.ora Parameters*

Using the Net8 Assistant

As of Net8, you can use the Net8 Assistant to manage your configuration files. If you use the default values for your configuration (for example, using the default UNIX port for your UNIX listeners), then you will be able to use the default configuration created by the Net8 Assistant.

As shown in Figure 13-3, the opening screen of the Net8 Assistant lists the three areas it supports: changing your local profile, managing the available service names, and managing the names servers. You can use the Net8 Assistant to manage your configuration file and test your connections.

For example, Figure 13-4 shows the different types of profile options you can change. Advanced options such as the Oracle Security Server can be managed via the Net8 Assistant. The Oracle Security Server and the Advanced Networking Option provide end-to-end encryption of data in a

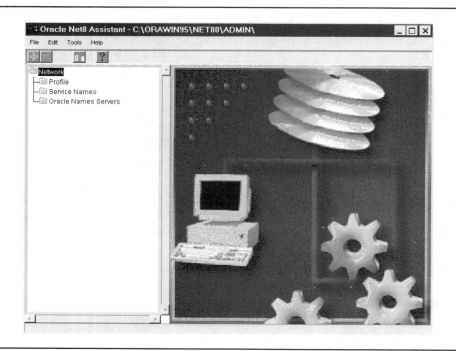

FIGURE 13-3. *Opening screen of the Net8 Assistant*

distributed environment. By default, your data will travel in clear text across your network unless you use ORACLE's encryption or a hardware-based encryption.

You can create new service names for your tnsnames.ora file via the ORACLE Service Names Wizard (see Figure 13-5). The Net8 Assistant will prompt you for each of the parameters required to establish a database connection, and will modify your local tnsnames.ora file to reflect the information you provide. If you use the default connectivity information (for example, using port 1521 for UNIX connections) then the wizard will be simplest to use. You can also use the Net8 Assistant to modify or test existing service names.

When you finish configuring a new service name, the Net8 Assistant will prompt you to test the service name. You can also test existing service

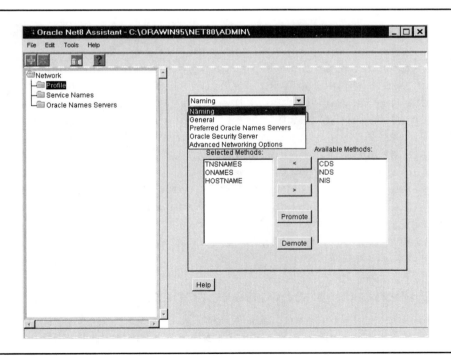

FIGURE 13-4.   *Profile options in the Net8 Assistant*

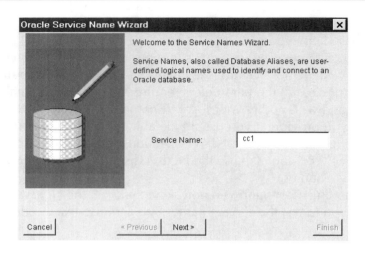

FIGURE 13-5. *The Service Names Wizard*

names by selecting the service name from the displayed list of services and selecting the test connection option from the menu options.

When you test your connections, the Net8 Assistant will prompt you for your username and password (see Figure 13-6). The username and password must be valid for the database identified by the current service name. The Net8 Assistant will attempt to log in to the database and will report the result of the connection attempt. The Net8 Assistant thus duplicates the functionality provided by the SQL*Net V2 TNSPING utility (see Chapter 14 for information on TNSPING).

The simpler you keep your client and server configurations, and the closer you adhere to the default values, the simpler the management of your configuration files will be. The Net8 Assistant simplifies your configuration file administration, but ideally you will accept the defaults for most of the prompted variables.

The MultiProtocol Interchange

The MultiProtocol Interchange portion of SQL*Net V2 is used to establish database communication links between otherwise incompatible network protocols. The concept of a network *community* is used to determine

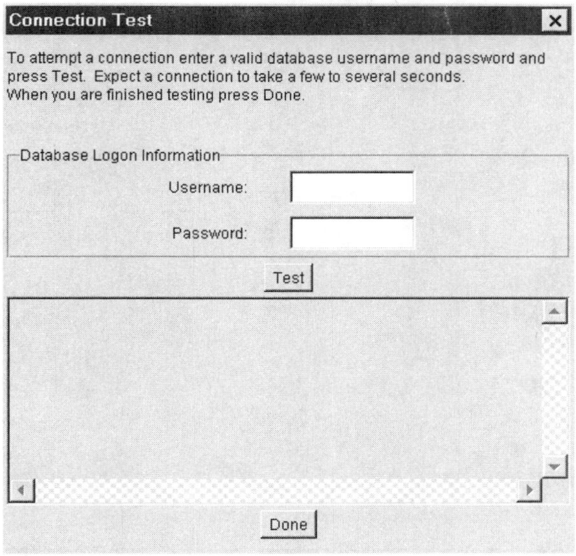

FIGURE 13-6.   *Connection test*

whether a MultiProtocol Interchange is necessary. The MultiProtocol
Interchange is obsolete as of Net8, replaced by the Connection Manager.

A network community is a set of servers that communicate with each
other via a single protocol. Examples of communities would include
networks of UNIX servers using TCP/IP, or of VAX servers using DECNet.
To transfer database requests from one community to another, a
MultiProtocol Interchange must be used. An interchange is shown
graphically in Figure 13-7.

The advantage of a MultiProtocol Interchange is that all servers do not
have to be using the same communications protocol. Because of this, each
server can use the communications protocol that is best suited to its
environment, and can still be able to transfer data back and forth with other
databases. This communication takes place regardless of the
communications protocols used on the remote servers; the MultiProtocol
Interchange takes care of the differences between the protocols.

In environments with three or more network communities, multiple
MultiProtocol Interchanges are used. They may be physically configured so

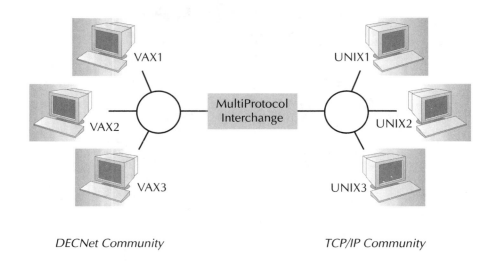

FIGURE 13-7. *A sample MultiProtocol Interchange*

that multiple access paths are available between servers. A multiple interchange configuration is shown in Figure 13-8.

Multiple access paths can be used to transfer data from one community to another. The MultiProtocol Interchanges will select the most appropriate path based on path availability and network load. The relative cost of each path is specified via the Network Manager utility when the MultiProtocol Interchanges are set up.

Each MultiProtocol Interchange has three components:

■ A Connection Manager, which manages a listener process to detect connection requests, and uses data pumps to transfer data

■ A Navigator, which chooses the best possible path through the TNS network

■ The Interchange Control Utility, which is used to manage the interchange's availability

You can use Network Manager to establish the configuration of each of these components when a new MultiProtocol Interchange is created.

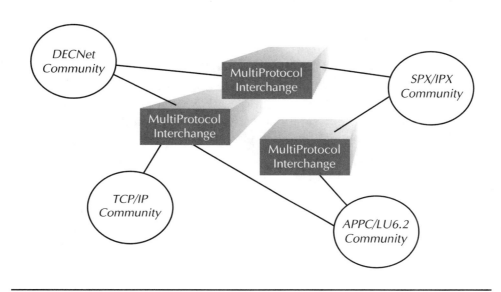

FIGURE 13-8.   *MultiProtocol Interchange configuration for three communities*

The network community in which a server exists should be added to the connect descriptors for its databases. A modified version of the connect descriptor shown earlier, with the COMMUNITY parameter added, is shown in the following listing. This is a modification to the tnsnames.ora files that are distributed throughout the network.

```
LOC =(DESCRIPTION=
        (ADDRESS=
             (COMMUNITY=TCP.HQ.COMPANY)
             (PROTOCOL=TCP)
             (HOST=HQ)
             (PORT=1521))
        (CONNECT DATA=
             (SID=loc)))
```

In this example, the host "HQ" is identified as being part of the TCP/IP community via the tnsnames.ora file. Other files that are generated from this tool for the MultiProtocol Interchanges are tnsnav.ora (community descriptions), tnsnet.ora (network overview), and intchg.ora (control parameters for the interchanges).

An additional file, sqlnet.ora, may be created to specify additional diagnostics beyond the default diagnostics provided.

Using Connection Manager

Net8 uses the Connection Manager in place of the MultiProtocol Interchange; it also supports connections within homogenous networks, reducing the number of physical connections maintained by the database. The Connection Manager is started via the **cmctl** command. The default start-up command is

```
cmctl start cman
```

If the Connection Manager has been started, then any client that has SOURCE_ROUTE set to YES in its tnsnames.ora file can use the Connection Manager. The Connection Manager reduces system resource requirements by maintaining logical connections while reusing physical connections.

Using ORACLE Names

With ORACLE Names, all of the tasks of managing distributed databases are handled via a global naming service available to all servers in a network. The service is used to store information about the following:

- Connect descriptors
- Database links
- Object aliases

ORACLE Names changes the way in which database links are resolved. Before, when a database link was specified, the database first looked at the user's private database links. If none with the matching name was found, then the available public database links were checked.

ORACLE Names adds an additional level to this. Now, if the first two checks do not return a match for the database link name, then the ORACLE Names server's list of global database link names is searched for the database link. If the link name is found there, ORACLE Names will return the link's specifications and resolve the query.

This greatly simplifies the administration of location transparency in a distributed environment. The information related to remote data access is now stored in a central location. The impact of this is felt every time a part of an FQON is modified. For example, if there were multiple links using specific connections to a single remote database, then a pre-Names modification to the user's password would require dropping and re-creating multiple database links. With Names, this change is made once.

ORACLE Names also supports the Domain Name Service (DNS) structure that ORACLE introduced with SQL*Net V2. ORACLE's DNS allows network hierarchies to be specified; thus, a server may be identified as HR.HQ.ACME.COM, which would be interpreted as the HR server in the HQ network of the ACME company.

If connect descriptors are also stored in ORACLE Names, then the need for manually maintaining multiple copies of the tnsnames.ora file diminishes. The centralized ORACLE Names server defines the relationships among the network objects. The database network may be divided into administrative regions, and the management tasks may be likewise divided. A change to one region will be transparently propagated to the other regions.

You can control an ORACLE Names server via the **namesctl** utility or via the Net8 Assistant.

Usage Example: Client-Server Applications

There are several ad hoc query tools available that work in a client-server fashion. Consider the example of a query tool operating in a Microsoft Windows environment on a PC. The PC is connected via a network card to a TCP/IP network, and is running a TCP/IP software package and SQL*Net V2 or Net8. The database that it will be accessing resides on a UNIX server on the same network. This configuration is depicted in Figure 13-9.

When the user runs the tool within Windows, a username, password, and service name for a database must be specified. When the user is connected to the database, he or she may then query from the tables available there. Every time a query is executed, the SQL statement for the query is sent to the server and executed. The data is then returned via SQL*Net V2 or Net8 and displayed on the client PC. See Chapter 16 for details of client-server implementation.

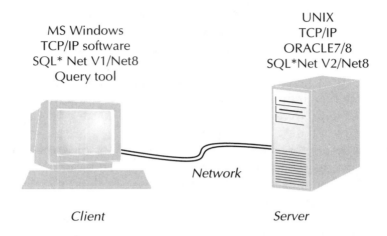

MS Windows
TCP/IP software
SQL* Net V1/Net8
Query tool

UNIX
TCP/IP
ORACLE7/8
SQL*Net V2/Net8

Network

Client   *Server*

FIGURE 13-9.   *Example client-server configuration*

Usage Example: Database Links

For frequently used connections to remote databases, *database links* should be established. Database links specify the connect descriptor to be used for a connection, and may also specify the username to connect to in the remote database.

A database link is typically used to create local objects (such as views or synonyms) that access remote databases via server-server communications. The local synonyms for remote objects provide location transparency to the local users. When a database link is referenced by a SQL statement, it opens a session in the remote database and executes the SQL statement there. The data is then returned, and the remote session may stay open in case it is needed again. Database links can be created as **public** links (by DBAs, making the link available to all users in the local database) or as private links.

The following example creates a private database link called HR_LINK:

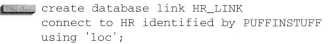

```
create database link HR_LINK
connect to HR identified by PUFFINSTUFF
using 'loc';
```

The **create database link** command, as shown in this example, has three parameters:

1. The name of the link (HR_LINK, in this example)

2. The account to connect to (if none is specified, then the local username and password will be used in the remote database)

3. The service name

A public database link can be created by adding the keyword **public** to the **create database link** command, as shown in the following example:

```
create public database link HR_LINK
connect to HR identified by PUFFINSTUFF
using 'loc';
```

Note that if the "LOC" instance is moved to a different server, then the database links can be redirected to LOC's new location simply by distributing a tnsnames.ora file that contains the modification. You can generate the revised tnsnames.ora file by using the Net8 Assistant tool described previously in this chapter.

To use these links, simply add them as suffixes to table names in commands. The following example creates a local view of a remote table, using the HR_LINK database link:

```
create view LOCAL_EMPLOYEE_VIEW
as
select * from EMPLOYEE@HR_LINK
where Office='ANNAPOLIS';
```

The **from** clause in this example refers to EMPLOYEE@HR_LINK. Since the HR_LINK database link specifies the server name, instance name, and owner name, the FQON for the table is known. If no account name had been specified, then the user's account name would have been used instead.

In this example, a view was created in order to limit the records that users could retrieve. If no such restriction is necessary, then a synonym can be used instead. This is shown in the following example:

```
create public synonym EMPLOYEE for EMPLOYEE@HR_LINK;
```

Local users who query the local public synonym EMPLOYEE will automatically have their queries redirected to the EMPLOYEE table in the LOC instance on the HQ server. Location transparency has thus been achieved.

By default, a single SQL statement can use up to four database links. This limit can be increased via the OPEN_LINKS parameter in the database's init.ora file.

Usage Example: The copy Command

The SQL*Plus **copy** command is an underutilitized, underappreciated command. The **copy** command allows data to be copied between databases (or within the same database) via SQL*Plus. Although it allows the user to select which columns to **copy**, it works best when all of the columns of a table are being chosen. The greatest benefit of this command is its ability to **commit** after each array of data has been processed; this in turn generates transactions that are of a manageable size.

Consider the case of a large table (again, using EMPLOYEE as the example). What if the EMPLOYEE table has 100,000 rows that use a total of 100MB of space, and you need to make a copy of that table into a different database? The easiest option, using a database link, involves the following steps:

```
create database link HR_LINK
connect to HR identified by PUFFINSTUFF
using 'loc';

create table EMPLOYEE
as
select * from EMPLOYEE@HR_LINK;
```

The first command creates the database link, and the second command creates a new table based on all of the data in the remote table.

Unfortunately, this option taxes your rollback segments. In order for it to work, a transaction the size of the entire remote table (100MB) must be supported. This in turn requires a rollback segment that is at least that large.

To break the transaction into smaller entries, use the SQL*Plus **copy** command. The syntax for this command is

```
copy from
remote_username/remote_password@service_name
to
username/password@service_name
[append|create|insert|replace]
TABLE_NAME
using subquery;
```

If the current account is to be the destination of the copied data, then the local username, password, and service name are not necessary.

To set the transaction entry size, use the SQL*Plus **set** command to set a value for the **arraysize** parameter. This determines the number of records that will be retrieved in each "batch." The **copycommit** parameter tells SQL*Plus how many batches should be **commit**ted at one time. Thus, the following SQL*Plus script accomplishes the same data-copying goal that the **create table as** command met; however, it breaks up the single transaction into multiple transactions. In this example, the data is committed after every 1,000 records. This reduces the transaction's rollback segment entry size needed from 100MB to 1MB—a much more manageable transaction size.

```
set copycommit 1
set arraysize 1000
copy from HR/PUFFINSTUFF@loc -
create EMPLOYEE -
using -
select * from EMPLOYEE
```

Except for the last line, each line in the **copy** command must be terminated with a dash (-), since this is a SQL*Plus command.

The different data options within the **copy** command are described in Table 13-2.

Option	Description
APPEND	Inserts the rows into the destination table. Automatically creates the table if it does not exist.
CREATE	Creates the table, then inserts the rows.
INSERT	Inserts the rows into the destination table if it exists; otherwise, returns an error. When using INSERT, all columns must be specified in the **using** subquery.
REPLACE	Drops the existing destination table and replaces it with a new table containing the copied data.

TABLE 13-2.   *Data Options for the* **copy** *Command*

The feedback provided by this command is confusing at first. After the final **commit** is complete, the database reports to the user the number of records that were **commit**ted in the *last* batch. The command feedback does not report the total number of records **committed** (unless they are all **commit**ted in a single batch).

Tuning SQL*Net and Net8

Tuning SQL*Net applications is fairly straightforward: wherever possible, reduce the amount of data that is sent across the network, particularly for online transaction-processing applications. The basic procedures that should be applied include

- The use of distributed objects, such as snapshots, to replicate static data to remote databases.

- The use of procedures to reduce the amount of data sent across the network. Rather than sending data back and forth, only the procedure's error status is returned.

- The use of the highest buffer size available for SQL*Net buffering.

- Using homogenous servers wherever possible to eliminate the need for protocol interchange.

The first of these topics is discussed in detail in Chapters 8 and 15.

The buffer size used by SQL*Net V2 and Net8 should take advantage of the packet sizes used by the network protocols (such as TCP/IP). If you send large packets of data across the network, then the packets may be fragmented. Since each packet contains header information, reducing packet fragmentation reduces network traffic.

As of SQL*Net V2.3, you can tune the size of the service layer and transport layer buffer sizes. The specification for the service layer data buffer is called SDU; it may be specified in your tnsnames.ora and listener.ora files. For example, the following listing shows a section of tnsnames.ora file for the LOC service name. In this example, the service layer buffer size is set to 2K via the SDU parameter. The transport layer buffer size, as defined the TDU parameter, is also set to 2K.

```
LOC =(DESCRIPTION=
        (SDU=2048)
        (TDU=2048)
        (ADDRESS=
              (PROTOCOL=TCP)
              (HOST=HQ)
              (PORT=1521))
        (CONNECT DATA=
              (SID=loc)))
```

The listener.ora file must contain matching entries:

```
LISTENER =
    (ADDRESS_LIST =
          (ADDRESS=
             (PROTOCOL=IPC)
             (KEY= loc.world)
          )
    )
SID_LIST_LISTENER =
    (SID_LIST =
      (SID_DESC =
        (SDU=2048)
        (TDU=2048)
        (SID_NAME = loc)
        (ORACLE_HOME = /orasw/app/oracle/product/8.0.3.1)
      )
    )
```

The listener.ora and tnsnames.ora SDU settings do not have to be identical; if they are different, then the lower of the two will be used for the communications. The default size of the SDU setting is 2K, as shown in the preceding listings.

The impact of changing the SDU and TDU settings is a reduction in network traffic and a shortening of the time required to connect to the database. However, you will need to know the size of the data being transferred in order to know whether increasing the SDU and TDU parameters can affect your performance. The buffer size for TCP/IP is 1,500 bytes; if your data exceeds this value, then you will be using multiple network packets no matter what the values are for the other parameters. The amount of data transferred at a time is determined by your **arraysize** setting and the size of the rows being read.

For example, if you **set arraysize 100** in SQL*Plus, and query rows that are 100 bytes each, then your data will require 10,000 bytes— so you will be using multiple packets. If you use an array size of 10 instead, then you will be transferring 1,000 bytes each time. Given the smaller array size, you can eliminate or reduce packet fragmentation by setting the SDU and TDU parameters to 2K, as shown in the previous examples. Setting SDU to higher values will not have a noticeable effect on your network traffic, since you will be limited by the buffer size supported by the underlying network protocol. If you regularly query tables with large row sizes, you may not be able to reduce the network traffic generated.

CHAPTER 14

Networking in UNIX

s a general rule, there is no general rule. And as for a
standard version of UNIX, there isn't one of those either.
This chapter will therefore concentrate on those networking
elements that are common to most UNIX versions.
Instructions for implementing SQL*Net V2 and Net8 in
UNIX will be provided. Both SQL*Net V2 and Net8 can be used to access
ORACLE8 databases (both work for ORACLE7 databases as well). Since the
TCP/IP communications protocol is commonly used for UNIX servers, that
protocol will be featured.

Before a process can connect to a database on a server, there are
several steps that the DBA must take in conjunction with the UNIX system
administrator. The following sections describe each of these steps.

Identification of Hosts

A *host*, for the purposes of this chapter, will be defined as a server that is
capable of communicating with another server via a network. Each host
maintains a list of the hosts with which it can communicate. This list is
maintained in a file called /etc/hosts. The "/etc" portion of the filename
signifies that it is located in the /etc directory. This file contains the Internet
address for the hosts, plus the host names. It may optionally include an
alias for each host name. A sample portion of an /etc/hosts file is shown in
the following listing:

```
127.0.0.1 nmhost
127.0.0.2 txhost
127.0.0.3 azhost  arizona
```

NOTE
*Your UNIX implementation may use a domain
name server instead, in which case the host IP
addresses may not all be listed in the /etc/hosts
file.*

In this example, there are three hosts listed. The first two entries assign
host names ("nmhost" and "txhost") to Internet addresses. The third entry
assigns both a host name ("azhost") and an alias ("arizona") to an Internet
address.

Most networking software for PC clients uses a similar file. Within the network software directory structure, a file called hosts is maintained. This file lists the IP address and host name for each host that the client can directly reach. The file is identical in structure to the UNIX /etc/hosts file.

The list of host names in the /etc/hosts file determines which host names can be accessed from this host. Therefore, you may wish to guarantee that no host's /etc/hosts file can be changed without distributing that change to all hosts on the network. Otherwise, you may create networks in which some hosts are dead ends.

Consider the /etc/hosts file shown in the previous listing. If that is the /etc/hosts file for the server known as txhost, then it will be able to reach two other servers (nmhost and azhost). However, what if no other server has txhost listed in *its* /etc/hosts file? The txhost server will be unreachable from the network.

That may be a desirable scenario from a security standpoint; it would serve to partially isolate the databases on txhost from the rest of the network. However, it is more often the case that hosts are added to the network in order to share information and resources. Inconsistent /etc/hosts files stand in the way of meeting that goal. The consistency of these files is usually maintained by a UNIX systems administrator.

Identification of Databases

All databases that are run on a host and are accessible to the network must be listed in a file named /etc/oratab. The "/etc" portion of the file name signifies that it is located in the /etc directory. This file is maintained by the DBA.

The components of an entry in this file are listed in Table 14-1.

The "Startup_Flag" component doesn't seem to fit; after all, why should a network connection care about the startup schedule for an instance? This flag is part of the entry because this file is also used (by default; it can be changed) during system startup to start the server's ORACLE databases.

The three components are listed all on one line, separated only by colons (:). A sample /etc/oratab file is shown in the following listing:

```
loc:/orasw/app/oracle/product/8.0.3.1:Y
cc1:/orasw/app/oracle/product/8.0.3.1:N
old:/orasw/app/oracle/product/8.0.3.0:Y
```

Component	Description
ORACLE_SID	Instance name (server ID).
ORACLE_HOME	Full path name of the root directory of the ORACLE software used by the database.
Startup_Flag	Flag to indicate whether the instance should be started when the host is started. If set to "Y", then it will be started. If set to "N", then it will not be started. This flag is used by the db_startup command file provided by ORACLE.

TABLE 14-1. *Entry Components for /etc/oratab*

This example shows entries for three instances, named loc, cc1, and old. The first two instances have the same ORACLE_HOME; the third uses an older version of the ORACLE kernel. Both loc and old will be automatically started when the server starts; cc1 will have to be manually started. To access the instances, you will first need to start the Listener process; the next section describes the configuration of the Listener process in UNIX.

Identification of Services

A *server process* listens for connection requests from clients. It directs those requests to the proper UNIX socket, and the connection can then take place. The method of managing the Listener server process—the server process for SQL*Net V2 and Net8—changed little between SQL*Net V2 and Net8.

The information needed by the Listener process (such as the port specifications and the host names) is stored in files that are distributed throughout the network. The tnsnames.ora file on each host will include listings of *service names,* with their associated connect descriptors. These descriptors contain the information needed to establish a connection with a UNIX listener process. A sample entry for tnsnames.ora is shown in the following listing:

```
HQ =(DESCRIPTION=
     (ADDRESS=
```

```
              (PROTOCOL=TCP)
              (HOST=HQ)
              (PORT=1521))
     (CONNECT DATA=
              (SID=loc)))
```

In this example, the service name HQ is given to a specific connect descriptor. That descriptor specifies the host ("HQ"), the protocol ("TCP"), the port ("1521"), and the instance ID ("loc").

In order for a client to connect to a database on a remote server, the remote server must be running a Listener process. This process, called TNSLSNR ("TNS listener"—"TNS" stands for "transparent network substrate"), waits for connection attempts to the databases listed in the listener.ora file. This file lists all of the Listeners on the server. The listener.ora file thus plays an important role in the server's ability to "listen" to outside connection requests. A sample portion of a listener.ora file is shown in the following listing:

```
LISTENER =
   (ADDRESS_LIST =
        (ADDRESS=
           (PROTOCOL=IPC)
           (KEY= loc.world)
        )
   )
SID_LIST_LISTENER =
   (SID_LIST =
     (SID_DESC =
       (SID_NAME = loc)
       (ORACLE_HOME = /orasw/app/oracle/product/8.0.3.1)
     )
   )
```

This listener.ora segment shows the instance that the Listener will service (in this case, the loc instance). The ORACLE software home directory for each instance must be listed in this file, as shown in the listing. As of ORACLE8, you can use the Net8 Assistant to manage your configuration files (see Chapter 13).

When you attempt to use either the tnsnames.ora or listener.ora files, ORACLE will look in the directory identified by the TNS_ADMIN environment variable. In most cases, the /etc directory is used as the TNS_ADMIN directory for these two files.

Starting the Listener process is described in the next section. When you migrate from SQL*Net V2 to Net8, there are several changes in the parameters of the listener control options.

Starting the Listener Server Process

The Listener process is controlled by the Listener Control Utility, executed via the **lsnrctl** command. The options available for the **lsnrctl** command are described in the next section, "Controlling the Listener Server Process." To start the Listener, use the command

```
> lsnrctl start
```

This will start the default Listener (named LISTENER). If you wish to start a Listener with a different name, include that Listener's name as the second parameter in the **lsnrctl** command. For example, if you created a Listener called MY_LSNR, then you could start it via the following command:

```
> lsnrctl start my_lsnr
```

In the next section you will find descriptions of the other parameters available for the Listener Control Utility.

After starting a Listener, you can check that it is running by using the **status** option of the Listener Control Utility.

The following command can be used to perform this check:

```
> lsnrctl status
```

Sample output for this command is shown in the following listing:

```
LSNRCTL for SUNOS: Version 2.3.3.0.0 -
Copyright (c) Oracle Corporation 1994.  All rights reserved.
Connecting to (ADDRESS=(PROTOCOL=IPC)(KEY=loc.world))

STATUS of the LISTENER
----------------------
Alias                    LISTENER
Version                  TNSLSNR for SUNOS: Version 2.3.3.0.0 - Production
Start Date               18-AUG-97 20:01:18
Uptime                   22 days 17 hr. 48 min. 26 sec
```

```
Trace Level              off
Security                 OFF
SNMP                     OFF
Listener Parameter File  /etc/listener.ora
Listener Log File        /orasw/app/oracle/product/7.3.3.2/network
                         /log/listener
.log
Services Summary...
  loc            has 1 service handler(s)
The command completed successfully.
```

The status output in the preceding listing shows that the Listener has been started, and that it is currently supporting only one service ("loc"), as defined by its listener.ora file. The Listener parameter file is identified as /etc/listener.ora and its log file location is shown.

If you wish to see the operating system-level processes that are involved, use the following command. It uses the UNIX **ps -ef** command to list the system's active processes. The **grep tnslsnr** command then eliminates those rows that do not contain the term "tnslsnr".

```
> ps -ef | grep tnslsnr
```

Sample output for this command:

```
oracle  4249     1  0  Aug 18  ?          1:14 /orasw/app/oracle/product/7.3.3.
                                          2/bin/tnslsnr LISTENER -inhe
oracle  2469  2419  1 13:56:23 ttypc      0:00 grep tns
```

This output shows two processes: the "LISTENER" process and the process that is checking for it. The first line of output is wrapped to the second line and truncated by the operating system. The term 'inherit' is truncated to 'inhe' because of the length limits on the data displayed by the **ps** command.

Controlling the Listener Server Process

It may be necessary to modify the Listener server processes periodically. Since you don't want to have to shut down and restart the server just to change the listener parameters, you can use the **lsnrctl** utility to manage them.

The Listener Control Utility, **lsnrctl**, is used to start, stop, and modify the Listener process on the server. Its command options are listed in Table 14-2. Each of these commands may be accompanied by a value; for all except the **set password** command, that value will be a Listener name. If no Listener name is specified, then the default ("LISTENER") will be used. Once within **lsnrctl**, you can change the Listener being modified via the **set current_listener** command.

NOTE
To use the Net8 Listener control utility, use **lsnrctl80** *in place of* **lsnrctl**.

Command	Description
CHANGE_PASSWORD	Sets a new password for the listener. You will be prompted for the old password for the listener.
DBSNMP_START	Starts the DBSNMP subagent for a database on the server. See Appendix B for information on DBSNMP.
DBSNMP_STATUS	Provides status information on the DBSNMP subagent.
DBSNMP_STOP	Stops the DBSNMP subagent on the server.
EXIT	Exits **lsnrctl**.
HELP	Displays a list of the **lsnrctl** command options. You can also see additional options via the **help set** and **help show** commands.
QUIT	Exits **lsnrctl**.
RELOAD	Allows you to modify the listener services after the listener has been started. It forces SQL*Net to read and use the most current listener.ora file.
SAVE_CONFIG	New as of Net8. Creates a backup of your existing listener.ora file, then updates your listener.ora with parameters you have changed via **lsnrctl**.

TABLE 14-2. *Listener Control Utility Commands*

Command	Description
SERVICES	Displays services available, along with its connection history. It also lists whether each service is enabled for remote DBA or autologin access.
SET	Set parameter values. Options are **connect_timeout** time, in seconds, the listener will wait for a valid connection request after the listener has been started. **current_listener** changes the listener process whose parameters are being set or shown. **log_directory** the directory for the listener log file. **log_file** the name of the listener log file. **log_status** whether logging is ON or OFF. **password** listener password **save_config_on_stop** new as of Net8. Saves your configuration changes to your listener.ora file when you exit **lsnrctl**. **startup_waittime** the number of seconds the listener sleeps before responding to a **lsnrctl start** command. **trc_directory** the directory for the listener trace file. **trc_file** the name for the listener trace file. **trc_level** the trace level (ADMIN, USER, SUPPORT, or OFF). See **lsnrctl trace**.
SHOW	Show current parameter settings. Options are the same as the **set** options with the sole omission of the **password** command.
SPAWN	Spawns a program that runs with an alias in the listener.ora file.
START	Starts the listener.
STATUS	Provides status information about the listener, including the time it was started, its parameter filename, its log file, and the services it supports. This can be used to query the status of a listener on a remote server.
STOP	Stops the listener.

TABLE 14-2. *Listener Control Utility Commands* (continued)

Command	Description
TRACE	Sets the trace level of the listener to one of three choices: OFF; USER (limited tracing); ADMIN (high level of tracing); and SUPPORT (for ORACLE Support).
VERSION	Displays version information for the listener, TNS, and the protocol adapters.

TABLE 14-2. *Listener Control Utility Commands* (continued)

You can enter the **lsnrctl** command by itself and enter the **lsnrctl** utility shell, from which all other commands can then be executed.

The commands options listed in Table 14-2 give you a great deal of control over the Listener process, as shown in the following examples. In most of these examples, the **lsnrctl** command is first entered by itself. This places the user in the **lsnrctl** utility (as indicated by the LSNRCTL prompt). The rest of the commands are entered from within this utility.

■ To stop the Listener:

```
> lsnrctl
LSNRCTL> set password lsnr_password
LSNRCTL> stop
```

■ To list status information for the Listener:

```
> lsnrctl status
```

To list the status of a Listener on another host, add a service name from that host as a parameter to the **status** command. The following example uses the "HQ" service name shown earlier in this chapter:

```
> lsnrctl status hq
```

■ To list version information about the Listener:

```
> lsnrctl version
```

■   To list information about the services supported by the Listener:

```
> lsnrctl
LSNRCTL> set password lsnr_password
LSNRCTL> services
```

■   To reload the services from the listener.ora file:

```
> lsnrctl
LSNRCTL> set password lsnr_password
LSNRCTL> reload
```

■   To save modified configuration parameters to the listener.ora file
(available as of Net8):

```
> lsnrctl
LSNRCTL> set password lsnr_password
LSNRCTL> save_config
```

■   To change the level of tracing performed:

```
> lsnrctl
LSNRCTL> set password lsnr_password
LSNRCTL> trace user
```

■   To start the Listener process:

```
> lsnrctl
LSNRCTL> set password lsnr_password
LSNRCTL> start
```

Most of these commands require passwords. Therefore, it is not
advisable to run them via batch commands, since that would involve either
storing the password in a file or passing it as a parameter to a batch program.

Debugging Connection Problems

As described in this chapter, SQL*Net/Net8 connections in UNIX require
that a number of communication mechanisms be properly configured. The
connections involve host-to-host communication, proper identification of
services and databases, and proper configuration of the listener server

processes. In the event of connection problems when using SQL*Net V2 or Net8, it is important to eliminate as many of these components as possible.

Start by making sure that the host the connection is trying to reach is accessible via the network. This can be checked via the following command:

```
> telnet host_name
```

If this command is successful, then you will be prompted for a username and password on the remote host. If the **ping** command is available to you, then you may use it instead. This command, shown in the following listing, will check to see if the remote host is available and will return a status message:

```
> ping host_name
```

If the host is available on the network, then the next step is to check if the Listener is running. At the same time, you can check to see what parameters it is currently using; this is important if you are attempting a remote autologin access. The **lsnrctl status** command will provide this information:

```
> lsnrctl status service_name
```

The *service_name* clause should refer to the name of a service on the remote server. If the *service_name* clause is not used, then the command will return the status of the Listener on the local server.

These two checks—of host availability and Listener availability—will resolve over 95 percent of SQL*Net and Net8 connection problems in server-server communications. The rest of the problems will result from difficulties with the database specification that is being used. These problems include invalid username/password combinations, down databases, and databases in need of recovery.

In client-server communications, the same principles for debugging connection problems apply. First, verify that the remote host is accessible; most communications software for clients includes a **telnet** or **ping** command. If it is not accessible, then the problem may be on the client side. Verify that *other* clients are able to access the host on which the database resides. If they can, then the problem is isolated to the client. If they cannot, then the problem lies on the server side, and the server, its Listener processes, and its databases should be checked.

From the client, you can use the **tnsping** command to test connection to a Listener. Execute the **tnsping** command with two parameters: the name of the service name to check and the number of connections to attempt. For example, if you run the command **tnsping hq 20**, then ORACLE will attempt to connect to the 'hq' service 20 consecutive times. The multiple connections are used because the output of the **tnsping** command may be displayed very quickly, and forcing it through multiple tests gives you time to read the output. The **tnsping** command is provided as part of the Windows client SQL*Net and Net8 connectivity software.

CHAPTER
15

Managing Distributed Databases

veryone knows somebody whose desk is a mess. Surely it wouldn't take too long to organize the papers by subject matter, file them in a comprehensible fashion, and clean up the mess. Of course, the desk's owner always replies that after everything was organized, it would never be found again.

Unless you want your databases to look like that desk, you need to plan their organization. As computers join ever-expanding local and wide area networks, local and remote databases will join in ever-expanding networks of databases. To take advantage of these distributed databases, you need to understand their capabilities, their management, and the monitoring and tuning considerations that are unique to them. The available data will then be organized *and* quickly retrievable—in stark contrast to the cluttered desk approach.

Overview of Distributed Databases

The *distributed database* architecture is based on the *server-server* configurations described in Chapter 13. In a distributed environment, databases on separate servers (hosts) share data with each other. Each server can then be physically isolated without being logically isolated from other servers.

A typical implementation of this type involves corporate headquarters servers that communicate with departmental servers in various locations. Each server supports client applications, but it also has the ability to communicate with other servers in the network. This architecture is shown in Figure 15-1.

When one of the servers sends a database request to another server, the sending server acts like a *client*. The receiving server executes the SQL statement that is passed to it and returns the results plus error conditions to the sender.

SQL*Net V2 and Net8 allow this architecture to become reality. When run on all of the servers, SQL*Net and Net8 allow database requests made from one database (or application) to be passed to another database on a separate server. Both distributed queries and distributed updates are supported.

With this functionality, you can communicate with all of the databases that are accessible via your network. You can then create synonyms that give applications true network transparency; the user who submits a query will not know the location of the data that is used to resolve it.

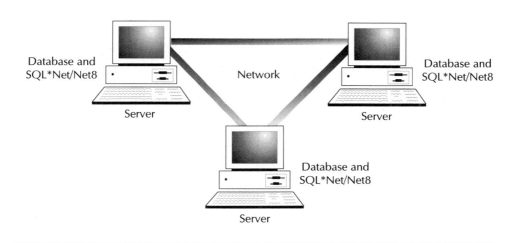

FIGURE 15-1. *Server-server architecture*

Remote Queries

The ability to perform remote queries is only one capability of a distributed database, and its usefulness is limited. It will only serve your needs if your data is isolated both logically and physically; that is, the "ownership" of the data can be ascribed to a single database, and there are no data dependencies between databases.

To query a remote database, a *database link* must be established. The database link specifies the service name that is to be used, and may also specify the username to connect to in the remote database. When a database link is referenced by an SQL statement, ORACLE opens a session in the remote database and executes the SQL statement there. The data is then returned, and the remote session stays open in case it is needed again. Database links can be created as public links (by DBAs, making the link available to all users in the local database) or as private links.

The following example creates a public database link called HR_LINK:

```
create public database link HR_LINK
connect to HR identified by PUFFINSTUFF
using 'hq';
```

The **create database link** command, as shown in this example, has several parameters:

- The optional keyword **public**, which allows DBAs to create links for all users in a database
- The name of the link (HR_LINK, in this example)
- The account to connect to (if none is specified, then the local username and password will be used in the remote database)
- The service name ('hq')

To use the newly created link, simply add it as a suffix to table names in commands. The following example queries a remote table by using the HR_LINK database link:

```
select * from EMPLOYEE@HR_LINK
 where Office='ANNAPOLIS';
```

When you execute this query, ORACLE will establish a session via the HR_LINK database link and query the EMPLOYEE table in that database. The **where** clause will be applied to the EMPLOYEE rows, and the matching records will be returned. The execution of the query is shown graphically in Figure 15-2.

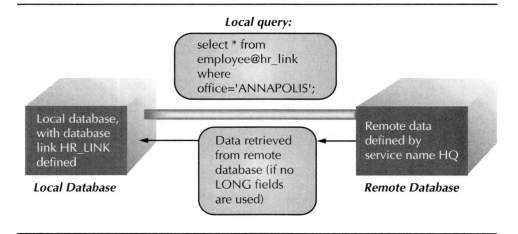

FIGURE 15-2. *Sample remote query*

NOTE
*Database links cannot be used to return values
from columns with LONG datatypes.*

The **from** clause in this example refers to EMPLOYEE@HR_LINK. Since the HR_LINK database link specifies the server name, instance name, and owner name, the full name of the table is known. If no account name had been specified in the database link, then the user's account name and password in the local database would have been used when attempting to log in to the remote database.

The detailed management of database links is described in the "Managing Distributed Data" section later in this chapter.

Remote Data Manipulation: Two-Phase Commit

To achieve remote data manipulation, you'll need to use *Two-Phase Commit (2PC)*—and that's where the ORACLE's distributed database capabilities come into play. 2PC allows groups of transactions across several nodes to be treated as a unit; either all of the transactions **commit**, or they all get rolled back. A set of distributed transactions is shown in Figure 15-3. In that figure, two **update** transactions are performed. The first **update** goes against a local table (EMPLOYEE); the second, against a remote table (EMPLOYEE@HR_LINK). After the two transactions are performed, a single **commit** is then executed. If either transaction cannot **commit**, then both transactions will be rolled back.

Distributed transactions yield two important benefits: databases on other servers can be **update**d, and those transactions can be grouped together with others in a logical unit. This second benefit occurs because of the database's use of 2PC. Its two phases are

1. The *Prepare* phase   An initiating node called the *global coordinator* notifies all sites involved in the transaction to be ready to either **commit** or roll back the transaction.

2. The *Commit* phase   If there is no problem with the Prepare phase, then all sites **commit** their transactions. If a network or node failure occurs, then all sites roll back their transactions.

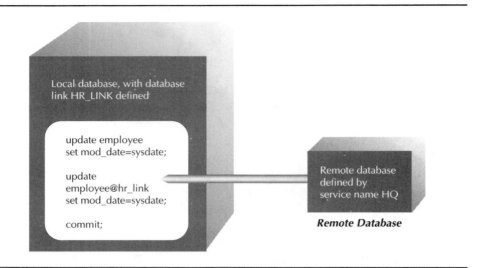

FIGURE 15-3. *Sample distributed transaction*

The use of 2PC is transparent to the users. The detailed management of distributed transactions is discussed in the "Managing Distributed Transactions" section later in this chapter.

Dynamic Data Replication

To improve the performance of queries that use data from remote databases, you may wish to replicate that data on the local server. There are several options for accomplishing this, depending on which ORACLE features you are using.

You can use *database triggers* to replicate data from one table into another. For example, after every **insert** into a table, a trigger may fire to **insert** that same record into another table—and that table may be in a remote database. Thus, triggers can be used to enforce data replication in simple configurations. If the types of transactions against the base table cannot be controlled, then the trigger code needed to perform the replication will be unacceptably complicated.

When using ORACLE's distributed features, you can use *snapshots* to replicate data between databases. You do not have to replicate an entire table or limit yourself to data from just one table. When replicating a single table, you may use a **where** clause to restrict which records are replicated, and may perform **group by** operations on the data. You can also join the table with other tables and replicate the result of the queries.

The data in the local snapshot of the remote table(s) will need to be refreshed. You can specify the refresh interval for the snapshot and the database will automatically take care of the replication procedures. If the snapshot is a one-to-one replication of records in a remote table (called a *simple snapshot*), then the database can use a *snapshot log* to send over only transaction data; otherwise, it is a *complex snapshot* and the database will perform complete refreshes on the local snapshot table. The dynamic replication of data via snapshots is shown in Figure 15-4.

Other methods may be used to replicate data, but they are not dynamically maintained by the database. For example, you can use the SQL*Plus **copy** command (see the "Usage Example: The **copy** Command" section of Chapter 13) to create copies of remote tables in local databases. However, the **copy** command would need to be repeated every time the data is changed; therefore, its use is limited to those situations in which large, static tables are replicated. Dynamic data requires dynamic replication.

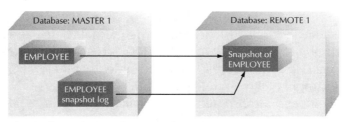

(a) A simple snapshot; snapshot logs can be used.

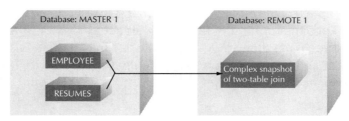

(b) A complex snapshot; the result of the join is replicated.

FIGURE 15-4.   *Simple and complex snapshots*

Managing Distributed Data

Before you can worry about managing transactions against remote databases, you have to get the data there—and make it globally accessible to other databases. The following sections describe the requisite management tasks: enforcing location transparency, and managing the database links, triggers, and snapshots that are used to access the data.

The Infrastructure: Enforcing Location Transparency

To properly design your distributed databases for long-term use, you must start by making the physical location of the data transparent to the application. The name of an object within a database is unique within the schema that owns it. Thus, within any single database, the combination of owner and object name will uniquely identify a table. However, a remote database may have an account with the same name, which may own an object with the same name. How can the object name be properly qualified?

Within distributed databases, two additional layers of object identification must be added. First, the name of the instance that accesses the database must be identified. Next, the name of the host on which that instance resides must be identified. Putting together these four parts of the object's name—its host, its instance, its owner, and its name—results in a *fully qualified object name* (*FQON*). The FQON is sometimes referred to as the *global object name*. To access a remote table, that table's FQON must be known. A sample is shown in Figure 15-5.

The goal of location transparency is to make the first three parts of the FQON—the host, the instance, and the schema—transparent to the user. It is even possible to make the object name itself transparent to the user (it may, for example, point instead to a view that joins two tables), but this chapter will keep that portion of the FQON intact as a point of reference.

The first three parts of the FQON are all specified via database links, so any effort at achieving location transparency should start there. First, consider a typical database link:

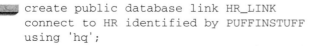

```
create public database link HR_LINK
connect to HR identified by PUFFINSTUFF
using 'hq';
```

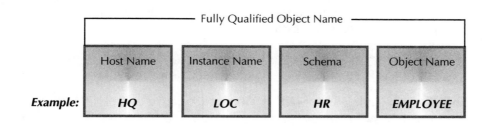

FIGURE 15-5. *Fully qualified object name*

By using a service name ('hq'), the host and instance names are kept transparent. They are translated into their actual values via the local host's tnsnames.ora file. A partial entry in this file, for this service name, is shown in the following listing:

```
hq =(DESCRIPTION=
        (ADDRESS=
              (PROTOCOL=TCP)
              (HOST=HQ)
              (PORT=1521))
        (CONNECT DATA=
              (SID=loc))))
```

The two lines in bold in this listing fill in the two missing pieces of the FQON: when the "HQ" service name is used, the host name is "HQ", and the instance name is "LOC". This tnsnames.ora file shows the parameters for the TCP/IP protocol; other protocols may use different keywords, but their usage is the same. They provide transparency for the server and instance names.

The HR_LINK database link, if created via the code given earlier in this section, will thus provide transparency for the first two parts of the FQON. But what if the data moves from the HR schema, or the HR account's password changes? The database link would have to be dropped and re-created. The same would be true if account-level security was required; it may be necessary to create and maintain multiple database links.

To resolve the transparency of the "schema" portion of the FQON, you can modify the way in which the database link is written. Consider the database link in the following listing:

```
create public database link HR_LINK
using 'hq';
```

This database link leaves out the **connect to** clause entirely. It will use what is known as a *default connection*. An example of this link being used is shown in the following listing:

```
select * from EMPLOYEE@HR_LINK;
```

When this link is used, the database will resolve the FQON in the following manner:

1. It will search the local tnsnames.ora file to determine the proper host name.

2. It will search the local tnsnames.ora file to determine the proper instance name.

3. It will search the database link for a **connect to** specification. If none is found, then it will attempt to connect to the specified database using the *current user's* username and password.

4. It will search the **from** clause of the query for the object name.

Default connections are often used to access tables whose rows can be restricted based on the username that is accessing the table. For example, if the remote database had a table named HR.EMPLOYEE, and every employee was allowed to see his or her own record, then a database link with a specific connection, such as

```
create public database link HR_LINK
connect to HR identified by PUFFINSTUFF
using 'hq';
```

would log in as the HR account (the owner of the table). If this specific connection is used, it is not possible to restrict the user's view of the records on the remote host. However, if a default connection is used, and a view is created on the remote host using the User pseudocolumn, then only that user's data would be returned from the remote host. A sample database link and view of this type is shown in the following listing:

```
create public database link HR_LINK
using 'hq';

create view REMOTE_EMP
as select * from EMPLOYEE@HR_LINK
where Ename=User;
```

The User pseudocolumn's value is the current ORACLE username. If you query the REMOTE_EMP view, you are using the HR_LINK database link. Since that link uses a default connection, your username and password will be used to connect to the 'hq' service name's database. You will therefore retrieve only those records from EMPLOYEE@HR_LINK for which your username is equal to the value of the Ename column in that table.

Either way, the data can be restricted. The difference is that when a default connection is used, the data can be restricted based on the username in the remote database; if a specific connection is used, then the data can be restricted after it has been returned to the local database. The default connection method thus reduces the amount of network traffic needed to resolve the query, as well as adding an additional level of location transparency to the data.

Using this method raises a different set of maintenance issues. The tnsnames.ora files must be synchronized across the servers, and the username/password combinations in multiple databases must be synchronized. These issues are addressed in the next section.

Managing Database Links

Information about public database links can be retrieved via the DBA_DB_LINKS data dictionary view. Private database links can be viewed via the USER_DB_LINKS data dictionary view. Whenever possible, separate your users among databases so that they may all share the same public database links. As a side benefit, these users will usually also be able to share public grants and synonyms.

The columns of the DBA_DB_LINKS data dictionary view are listed in Table 15-1. The password for the link to use is not viewable via DBA_DB_LINKS; it is stored unencrypted in the SYS.LINK$ table.

Column Name	Description
OWNER	Owner of the database link
DB_LINK	Name of the database link (such as "HR_LINK" in this chapter's examples)
USERNAME	The name of the account that should be used to open a session in the remote database, if a specific connection is used
HOST	The SQL*Net connect string that will be used to connect to the remote database
CREATED	A timestamp that marks the creation date for the database link

TABLE 15-1. *Columns of DBA_DB_LINKS*

NOTE
The number of database links that can be used by a single query is limited by the OPEN_LINKS parameter in the database's init.ora file. Its default value is 4.

The managerial tasks involved for database links depend on the level to which you have implemented location transparency in your databases. They also depend on the version of SQL*Net you are using—users of Net8 should see Chapter 13 for details on the use of the Net8 Assistant.

In the best-case scenario, default connections are used along with service names or aliases. In this case, the only requirements for successful maintenance are that the tnsnames.ora file be consistent across hosts and that user account/password combinations be maintained globally. The file synchronization can be accomplished via the operating system—for example, by use of the UNIX **rcp** (remote copy) command to copy files to remote hosts.

Synchronizing account/password combinations is more difficult, but there are several alternatives. First, you may force all changes to user account passwords to go through a central authority. This central authority would have the responsibility for updating the password for the account in all databases in the network—a time-consuming task, but a valuable one.

Second, you may audit all user password changes by auditing all **alter user** commands. If a user's password changes in one database, then it is changed on all databases available in the network that are accessed via default connections. Synchronizing database password changes is more difficult if you use the password management features available as of ORACLE8, since you can force passwords to expire and force frequent password changes.

If any part of the FQON—such as a username—is embedded in the database link, then a change affecting that part of the FQON requires that the database link be dropped and re-created. For example, if the HR user's password was changed, then the HR_LINK database link with a specific connection defined earlier would be dropped:

```
drop database link HR_LINK;
```

and the link would then be re-created, using the new account specification:

```
create public database link HR_LINK
connect to HR identified by NEWPASSWORD
using 'hq';
```

You cannot create a database link in another user's account. If you attempt to create a database link in SCOTT's account, as in the following:

```
create database link SCOTT.HR_LINK
connect to HR identified by PUFFINSTUFF
using 'hq';
```

then ORACLE will not create the HR_LINK database link in SCOTT's account. Instead, ORACLE will create a database link named SCOTT.HR_LINK in the account that executed the **create database link** command. To create private database links, you must be logged into the database in the account that will own the link.

Managing Database Triggers

If your data replication needs are fairly limited, then you can use database triggers to replicate data from one table into another. In general, this method is only used when the only type of data being sent to the remote database is either an **insert** or a **delete**. The code necessary to support **update** transactions is usually much more complex than a comparable snapshot; see the following sections for details on implementing snapshots.

Database triggers are executed when specific actions happen to specific tables. They can be executed for each row of a transaction, or for an entire transaction as a unit. When dealing with data replication, you will usually be concerned with each row of data.

Before creating the trigger, you must create a database link for the trigger to use. In this case, the link is created in the database that *owns* the data, accessible to the owner of the table being replicated.

```
create public database link TRIGGER_LINK
using 'remote1';
```

This link, named TRIGGER_LINK, uses a service name ('remote1') to specify the connection to a remote database. Since no specific **connect** clause is specified, a default connection will be attempted instead. The default connection will attempt to log into the 'remote1' database using the same username and password as the account that calls the link.

The trigger shown in the following listing uses this link. It is fired after every row is **insert**ed into the EMPLOYEE table. Since it executes after the row has been **insert**ed, the row's data has already been validated. It then **insert**s the same row into a remote table with the same structure, using the TRIGGER_LINK database link just defined. The remote table must already exist.

```
create trigger COPY_DATA
after insert on EMPLOYEE
for each row
begin
      insert into EMPLOYEE@TRIGGER_LINK
      values
      (:new.Empno, :new.Ename, :new.Deptno,
      :new.Salary, :new.Birth_Date, :new.Soc_Sec_Num);
end;
/
```

This trigger uses the **new** keyword to reference the values from the row that was just **insert**ed into the local EMPLOYEE table.

To list information about triggers, use the DBA_TRIGGERS data dictionary view. The following query will list the "header" information about the trigger—its type, the statement that calls it, and the table on which it calls. This example shows the header information for the COPY_DATA trigger just created:

```
select Trigger_Type,
       Triggering_Event,
       Table_Name
  from DBA_TRIGGERS
 where Trigger_Name = 'COPY_DATA';
```

Sample output from this query is shown here:

```
TYPE              TRIGGERING_EVENT        TABLE_NAME
---------------   ---------------------   ------------
AFTER EACH ROW    INSERT                  EMPLOYEE
```

The text of the trigger can also be queried from this view, as shown in the following listing:

```
select Trigger_Body
  from DBA_TRIGGERS
 where Trigger_Name = 'COPY_DATA';
```

Sample output from this query is shown in the following listing:

```
TRIGGER_BODY
-------------------------------------------------------
begin
     insert into EMPLOYEE@TRIGGER_LINK
     values
     (:new.Empno, :new.Ename, :new.Deptno,
      :new.Salary, :new.Birth_Date, :new.Soc_Sec_Num);
end;
```

It is theoretically possible to create a trigger to replicate all possible permutations of data manipulation actions on the local database, but this quickly becomes difficult to manage. For a complex environment, it is best to consider the use of snapshots or manual data copies. However, for the limited circumstances described earlier, triggers are a very easy solution to implement.

Managing Snapshots

Snapshots are used to dynamically replicate data between distributed databases. The master table will be updatable, but the snapshots will be either read-only or updatable. Read-only snapshots are the most common types of snapshots implemented. There are two types of snapshots available: *complex snapshots* and *simple snapshots*.

In a simple snapshot, each row is based on a single row in a single remote table. A row in a complex snapshot may be based on more than one row in a remote table—such as via a **group by** operation—or on the result of a multitable join. Simple snapshots are thus a specific subset of the snapshots that can be created.

Since the snapshot will create several objects in the local database, the user creating the snapshot must have CREATE TABLE, CREATE VIEW, and CREATE INDEX privileges.

Before creating a snapshot, a database link to the source database should first be created in the local database. The following example creates a private database link called HR_LINK (which has been used as an example throughout this chapter):

```
create database link HR_LINK
connect to HR identified by PUFFINSTUFF
using 'hq';
```

The syntax used to create the snapshot on the local server is shown in the following listing. In this example, the snapshot is given a name (EMP_DEPT_COUNT), and its storage parameters are specified. Its base query is given, as well as its refresh interval. In this case, the snapshot is told to immediately retrieve the master data, then to perform the snapshot operation again in seven days (SysDate+7).

```
create snapshot EMP_DEPT_COUNT
pctfree 5
tablespace SNAP
storage (initial 100K next 100K pctincrease 0)
refresh complete
      start with SysDate
      next SysDate+7
as select Deptno, COUNT(*) Dept_Count
    from EMPLOYEE@HR_LINK
   group by Deptno;
```

NOTE
Because ORACLE uses the name of the snapshot in the names of the database objects that support it, the snapshot's name should be kept to fewer than 19 characters.

NOTE
*A snapshot query cannot reference tables or
views owned by the user SYS.*

See Appendix C for the full syntax options for the **create snapshot** command.
Because the records in this snapshot will not correspond one to one
with the records in the master table (since the query contains a **group by**
clause), this is a complex snapshot. Since the snapshot is a complex
snapshot, the snapshot will need to be completely re-created every time it
is refreshed.

When this snapshot is created, a table is created in the local database.
ORACLE will create a table— the local base table for the snapshot— called
SNAP$_*snapshotname* to store the records from the snapshot's query. This
table should not be altered in any way, although it may be indexed. A
read-only view of this table, named after the snapshot, will be created as
well. A second view, named MVIEW$_*snapshotname*, will be created as a
view of the remote master table(s). This view will be used during refreshes.

To drop a snapshot, use the **drop snapshot** command. An example of
this is shown in the following listing:

```
drop snapshot EMP_DEPT_COUNT;
```

The snapshot's storage parameters can be altered via the **alter snapshot**
command, as shown in the following listing:

```
alter snapshot EMP_DEPT_COUNT pctfree 5;
```

To improve the snapshot's performance, you may wish to add an index
to its local base table. To do this, create the appropriate index on the
underlying SNAP$_*snapshotname* table via the **create index** command.

To view data about snapshots, query the DBA_SNAPSHOTS data
dictionary view. A sample query against this view is shown in the
following listing:

```
select
  Name,          /*Name of the view used for the snapshot*/
  Last_Refresh,  /*Timestamp for the last refresh*/
  Type,          /*Type of refresh used for automatic refreshes*/
  Query          /*Query used to create the snapshot*/
from DBA_SNAPSHOTS;
```

This query will return the most-used information for the snapshot. Other information, such as the master table name and the name of the database link used, can also be retrieved via this view.

Dealing with Media Failures

Once you create a snapshot, its data is linked (logically, not physically) to the master data. If there is a problem with the server on which their master data resides, then you may need to re-create or completely refresh the snapshot.

For example, the EMP_DEPT_COUNT snapshot described in the previous section of this chapter is based on data in the remote EMPLOYEE table. If there is a media failure on the server that is used by the EMPLOYEE table, then you may need to perform database recovery on that server. Unless you can recover all of the lost data, your master EMPLOYEE table may not contain all of the records it contained when the snapshot was created. As a result, the data in the base (EMPLOYEE) table and its snapshot may be out of sync.

If the snapshot is a simple snapshot, you can create it using the **with rowid** clause. The **with rowid** clause tells ORACLE to use the RowIDs of the master table records as the means of correlating rows in the master table with rows in the snapshot (during fast refreshes). If you have to perform a recovery on the master table, then its RowID values may change, even if you perform a full recovery. If you have to perform recovery on the master table's database, you should completely refresh the snapshot. If you have to perform recovery on the snapshot's database, you should perform a complete refresh of the snapshot after the recovery has completed.

Enforcing Referential Integrity in Snapshots

The referential integrity between two related tables, both of which have simple snapshots to a remote database, may not be enforced in their snapshots. If the tables are refreshed at different times, or if transactions are occurring on the master tables during the refresh, then it is possible for the snapshots of those tables to not reflect the referential integrity of the master tables.

If, for example, EMPLOYEE and DEPT are related to each other via a primary key-foreign key relationship, then simple snapshots of these tables may contain violations of this relationship. These violations may include foreign keys without matching primary keys. In this example, that could mean employees in the EMPLOYEE snapshot with DEPTNO values that do not exist in the DEPT snapshot.

There are a number of potential solutions to this problem. First, time the refreshes to occur when the master tables are not in use. Second, perform the refreshes manually (see the following section for information on this) immediately after locking the master tables. Third, you may join the tables in the snapshot, creating a complex snapshot that will be based on the master tables (which will be properly related to each other).

Related snapshots can be collected into *refresh groups*. The purpose of a refresh group is to coordinate the refresh schedules of its members. Snapshots whose master tables have relationships with other snapshot master tables are good candidates for membership in refresh groups. Coordinating the refresh schedules of the snapshots will maintain the master tables' referential integrity in the snapshots as well. If refresh groups are not used, then the data in the snapshots may be inconsistent with regard to the master tables' referential integrity.

All manipulation of refresh groups is achieved via the DBMS_REFRESH package. The procedures within that package are MAKE, ADD, SUBTRACT, CHANGE, DESTROY, and REFRESH, as shown in the following examples. Information about existing refresh groups can be queried from the USER_REFRESH and USER_REFRESH_CHILDREN data dictionary views.

NOTE
Snapshots that belong to a refresh group do not have to belong to the same schema, but they do have to be all stored within the same database.

Create a refresh group by executing the MAKE procedure in the DBMS_REFRESH package, whose structure is shown in the following listing:

```
DBMS_REFRESH.MAKE
( name      IN VARCHAR2,
  list      IN VARCHAR2,
  next_date IN DATE,
  interval  IN VARCHAR2,
  implicit_destroy     IN BOOLEAN DEFAULT FALSE,
  lax                  IN BOOLEAN DEFAULT FALSE,
  job                  IN BINARY_INTEGER DEFAULT 0,
  rollback_seg         IN VARCHAR2 DEFAULT NULL,
  push_deferred_rpc    IN BOOLEAN DEFAULT TRUE,
  refresh_after_errors IN BOOLEAN DEFAULT FALSE );
```

The last six of the parameters for this procedure have default values that are usually acceptable. You can use the following command to create a refresh group for snapshots named LOCAL_EMP and LOCAL_DEPT:

```
execute DBMS_REFRESH.MAKE
(name => 'emp_group',
 list => 'local_emp, local_dept',
 next_date => SysDate,
 interval => SysDate+7)
```

NOTE
The snapshot list parameter, which is the second parameter in the listing, has a single quote at its beginning and at its end, with none between. In this example, two snapshots, LOCAL_EMP and LOCAL_DEPT, are passed to the procedure via a single parameter.

The preceding command will create a refresh group named EMP_GROUP, with two snapshots as its members. The refresh group name is enclosed in single quotes, as is the *list* of snapshot members—but not each member.

If the refresh group is going to contain a snapshot that is already a member of another refresh group (for example, during a move of a snapshot from an old refresh group to a newly created refresh group), then you must set the lax parameter to TRUE. A snapshot can only belong to one refresh group at a time.

To add snapshots to an existing refresh group, use the ADD procedure of the DBMS_REFRESH package, whose structure is

```
DBMS_REFRESH.ADD
( name        IN VARCHAR2,
  list        IN VARCHAR2,
  lax         IN BOOLEAN  DEFAULT FALSE );
```

As with the MAKE procedure, the ADD procedure's *lax* parameter does not have to be specified unless a snapshot is being moved between two refresh groups. When this procedure is executed with the lax parameter set to TRUE, the snapshot is moved to the new refresh group and is automatically deleted from the old refresh group.

To remove snapshots from an existing refresh group, use the SUBTRACT procedure of the DBMS_REFRESH package, as in the following:

```
DBMS_REFRESH.SUBTRACT
( name       IN VARCHAR2,
  list       IN VARCHAR2,
  lax        IN BOOLEAN  DEFAULT FALSE );
```

As with the MAKE and ADD procedures, a single snapshot or a list of snapshots (separated by commas) may serve as input to this procedure.

The refresh schedule for a refresh group may be altered via the CHANGE procedure of the DBMS_REFRESH package.

```
DBMS_REFRESH.CHANGE
( name                 IN VARCHAR2,
  next_date            IN DATE DEFAULT NULL,
  interval             IN VARCHAR2 DEFAULT NULL,
  implicit_destroy     IN BOOLEAN  DEFAULT NULL,
  rollback_seg         IN VARCHAR2 DEFAULT NULL,
  push_deferred_rpc    IN BOOLEAN DEFAULT NULL,
  refresh_after_errors IN BOOLEAN DEFAULT NULL);
```

The *next_date* parameter is analogous to the **start with** clause in the **create snapshot** command. The *interval* parameter is analogous to the **next** clause in the **create snapshot** command.

For example, to change the EMP_GROUP's schedule so that it will be replicated every three days, you can execute the following command (which specifies a null value for the *next_date* parameter, leaving that value unchanged):

```
execute DBMS_REFRESH.CHANGE
(name => 'emp_group',
 next_date => null,
 interval => SysDate+3);
```

After this command is executed, the refresh cycle for the EMP_GROUP refresh group will be changed to every three days.

To delete a refresh group, use the DESTROY procedure of the DBMS_REFRESH package, as shown in the following example. Its only parameter is the name of the refresh group.

```
execute DBMS_REFRESH.DESTROY(name => 'emp_group');
```

You may also implicitly destroy the refresh group. If you set the *implicit_destroy* parameter to TRUE when you create the group with the MAKE procedure, then the refresh group will be deleted (destroyed) when its last member is removed from the group (usually via the SUBTRACT procedure).

Sizing and Storing Snapshots

The appropriate storage parameters for snapshots are derived from the data being selected. Since the data is being replicated, the source data is known and can be sized. Use the space calculations in Chapter 5 to size the snapshot's local base table.

If a complex snapshot is used, then the storage needs will vary. For example, the EMP_DEPT_COUNT snapshot shown in the previous section should use less space than its master table since it performs a **group by** on the table and only returns two columns. For other complex snapshots—such as those involving joins and returning columns from multiple tables—the space needs for the snapshot may exceed those of any of the master tables involved. Therefore, always calculate the space for the local snapshot rather than relying on the storage parameters for the master tables.

Because of the nature of the snapshot data and objects, you may wish to create a tablespace that is dedicated to supporting them. The emphasis should be on providing enough contiguous space so that no snapshot refresh attempt will ever fail due to space availability problems.

Automatic and Manual Snapshot Refreshes

The EMP_DEPT_COUNT snapshot defined earlier contained the following specifications about its refresh interval:

```
refresh complete
      start with SysDate
      next SysDate+7
```

The **refresh complete** clause indicates that each time the snapshot is refreshed, it should be completely re-created. The available **refresh** options are listed in Table 15-2.

The **start with** clause tells the database when the snapshot should be refreshed. In this example, that is specified as SysDate, so the database will replicate the data when the snapshot is created.

Refresh Option	Description
COMPLETE	The snapshot tables are completely regenerated using the snapshot's query and the master tables every time the snapshot is refreshed.
FAST	If a simple snapshot is used, then a snapshot log can be used to send only the changes to the snapshot table.
FORCE	The default value. If possible, it performs a FAST refresh; otherwise, it will perform a COMPLETE refresh.

TABLE 15-2.   *Snapshot Refresh Options*

The **next** clause sets the interval for the refreshes. This period will be measured from the time of the last refresh, whether it was done automatically by the database or manually by the DBA. In this example, a refresh will occur seven days after the most recent snapshot.

For automatic snapshot refreshes to occur, you must tell ORACLE to create the SNP background processes that perform the snapshot refreshes. The number of SNP processes to create is determined by the JOB_QUEUE_PROCESSES init.ora parameter. If you do not set a value for this parameter, then it will default to 0 and no automatic refreshes will ever occur. You will not typically need more than one background process (called SNP0) unless you have many snapshots being refreshed simultaneously. You can create up to 36 SNP processes.

The interval, in seconds, between "wake-up calls" to the SNP*n* processes is set by the JOB_QUEUE_INTERVAL parameter in the init.ora parameter file. The default interval is 60 seconds.

NOTE
The JOB_QUEUE_PROCESSES and JOB_QUEUE_INTERVAL parameters create background processes that are used for job queue management as well as snapshot refreshes. Job queue management is described later in this chapter.

You may manually refresh the snapshot via the DBMS_SNAPSHOT package provided by ORACLE. There is a procedure named REFRESH within this package that can be used to refresh a single snapshot. An example of the command's usage is shown in the following listing. In this example, the user uses the **execute** command to execute the procedure. The parameters passed to the procedure are described following the example.

```
execute DBMS_SNAPSHOT.REFRESH('emp_dept_count','?');
```

The REFRESH procedure of the DBMS_SNAPSHOT package, as shown in this listing, takes two parameters. The first is the name of the snapshot, which should be prefixed by the name of the snapshot's owner (if other than the user executing this command). The second parameter is the manual refresh option. The available values for the manual refresh option parameter are listed in Table 15-3.

Another procedure in the DBMS_SNAPSHOT package can be used to refresh all of the snapshots that are scheduled to be automatically refreshed. This procedure, named REFRESH_ALL, will refresh each snapshot separately. It does not accept any parameters. The following listing shows an example of its execution:

```
execute DBMS_SNAPSHOT.REFRESH_ALL;
```

Since the snapshots will be refreshed via REFRESH_ALL consecutively, they are not all refreshed at the same time. Therefore, a database or server failure during the execution of this procedure may cause the local

Manual Refresh Option	Description
F	Fast refresh
f	Fast refresh
C	Complete refresh
c	Complete refresh
?	Indicates that the default refresh option for the snapshot should be used

TABLE 15-3. *Manual Refresh Option Values for the DBMS_SNAPSHOT.REFRESH Procedure*

snapshots to be out of sync with each other. If that happens, simply rerun this procedure after the database has been recovered.

A refresh group may be manually refreshed via the REFRESH procedure of the DBMS_REFRESH package. The REFRESH procedure accepts the name of the refresh group as its only parameter. The command shown in the following listing will refresh the refresh group named EMP_GROUP:

```
execute DBMS_REFRESH.REFRESH('emp_group');
```

Managing Snapshot Logs

A snapshot log is a table that maintains a record of modifications to the master table in a snapshot. It is stored in the same database as the master table and is only used by simple snapshots. The data in the snapshot log is used during fast refreshes of the table's snapshots. If you are going to use this method, create the snapshot log before creating the snapshot.

To create a snapshot log, you must be able to create an AFTER ROW trigger on the table. This implies that you have CREATE TRIGGER and CREATE TABLE privileges. You cannot specify a name for the snapshot log.

NOTE
Because ORACLE uses the name of the master table in the names of the database objects that support its snapshot log, the master table's name should be kept to fewer than 19 characters.

Since the snapshot log is a table, it has the full set of table storage clauses available to it. The example in the following listing shows the creation of a snapshot log on a table named EMPLOYEE. The log will be placed in the DATA_2 tablespace, with the specified storage parameters.

```
create snapshot log on EMPLOYEE
tablespace DATA_2
storage(initial 100K next 50K pctincrease 0)
pctfree 5 pctused 90;
```

The **pctfree** value for this table can be set very low, and the **pctused** value should be set very high, as shown in this example. The size of the snapshot log depends on the number of changes that will be processed during each refresh. The more frequently the snapshot is refreshed, the less space is needed for the snapshot log.

Just as snapshots create underlying tables, snapshot logs create a set of database structures. In the master table's database, the snapshot log creates a table named MLOG$_*tablename* to store the RowID and a timestamp for the rows in the master table. This table will be used to identify the rows that have changed since the last refresh. An AFTER ROW trigger named TLOG$_*tablename*, which will populate the MLOG$_*tablename* table, is created on the master table. Do not alter either of these objects. If the snapshot is based on primary keys instead of RowIDs, then the snapshot log will contain the primary key values instead of the RowID values.

The storage parameters for the snapshot log can be modified via the **alter snapshot log** command. When using this command, specify the name of the master table, not its snapshot log table name. An example of altering the EMPLOYEE table's snapshot log is shown in the following listing:

```
alter snapshot log EMPLOYEE
pctfree 10;
```

Information about snapshot logs can be retrieved via the DBA_SNAPSHOT_ LOGS data dictionary view. This view lists the owner of the snapshot log, its master table, its snapshot log table, and the trigger used. Since the snapshot log table is a segment in the database, and its name is known (MLOG$_*tablename*), its space usage can be tracked via the extent monitoring scripts provided in Chapter 6.

To drop a snapshot log, use the **drop snapshot log** command, as shown in the following example:

```
drop snapshot log on EMPLOYEE;
```

This command will drop the snapshot log and its associated objects from the database.

Choosing the Refresh Type

Which type of refresh is best for your snapshots? The correct answer may change from snapshot to snapshot within your database. The deciding factors should be

■ *The network traffic*   Complete refreshes send a large volume of data across the network.

■ *The transaction size* A complete refresh generates a very large transaction (an **insert as select** command based on the base query for the snapshot). Fast refreshes typically generate smaller transaction sizes.

■ *The volatility of the data* If more than 25 percent of the rows have changed, then a complete refresh will typically perform better than a fast refresh.

■ *The number of indexes on the local base table for the snapshot* A complete refresh truncates the local base table and then performs an **insert as select** into the local base table. All of the local base table's indexes are left in place during the complete refresh. If there are many indexes on the local base table, then the refresh performance will be adversely affected.

■ *The storage requirements for the snapshot log* In order to use fast refreshes, you have to create and maintain a snapshot log. The snapshot log will grow in size and will not automatically release freed space.

For low-volatility data, fast refreshes may be the most appropriate method to use. Since multiple snapshots can use the same snapshot log, the space requirements for the snapshot log data may be shared by many snapshots. If you use fast refreshes, see the "Purging the Snapshot Log" section later in this chapter for details on snapshot log space management.

Offline Instantiation of Snapshots

When you create a snapshot, ORACLE issues a single **create table as select** command to create and populate the snapshot. If you have a great deal of data to replicate, this may be an unacceptable solution since it generates a very large transaction and a great deal of network traffic. If the transaction does not fit within one of your rollback segments (see Chapter 7), then the snapshot creation will fail.

To work around this problem, you can use Import to bring the data into the snapshot's database. In order to use this method (called *offline instantiation*), you need to trick ORACLE by creating the proper objects in the master database first, and then exporting them. This method requires that the rollback segments of the master database be large enough to support the snapshot creation.

First, create an account at the master site that has privileges on the master table, the ability to create database links, and the ability to create snapshots. Within that account, create a database link with the same name as you will use in the remote database when accessing the master database. Next, create the snapshot within this new master database account, using the database link you just created.

For example, the following commands create the HR_LINK database link and the EMP_DEPT_COUNT snapshot within an account in the master database:

```
create database link HR_LINK
connect to HR identified by PUFFINSTUFF
using 'hq';

create snapshot EMP_DEPT_COUNT
refresh complete
     start with SYSDATE
     next SYSDATE+7
as select Deptno, COUNT(*) Dept_Count
   from EMPLOYEE@HR_LINK
   group by Deptno;
```

When these commands complete, you will have an account that has the HR_LINK database link, the EMP_DEPT_COUNT snapshot (with its related objects), and the data for the snapshot.

Next, Export the user who owns the snapshot in the master database. You can now transfer the Export dump file to the remote server and Import that file's data into the remote database. During the Import, the database link will be created, the snapshot will be created, and the snapshot's local base table will be populated. You can control the size of the transactions created during the Import (and thus the size of the rollback segments required) via the COMMIT and BUFFER parameters of the Import utility. See Chapter 10 for details on the use of Import and Export.

Purging the Snapshot Log

The snapshot log contains transient data; records are **insert**ed into the snapshot log, used during refreshes, and then **delete**d. Therefore, you should encourage reuse of the snapshot log's blocks by setting a high value for **pctused** when creating the snapshot log.

If multiple snapshots use the same master table, then they share the same snapshot log. If one of the snapshots is not refreshed for a long period, then the snapshot log may never delete any of its records. As a result, the space requirements of the snapshot log will grow.

To reduce the space used by snapshot log entries, you can use the PURGE_LOG procedure of the DBMS_SNAPSHOT package. PURGE_LOG takes three parameters: the name of the master table, a "num" variable, and a 'DELETE' flag. The 'num' variable specifies the number of least recently refreshed snapshots whose rows will be removed from the snapshot log. For example, if you have three snapshots that use the snapshot log and one of them has not been refreshed for a very long time, then you would use a 'num' value of 1.

The following listing shows an example of the PURGE_LOG procedure. In this example, the EMPLOYEE table's snapshot log will be purged of the entries required by the least recently used snapshot.

```
execute DBMS_SNAPSHOT.PURGE_LOG
(master => 'EMPLOYEE',
    num => 1,
    flag => 'DELETE');
```

You can manage the rows within the snapshot log the same way you manage the rows in any other table, as long as you can guarantee that rows are not being written to the master table while you manage the snapshot log. For example, you can Export the snapshot log's data, **truncate** the log's table, and then Import the data back into the snapshot log in order to reduce its space requirements.

To further support snapshot maintenance, ORACLE provides two snapshot-specific options for the **truncate** command. If you want to **truncate** the master table without losing its snapshot log entries, you can enter the command

```
truncate table EMPLOYEE preserve snapshot log;
```

If the EMPLOYEE table's snapshots are based on primary key values, then the snapshot log values will still be valid following an Export/Import of the EMPLOYEE tables. However, if the EMPLOYEE table's snapshots are based on RowID values, then the snapshot log would be invalid following an Export/Import of the base table (since different RowIDs may be assigned during the Import). In that case, you should **truncate** the snapshot log when you **truncate** the base table.

```
truncate table EMPLOYEE purge snapshot log;
```

Managing Distributed Transactions

A single logical unit of work may include transactions against multiple databases. The example shown earlier in Figure 15-3 illustrates this: a **commit** is submitted after two tables in separate databases have been **update**d. ORACLE will transparently maintain the integrity between the two databases by ensuring that all of the transactions involved either **commit** or roll back as a group. This is accomplished automatically via ORACLE's Two-Phase Commit (2PC) mechanism.

The first phase of the 2PC is the Prepare phase. In this phase, each node involved in a transaction prepares the data that it will need to either **commit** or roll back the data. Once prepared, a node is said to be *in doubt*. The nodes notify the initiating node for the transaction (known as the *global coordinator*) of their status.

Once all nodes are prepared, the transaction enters the Commit phase, and all nodes are instructed to **commit** their portion of the logical transaction. The databases all **commit** the data at the same logical time, preserving the integrity of the distributed data.

Resolving In-Doubt Transactions

Transactions against stand-alone databases may fail due to problems with the database server; for example, there may be a media failure. Working with distributed databases increases the number of potential failure causes. For example, a transaction against a remote database requires that the network used to access that database, and the remote host itself, be available.

When a distributed transaction is pending, an entry for that transaction can be viewed via the DBA_2PC_PENDING data dictionary view. When the transaction completes, its record is removed from that table. If the transaction is pending, but is not able to complete, then its record stays in DBA_2PC_PENDING.

The RECO (Recoverer) background process periodically checks the DBA_2PC_PENDING view for distributed transactions that failed to complete. Using the information there, the RECO process on a node will automatically attempt to recover the local portion of an in-doubt transaction. It then attempts to establish connections to any other databases involved in the transaction and resolves the distributed portions of the transaction. The related rows in the DBA_2PC_PENDING views in each database are then removed.

NOTE
The RECO background process will not be started unless the DISTRIBUTED_ TRANSACTIONS parameter in your instance's init.ora file is set to a nonzero value prior to startup. This parameter should be set to the anticipated maximum number of concurrent distributed transactions.

The recovery of distributed transactions is performed automatically by the RECO process. You can manually recover the local portions of a distributed transaction, but this will usually result in inconsistent data between the distributed databases. Data inconsistency is counter to the purpose of distributed transactions, since they serve to enforce relationships between local and remote data. If a local recovery is performed, then the remote data will be out of sync.

To minimize the number of distributed recoveries necessary, you can influence the way that the distributed transaction is processed. The transaction processing is influenced via the use of *commit point strengths* to tell the database how to structure the transaction.

Commit Point Strength

Each set of distributed transactions, by its nature, references multiple hosts and databases. Of those, one host and database can normally be singled out as being the most reliable, or as owning the most critical data. This database is known as the *commit point site;* if data is committed there, then it is committed for all databases. If the transaction against the commit point site fails, then the transactions against the other nodes are rolled back. This site also stores information about the status of the distributed transaction.

The commit point site will be selected by ORACLE based on each database's *commit point strength*. This is set via the init.ora file, as shown in the following listing:

```
COMMIT_POINT_STRENGTH=100
```

The values set for the COMMIT_POINT_STRENGTH parameter are set on a relative scale, not on an absolute scale. In the preceding example, it was set to 100. If another database has a commit point strength of 200, then that database would be the commit point site for a distributed transaction involving those two databases. The value cannot exceed 255.

Since the scale is relative, set up a site-specific scale. Set the commit point on your most reliable database to 200. Then grade the other servers and databases relative to that one. If, for example, another database is only 80 percent as reliable as the most reliable database, then assign it a commit point strength of 160 (80 percent of 200). Fixing a single database at a definite point (in this case, 200) allows the rest of the databases to be graded on an even scale. This should result in the proper commit point site being used for each transaction.

Database Domains and Communities

All of the examples in this chapter have used the standard method for evaluating an object's FQON—using the object name in the query and resolving the rest of the object name via a database link. This method will work across all platforms and networking options. However, networks that use a domain name service (DNS) to name their hosts can take advantage of additional networking features within ORACLE.

A *domain name service* allows hosts within a network to be hierarchically organized. Each node within the organization is called a *domain*, and each domain is labeled by its function. These functions may include "COM" for companies and "EDU" for schools. Each domain may have many subdomains. Therefore, each host will be given a unique name within the network; its name contains information about how it fits into the network hierarchy. Host names within a network typically have up to four parts; the left-most portion of the name is the host's name, and the rest of the name shows the domain to which the host belongs.

For example, a host may be named "HQ.MYCORP.COM". In this example, the host is named "HQ". It is identified as being part of the "MYCORP" subdomain of the "COM" domain.

This is significant for two reasons. First, the host name is part of the FQON. Second, ORACLE allows you to specify the DNS version of the host name in database link names, thus simplifying the management of distributed database connections.

To implement this, you first need to add two parameters to your init.ora file for the database. The first of these, DB_NAME, may already be there. It should be set to the instance name. The second parameter is DB_DOMAIN, which is set to the DNS name of the database's host. It specifies the network domain in which the host resides. If a database named "LOC" was created on the "HQ.MYCORP.COM" server, then its init.ora entries would be the ones shown in the following listing:

```
DB_NAME = loc
DB_DOMAIN = hq.mycorp.com
```

To enable the usage of the database domain name, the GLOBAL_NAMES parameter must be set to TRUE in your init.ora file, as shown in the following listing. If it is not set, then it will default to FALSE, and the database link names will not correspond to global database names (as shown earlier in this chapter).

```
GLOBAL_NAMES = true
```

Once these parameters have been set, the database must be shut down and restarted using this init.ora file for the settings to take effect.

NOTE
*If you set GLOBAL_NAMES to TRUE, then **all** of your database link names must follow the rules described in this section.*

When using this method of creating global database names, the names of the database links that are created are the same as the databases to which they point. Thus, a database link that pointed to the "LOC" database listed earlier would be named LOC.HQ.MYCORP.COM. This is shown in the following listing:

```
CREATE PUBLIC DATABASE LINK loc.hq.mycorp.com
USING 'connect string';
```

In this configuration, it is still possible to create database links that do not contain the global database name of the database to which they point. In those cases, ORACLE appends the local database's DB_DOMAIN value to the name of the database link. For example, if the database was within the "HQ.MYCORP.COM" domain, and the database link was named "LOC", then the database link name, when used, would be automatically expanded to "LOC.HQ.MYCORP.COM".

Using global database names thus establishes a link between the database name, database domain, and database link names. This, in turn, makes it easier to identify and manage database links. For example, you can create a public database link (with no connect string) in each database that points to every other database. Users within a database no longer need to guess at the proper database link to use; if they know the global database name, then they know the database link name. If a table is moved from one database to another, or if a database is moved from one host to another, it is easy to determine which of the old database links must be dropped and re-created. Using global database names is part of migrating from stand-alone databases to true networks of databases.

Database domains are often confused with communities. *Communities* are used by SQL*Net V2 to identify a group of servers that communicate via the same communications protocol. For example, a community may be named "TCP.HQ.MYCORP.COM". That name would identify the community as being the community of servers using the TCP/IP protocol to communicate within the "HQ.MYCORP.COM" network domain. Thus, the network domain serves to help enforce the uniqueness of the SQL*Net community's name. The "TCP" portion of the community's name refers not to a host or database name, but to the communication protocol that the hosts share.

Since it is common for hosts in the same domain to share the same communications protocol, it is useful to make the network domain part of the SQL*Net community name. The ".COM" portion of the network domain name is usually left off the community name since communities usually do not span that level of the network hierarchy. Thus, the TCP/IP community in this example would be named "TCP.HQ.MYCORP". Using a three-part community name also helps to reduce potential confusion between community names and network domain names.

Monitoring Distributed Databases

Most database-level monitoring systems, such as the Command Center database described in Chapter 6, analyze the performance of databases without taking their environments into account. However, there are several other key performance measures that must be taken into account for databases:

- The performance of the host
- The distribution of I/O across disks and controllers
- The usage of available memory

For distributed databases, you must also consider the following:

- The capacity of the network and its hardware
- The load on the network segments
- The usage of different physical access paths between hosts

None of these can be measured from within the database. The focus of monitoring efforts shifts from being database-centric to network-centric. The database becomes one part of the monitored environment, rather than the only part that is checked.

You still need to monitor those aspects of the database that are critical to its success—such as the extensions of its segments and the free space in tablespaces. However, the *performance* of distributed databases cannot be measured except as part of the performance of the network that supports them. Therefore, all performance-related tests, such as stress tests, must be coordinated with the network management staff. That staff can also verify the effectiveness of your attempts to reduce the database load on the network.

The performance of the individual hosts can usually be monitored via a network monitoring package. This monitoring is thus performed in a top-down fashion—network to host to database. Use the monitoring system described in Chapter 6 as an extension to the network and host monitors.

Tuning Distributed Databases

When tuning a stand-alone database, the goal is to reduce the amount of time it takes to find data. The DBA can use a number of database structures and options to increase the likelihood that the data will be found in memory or in the first place that the database looks. These are described in Chapter 8.

When working with distributed databases, there is an additional consideration. Since data is now not only being found but also being shipped across the network, the performance of a query is now made up of the performance of these two steps. You must therefore consider the ways in which data is being transferred across the network, with a goal of reducing the network traffic.

A simple way to reduce network traffic is to replicate data from one node to another. You can do this manually (via the SQL*Plus **copy** command), or automatically by the database (via snapshots). Replicating data improves the performance of queries against remote databases by bringing the data across the network once—usually during a slow period on the local host. Local queries can then use the local copy of the data, eliminating the network traffic that would otherwise be required.

There are two problems with this solution: first, the local data may become out of sync with the remote data. This is an historic problem with derived data; it limits the usefulness of this option to tables whose data is fairly static. Even if a simple snapshot is used with a snapshot log, the data will not be refreshed continuously, only when scheduled.

The second problem with the replicated data solution is that the copy of the table may not be able to pass **update**s back to the master table. That is, if a read-only snapshot is used to make a local copy of a remote table, then the snapshot cannot be **update**d. The same must hold true for tables created with the SQL*Plus **copy** command; they are not the master tables and should be treated as read-only tables.

Thus, any **update**s against those tables must be performed against the master tables. If the table is frequently **update**d, then replicating the data will not improve your performance unless you are using ORACLE's Advanced Replication Option. This option supports multisite ownership of data, and users can make changes in any database designated as an owner of the data. The management of ORACLE's Advanced Replication Option is very involved, and requires creating a database environment (with database links, etc.) specifically geared toward supporting the two-way replication of data. See the ORACLE manuals for the Advanced Replication Option for details.

The type of snapshot to use depends on the nature of the application. Simple snapshots do not involve any data manipulation with the query—they are simply copies of rows from remote tables. Complex snapshots perform operations such as **group by**, **connect by**, or joins on the remote tables. Knowing which to use requires that you know the way in which the data is to be used by the local database.

If you use simple snapshots, you can use snapshot logs. These are logs of the transactions made against the remote table. When it is time to refresh that table's snapshots, only the transactions from the snapshot log are sent across the network. Therefore, if the remote table is frequently modified, and you need frequent refreshes of less than 25 percent of the table's rows, then using a simple snapshot will improve the performance of the snapshot refresh process.

When a complex snapshot is refreshed, it has to completely rebuild the snapshot tables. This seems at first like a tremendous burden to put on the system—why not find a way to use simple snapshots instead? However, there are a number of advantages to complex snapshots:

■ Tables chosen for replication are typically modified infrequently. Therefore, the refreshes can normally be scheduled for low-usage times in the local database, lessening the impact of full refreshes.

■ Complex snapshots may replicate less data than simple snapshots.

The second point seems a little cryptic. After all, a complex snapshot involves more processing than a simple snapshot, so shouldn't it require more work for the network? Actually, it may require *less* work for the network, because more work is being done by the database.

Consider the case of two tables being replicated via snapshots. The users on the local database will always query the two tables together, via a join. As shown in Figure 15-6, there are two options. You can either use two simple snapshots (Figure 15-6a), or you can perform the join via a complex snapshot (Figure 15-6b). What is the difference in performance between the two?

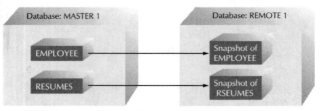

(a) Multiple simple snapshots; snapshot logs and REFRESH FAST can be used.

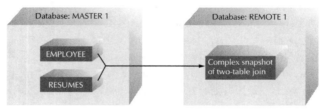

(b) A complex snapshot; the join is already performed.

FIGURE 15-6. *Data replication options for joins*

If the tables are joined properly, then the complex snapshot, even if it returns all columns from both tables, should not send any more data across the network than the two simple snapshots will when they are first created. In fact, it will most likely send less data during its creation. When choosing between these two alternatives on the basis of performance, you need to consider two factors:

1. The performance of the refreshes
2. The performance of queries against the snapshots

The second of these criteria is usually the more important of the two. After all, the data is being replicated to improve query performance. If the users only access the tables via a specific join, then the complex snapshot has already performed the join for them. Performing the join against two simple snapshots will take longer. You cannot determine which of these options is preferable until the access paths that the users will use have been fully defined. If the tables are sometimes queried separately, or via a different join path, then you will need to use simple snapshots or multiple complex snapshots.

The performance of the refreshes won't concern your users. What may concern them is the validity of the data. If the remote tables are frequently modified, and are of considerable size, then you are almost forced to use simple snapshots with snapshot logs. Performing complete refreshes in the middle of a workday is generally unacceptable. Thus, it is the *frequency* of the refreshes, rather than the size of them, that determines which type of snapshot will have the better performance for the users. After all, they are most concerned about the performance of the system while they are using it; refreshes performed late at night do not affect them. If the tables need to be frequently synchronized, use simple snapshots with snapshot logs. Otherwise, custom complex snapshots should be used.

As was noted previously in this chapter, you may index the underlying SNAP$_*tablename* tables that are created by the snapshot in the local database. This should also help to improve query performance, at the expense of slowing down the refreshes.

Another means of reducing network traffic, via remote procedure calls, is described in Chapter 8. That chapter also includes information on tuning SQL and the application design. If the database was properly structured, then tuning the way the application processes data will yield the most significant performance improvements.

Using the Job Queues

In order to support snapshot refreshes and other replication functions, ORACLE manages a set of internal job queues. If you have enabled job queues within your database (via the JOB_QUEUE_PROCESSES and JOB_QUEUE_INTERVAL parameters described previously in this chapter), then you can submit jobs of your own to the queues. You can use these queues in place of operating system job queues.

To manage the internal job queue, you can use the SUBMIT, REMOVE, CHANGE, WHAT, NEXT_DATE, INTERVAL, BROKEN, and RUN procedures of the DBMS_JOB package. The most important are the SUBMIT, REMOVE, and RUN procedures.

The SUBMIT procedure has five parameters, as follows:

```
PROCEDURE SUBMIT
   ( job        OUT  BINARY_INTEGER,
     what       IN   VARCHAR2,
     next_date  IN   DATE DEFAULT sysdate,
     interval   IN   VARCHAR2 DEFAULT 'null',
     no_parse   IN   BOOLEAN DEFAULT FALSE);
```

The *job* parameter is an output parameter; ORACLE generates a job number for the job via the SYS.JOBSEQ sequence. When you submit a job, you should first define a variable that will accept the job number as the output. For example, the following listing defines a variable and submits a job to execute 'myproc' every day:

```
variable jobno number;
begin
   DBMS_JOB.SUBMIT(:jobno,'myproc',SysDate,SysDate+1);
   commit;
end;
/

print jobno

JOBNO
-----------
      8791
```

The submitter of a job can later alter the job (via the BROKEN, CHANGE, INTERVAL, NEXT_DATE and WHAT procedures), remove it from the queue (the REMOVE procedure), or force it to run (the RUN procedure). For each of these procedures, you will need to know the job number.

If you did not record the job number when you submitted your job, you can query DBMS_JOBS to see the jobs submitted in your database.

Managing Jobs

You can alter a job to 'broken' state via the BROKEN procedure. If you mark a job as being broken, then it will not be run the next time it is scheduled to run. The structure of the BROKEN procedure is

```
PROCEDURE BROKEN
( job       IN   BINARY_INTEGER,
  broken    IN   BOOLEAN,
  next_date IN   DATE DEFAULT SYSDATE );
```

If you have previously set a job to be broken (by setting the *broken* variable to TRUE), then you can set it to be not broken by setting the *broken* variable to FALSE.

The CHANGE procedure lets you change the code you want to have executed via the *what* parameter, the next date on which the job will be run, and the interval between job runs. Its structure is

```
PROCEDURE CHANGE
( job       IN  BINARY_INTEGER,
  what      IN  VARCHAR2,
  next_date IN  DATE,
  interval  IN  VARCHAR2);
```

If you do not specify a value for the CHANGE variables (or set them to **NULL**), they will be left at their former settings. Thus, you can change part of the job specification via the CHANGE procedure without having to change all of the job's settings.

If you only want to change the interval between job executions, you can use the INTERVAL procedure, whose two parameters are the job number and the new interval function. You can use the NEXT_DATE procedure to change the next date on which the job is to be run; its two parameters are the job number and the date on which the job should be run.

If you want to change the PL/SQL code that is executed, you can use the WHAT procedure. Its two parameters are the job number and the PL/SQL code to be executed. The INTERVAL, NEXT_DATE, and WHAT procedures do not provide any capabilities that are not already provided via the CHANGE procedure described previously. When using CHANGE, just set to **NULL** the variables you don't want to change.

You can remove a job from the job queue via the REMOVE procedure. This procedure has the job number as its sole parameter. If you have many features of the job to change, you may wish to completely remove the job from the job queue and resubmit it.

To force a job to run at any time, use the RUN procedure. The RUN procedure, which takes the job number as its input variable, is the only way you can run a 'broken' job.

Job queues are typically used to manage internal database functions (such as analyzing database objects). If the jobs are to be part of the regular production maintenance of the database, then they should be run via the normal scheduling mechanism for the system on which the database resides. Even though you can run these jobs via the ORACLE job queues, it may be more appropriate to run them via a centrally controlled job management facility that is maintained outside of the database. Use the internal ORACLE job queues for small jobs that are not part of the production control of the database.

For further details on the DBMS_JOB procedures, see the dbmsjob.sql file, which is located in the /rdbms/admin subdirectory under the ORACLE software home directory.

CHAPTER
16

Configuring
Client-Server and
Network Computing
Environments

ince ORACLE supports so many different configurations and platforms, there is no single set of specifications that will be valid for every client-server or network computing environment. However, there are a number of general procedures that apply to the configuration of networked environments. These guidelines are based on the communications details from Chapters 13 and 14.

Overview of Client-Server Processing

Using a *client-server* configuration allows the CPU and processing load of an application to be distributed between two machines. The first, called the *client,* supports the application that initiates the request from the database. The back-end machine on which the database resides is called the *server.* The client may bear most of the CPU load, while the database server is dedicated to supporting queries, not applications. This distribution of resource requirements is shown in Figure 16-1.

When the client sends a database request to the server (via SQL*Net or Net8), the server receives and executes the SQL statement that is passed to it. The results of the SQL statement, plus any error conditions that are returned, are then sent back to the client.

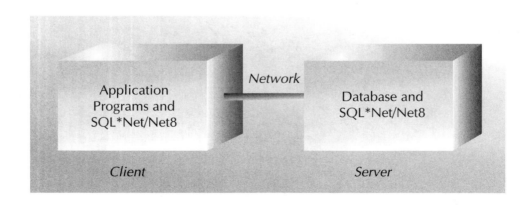

FIGURE 16-1. *Client-server architecture*

To use a client-server architecture, the client and server machines must be capable of communicating with each other. This implies that there is a hardware connection between the two machines. Each machine must support a communications protocol that allows them to interchange data. You can use the SQL*Net V2 Multiprotocol Interchange or the Net8 Connection Manager to resolve compatibility problems between various protocol communities (see Chapter 13).

Two examples will be used in this chapter. First, consider a client that is running Microsoft Windows and SQL*Net V2. It is connected via a *NIC* (*network interface card*) to an Ethernet network. The server with which it hopes to communicate is also located on that network. To make this example generic, assume that the server is running UNIX and both machines are running the TCP/IP protocol. This generic configuration will be used as an illustration throughout this chapter.

This configuration is shown graphically in Figure 16-2.

A second architecture, which involves adding a file server to the configuration, will be described as a modification to this configuration.

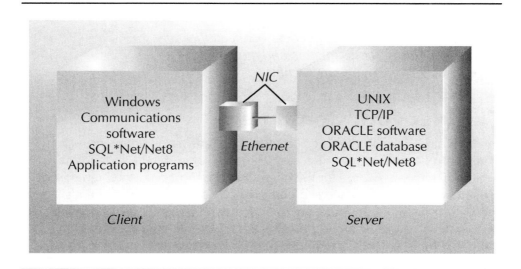

FIGURE 16-2. *Sample client-server configuration*

For the client and server to communicate, several steps must be taken:

- The server must be configured to accept communications via the network.

- The server must identify which databases are available for network logins.

- The server must be running SQL*Net/Net8.

- The client must be configured to communicate via the network.

- The client must have adequate memory and disk resources available.

- The client must have SQL*Net/Net8 installed and specify a connect string.

If any of these steps is skipped, then the client application will be unable to communicate with the database on the server.

NOTE
*Both SQL*Net V2 and Net8 can be used to access ORACLE8 databases in networked environments. From a client-server perspective, the major differences between the two are the ease of installation and the parameters used in parameter files.*

The Network Computer

The Network Computer (NC) concept is an extension of the client-server architecture. Traditionally, a two-tier client-server architecture tends to lead to high maintenance costs for the client. For the most part, the high cost of client machine maintenance is based on the complexity of the client's operating system. If you focus on the networking capabilities of the client, then you can create a much "thinner," less expensive, and simpler to maintain client. An NC is such a device—a very simple client.

If the client is much simpler, then some of its former tasks must be performed somewhere else. Normally, they are performed by an application server elsewhere on the network. Thus, an NC architecture may have three tiers instead of two. Centralizing the application tasks may also help to reduce the cost of application and system maintenance.

In this chapter, you will see a description of traditional client-server computing, followed by examples of NC extensions to the client-server architecture.

Configuring the Server

Server configurations are described in Chapter 14. The server must identify which hosts it can communicate with, specify which databases are available, and run the SQL*Net server process.

Identifying Available Hosts

A *host,* for the purposes of this example, will be defined as a server that is capable of communicating with another server via a network. Each host may maintain a list of the hosts with which it can communicate. This list is usually maintained in a file called /etc/hosts. The "/etc" portion of the filename signifies that it is located in the /etc directory. This file contains the Internet address for the hosts, plus the host names. It may optionally include an alias for each host name. A sample portion of an /etc/hosts file is shown in Figure 16-3.

In this example, there are five hosts listed. The first two entries assign host names ("nmhost" and "txhost") to Internet addresses. The third entry assigns both a host name ("azhost") and an alias ("arizona") to an Internet address. The fourth entry maps the "hq" server to its Internet address. The fifth entry, "mypc", maps the client PC's Internet address to its host name.

```
127.0.0.1    nmhost
127.0.0.2    txhost
127.0.0.3    azhost arizona
127.0.0.4    hq
127.4.2.11   mypc
```

FIGURE 16-3. *Sample portion of an /etc/hosts file*

Identifying Available Services

A *server process* listens for connection requests from clients. The server process directs those requests to the proper UNIX socket, and the connection can then take place. The services for both SQL*Net V2 and Net8 are described in Chapters 13 and 14. The examples in this chapter will focus on the SQL*Net V2 installation.

Services on a UNIX server are listed in a file called /etc/services. The "/etc" portion of the filename signifies that it is located in the /etc directory. Like the /etc/hosts file, this file is typically maintained by a UNIX systems administrator.

The SQL*Net service is called the *listener* for SQL*Net V2. In SQL*Net V2, it should be assigned to port 1521. The SQL*Net V2 entry in the /etc/services file is shown in the following listing. As shown, there are two parts to the entry: the service name and the port number.

```
listener   1521
```

Identifying Available Databases

All databases that are run on a UNIX host and are accessible to the network must be listed in a file named /etc/oratab. The "/etc" portion of the filename signifies that it is located in the /etc directory. This file is maintained by the DBA. Each database used in a client-server application must be listed in the /etc/oratab file.

A sample /etc/oratab file is shown in the following listing:

```
loc:/orasw/app/oracle/product/8.0.3.1:Y
cc1:/orasw/app/oracle/product/8.0.3.1:N
old:/orasw/app/oracle/product/8.0.3.0:Y
```

There are three components to each entry in the /etc/oratab file, separated only by colons (:). The entries' components, which are fully described in Chapter 14, are the instance name (ORACLE_SID), ORACLE software root directory (ORACLE_HOME), and a flag to indicate if the instance should be started on host startup (which is a necessary flag, but irrelevant to SQL*Net communications).

This example shows entries for three instances: LOC, CC1, and OLD (the first components in each entry). The first two instances have the same

ORACLE_HOME; the third uses an older version of the ORACLE kernel (as shown in the second component of the entries). Both LOC and OLD will be automatically started when the server starts; CC1 will have to be manually started (by virtue of the "Y" and "N" flags in the third component of each entry).

Once an instance is listed in the /etc/oratab file on an identified host on the network (via /etc/hosts), it can be accessed via SQL*Net connect descriptors. However, SQL*Net must be enabled for this to work. The next section describes the configuration of the SQL*Net server process in UNIX.

Starting SQL*Net

In the Windows-to-UNIX example, if the database application will be using SQL*Net V2, then the listener process must be started on the server. All of the available parameters for this process are listed in Chapter 14.

The following command starts the Listener process:

```
> lsnrctl start
```

To verify the status of the Listener, execute the **lsnrctl status** command, as shown in the following listing:

```
> lsnrctl status
```

For a full description of the options for the **lsnrctl** command, see Chapter 14.

Configuring the Client

Before any communications can begin, the client machine must be physically connected to a network, and must have network communications software installed on it. The NIC in your client machine must be supported by the communications software. See the *Setting up SQL*Net* guide for your client operating system for a list of the supported communications packages. Be sure to check this listing every time you upgrade either the communications package or the client's SQL*Net version.

Identifying Available Hosts

Just as the server machine must identify its available hosts, the client machine must also specify the hosts to which it can connect. This is typically done via the use of a file identical in structure to the server's /etc/hosts file.

The hosts file contains the Internet address for the hosts, plus the host names. It may optionally include an alias for each host name. A sample portion of a hosts file is shown in the following listing:

```
127.0.0.1 nmhost
127.0.0.2 txhost
127.0.0.3 azhost arizona
127.0.0.4 hq
```

In this example, there are four hosts listed. The first two entries assign host names ("nmhost" and "txhost") to Internet addresses. The third entry assigns both a host name ("azhost") and an alias ("arizona") to an Internet address. The fourth entry assigns an Internet address to the "hq" server.

The location of this file in the client's directory structure is dependent on the communications package in use.

Identifying Available Services

Just as the server machine may have a file to define the services it uses, the client machine may also have a way of specifying the services that it will connect to. On the server machine, this file is called /etc/services. On the client machine, it is called services. The SQL*Net portion of the services file should be identical on both machines. The services file for the sample configuration is shown in the following listing:

```
listener   1521
```

This file will be used by the communications software to attach to the proper communications socket on the UNIX server when an SQL*Net connection is attempted.

Client Machine Specifications

Can your Windows client support these requirements? To do so, it will have to meet the following minimum specifications.

Hardware:

- IBM, Compaq, or 100-percent compatible PC with an 80286 processor (or higher)
- Enough hard-disk space to store the files for your operating system, SQL*Net, your communications software, and your applications software
- A disk drive to use during installations
- A NIC for network communications

Memory:

- Enough memory to run your network software, SQL*Net, and your application software; a minimum of 5MB is recommended

Software:

- Microsoft Windows
- SQL*Net for Windows, with the TCP/IP protocol adapter
- Network communications software

The SQL*Net TCP/IP for Windows software takes 100K of disk space, and approximately 120K of memory. When sizing your client machine, keep in mind that the application front-end programs, operating system, and communications software will require far greater resources than SQL*Net will.

If your processor is slow, then programs will usually run (just slower than you'd like). If not enough memory is available, then applications may not run at all. For that reason, be sure that you have at least 5MB of memory on the PC—the more, the better.

Running SQL*Net

Now that the machines are set up and ready to talk, all you have to do is make sure that the tool you will be using to communicate with the remote database is properly configured. As noted in Chapter 11, there are often changes required to tools when you migrate from one version of ORACLE to another. There may also be differences between tools in the syntax of the database service name. For example, some tools require that the entire service name be entered in lowercase and enclosed in double quotes (though this is an isolated case). Be sure to test the connections thoroughly each time the network hardware, communications software, operating system, or SQL*Net version is changed.

Toward a Network Computer Configuration

To better distribute the resources required for a database application, you may choose to add a *file server* to the architecture. In this design, the ORACLE software and application software may be stored on the file server. The result of this design is that no direct logins are made to the database server; rather, it exists solely to service database requests. This allows the database server to be tuned for this purpose.

In this architecture, it is usually preferable to use UNIX workstations for clients instead of PC clients. As shown in Figures 16-4 and 16-5, this allows two different architectures to be considered. In Figure 16-4, the workstations send SQL*Net requests to the database server. The file server, which is *NFS-mounted* to the database server, handles all requests for application and ORACLE software. The "mounting" process enables the files on the file server to be accessed as if they were on the database server.

The second option is to have the client workstations NFS mounted on the file servers. The file servers would still contain the ORACLE software and application software. The clients would thus be mounted as part of the file server that contains the ORACLE code. The file server would communicate with the database server via the network, as shown in Figure 16-5.

The configuration shown in Figure 16-5 approximates an NC architecture. In an NC architecture, the clients are as simple as possible. As a result, the maintenance of the application software is centralized. The simple architectures of the client reduce the overall support and configuration costs of the system. In a true NC architecture, the clients are not NFS-mounted to the file/application server. Instead, they communicate

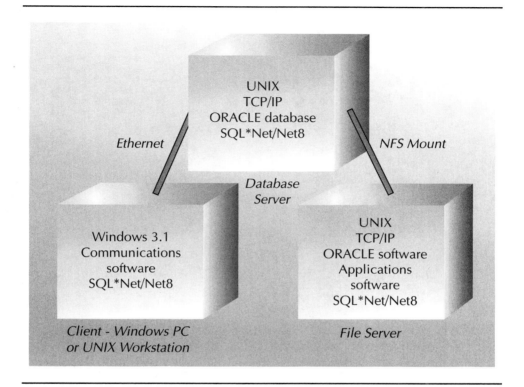

FIGURE 16-4. *Client-server architecture with a file server networked to the server*

with the application server via communications protocols and programs (such as Java applets).

Using either of these configurations adds a great many capabilities to your architecture. For example:

■ No users log directly into the database server. Therefore, memory and system resources can be tuned exclusively to handle database requests.

■ Users can be separated by class. That is, developers can be physically separated from users.

■ Different user classes can access different executables. This can be used to test new versions of code or to prevent user access to development tools (see Chapter 9).

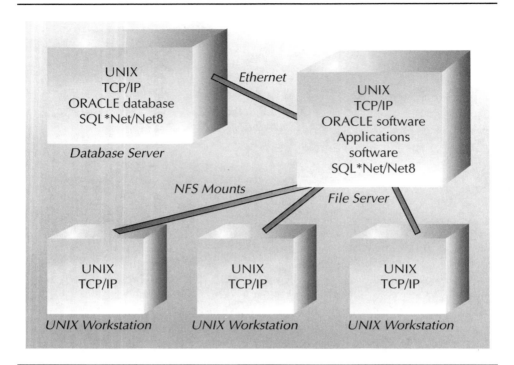

FIGURE 16-5.   *Client-server architecture with a file server networked to the clients*

These capabilities add a layer of complexity to the administration of the system. When designing the administrative tools for this type of system, consider

- The mechanisms you will use to keep the files on the file servers in sync.

- The mechanisms you will use to keep the operating system parameters of the file servers in sync.

- The network capacity. Now that the servers can be tuned for specific uses, do not skimp on the network that allows them to communicate.

- The security issues inherent in distributed environments.

■ The memory and disk capacity of the file servers. Having introduced them as a benefit to the architecture, do not turn them into a system bottleneck.

If you implement a network computing architecture, you cannot allow the middle components of the architecture— the application server and the network— to be the performance bottlenecks. The network infrastructure is the area over which DBAs typically have the least control. Therefore, you should make sure the network architecture already in place has adequate capacity to handle the requirements of your application. If there is a bottleneck, it should be on the database server—which is the most tunable portion of the application. Your application server and network should be able to fully support the application without tuning or upgrades.

The client may be extremely simple. An NC needs an Internet address, a small operating system, and the ability to accept and display input. Every other function may be handled by the application server and the database server, freeing the resources previously spent on client configuration maintenance.

PART
IV

Appendixes

APPENDIX A

Migrating from ORACLE7 to ORACLE8

ou can migrate from ORACLE7 to ORACLE8 without taking advantage of any of the new features of ORACLE8 (such as partitions or abstract datatypes). Even if you do not use the new features, your database will change as the new RowID format is applied to your rows. In this chapter, you will see the changes you will need to be aware of regardless of the ORACLE8 features you implement. You will also see the management issues related to the new ORACLE8 features.

Installing ORACLE8

The installation process for ORACLE8 (run via the ORACLE installation software programs) creates a database whose internal and external structures are based on the Optimal Flexible Architecture (OFA). If you had previously used ORACLE7, you will need to know where the administration and configuration files now reside. There is no problem with running ORACLE7 and ORACLE8 on the same host. As long as the host can support two versions of the software, you can run ORACLE7 and ORACLE8 databases concurrently. The ability to run both versions concurrently simplifies the database upgrade process and improves your ability to undo changes.

Where Did init.ora Go?

Most of the ORACLE8 OFA changes at the operating system level were introduced with ORACLE7.3. The init.ora and config.ora files are no longer stored under the ORACLE software version directory. In earlier versions of ORACLE, the init.ora and config.ora files were stored under the software version directories. For example, for the CC1 database running under ORACLE7.2, there would be two files, named initCC1.ora and configCC1.ora, and they would be stored in the directory named /orasw/v7.2.3/dbs (where /orasw/v7.2.3 is the ORACLE software home directory).

In ORACLE8, these files are stored in a directory that is specific to the instance and not specific to the software version. The directory for the initCC1.ora and configCC1.ora files will be named /orasw/app/oracle/admin/CC1/pfile (where CC1 is the instance name). The 'pfile' directory is used to store the parameter files for the CC1 instance. If you upgrade the CC1 database to use a different version of the database software, you do not need to move the configuration files.

In many UNIX-based operating systems, the /dbs directory under the ORACLE software home directory will point users to the correct /orasw/app/oracle/admin/CC1/pfile directory.

Where Is the Alert Log?

The alert log records the major events and errors encountered in the life of the database. In ORACLE8, the alert log is located in the directory /orasw/app/oracle/admin/*INSTANCE_NAME*/bdump. For example, for the CC1 database, the alert log is named alertcc1.log, and is stored in /orasw/app/oracle/admin/CC1/bdump.

The dump files for the ORACLE server background processes (such as DBWR and PMON) are also written to the /orasw/app/oracle/admin/CC1/bdump directory.

Where Are the User Dump Files?

The user dump files record the major core-related errors encountered by users. In ORACLE8, the user dump file directory is /orasw/app/oracle/admin/INSTANCE_NAME/udump. For example, for the CC1 database, the user dump files are stored in /orasw/app/oracle/admin/CC1/udump.

Because the user dump files are separated from the alert log and the background dump files, you can set different security levels for the directories. You can set the security to allow users to read the contents of the user dump file directory without giving them the rights to read the contents of the background process dump file directory.

Obsolete and Changed init.ora Parameters

The following init.ora parameters are obsolete as of ORACLE8. You should remove their entries from your init.ora and config.ora files.

```
INIT_SQL_FILES
LM_DOMAINS
LM_NON_FAULT_TOLERANT
```

PARALLEL_DEFAULT_MAX_SCANS
PARALLEL_DEFAULT_SCANSIZE
SEQUENCE_CACHE_HASH_BUCKETS
SERIALIZABLE
SESSION_CACHED_CURSORS
V733_PLANS_ENABLED

Your entries for the following init.ora parameters should be modified after upgrading to ORACLE8:

COMPATIBLE	Change to reflect the current version (ex: 8.0.3).
SNAPSHOT_REFRESH_INTERVAL	Change parameter name to JOB_QUEUE_INTERVAL.
SNAPSHOT_REFRESH_PROCESS	Change parameter name to JOB_QUEUE_PROCESSES.
USER_DUMP_DEST	Point to new user dump file destination area; usually /orasw/app/oracle/ admin/*INSTANCE_NAME*/udump. Be sure to list the full directory specification.
BACKGROUND_DUMP_DEST	Point to new background dump file destination area; usually /orasw/app/ oracle/admin/*INSTANCE_NAME*/bdump. Be sure to list the full directory specification.
IFILE	Update to point to the new location of config.ora.
DB_WRITERS	Remove this entry; replace with an entry for DBWR_IO_SLAVES.

In addition to DBWR_IO_SLAVES, you can create slaves for the LGWR and ARCH processes via the LGWR_IO_SLAVES and ARCH_IO_SLAVES parameters, respectively.

If you use NLS, use ORA_NLS32 for ORACLE7.3 databases and ORA_NLS33 for ORACLE8 databases.

Obsolete sqlnet.ora Parameters

The following sqlnet.ora parameters are obsolete as of Net8:

    SQLNET.AUTHENTICATION_SERVICES
    SQLNET.EXPIRE_TIME
    SQLNET.CRYPTO_SEED

   If you have these parameters in your SQLNET.ORA files, you should
either delete their entries or comment out their lines in the file.

Obsolete tnsnames.ora and listener.ora Parameters

The following tnsnames.ora and listener.ora parameters are obsolete
as of Net8:

    COMMUNITY
    NAMES.DEFAULT_ZONE
    NAMES.PREFERRED_SERVERS

   You do not have to use Net8 in order to access an ORACLE8 database;
you can continue to use SQL*Net Version 2. If you upgrade to Net8,
however, you should remove the obsolete parameters from your
configuration files.

Obsolete Parameter Files for Net8

As of Net8, the following configuration files are obsolete:

    intchg.ora
    tnsnav.ora
    tnsnet.ora

   These three files are used by the SQL*Net Version 2 Multi-Protocol
Interchange. The Multi-Protocol Interchange is no longer used as of Net8.

How to Migrate

When migrating an ORACLE7 database to ORACLE8, you can either use the Export/Import method or the Migration Utility provided with ORACLE8. In the following sections, you will see descriptions of each method. In general, the Migration Utility will minimize the time required for the migration. If you use the Export/Import method, you will reinsert all of your data, potentially improving your space usage within the database.

The Export/Import Method

In the Export/Import method, you perform a full database export of an ORACLE7 database and then use the Export dump file as the data source for an import into an ORACLE8 database. The ORACLE7 and ORACLE8 databases do not have to be on the same host. If they are on the same host, then they will have to have different instance names (you can reuse the same instance name, but doing so will make it more difficult to revert to your old database, should that be necessary).

Step 1: Point your environment variables to the old instance and perform a full Export.

For example:

```
> ORACLE_SID=olddb; export ORACLE_SID
> ORAENV_ASK=NO; export ORAENV_ASK
> . oraenv
> exp system/manager file=olddb.dmp rows=Y grants=Y indexes=Y
```

Step 2: Point your environment variables to the new instance, and perform a full Import.

For example:

```
> ORACLE_SID=newdb; export ORACLE_SID
> ORAENV_ASK=NO; export ORAENV_ASK
> . oraenv
> imp system/manager file=olddb.dmp full=Y buffer=1000000
                      commit=Y ignore=Y
```

To make the Import process run faster, you can execute it in two steps. In the first step, import the tables and data, without the indexes. In the second step, import just the indexes. Replace the single Import command in the preceding listing with the following two commands:

```
> imp system/manager file=olddb.dmp full=Y buffer=1000000 commit=Y
                                    ignore=Y rows=Y indexes=N
> imp system/manager file=olddb.dmp full=Y ignore=Y rows=N indexes=Y
```

The data from the olddb.dmp Export dump file will be imported into the "newdb" instance. After the Import completes, you should reexecute the scripts that create the database catalog in the ORACLE8 database. Change your directory so you are in the /rdbms/admin subdirectory under the ORACLE8 software directory and run the catalog.sql script from within Server Manager:

```
> svrmgrl
SVRMGR> connect internal;
SVRMGR> @catalog
```

Your database has now been migrated from ORACLE7 to ORACLE8.

Using the Migration Utility

If you use the ORACLE8 Migration Utility, then your data's RowID values will not be changed automatically. The Migration Utility does not change the RowID values; the RowID values are not altered until the blocks are accessed by your users. Because it does not modify RowID values, the Migration Utility provides a quick upgrade path. However, because the RowIDs will be updated later during database usage, it places a potential performance burden on the users of your database applications.

Because you cannot always predict when all of your tables will be accessed by users, you should use the Export/Import method if possible during the database upgrade. If, however, the time required to perform the upgrade is extremely limited, then you should consider using the Migration Utility provided with ORACLE8.

The Migration Utility is one of the software modules provided with the ORACLE8 software. You should install this software during your ORACLE8 software installation. You can run the Migration Utility from within the Installer by choosing the "Migrate from ORACLE7 to ORACLE8" option of the Installation Options screen. When you then choose "Run Migration Utility", you will be prompted for the name of the instance to migrate.

After you run the Migration Utility from within the ORACLE Installer, move the conversion file created by the utility. The conversion file will be named conv*INSTANCE_NAME*.dbf (for example, convcc1.dbf). The file should be moved from the /dbs subdirectory under the ORACLE7 software directory to the /dbs subdirectory under the ORACLE8 software directory. If you are changing the name of the instance, then you should change the name of the conversion file to match the name of the new ORACLE8 instance.

At this time, you should make sure that the CONTROL_FILES parameter in the config.ora (or init.ora) file for your ORACLE8 database points to a location that does not presently contain control files (the migration process will create new control files). Then, convert the database by issuing the **alter database convert** command within Server Manager (while your environment variables are pointed to the new instance), as shown in the following listing:

```
> svrmgrl
SVRMGR> startup nomount;
SVRMGR> alter database convert;
SVRMGR> alter database open resetlogs;
```

The **alter database convert** command uses the conversion file to create new control files for the ORACLE8 instance. The conversion file contains all of the information ORACLE needs to create the control files, so the conversion operation completes very quickly.

You should then run the cat8000.sql script found in the /rdbms/admin subdirectory under the ORACLE8 software home directory. Go to that directory and execute the following commands:

```
> svrmgrl
SVRMGR> connect internal
SVRMGR> @cat8000.sql
```

As a result of these actions, the Migration Utility will create new control files for the ORACLE8 database, and the datafiles from the ORACLE7 instance will be used for the ORACLE8 database. As noted earlier, however, the RowIDs in the ORACLE7 database will not be converted to the extended RowID format until they are first used. Thus, while the Migration Utility may complete quickly, the migration may cause performance impacts for your users while they are first accessing data in the ORACLE8 database. In the next section, you will see details on the changes to the RowID format.

Changes to ROWID

As of ORACLE8, the formats for RowIDs have been changed. The changed format for the RowID allows ORACLE to support more files per database and more blocks per file. As a result of the RowID changes, ORACLE can now store petabytes of data instead of terabytes (1 petabyte = 1,024 terabytes). A terabyte, in turn, is 1,024 gigabytes (Gb).

The new format for the RowIDs is called the "extended" format. The format used in earlier versions of ORACLE is now referred to as the "restricted" format. You can use a number of ORACLE-provided functions to translate the extended format RowID values into the more familiar restricted format.

In the following sections, you will see examples of the functions provided via the DBMS_ROWID package. The full package description is located in the dbmsutil.sql file, usually located in the /rdbms/admin subdirectory under your ORACLE software home directory.

You can select the extended RowID values the same way you selected the restricted RowID values in ORACLE7:

```
select RowID
  from NUMBERTEST
 where Rownum=1;

ROWID
-----------------
AAAArfABQAAAALBAAA
```

The preceding query selects the RowID of a single row in the NUMBERTEST table. The extended RowID does not immediately appear to provide useful information. However, if you use the functions provided by ORACLE, you will find that the extended RowID values contain data not provided via the restricted RowID. As you will see in the next section, you can use the extended RowID to determine the Object_ID value for the object to which the row belongs.

What Is the Object_ID Value?

To see the Object_ID for an object based on its extended RowID, use the ROWID_OBJECT function within the DBMS_ROWID package. In the following listing, a row is selected from the NUMBERTEST table; its extended RowID value is used as the input to the ROWID_OBJECT function:

```
select DBMS_ROWID.ROWID_OBJECT(RowID)
  from NUMBERTEST
 where RowNum=1;

DBMS_ROWID.ROWID_OBJECT(ROWID)
------------------------------
                          2783
```

The ROWID_OBJECT function helps you identify an object if you only have a RowID of a row within the object. If you already have the Object_ID value, you can query the object's name from DBA_OBJECTS.

```
select Object_Name
  from DBA_OBJECTS
 where Object_ID = 2783;

OBJECT_NAME
----------------------------------------
NUMBERTEST
```

With the restricted RowID format, determining the object ID for an object required comparing the RowID's block and file number values to entries in DBA_EXTENTS. The extended RowID format greatly simplifies the translation of RowIDs to object ID values.

Converting RowIDs to the Restricted Format

You can use the ROWID_TO_RESTRICTED function of the DBMS_ROWID package to display extended RowIDs in the restricted format. The ROWID_TO_RESTRICTED function has two parameters: the extended RowID value and the type of conversion. Use '0' for the conversion type value, as shown in the following listing. In the example, the RowID values from the NUMBERTEST table are converted to restricted format.

```
select DBMS_ROWID.ROWID_TO_RESTRICTED(RowID,0)
  from NUMBERTEST;
```

```
DBMS_ROWID.ROWID_T
------------------
000002C1.0000.0050
000002C1.0001.0050
000002C1.0002.0050
000002C1.0003.0050
000002C1.0004.0050
000002C1.0005.0050
000002C1.0006.0050
000002C1.0007.0050
```

In the restricted format, the first eight bytes constitute the block number, in hexadecimal. Hex "2C1" is equivalent to decimal "705", so the data is stored in block #705 of its file. The file ID is the last four digits of the restricted RowID (in hexadecimal).

NOTE
The file ID portion of the converted RowID is the relative file number, not the absolute file number. As of ORACLE8, there are two classes of file numbers, as described in the next section.

The relative file number, the last part of the restricted RowID, is displayed as '0050'. The relative file number portion, like the block ID portion, is in hexadecimal. Hexadecimal "50" is equivalent to decimal "80", so the relative file number is 80.

The middle part of the restricted RowID is the sequence number of the row within the block, starting with 0. The eight rows in the NUMBERTEST table are all stored in the same block.

What File Is the Row in?

As of ORACLE8, there are two different types of file numbers: relative file numbers and absolute file numbers. The expanded types of file numbers allow ORACLE to support a greater number of files per database.

The ROWID_TO_RESTRICTED function shown in the previous section displayed the relative file number for the file in which the rows are stored.

You can also select the relative file number directly from the RowID values via the ROWID_RELATIVE_FNO function of the DBMS_ROWID package. As shown in the following listing, the ROWID_RELATIVE_FNO function returns the relative file number (in decimal) of the file in which the row is stored:

```
select DBMS_ROWID.ROWID_RELATIVE_FNO(RowID)
  from NUMBERTEST
 where RowNum=1;

DBMS_ROWID.ROWID_RELATIVE_FNO(ROWID)
------------------------------------
                                  80
```

You can verify the relative file number by querying the file information from DBA_DATA_FILES. When querying with the new relative file numbers, use the decimal version of the Relative_FNO value. The following example shows the DBA_DATA_FILES entry for the NUMBERTEST row queried in the preceding listing:

```
select File_Name, File_ID
  from DBA_DATA_FILES
 where Relative_FNO = 80;

FILE_NAME                                   FILE_ID
------------------------------------------- ----------
/db02/oracle/CC1/users01.dbf                      5
```

The File_ID value of 5 represents the *absolute* file number for the data file; 80 is the *relative* file number. In general, it is simpler to deal with relative file numbers than absolute file numbers. If you want to derive absolute file numbers from the RowID values, you can use the ROWID_TO_ABSOLUTE_FNO function of the DBMS_ROWID package.

The ROWID_TO_ABSOLUTE_FNO function requires three inputs. They are, in order:

1. The RowID

2. The name of the schema that owns the table

3. The name of the table

In the following listing, the absolute file number for the NUMBERTEST table owned by a user named Talbot is queried:

```
select DBMS_ROWID.ROWID_TO_ABSOLUTE_FNO(RowID,'TALBOT','NUMBERTEST')
  from NUMBERTEST
 where RowNum=1;

DBMS_ROWID.ROWID_TO_ABSOLUTE_FNO(ROWID,'TALBOT','NUMBERTEST')
-------------------------------------------------------------
                                                            5
```

The absolute file number of 5 corresponds to the datafile's File_ID value in DBA_DATA_FILES, as shown in the previous query of DBA_DATA_FILES.

What Block Is the Row in?

You can query the block number for a row directly from the RowID by using the ROWID_BLOCK_NUMBER function of the DBMS_ROWID package. As shown in the following listing, the ROWID_BLOCK_NUMBER has one input (the RowID) and returns the block number in decimal format.

```
select DBMS_ROWID.ROWID_BLOCK_NUMBER(RowID)
  from NUMBERTEST
 where RowNum=1;

DBMS_ROWID.ROWID_BLOCK_NUMBER(ROWID)
------------------------------------
                                 705
```

The row is stored in block 705 of the file whose relative file number (from the previous section of this chapter) is 80. Since the NUMBERTEST table is very small and has only a single extent, it is easy to verify this block number by querying DBA_EXTENTS. The following query selects the header block for the NUMBERTEST extent:

```
select Relative_FNO, Block_ID
  from DBA_EXTENTS
 where Segment_Name = 'NUMBERTEST';

RELATIVE_FNO    BLOCK_ID
------------    ----------
          80          704
```

The header block for the table is block number 704; rows are stored starting with the next block (705).

You normally query file numbers and block numbers together. The following query selects both the relative file number and the block number for a row via function calls:

```
select DBMS_ROWID.ROWID_RELATIVE_FNO(RowID),
       DBMS_ROWID.ROWID_BLOCK_NUMBER(RowID)
  from NUMBERTEST
 where RowNum=1;
```

What Is the Row's Sequence Number?

Multiple rows may be stored in a single block. ORACLE assigns a sequence number to each row within a block, starting with a sequence number of 0. You can select the sequence number directly from the extended RowID value. ORACLE provides a function named ROWID_ROW_NUMBER within the DBMS_ROWID package to extract row sequence numbers from extended RowID values.

In the following listing, the ROWID_ROW_NUMBER function is used to determine the sequence numbers of the rows in the NUMBERTEST table:

```
select DBMS_ROWID.ROWID_ROW_NUMBER(RowID)
  from NUMBERTEST;

DBMS_ROWID.ROWID_ROW_NUMBER(ROWID)
----------------------------------
                                 0
                                 1
                                 2
                                 3
                                 4
                                 5
                                 6
                                 7
```

The query output in the preceding listing shows the sequence numbers within block 705 for the rows of the NUMBERTEST table. Row sequence numbers are usually selected along with their block numbers (via ROWID_BLOCK_NUMBER) and relative file numbers (via ROWID_RELATIVE_FNO).

There is no loss of functionality in RowIDs when going from ORACLE7 to ORACLE8. When you first migrate, you may find it simplest to use the ROWID_TO_RESTRICTED function to display the data in the familiar old format. However, you should learn to use the DBMS_ROWID functions to extract the data you need from the RowID values.

ORACLE provides several additional procedures and functions in the DBMS_ROWID package. The additional options are useful if you develop applications that use ROWID as a datatype, in which case you will need to convert that data when you migrate to ORACLE8. See the dbmsutil.sql file in the /rdbms/admin directory under the ORACLE software home directory for further details on these additional options.

Managing Passwords

As of ORACLE8, there are several significant improvements to your ability to manage users' passwords. For example, you can enforce a minimum length for passwords, you can prevent users from using simple passwords, and you can prevent the reuse of passwords. If a user repeatedly fails to access an account, you can lock the account to prevent further login attempts. See Chapter 9 for details on the administration of these features.

Partitions

As of ORACLE8, you can define the partition ranges used for your tables and indexes. Partitioning splits the rows of a table across multiple smaller tables, potentially simplifying the management of the table's data and improving performance for queries of the table. See Chapter 12 for details on the implementation of partitioned tables and indexes.

Large Objects (LOBs)

As of ORACLE8, four new large object (LOB) datatypes are supported: one external LOB datatype (BFILE) and three internal LOB datatypes (BLOB, CLOB, and NCLOB). If you use the BFILE datatype, the database only stores a locator value that points to the external binary file. ORACLE does not manage read consistency or recoverability for the external data. In order to create a BFILE entry, you must first create a directory via the **create directory** command.

If the data is stored using a BLOB, CLOB, or NCLOB datatype, then it is stored inside the database. A single internal LOB column can be up to 4Gb in length, and you can have multiple LOB columns *per table*. A BLOB datatype is used for binary large objects, a CLOB datatype is used for character large objects, and NCLOB is a CLOB datatype for multibyte character sets. Since they quickly consume large quantities of space, you should avoid using the BLOB, CLOB, and NCLOB datatypes except when there is no alternative.

If you use LOB datatypes, you can specify where the LOB data is stored. Rather than storing LOB data with the rest of the table, ORACLE allows you to specify a separate storage area for the LOB data. This separation greatly simplifies the table sizing and data administration activities for the table that contains the LOB data. You can also specify whether or not changes to the LOB data should be recorded on the online redo log files via the **nologging** parameter. The storage and logging parameters for LOBs are set via the **lob** clause of the **create table** command. The **nologging** clause is described in the next section of this chapter.

The nologging Clause

ORACLE7.2 introduced the concept of an *unrecoverable* operation. During an unrecoverable operation, no entries are written to the online redo log files. The only two operations that could use the **unrecoverable** option were the **create table as select** command and the **create index** command. Since both of those operations store redundant data, you could conceivably recover them following a media failure without needing to restore their data via archived redo logs.

The **unrecoverable** option improves the performance of **create table as select** commands and **create index** commands significantly. In most cases, the time required for the operations to complete is cut in half.

As of ORACLE8, the **unrecoverable** option is replaced by the **nologging** option. When you create a table with the **nologging** option, its initial creation is not logged and neither are any subsequent transactions against the table. The **nologging** option is particularly useful when storing large objects (LOBs) in the database. When you create a table that contains a BLOB (binary large object) or CLOB (character large object), you can specify via the **lob** clause of the **create table** command whether changes to the LOB data are logged. Similarly, you can specify the **nologging** option for specific partitions within a table (see Chapter 12). You can therefore control the logging of transactions for all transactions against either an entire table or part of a table.

Managing Abstract Datatypes

As of ORACLE8, you can use abstract datatypes to group related columns into objects. For example, columns that are part of address information can be grouped into an ADDRESS_TY datatype via the **create type** command.

```
create type ADDRESS_TY as object
(Street  VARCHAR2(50),
 City    VARCHAR2(25),
 State   CHAR(2),
 Zip     NUMBER);
```

The **create type** command in the preceding listing creates an ADDRESS_TY abstract datatype. You can use ADDRESS_TY when creating additional database objects. For example, the following **create type** command creates the PERSON_TY datatype, using the ADDRESS_TY datatype as the datatype for its Address column:

```
create type PERSON_TY as object
(Name     VARCHAR2(25),
 Address  ADDRESS_TY);
```

Because the Address column of the PERSON_TY datatype uses the ADDRESS_TY datatype, it holds not one value but four—the four related attributes that constitute the ADDRESS_TY datatype.

You can use an abstract datatype when creating a table, as shown in the following listing:

```
create table CUSTOMER
(Customer_ID  NUMBER,
 Person       PERSON_TY);
```

The CUSTOMER table has only two columns. When you insert data into the CUSTOMER table, you use the *constructor methods* ORACLE creates for the datatype, as shown in the following example. The constructor methods are named after the datatypes; their parameters are the attributes of the datatypes.

```
insert into CUSTOMER values
(444,
 PERSON_TY('JANET NORWOOD',
    ADDRESS_TY('100 RIVER RD', 'RIDGE', 'MA', 10002)));
```

The preceding **insert** command uses the PERSON_TY constructor method to insert data into the Person column of the CUSTOMER table. The second attribute within Person is Address, which uses the ADDRESS_TY datatype. Therefore, a call to ADDRESS_TY is nested within the call to PERSON_TY. Developers can create additional methods that apply to each datatype.

Security for Abstract Datatypes

The previous example assumed that the same user owned both the ADDRESS_TY datatype and the PERSON_TY datatype. What if the owner of the PERSON_TY datatype were different from the ADDRESS_TY datatype's owner?

For example, what if the account named "Dora" owns the ADDRESS_TY datatype, and the user of the account named "George" tries to create the PERSON_TY datatype? George executes the following command:

```
create type PERSON_TY as object
(Name     VARCHAR2(25),
 Address  ADDRESS_TY);
```

If George does not own the ADDRESS_TY abstract datatype, then ORACLE will respond to this **create type** command with the following message:

```
Warning: Type created with compilation errors.
```

The compilation errors are caused by problems creating the constructor method when the datatype is created. ORACLE cannot resolve the reference to the ADDRESS_TY datatype since George does not own a datatype with that name. He could issue the **create type** command again (using the **or replace** clause) to specifically reference Dora's ADDRESS_TY datatype.

```
create or replace type PERSON_TY as object
(Name     VARCHAR2(25),
 Address  Dora.ADDRESS_TY);

Warning: Type created with compilation errors.
```

To see the errors associated with the datatype creation, use the **show errors** command:

```
show errors
Errors for TYPE PERSON_TY:

LINE/COL ERROR
-------- -----------------------------------------------------------
0/0      PL/SQL: Compilation unit analysis terminated
3/11     PLS-00201: identifier 'DORA.ADDRESS_TY' must be declared
```

George will not be able to create the PERSON_TY datatype (which includes the ADDRESS_TY datatype) unless Dora first **grant**s him EXECUTE privilege on her type. The following listing shows this grant:

```
grant EXECUTE on ADDRESS_TY to George;
```

Now that the proper grants are in place, George can create a datatype that is based on Dora's ADDRESS_TY datatype.

```
create or replace type PERSON_TY as object
(Name      VARCHAR2(25),
 Address   Dora.ADDRESS_TY);
```

George's PERSON_TY datatype will now be successfully created. However, using datatypes based on another user's datatypes is not trivial. For example, during **insert** operations, you must fully specify the name of the owner of each type. George can create a table based on his PERSON_TY datatype (which includes Dora's ADDRESS_TY datatype), as shown in the following listing:

```
create table CUSTOMER
(Customer_ID  NUMBER,
 Person       PERSON_TY);
```

If George owned PERSON_TY and ADDRESS_TY datatypes, then an **insert** into CUSTOMER would use the format:

```
insert into CUSTOMER values
(1,PERSON_TY('SomeName',
    ADDRESS_TY('StreetValue','CityValue','ST',11111)));
```

Since George does not own the ADDRESS_TY datatype, this command will fail. During the **insert**, the ADDRESS_TY constructor method is used, and Dora owns it. Therefore, the **insert** command must be modified to specify Dora as the owner of ADDRESS_TY. The following example shows the corrected **insert** statement, with the reference to Dora shown in bold:

```
insert into CUSTOMER values
(1,PERSON_TY('SomeName',
   Dora.ADDRESS_TY('StreetValue','CityValue','ST',11111)));
```

Can George use a synonym for Dora's datatype? No. George *can* create a synonym named ADDRESS_TY:

```
create synonym ADDRESS_TY for Dora.ADDRESS_TY;
```

but this synonym cannot be used.

```
create type PERSON2_TY
(Name      VARCHAR2(25),
 Address   ADDRESS_TY);

create type PERSON2_TY
*
ERROR at line 1:
ORA-22863: synonym for datatype DORA.ADDRESS_TY not allowed
```

As shown by the error message, you cannot use a synonym for another user's datatype. Therefore, you will need to refer to the datatype's owner during each **insert** command.

NOTE
When you create a synonym, ORACLE does not check the validity of the object for which you are creating a synonym. If you **create synonym x for y**, *ORACLE does not check to make sure that "y" is a valid object name or valid object type. The validation of that object's accessibility via synonyms is only checked when the object is accessed via the synonym.*

In a relational-only implementation of ORACLE, you grant the EXECUTE privilege on procedural objects, such as procedures and packages. Within the object-relational implementation of ORACLE, the EXECUTE privilege is extended to cover abstract datatypes as well. The EXECUTE privilege is used because abstract datatypes can include *methods*—PL/SQL functions and procedures that operate on the datatype. If you grant someone the privilege to use your datatype, you are granting the user the privilege to execute the methods you have defined on the datatype. Therefore, the proper privilege to grant is EXECUTE. Although Dora did not yet define any methods on the ADDRESS_TY datatype, ORACLE automatically creates special procedures called constructor methods that are used to access the data. Any object (such as PERSON_TY) that uses the ADDRESS_TY datatype uses the constructor method associated with ADDRESS_TY. So, even if you haven't created any methods for your abstract datatype, there are still procedures associated with it.

You cannot create public types, and you cannot create public synonyms for your types. Therefore, you will need to either reference the owner of the type or create the type under each account that can create tables in your database. Neither of these is a simple solution to the problem of datatype management.

Indexing Abstract Datatype Attributes

In the preceding example, the CUSTOMER table was created based on a PERSON_TY datatype and an ADDRESS_TY datatype. As shown in the following listing, the CUSTOMER table contains a normal column—Customer_ID—and a Person column that is defined by the PERSON_TY abstract datatype:

```
create table CUSTOMER
(Customer_ID    NUMBER,
 Person         PERSON_TY);
```

From the datatype definitions shown in the previous section of this chapter, you can see that PERSON_TY has one column—Name—followed by an Address column defined by the ADDRESS_TY datatype.

When referencing columns within the abstract datatypes during queries, **update**s, and **delete**s, specify the full path to the datatype attributes. For example, the following query returns the Customer_ID column along with the Name column. The Name column is an attribute of the datatype that defines the Person column, so you refer to the attribute as Person.Name.

```
select Customer_ID, Person.Name
   from CUSTOMER;
```

You can refer to attributes within the ADDRESS_TY datatype by specifying the full path through the related columns. For example, the Street column is referred to as Person.Address.Street, which fully describes its location within the structure of the table. In the following example, the City column is referenced twice; once in the list of columns to select and once within the **where** clause.

```
select Person.Name,
       Person.Address.City
  from CUSTOMER
 where Person.Address.City like 'F%';
```

Because the City column is used with a range search in the **where** clause, the ORACLE optimizer may be able to use an index when resolving the query. If an index is available on the City column, then ORACLE can quickly find all of the rows that have City values starting with the letter 'F' as requested by the query.

To create an index on a column that is part of an abstract datatype, you need to specify the full path to the column as part of the **create index** command. To create an index on the City column (which is part of the Address column), you can execute the following command:

```
create index I_CUSTOMER$CITY
on CUSTOMER(Person.Address.City);
```

This command will create an index named I_CUSTOMER$CITY on the Person.Address.City column. Whenever the City column is accessed, the ORACLE optimizer will evaluate the SQL used to access the data and determine if the new index can be useful to improve the performance of the access.

When creating tables based on abstract datatypes, you should consider how the columns within the abstract datatypes will be accessed. If, like the City column in the previous example, certain columns will commonly be used as part of limiting conditions in queries, then they should be indexed. In this regard, the representation of multiple columns in a single abstract datatype may hinder your application performance, since it may obscure the need to index specific columns within the datatype.

When you use abstract datatypes, you become accustomed to treating a group of columns as single entity, such as the Address columns or the Person columns. It is important to remember that the optimizer, when evaluating query access paths, will consider the columns individually. You therefore need to address the indexing requirements for the columns even when you are using abstract datatypes. In addition, remember that indexing the City column in one table that uses the ADDRESS_TY datatype does not affect the City column in a second table that uses the ADDRESS_TY datatype. For example, if there is a second table named BRANCH that uses the ADDRESS_TY datatype, then *its* City column will not be indexed unless you create an index for it. The fact that there is an index on the City column in the CUSTOMER table will not impact the City column in the BRANCH table.

Using Object Views

The CUSTOMER table created in the previous section of this chapter assumed that a PERSON_TY datatype already existed. But what if your tables already exist? What if you had previously created a relational database application and are trying to implement object-relational concepts in your application without rebuilding and recreating the entire application? What you would need is the ability to overlay object-oriented (OO) structures such as abstract datatypes on existing relational tables. ORACLE provides *object views* as a means for defining objects used by existing relational tables.

If the CUSTOMER table already existed, you could create the ADDRESS_TY and PERSON_TY datatypes, and use object views to relate them to the CUSTOMER table. In the following listing, the CUSTOMER table is created as a relational table, using only the normally provided datatypes:

```
create table CUSTOMER
(Customer_ID NUMBER    primary key,
 Name         VARCHAR2(25),
 Street       VARCHAR2(50),
 City         VARCHAR2(25),
 State        CHAR(2),
 Zip          NUMBER);
```

If you want to create another table or application that stores information about people and addresses, you may choose to create the ADDRESS_TY and PERSON_TY datatypes. However, for consistency, they should be applied to the CUSTOMER table as well. In the following examples, the ADDRESS_TY and PERSON_TY datatypes created earlier in this chapter will be used.

You can create an object view based on the CUSTOMER table, using the datatypes you have defined. An object view is created via the **create view** command. Within the **create view** command, you specify the query that will form the basis of the view. To use the abstract datatypes you've just created, you'll use the datatypes you just created. The code for creating the CUSTOMER_OV object view is shown in the following listing:

```
create view CUSTOMER_OV (Customer_ID, Person) as
select Customer_ID,
       PERSON_TY(Name,
       ADDRESS_TY(Street, City, State, Zip))
  from CUSTOMER;
```

The CUSTOMER_OV view will have two columns: the Customer_ID and the Person column (the latter is defined by the PERSON_TY datatype). Note that you cannot specify "object" as an option within the **create view** command.

There are several important syntax issues presented in this example. When a table is built upon existing abstract datatypes, you select column values from the table by referring to the names of the columns (such as Person and Address) instead of their constructor methods. When creating the object view, however, you refer to the names of the constructor methods (PERSON_TY and ADDRESS_TY) instead. Also, you can use **where** clauses in the query that forms the basis of the object view. You can therefore limit the rows that are accessible via the object view.

If you use object views, then DBAs administer relational tables, the same way they did before object-relational features were introduced in the database. You will still need to manage the privileges for the datatypes, but the table and index structures will be the same as they were in ORACLE7. Using the old structures may simplify your administration tasks while allowing developers to access "objects" via the object views of the tables.

You can also use object views to simulate the references used by row objects. Row objects are rows within an object table. To create an object view that supports row objects, you need to first create a datatype that has the same structure as the table:

```
create or replace type CUSTOMER_TY as object
(Customer_ID NUMBER,
 Name         VARCHAR2(25),
 Street       VARCHAR2(50),
 City         VARCHAR2(25),
 State        CHAR(2),
 Zip          NUMBER);
```

Next, create an object view based on the CUSTOMER_TY type, while assigning OID values to the records in CUSTOMER.

```
create view CUSTOMER_OV of CUSTOMER_TY
with object OID (Customer_ID) as
select Customer_ID, Name, Street, City, State, Zip
  from CUSTOMER;
```

The first part of this **create view** command gives the view its name (CUSTOMER_OV) and tells ORACLE that the view's structure is based on the CUSTOMER_TY datatype. An OID is an object identifier (for a row object). In this object view, the Customer_ID column will be used as the OID.

If you have a second table that references CUSTOMER via a foreign key/primary key relationship, then you can set up an object view that contains references to CUSTOMER_OV. For example, the CUSTOMER_CALL table contains a foreign key to the CUSTOMER table:

```
create table CUSTOMER_CALL
(Customer_ID    NUMBER,
 Call_Number    NUMBER,
 Call_Date      DATE,
 constraint CUSTOMER_CALL_PK
     primary key (Customer_ID, Call_Number),
 constraint CUSTOMER_CALL_FK foreign key (Customer_ID)
   references CUSTOMER(Customer_ID));
```

The Customer_ID column of CUSTOMER_CALL references the same column in the CUSTOMER table. Since you have simulated OIDs (called pkOIDs) based on the primary key of CUSTOMER, you need to create references to those OIDs. ORACLE provides an operator called **MAKE_REF** that creates the references (called pkREFs). In the following listing, the **MAKE_REF** operator is used to create references from the object view of CUSTOMER_CALL to the object view of CUSTOMER:

```
create view CUSTOMER_CALL_OV as
select MAKE_REF(CUSTOMER_OV, Customer_ID) Customer_ID,
       Call_Number,
       Call_Date
  from CUSTOMER_CALL;
```

Within the CUSTOMER_CALL_OV view, you tell ORACLE the name of the view to reference and the columns that constitute the pkREF. You could now query CUSTOMER_OV data from within CUSTOMER_CALL_OV by using the DEREF operator on the Customer_ID column.

```
select DEREF(CCOV.Customer_ID)
  from CUSTOMER_CALL_OV CCOV
 where Call_Date = TRUNC(SysDate);
```

You can thus return CUSTOMER data from your query without directly querying the CUSTOMER table. In this example, the Call_Date column is used as a limiting condition for the rows returned by the query.

As with abstract datatypes, you can use object views to shield your tables from the object relationships. The tables are not modified; you administer them the way you always did. The difference is that the users can now access the rows of CUSTOMER as if they are row objects.

Using Nested Tables and Varying Arrays

As of ORACLE8, you can use two different types of collectors within your database. A collector allows you to have multiple values for a single row in your database. For example, if you had multiple addresses for a person, you could either have multiple address rows for that person or you could have a single row for the person with multiple occurrences of the address data within that row.

The two types of collectors you can use are called varying arrays and nested tables. A varying array is a limited set of values that repeat for a row. You can set the maximum number of values allowed for the array. The varying array's data is stored with the table that contains the array. A nested table, on the other hand, has no upper limit to its number of records and is stored apart from the main table.

You can use nested tables and varying arrays to model repeating attributes along with master records as part of a single 'object'. However, the SQL and PL/SQL used to query and manipulate their records represents a departure from ORACLE's normal SQL, since you now need to be concerned about columns that may contain multiple values per row. In general, you should first attempt to implement these features via object views to simplify their data administration. If you decide to implement collectors, you should favor nested tables over varying arrays. Since nested tables are stored in a separate table, their data is easier to manage, and their entries may be indexed. Also, in the first release of ORACLE8, you can only query varying arrays via PL/SQL, making them difficult to use effectively.

ORACLE Enterprise Manager

As of ORACLE8, the ORACLE Enterprise Manager (OEM) has been enhanced to include a new Recovery Manager utility. Although you do not need to use OEM to perform almost all database administration tasks, some database backup capabilities are only available via OEM. For an overview of the OEM capabilities, see Appendix B.

APPENDIX B

Managing the ORACLE Enterprise Manager

RACLE first introduced the ORACLE Enterprise Manager (OEM) in later versions of ORACLE7. Since its introduction, it has grown in features and complexity. Version 1.4 of OEM has been introduced to support ORACLE8. You can use OEM to perform many of the database administration tasks described in this book—such as creating users, adding datafiles, and dropping objects. OEM provides a graphical user interface in place of the traditional line-mode command interface used by DBAs. The traditional command mode is still supported via the line-mode interface of Server Manager.

Although the user interface for DBA commands is simpler in OEM than in line-mode (Server Manager) commands, OEM places a management burden on the DBA. In this appendix, you will see the management issues associated with OEM; for as OEM has grown in complexity, the number of potential management issues associated with OEM has increased.

Unique Features of OEM

In addition to supporting the traditional DBA commands, OEM provides several unique features. For example, you can use OEM to easily create a new user whose objects and privileges are the same as those of an existing user. You can also create objects in one schema that are based on the definitions of objects in a second schema, without having to manually execute all of the required SQL commands.

For many of its actions, OEM uses the internal ORACLE job queue management facility described in Chapter 15. In order to use the internal job queues, you must start job queue processes and set a time interval for their execution. The number of job queue processes to start is specified via the JOB_QUEUE_PROCESSES init.ora parameter. You can start up to 36 concurrent job queue processes. The time interval (in seconds) that passes before the processes "wake up" to check for pending jobs is set via the JOB_QUEUE_INTERVAL parameter. See Chapter 15 for examples of manually managing the job queue.

Recovery Manager

As of ORACLE8, OEM includes Recovery Manager, a utility that keeps track of your backups and adds new backup capabilities. Recovery Manager gives you new backup and recovery features, such the ability to perform incremental physical backups of your datafiles. During a full (called a *level 0*) datafile backup, all of the blocks ever used in the datafile are backed up. During a cumulative (*level 1*) datafile backup, all of the blocks used since the last full datafile backup are backed up. An incremental (*level 2*) datafile backup backs up only those blocks that have changed since the most recent cumulative or full backup.

Since you may be backing up a smaller amount of data with each backup, the performance of your backups may improve. However, you need to consider the potential impact of your backup strategies on your recovery operations. During a recovery, you will need to have available all of the data that ORACLE needs to recreate the lost data. Using the traditional backup methods (see Chapter 10), there is no confusion about the data required; if you lose a datafile, you need to recover the datafile. If you perform incremental physical backups via Recovery Manager, however, the data required during recoveries includes the most recent full backup of the datafile and the partial backups performed since that time. Unless you clearly document your recovery procedures and account for the disk space required by the additional backup files, you may not be able to effectively use Recovery Manager. Also, note that Recovery Manager does not shield you from the commands needed to recover the database.

The information that Recovery Manager uses to perform backups and recoveries is stored in an ORACLE database. Thus, if that repository of information is lost, then your ability to back up and recover your databases is effectively eliminated. You must back up your repository database in order to ensure that your repository data is recoverable.

The larger concern when implementing Recovery Manager is the potential loss of process integration between the DBA community and the systems management personnel. As noted in Chapter 10, the backup processes executed by the DBA team should be part of an enterprise backup plan. If you use Recovery Manager and ORACLE's internal job queues to manage your backup processes, how will the system management personnel control the ORACLE backups? If you have multiple teams that own the same process, then you will almost always have problems implementing the process in a consistent and effective fashion.

Most systems management teams use batch programs at the operating system level to perform backups of the operating system and its directories. If you use a script-based method (see Chapter 10) for your backups, your scripts can usually be tightly integrated with the operating system backups. If you use Recovery Manager, you will need to document the standard operating procedures for the backup and recovery operations to minimize the impact of the loss of backup integration.

Performance Pack and ORACLE Trace

By default, OEM does not come with the Performance Pack installed. The Performance Pack is a set of add-on utilities designed to help with the tuning and performance management aspects of the database. The Performance Pack includes tools such as Top Sessions and ORACLE Expert.

One of the Performance Pack tools, ORACLE Trace, may impact your performance even if you do not use it. ORACLE Trace evaluates database-level trace information to identify potential performance problems. To generate the information it needs in order to perform this evaluation, ORACLE Trace collects trace information about the database activity.

You should not run ORACLE Trace constantly; however, it is enabled by default in many installations. As a result, your database is constantly generating trace data that you may never use. Because you are generating and maintaining this trace information, your database may exhibit performance-related problems, such as poor query response time, aborted sessions, and database connection attempts that take a very long time to establish a connection. This problem is most prevalent in the UNIX implementations of ORACLE Trace.

To determine if ORACLE Trace is collecting data on your server, check for the existence of the process.dat and regid.dat files in the /otrace/admin subdirectory of your ORACLE software home directory. An example of this check, as performed on a UNIX server, is shown in the following listing. The **cd** command changes the directory, and the **ls** command lists the files that match the *.dat filename format.

```
> cd $ORACLE_HOME/otrace/admin
> ls -alt *.dat
-rw-rw-rw-   1 oracle   dba      11948576 Sep 16 10:40 process.dat
-rw-rw-rw-   1 oracle   dba       1023292 Sep 16 10:40 regid.dat
```

The listing shows that the process.dat file has grown to over 11MB. In general, the performance of database connections is affected when the process.dat file exceeds 5MB in size. Before beginning to resolve the problem, you should first shut down the databases on the server. To resolve the problem, delete the process.dat and regid.dat files and run the **otrccref** command (which re-initializes the ORACLE Trace files). These actions are shown in the following example:

```
> cd $ORACLE_HOME/otrace/admin
> rm -f process.dat regid.dat
> otrccref
```

In the listing, the UNIX **rm** command is used to delete the trace files created by ORACLE Trace. To prevent new entries from being written to the trace files, you should set the EPC_DISABLED environment variable to TRUE in the profile (login) file for the user account that owns the ORACLE software (usually named oracle). For example, the following Bourne shell command set this variable:

```
EPC_DISABLED=TRUE; export EPC_DISABLED
```

You can also disable ORACLE Trace log generation by modifying the listener.ora file. Each listener.ora file includes a section that lists the instances to listen for and the ORACLE software home directory for the instances. A sample listener.ora section for the 'loc' instance is shown in the following listing:

```
SID_LIST_LISTENER =
  (SID_LIST =
   (SID_DESC =
     (SID_NAME = loc)
     (ORACLE_HOME = /orasw/app/oracle/product/8.0.3.1)
   )
  )
```

To make sure SQL*Net V2 and Net8 connections to your database do not enable ORACLE Trace, you can add a clause to the listener.ora file. The new clause, which sets a value for the ENVS variable, should follow the ORACLE_HOME variable setting, as shown in the following listing:

```
SID_LIST_LISTENER =
  (SID_LIST =
   (SID_DESC =
     (SID_NAME = loc)
     (ORACLE_HOME = /orasw/app/oracle/product/8.0.3.1)
     (ENVS='EPC_DISABLED=TRUE')
   )
  )
```

For all of the environment variables to take effect, you should log in to the server again, shut down and restart the listener process, and restart the databases.

Managing the Repository

OEM stores data in a repository. The OEM repository is a collection of tables and views; when you first enter OEM, you will be asked for a username, password, and the name of the database in which your repository is stored. The number of objects that constitute the repository changes with each version of OEM. In general, there are about 140 tables, 150 indexes, and 45 views in the repository.

Any application that has 140 tables should be carefully planned and closely monitored. Unfortunately, you are not given much control over the initial space allocation of the repository tables. When managing your repository, you should use the following guidelines:

1. Create a new user who will own the repository. Do not create the repository under an existing user, or the repository objects may be more difficult to distinguish and manage. The name of the repository owner should be unique across all OEM repositories in your database environment.

2. Assign the repository owner a default tablespace to hold the repository objects. All of the repository tables and indexes will be stored in the same tablespace when the repository is created.

3. Alter the default storage parameters for the repository tablespace before creating the repository. ORACLE will be creating about 290 objects in the tablespace, and you will have *no* ability to specify the **storage** parameters for those objects. Therefore, you should set very low values for the **initial** and **next** extent sizes for the tablespace. For example:

```
alter tablespace REPOS_TS
default storage (initial 20K next 20K pctincrease 0
                 maxextents 250);
```

4. In order for this tablespace to hold the repository tables, its datafiles must have at least 5,800K (20K minimum per object * 290 tables

and indexes) of free space in its datafiles. Set **pctincrease** to 0 (as shown in the example) to minimize the increase in extent sizes as tables grow.

After you upgrade OEM on your client machine, OEM will detect that the repository needs to be upgraded as well. This may present a problem if other DBAs have not upgraded their versions of OEM as well. For example, suppose that one DBA is using OEM version 1.2.2 (which was shipped with ORACLE version 7.3.2) and a second DBA has upgraded to OEM version 1.4 (which is available as of ORACLE version 8.0.3). When the DBA using OEM 1.4 accesses the repository, the repository will be upgraded to reflect the data structures used by OEM 1.4. When the DBA using OEM version 1.2.2 attempts to access the same repository, OEM may detect that the repository is from a later version, and the results may be unpredictable.

To avoid this potential problem, you should maintain different repositories for the different DBAs if they may be using different versions of the OEM client software.

Managing Remote Security

In order to administer a remote database from a client PC, you must create a password file. Password files are created by the **orapwd** utility provided with your ORACLE software. The password files are stored in the /dbs subdirectory of the ORACLE software home directory.

When you connect to OEM, you can connect in three modes: NORMAL, SYSDBA, and SYSOPER. The SYSOPER mode allows you to shut down and start up the database; the SYSDBA mode gives you the same privileges as the SYS user. Thus, you can use these modes to **connect internal** with different privilege levels via an OEM connection.

To create the password file, you must be logged into the server on which the remote database has been created. Execute the **orapwd** command, specifying the output filename, the password, and the number of entries to create. The number of entries to create is an optional parameter that reflects the number of distinct DBA and operator accounts. In the following listing, the output file is placed in a file named orapwCC1 in the /dbs subdirectory of the ORACLE software directory (via the ORACLE_HOME environment variable), and the SYS password is specified:

```
orapwd file=$ORACLE_HOME/dbs/orapwCC1 password=wwywwyl
```

You will now be able to connect to the SYSDBA and SYSOPER modes, provided the following entry is in the database's init.ora file:

```
REMOTE_LOGIN_PASSWORDFILE=EXCLUSIVE
```

Managing Configuration Files

You will need to modify several of your existing configuration files to support the intelligent agents used by OEM to perform administrative tasks on the server from which you have chosen to run the OEM console. OEM uses SNMP (a network management communications protocol) to send communications when predefined events occur. The SNMP configuration information is stored in some of your existing configuration files (such as tnsnames.ora) and new files (such as topology.ora and snmp.ora).

You need to modify your tnsnames.ora file to include a service name entry for your SNMP service. A sample SNMP entry in tnsnames.ora is shown in the following listing:

```
dbsnmp.world =
(DESCRIPTION=(ADDRESS=(PROTOCOL=tcp)(HOST=hq)(PORT=1528)))
```

The entry for the dbsnmp.world service name identifies the host to connect to, the protocol to use, and the port to use for the SNMP agent communications.

You can use the Topology Generator utility in OEM to generate a topology.ora file on the machine from which the OEM console is run. The topology.ora file contains entries for service names, remote agents, and Listeners. OEM uses the topology.ora file to locate and display the database services via the OEM console. The service names entries will be automatically generated by the Topology Generator. The entries for the Listeners and remote agents must be added manually.

The following listing shows a sample set of entries in the topology.ora file. The first entry is the service name for the CC1 database. Its type is identified as ORACLE_DATABASE, and it resides on the 'hq' server, accessed via the Listener process on that server. The second entry identifies dbsnmp.world as an ORACLE_AGENT process running on the 'hq' server. The third entry specifies the name of the Listener on the 'hq' server.

```
cc1.world = (ORACLE_DATABASE,hq, LISTENER_hq.world)
dbsnmp.world = (ORACLE_AGENT,hq)
listener.world = (ORACLE_LISTENER, hq)
```

The snmp.ora file defines the connection information used by the SNMP agent processes. The snmp.ora file is usually generated manually. If there is more than one community in your database environment (see Chapter 13), then you will need to use the COMMUNITY parameter. The following listing shows sample entries for the snmp.ora file:

```
snmp.visibleservices = (cc1.world)
snmp.ORACLE_HOME.cc1.world=/orasw/app.oracle/product/8.0.3.0
snmp.INDEX.cc1.world = 1
snmp.CONTACT.cc1.world = "Your Name Here"
snmp.SID.cc1.world = cc1
snmp.CONNECT.cc1.world.name = dbsnmp
snmp.CONNECT.cc1.world = dbsnmp
nmi.trace_level = off
nmi.trace_mask = (106)
dbsnmp.address =
(DESCRIPTION=(ADDRESS=(PROTOCOL=tcp)(HOST=hq)(PORT=1528)))
dbsnmp.spawnaddress=(DESCRIPTION=(ADDRESS=(PROTOCOL=tcp)(HOST=hq)
(PORT=1529)))
```

If you are using communities, then the last two entries of the snmp.ora file should be modified to include the COMMUNITY parameter, as shown in the following listing:

```
dbsnmp.address = (DESCRIPTION=(ADDRESS=
(COMMUNITY=unix.world)(PROTOCOL=tcp)(HOST=hq)(PORT=1528)))
dbsnmp.spawnaddress=(DESCRIPTION=(ADDRESS=
(COMMUNITY=unix.world)(PROTOCOL=tcp)(HOST=hq)(PORT=1529)))
```

When you install OEM, there are three files created to support your SNMP configuration. The three files are snmp_ro.ora, snmp_rw.ora, and snmp.ora. You can modify the snmp.ora file (as shown in the preceding listings), but you should not edit the snmp_ro.ora file (the "_ro" in its filename stands for "read only"). The snmp.ora file shows the services it supports (cc1.world in this example) and the ORACLE software home directory. The snmp.CONNECT variables specify the username and password to use when logging into the database. This is a potential security issue, since you are storing the password for a database account in a text file. The dbsnmp.address entry must match the address entry in the tnsnames.ora file. The dbsnmp.spawnaddress entry, which provides port details for spawned processes, must be assigned to a different port. See your operating-system-specific documentation for the recommended port numbers to use for SNMP communications.

If you change your ORACLE software home directory for a database, then you need to coordinate the changes to your configuration files. For example, if you upgrade the CC1 instance from 8.0.3 to 8.0.4, then you will need to update the ORACLE_HOME entry in three places: the /etc/oratab file, the listener.ora file, and the snmp.ora file. You should create a checklist of actions to follow when upgrading your databases, since ORACLE will not update any of these files for you. To effectively use OEM, you must keep your configuration files updated and control the file modification process.

APPENDIX C

SQL Reference for DBA Commands

ALTER DATABASE

Purpose

To alter an existing database in one of these ways:

- mount the database, clone, or standby database
- convert an Oracle Version 7 data dictionary when migrating to Oracle8
- open the database
- choose archivelog or noarchivelog mode for redo log file groups
- perform media recovery
- add or drop a redo log file group or a member of a redo log file group
- clear and initialize an online redo log file
- rename a redo log file member or a datafile
- backup the current control file
- backup SQL commands (that can be used to re-create the database) to the database's trace file
- take a datafile online or offline
- enable or disable a thread of redo log file groups
- change the database's global name
- prepare to downgrade to an earlier release of Oracle
- resize one or more datafiles
- create a new datafile in place of an old one for recovery purposes
- enable or disable the autoextending of the size of datafiles

Prerequisites

You must have ALTER DATABASE system privilege.

Syntax

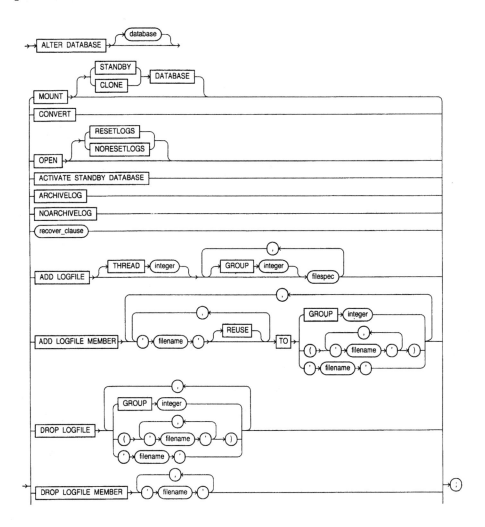

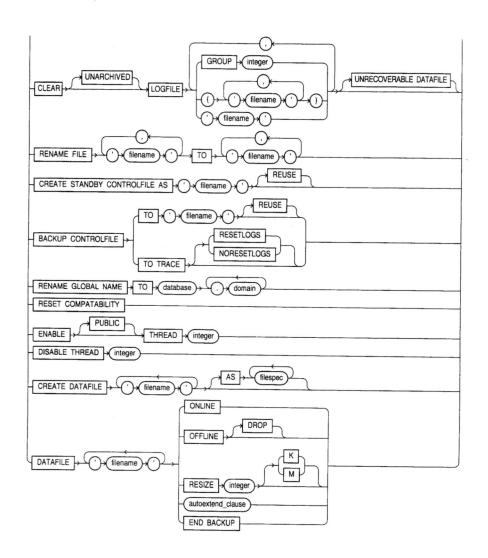

autoextend_clause ::=

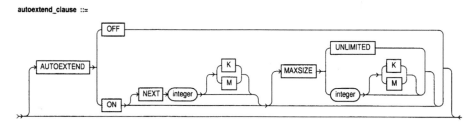

Keywords and Parameters

database	identifies the database to be altered. If you omit database, Oracle alters the database identified by the value of the initialization parameter DB_NAME. You can only alter the database whose control files are specified by the initialization parameter CONTROL_FILES. Note that the database identifier is not related to the Net8 database specification.

You can only use the following options when the database is not mounted by your instance:

MOUNT	mounts the database.
STANDBY DATABASE	mounts the standby database. For more information, see the *Oracle8 Server Administrator's Guide*.
CLONE DATABASE	mounts the clone database. For more information, see the *Oracle8 Server Backup and Recovery Guide*.
CONVERT	completes the conversion of the Oracle Version 7 data dictionary. After you use this option, the Version 7 data dictionary no longer exists in the Oracle database. Only use this option when you are migrating to Oracle8. For more information on using this option, see *Oracle8 Server Migration*.
OPEN	opens the database, making it available for normal use. You must mount the database before you can open it. You cannot open a standby database that has not been activated.
	RESETLOGS	resets the current log sequence number to 1 and discards any redo information that was not applied during recovery; ensuring that it will never be applied. This effectively discards all changes that are in the redo log, but not in the database. You must use this option to open the database after performing media recovery with an incomplete recovery using the RECOVER UNTIL clause or with a backup controlfile. After opening the database with this option, you should perform a complete database backup.

NORESETLOGS	leaves the log sequence number and redo log files in their current state.

You can only specify the above options after performing incomplete media recovery or complete media recovery with a backup controlfile. In any other case, Oracle uses the NORESETLOGS automatically.

ACTIVATE STANDBY DATABASE changes the state of a standby database to an active database. For more information, see *Oracle8 Server Administrator's Guide*.

You can only use the following options when your instance has the database mounted in parallel server disabled mode, but not open:

ARCHIVELOG	establishes archivelog mode for redo log file groups. In this mode, the contents of a redo log file group must be archived before the group can be reused. This option prepares for the possibility of media recovery. You can only use this option after shutting down your instance normally or immediately with no errors and then restarting it, mounting the database in parallel server disabled mode.
NOARCHIVELOG	establishes noarchivelog mode for redo log files. In this mode, the contents of a redo log file group need not be archived so that the group can be reused. This mode does not prepare for recovery after media failure.

You can use any of the following options when your instance has the database mounted, open, or closed, and the files involved are not in use:

recover_clause	performs media recovery. You only recover the entire database when the database is closed. You can recover tablespaces or datafiles when the database is open or closed, provided the tablespaces or datafiles to be recovered are offline. You cannot perform media recovery if you are connected to Oracle through the multi-threaded server architecture. You can also perform media recovery with the Server Manager recovery dialog box.

ADD LOGFILE	adds one or more redo log file groups to the specified thread, making them available to the instance assigned the thread. If you omit the THREAD parameter, the redo log file group is added to the thread assigned to your instance. You need only use the THREAD parameter if you are using Oracle with the Parallel Server option in parallel mode. Each *filespec* specifies a redo log file group containing one or more members, or copies. You can choose the value of the GROUP parameter for each redo log file group. Each value uniquely identifies the redo log file group among all groups in all threads and can range from 1 to the MAXLOGFILES value. You cannot add multiple redo log file groups having the same GROUP value. If you omit this parameter, Oracle generates its value automatically. You can examine the GROUP value for a redo log file group through the dynamic performance table V$LOG.
ADD LOGFILE MEMBER	adds new members to existing redo log file groups. Each new member is specified by '*filename*'. If the file already exists, it must be the same size as the other group members and you must specify the REUSE option. If the file does not exist, Oracle creates a file of the correct size. You cannot add a member to a group if all of the group's members have been lost through media failure. You can specify an existing redo log file group in one of these ways:

GROUP *parameter*	You can specify the value of the GROUP parameter that identifies the redo log file group.
list of filenames	You can list all members of the redo log file group. You must fully specify each filename according to the conventions for your operating system.

DROP LOGFILE	drops all members of a redo log file group. You can specify a redo log file group in the same manner as the ADD LOGFILE MEMBER clause. You cannot drop a redo log file group if it needs archiving or is the currently active group. Nor can you drop a redo log file group if doing so would cause the redo thread to contain less than two redo log file groups.

DROP LOGFILE MEMBER	drops one or more redo log file members. Each 'filename' must fully specify a member using the conventions for filenames on your operating system. You cannot use this clause to drop all members of a redo log file group that contain valid data. To perform this operation, use the DROP LOGFILE clause.
CLEAR LOGFILE	reinitialize an online redo log and optionally not archive the redo log. CLEAR LOGFILE is similar to adding and dropping a redo log except that the command may be issued even if there are only two logs for the thread and also may be issued for the current redo log of a closed thread.

CLEAR LOGFILE cannot be used to clear a log needed for media recovery. If it is necessary to clear a log containing redo after the database checkpoint, then incomplete media recovery will be necessary. The current redo log of an open thread can be cleared. The current log of a closed thread can be cleared by switching logs in the closed thread.

If the CLEAR LOGFILE command is interrupted by a system or instance failure, then the database may hang. If so, command must be reissued once the database is restarted. If the failure occurred because of I/O errors accessing one member of a log group, then that member can be dropped and other members added.

UNARCHIVED	you must specify UNARCHIVED if you want to reuse a redo log that was not archived.

WARNING
Specifying UNARCHIVED will make backups unusable if the redo log is needed for recovery.

UNRECOVERABLE DATAFILE	you must specify UNRECOVERABLE DATAFILE if the database has a datafile that is offline (not for drop) and if the unarchived log to be cleared is needed to recover the datafile before bringing it back online. If so, then the datafile and the entire tablespace must be dropped once the CLEAR LOGFILE command completes.

RENAME FILE	renames datafiles or redo log file members. This clause only renames files in the control file, it does not actually rename them on your operating system. You must specify each filename using the conventions for filenames on your operating system.	
CREATE STANDBY CONTROLFILE	create a controlfile to be used to maintain a standby database. For more information, see *Oracle8 Server Administrator's Guide*.	
BACKUP CONTROLFILE	backs up the current control file.	
	TO '*filename*'	specifies the file to which the control file is backed up. You must fully specify the 'filename' using the conventions for your operating system. If the specified file already exists, you must specify the REUSE option.
	TO TRACE	writes SQL statements to the database's trace file, rather than making a physical backup of the control file.
		The SQL commands can be used to start up the database, re-create the control file, and recover and open the database appropriately, based on the created control file.
		You can copy the commands from the trace file into a script file, edit the commands as necessary, and use the database if all copies of the control file are lost (or to change the size of the control file).
	RESETLOGS	the SQL statement written to the trace file for starting the database is ALTER DATABASE OPEN RESETLOGS.
	NORESETLOGS	the SQL statement written to the trace file for starting the database is ALTER DATABASE OPEN NORESETLOGS.

You can only use the following options when your instance has the database open:

ENABLE in a parallel server, enables the specified thread of redo log file groups. The thread must have at least two redo log file groups before you can enable it.

PUBLIC makes the enabled thread available to any instance that does not explicitly request a specific thread with the initialization parameter THREAD.

If you omit the PUBLIC option, the thread is only available to the instance that explicitly requests it with the initialization parameter THREAD.

DISABLE disables the specified thread, making it unavailable to all instances. You cannot disable a thread if an instance using it has the database mounted.

RENAME GLOBAL_NAME changes the global name of the database. The *database* is the new database name and can be as long as eight bytes. The optional *domains* specifies where the database is effectively located in the network hierarchy. Renaming your database automatically clears all data from the shared pool in the SGA. However, renaming your database does not change global references to your database from existing database links, synonyms, and stored procedures and functions on remote databases. Changing such references is the responsibility of the administrator of the remote databases. For more information on global names, see *Oracle8 Server Distributed Systems*.

RESET COMPATIBILITY marks the database to be reset to an earlier version of Oracle when the database is next restarted.

NOTE
RESET COMPATIBILITY will not work unless you have successfully disabled Oracle features that affect backward compatibility. For more information on downgrading to an earlier version of Oracle, see Oracle8 Server Migration.

You can use any of the following options when your instance has the database mounted, open or closed, and the files involved are not in use:

CREATE DATAFILE	creates a new empty datafile in place of an old one. You can use this option to re-create a datafile that was lost with no backup. The '*filename*' must identify a file that is or was once part of the database. The *filespec* specifies the name and size of the new datafile. If you omit the AS clause, Oracle creates the new file with the name and size as the file specified by '*filename*'. During recovery, all archived redo logs written to since the original datafile was created must be applied to the new, empty version of the lost datafile. Oracle creates the new file in the same state as the old file when it was created. You must perform media recovery on the new file to return it to the state of the old file at the time it was lost. You cannot create a new file based on the first datafile of the SYSTEM tablespace.
DATAFILE	changes one of the following for your database:

	ONLINE	brings the datafile online.
	OFFLINE	takes the datafile offline. If the database is open, then you must perform media recovery on the datafile before bringing it back online. This is because a checkpoint is not performed on the datafile before it is taken offline.
	DROP	takes a datafile offline when the database is in NOARCHIVELOG mode.
	RESIZE	attempts to change the size of the datafile to the specified absolute size in bytes. You can also use K or M to specify this size in kilobytes or megabytes. There is no default, so you must specify a size.

AUTOEXTEND	enables or disables the automatic extension of a datafile.

	OFF	disables autoextend if it is turned on. NEXT and MAXSIZE are set to zero. Values for NEXT and MAXSIZE must be respecified in further ALTER DATABASE AUTOEXTEND commands.
	ON	enables autoextend.
	NEXT	the size in bytes of the next increment of disk space to be automatically allocated to the datafile when more extents are required. You can also use K or M to specify this size in kilobytes or megabytes. The default is one data block.

| MAXSIZE | maximum disk space allowed for automatic extension of the datafile. |
| UNLIMITED | sets no limit on allocating disk space to the datafile. |

END BACKUP   avoids media recovery on database startup after an online tablespace backup was interrupted by a system failure or instance failure or SHUTDOWN ABORT.

WARNING
Do not use ALTER TABLESPACE ... END BACKUP if you have restored any of the files affected from a backup. Media recovery is fully described in the Oracle8 Server Backup and Recovery Guide and Oracle8 Server Administrator's Guide.

Usage Notes

For more information on using the ALTER DATABASE command for database maintenance, see the *Oracle8 Server Administrator's Guide*.

ALTER INDEX

Purpose

Use ALTER INDEX to:

- change storage allocation for, rebuild, or rename an index
- rename, split, remove, mark as unusable, rebuild, or modify physical or logging attributes of a partition of a partitioned index
- modify the physical, parallel, or logging attributes of a non-partitioned index
- modify the default physical, parallel, or logging attributes of a partitioned index
- modify the default phsyical, logging attributes of index partition(s)
- rebuild an index to store the bytes of the index block in reverse order
- modify a nested table index

Prerequisites

The index must be in your own schema or you must have ALTER ANY INDEX system privilege.

Schema object privileges are granted on the parent index, not on individual index partitions. The following index partition operations require tablespace quota:

- modify
- rebuild
- split

Syntax

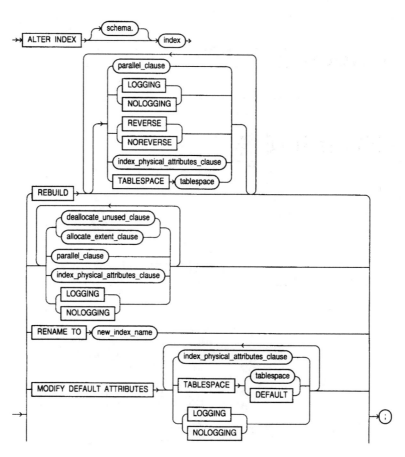

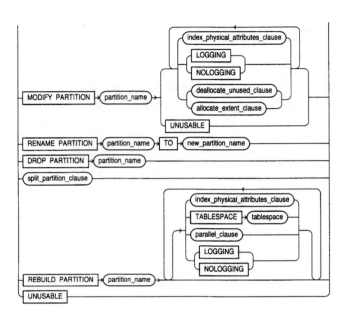

index_physical_attributes_clause ::=

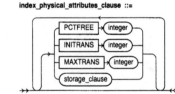

allocate_extent_clause ::=

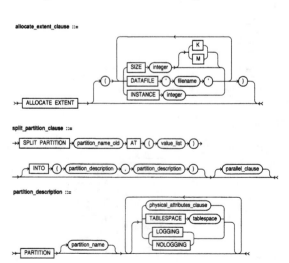

split_partition_clause ::=

partition_description ::=

Keywords and Parameters

schema	is the schema containing the index. If you omit schema, Oracle assumes the index is in your own schema.
index	is the name of the index to be altered.
	The following operations can only be performed on partitioned global indexes: *drop partition *split partition *rename partition *rebuild partition *modify partition
partition_name	is the name of the index partition to be altered. It must be a partition in *index*.
MODIFY DEFAULT ATTRIBUTES	is a valid option only for a partitioned index. Use this option to specify new values for the default attributes of a partitioned index.
PCTFREE INITRANS MAXTRANS	changes the values of these parameters for a non-partitioned index, index partition, or all partitions of a partitioned index, or default values of these parameters for a partitioned index.
storage_clause	changes the storage parameters for a non-partitioned index, index partition, or all partitions of a partitioned index, or default values of these parameters for a partitioned index.
ALLOCATE EXTENT	explicitly allocates a new extent for the index.

	SIZE	specifies the size of the extent in bytes. You can use K or M to specify the extent size in kilobytes or megabytes. If you omit this parameter, Oracle determines the size based on the values of the index's STORAGE parameters.
	DATAFILE	specifies one of the data files in the index's tablespace to contain the new extent. If you omit this parameter, Oracle chooses the data file.
	INSTANCE	makes the new extent available to the specified instance. An instance is identified by the value of its initialization parameter INSTANCE_NUMBER. If you omit this parameter, the extent is available to all instances. Only use this parameter if you are using Oracle with the Parallel Server option in parallel mode.

	Explicitly allocating an extent with this clause does affect the size for the next extent to be allocated as specified by the NEXT and PCTINCREASE storage parameters.
DEALLOCATE UNUSED	explicitly deallocates unused space at the end of the index and makes the freed space available for other segments. Only unused space above the high-water mark can be freed. If KEEP is omitted, all unused space is freed.

	KEEP	specifies the number of bytes above the high-water mark that the index will have after deallocation. If the number of remaining extents are less than MINEXTENTS, then MINEXTENTS is set to the current number of extents. If the initial extent becomes smaller than INITIAL, then INITIAL is set to the value of the current initial extent.

REBUILD	recreates an existing index.

	REVERSE	stores the bytes of the index block in reverse order, excluding the ROWID when the index is rebuilt.
	NOREVERSE	stores the bytes of the index block without reversing the order when the index is rebuilt. Rebuilding a REVERSE index without the NOREVERSE keyword produces a rebuilt, reverse keyed index.

parallel_clause	specifies that rebuilding the index, or some queries against the index or the index partition, is performed either in serial or parallel execution. For more information about parallelized operations see *Oracle8 Parallel Server and Administration Guide.*

LOGGING
NOLOGGING

LOGGING/NOLOGGING specifies that subsequent Direct Loader (SQL*Loader) and Direct-Load INSERT operations against a non-partitioned index, index partition, or all partitions of a partitioned index will be logged (LOGGING) or not logged (NOLOGGING) in the redo log file.

LOGGING/NOLOGGING also specifies if ALTER INDEX...REBUILD and ALTER INDEX...SPLIT operations will be logged.

If used with MODIFY DEFAULT ATTRIBUTES, specifies the default logging attribute of a partitioned index.

In NOLOGGING mode, data is modified without redo logging. Some minimal logging is still done for marking new extents invalid, and dictionary changes are always fully logged. When applied during media recovery, the extent invalidation records mark a range of blocks as logically corrupt, since the redo data is not logged. Thus if you cannot afford to lose this index, it is important to take a backup after the NOLOGGING operation.

If the database is run in ARCHIVELOG mode, media recovery from a backup taken before the LOGGING operation will recreate the index. However, media recovery from a backup taken before the NOLOGGING operation will not recreate the index. The logging attribute of the index is independent to that of its base table. For more information about the LOGGING option and Parallel DML, see *Oracle8 Server Concepts and the Oracle8 Parallel Server and Administration Guide.*

NOTE

In future versions of Oracle, the LOGGING/NOLOGGING keywords will replace the RECOVERABLE/UNRECOVERABLE option. RECOVERABLE is still available as a valid keyword in Oracle when altering or rebuilding non-partitioned indexes; however, it is not recommended.

RECOVERABLE	is a deprecated option in Oracle8. You cannot use RECOVERABLE for partitioned indexes or index partitions.
UNRECOVERABLE	is a deprecated option in Oracle8. You cannot use UNRECOVERABLE for partitioned indexes or index partitions.
TABLESPACE	specifies the tablespace where the rebuilt index, or index partition will be stored or the default tablespace of a partitioned index. The default is the default tablespace of the user issuing the command.
RENAME	renames index to *new_index_name*. The *new_index_name* is a single identifier and does not include the schema name.
RENAME PARTITION	renames index *partition_name* to *new_partition_name*.
MODIFY PARTITION	modifies the real physical attributes, logging option, or storage characteristics of index partition *partition_name*.
UNUSABLE	marks the index or index partition(s) as unusable. An unusable index must be rebuilt, or dropped and recreated before it can be used. While one partition is marked unusable, the other partitions of the index are still valid, and you can execute statements that require the index if the statements do not access the unusable partition. You can also split or rename the unusable partition before rebuilding it.
REBUILD PARTITION	rebuilds one partition of an index. You can also use this option to move an index partition to another tablespace or to change a create-time physical attribute. For more information about partition maintenance operations, see the *Oracle8 Server Administrator's Guide*.
DROP PARTITION	removes a partition and the data in it from a partitioned global index. Dropping a partition of a global index marks the index's next partition as unusable. You cannot drop the highest partition of a global index.
SPLIT PARTITION	splits a global partitioned index into two partitions, adding a new partition to the index. Splitting a partition marked as unusable, results in two partitions, both marked as unusable. The partitions must be rebuilt before using them. Splitting a usable partition results in two partitions populated with index data that are both marked as usable.

AT (*value_list*)	specifies the new non-inclusive upper bound for *split_partition_1*. The *value_list* must compare less than the pre-split partition bound for *partition_name_old* and greater than the partition bound for the next lowest partition (if there is one).
INTO	describes the two partitions resulting from the split.
PARTITION *partition_name*, PARTITION *partition_name*	specifies the names and physical attributes of the two partitions resulting from the split.

Usage Notes

The INITRANS and MAXTRANS parameters as well as the STORAGE and ALLOCATE EXTENT clauses, all have the same function as in the CREATE TABLE command.

An index segment can have logging attributes that are different than those of the base table, and which are different from other index segments for the same base table.

Partitioned Indexes

You can combine several operations on the base index into one ALTER INDEX statement (except RENAME), but you cannot combine partition operations with other partition operations or with operations on the base index.

ALTER PROFILE

Purpose

To add, modify, or remove a resource limit or password management in a profile.

Prerequisites

You must have ALTER PROFILE system privilege to change profile resource limits. To modify password limits and protection, you must have ALTER PROFILE and ALTER USER system privleges.

Syntax

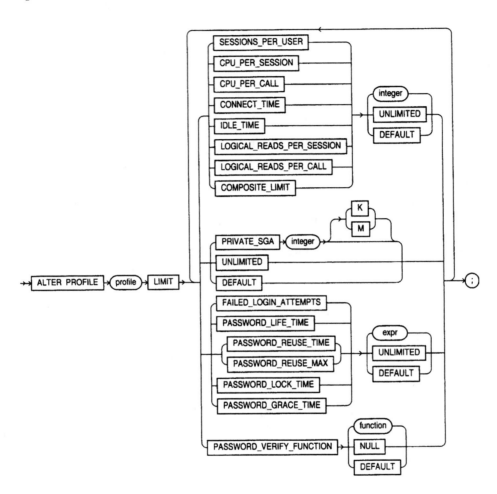

Keywords and Parameters

profile   is the name of the profile to be altered.

integer   defines a new limit for a resource in this profile.

Usage Notes

Changes made to a profile with an ALTER PROFILE statement only affect users in their subsequent sessions, not in their current sessions. You cannot remove a limit from the DEFAULT profile. You can use fractions of days for all parameters with days as units. Fractions are expressed as *x/y*. For example, 1 hour is 1/24 and 1 minute is 1/1440.

Using Password History

The following restrictions apply when specifying password history parameters:

- If PASSWORD_REUSE_TIME is set to an integer value, PASSWORD_REUSE_MAX must be set to UNLIMITED. If PASSWORD_REUSE_MAX is set to an integer value, PASSWORD_REUSE_TIME must be set to UNLIMITED.

- If both PASSWORD_REUSE_TIME and PASSWORD_REUSE_MAX are set to UNLIMITED, then Oracle uses neither of these password resources.

- If PASSWORD_REUSE_MAX is set to DEFAULT and PASSWORD_REUSE_TIME is set to UNLIMITED, then Oracle uses the PASSWORD_REUSE_MAX value defined in the default profile.

- If PASSWORD_REUSE_TIME is set to DEFAULT and PASSWORD_REUSE_MAX is set to UNLIMITED, then Oracle uses the PASSWORD_REUSE_TIME value defined in the default profile.

- If both PASSWORD_REUSE_TIME and PASSWORD_REUSE_MAX are set to DEFAULT, then Oracle uses whichever value is defined in the default profile.

ALTER ROLE

Purpose

To change the authorization needed to enable a role.

Prerequisites

You must either have been granted the role with the ADMIN OPTION or have ALTER ANY ROLE system privilege.

Syntax

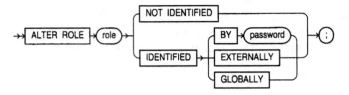

Keywords and Parameters

The keywords and parameters in the ALTER ROLE command all have the same meaning as in the CREATE ROLE command.

Usage Notes

You must revoke all grants of roles identified externally to the role before you alter a role to IDENTIFIED GLOBALLY. You must also revoke the grant of the role from all users, roles, and PUBLIC before you alter a role to IDENTIFIED GLOBALLY. The one exception to this rule is that you should not revoke the role from the user who is currently altering the role.

If a user with ALTER ANY ROLE changes a role which is IDENTIFIED GLOBALLY to any of the following, then Oracle grants the role with the ADMIN OPTION:

■ to IDENTIFIED BY password

■ to IDENTIFIED EXTERNALLY

■ to NOT IDENTIFIED

ALTER ROLLBACK SEGMENT

Purpose

To alter a rollback segment in one of these ways:

■ by bringing it online

■ by taking it offline

- by changing its storage characteristics
- by shrinking it to an optimal or given size

Prerequisites

You must have ALTER ROLLBACK SEGMENT system privilege.

Syntax

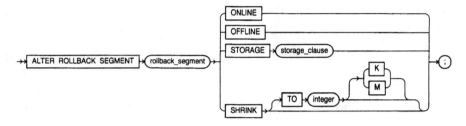

Keywords and Parameters

rollback_segment	specifies the name of an existing rollback segment.
ONLINE	brings the rollback segment online.
OFFLINE	takes the rollback segment offline.
STORAGE	changes the rollback segment's storage characteristics.
SHRINK	attempts to shrink the rollback segment to an optimal or given size.

Usage Notes

When you create a rollback segment, it is initially offline. An offline rollback segment is not available for transactions.

The ONLINE option brings the rollback segment online making it available for transactions by your instance. You can also bring a rollback segment online when you start your instance with the initialization parameter ROLLBACK_SEGMENTS.

The OFFLINE option takes the rollback segment offline. If the rollback segment does not contain information necessary to roll back any active transactions, Oracle takes it offline immediately. If the rollback segment does contain information for active transactions, Oracle makes the rollback segment unavailable for future transactions and takes it offline after all the active transactions are committed or rolled back. Once the rollback segment is offline, it can be brought online by any instance.

You cannot take the SYSTEM rollback segment offline.

You can tell whether a rollback segment is online or offline by querying the data dictionary view DBA_ROLLBACK_SEGS. Online rollback segments are indicated by a STATUS value of 'IN_USE'. Offline rollback segments are indicated by a STATUS value of 'AVAILABLE'.

For more information on making rollback segments available and unavailable, see the "Managing Rollback Segments" chapter of *Oracle8 Server Administrator's Guide*.

The STORAGE clause of the ALTER ROLLBACK SEGMENT command affects future space allocation in the rollback segment. You cannot change the values of the INITIAL and MINEXTENTS for an existing rollback segment.

The SHRINK clause of the ALTER ROLLBACK SEGMENT command initiates an attempt to reduce the specified rollback segment to an optimum size. If size is not specified, then the size defaults to the OPTIMAL value of the STORAGE clause of the CREATE ROLLBACK SEGMENT command that created the rollback segment. If the OPTIMAL value was not specified, then the size defaults to the MINEXTENTS value of the STORAGE clause. The specified size in a SHRINK is valid for the execution of the command; thereafter, OPTIMUM remains unchanged. Regardless of whether a size is specified or not, the rollback segment cannot shrink to less than two extents.

You can query the DBA_ROLLBACK_SEGS tables to determine the actual size of a rollback segment after attempting to shrink a rollback segment.

For a parallel server, you can only shrink rollback segments that are online to your instance.

The SHRINK option is an *attempt* to shrink the size of the rollback segment; the success and amount of shrinkage depends on the following:

- available free space in the rollback segment
- how active transactions are holding space in the rollback segment

ALTER SYSTEM

Purpose

To dynamically alter your Oracle instance in one of the following ways:

- to restrict logons to Oracle to only those users with RESTRICTED SESSION system privilege
- to clear all data from the shared pool in the System Global Area (SGA)
- to explicitly perform a checkpoint

- to verify access to data files
- to enable or disable resource limits
- to enable or disable global name resolution
- to manage shared server processes or dispatcher processes for the multi-threaded server architecture
- to dynamically change or disable limits or thresholds for concurrent usage licensing and named user licensing
- to explicitly switch redo log file groups
- to enable distributed recovery in a single-process environment
- to disable distributed recovery
- to manually archive redo log file groups or to enable or disable automatic archiving
- to terminate a session

Prerequisites

You must have ALTER SYSTEM system privilege.

Syntax

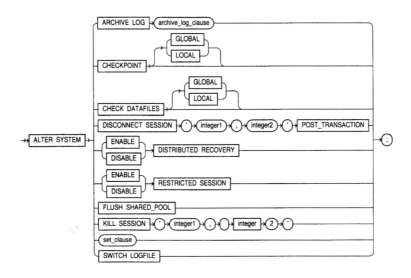

set_clause ::=

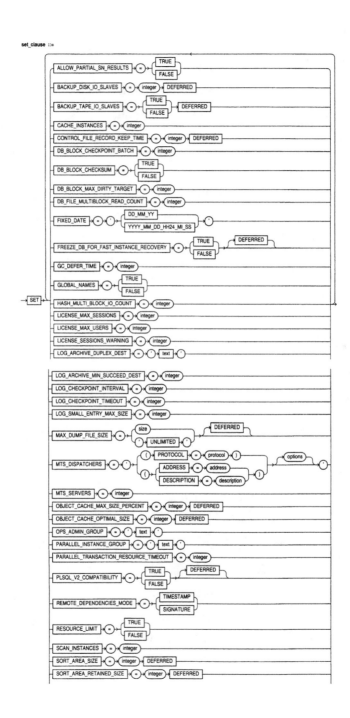

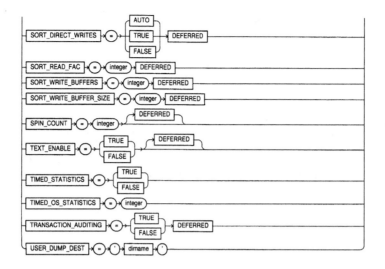

opts_clause ::=

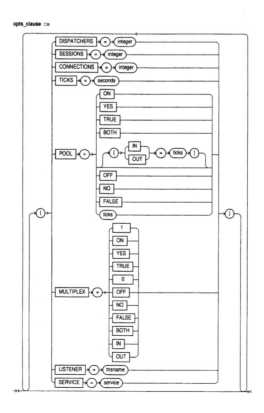

Keywords and Parameters

You can use the following options regardless of whether your instance has the database dismounted or mounted, open or closed:

ENABLE RESTRICTED SESSION	allows only users with RESTRICTED SESSION system privilege to log on to Oracle.
DISABLE RESTRICTED SESSION	reverses the effect of the ENABLE RESTRICTED SESSION option, allowing all users with CREATE SESSION system privilege to log on to Oracle.
FLUSH SHARED_POOL	clears all data from the shared pool in the System Global Area (SGA).

You can use the following options when your instance has the database mounted, open or closed:

CHECKPOINT		performs a checkpoint.
	GLOBAL	performs a checkpoint for all instances that have opened the database.
	LOCAL	performs a checkpoint only for the thread of redo log file groups for your instance. You can only use this option when your instance has the database open.

If you omit both the GLOBAL and LOCAL options, Oracle performs a global checkpoint.

CHECK DATAFILES		
	GLOBAL	verifies that all instances that have opened the database can access all online data files.
	LOCAL	verifies that your instance can access all online data files.

If you omit both the GLOBAL and LOCAL options, Oracle uses GLOBAL by default.

You can only use the following parameters and options when your instance has the database open:

RESOURCE_LIMIT	controls resource limits.	
	TRUE	enables resource limits.
	FALSE	disables resource limits.
GLOBAL_NAMES		
	TRUE	enables the enforcement of global names.
	FALSE	disables the enforcement of global names.
SCAN_INSTANCES	in a parallel server, specifies the number of instances to participate in parallelized operations. This syntax will be obsolete in the next major release.	
CACHE_INSTANCES	in a parallel server, specifies the number of instances that will cache a table. This syntax will be obsolete in the next major release.	
	For more information on parallel operations, see *Oracle8 Server Tuning*.	
MTS_SERVERS	specifies a new minimum number of shared server processes.	
MTS_DISPATCHERS	specifies a new number of dispatcher processes:	
	protocol	is the network protocol of the dispatcher processes.
	integer	is the new number of dispatcher processes of the specified protocol.
	You can specify multiple MTS_DISPATCHERS parameters in a single command for multiple network protocols.	
LICENSE_MAX_SESSIONS	limits the number of sessions on your instance. A value of 0 disables the limit.	
LICENSE_SESSIONS_WARNING	establishes a threshold of sessions over which Oracle writes warning messages to the ALERT file for susequent sessions. A value of 0 disables the warning threshold.	

LICENSE_MAX_USERS	limits number of concurrent users on your database. A value of 0 disables the limit.
REMOTE_DEPENDENCIES_ MODE	specifies how dependencies of remote stored procedures are handled by the server. For more information, refer to the *Oracle8 Server Application Developer's Guide*.
SWITCH LOGFILE	switches redo log file groups.
ENABLE DISTRIBUTED RECOVERY	enables distributed recovery. In a single-process environment, you must use this option to initiate distributed recovery.
DISABLE DISTRIBUTED RECOVERY	switches redo log files.
ARCHIVE LOG	manually archives redo log files or enables or disables automatic archiving.
KILL SESSION	terminates a session and any ongoing transactions. You must identify the session with both of the following values from the V$SESSION view:

integer1	is the value of the SID column.
integer2	is the value of the SERIAL# column.

DISCONNECT SESSION	disconnects the current session by destroying the dedicated server process (or virtual circuit if the connection was made via MTS). If configured, application failover will take effect. For more information about application failover see *Oracle8 Server Tuning* and *Oracle8 Parallel Server Concepts & Administration*. You must identify the session with both of the following values from the V$SESSION view:

integer1	is the value of the SID column.
integer2	is the value of the SERIAL# column.

POST_TRANSACTION allows ongoing transactions to complete before the session is disconnected. You must include this keyword when the DISCONNECT SESSION clause is specified.

PLSQL_V2_COMPATIBILITY	modifies the compile-time behavior of PL/SQL programs to allow language constructs that are illegal in Oracle8 (PL/SQL V3), but were legal in Oracle7 (PL/SQL V2). See the *PL/SQL User's Guide and Reference* and *Oracle8 Server Reference Manual* for more information about this system parameter.

TRUE	enables Oracle8 PL/SQL V3 programs to execute Oracle7 PL/SQL V2 constructs.
FALSE	disallows illegal Oracle7 PL/SQL V2 constructs. This is the default.

MAX_DUMP_FILE_SIZE	specifies the trace dump file size upper limit for all user sessions. Specifies the maximum *size* as either a non-negative integer that represents the number of blocks , or as 'UNLIMITED'. If 'UNLIMITED' is specified, no upper limit is imposed.

DEFERRED	modifies the trace dump file size upper limit for future user sessions only.

Restricting Logons

By default, any user granted CREATE SESSION system privilege can log on to Oracle. The ENABLE RESTRICTED SESSION option of the ALTER SYSTEM command prevents logons by all users except those having RESTRICTED SESSION system privilege. Existing sessions are not terminated.

You may want to restrict logons if you are performing application maintenance and you want only application developers with RESTRICTED SESSION system privilege to log on. To restrict logons, issue the following statement:

```
ALTER SYSTEM
    ENABLE RESTRICTED SESSION;
```

You can then terminate any existing sessions using the KILL SESSION clause of the ALTER SYSTEM command.

After performing maintenance on your application, issue the following statement to allow any user with CREATE SESSION system privilege to log on:

```
ALTER SYSTEM
    DISABLE RESTRICTED SESSION;
```

Clearing the Shared Pool

The FLUSH SHARED_POOL option of the ALTER SYSTEM command clears all information from the shared pool in the System Global Area (SGA). The shared pool stores this information:

- cached data dictionary information
- shared SQL and PL/SQL areas for SQL statements, stored procedures, functions, packages, and triggers

You might want to clear the shared pool before beginning performance analysis. To clear the shared pool, issue the following statement:

```
ALTER SYSTEM
    FLUSH SHARED_POOL;
```

The above statement does not clear shared SQL and PL/SQL areas for SQL statements, stored procedures, functions, packages, or triggers that are currently being executed or for SQL SELECT statements for which all rows have not yet been fetched.

Performing a Checkpoint

The CHECKPOINT clause of the ALTER SYSTEM command explicitly forces Oracle to perform a checkpoint. You can force a checkpoint if you want to ensure that all changes made by committed transactions are written to the data files on disk. For more information on checkpoints, see the "Recovery Structures" chapter of *Oracle8 Server Concepts*.

If you are using Oracle with the Parallel Server option in parallel mode, you can specify either the GLOBAL option to perform a checkpoint on all instances that have opened the database or the LOCAL option to perform a checkpoint on only your instance.

The following statement forces a checkpoint:

```
ALTER SYSTEM
    CHECKPOINT;
```

Oracle does not return control to you until the checkpoint is complete.

Checking Data Files

The CHECK DATAFILES clause of the ALTER SYSTEM command verifies access to all online data files. If any data file is not accessible, Oracle writes a message to an ALERT file. You may want to perform this operation after fixing a hardware problem that prevented an instance from accessing a data file. For more information on using this clause, see *Oracle8 Parallel Server Concepts & Administration*.

The following statement verifies that all instances that have opened the database can access all online data files:

```
ALTER SYSTEM
   CHECK DATAFILES GLOBAL;
```

Using Resource Limits

When you start an instance, Oracle enables or disables resource limits based on the value of the initialization parameter RESOURCE_LIMIT. You can issue an ALTER SYSTEM statement with the RESOURCE_LIMIT option to enable or disable resource limits for subsequent sessions.

Enabling resource limits only causes Oracle to enforce the resource limits assigned to users. To choose resource limit values for a user, you must create a *profile*, or a set of limits, and assign that profile to the user.

This ALTER SYSTEM statement dynamically enables resource limits:

```
ALTER SYSTEM
   SET RESOURCE_LIMIT = TRUE;
```

Enabling and Disabling Global Name Resolution

When you start an instance, Oracle determines whether to enforce global name resolution for remote objects accessed in SQL statements based on the value of the initialization parameter GLOBAL_NAMES. You can subsequently enable or disable global names resolution while your instance is running with the GLOBAL_NAMES parameter of the ALTER SYSTEM command. You can also enable or disable global name resolution for your session with the GLOBAL_NAMES parameter of the ALTER SESSION command discussed earlier in this chapter.

It is recommended that you enable global name resolution.

Managing Processes for the Multi-Threaded Server

When you start your instance, Oracle creates shared server processes and dispatcher processes for the multi-threaded server architecture based on the values of the following initialization parameters:

MTS_SERVERS   This parameter specifies the initial and minimum number of shared server processes. Oracle may automatically change the number of shared server processes if the load on the existing processes changes. While your instance is running, the number of shared server processes can vary between the values of the initialization parameters MTS_SERVERS and MTS_MAX_SERVERS.

MTS_DISPATCHERS   This parameters specifies one or more network protocols and the number of dispatcher processes for each protocol.

For more information on the multi-threaded server architecture, see *Oracle8 Server Concepts*.

You can subsequently use the MTS_SERVERS and MTS_DISPATCHERS parameters of the ALTER SYSTEM command to perform one of the following operations while the instance is running:

To create additional shared server processes: You can cause Oracle to create additional shared server processes by increasing the minimum number of shared server processes.

To terminate existing shared server processes: Oracle terminates the shared server processes after finishing processing their current calls, unless the load on the server processes is so high it cannot be managed by the remaining processes.

To create more dispatcher processes for a specific protocol: You can create additional dispatcher processes up to a maximum across all protocols specified by the initialization parameter MTS_MAX_DISPATCHERS.

You cannot use this command to create dispatcher processes for network protocols that are not specified by the initialization parameter MTS_DISPATCHERS. To create dispatcher processes for a new protocol, you must change the value of the initialization parameter.

To terminate existing dispatcher processes for a specific protocol: Oracle terminates the dispatcher processes only after their current user processes disconnect from the instance.

Using Licensing Limits

Oracle enforces concurrent usage licensing and named user licensing limits specified by your Oracle license. When you start your instance, Oracle establishes the licensing limits based on the values of the following initialization parameters:

LICENSE_MAX_SESSIONS	This parameter establishes the concurrent usage licensing limit, or the limit for concurrent sessions. Once this limit is reached, only users with RESTRICTED SESSION system privilege can connect.
LICENSE_SESSIONS_WARNING	This parameter establishes a warning threshold for concurrent usage. Once this threshold is reached, Oracle writes warning messages to the database ALERT file for each subsequent session. Also, users with RESTRICTED SESSION system privilege receive warning messages when they begin subsequent sessions.

LICENSE_MAX_USERS	This parameter establishes the limit for users connected to your database. Once this limit for users is reached, more users cannot connect.

You can subsequently use the LICENSE_MAX_SESSIONS, LICENSE_SESSIONS_WARNING, and LICENSE_MAX_USERS parameters of the ALTER SYSTEM command to dynamically change or disable limits or thresholds while your instance is running. Do not disable or raise session or user limits unless you have appropriately upgraded your Oracle license. For information on upgrading your license, contact your Oracle sales representative.

New limits apply only to future sessions and users:

- If you reduce the limit on sessions below the current number of sessions, Oracle does not end existing sessions to enforce the new limit. Users without RESTRICTED SESSION system privilege can only begin new sessions when the number of sessions falls below the new limit.

- If you reduce the warning threshold for sessions below the current number of sessions, Oracle writes a message to the ALERT file for all subsequent sessions.

- You cannot reduce the limit on users below the current number of users created for the database.

Switching Redo Log File Groups

The SWITCH LOGFILE option of the ALTER SYSTEM command explicitly forces Oracle to begin writing to a new redo log file group, regardless of whether the files in the current redo log file group are full. You may want to force a log switch to drop or rename the current redo log file group or one of its members, since you cannot drop or rename a file while Oracle is writing to it. The forced log switch only affects your instance's redo log thread. Note that when you force a log switch, Oracle begins to perform a checkpoint. Oracle returns control to you immediately rather than when the associated checkpoint is complete.

The following statement forces a log switch:

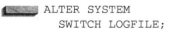
```
ALTER SYSTEM
   SWITCH LOGFILE;
```

Enabling Distributed Recovery

Oracle allows you to perform distributed transactions, or transactions that modify data on multiple databases. If a network or machine failure occurs during the commit process for a distributed transaction, the state of the transaction may be unknown, or *in-doubt*. Once the failure has been corrected and the network and its nodes are back online, Oracle recovers the transaction.

If you are using Oracle in multiple-process mode, this distributed recovery is performed automatically. If you are using Oracle in single-process (single user) mode, such as on the MS-DOS operating system, you must explicitly initiate distributed recovery with the following statement.

```
ALTER SYSTEM ENABLE DISTRIBUTED RECOVERY;
```

You may need to issue the above statement more than once to recover an in-doubt transaction, especially if the remote node involved in the transaction is not accessible. In-doubt transactions appear in the data dictionary view DBA_2PC_PENDING. You can tell that the transaction is recovered when it no longer appears in DBA_2PC_PENDING. For more information about distributed transactions and distributed recovery, see *Oracle8 Server Distributed Systems*.

Disabling Distributed Recovery

You can use the following statement to disable distributed recovery in both single-process and multiprocess mode:

```
ALTER SYSTEM DISABLE DISTRIBUTED RECOVERY;
```

You may want to disable distributed recovery for demonstration purposes. You can then enable distributed recovery again by issuing an ALTER SYSTEM statement with the ENABLE DISTRIBUTED RECOVERY clause.

Terminating a Session

The KILL SESSION clause of the ALTER SYSTEM command terminates a session, immediately performing the following tasks:

- rolling back its current transactions
- releasing all of its locks
- freeing all of its resources

You may want to kill the session of a user that is holding resources needed by other users. The user receives an error message indicating that the session has been killed and can no longer make calls to the database without beginning a new session. You can only kill a session on the same instance as your current session.

If you try to kill a session that is performing some activity that must be completed, such as waiting for a reply from a remote database or rolling back a transaction, Oracle waits for this activity to complete, kills the session, and then returns control to you. If the waiting lasts as long as a minute, Oracle marks the session to be killed and returns control to you with a message indicating that the session is marked to be killed. Oracle then kills the session when the activity is complete.

Disconnecting a Session

The DISCONNECT SESSION clause is similar to the KILL SESSION clause, but with two distinct differences.

First, the ALTER SYSTEM DISCONNECT SESSION 'X, Y' POST_TRANSACTION command waits until any current transaction that the session is working on completes before taking effect.

Second, the session is disconnected rather than killed, which means that the dedicated server process (or virtual circuit if the connection was made via MTS) is destroyed by this command. Termination of a session's connection causes application failover to take effect if the appropriate system parameters are configured.

Disconnecting a session essentially allows you to perform a manual application failover. Using this command in a parallel server environment allows you to disconnect sessions on an overloaded instance and shift them to another.

The POST_TRANSACTION keyword is required.

ALTER TABLE

Purpose

To alter the definition of a table in one of the following ways:

- to add a column
- to add an integrity constraint

- to redefine a column (datatype, size, default value)
- to modify storage characteristics or other parameters
- to modify the real storage attributes of a non-partitioned table or the default attributes of a partitioned table
- to enable, disable, or drop an integrity constraint or trigger
- to explicitly allocate an extent
- to explicitly deallocate the unused space of a table
- to allow or disallow writing to a table
- to modify the degree of parallelism for a table
- to modify the logging attributes of a non-partitioned table, partitioned table or table partition(s)
- to modify the CACHE/NOCACHE attributes
- to add, modify, split, move, drop, or truncate table partitions
- to rename a table or a table partition
- to add or modify index-organized table characteristics
- to add or modify LOB columns
- to add or modify object type, nested table type, or VARRAY type column to a table
- to add integrity constraints to object type columns

Prerequisites

The table must be in your own schema or you must have ALTER privilege on the table or you must have ALTER ANY TABLE system privilege. To use an object type in a column definition when modifying a table, either that object must belong to the same schema as the table being altered, or you must have either the EXECUTE ANY TYPE system privilege or the EXECUTE schema object privilege for the object type.

Syntax

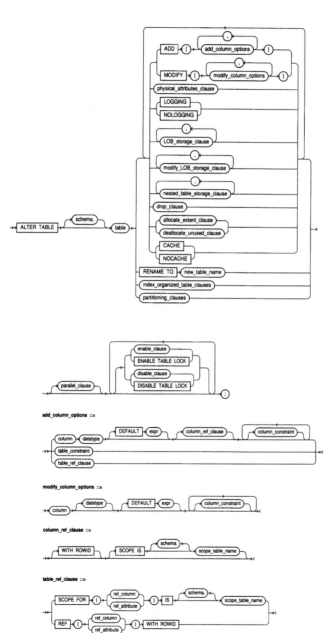

add_column_options ::=

modify_column_options ::=

column_ref_clause ::=

table_ref_clause ::=

physical_attributes_clause ::=

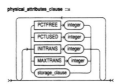

LOB_storage_clause ::=

lob_parameters ::=

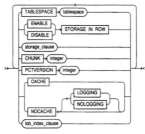

lob_index_clause ::=

lob_index_parameters ::=

modify_LOB_storage_clause ::=

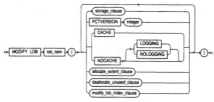

modify_lob_index_clause ::=

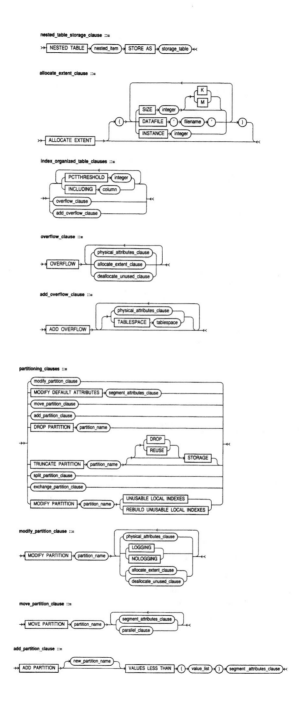

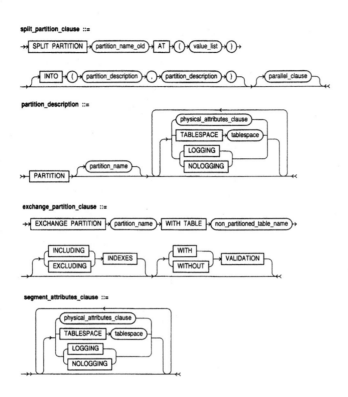

Keywords and Parameters

schema	is the schema containing the table. If you omit schema, Oracle assumes the table is in your own schema.
table	is the name of the table to be altered. You can alter the definition of an index-organized *table*.
ADD	adds a column or integrity constraint. You cannot ADD columns to an index-organized table.
MODIFY	modifies the definition of an existing column. If you omit any of the optional parts of the column definition (datatype, default value, or column constraint), these parts remain unchanged.You cannot MODIFY column definitions of index-organized tables.
column	is the name of the column to be added or modified.

datatype	specifies a datatype for a new column or a new datatype for an existing column. You can only omit the datatype if the statement also designates the column as part of the foreign key of a referential integrity constraint. Oracle automatically assigns the column the same datatype as the corresponding column of the referenced key of the referential integrity constraint.
DEFAULT	specifies a default value for a new column or a new default for an existing column. Oracle assigns this value to the column if a subsequent INSERT statement omits a value for the column. The datatype of the default value must match the datatype specified for the column. The column must also be long enough to hold the default value. A DEFAULT expression cannot contain references to other columns, the pseudocolumns CURRVAL, NEXTVAL, LEVEL, and ROWNUM, or date constants that are not fully specified.
column_constraint	adds or removes a NOT NULL constraint to or from an existing column.
table_constraint	adds an integrity constraint to the table.
MODIFY DEFAULT ATTRIBUTES	is a valid option only for partitioned tables. Use this option to specify new values for the default attributes of a partitioned table.
PCTFREE PCTUSED INITRANS MAXTRANS	changes the value of specified parameters for the table, partition, the overflow data segment, or the default characteristics of a partitioned table.
STORAGE	changes the storage characteristics of the table, partition, overflow data segment, or the default characteristics of a partitioned table.
PCTTHRESHOLD	specifies the percentage of space reserved in the index block for an index-organized table row. Any portion of the row that exceeds the specified threshold is stored in the overflow area. If OVERFLOW is not specified, then rows exceeding the THRESHOLD limit are rejected. PCTTHRESHOLD must be a value from 0 to 50. INCLUDING *column_name* specifies a column at which to divide an index-organized table row into index and overflow portions. All columns which follow *column_name* are stored in the overflow data segment. A *column_name* is either the name of the last primary key column or any non-primary key column.
LOB	specifies the LOB storage characteristics.
lob_item	is the LOB column name or LOB object attribute for which you are explicitly defining tablespace and storage characteristics that are different from those of the table.
STORE AS	

lob_segname	specifies the name of the LOB data segment. You cannot use *lob_segname* if more than one *lob_item* is specified.
ENABLE STORAGE IN ROW	specifies that the LOB value is stored in the row (inline) if its length is less than approximately 4000 bytes minus system control information. This is the default.
DISABLE STORAGE IN ROW	specifies that the LOB value is stored outside of the row regardless of the length of the LOB value.

NOTE
The LOB locator is always stored in the row regardless of where the LOB value is stored. You cannot change the STORAGE IN ROW once it is set.

CHUNK *integer*	is the unit of LOB value allocation and manipulation. Oracle allocates each unit of LOB storage as CHUNK *integer*. This unit of LOB storage is calculated as (*integer* * data block size). For example, if *integer* is 4 and the data block size is 4K, then each unit of LOB storage is 16K. The maximum value is 32K, which is the largest Oracle block size allowed.
PCTVERSION *integer*	is the maximum percentage of overall LOB storage space used for creating new versions of the LOB. The default value is 10, meaning that older versions of the LOB data are not overwritten until 10% of the overall LOB storage space is used.

INDEX *lob_index_name*	is the name of the LOB index segment. You cannot use *lob_index_name* if more than one *lob_item* is specified.

MODIFY LOB (*lob_item*)	modifies the physical attributes of the LOB attribute *lob_item* or LOB object attribute. You can only specify one LOB column for each MODIFY LOB clause.

NESTED TABLE *nested_item* STORE AS *storage_table*	specifies *storage_table* as the name of the storage table in which the rows of all *nested_item* values reside. You must include this clause when modifying a table with columns or column attributes whose type is a nested table.
	
	    The *nested_item* is the name of a column or a column-qualified attribute whose type is a nested table.
	    The *storage_table* is the name of the storage table. The storage table is modified in the same schema and the same tablespace as the parent table.

DROP	drops an integrity constraint.
ALLOCATE EXTENT	explicitly allocates a new extent for the table, the partition, the overflow data segment, the LOB data segment, or the LOB index.

SIZE	specifies the size of the extent in bytes. You can use K or M to specify the extent size in kilobytes or megabytes. If you omit this parameter, Oracle determines the size based on the values of the table's overflow data segment's, or LOB index's, STORAGE parameters.
DATAFILE	specifies one of the data files in the table's, overflow data segment's, LOB data's, tablespace, or LOB index's tablespace to contain the new extent. If you omit this parameter, Oracle chooses the data file.

INSTANCE makes the new extent available to the freelist group associated with the specified instance. If the instance number exceeds the maximum number of freelist groups, the former is divided by the latter, and the remainder is used to identify the freelist group to be used. An instance is identified by the value of its initialization parameter INSTANCE_NUMBER. If you omit this parameter, the space is allocated to the table, but is not drawn from any particular freelist group. Rather the master freelist is used, and space is allocated as needed. For more information, see *Oracle8 Server Concepts*. Only use this parameter if you are using Oracle with the Parallel Server option in parallel mode.

Explicitly allocating an extent with this clause does affect the size for the next extent to be allocated as specified by the NEXT and PCTINCREASE storage parameters.

DEALLOCATE UNUSED explicitly deallocates unused space at the end of the table, partition, overflow data segment, LOB data segment, or LOB index and makes the space available for other segments. You can free only unused space above the high-water mark. If KEEP is omitted, all unused space is freed.

KEEP specifies the number of bytes above the high-water mark that the table, overflow data segment, LOB data segment, or LOB index will have after deallocation. If the number of remaining extents are less than MINEXTENTS, then MINEXTENTS is set to the current number of extents. If the initial extent becomes smaller than INITIAL, then INITIAL is set to the value of the current initial extent.

OVERFLOW	specifies the overflow data segment physical storage attributes to be modified for the index-organized table. Parameters specified in this clause are only applicable to the overflow data segment.
ADD OVERFLOW	adds an overflow data segment to the specified index-organized table.
enable_clause	enables a single integrity constraint or all triggers associated with the table.
ENABLE TABLE LOCK	enables DML and DDL locks on a table in a parallel server environment. For more information, see *Oracle8 Parallel Server Concepts & Administration*.
disable_clause	disables a single integrity contraint or all triggers associated with the tables. Integrity constraints specified in DISABLED clauses must be defined in the ALTER TABLE statements or in a previously issued statement. You can also enable and disable integrity constraints with the ENABLE and DISABLE keywords of the CONSTRAINT clause. If you define an integrity constraint but do not explicitly enable or disable it, Oracle enables it by default. DISABLE TABLE LOCK disables DML and DDL locks on a table to improve performance in a parallel server environment.
parallel_clause	specifies the degree of parallelism for the table. PARALLEL is not a valid option for index-organized tables.
CACHE	specifies that the data is accessed frequently, therefore the blocks retrieved for this table are placed at the most recently used end of the LRU list in the buffer cache when a full table scan is performed. This option is useful for small lookup tables. CACHE is not a valid option for index-organized tables.
NOCACHE	specifies that the data is not accessed frequently, therefore the blocks retrieved for this table are placed at the least recently used end of the LRU list in the buffer cache when a full table scan is performed. For LOBs, the LOB value is either *not brought into the buffer cache or *brought into the buffer cache and placed at the least recently used end of the LRU list. This is the default behavior. NOCACHE is not a valid option for index-organized tables.

LOGGING NOLOGGING	LOGGING/NOLOGGING specifies that subsequent Direct Loader (SQL*Loader) and Direct-Load INSERT operations against a non-partitioned table, table partition, or all partitions of a partitioned table will be logged (LOGGING) or not logged (NOLOGGING) in the redo log file. LOGGING/NOLOGGING also specifies if ALTER TABLE...MOVE and ALTER TABLE...SPLIT operations will be logged or not logged.
	In NOLOGGING mode, data is modified without redo logging. Some minimal logging is still done for marking new extents invalid, and dictionary changes are always fully logged. When applied during media recovery, the extent invalidation records mark a range of blocks as logically corrupt, since the redo data is not logged. Thus if you cannot afford to lose this table, it is important to take a backup after the NOLOGGING operation.
	If the database is run in ARCHIVELOG mode, media recovery from a backup taken before the LOGGING operation will restore the table. However, media recovery from a backup taken before the NOLOGGING operation will not restore the table.
	The logging attribute of the base table is independent of that of its indexes.
	For more information about the LOGGING option and Parallel DML, see *Oracle8 Parallel Server Concepts & Administration.*
	NOLOGGING is not a valid keyword for altering index-organized tables.
RENAME TO *new_table_name*	renames *table* to *new_table_name.*
MODIFY PARTITION *partition_name*	modifies the real physical attributes of a table partition. You can specify any of the following as new physical attributes for the partition: *logging attribute *PCTFREE *PCTUSED *INITRANS *MAXTRANS *STORAGE
RENAME PARTITION *partition_name* TO *new_partition_name*	renames table partition *partition_name* to *new_partition_name.*
MOVE PARTITION *partition_name*	moves table partition *partition_name* to another segment. You can move partition data to another tablespace, recluster data to reduce fragmentation, or change a create-time physical attribute.

ADD PARTITION *new_partition_name*	adds a new partition *new_partition_name* to the "high" end of a partitioned table. You can specify any of the following as new physical attributes for the partition: logging attribute PCTFREE PCTUSED INITRANS MAXTRANS STORAGE	
	VALUES LESS THAN (*value_list*)	specifies the upper bound for the new partition. The *value_list* is a comma-separated, ordered list of literal values corresponding to *column_list*. The *value_list* must collate greater than the partition bound for the highest existing partition in the table.
DROP PARTITION *partition_name*	removes partition *partition_name*, and the data in that partition, from a partitioned table.	
TRUNCATE PARTITION *partition_name*	removes all rows from a partition in a table.	
	DROP STORAGE	specifies that space from the deleted rows be deallocated and made available for use by other schema objects in the tablespace.
	REUSE STORAGE	specifies that space from the deleted rows remains allocated to the partition. The space is subsequently only available for inserts and updates to the same partition.
SPLIT PARTITION *partition_name_old*	creates two new partitions, each with a new segment and new physical attributes, and new initial extents. The segment associated with the old partition is discarded.	

	AT (*value_list*)	specifies the new non-inclusive upper bound for *split_partition_1*. The *value_list* must compare less than the pre-split partition bound for *partition_name_old* and greater than the partition bound for the next lowest partition (if there is one).
	INTO	describes the two partitions resulting from the split.
	PARTITION *split_partition_1*, PARTITION *split_partition_2*	specifies the names and physical attributes of the two partitions resulting from the split.
EXCHANGE PARTITION *partition_name*		converts partition *partition_name* into a non-partitioned table, and a non-partitioned table into a partition of a partitioned table by exchanging their data (and index) segments.
	WITH TABLE *table*	specifies the table with which the partition will be exchanged.
	INCLUDING INDEXES	specifies that the local index partitions be exchanged with the corresponding regular indexes.
	EXCLUDING INDEXES	specifies that all the local index partitions corresponding to the partition and all the regular indexes on the exchanged table are marked as unusable.
	WITH VALIDATION	specifies that any rows in the exchanged table that do not collate properly return an error.
	WITHOUT VALIDATION	specifies that the proper collation of rows in the exchanged table is not checked.

UNUSABLE LOCAL INDEXES	marks all the local index partitions associated with *partition_name* as unusable.
REBUILD UNUSABLE LOCAL INDEXES	rebuilds the unusable local index partitions associated with *partition_name*.

Adding Columns

If you use the ADD clause to add a new column to the table, then the initial value of each row for the new column is null. You can add a column with a NOT NULL constraint only to a table that contains no rows.

If you create a view with a query that uses the asterisk (*) in the select list to select all columns from the base table and you subsequently add columns to the base table, Oracle will not automatically add the new column to the view. To add the new column to the view, you can re-create the view using the CREATE VIEW command with the OR REPLACE option.

Operations performed by the ALTER TABLE command can cause Oracle to invalidate procedures and stored functions that access the table. For information on how and when Oracle invalidates such objects, see the "Dependencies Among Schema Objects" chapter of *Oracle8 Server Concepts*.

Modifying Column Definitions

You can use the MODIFY clause to change any of the following parts of a column definition:

- datatype
- size
- default value
- NOT NULL column constraint

The MODIFY clause need only specify the column name and the modified part of the definition, rather than the entire column definition.

DATATYPES AND SIZES   You can change a CHAR column to VARCHAR2 (or VARCHAR) and a VARCHAR2 (or VARCHAR) to CHAR only if the column contains nulls in all rows or if you do not attempt to change the column size. You can change any column's datatype or decrease any column's size if all rows for the column contain nulls. However, you can always increase the size of a character or raw column or the precision of a numeric column.

You cannot change a column's datatype to a LOB or REF datatype.

DEFAULT VALUES   A change to a column's default value only affects rows subsequently inserted into the table. Such a change does not change default values previously inserted.

INTEGRITY CONSTRAINTS   The only type of integrity constraint that you can add to an existing column using the MODIFY clause with the column constraint syntax is a NOT NULL constraint. However, you can define other types of integrity constraints (UNIQUE, PRIMARY KEY, referential integrity, and CHECK constraints) on existing columns using the ADD clause and the table constraint syntax.

You can define a NOT NULL constraint on an existing column only if the column contains no nulls.

Index-organized Tables

Index-organized tables are special kinds of tables that keep data sorted on the primary key and are therefore best suited for primary key-based access and manipulation.

You cannot ADD columns to an index-organized table, but you can alter the definition of an index-organized table.

LOB Columns

You can add a LOB column to a table, or modify the LOB data segment or index storage charactersitics.

Nested Table Columns

You can add a nested table type column to a table. Specify a nested table storage clause for each column added.

You can also modify a nested table's storage characteristics. Use the name of the storage table specified in the nested table storage clause to make the modification. You *cannot* query or perform DML statements on the storage table; only use the storage table to modify the nested table column storage characteristics.

REFs

A REF value is a reference to a row in an object table. A table can have top-level REF columns or it can have REF attributes embedded within an object column. In general, if a table has a REF column, each REF value in the column could reference a row in a different object table. A SCOPE clause restricts the scope of references to a single table.

Use the ALTER TABLE command to add new REF columns or to add REF clauses to existing REF columns. You can modify any table, including named inner nested tables (storage tables). If a REF column is created WITH ROWID or with a scope table, you cannot modify the column to drop these options.

However, if a table is created without any REF clauses, you can add them later with an ALTER TABLE statement.

NOTE
You can only add a SCOPE clause to existing REF columns of a table if the table is empty. The scope_table_name must be in your own schema or you must have SELECT privilege on the table, or the SELECT ANY TABLE system privilege. This privilege is only needed while altering the table with the REF column.

Modifying Table Partitions

You can modify a table or table partition in any of the following ways. You cannot combine partition operations with other partition operations or with operations on the base table in one ALTER TABLE statement.

ADD PARTITION   Use ALTER TABLE ADD PARTITION to add a partition to the high end of the table (after the last existing partition). If the first element of the partition bound of the high partition is MAXVALUE, you cannot add a partition to the table. You must split the high partition.

You can add a partition to a table even if one or more of the table indexes or index partitions are marked UNUSABLE.

You must use the SPLIT PARTITION clause to add a partition at the beginning or the middle of the table.

The following example adds partition JAN97 to tablespace TSX:

```
ALTER TABLE sales
    ADD PARTITION jan97 VALUES LESS THAN( '970201' )
    TABLESPACE tsx;
```

DROP PARTITION   ALTER TABLE DROP PARTITION drops a partition and its data. If you want to drop a partition but keep its data in the table, you must merge the partition into one of the adjacent partitions. For information about merging two tables partitions, see the *Oracle8 Server Administrator's Guide.*

If you drop a partition and later insert a row that would have belonged to the dropped partition, the row will be stored in the next higher partition. However, if you drop the highest partition, the insert will fail because the range of values represented by the dropped partition is no longer valid for the table.

This statement also drops the corresponding partition in each local index defined on *table*. The index partitions are dropped even if they are marked as unusable.

If there are global indexes defined on *table*, and the partition you want to drop is *not* empty, dropping the partition marks all the global, non-partitioned indexes, and all the partitions of global partitioned indexes as unusable.

When a table contains only one partition, you cannot drop the partition. You must drop the table.

The following example drops partition DEC95:

```
ALTER TABLE sales DROP PARTITION dec95;
```

EXCHANGE PARTITION This form of ALTER TABLE converts a partition to a non-partitioned table and a table to a partition by exchanging their data segments. You must have ALTER TABLE privileges on both tables to perform this operation.

The statistics of the table and partition, including table, column, index statistics and histograms are exchanged. The aggregate statistics of the partitioned table are recalculated.

The logging attribute of the table and partition is exchanged.

The following example converts partition FEB97 to table SALES_FEB97:

```
ALTER TABLE sales
   EXCHANGE PARTITION feb97 WITH TABLE sales_feb97
   WITHOUT VALIDATION;
```

MODIFY PARTITION Use the MODIFY PARTITION options of ALTER TABLE to

- mark local index partitions corresponding to a table partition as unusable.

- rebuild all the unusable local index partitions corresponding to a table partition.

- modify the physical attributes of a table partition.

The following example marks all the local index partitions corresponding to the NOV96 partition of the sales table UNUSABLE:

```
ALTER TABLE sales MODIFY PARTITION nov96
   UNUSABLE LOCAL INDEXES;
```

The following example rebuilds all the local index partitions which were marked UNUSABLE:

```
ALTER TABLE sales MODIFY PARTITIION jan97
   REBUILD UNUSABLE LOCAL INDEXES;
```

The following example changes MAXEXTENTS for partition BRANCH_NY:

```
ALTER TABLE branch MODIFY PARTITION branch_ny
   STORAGE(MAXEXTENTS 75) LOGGING;
```

MOVE PARTITION   This ALTER TABLE option moves a table partition to another segment. MOVE PARTITION always drops the partition's old segment and creates a new segment, even if you do not specify a new tablespace.

If *partition_name* is not empty, MOVE PARTITION marks all corresponding local index partitions and all global non-partitioned indexes, and all the partitions of global partitioned indexes as unusable.

ALTER TABLE MOVE PARTITION obtains its parallel attribute from the PARALLEL clause, if specified. If not specified, the default PARALLEL attributes of the table, if any, are used. If neither is specified, it performs the move without using parallelism.

The PARALLEL clause on MOVE PARTITION does not change the default PARALLEL attributes of *table*.

The following example moves partition DEPOT2 to tablespace TS094:

```
ALTER TABLE parts
   MOVE PARTITION depot2 TABLESPACE ts094 NOLOGGING;
```

RENAME   Use the RENAME option of ALTER TABLE to rename a table or to rename a partition.

The following example renames a table:

```
ALTER TABLE emp RENAME TO employee;
```

In the following example, partition EMP3 is renamed:

```
ALTER TABLE employee RENAME PARTITION emp3 TO employee3;
```

SPLIT PARTITION   The SPLIT PARTITION option divides a partition into two partitions, each with a new segment, new physical attributes, and new initial extents. The segment associated with the old partition is discarded.

This statement also performs a matching split on the corresponding partition in each local index defined on *table*. The index partitions are split even if they are marked unusable.

With the exception of the TABLESPACE attribute, the physical attributes of the LOCAL index partition being split are used for both new index partitions.

If the parent LOCAL index lacks a default TABLESPACE attribute, new LOCAL index partitions will reside in the same tablespace as the corresponding newly created partitions of the underlying table.

If you do not specify physical attributes (PCTFREE, PCTUSED, INITRANS, MAXTRANS, STORAGE) for the new partitions, the current values of the partition being split are used as the default values for both partitions.

If *partition_name* is not empty, SPLIT PARTITION marks all affected index partitions as unusable. This includes all global index partitions as well as the local index partitions which result from the split.

The PARALLEL clause on SPLIT PARTITION does not change the default PARALLEL attributes of *table*.

The following example splits the old partition DEPOT4 creating a new partition for DEPOT9:

```
ALTER TABLE parts
   SPLIT PARTITION depot4 AT ( '40-001' )
   INTO ( PARTITION depot4 TABLESPACE ts009 (MINEXTENTS 2),
          PARTITION depot9 TABLESPACE ts010 )
   PARALLEL ( DEGREE 10 );
```

TRUNCATE PARTITION   Use TRUNCATE PARTITION to remove all rows from a partition in a table. Freed space is deallocated or reused depending on whether DROP STORAGE or REUSE STORAGE is specified in the clause.

This statement truncates the corresponding partition in each local index defined on *table*. The local index partitions are truncated even if they are marked as unusable. The unusable local index partitions are marked valid, resetting the UNUSABLE indicator.

If there are global indexes defined on *table*, and the partition you want to truncate is *not* empty, truncating the partition marks all the global non-partitioned indexes, and all the partitions of global partitioned indexes as unusable.

If you want to truncate a partition that contains data, you must first disable any referential integrity constraints on the table. Alternatively, you can delete the rows and then truncate the partition.

The following example deletes all the data in the SYS_P017 partition and deallocates the freed space:

```
ALTER TABLE deliveries
   TRUNCATE PARTITION sys_p017 DROP STORAGE;
```

ALTER TABLESPACE

Purpose

To alter an existing tablespace in one of the following ways:

- to add datafile(s)
- to rename datafiles
- to change default storage parameters
- to take the tablespace online or offline
- to begin or end a backup
- to allow or disallow writing to a tablespace
- to change the default logging attribute of the tablespace
- to change the minimum tablespace extent length

Prerequisites

If you have ALTER TABLESPACE system privilege, you can perform any of this command's operations. If you have MANAGE TABLESPACE system privilege, you can only perform the following operations:

- to take the tablespace online or offline
- to begin or end a backup
- to make the tablespace read-only or read-write

Before you can make a tablespace read-only, the following conditions must be met. It may be easiest to meet these restrictions by performing this function in restricted mode, so that only users with the RESTRICTED SESSION system privilege can be logged on.

- The tablespace must be online.
- There must not be any active transactions in the entire database. This is necessary to ensure that there is no undo information that needs to be applied to the tablespace.

- The tablespace must not contain any active rollback segments. For this reason, the SYSTEM tablespace can never be made read-only, since it contains the SYSTEM rollback segment. Additionally, because the rollback segments of a read-only tablespace are not accessible, it is recommended that you drop the rollback segments before you make a tablespace read-only.

- The tablespace must not be involved in an open backup, since the end of a backup updates the header file of all datafiles in the tablespace.

- The COMPATIBLE initialization parameter must be set to 7.1.0 or greater.

Syntax

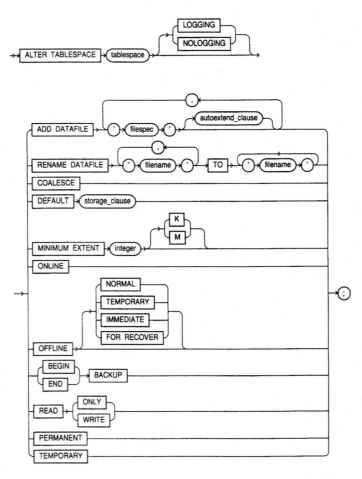

autoextend_clause ::=

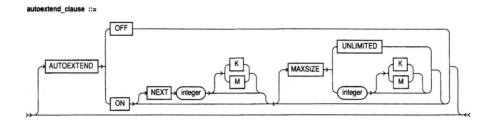

Keywords and Parameters

tablespace	is the name of the tablespace to be altered.
LOGGING NOLOGGING	specifies the logging attribute of all tables, indexes, and partitions within the tablespace.

The tablespace-level logging attribute can be overridden by logging specifications at the table, index, and partition levels.

When an existing tablespace logging attribute is changed by an ALTER TABLESPACE statement, all tables, indexes, and partitions created after the statement will have the new logging attribute; the logging attributes of existing objects are not changed.

Only the following operations support NOLOGGING mode:

DML:
*direct-load INSERT (serial or parallel)
*Direct Loader (SQL*Loader)

DDL:
CREATE TABLE ... AS SELECT
CREATE INDEX
ALTER INDEX ... REBUILD
ALTER INDEX ... REBUILD PARTITION
ALTER INDEX ... SPLIT PARTITION
ALTER TABLE ... SPLIT PARTITION
ALTER TABLE ... MOVE PARTITION

In NOLOGGING mode, data is modified without redo logging. Some minimal logging is still done for marking new extents invalid, and dictionary changes are always fully logged. When applied during media recovery, the extent invalidation records mark a range of blocks as logically corrupt, since the redo data is not logged. Thus if you cannot afford to lose the object, it is important to take a backup after the NOLOGGING operation.

ADD DATAFILE		adds the datafile specified by filespec to the tablespace. You can add a datafile while the tablespace is online or offline. Be sure that the datafile is not already in use by another database.
AUTOEXTEND		enables or disables the autoextending of the size of the datafile in the tablespace.
	OFF	disables autoextend if it is turned on. NEXT and MAXSIZE are set to zero. Values for NEXT and MAXSIZE must be respecified in further ALTER TABLESPACE AUTOEXTEND commands.
	ON	enables autoextend.
	NEXT	the size in bytes of the next increment of disk space to be automatically allocated to the datafile when more extents are required. You can also use K or M to specify this size in kilobytes or megabytes. The default is one data block.
	MAXSIZE	maximum disk space allowed for automatic extension of the datafile.
	UNLIMITED	sets no limit on allocating disk space to the datafile.
RENAME DATAFILE		renames one or more of the tablespace's datafile. Takes the tablespace offline before renaming the datafile. Each 'filename' must fully specify a datafile using the conventions for filenames on your operating system. This clause only associates the tablespace with the new file rather than the old one. This clause does not actually change the name of the operating system file. You must change the name of the file through your operating system.
COALESCE		for each datafile in the tablespace, coalesces all contiguous free extents into larger contiguous extents. COALESCE cannot be specified with any other command option.
DEFAULT *storage_clause*		specifies the new default storage parameters for objects subsequently created in the tablespace.

MINIMUM EXTENT *integer*	controls free space fragmentation in the tablespace by ensuring that every used and/or free extent size in a tablespace is at least as large as, and is a multiple of, *integer*. For more information about using MINIMUM EXTENT to control space fragmentation, see the *Oracle8 Server Administrator's Guide*.
ONLINE	brings the tablespace online.
OFFLINE	takes the tablespace offline and prevents further access to its segments.

NORMAL	performs a checkpoint for all datafiles in the tablespace. All of these datafiles must be online. You need not perform media recovery on this tablespace before bringing it back online. You must use this option if the database is in noarchivelog mode.
TEMPORARY	performs a checkpoint for all online datafiles in the tablespace but does not ensure that all files can be written. Any offline files may require media recovery before you bring the tablespace back online.
IMMEDIATE	does not ensure that tablespace files are available and does not perform a checkpoint. You must perform media recovery on the tablespace before bringing it back online.
FOR RECOVER	takes the production database tablespaces in the recovery set offline. Use this option when one or more datafiles in the tablespace are unavailable.

The default is NORMAL.

It is suggested that before taking a tablespace offline for a long time, you may want to alter any users who have been assigned the tablespace as either a default or temporary tablespace. When the tablespace is offline, these users cannot allocate space for objects or sort areas in the tablespace. You can reassign users new default and temporary tablespaces with the ALTER USER command.

BEGIN BACKUP	signifies that an open backup is to be performed on the datafiles that comprise this tablespace. This option does not prevent users from accessing the tablespace. You must use this option before beginning an open backup. You cannot use this option on a read-only tablespace.
	While the backup is in progress, you cannot:
	*take the tablespace offline normally
	*shut down the instance
	*begin another backup of the tablespace
END BACKUP	signifies that an open backup of the tablespace is complete. Use this option as soon as possible after completing an open backup. You cannot use this option on a read-only tablespace.
READ ONLY	signifies that no further write operations are allowed on the tablespace. The tablespace becomes read-only.
READ WRITE	signifies that write operations are allowed on a previously read-only tablespace.
PERMANENT	specifies that the tablespace is to be converted from a temporary to a permanent one. A permanent tablespace is one wherein permanent database objects can be stored. This is the default when a tablespace is created.
TEMPORARY	specifies that the tablespace is to be converted from a permanent to a temporary one. A temporary tablespace is one wherein no permanent database objects can be stored.

Usage Notes

Before taking a tablespace offline for a long time, you may want to alter any users who have been assigned the tablespace as either a default or temporary tablespace. When the tablespace is offline, these users cannot allocate space for objects or sort areas in the tablespace. You can reassign users new default and temporary tablespaces with the ALTER USER command.

Once a tablespace is read-only, you can copy its files to read-only media. You must then rename the datafiles in the control file to point to the new location by using the SQL command ALTER DATABASE RENAME.

If you forget to indicate the end of an online tablespace backup, and an instance failure or SHUTDOWN ABORT occurs, Oracle assumes that media recovery (possibly requiring archived redo log) is necessary at the next instance start up. To restart the database without media recovery, see *Oracle8 Server Administrator's Guide.*

ALTER USER

Purpose

To change any of the following characteristics of a database user:

- authentication mechanism of the user
- password
- default tablespace for object creation
- tablespace for temporary segments created for the user
- tablespace access and tablespace quotas
- limits on database resources
- default roles

Prerequisites

You must have the ALTER USER system privilege. However, you can change your own password without this privilege.

Syntax

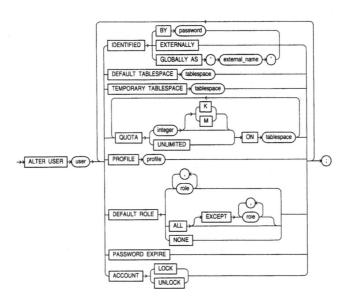

Keywords and Parameters

The keywords and parameters in the ALTER USER command all have the same meaning as in the CREATE USER command.

Establishing Default Roles

The DEFAULT ROLE clause can only contain roles that have been granted directly to the user with a GRANT statement. You cannot use the DEFAULT ROLE clause to enable:

■ roles not granted to the user

■ roles granted through other roles

■ roles managed by an external service (such as the operating system), or by the Oracle Security Service Certification Authority

NOTE
Oracle enables default roles at logon without requiring the user to specify their passwords.

Security Domains

You can only change a user's access verification method to IDENTIFIED GLOBALLY AS 'external_name' if all external roles granted directly to the user are revoked.

You can change a user created as IDENTIFIED GLOBALLY AS 'external_name' to IDENTIFIED BY password or IDENTIFIED EXTERNALLY.

ANALYZE

NOTE
Descriptions of commands and clauses preceded by are only available if the Oracle objects option is installed on your database server.

Purpose

To perform one of the following functions on an index or index partition, table or table partition, index-organized table, or cluster:

- collect statistics about the schema object used by the optimizer and store them in the data dictionary
- delete statistics about the schema object from the data dictionary
- validate the structure of the schema object
- identify migrated and chained rows of the table or cluster
- collect statistics on scalar object attributes
- validate and update object references (REFs)

Prerequisites

The schema object to be analyzed must be in your own schema or you must have the ANALYZE ANY system privilege.

If you want to list chained rows of a table or cluster into a list table, the list table must be in your own schema or you must have INSERT privilege on the list table or you must have INSERT ANY TABLE system privilege. If you want to validate a partitioned table, you must have INSERT privilege on the table into which you list analyzed ROWIDS, or you must have INSERT ANY TABLE system privilege.

Syntax

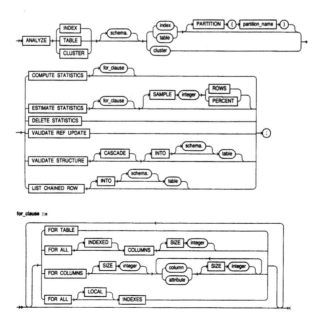

Keywords and Parameters

attribute	specifies the qualified column name of an item in an object.
INDEX	identifies an index to be analyzed (if no FOR clause is used). If you omit schema, Oracle assumes the index is in your own schema.
TABLE	identifies a table to be analyzed. If you omit schema, Oracle assumes the table is in your own schema. When you collect statistics for a table, Oracle also automatically collects the statistics for each of the table's indexes, provided that no FOR clauses are used.
PARTITION (*partition_name*)	specifies that statistics will be gathered for (*partition_name*). You cannot use this option when analyzing clusters.
CLUSTER	identifies a cluster to be analyzed. If you omit schema, Oracle assumes the cluster is in your own schema. When you collect statistics for a cluster, Oracle also automatically collects the statistics for all the cluster's tables and all their indexes, including the cluster index.
VALIDATE REF UPDATE	validates the REFs in the specified table, checks the ROWID portion in each REF, compares it with the true ROWID, and corrects, if necessary. You can only use this option when analyzing a table.
COMPUTE STATISTICS	computes exact statistics about the analyzed object and stores them in a data dictionary.
ESTIMATE STATISTICS	estimates statistics about the analyzed object and stores them in the data dictionary.

	SAMPLE	specifies the amount of data from the analyzed object Oracle samples to estimate statistics. If you omit this parameter, Oracle samples 1064 rows. If you specify more than half of the data, Oracle reads all the data and computes the statistics.
	ROWS	causes Oracle to sample integer rows of the table or cluster or integer entries from the index. The integer must be at least 1.
	PERCENT	causes Oracle to sample integer percent of the rows from the table or cluster or integer percent of the index entries. The integer can range from 1 to 99.

Histogram statistics are described in *Oracle Server Tuning*. The following clauses only apply to the ANALYZE TABLE version of this command:

FOR TABLE	collects table statistics for the table.
FOR ALL COLUMNS	collects column statistics for all columns and scalar attributes.
FOR ALL INDEXED COLUMNS	collects column statistics for all indexed columns in the table.
FOR COLUMNS	collects column statistics for the specified columns and scalar object attributes.
FOR ALL INDEXES	all indexes associated with the table will be analyzed.
FOR ALL LOCAL INDEXES	specifies that all local index partitions are analyzed. You must specify the keyword LOCAL if the PARTITION (*partition_name*) clause and the index option are specified.
SIZE	specifies the maximum number of partitions in the histogram. The default value is 75, minimum value is 1, and maximum value is 254.

DELETE STATISTICS	deletes any statistics about the analyzed object that are currently stored in the data dictionary.
VALIDATE STRUCTURE	validates the structure of the analyzed object. If you use this option when analyzing a cluster, Oracle automatically validates the structure of the cluster's tables.

INTO	specifies a table into which Oracle lists the rowids of the partitions whose rows do not collate correctly. If you omit *schema*, Oracle assumes the list is in your own schema. If you omit this clause altogether, Oracle assumes that the table is named INVALID_ROWS. The SQL script used to create this table is UTLVALID.SQL.

CASCADE	validates the structure of the indexes associated with the table or cluster. If you use this option when validating a table, Oracle also validates the table's indexes. If you use this option when validating a cluster, Oracle also validates all the clustered tables' indexes, including the cluster index.
LIST CHAINED ROWS	identifies migrated and chained rows of the analyzed table or cluster. You cannot use this option when analyzing an index.

INTO	specifies a table into which Oracle lists the migrated and chained rows. If you omit schema, Oracle assumes the list table is in your own schema. If you omit this clause altogether, Oracle assumes that the table is named CHAINED_ROWS. The script used to create this table is UTLCHAIN.SQL. The list table must be on your local database.
	To analyze index-organized tables, you must create a separate chained rows table for each index-organized table created to accomodate the primary key storage of index-organized tables. Use the SQL scripts DBMSIOTC.SQL and PRVTIOTC.PLB to define the BUILD_CHAIN_ROWS_TABLE package and then execute this procedure to create an IOT_CHAINED_ROWS table for an index-organized table.

Usage Notes

Do not use ANALYZE to collect statistics on data dictionary tables.

You cannot compute or estimate statistics for the following column types:

- REFs
- VARRAYs
- nested tables
- LOBs (LOBs are not analyzed, they are skipped)
- LONGs
- object types

Collecting Statistics

You can collect statistics about the physical storage characteristics and data distribution of an index, table, column, or cluster and store them in the data dictionary. For computing or estimating statistics

- Computation always provides exact values, but can take longer than estimation.

- Estimation is often much faster than computation and the results are usually nearly exact.

Use estimation, rather than computation, unless you feel you need exact values. Some statistics are always computed exactly, regardless of whether you specify computation or estimation. If you choose estimation and the time saved by estimating a statistic is negligible, Oracle computes the statistic exactly.

If the data dictionary already contains statistics for the analyzed object, Oracle updates the existing statistics with the new ones.

The following sections list the statistics for indexes, tables, columns, and clusters.

INDEXES   For an index, Oracle collects the following statistics:

- depth of the index from its root block to its leaf blocks*

- number of leaf blocks

- number of distinct index values

- average number of leaf blocks per index value

- average number of data blocks per index value (for an index on a table)

- clustering factor (how well ordered are the rows about the indexed values)

The statistics marked with asterisks (*) are always computed exactly.

Index statistics appear in the data dictionary views USER_INDEXES, ALL_INDEXES, and DBA_INDEXES.

TABLES   For a table, Oracle collects the following statistics:

- number of rows

- number of data blocks currently containing data *

- number of data blocks allocated to the table that have never been used *

- average available free space in each data block in bytes
- number of chained rows
- average row length, including the row's overhead, in bytes

The statistics marked with asterisks (*) are always computed exactly.

Table statistics appear in the data dictionary views USER_TABLES, ALL_TABLES, and DBA_TABLES.

COLUMNS   Column statistics can be based on the entire column or can use a histogram. A histogram partitions the values in the column into bands, so that all column values in a band fall within the same range. In some cases, it is useful to see how many values fall in various ranges. Oracle's histograms are height balanced as opposed to width balanced. This means that the column values are divided into bands so that each band contains approximately the same number of values. The useful information the histogram provides, then, is where in the range of values the endpoints fall. Width-balanced histograms, on the other hand, divide the data into a number of ranges, all of which are the same size, and then count the number of values falling into each range.

- number of distinct values in the column as a whole
- maximum and minimum values in each band

When to Use Histograms

For uniformly distributed data, the cost-based approach makes fairly accurate guesses at the cost of executing a particular statement. For non-uniformly distributed data, Oracle allows you to store histograms describing the data distribution of a particular column. These histograms are stored in the dictionary and can be used by the cost-based optimizer.

Since they are persistent objects, there is a maintenance and space cost for using histograms. You should only compute histograms for columns that you know have highly skewed data distribution. Also, be aware that histograms, as well as all optimizer statistics, are static. If the data distribution of a column changes frequently, you must reissue the ANALYZE command to recompute the histogram for that column.

Histograms are not useful for columns with the following characteristics:

- all predicates on the column use bind variables
- the column data is uniformly distributed
- the column is not used in WHERE clauses of queries
- the column is unique and is used only with equality predicates

Create histograms on columns that are frequently used in WHERE clauses of queries and have a highly skewed data distribution. You create a histogram by using the ANALYZE TABLE option of this command. For example, if you want to create a 10-band histogram on the SAL column of the EMP table, issue the following statement:

```
ANALYZE TABLE emp
    COMPUTE STATISTICS FOR COLUMNS sal SIZE 10;
```

You can also collect histograms for a single partition of a table. The following statement analyzes the EMP table partition P1:

```
ANALYZE TABLE emp PARTITION (p1) COMPUTE STATISTICS;
```

Column statistics appear in the data dictionary views:

- USER_TAB_COLUMNS
- ALL_TAB_COLUMNS
- DBA_TAB_COLUMNS

Histograms appear in the data dictionary views USER_HISTOGRAMS, DBA_HISTOGRAMS, and ALL_HISTOGRAMS.

CLUSTERS   For an indexed cluster, Oracle collects the average number of data blocks taken up by a single cluster key value and all of its rows. For a hash cluster, Oracle collects the average number of data blocks taken up by a single hash key value and all of its rows. These statistics appear in the data dictionary views USER_CLUSTERS and DBA_CLUSTERS.

Deleting Statistics

With the DELETE STATISTICS option of the ANALYZE command, you can remove existing statistics about an object from the data dictionary. You may want to remove statistics if you no longer want the Oracle optimizer to use them.

When you use the DELETE STATISTICS option on a table, Oracle also automatically removes statistics for all the table's indexes. When you use the DELETE STATISTICS option on a cluster, Oracle also automatically removes statistics for all the cluster's tables and all their indexes, including the cluster index.

Validating Structures

With the VALIDATE STRUCTURE option of the ANALYZE command, you can verify the integrity of the structure of an index, table, or cluster. If Oracle successfully validates the structure, a message confirming its validation is returned to you. If Oracle encounters corruption in the structure of the object, an error message is returned to you. In this case, drop and recreate the object.

Since validating the structure of a object prevents SELECT, INSERT, UPDATE, and DELETE statements from concurrently accessing the object, do not use this option on the tables, clusters, and indexes of your production applications during periods of high database activity.

INDEXES   For an index, the VALIDATE STRUCTURE option verifies the integrity of each data block in the index and checks for block corruption. Note that this option does not confirm that each row in the table has an index entry or that each index entry points to a row in the table. You can perform these operations by validating the structure of the table.

When you use the VALIDATE STRUCTURE option on an index, Oracle also collects statistics about the index and stores them in the data dictionary view INDEX_STATS. Oracle overwrites any existing statistics about previously validated indexes. At any time, INDEX_STATS can contain only one row describing only one index. The INDEX_STATS view is described in the *Oracle8 Server Reference*.

The statistics collected by this option are not used by the Oracle optimizer. Do not confuse these statistics with the statistics collected by the COMPUTE STATISTICS and ESTIMATE STATISTICS options.

TABLES   For a table, the VALIDATE STRUCTURE option verifies the integrity of each of the table's data blocks and rows. You can use the CASCADE option to also validate the structure of all indexes on the table and to perform cross-referencing between the table and each of its indexes. For each index, the cross-referencing involves the following validations:

- Each value of the tables' indexed column must match the indexed column value of an index entry. The matching index entry must also identify the row in the table by the correct ROWID.

- Each entry in the index identifies a row in the table. The indexed column value in the index entry must match that of the identified row.

CLUSTERS   For a cluster, the VALIDATE STRUCTURE option verifies the integrity of each row in the cluster and automatically validates the structure of each of the cluster's tables. You can use the CASCADE option to also validate the structure of all indexes on the cluster's tables, including the cluster index.

PARTITIONED TABLES   There is no rule-based optimizer for partitioned tables, so it is important to analyze partitioned tables and indexes regularly.

For a partitioned table, the VALIDATE STRUCTURE option verifies each row in the partition to check if the column values of the partitioning columns collate less than the partition bound of that partition and greater than the partition bound of the previous partition (except the first partition). If the row does not collate correctly, the ROWID is inserted into the INVALID_ROWS table.

Listing Chained Rows

With the LIST option of the ANALYZE command, you can collect information about the migrated and chained rows in a table or cluster. A *migrated row* is one that has been moved from one data block to another. For example, Oracle migrates a row in a cluster if its cluster key value is updated. A *chained row* is one that is contained in more than one data block. For example, Oracle chains a row of a table or cluster if the row is too long to fit in a single data block. Migrated and chained rows may cause excessive I/O. You may want to identify such rows to eliminate them. For information on eliminating migrated and chained rows, see *Oracle8 Server Tuning*.

You can use the INTO clause to specify an output table into which Oracle places this information. The definition of a sample output table CHAINED_ROWS is provided in a SQL script available on your distribution media. Your list table must have the same column names, types, and sizes as the CHAINED_ROWS table. On many operating systems, the name of this script is UTLCHAIN.SQL. The actual name and location of this script may vary depending on your operating system.

ARCHIVE LOG clause

Purpose

To manually archive redo log file groups or to enable or disable automatic archiving.

Prerequisites

The ARCHIVE LOG clause must appear in an ALTER SYSTEM command. You must have the privileges necessary to issue this statement.

You must also have the OSDBA or OSOPER role enabled.

You can use most of the options of this clause when your instance has the database mounted, open or closed. Options that require your instance to have the database open are noted.

Syntax

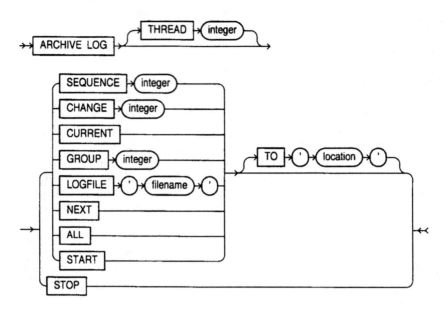

Keywords and Parameters

THREAD   specifies thread containing the redo log file group to be archived. You only need to specify this parameter if you are using Oracle with the Parallel Server option in parallel mode.

SEQ   manually archives the online redo log file group identified by the log sequence number integer in the specified thread. If you omit the THREAD parameter, Oracle archives the specified group from the thread assigned to your instance.

CHANGE   manually archives the online redo log file group containing the redo log entry with the system change number (SCN) specified by integer in the specified thread. If the SCN is in the current redo log file group, Oracle performs a log switch. If you omit the THREAD parameter, Oracle archives the groups containing this SCN from all enabled threads. You can only use this option when your instance has the database open.

CURRENT   manually archives the current redo log file group of the specified thread, forcing a log switch. If you omit the THREAD parameter, Oracle archives all redo log file groups from all enabled threads, including logs previous to current logs. You can only use this option when your instance has the database open.

GROUP   manually archives the online redo log file group with the specified GROUP value. You can determine the GROUP value for a redo log file group by examining the data dictionary view DBA_LOG_FILES. If you specify both the THREAD and GROUP parameters, the specified redo log file group must be in the specified thread.

LOGFILE   manually archives the online redo log file group containing the redo log file member identified by 'filename'. If you specify both the THREAD and LOGFILE parameters, the specified redo log file group must be in the specified thread.

NEXT   manually archives the next online redo log file group from the specified thread that is full but has not yet been archived. If you omit the THREAD parameter, Oracle archives the earliest unarchived redo log file group from any enabled thread.

ALL   manually archives all online redo log file groups from the specified thread that are full but have not been archived. If you omit the THREAD parameter, Oracle archives all full unarchived redo log file groups from all enabled threads.

START   enables automatic archiving of redo log file groups. You can only enable automatic archiving for the thread assigned to your instance.

TO   specifies the location to which the redo log file group is archived. The value of this parameter must be a fully specified file location following the conventions of your operating system. If you omit this parameter, Oracle archives the redo log file group to the location specified by the initialization parameter LOG_ARCHIVE_DEST.

STOP   disables automatic archiving of redo log file groups. You can only disable automatic archiving for the thread assigned to your instance.

Usage Notes

You must archive redo log file groups in the order in which they are filled. If you specify a redo log file group for archiving with these or LOGFILE parameter and earlier redo log file groups are not yet archived, Oracle returns an error. If you specify a redo log file group for archiving with the CHANGE parameter or CURRENT option and earlier redo log file groups are not yet archived, Oracle archives all unarchived groups up to and including the specified group.

You can also manually archive redo log file groups with the ARCHIVE LOG Server Manager command. For information on this command, see the *Oracle Server Manager User's Guide*.

You can also choose to have Oracle archive redo log files groups automatically. For information on automatic archiving, see the "Archiving Redo Information" chapter of the *Oracle8 Server Administrator's Guide*. Note that you can always manually archive redo log file groups regardless of whether automatic archiving is enabled.

AUDIT (SQL Statements)

NOTE
Descriptions of commands and clauses preceded by are only available if the Oracle objects option is installed on your database server.

Purpose

To choose specific SQL statements for auditing in subsequent user sessions. To choose particular schema objects for auditing, use the AUDIT command (Schema Objects).

Prerequisites

You must have AUDIT SYSTEM system privilege.

Syntax

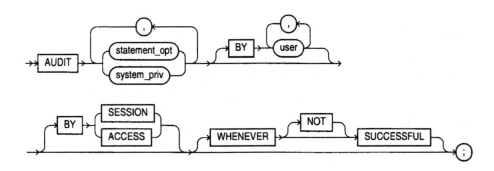

Keywords and Parameters

statement_opt	chooses specific SQL statements for auditing. For a list of these statement options and the SQL statements they audit, see Table C-1 and Table C-2.
system_priv	chooses SQL statements that are authorized by the specified system privilege for auditing. For a list of all system privileges and the SQL statements that they authorize, see Table C-5.
BY *user*	chooses only SQL statements issued by specified users for auditing. If you omit this clause, Oracle audits all users' statements.
BY SESSION	causes Oracle to write a single record for all SQL statements of the same type issued in the same session.
BY ACCESS	causes Oracle to write one record for each audited statement.

If you specify statement options or system privileges that audit Data Definition Language statements, Oracle automatically audits by access regardless of whether you specify the BY SESSION or BY ACCESS option.

For statement options and system privileges that audit other types of SQL statements, you can specify either the BY SESSION or BY ACCESS option. BY SESSION is the default.

WHENEVER SUCCESSFUL chooses auditing only for statements that succeed.

NOT	chooses auditing only for statements that fail, or result in errors.

If you omit the WHENEVER clause, Oracle audits SQL statements regardless of success or failure.

Auditing

Auditing keeps track of operations performed by database users. For each audited operation, Oracle produces an audit record containing this information:

- user performing the operation
- type of operation

- object involved in the operation
- date and time of the operation

Oracle writes audit records to the audit trail. The audit trail is a database table that contains audit records. You can review database activity by examining the audit trail through data dictionary views. For information on these views, see the *Oracle8 Server Reference*.

How to Audit
To generate audit records, you must perform the following steps:

- **Enable auditing:** You must enable auditing with the initialization parameter AUDIT_TRAIL.

- **Specify auditing options:** To specify auditing options, you must use the AUDIT command. Auditing options choose which SQL commands, operations, database objects, and users Oracle audits. After you specify auditing options, they appear in the data dictionary. For more information on data dictionary views containing auditing options see the *Oracle8 Server Reference*.

You can specify auditing options regardless of whether auditing is enabled. However, Oracle does not generate audit records until you enable auditing.

Auditing options specified by the AUDIT command (SQL Statements) apply only to subsequent sessions, rather than to current sessions.

Statement Options
Table C-1 lists the statement options and the statements that they audit.

Statement Option	SQL Statements and Operations
CLUSTER	CREATE CLUSTER
	AUDIT CLUSTER
	DROP CLUSTER
	TRUNCATE CLUSTER
DATABASE LINK	CREATE DATABASE LINK
	DROP DATABASE LINK
DIRECTORY	CREATE DIRECTORY
	DROP DIRECTORY
INDEX	CREATE INDEX
	ALTER INDEX
	DROP INDEX
NOT EXISTS	All SQL statements that fail because a specified object does not exist.
PROCEDURE	CREATE FUNCTION
	CREATE LIBRARY
	CREATE PACKAGE
	CREATE PACKAGE BODY
	CREATE PROCEDURE
	DROP FUNCTION
	DROP LIBRARY
	DROP PACKAGE
	DROP PROCEDURE
PROFILE	CREATE PROFILE
	ALTER PROFILE
	DROP PROFILE
PUBLIC DATABASE LINK	CREATE PUBLIC DATABASE LINK
	DROP PUBLIC DATABASE LINK
PUBLIC SYNONYM	CREATE PUBLIC SYNONYM
	DROP PUBLIC SYNONYM
ROLE	CREATE ROLE
	ALTER ROLE
	DROP ROLE
	SET ROLE

TABLE C-1.   *Statement Auditing Options*

Statement Option	SQL Statements and Operations
ROLLBACK STATEMENT	CREATE ROLLBACK SEGMENT
	ALTER ROLLBACK SEGMENT
	DROP ROLLBACK SEGMENT
SEQUENCE	CREATE SEQUENCE
	DROP SEQUENCE
SESSION	Logons
SYNONYM	CREATE SYNONYM
	DROP SYNONYM
SYSTEM AUDIT	AUDIT (SQL Statements)
	NOAUDIT (SQL Statements)
SYSTEM GRANT	GRANT (System Privileges and Roles)
	REVOKE (System Privileges and Roles)
TABLE	CREATE TABLE
	DROP TABLE
	TRUNCATE TABLE
TABLESPACE	CREATE TABLESPACE
	ALTER TABLESPACE
	DROP TABLESPACE
TRIGGER	CREATE TRIGGER
	ALTER TRIGGER (with ENABLE and DISABLE options)
	DROP TRIGGER
	ALTER TABLE (with ENABLE ALL TRIGGERS and DISABLE ALL TRIGGERS clauses)
TYPE	CREATE TYPE
	CREATE TYPE BODY
	ALTER TYPE
	DROP TYPE
	DROP TYPE BODY
USER	CREATE USER
	ALTER USER
	DROP USER
VIEW	CREATE VIEW
	DROP VIEW

TABLE C-I. *Statement Auditing Options* (continued)

Shortcuts for System Privileges and Statement Options

Oracle provides shortcuts for specifying system privileges and statement options. With these shortcuts, you can specify auditing for multiple system privileges and statement options at once:

CONNECT	This shortcut is equivalent to specifying the CREATE SESSION system privilege.
RESOURCE	This shortcut is equivalent to specifying the following system privileges: *ALTER SESSION *CREATE CLUSTER *CREATE DATABASE LINK *CREATE PROCEDURE *CREATE ROLLBACK SEGMENT *CREATE SEQUENCE *CREATE SYNONYM *CREATE TABLE *CREATE TABLESPACE *CREATE VIEW
DBA	This shortcut is equivalent to the SYSTEM GRANT statement option and the following system privileges: *AUDIT SYSTEM *CREATE PUBLIC DATABASE LINK *CREATE PUBLIC SYNONYM *CREATE ROLE *CREATE USER
ALL	This shortcut is equivalent to specifying all statement options shown in Table C-1, but not the additional statement options shown in Table C-2.
ALL PRIVILEGES	This shortcut is equivalent to specifying all system privileges.

Oracle Corporation encourages you to choose individual system privileges and statement options for auditing, rather than these shortcuts. These shortcuts may not be supported in future versions of Oracle.

Additional Statement Options

Table C-2 lists additional statement options and the SQL statements and operations that they audit. Note that these statement options are not included in the ALL shortcut.

Statement Option	SQL Statements and Operations
ALTER SEQUENCE	ALTER SEQUENCE
ALTER TABLE	ALTER TABLE
COMMENT TABLE	COMMENT ON TABLE table, view, snapshot COMMENT ON COLUMN table.column, view.column, snapshot.column
DELETE TABLE	DELETE FROM table, view
EXECUTE PROCEDURE	Execution of any procedure or function or access to any variable, library, or cursor inside a package
GRANT DIRECTORY	GRANT privilege ON directory REVOKE privilege ON directory
GRANT PROCEDURE	GRANT privilege ON procedure, function, package REVOKE privilege ON procedure, function, package
GRANT SEQUENCE	GRANT privilege ON sequence REVOKE privilege ON sequence
GRANT TABLE	GRANT privilege ON table, view, snapshot REVOKE privilege ON table, view, snapshot
GRANT TYPE	GRANT privilege ON TYPE REVOKE privilege ON TYPE
INSERT TABLE	INSERT INTO table, view
LOCK TABLE	LOCK TABLE table, view
SELECT SEQUENCE	Any statement containing sequence.CURRVAL or sequence.NEXTVAL
SELECT TABLE	SELECT FROM table, view, snapshot
UPDATE TABLE	UPDATE table, view

TABLE C-2. *Additional Statement Auditing Options*

AUDIT (Schema Objects)

Purpose

To choose a specific schema object for auditing. To choose particular SQL commands for auditing, use the AUDIT command (SQL Statements) described in the previous section of this chapter.

Prerequisites

The object you choose for auditing must be in your own schema or you must have AUDIT ANY system privilege.

Syntax

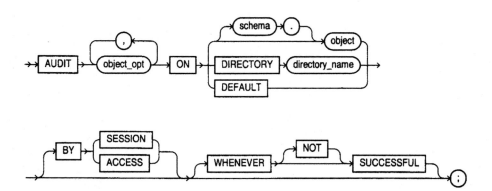

Keywords and Parameters

object_opt	specifies a particular operation for auditing. Table C-3 shows each object option and the types of objects for which it applies.
schema	is the schema containing the object chosen for auditing. If you omit schema, Oracle assumes the object is in your own schema.
object	identifies the object chosen for auditing. The object must be one of the following types: *table *view *sequence *stored procedure, function, or package *snapshot *library You can also specify a synonym for a table, view, sequence, procedure, stored function, package, or snapshot.

| DIRECTORY *directory_name* | identifies the name of the directory on which auditing is being stopped. |

If you omit both of the following options, Oracle audits by session.

BY SESSION	means that Oracle writes a single record for all operations of the same type on the same object issued in the same session.
BY ACCESS	means that Oracle writes one record for each audited operation.
WHENEVER SUCCESSFUL	chooses auditing only for SQL statements that complete successfully.
NOT	chooses auditing only for statements that fail, or result in errors. If you omit the WHENEVER clause entirely, Oracle audits all SQL statements, regardless of success or failure.

Auditing

Auditing keeps track of operations performed by database users. Note that auditing options established by the AUDIT command (Schema Objects) apply to current sessions as well as to subsequent sessions.

Object Options

Table C-3 shows the object options you can choose for each type of object.

The name of each object option specifies a command to be audited. For example, if you choose to audit a table with the ALTER option, Oracle audits all ALTER TABLE statements issued against the table. If you choose to audit a sequence with the SELECT option, Oracle audits all statements that use any of the sequence's values.

SHORTCUTS FOR OBJECT OPTIONS   Oracle provides a shortcut for specifying object auditing options:

| ALL | This shortcut is equivalent to specifying all object options applicable for the type of object. You can use this shortcut rather than explicitly specifying all options for an object. |

Object Option	Table	View	Sequence	Procedure Function Package	Snapshot	Library	Directory
ALTER	X		X		X		
AUDIT	X	X	X	X	X		X
COMMENT	X	X			X		
DELETE	X	X			X		
EXECUTE				X		X	
GRANT	X	X	X	X	X	X	X
INDEX	X				X		
INSERT	X	X			X		
LOCK	X	X			X		
READ							X
RENAME	X	X		X	X		
SELECT	X	X	X		X		
UPDATE	X	X			X		

TABLE C-3. *Object Auditing Options*

Default Auditing

You can use the DEFAULT option of the AUDIT command to specify auditing options for objects that have not yet been created. Once you have established these default auditing options, any subsequently created object is automatically audited with those options. Note that the default auditing options for a view are always the union of the auditing options for the view's base tables.

If you change the default auditing options, the auditing options for previously created objects remain the same. You can only change the auditing options for an existing object by specifying the object in the ON clause of the AUDIT command.

CREATE CONTROLFILE

Purpose

To recreate a control file in one of the following cases:

- All copies of your existing control files have been lost through media failure.

- You want to change the name of the database.

- You want to change the maximum number of redo log file groups, redo log file members, archived redo log files, data files, or instances that can concurrently have the database mounted and open.

WARNING
It is recommended that you perform a full backup of all files in the database before using this command.

Prerequisites

You must have the OSDBA role enabled. The database must not be mounted by any instance.

Syntax

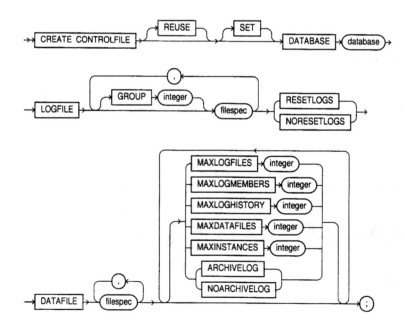

Keywords and Parameters

REUSE

specifies that existing control files identified by the initialization parameter CONTROL_FILES can be reused, thus ignoring and overwriting any information they may currently contain. If you omit this option and any of these control files already exist, Oracle returns an error.

SET DATABASE

changes the name of the database. The name of a database can be as long as eight bytes.

DATABASE

specifies the name of the database. The value of this parameter must be the existing database name established by the previous CREATE DATABASE statement or CREATE CONTROLFILE statement.

LOGFILE

specifies the redo log file groups for your database. You must list all members of all redo log file groups.

RESETLOGS

ignores the contents of the files listed in the LOGFILE clause. These files do not have to exist. Each filespec in the LOGFILE clause must specify the SIZE parameter. Oracle assigns all redo log file groups to thread 1 and enables this thread for public use by any instance. After using this option, you must open the database using the RESETLOGS option of the ALTER DATABASE command.

NORESETLOGS

specifies that all files in the LOGFILE clause should be used as they were when the database was last opened. These files must exit and must be the current redo log files rather than restored backups. Oracle reassigns the redo log file groups to the threads to which they were previously assigned and re-enables the threads as they were previously enabled. If you specify GROUP values, Oracle verifies these values with the GROUP values when the database was last opened.

DATAFILE

specifies the data files of the database. You must list all data files. These files must all exist, although they may be restored backups that require media recovery.

MAXLOGFILES

specifies the maximum number of redo log file groups that can ever be created for the database. Oracle uses this value to determine how much space in the control file to allocate for the names of redo log files. The default and maximum values depend on your operating system. The value that you specify should not be less than the greatest GROUP value for any redo log file group.

Note that the number of redo log file groups accessible to your instance is also limited by the initialization parameter LOG_FILES.

MAXLOGMEMBERS	specifies the maximum number of members, or copies, for a redo log file group. Oracle uses this value to determine how much space in the control file to allocate for the names of redo log file. The minimum value is 1. The maximum and default values depend on your operating system.
MAXLOGHISTORY	specifies the maximum number of archived redo log file groups for automatic media recovery of the Oracle8 Parallel Server. Oracle uses this value to determine how much space in the control file to allocate for the names of archived redo log files. The minimum value is 0. The default value is a multiple of the MAXINSTANCE value and varies depending on your operating system. The maximum value is limited only by the maximum size of the control file. Note that this parameter is only useful if you are using Oracle with the Parallel Server option in both parallel mode and archivelog mode.
MAXDATAFILES	specifies the initial sizing of the datafiles section of the controlfile at CREATE DATABASE or CREATE CONTROLFILE time. Attempting to add a file whose number will be greater than MAXDATAFILES, but less than or equal to DB_FILES, causes the Oracle controlfile to expand automatically so that the datafiles section accommodates more files. The minimum value is 1. The maximum and default values depend on your operating system. The value you specify should not be less than the total number of data files ever in the database, including those for tablespaces that have been dropped.
	Note that the number of data files accessible to your instance is also limited by the initialization parameter DB_FILES.
MAXINSTANCES	specifies the maximum number of instances that can simultaneously have the database mounted and open. This value takes precedence over the value of the initialization parameter INSTANCES. The minimum value is 1. The maximum and default values depend on your operating system.
ARCHIVELOG	establishes the mode of archiving the contents of redo log files before reusing them. This option prepares for the possibility of media recovery as well as instance recovery.
NOARCHIVELOG	If you omit both the ARCHIVELOG and NOARCHIVELOG options, Oracle chooses noarchivelog mode by default. After creating the control file, you can change between archivelog mode and noarchivelog mode with the ALTER DATABASE command.

Usage Notes

It is recommended that you take a full backup of all files in the database before issuing a CREATE CONTROLFILE statement.

When you issue a CREATE CONTROLFILE statement, Oracle creates a new control file based on the information you specify in the statement. If you omit any of the options from the statement, Oracle uses the default options, rather than the options for the previous control file. After successfully creating the control file, Oracle mounts the database in the mode specified by the initialization parameter, PARALLEL_SERVER. You then must perform media recovery before opening the database. It is recommended that you then shut down the instance and take a full backup of all files in the database.

For more information about using this command, see the *Oracle8 Server Administrator's Guide.*

CREATE DATABASE

Purpose

To create a database, making it available for general use, with the following options:

- to establish a maximum number of instances, data files, redo log files groups, or redo log file members

- to specify names and sizes of data files and redo log files

- to choose a mode of use for the redo log

- to specify the national and database character sets

WARNING
This command prepares a database for initial use and erases any data currently in the specified files. Only use this command when you understand its ramifications.

Prerequisites

You must have the OSDBA role enabled.

Syntax

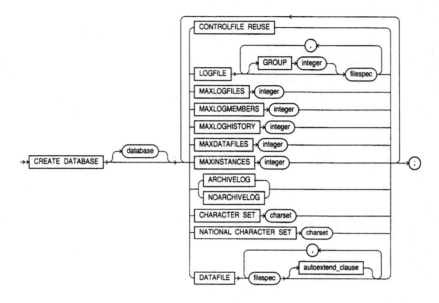

autoextend_clause ::=

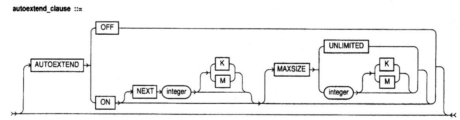

Keywords and Parameters

database

is the name of the database to be created and can be up to eight bytes long. Oracle writes this name into the control file. If you subsequently issue an ALTER DATABASE statement and that explicitly specifies a database name, Oracle verifies that name with the name in the control file.

NOTE
You cannot use special characters from European or Asian character sets in a database name. For example, the umlaut is not allowed.

	If you omit the database name from a CREATE DATABASE statement, the name specified by the initialization parameter DB_NAME is used.
CONTROLFILE REUSE	reuses existing control files identified by the initialization parameter CONTROL_FILES, thus ignoring and overwriting any information they currently contain. This option is usually used only when you are recreating a database, rather than creating one for the first time. You cannot use this option if you also specify a parameter value that requires that the control file be larger than the existing files. These parameters are MAXLOGFILES, MAXLOGMEMBERS, MAXLOGHISTORY, MAXDATAFILES, and MAXINSTANCES.
	If you omit this option and any of the files specified by CONTROL_FILES already exist, Oracle returns an error message.
LOGFILE	specifies one or more files to be used as redo log files. Each filespec specifies a redo log file group containing one or more redo log file members, or copies. All redo log files specified in a CREATE DATABASE statement are added to redo log thread number 1.
	You can also choose the value of the GROUP parameter for the redo log file group. Each value uniquely identifies a redo log file group and can range from 1 to the value of the MAXLOGFILES parameter. You cannot specify multiple redo log file groups having the same GROUP value. If you omit this parameter, Oracle generates its value automatically. You can examine the GROUP value for a redo log file group through the dynamic performance table V$LOG.
	If you omit the LOGFILE clause, Oracle creates two redo log file groups by default. The names and sizes of the default files vary depending on your operating system.
MAXLOGFILES	specifies the maximum number of redo log file groups that can ever be created for the database. Oracle uses this value to determine how much space in the control file to allocate for the names of redo log files. The default, minimum, and maximum values vary depending on your operating system.
	The number of redo log file groups accessible to your instance is also limited by the initialization parameter LOG_FILES.

MAXLOGMEMBERS   specifies the maximum number of members, or copies, for a
                     redo log file group. Oracle uses this value to determine how
                     much space in the control file to allocate for the names of
                     redo log files. The minimum value is 1. The maximum and
                     default values vary depending on your operating system.

MAXLOGHISTORY   specifies the maximum number of archived redo log files for
                     automatic media recovery of Oracle with the Parallel Server
                     option. Oracle uses this value to determine how much space
                     in the control file to allocate for the names of archived redo
                     log files. The minimum value is 0. The default value is a
                     multiple of the MAXINSTANCES value and varies depending
                     on your operating system. The maximum value is limited only
                     by the maximum size of the control file. Note that this
                     parameter is only useful if you are using Oracle with the
                     Parallel Server option in parallel mode, and archivelog
                     mode enabled.

MAXDATAFILES   specifies the initial sizing of the datafiles section of the
                     controlfile at CREATE DATABASE or CREATE CONTROLFILE
                     time. Attempts to add a file whose number will be greater than
                     MAXDATAFILES, but less than or equal to DB_FILES, cause
                     the Oracle8 controlfile to expand automatically so that the
                     datafiles section accomodates more files.

MAXINSTANCES   specifies the maximum number of instances that can
                     simultaneously have this database mounted and open.
                     This value takes precedence over the value of intialization
                     parameter INSTANCES. The minimum value is 1.
                     The maximum and default values depend on your
                     operating system.

ARCHIVELOG   establishes archivelog mode for redo log file groups. In this
                     mode, the contents of a redo log file group must be archived
                     before the group can be reused. This option prepares for the
                     possibility of media recovery.

NOARCHIVELOG   establishes noarchivelog mode for redo log files groups. In this
                     mode, the contents of a redo log file group need not be
                     archived before the group can be reused. This option does not
                     prepare for the possibility of media recovery.
                        The default is noarchivelog mode. After creating the
                     database, you can change between archivelog mode and
                     noarchivelog mode with the ALTER DATABASE command.

CHARACTER SET	specifies the character set the database uses to store data. You cannot change the database character set after creating the database. The supported character sets and default value of this parameter depends on your operating system. You can specify any supported character set except the following fixed-width, multi-byte character sets, which can only be used as the national character set: *JA16SJISFIXED *JA16EUCFIXED *JA16DBCSFIXED For more information about valid character sets, see the chapter "National Language Support" in the *Oracle8 Server Reference Manual.*
NATIONAL CHARACTER SET	specifies the national character set used to store data in columns specifically defined as NCHAR, NCLOB, or NVARCHAR2. You cannot change the national character set after creating the database. If not specified, the national character set defaults to the database character set. See the *Oracle Server Reference Manual* for valid character set names.
DATAFILE	specifies one or more files to be used as data files. These files all become part of the SYSTEM tablespace. If you omit this clause, Oracle creates one data file by default. The name and size of this default file depends on your operating system.
AUTOEXTEND	enables or disables the automatic extension of a datafile.

OFF	disables autoextend if it is turned on. NEXT and MAXSIZE are set to zero. Values for NEXT and MAXSIZE must be respecified in ALTER DATABASE AUTOEXTEND or ALTER TABLESPACE AUTOEXTEND commands.
ON	enables autoextend.
NEXT	the size in bytes of the next increment of disk space to be automatically allocated to the datafile when more extents are required. You can also use K or M to specify this size in kilobytes or megabytes. The default is one data block.
MAXSIZE	maximum disk space allowed for automatic extension of the datafile.
UNLIMITED	sets no limit on allocating disk space to the datafile.

Usage Notes

This command erases all data in any specified data files that already exist to prepare them for initial database use. If you use the command on an existing database, all data in the data files is lost.

After creating the database, this command mounts it in the mode specified by the initialization parameter, PARALLEL_SERVER, and opens it, making it available for normal use.

CREATE DATABASE LINK

Purpose

To create a database link. A *database link* is a schema object in the local database that allows you to access objects on a remote database. The remote database can be either an Oracle or a non-Oracle system.

Prerequisites

To create a private database link, you must have CREATE DATABASE LINK system privilege. To create a public database link, you must have CREATE PUBLIC DATABASE LINK system privilege. Also, you must have CREATE SESSION privilege on the remote Oracle database. Net8 must be installed on both the local and remote Oracle databases. To access non-Oracle systems you must use the Oracle8 Heterogeneous Services.

Syntax

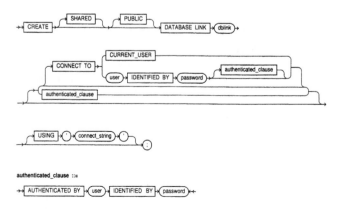

Keywords and Parameters

SHARED   uses a single network connection to create a public database link that can be shared between multiple users. This option is only available with the multi-threaded server configuration. For more information about shared database links, see *Oracle8 Server Distributed Database Systems*.

PUBLIC   creates a public database link available to all users. If you omit this option, the database link is private and is available only to you.

dblink   is the complete or partial name of the database link.

CONNECT TO   enables a connection to the remote database.

         CURRENT_USER   creates a current user database link. To use a current database link, the current user must be a global user authenticated by the Oracle Security Server.

         user IDENTIFIED BY *password*   is the username and password used to connect to the remote database (fixed user database link). If you omit this clause, the database link uses the username and password of each user who is connected to the database (connected user database link).

AUTHENTICATED BY *user* IDENTIFIED BY *password*   specifies the username and password on the target instance. This clause authenticates the user to the remote server and is required for security. The specified username and password must be a valid username and password on the remote instance. The username and password are only used for authentication; no other operations are performed on behalf of this user.
You must specify this clause when using the SHARED option.

USING '*connect string*'   specifies the service name of a remote database.
For information on specifying remote databases, see the *Net8 Administrator's Guide*.

Usage Notes

You cannot create a database link in another user's schema and you cannot qualify *dblink* with the name of a schema. Since periods are permitted in names of database links, Oracle interprets the entire name, such as RALPH.LINKTOSALES, as the name of a database link in your schema rather than as a database link named LINKTOSALES in the schema RALPH.

Once you have created a database link, you can use it to refer to tables and views on the remote database. You can refer to a remote table or view in a SQL statement by appending *@dblink* to the table or view name. You can query a remote table or view with the SELECT command. If you are using Oracle with the distributed option, you can also access remote tables and views in any of the following commands:

- DELETE command
- INSERT command
- LOCK TABLE command
- UPDATE command

See the *PL/SQL User's Guide and Reference* for information about accessing remote tables or views with PL/SQL functions, procedures, packages, and datatypes.

The number of different database links that can appear in a single statement is limited to the value of the initialization parameter OPEN_LINKS.

Current User Database Links

A privileged database link is one that contains no user credentials and that enables a connection to a remote database as the current user. To use the link, the current user must be a global user with global accounts on both the local and remote databases. Both databases must be members of the same security domain.

CURRENT USER   When executing a stored object (such as a procedure, view, or trigger) that initiates a database link, CURRENT_USER is the username that created the stored object, and not the username that called the object. For example if the database link appears inside procedure SCOTT.P (created by SCOTT), and user JANE calls procedure SCOTT.P, the current user is SCOTT.

If the database link is used directly, that is, NOT from within a stored object, then the current user is the same as the connected user.

CREATE INDEX

Purpose

To create an index on

- one or more columns of a table, a partitioned table, or a cluster.

- one or more scalar typed object attributes of a table or a cluster.

- a nested table storage table for indexing a nested table column.

An *index* is a schema object that contains an entry for each value that appears in the indexed column(s) of the table or cluster and provides direct, fast access to rows. A *partitioned index* consists of partitions containing an entry for each value that appears in the indexed column(s) of the table.

Prerequisites

To create an index in your own schema, one of the following conditions must be true:

- The table or cluster to be indexed must be in your own schema.

- You must have INDEX privilege on the table to be indexed.

- You must have CREATE ANY INDEX system privilege.

To create an index in another schema, you must have CREATE ANY INDEX system privilege.

Also, the owner of the schema to contain the index must have either space quota on the tablespaces to contain the index or index partitions, or UNLIMITED TABLESPACE system privilege.

Syntax

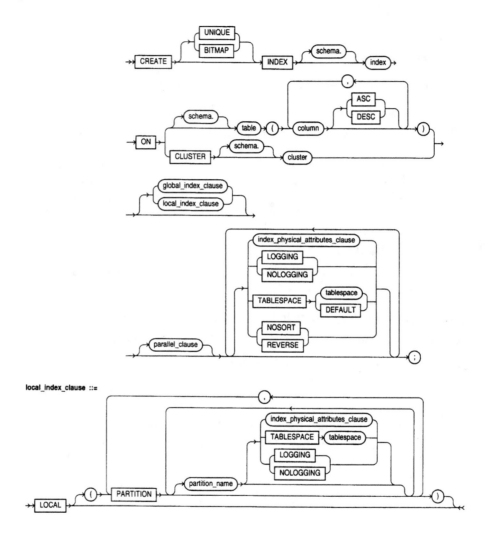

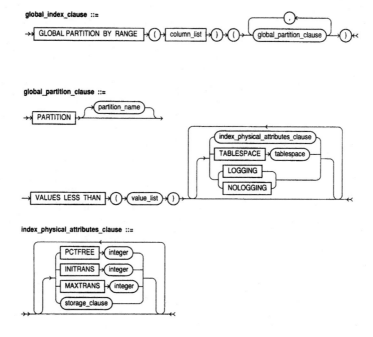

global_index_clause ::=

global_partition_clause ::=

index_physical_attributes_clause ::=

Keywords and Parameters

UNIQUE
: specifies that the value of the column (or combination of columns) in the table to be indexed must be unique.
If the index is local non-prefixed (see LOCAL clause below), then the index key must contain the partitioning key.

BITMAP
: specifies that *index* is to be created as a bitmap, rather than as a B-tree. You cannot use this keyword when creating a global partitioned index.

schema
: is the schema to contain the index. If you omit schema, Oracle creates the index in your own schema.

index
: is the name of the index to be created. An *index* can contain several partitions.
You cannot range partition a cluster index or an index defined on a clustered table.

table
: is the name of the table for which the index is to be created. If you do not qualify table with schema, Oracle assumes the table is contained in your own schema.
If the index is LOCAL, then *table* must be partitioned.
You cannot create an index on an index-organized table.
You can create an index on a nested table storage table.

column	is the name of a column in the table. An index can have as many as 32 columns. A column of an index cannot be of datatype LONG or LONG RAW.
	You can create an index on a scalar object attribute column or on the system-defined NESTED_TABLE_ID column of the nested table storage table. If an object attribute column is specified, the column name must be qualified with the table name. If a nested table column attribute is specified, then it must be qualified with the outermost table name, the containing column name, and all intermediate attribute names leading to the nested table column attribute.
ASC DESC	are allowed for DB2 syntax compatibility, although indexes are always created in ascending order. Indexes on character data are created in ascending order of the character values in the database character set.
CLUSTER	specifies the cluster for which a cluster index is to be created. If you do not qualify cluster with schema, Oracle assumes the cluster is contained in your current schema. You cannot create a cluster index for a hash cluster.
INITRANS MAXTRANS	establishes values for these parameters for the index.
TABLESPACE	is the name of the tablespace to hold the index or index partition. If you omit this option, Oracle creates the index in the default tablespace of the owner of the schema containing the index. For a partitioned index, this is the tablespace name. For a LOCAL index, you can specify the keyword DEFAULT in place of a tablespace name. New partitions added to the LOCAL index will be created in the same tablespace(s) as the corresponding partition(s) of the underlying table.
STORAGE	establishes the storage characteristics for the index.
PCTFREE	is the percentage of space to leave free for updates and insertions within each of the index's data blocks.
NOSORT	indicates to Oracle that the rows are stored in the database in ascending order and therefore Oracle does not have to sort the rows when creating the index. You cannot specify REVERSE with this option.
REVERSE	stores the bytes of the index block in reverse order, excluding the ROWID. You cannot specify NOSORT with this option. You cannot reverse a bitmap index.

LOGGING   specifies that the creation of the index will be logged (LOGGING) or
NOLOGGING   not logged (NOLOGGING) in the redo log file. It also specifies that
             subsequent Direct Loader (SQL*Loader) and Direct-Load INSERT
             operations against the index are logged or not logged. LOGGING is
             the default.

                If *index* is non-partitioned, this is the logging attribute of the index.
             For partitioned index, the logging attribute specified is the default
             physical attribute of the segments associated with the index partitions.
             The default logging value applies to all partitions specified in the
             CREATE statement (and on subsequent ALTER TABLE ADD PARTITION
             statements) unless you specify LOGGING/NOLOGGING in the
             PARTITION description clause.

                In NOLOGGING mode, data is modified without redo logging.
             Some minimal logging is still done for marking new extents invalid, and
             dictionary changes are always fully logged. When applied during media
             recovery, the extent invalidation records mark a range of blocks as
             logically corrupt, since the redo data is not logged. Thus if you cannot
             afford to lose this index, it is important to take a backup after the
             NOLOGGING operation.

                If the database is run in ARCHIVELOG mode, media recovery from a
             backup taken before the LOGGING operation will recreate the index.
             However, media recovery from a backup taken before the
             NOLOGGING operation will not recreate the index.
             The logging attribute of the index is independent to that of its base table.
             If the [NO]LOGGING clause is omitted, the logging attribute of
             the index defaults to the logging attribute of the tablespace in which
             it resides.

                For more information about the LOGGING option and Parallel DML,
             see *Oracle8 Server Concepts and the Oracle8 Parallel Server and
             Administration Guide.*

GLOBAL   specifies that the partitioning of the index is user-defined and is not
             equi-partitioned with the underlying table. By default, non-partitioned
             indexes are global indexes.

PARTITION   specifies that the global index is partitioned on the ranges of values
BY RANGE   from the columns specified in *column_list*. You cannot specify this
             clause for a LOCAL index.

(*column_list*)   is the name of the column(s) of a table on which the index is
             partitioned. *The column_list* must specify a left prefix of the index
             column list.

                You cannot specify more than 32 columns in *column_list* and the
             columns cannot contain the ROWID pseudocolumn or a column of
             type ROWID.

LOCAL   specifies that the index is range partitioned on the same columns, with
             the same number of partitions, and the same partition bounds as *table*.
             Oracle automatically maintains LOCAL index partitioning as the
             underlying table is repartitioned.

PARTITION *partition_name*	describes the individual partitions. The number of clauses determines the number of partitions. If the index is local, the number of index partitions must be equal to the number, and will correspond to the order of the table partitions. The *partition_name* is the name of the physical index partition. If *partition_name* is omitted Oracle generates a name with the form SYS_P*n*. For LOCAL indexes, if *partition_name* is omitted Oracle generates a name that is consistent with the corresponding table partition. If the name conflicts with an existing index partition name, the form SYS_P*n* is used.
VALUES LESS THAN (*value_list*)	specifies the (non-inclusive) upper bound for the current partition in a global index. *The value_list* is a comma-separated, ordered list of literal values corresponding to *column_list* in the PARTITION BY RANGE clause. Always specify MAXVALUE as the *value_list* of the last partition. You cannot specify this clause for a local index.
PARALLEL	specifies the degree of parallelism for creating the index.

Usage Notes

An index is an ordered list of all the values that reside in a group of one or more columns at a given time. Such a list makes queries that test the values in those columns vastly more efficient. Indexes also take up data storage space, however, and must be changed whenever the data is, so a cost-benefit analysis must be made in each case to determine whether and how indexes should be used. Oracle can use indexes to improve performance when:

- searching for rows with specified index column values
- accessing tables in index column order

When you initially insert rows into a new table, it is generally faster to create the table, insert the rows, and then create the index. If you create the index before inserting the rows, Oracle must update the index for every row inserted.

Oracle recommends that you do not explicitly define UNIQUE indexes on tables; uniqueness is strictly a logical concept and should be associated with the definition of a table. Alternatively, define UNIQUE integrity constraints on the desired columns. Oracle enforces UNIQUE integrity constraints by automatically defining a unique index on the unique key. Exceptions to this recommendation are usually performance related. For example, using a CREATE TABLE ... AS SELECT with a UNIQUE constraint is very much slower than creating the table without the constraint and then manually creating the UNIQUE index.

If indexes contain NULLs, the NULLs generally are considered distinct values. There is, however, one exception: if all the non-NULL values in two or more rows of an index are identical, the rows are considered identical; therefore, UNIQUE indexes prevent this from occurring. This does not apply if there are no non-NULL values—in other words, if the rows are entirely NULL.

Index Columns

An index can contain a maximum of 32 columns. The index entry becomes the concatenation of all data values from each column. You can specify the columns in any order. The order you choose is important to how Oracle uses the index.

When appropriate, Oracle uses the entire index or a leading portion of the index. Assume an index named IDX1 is created on columns A, B, and C of table TAB1 (in the order A, B, C). Oracle uses the index for references to columns A, B, C (the entire index); A, B; or just column A. References to columns B and C do not use the IDX1 index. Of course, you can also create another index just for columns B and C.

Multiple Indexes Per Table

Unlimited indexes can be created for a table provided that the combination of columns differs for each index. You can create more than one index using the same columns provided that you specify distinctly different combinations of the columns. For example, the following statements specify valid combinations:

```
CREATE INDEX emp_idx1 ON emp (ename, job);
CREATE INDEX emp_idx2 ON emp (job, ename);
```

You cannot create an index that references only one column in a table if another such index already exists.

Note that each index increases the processing time needed to maintain the table during updates to indexed data. There is overhead in maintaining indexes when a table is updated. Thus, updating a table with a single index will take less time than if the table had five indexes.

The NOSORT Option

The NOSORT option can substantially reduce the time required to create an index. Normal index creation first sorts the rows of the table based on the index columns and then builds the index. The sort operation is often a substantial portion of the total work involved. If the rows are physically stored in ascending order (based on the indexed column values), then the NOSORT option causes Oracle to bypass the sort phase of the process.

You cannot use the NOSORT option to create a cluster index, partitioned index, or a bitmap index.

The NOSORT option also reduces the amount of space required to build the index. Oracle uses temporary segments during the sort. Since a sort is not performed, the index is created with much less temporary space.

To use the NOSORT option, you must guarantee that the rows are physically sorted in ascending order. Because of the physical data independence inherent in relational database management systems, especially Oracle, there is no way to force a physical internal order on a table. The CREATE INDEX command with the NOSORT option should be used immediately after the initial load of rows into a table.

You run no risk by trying the NOSORT option. If your rows are not in the ascending order, Oracle returns an error. You can issue another CREATE INDEX without the NOSORT option.

NOLOGGING

The NOLOGGING option may substantially reduce the time required to create a large index. This feature is particularly useful after creating a large index in parallel. For backup and recovery considerations, see *Oracle8 Server Backup and Recovery Guide* and *Oracle8 Server Administrator's Guide*.

Nulls

Table rows in which all key columns are NULL are not indexed.

Creating Cluster Indexes

Oracle does not automatically create an index for a cluster when the cluster is initially created. Data Manipulation Language statements cannot be issued against clustered tables until a cluster index has been created.

Note that no index columns are specified since the index is automatically built on all the columns of the cluster key. For cluster indexes, all rows are indexed.

Creating Partitioned Indexes

Indexes can be local prefixed (unique or non-unique), local non-prefixed (unique, but only when the partitioning key is a subset of the index key or non-unique), or global prefixed (unique or non-unique). Global non-prefixed indexes are not supported. Local indexes are always partitioned. Global indexes can be non-partitioned or partitioned.

Index partitions must be listed in order. For a global index, this means that the partition bound of the first partition listed must be *less than* the partition bound of the second partition listed, and the partition bound of the second partition listed must be *less than* the third, and so on. For a local index, you must list the partitions in the same order as the partitions of the underlying table to which they correspond.

Creating Bitmap Indexes

Bitmap indexes store the rowids associated with a key value as a bitmap. Each bit in the bitmap corresponds to a possible ROWID, and if the bit is set, it means that the row with the corresponding ROWID contains the key value. The internal representation of bitmaps is best suited for applications with low levels of concurrent transactions, such as data warehousing. See the *Oracle8 Server Concepts* and *Oracle8 Server Tuning* for more information about using bitmap indexes.

You cannot create bitmap indexes, unique bitmap indexes, or global partitioned indexes.

Creating Indexes on Nested Table Columns

Creating a table with nested table columns implicitly creates a storage table for each nested table column. The storage table stores the rows of the nested table values and the nested table identifier values assigned to each row. These identifier values are contained in a storage table pseuocolumn called NESTED_TABLE_ID.

You create an index on a nested table column by creating the index on the nested table storage table. You can include the NESTED_TABLE_ID psuedocolumn to create a UNIQUE index which effectively ensures that the rows of a nested table value are distinct.

CREATE PROFILE

Purpose

To create a profile. A *profile* is a set of limits on database resources. If you assign the profile to a user, that user cannot exceed these limits.

Prerequisites

You must have CREATE PROFILE system privilege.

Syntax

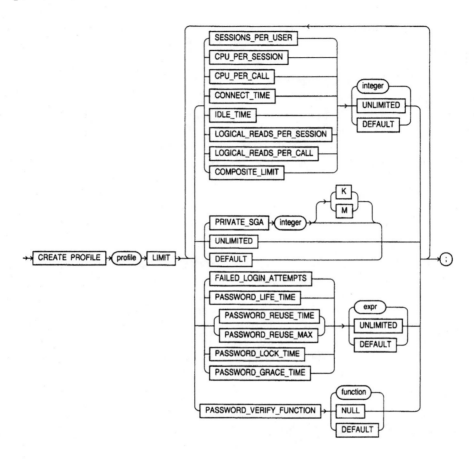

Keywords and Parameters

profile	is the name of the profile to be created.
SESSIONS_PER_USER	limits a user *integer* concurrent sessions.
CPU_PER_SESSION	limits the CPU time for a session. This value is expressed in hundredth of seconds CPU_PER_CALL limits the CPU time for a call (a parse, execute, or fetch). This value is expressed in hundredths of seconds.

CONNECT_TIME	limits the total elapsed time of a session. This value is expressed in minutes.
IDLE_TIME	limits periods of continuous inactive time during a session. This value is expressed in minutes. Long-running queries and other operations are not subject to this limit.
LOGICAL_READS_PER_SESSION	limits the number of data blocks read in a session including blocks read from memory and disk, to integer blocks.
LOGICAL_READS_PER_CALL	limits the number of data blocks read for a call to process a SQL statement (a parse, execute, or fetch) to *integer* blocks.
PRIVATE_SGA	limits the amount of private space a session can allocate in the shared pool of the System Global Area (SGA) to integer bytes. You can also use the K or M to specify this limit in kilobytes or megabytes. This limit only applies if you are using the multi-threaded server architecture. The private space for a session in the SGA includes private SQL and PL/SQL areas, but not shared SQL and PL/SQL areas.
FAILED_LOGIN_ATTEMPTS	specifies the number of failed attempts to log in to the user account before the account is locked.
PASSWORD_LIFE_TIME	limits the number of days the same password can be used for authentication. The password expires if it is not changed within this period, and further connections are rejected.
PASSWORD_REUSE_TIME	specifies the number of days before which a password cannot be reused. If you set PASSWORD_REUSE_TIME to an integer value, then you must set PASSWORD_REUSE_MAX to UNLIMITED.
PASSWORD_REUSE_MAX	specifies the number of password changes required before the current password can be reused. If you set PASSWORD_REUSE_MAX to an integer value, then you must set PASSWORD_REUSE_TIME to UNLIMITED.
PASSWORD_LOCK_TIME	specifies the number of days an account will be locked after the specified number of consecutive failed login attempts.
PASSWORD_GRACE_TIME	specifies the number of days after the grace period begins during which a warning is issued and login is allowed. If the password is not changed during the grace period, the password expires.

PASSWORD_VERIFY_FUNCTION allows a PL/SQL password complexity verification script to be passed as an argument to the CREATE PROFILE command. Oracle provides a default script, but you can create your own routine or use third party software instead.

function	is the name of the password complexity verification routine.
NULL	indicates that no password verification is performed.
DEFAULT	omits a limit for this resource in this profile. A user assigned this profile is subject to the limit on the resource specified in the default profile.

COMPOSITE_LIMIT	limits the total resources cost for a session. You must express the value of this parameter in service units. Oracle calculates the total resource cost as a weighted sum of the following resources: *CPU_PER_SESSION *CONNECT_TIME *LOGICAL_READS_PER_SESSION *PRIVATE_SGA
UNLIMITED	indicates that a user assigned this profile can use an unlimited amount of this resource.
DEFAULT	omits a limit for this resource in this profile. A user assigned this profile is subject to the limit for this resource specified in the DEFAULT profile.

Usage Notes

You can use fractions of days for all parameters with days as units. Fractions are expressed as x/y. For example, 1 hour is 1/24 and 1 minute is 1/1440.

For a detailed description and explanation of how to use password management and protection, see the *Oracle8 Server Administrator's Guide*.

Using Profiles

A *profile* is a set of limits on database resources. You can use profiles to limit the database resources available to a user for a single call or a single session. Oracle enforces resource limits in the following ways:

- If a user exceeds the CONNECT_TIME or IDLE_TIME session resource limit, Oracle rolls back the current transaction and ends the session. When the user process next issues a call to Oracle, an error message is returned.

- If a user attempts to perform an operation that exceeds the limit for other session resources, Oracle aborts the operation, rolls back the current statement, and immediately returns an error. The user can then commit or roll back the current transaction. The user must then end the session.

- If a user attempts to perform an operation that exceeds the limit for a single call, Oracle aborts the operation, rolls back the current statement, and returns an error message, leaving the current transaction intact.

How to Limit Resources

To specify resource limits for a user, you must perform both of the following operations:

Enable resource limits: You can enable resource limits through one of the following ways:

- You can enable resources limits with the initialization parameter RESOURCE_LIMIT. Note that this parameter does not apply to password resources. Password resources are always enabled.

- You can enable resource limits dynamically with the ALTER SYSTEM command.

Specify resource limits: To specify a resource limit for a user, you must perform the following steps:

1. Create a profile that defines the limits using the CREATE PROFILE command.

2. Assign the profile to the user using the CREATE USER or ALTER USER command.

Note that you can specify resource limits for users regardless of whether resource limits are enabled. However, Oracle does not enforce these limits until you enable them.

The DEFAULT Profile

Oracle automatically creates a default profile named DEFAULT. This profile initially defines unlimited resources. You can change the limits defined in this profile with the ALTER PROFILE command.

Any user who is not explicitly assigned a profile is subject to the limits defined in the DEFAULT profile. Also, if the profile that is explicitly assigned to a user omits limits for some resources or specifies DEFAULT for some limits, the user is subject to the limits on those resources defined by the DEFAULT profile.

CREATE ROLE

Purpose

To create a role. A *role* is a set of privileges that can be granted to users or to other roles.

Prerequisites

You must have CREATE ROLE system privilege.

Syntax

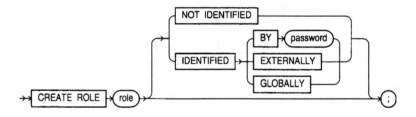

Keywords and Parameters

role	is the name of the role to be created. It is recommended that the role contain at least one single-byte character regardless of whether the database character set also contains multi-byte characters.
NOT IDENTIFIED	indicates that this role is authorized by the database and that no password is required to enable the role.
IDENTIFIED	indicates that a user must be authorized by the specified method before the role is enabled with the SET ROLE command.

BY *password*	The user must specify the password to Oracle when enabling the role. The password can only contain single-byte characters from your database character set regardless of whether this character set also contains multi-byte characters.
EXTERNALLY	indicates that a user must be authorized by an external service (such as the operating system or a third party service) before enabling the role. Depending on the operating system, the user may have to specify a password to the operating system before the role is enabled. For more information about third party service, see *The Oracle Security Server Guide*.
GLOBALLY	indicates that a user must be authorized to use the role by the Oracle Security Service before the role is enabled with the SET ROLE command, or at login.

If you omit both the NOT IDENTIFIED option and the IDENTIFIED clause, the role defaults to NOT IDENTIFIED.

Usage Notes

For a detailed description and explanation of using global roles, see *Oracle8 Server Distributed Systems*.

Using Roles

A *role* is a set of privileges that can be granted to users or to other roles. You can use roles to administer database privileges. You can add privileges to a role and then grant the role to a user. The user can then enable the role and exercise the privileges granted by the role.

A role contains all privileges granted to the role and all privileges of other roles granted to it. A new role is initially empty. You add privileges to a role with the GRANT command.

When you create a role, Oracle grants you the role with ADMIN OPTION. The ADMIN OPTION allows you to perform the following operations:

- grant the role to another user or role, unless the role is a GLOBAL role
- revoke the role from another user or role
- alter the role to change the authorization needed to access it
- drop the role

NOTE
When you create a role IDENTIFIED GLOBALLY, Oracle does not grant you the role as it does with non-global roles.

Roles Predefined by Oracle

Some roles are defined by SQL scripts provided on your distribution media. The following roles are predefined:

- CONNECT
- RESOURCE
- DBA
- EXP_FULL_DATABASE
- IMP_FULL_DATABASE
- DELETE_CATALOG_ROLE
- EXECUTE_CATALOG_ROLE
- SELECT_CATALOG_ROLE

The SELECT_CATALOG_ROLE, EXECUTE_CATALOG_ROLE, and DELETE_CATALOG_ROLE roles are provided for accessing exported data dictionary views and packages. For more information on these roles, see the *Oracle8 Server Administrator's Guide.*

The CONNECT, RESOURCE, and DBA roles are provided for compatibility with previous versions of Oracle. You should not rely on these roles; rather, it is recommended that you to design your own roles for database security. These roles may not be created automatically by future versions of Oracle.

The EXP_FULL_DATABASE and IMP_FULL_DATABASE roles are provided for convenience in using the Import and Export utilities.

Oracle also creates other roles that authorize you to administer the database. On many operating systems, these roles are called OSOPER and OSDBA. Their names may be different on your operating system.

CREATE ROLLBACK SEGMENT

Purpose

To create a rollback segment. A *rollback segment* is an object that Oracle uses to store data necessary to reverse, or undo, changes made by transactions.

Prerequisites

You must have CREATE ROLLBACK SEGMENT system privilege. Also, you must have either space quota on the tablespace to contain the rollback segment or UNLIMITED TABLESPACE system privilege.

Syntax

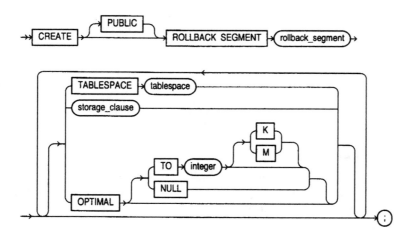

Keywords and Parameters

PUBLIC specifies that the rollback segment is public and is available to any instance. If you omit this option, the rollback segment is private and is only available to the instance naming it in its initialization parameter ROLLBACK_SEGMENTS.

rollback_segment is the name of the rollback segment to be created.

TABLESPACE	identifies the tablespace in which the rollback segment is created. If you omit this option, Oracle creates the rollback segment in the SYSTEM tablespace.
STORAGE	specifies the characteristics for the rollback segment.
OPTIMAL	specifies an optimal size in bytes for a rollback segment. You can also use K or M to specify this size in kilobytes or megabytes. Oracle tries to maintain this size for the rollback segment by dynamically deallocating extents when their data is no longer needed for active transactions. Oracle deallocates as many extents as possible without reducing the total size of the rollback segment below the OPTIMAL value.

NULL	specifies no optimal size for the rollback segment, meaning that Oracle never deallocates the rollback segment's extents. This is the default behavior.
	The value of this parameter cannot be less than the space initially allocated for the rollback segment specified by the MINEXTENTS, INITIAL, NEXT, and PCTINCREASE parameters. The maximum value varies depending on your operating system. Oracle rounds values to the next multiple of the data block size.

Usage Notes

The tablespace must be online for you to add a rollback segment to it.

When you create a rollback segment, it is initially offline. To make it available for transactions by your Oracle instance, you must bring it online using one of the following:

- ALTER ROLLBACK SEGMENT command
- ROLLBACK_SEGMENTS initialization parameter

For more information on creating rollback segments and making them available, see the "Managing Rollback Segments" chapter of the *Oracle8 Server Administrator's Guide*.

A tablespace can have multiple rollback segments. Generally, multiple rollback segments improve performance.

CREATE SYNONYM

Purpose

To create a synonym. A *synonym* is an alternative name for a table, view, sequence, procedure, stored function, package, snapshot, or another synonym.

Prerequisites

To create a private synonym in your own schema, you must have CREATE SYNONYM system privilege.

To create a private synonym in another user's schema, you must have CREATE ANY SYNONYM system privilege.

To create a PUBLIC synonym, you must have CREATE PUBLIC SYNONYM system privilege.

Syntax

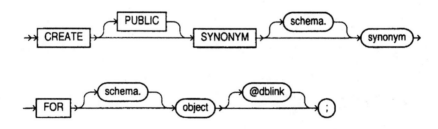

Keywords and Parameters

PUBLIC	creates a public synonym. Public synonyms are accessible to all users. If you omit this option, the synonym is private and is accessible only within its schema.
schema	is the schema to contain the synonym. If you omit schema, Oracle creates the synonym in your own schema. You cannot specify schema if you have specified PUBLIC.
synonym	is the name of the synonym to be created.

FOR   identifies the object for which the synonym is created. If you do not
qualify object with schema, Oracle assumes that the schema object is
in your own schema. The schema object can be of the following types:
*table
*object table
*view
*object view
*sequence
*stored procedure, function, or package
*snapshot
*synonym
You can create a synonym for an object table or an object view, but
not for object types.
The schema object cannot be contained in a package.
Note that the schema object need not currently exist and you need not
have privileges to access the object.
You can use a complete or partial *dblink* to create a synonym for a
schema object on a remote database where the object is located. If
you specify *dblink* and omit *schema*, the synonym refers to an object
in the schema specified by the database link. It is recommended that
you specify the schema containing the object in the remote database.
If you omit *dblink*, Oracle assumes the object is located on the
local database.

Usage Notes

A synonym can be used to stand for its base object in any of the following Data
Manipulation Language statements:

- SELECT

- INSERT

- UPDATE

- DELETE

- EXPLAIN PLAN

- LOCK TABLE

Synonyms can also be used in the following Data Definition Language
statements:

- AUDIT
- NOAUDIT
- GRANT
- REVOKE
- COMMENT

Synonyms are used for security and convenience. Creating a synonym for an object allows you to:

- reference the object without specifying its owner
- reference the object without specifying the database on which it is located
- provide another name for the object

Synonyms provide both data independence and location transparency; synonyms permit applications to function without modification regardless of which user owns the table or view and regardless of which database holds the table or view.

Scope of Synonyms

A private synonym name must be distinct from all other objects in its schema. Oracle attempts to resolve references to objects at the schema level before resolving them at the PUBLIC synonym level. Oracle only uses a public synonym when resolving references to an object if both of the following cases are true:

- the object is not prefaced by a schema
- the object is not followed by a database link

For example, assume the schemas SCOTT and BLAKE each contain tables named DEPT and the user SYSTEM creates a PUBLIC synonym named DEPT for BLAKE.DEPT. If the user SCOTT then issues the following statement, Oracle returns rows from SCOTT.DEPT:

```
SELECT *
   FROM dept
```

To retrieve rows from BLAKE.DEPT, the user SCOTT must preface DEPT with the schema name:

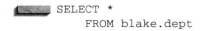

```
SELECT *
    FROM blake.dept
```

If the user ADAM's schema does not contain an object named DEPT, then ADAM can access the DEPT table in BLAKE's schema by using the public synonym DEPT:

```
SELECT *
    FROM dept
```

CREATE TABLE

Purpose

To create a *table*, the basic structure to hold user data, specifying the following information:

- column definitions
- table organization definition
- column definitions using objects
- integrity constraints
- the table's tablespace
- storage characteristics
- an optional cluster
- data from an arbitrary query

- degree of parallelism used to create the table and the default degree of parallelism for queries on the table
- partitioning definitions
- index-organized or heap-organized

Use CREATE TABLE to create an object table or a table that uses an object type for a column definition. An *object table* is a table explicitly defined to hold object instances of a particular type.

You can also create an object type and then use it in a column when creating a relational table.

Prerequisites

To create a relational table in your own schema, you must have CREATE TABLE system privilege. To create a table in another user's schema, you must have CREATE ANY TABLE system privilege. Also, the owner of the schema to contain the table must have either space quota on the tablespace to contain the table or UNLIMITED TABLESPACE system privilege.

In addition to the table privileges above, to create a table that uses types, the owner of the table must be explicitly granted the EXECUTE object privilege in order to access all types referenced by the table, or you must have the EXECUTE ANY TYPE system privilege. These privileges must be granted explicitly and not acquired through a role.

Additionally, if the table owner intends to grant access to the table to other users, the owner must have received the EXECUTE privileges to the referenced types with the GRANT OPTION, or have the EXECUTE ANY TYPE system privilege with the ADMIN OPTION. If not, the table owner has insufficient privileges to grant access on the table to other users.

For more information about the privileges required to create tables using types, see the *Oracle8 Server Application Developer's Guide*.

Syntax

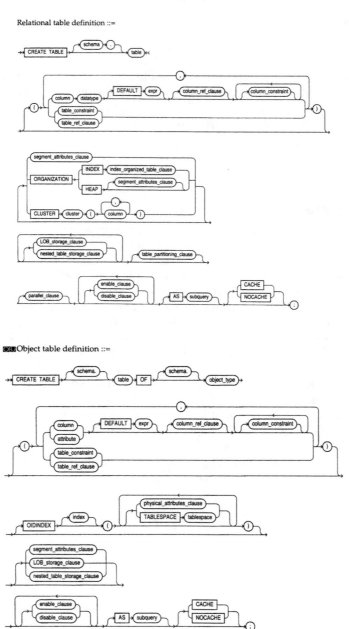

Relational table definition ::=

Object table definition ::=

column_ref_clause ::=

table_ref_clause ::=

segment_attributes_clause ::=

physical_attributes_clause ::=

index_organized_table_clause ::=

index_organized_overflow_clause ::=

LOB_storage_clause ::=

lob_parameters ::=

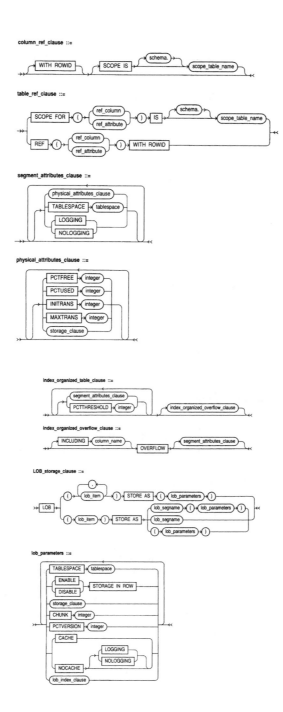

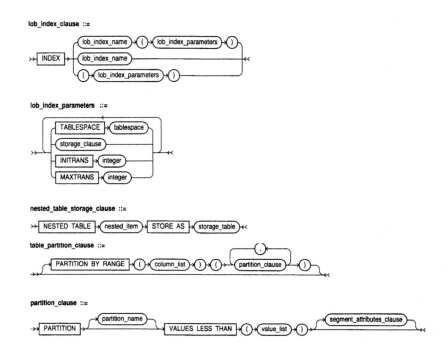

lob_index_clause ::=

lob_index_parameters ::=

nested_table_storage_clause ::=

table_partition_clause ::=

partition_clause ::=

Keywords and Parameters

schema	is the schema to contain the table. If you omit schema, Oracle creates the table in your own schema.
table	is the name of the table (or object table) to be created. A partitioned *table* cannot be a clustered table or an object table.
OF *object_type*	explicitly creates an object table of type *object_type*. The columns of an object table correspond to the top-level attributes of type *object_type*. Each row will contain an object instance and each instance will be assigned a unique, system-generated object identifier (OID) when a row is inserted. If you omit schema, Oracle creates the object table in your own schema.
column	specifies the name of a column of the table. A table can have up to 1000 columns. You may only omit column definitions when using the AS subquery clause.

attribute	specifies the qualified column name of an item in an object.
datatype	is the datatype of a column. You can omit the datatype only if the statement also designates the column as part of a foreign key in a referential integrity constraint. Oracle automatically assigns the column the datatype of the corresponding column of the referenced key of the referential integrity constraint. Object types, REF *object_type*, VARRAYs, and nested tables are valid datatypes.
DEFAULT	specifies a value to be assigned to the column if a subsequent INSERT statement omits a value for the column. The datatype of the expression must match the datatype of the column. The column must also be long enough to hold this expression. A DEFAULT expression cannot contain references to other columns, the pseudocolumns CURRVAL, NEXTVAL, LEVEL, and ROWNUM, or date constants that are not fully specified.
WITH ROWID	stores the ROWID and the REF value in *column* or *attribute*. Storing a REF value with a ROWID can improve the performance of dereferencing operations, but will also use more space. Default storage of REF values is without ROWIDs.
SCOPE IS *scope_table_name*	restricts the scope of the column REF values to *scope_table_name*. The REF values for the column must come from REF values obtained from the object table specified in the clause. You can only specify one scope table per REF column. The *scope_table_name* is the name of the object table in which object instances (of the same type as the REF column) are stored. The values in the REF column point to objects in the scope table. You must have SELECT privileges on the table or SELECT ANY TABLE system privileges.
SCOPE FOR (*ref_column_name*) IS *scope_table_name*	restricts the scope of the REF values in *ref_column_name to scope_table_name*. The REF values for the column must come from REF values obtained from the object table specified in the clause. The *ref_column_name* is the name of a REF column in an object table or an embedded REF attribute within an object column of a relational table. The values in the REF column point to objects in the scope table.

REF (*ref_column_name*)   is a reference to a row in an object table. You can specify either a REF column name of an object or relational table or an embedded REF attribute within an object column as *ref_column_name*.

OIDINDEX   specifies an index on the hidden object identifier column and/or the storage specification for the index. Either *index* or *storage_specification* must be specified.

index   is the name of the index on the hidden object identifier column. If not specified, a name is generated by the system.

column_constraint   defines an integrity constraint as part of the column definition.

table_constraint   defines an integrity constraint as part of the table definition.

ORGANIZATION INDEX   specifies that *table* is created as an index-organized table. In an index-organized table, the data rows are held in an index defined on the primary key for the table.

ORGANIZATION HEAP   specifies that the data rows of *table* are stored in no particular order. This is the default.

PCTTHRESHOLD *integer*   specifies the percentage of space reserved in the index block for an index-organized table row. Any portion of the row that exceeds the specified threshold is stored in the area. If OVERFLOW is not specified, then rows exceeding the THRESHOLD limit are rejected. PCTTHRESHOLD must be a value from 0 to 50.

INCLUDING *column_name*   specifies a column at which to divide an index organized table row into index and overflow portions. All columns which follow *column_name* are stored in the overflow data segment. A *column_name* is either the name of the last primary key column or any non primary key column.

PCTFREE

specifies the percentage of space in each of the table's, object table's OIDINDEX, or partition's data blocks reserved for future updates to the table's rows. The value of PCTFREE must be a value from 0 to 99. A value of 0 allows the entire block to be filled by inserts of new rows. The default value is 10. This value reserves 10% of each block for updates to existing rows and allows inserts of new rows to fill a maximum of 90% of each block.

PCTFREE has the same function in the PARTITION description clause and in the commands that create and alter clusters, indexes, snapshots, and snapshot logs. The combination of PCTFREE and PCTUSED determines whether inserted rows will go into existing data blocks or into new blocks.

For non-partitioned tables, the value specified for PCTFREE is the actual physical attribute of the segment associated with the table. For partitioned tables, the value specified for PCTFREE is the default physical attribute of the segments associated with the table partitions. The default value of PCTFREE applies to all partitions specified in the CREATE statement (and on subsequent ALTER TABLE ADD PARTITION statements) unless you specify PCTFREE in the PARTITION description clause.

PCTUSED

specifies the minimum percentage of used space that Oracle maintains for each data block of the table, object table OIDINDEX, or index-organized table overflow data segment. A block becomes a candidate for row insertion when its used space falls below PCTUSED. PCTUSED is specified as a positive integer from 1 to 99 and defaults to 40.

PCTUSED has the same function in the PARTITION description clause and in the commands that create and alter clusters, snapshots, and snapshot logs.

For non-partitioned tables, the value specified for PCTUSED is the actual physical attribute of the segment associated with the table. For partitioned tables, the value specified for PCTUSED is the default physical attribute of the segments associated with the table partitions. The default value of PCTUSED applies to all partitions specified in the CREATE statement (and on subsequent ALTER TABLE ADD PARTITION statements) unless you specify PCTUSED in the PARTITION description clause.

PCTUSED is not a valid table storage characteristic if creating an index-organized table (ORGANIZATION INDEX).

The sum of PCTFREE and PCTUSED must be less than 100. You can use PCTFREE and PCTUSED together to use space within a table more efficiently. For information on the performance effects of different values PCTUSED and PCTFREE, see *Oracle8 Server Tuning*.

INITRANS specifies the initial number of transaction entries allocated within each data block allocated to the table, object table OIDINDEX, partition, LOB index segment, or overflow data segment. This value can range from 1 to 255 and defaults to 1. In general, you should not change the INITRANS value from its default.

Each transaction that updates a block requires a transaction entry in the block. The size of a transaction entry depends on your operating system.

This parameter ensures that a minimum number of concurrent transactions can update the block and helps avoid the overhead of dynamically allocating a transaction entry.

The INITRANS parameter serves the same purpose in the PARTITION description clause and in clusters, indexes, snapshots, and snapshot logs as in tables. The minimum and default INITRANS value for a cluster or index is 2, rather than 1.

For non-partitioned tables, the value specified for INITRANS is the actual physical attribute of the segment associated with the table. For partitioned tables, the value specified for INITRANS is the default physical attribute of the segments associated with the table partitions. The default value of INITRANS applies to all partitions specified in the CREATE statement (and on subsequent ALTER TABLE ADD PARTITION statements) unless you specify INITRANS in the PARTITION description clause.

MAXTRANS specifies the maximum number of concurrent transactions that can update a data block allocated to the table, object table OIDINDEX, partition, LOB index segment, or index-organized overflow data segment. This limit does not apply to queries. This value can range from 1 to 255 and the default is a function of the data block size. You should not change the MAXTRANS value from its default.

If the number of concurrent transactions updating a block exceeds the INITRANS value, Oracle dynamically allocates transaction entries in the block until either the MAXTRANS value is exceeded or the block has no more free space.

The MAXTRANS parameter serves the same purpose in the PARTITION description clause, clusters, snapshots, and snapshot logs as in tables.

For non-partitioned tables, the value specified for MAXTRANS is the actual physical attribute of the segment associated with the table.

For partitioned tables, the value specified for MAXTRANS is the default physical attribute of the segments associated with the table partitions. The default value of MAXTRANS applies to all partitions specified in the CREATE statement (and on subsequent ALTER TABLE ADD PARTITION statements) unless you specify MAXTRANS in the PARTITION description clause.

TABLESPACE	specifies the tablespace in which Oracle creates the table, object table OIDINDEX, partition, LOB storage, LOB index segment, or index-organized table overflow data segment. If you omit this option, then Oracle creates the table, partition, LOB storage, LOB index segment, or partition in the default tablespace of the owner of the schema containing the table.
	For non-partitioned tables, the value specified for TABLESPACE is the actual physical attribute of the segment associated with the table.
	For partitioned tables, the value specified for TABLESPACE is the default physical attribute of the segments associated with the table partitions. The default value of TABLESPACE applies to all partitions specified in the CREATE statement (and on subsequent ALTER TABLE ADD PARTITION statements) unless you specify TABLESPACE in the PARTITION description clause.
STORAGE	specifies the storage characteristics for the table, object table OIDINDEX, partition, LOB storage, LOB index segment, or index-organized table overflow data segment. This clause has performance ramifications for large tables. Storage should be allocated to minimize dynamic allocation of additional space. For non-partitioned tables, the value specified for STORAGE is the actual physical attribute of the segment associated with the table. For partitioned tables, the value specified for STORAGE is the default physical attribute of the segments associated with the table partitions. The default value of STORAGE applies to all partitions specified in the CREATE statement (and on subsequent ALTER TABLE ADD PARTITION statements) unless you specify STORAGE in the PARTITION description clause.
OVERFLOW	specifies that index-organized table data rows exceeding the specified threshold are placed in the data segment listed in this clause.
LOGGING NOLOGGING	specifies that the creation of the table (and any indexes required because of constraints), partition, or LOB storage characteristics will be logged or otherwise in the redo log file. It also specifies that subsequent Direct Loader (SQL*Loader) and Direct-Load INSERT operations against the table, partition, or LOB storage are logged (LOGGING) or not logged (NOLOGGING). LOGGING is the default.

For non-partitioned tables, the value specified for LOGGING is the actual physical attribute of the segment associated with the table. For partitioned tables, the logging attribute value specified is the default physical attribute of the segments associated with the table partitions. The default logging value applies to all partitions specified in the CREATE statement (and on subsequent ALTER TABLE ADD PARTITION statements) unless you specify LOGGING/NOLOGGING in the PARTITION description clause. In NOLOGGING mode, data is modified without redo logging. Some minimal logging is still done for marking new extents invalid, and dictionary changes are always fully logged. When applied during media recovery, the extent invalidation records mark a range of blocks as logically corrupt, since the redo data is not logged. Thus if you cannot afford to lose this table, it is important to take a backup after the NOLOGGING operation.

If the database is run in ARCHIVELOG mode, media recovery from a backup taken before the LOGGING operation will restore the table. However, media recovery from a backup taken before the NOLOGGING operation will not restore the table.

The logging attribute of the table is independent to that of its indexes.

If the [NO]LOGGING clause is omitted, the logging attribute of the table defaults to the logging attribute of the tablespace in which it resides.

NOLOGGING is not a valid keyword for creating index-organized tables.

For more information about the LOGGING option and Parallel DML, see *Oracle8 Server Concepts* and the *Oracle8 Parallel Server and Administration Guide*.

NOTE

In future versions of Oracle, the LOGGING keyword will replace the RECOVERABLE option. RECOVERABLE is still available as a valid keyword in Oracle when creating non-partitioned tables; however, it is not recommended.

RECOVERABLE   is a deprecated option. RECOVERABLE is not a valid keyword for creating partitioned tables or LOB storage characteristics.

UNRECOVERABLE   is a deprecated option. It specifies that the creation of the table (and any indices required because of constraints) will not be logged in the redo log file.
This keyword can only be specified with the AS subquery clause. UNRECOVERABLE is not a valid keyword for creating partitioned or index-organized tables.

LOB

specifies the LOB storage characteristics. For detailed information about LOBs, see *Oracle8 Server Application Developer's Guide.*

lob_item

is the LOB column name or LOB object attribute for which you are explicitly defining tablespace and storage characteristics that are different from those of the table.

STORE AS

lob_segname	specifies the name of the LOB data segment. You cannot use *lob_segname* if more than one *lob_item* is specified.
ENABLE STORAGE IN ROW	specifies that the LOB value is stored in the row (inline) if its length is less than approximately 4000 bytes minus system control information. This is the default.
DISABLE STORAGE IN ROW	specifies that the LOB value is stored outside of the row regardless of the length of the LOB value.

Note that the LOB locator is always stored in the row regardless of where the LOB value is stored. You cannot change the STORAGE IN ROW once it is set.

CHUNK *integer*	is the unit of LOB value allocation and manipulation. Oracle allocates each unit of LOB storage as CHUNK *integer*. This unit of LOB storage is calculated as (*integer* * data block size). For example, if *integer* is 4 and the data block size is 4K, then each unit of LOB storage is 16K. The maximum value is 32K, which is the largest Oracle block size allowed.
PCTVERSION *integer*	is the maximum percentage of overall LOB storage space used for creating new versions of the LOB. The default value is 10, meaning that older versions of the LOB data are not overwritten until 10% of the overall LOB storage space is used.
INDEX *lob_index_name*	is the name of the LOB index segment. You cannot use *lob_index_name* if more than one *lob_item* is specified.
NESTED TABLE *nested_item* STORE AS *storage_table*	specifies *storage_table* as the name of the storage table in which the rows of all *nested_item* values reside. You must include this clause when creating a table with columns or column attributes whose type is a nested table. The *nested_item* is the name of a column or a column-qualified attribute whose type is a nested table. The *storage_table* is the name of the storage table. The storage table is created in the same schema and the same tablespace as the parent table.

CLUSTER	specifies that the table is to be part of the cluster. The columns listed in this clause are the table columns that correspond to the cluster's columns. Generally, the cluster columns of a table are the column or columns that comprise its primary key or a portion of its primary key.
	Specifies one column from the table for each column in the cluster key. The columns are matched by position, not by name. Since a clustered table uses the cluster's space allocation, do not use the PCTFREE, PCTUSED, INITRANS, or MAXTRANS parameters, the TABLESPACE option, or the STORAGE clause with the CLUSTER option.
	Object tables cannot be part of a cluster.
parallel_clause	specifies the degree of parallelism for creating the table and the default degree of parallelism for queries on the table once created.
	This is not a valid option when creating index-organized tables.
PARTITION BY RANGE	specifies that the table is partitioned on ranges of values from *column_list*.
column_list	is an ordered list of columns used to determine into which partition a row belongs. You cannot specify more than 16 columns in *column_list*. The *column_list* cannot contain the ROWID pseudocolumn or any columns of datatype ROWID or LONG.
PARTITION *partition_name*	specifies the physical partition clause. If *partition_name* is omitted, Oracle generates a name with the form SYS_P*n* for the partition.
VALUES LESS THAN	specifies the non-inclusive upper bound for the current partition.
value_list	is an ordered list of literal values corresponding to *column_list* in the PARTITION BY RANGE clause. You can substitute the keyword MAXVALUE for any literal in *value_list*. Specifying a value other than MAXVALUE for the highest partition bound imposes an implicit integrity constraint on the table. See *Oracle8 Server Concepts* for more information about partition bounds.
MAXVALUE	specifies a maximum value that will always sort higher than any other value, including NULL.
ENABLE	enables an integrity constraint.

DISABLE	disables an integrity constraint.
	Constraints specified in the ENABLE and DISABLE clauses of a CREATE TABLE statement must be defined in the statement. You can also enable and disable constraints with the ENABLE and DISABLE keywords of the CONSTRAINT clause. If you define a constraint but do not explicitly enable or disable it, Oracle enables it by default.
	You cannot use the ENABLE and DISABLE clauses in a CREATE TABLE statement to enable and disable triggers.
AS *subquery*	inserts the rows returned by the subquery into the table upon its creation.
	The number of columns in the table must equal the number of expressions in the subquery. The column definitions can only specify column names, default values, and integrity constraints, not datatypes. Oracle derives datatypes and lengths from the subquery. Oracle also follows the following rules for integrity constraints:
	Oracle also automatically defines any NOT NULL constraints on columns in the new table that existed on the corresponding columns of the selected table if the subquery selects the column rather than an expression containing the column.
	A CREATE TABLE statement cannot contain both AS clause and a referential integrity constraint definition.
	If a CREATE TABLE statement contains both the an AS clause and a CONSTRAINT clause or an ENABLE clause with the EXCEPTIONS option, Oracle ignores the EXCEPTIONS option. If any rows violate the constraint, Oracle does not create the table and returns an error message.
	If all expressions in the subquery are columns, rather than expressions, you can omit the columns from the table definition entirely. In this case, the names of the columns of table are the same as the columns in the subquery.
	For object tables, *subquery* can contain either one expression corresponding to the table type, or the number of top-level attributes of the table type.
CACHE	specifies that the data will be accessed frequently, therefore the blocks retrieved for this table are placed at the most recently used end of the LRU list in the buffer cache when a full table scan is performed. This option is useful for small lookup tables. CACHE as a parameter in the LOB storage clause specifies that Oracle preallocates and retains LOB data values in memory for faster access.
	This is not a valid keyword when creating index-organized tables.

NOCACHE   specifies that the data will not be accessed frequently, therefore
                     the blocks retrieved for this table are placed at the least recently
                     used end of the LRU list in the buffer cache when a full table
                     scan is performed. For LOBs, the LOB value is either
                     *not brought into the buffer cache
                     or
                     *brought into the buffer cache and placed at the least recently
                     used end of the LRU list
                     This is the default behavior except when creating
                     index-organized tables. This is not a valid keyword when
                     creating index-organized tables.
                     NOCACHE as a parameter in the LOB storage clause specifies
                     that LOB values are not pre-allocated in memory. This is the
                     LOB storage default.

Usage Notes

Tables are created with no data unless a query is specified. You can add rows to a
table with the INSERT command.

After creating a table, you can define additional columns, partitions, and
integrity constraints with the ADD clause of the ALTER TABLE command. You can
change the definition of an existing column or partition with the MODIFY clause of
the ALTER TABLE command. To modify an integrity constraint, you must drop the
constraint and redefine it.

Index-organized Tables

Index-organized tables are special kinds of tables that keep data sorted on the
primary key and are therefore best suited for primary key-based access and
manipulation.

An index-organized table is an alternative to

- a non-clustered table which is indexed on the primary key by using the
  CREATE INDEX command.

- a clustered table stored in an indexed cluster that has been created using
  the CREATE CLUSTER command that maps the primary key for the table to
  the cluster key.

Index-organized tables differ from other kinds of tables in that Oracle maintains
the table rows in a B-Tree index built on the primary key. However, the index row
contains both the primary key column values and the associated non-key column
values for the corresponding row.

You must specify a primary key for an index-organized table, the primary key uniquely identifies a row. Use the primary key instead of the ROWID for directly accessing index-organized rows.

Partitioned Tables

A partitioned table consists of a number of pieces all of which have the same logical attributes. For example, all partitions share the same column and constraint definitions.

You can create a partitioned table with just one partition. Note that there is a difference between a partitioned table with one partition and a non-partitioned table. For instance, you cannot add a partition to a non-partitioned table.

For information about partitioned table maintenance operations, see the *Oracle8 Server Administrator's Guide*.

Object Tables

In order to have Oracle assign an object identifier to an object, the object must reside in a special kind of table called an object table. Objects residing in an object table are referenceable.

The columns of an object table correspond to the top-level attributes of the corresponding type. Each row will contain an object instance and each instance will be assigned a unique, system-generated object identifier (OID) when a row is inserted. For example, consider object type DEPT_T:

```
CREATE TYPE dept_t AS OBJECT
( dname VARCHAR2(100),
address VARCHAR2(200) );
```

Object table DEPT holds department objects of type DEPT_T:

```
CREATE TABLE dept OF dept_t;
```

Nested Table Storage

Creating a table with columns of type TABLE implicitly creates a storage table for each nested table column. The storage table is created in the same tablespace as its parent table (using the default storage characteristics) and stores the nested table values of the column for which it was created.

You *cannot* query or perform DML statements on the storage table directly, but you can modify the nested table column storage characteristics by using the name of storage table in an ALTER TABLE statement.

REFs

A REF value is a reference to a row in an object table. A table can have top-level REF columns or REF attributes embedded within an object type column. In general, if a table has a REF column, each REF value in the column could reference a row in a different object table. A SCOPE clause restricts the scope of references to a single table.

For example, if you create an object table DEPT which stores all the departments in an organization, you could then create table EMP that contains a REF column (E_DEPT) to point to the department in which each employee works. Because all employees work in some department stored in the DEPT table, a scope clause can be specified on the E_DEPT column of EMP to restrict the scope of references to the DEPT table.

You can increase the performance of queries with dereference operations and decrease the amount of storage needed for REF values by using the SCOPE clause. Note that a SCOPE clause does not have the same semantics as referential constraints. Referential constraints do not allow dangling references. Also, referential constraints do not necessarily restrict the scope of references to a single table (one can specify multiple referential constraints on the same foreign key with each one of them pointing to a different table).

You can also store REF values with or without ROWIDs. Storing REF values WITH ROWID can enhance the performance of dereference operations, but takes up more space. The default behavior is to store REF values without the ROWID.

REF clauses cannot be specified on REF columns in nested tables through the CREATE TABLE statement. To specify REF clauses on REF columns in nested tables, use the ALTER TABLE to modify the nested table's storage table.

CREATE TABLESPACE

Purpose

To create a tablespace. A *tablespace* is an allocation of space in the database that can contain schema objects.

Prerequisites

You must have CREATE TABLESPACE system privilege. Also, the SYSTEM tablespace must contain at least two rollback segments including the SYSTEM rollback segment.

Syntax

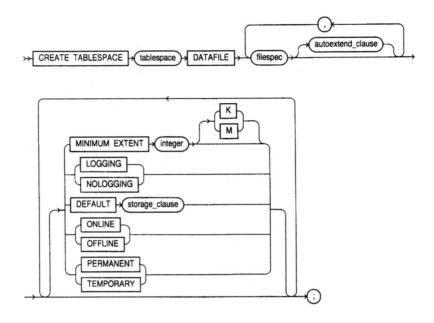

autoextend_clause ::=

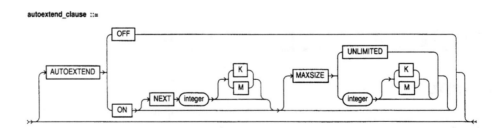

Keywords and Parameters

tablespace	is the name of the tablespace to be created.
DATAFILE	specifies the data file or files to comprise the tablespace. See "Filespec."

MINIMUM EXTENT *integer*   controls free space fragmentation in the tablespace by ensuring that every used and/or free extent size in a tablespace is at least as large as, and is a multiple of, *integer*. For more information about using MINIMUM EXTENT to control space fragmentation, see the *Oracle8 Server Administrator's Guide*.

AUTOEXTEND   enables or disables the automatic extension of data file.

OFF	disables autoextend if it is turned on. NEXT and MAXSIZE are set to zero. Values for NEXT and MAXSIZE must be respecified in further ALTER TABLESPACE AUTOEXTEND commands.
ON	enables autoextend.
NEXT	disk space to allocate to the data file when more extents are required.
MAXSIZE	maximum disk space allowed for allocation to the data file.
UNLIMITED	sets no limit on allocating disk space to the data file.

LOGGING
NOLOGGING   specifies the default logging attributes of all tables, indexes, and partitions within the tablespace. LOGGING is the default. The tablespace-level logging attribute can be overridden by logging specifications at the table, index, and partition levels. Only the following oprations support the NOLOGGING mode:
DML:
*direct-load INSERT (serial or parallel)
*Direct Loader (SQL*Loader)
DDL:
*CREATE TABLE ... AS SELECT
*CREATE INDEX
*ALTER INDEX ... REBUILD
*ALTER INDEX ... REBUILD PARTITION
*ALTER INDEX ... SPLIT PARTITION
*ALTER TABLE ... SPLIT PARTITION
*ALTER TABLE ... MOVE PARTITION
In NOLOGGING mode, data is modified without redo logging. Some minimal logging is still done for marking new extents invalid, and dictionary changes are always fully logged. When applied during media recovery, the extent invalidation records mark a range of blocks as logically corrupt, since the redo data is not logged. Thus if you cannot afford to lose the object, it is important to take a backup after the NOLOGGING operation.

DEFAULT STORAGE	specifies the default storage parameters for all objects created in the tablespace.
ONLINE	makes the tablespace available immediately after creation to users who have been granted access to the tablespace.
OFFLINE	makes the tablespace unavailable immediately after creation. If you omit both the ONLINE and OFFLINE options, Oracle creates the tablespace online by default. The data dictionary view DBA_TABLESPACES indicates whether each tablespace is online or offline.
PERMANENT	specifies that the tablespace will be used to hold permanent objects. This is the default.
TEMPORARY	specifies that the tablespace will only be used to hold temporary objects. For example, segments used by implicit sorts to handle ORDER BY clauses.

Usage Notes

A *tablespace* is an allocation of space in the database that can contain any of the following segments:

- data segments
- index segments
- rollback segments
- temporary segments

All databases have at least one tablespace, SYSTEM, which Oracle creates automatically when you create the database.

When you create a tablespace, it is initially a read-write tablespace. After creating the tablespace, you can subsequently use the ALTER TABLESPACE command to take it offline or online, add data files to it, or make it a read-only tablespace.

Many schema objects have associated segments that occupy space in the database. These objects are located in tablespaces. The user creating such an object can optionally specify the tablespace to contain the object. The owner of the schema containing the object must have space quota on the object's tablespace. You can assign space quota on a tablespace to a user with the QUOTA clause of the CREATE USER or ALTER USER command.

WARNING
For operating systems that support raw devices, be aware that the STORAGE clause REUSE keyword has no meaning when specifying a raw device as a data file in a CREATE TABLESPACE command; such a command will always succeed even if REUSE is not specified.

CREATE USER

Purpose

Use CREATE USER to create a database *user,* or an account through which you can log in to the database, and establish the means by which Oracle permits access by the user. You can optionally assign the following properties to the user:

- default tablespace
- temporary tablespace
- quotas for allocating space in tablespaces
- profile containing resource limits

Prerequisites

You must have CREATE USER system privilege.

Syntax

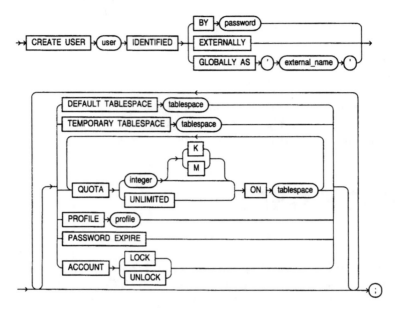

Keywords and Parameters

user	is the name of the user to be created. This name can only contain characters from your database character set. It is recommended that the user contain at least one single-byte character regardless of whether the database character set also contains multi-byte characters.
IDENTIFIED	indicates how Oracle permits user access:

	BY *password*	The user must specify this password to logon. Password can only contain single-byte characters from your database character set regardless of whether this character set also contains multi-byte characters.
	EXTERNALLY	Oracle verifies that the operating system username matches the database username specified in a database connection.

GLOBALLY AS 'external_name'	indicates that Oracle permits user access by obtaining the username and required authorizations from the security domain central authority. The 'external_name' string denotes the external name of the database user. This string can be the user's identity at any external authentication service, such as Oracle Security Server.
DEFAULT TABLESPACE	identifies the default tablespace for objects that the user creates. If you omit this clause, objects default to the SYSTEM tablespace.
TEMPORARY TABLESPACE	identifies the tablespace for the user's temporary segments. If you omit this clause, temporary segments default to the SYSTEM tablespace.
QUOTA	allows the user to allocate space in the tablespace and optionally establishes a quota of integer bytes. This quota is the maximum space in the tablespace the user can allocate. You can also use the K or M to specify the quota in kilobytes or megabytes. Note that a CREATE USER command can have multiple QUOTA clauses for multiple tablespaces.

	UNLIMITED	allows the user to allocate space in the tablespace without bound.

PROFILE	reassigns the profile named to the user. The profile limits the amount of database resources the user can use. If you omit this clause, Oracle assigns the DEFAULT profile to the user.
PASSWORD EXPIRE	causes the user's *password* to expire. Change the password before attempting to log in to the database.
ACCOUNT LOCK	locks the user's account and disables access.
ACCOUNT UNLOCK	unlocks the user's account and enables access to the account.

Usage Notes

For a detailed description and explanation of how to use password management and protection, see the *Oracle8 Server Administrator's Guide.*

Verifying Users Through Your Operating System

Using CREATE USER ... IDENTIFIED EXTERNALLY allows a database administrator to create a database user that can only be accessed from a specific operating system account. Effectively, you are relying on the login authentication of the operating system to ensure that a specific operating system user has access to a specific database user. Thus, the effective security of such database accounts is entirely dependent on the strength of that security mechanism. For more information, see *Oracle8 Server Administrator's Guide*.

Oracle Corporation strongly recommends that you do not use IDENTIFIED EXTERNALLY with operating systems that have inherently weak login security.

Verifying Users Through the Network

Using CREATE USER ... IDENTIFIED GLOBALLY enables a database administrator to create a database user that can only be authorized by an external authentication service, such as Oracle Security Server (OSS), or any external authentication system. For more information about OSS, see *The Oracle Security Server Guide* and *Oracle8 Server Distributed Systems*.

Establishing Tablespace Quotas for Users

To create an object or a temporary segment, the user must allocate space in some tablespace. To allow the user to allocate space, use the QUOTA clause. A CREATE USER statement can have multiple QUOTA clauses, each for a different tablespace. Other clauses can appear only once.

Note that you need not have a quota on a tablespace to establish a quota for another user on that tablespace.

Granting Privileges to a User

For a user to perform any database operation, the user's privilege domain must contain a privilege that authorizes that operation. A user's privilege domain contains all privileges granted to the user and all privileges in the privilege domains of the user's enabled roles. When you create a user with the CREATE USER command, the user's privilege domain is empty.

NOTE
To log on to Oracle, a user must have CREATE SESSION system privilege. After creating a user, you should grant the user this privilege.

EXPLAIN PLAN

Purpose

To determine the execution plan Oracle follows to execute a specified SQL statement. This command inserts a row describing each step of the execution plan into a specified table. If you are using cost-based optimization, this command also determines the cost of executing the statement.

Prerequisites

To issue an EXPLAIN PLAN statement, you must have the privileges necessary to insert rows into an existing output table that you specify to hold the execution plan.

    You must also have the privileges necessary to execute the SQL statement for which you are determining the execution plan. If the SQL statement accesses a view, you must have privileges to access any tables and views on which the view is based. If the view is based on another view that is based on a table, you must have privileges to access both the other view and its underlying table.

    To examine the execution plan produced by an EXPLAIN PLAN statement, you must have the privileges necessary to query the output table.

Syntax

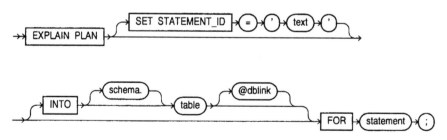

Keywords and Parameters

SET   specifies the value of the STATEMENT_ID column for the rows of the execution plan in the output table. If you omit this clause, the STATEMENT_ID value defaults to null.

INTO   specifies the schema, name, and database containing the output table. This table must exist before you use the EXPLAIN PLAN command. If you omit schema, Oracle assumes the table is in your own schema.

The *dblink* can be a complete or partial name of a database link to a remote Oracle database where the output table is located. You can only specify a remote output table if you are using Oracle with the distributed option.

If you omit *dblink*, Oracle assumes the table is on your local database. If you omit the INTO clause altogether, Oracle assumes an output table named PLAN_TABLE in your own schema on your local database.

FOR   specifies a SELECT, INSERT, UPDATE, or DELETE statement for which the execution plan is generated.

Usage Notes

The definition of a sample output table PLAN_TABLE is available in SQL script on your distribution media. Your output table must have the same column names and datatypes as this table. The common name of this script is UTLXPLAN.SQL, although the exact name and location may vary depending on your operating system.

The value you specify in the SET clause appears in the STATEMENT_ID column in the rows of the execution plan. You can then use this value to identify these rows among others in the output table. Be sure to specify a STATEMENT_ID value if your output table contains rows from many execution plans.

Since the EXPLAIN PLAN command is a Data Manipulation Language command, rather than a Data Definition Language command, Oracle does not implicitly commit the changes made by an EXPLAIN PLAN statement. If you want to keep the rows generated by an EXPLAIN PLAN statement in the output table, you must commit the transaction containing the statement.

You should not use the EXPLAIN PLAN command to determine the execution plans of SQL statements that access data dictionary views or dynamic performance tables.

You can also issue the EXPLAIN PLAN command as part of the SQL trace facility. For information on how to use the SQL trace facility and how to interpret execution plans, see *Oracle8 Server Tuning*.

Partitioned Tables

Information for partitioning is provided in the steps (rows of the Explain table) of the Explain plan for a SQL statement. The information consists of:

- Three columns of the Explain table: partition_start, partition_stop, partition_id.
- Step: PARTITION.

■ Enhancements to the TABLE ACCESS and INDEX steps when such steps refer to partitioned objects.

PARTITIONING COLUMNS OF EXPLAIN TABLE   The partition_start and partition_stop columns describe how the partitions being accessed are computed by Oracle and provide the range of accessible partitions (if known).

The **partition_start** column describes the start partition of a range of accessed partitions. It can take these values:

■ NUMBER(n) indicating that the start partition has been identified by the SQL compiler and its partition number is given by *n*.

■ KEY indicating that the start partition will be identified at execution time from partitioning key values.

■ ROW LOCATION indicating that the start partition (same as the stop partition) is computed at execution time from the location of each record being retrieved. The record location is obtained by a user or from a global index.

■ INVALID if the range of accessed partitions is empty.

The **partition_stop** column describes the stop partition of a range of accessed partitions. It can take these values:

■ NUMBER(n) indicating that the stop partition has been identified by the SQL compiler and its partition number is given by *n*.

■ KEY indicating that the stop partition will be identified at execution time from partitioning key values.

■ ROW LOCATION indicating that the stop partition (same as the start partition) will be computed at execution time from the location of each record being retrieved. The record location is obtained by a user or from a global index.

■ INVALID if the range of accessed partitions is empty.

The **partition_id** column identifies the step that has computed a pair of values of the partition_start and partition_stop columns.

PARTITION STEP OF EXPLAIN TABLE   The PARTITION step describes partition boundaries applicable to a single partitioned object (table or index) or to a set of equi-partitioned objects (a partitioned table and its local

indexes). The partition boundaries are provided by the values of partition_start and partition_stop of the PARTITION step. Possible values for partition_start and partition_stop are NUMBER(*n*), KEY, INVALID.

The options column of a PARTITION step can take these values:

- CONCATENATED indicating that the PARTITION step concatenates the result sets returned from accessed partitions.

- SINGLE indicating the set of partitions to be accessed consists of a single partition to be determined at execution time.

- EMPTY indicating that the set of partitions to be accessed is empty.

MODIFIED STEPS (ROWS) OF EXPLAIN TABLE   The TABLE ACCESS and INDEX steps describing access to a partitioned table or index are enhanced to provide partition boundary information in the partition_start, partition_stop, and partition_id columns.

The partition boundaries may have been computed by:

- A previous PARTITION step, in which case the partition_start and partition_stop column values replicate the values present in the PARTITION step, and the partition_id contains the id of the PARTITION step. Possible values for partition_start and partition_stop are NUMBER(*n*), KEY, INVALID.

- The TABLE ACCESS or INDEX step itself, in which case the partition_id contains the id of the step. Possible values for partition_start and partition_stop are NUMBER(*n*), KEY, ROW LOCATION (TABLE ACCESS only), INVALID.

The options column of a TABLE ACCESS step describing access by rowid to a table may contain the following values:

- "BY USER ROWID" if the table rows are located using user supplied rowids.

- "BY INDEX ROWID" if the table is non partitioned and rows are located using index(es).

- "BY GLOBAL INDEX ROWID" if the table is partitioned and rows are located using only global indexes.

- "BY LOCAL INDEX ROWID" if the table is partitioned and rows are located using one or more local indexes and possibly some global indexes.

Filespec

Purpose

To either specify a file as a data file or to specify a group of one or more files as a redo log file group.

Prerequisites

A filespec can appear in either CREATE DATABASE, ALTERDATABASE, CREATE TABLESPACE, or ALTER TABLESPACE commands. You must have the privileges necessary to issue one of these commands.

Syntax

filespec_data_files ::=

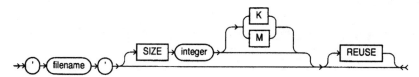

filespec_redo_log_file_groups ::=

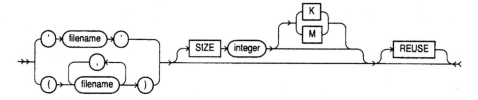

Keywords and Parameters

'*filename*'   is the name of either a data file or a redo log file member. A '*filename*' can only contain single-byte such as characters from 7-bit ASCII or EBCDIC character sets. Multi-byte characters are not valid.
A redo log file group can have one or more members, or copies. Each '*filename*' must be fully specified according to the conventions for your operating system.

SIZE	specifies the size of the file. If you omit this parameter, the file must already exist. Note that the tablespace size must be one block greater than the sum of the sizes of the objects contained in it.

K	specifies the size in kilobytes.
M	specifies the size in megabytes.

If you omit K and M, the size is specified in bytes.

REUSE	allows Oracle to reuse an existing file. If the file already exists, Oracle verifies that its size matches the value of the SIZE parameter. If the file does not exist, Oracle creates it. If you omit this option, the file must not already exist and Oracle creates the file. The REUSE option is only significant when used with the SIZE option. If you omit the SIZE option, Oracle expects the file to exist already. Note that whenever Oracle uses an existing file, the file's previous contents are lost.

GRANT
(System Privileges and Roles)

Purpose

To grant system privileges and roles to users and roles.

Prerequisites

To grant a system privilege, you must either have been granted the system privilege with the ADMIN OPTION or have been granted GRANT ANY PRIVILEGE system privilege.

To grant a role, you must either have been granted the role with the ADMIN OPTION or have been granted GRANT ANY ROLE system privilege or have created the role.

Syntax

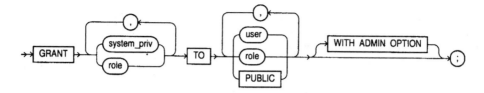

Keywords and Parameters

system_priv	is a system privilege to be granted.
role	is a role to be granted.
TO	identifies users or roles to which system privileges and roles are granted.
PUBLIC	grants system privileges or roles to all users.
WITH ADMIN OPTION	allows the grantee to grant the system privilege or role to other users or roles. If you grant a role with ADMIN OPTION, the grantee can also alter or drop the role.

Usage Notes

You can use this form of the GRANT command to grant both system privileges and roles to users, roles, and PUBLIC:

If you grant a privilege to a user: Oracle adds the privilege to the user's privilege domain. The user can immediately exercise the privilege.

If you grant a privilege to a role: Oracle adds the privilege to the role's privilege domain. Users who have been granted and have enabled the role can immediately exercise the privilege. Other users who have been granted the role can enable the role and exercise the privilege.

If you grant a privilege to PUBLIC: Oracle adds the privilege to the privilege domains of each user. All users can immediately perform operations authorized by the privilege.

If you grant a role to a user: Oracle makes the role available to the user. The user can immediately enable the role and exercise the privileges in the role's privilege domain.

You cannot grant:

■   a global role to a user

■ a role IDENTIFIED EXTERNALLY to a global user

If you grant a role to another role: Oracle adds the granted role's privilege domain to the grantee role's privilege domain. Users who have been granted the grantee role can enable it and exercise the privileges in the granted role's privilege domain.

You cannot grant:

■ a global role to another role or to another global role

■ a role IDENTIFIED EXTERNALLY to a global role

If you grant a role to PUBLIC: Oracle makes the role available to all users. All users can immediately enable the role and exercise the privileges in the roles privilege domain.

You cannot grant a global role to PUBLIC.

A privilege or role cannot appear more than once in the list of privileges and roles to be granted. A user, role, or PUBLIC cannot appear more than once in the TO clause.

You cannot grant roles circularly. For example, if you grant the role BANKER to the role TELLER, you cannot subsequently grant TELLER to BANKER. Also, you cannot grant a role to itself.

Table C-4 should clarify which user can be given which authorizations.

System Privileges

Table C-5 lists system privileges and the operations that they authorize. You can grant any of these system privileges with the GRANT command.

ADMIN OPTION

A grant with the ADMIN OPTION supersedes a previous identical grant without the ADMIN OPTION. If you grant a system privilege or role to user without the ADMIN OPTION, and then subsequently grant the privilege or role to the user with the ADMIN OPTION, the user has the ADMIN OPTION on the privilege or role.

A grant without the ADMIN OPTION does not supersede a previous grant with the ADMIN OPTION. To revoke the ADMIN OPTION on a system privilege or role from a user, you must revoke the privilege or role from the user altogether and then grant the privilege or role to the user without the ADMIN OPTION.

Other Authorization Methods

Database users may be authorized to use roles through other means than the database and the GRANT statement. For example, some operating systems have

User Type -> ——————— Type of Role	Grant to User Identified by Password	Grant to User Identified Externally	Grant to User Identified Globally	Grant to Local Role	Grant to External Role	Grant to Global Role
Local Role	Yes	Yes	Yes	Yes	Yes	Yes
External Role	Yes	Yes	No	Yes	Yes	No
Global Role	No	No	No	No	No	No
Privileges	Yes	Yes	Yes	Yes	Yes	Yes

TABLE C-4. *DB GRANTS Allowed*

System Privilege	Operations Authorized
ALTER ANY CLUSTER	Allows grantee to alter any cluster in any schema.
ALTER ANY INDEX	Allows grantee to alter any index in any schema.
ALTER ANY PROCEDURE	Allows grantee to alter any stored procedure, function, or package in any schema.
ALTER ANY ROLE	Allows grantee to alter any role in the database.
ALTER ANY SEQUENCE	Allows grantee to alter any sequence in the database.
ALTER ANY SNAPSHOT	Allows grantee to alter any snapshot in the database.
ALTER ANY TABLE	Allows grantee to alter any table or view in the schema.
ALTER ANY TYPE	Allows grantee to alter any type in any schema.
ALTER ANY TRIGGER	Allows grantee to enable, disable, or compile any database trigger in any schema.
ALTER DATABASE	Allows grantee to alter the database.
ALTER PROFILE	Allows grantee to alter profiles.
ALTER RESOURCE COST	Allows grantee to set costs for session resources.
ALTER ROLLBACK SEGMENT	Allows grantee to alter rollback segments.
ALTER SESSION	Allows grantee to issue ALTER SESSION statements.
ALTER SYSTEM	Allows grantee to issue ALTER SYSTEM statements.
ALTER TABLESPACE	Allows grantee to alter tablespaces.

TABLE C-5. *System Privileges*

System Privilege	Operations Authorized
ALTER USER	Allows grantee to alter any user. This privilege authorizes the grantee to change another user's password or authentication method, assign quotas on *any* tablespace, set default and temporary tablespaces, and assign a profile and default roles.
ANALYZE ANY	Allows grantee to analyze any table, cluster, or index in any schema.
AUDIT ANY	Allows grantee to audit any object in any schema using AUDIT (Schema Objects) statements.
AUDIT SYSTEM	Allows grantee to issue AUDIT (SQL Statements) statements.
BACKUP ANY TABLE	Allows grantee to use the Export utility to incrementally export objects from the schema of other users.
BECOME USER	Allows grantee to become another user. (Required by any user performing a full database import.)
COMMENT ANY TABLE	Allows grantee to Comment on any table, view, or column in any schema.
CREATE ANY CLUSTER	Allows grantee to create a cluster in any schema. Behaves similarly to CREATE ANY TABLE.
CREATE ANY DIRECTORY	Allows the grantee to create a directory database object in any schema.
CREATE ANY INDEX	Allows grantee to create an index in any schema on any table in any schema.
CREATE ANY LIBRARY	Allows grantee to create external procedure/function libraries in any schema.
CREATE ANY PROCEDURE	Allows grantee to create stored procedures, functions, and packages in any schema.
CREATE ANY SEQUENCE	Allows grantee to create a sequence in any schema.
CREATE ANY SNAPSHOT	Allows grantee to create snapshots in any schema.
CREATE ANY SYNONYM	Allows grantee to create private synonyms in any schema.
CREATE ANY TABLE	Allows grantee to create tables in any schema. The owner of the schema containing the table must have space quota on the tablespace to contain the table.
CREATE ANY TRIGGER	Allows grantee to create a database trigger in any schema associated with a table in any schema.

TABLE C-5. *System Privileges* (continued)

System Privilege	Operations Authorized
CREATE ANY TYPE	Allows grantee to create types and type bodies in any schema.
CREATE ANY VIEW	Allows grantee to create views in any schema.
CREATE CLUSTER	Allows grantee to create clusters in own schema.
CREATE DATABASE LINK	Allows grantee to create private database links in own schema.
CREATE ANY LIBRARY	Allows grantee to create external procedure/function libraries in own schema.
CREATE PROCEDURE	Allows grantee to create stored procedures, functions, and packages in own schema.
CREATE PROFILE	Allows grantee to create profiles.
CREATE PUBLIC DATABASE LINK	Allows grantee to create public database links.
CREATE PUBLIC SYNONYM	Allows grantee to create public synonyms.
CREATE ROLE	Allows grantee to create roles.
CREATE ROLLBACK SEGMENT	Allows grantee to create rollback segments.
CREATE SEQUENCE	Allows grantee to create sequences in own schema.
CREATE SESSION	Allows grantee to connect to the database.
CREATE SNAPSHOT	Allows grantee to create snapshots in own schema.
CREATE SYNONYM	Allows grantee to create synonyms in own schema.
CREATE TABLE	Allows grantee to create tables in own schema. To create a table, the grantee must also have space quota on the tablespace to contain the table.
CREATE TABLESPACE	Allows grantee to create tablespaces.
CREATE TRIGGER	Allows grantee to create a database trigger in own schema.
CREATE TYPE	Allows grantee to create types and type bodies in own schema.
CREATE USER	Allows grantee to create users. This privilege also allows the creator to assign quotas on *any* tablespace, set default and temporary tablespaces, and assign a profile as part of a CREATE USER statement.
CREATE VIEW	Allows grantee to create views in own schema.
DELETE ANY TABLE	Allows grantee to delete rows from tables or views in any schema or truncate tables in any schema.
DROP ANY CLUSTER	Allows grantee to drop clusters in any schema.

TABLE C-5. *System Privileges* (continued)

System Privilege	Operations Authorized
DROP ANY DIRECTORY	Allows grantee to drop directory database objects.
DROP ANY INDEX	Allows grantee to drop indexes in any schema.
DROP ANY LIBRARY	Allows grantee to drop external procedure/function libraries in any schema.
DROP ANY PROCEDURE	Allows grantee to drop stored procedures, functions, or packages in any schema.
DROP ANY ROLE	Allows grantee to drop roles.
DROP ANY SEQUENCE	Allows grantee to drop sequences in any schema.
DROP ANY SNAPSHOT	Allows grantee to drop snapshots in any schema.
DROP ANY SYNONYM	Allows grantee to drop private synonyms in any schema.
DROP ANY TABLE	Allows grantee to drop tables in any schema.
DROP ANY TRIGGER	Allows grantee to drop database triggers in any schema.
DROP ANY TYPE	Allows grantee to drop object types and object type bodies in any schema.
DROP ANY VIEW	Allows grantee to drop views in any schema.
DROP LIBRARY	Allows grantee to drop external procedure/ function libraries.
DROP PROFILE	Allows grantee to drop profiles.
DROP PUBLIC DATABASE LINK	Allows grantee to drop public database links.
DROP PUBLIC SYNONYM	Allows grantee to drop public synonyms.
DROP ROLLBACK SEGMENT	Allows grantee to drop rollback segments.
DROP TABLESPACE	Allows grantee to drop tablespaces.
DROP USER	Allows grantee to drop users.
EXECUTE ANY PROCEDURE	Allows grantee to execute procedures or functions (stand-alone or packaged) or reference public package variables in any schema.
EXECUTE ANY TYPE	Allows grantee to use and reference object types, and invoke methods of any type in any schema. You cannot grant EXECUTE ANY TYPE to a role. You must grant EXECUTE ANY TYPE to a specific user.
FORCE ANY TRANSACTION	Allows grantee to force the commit or rollback of any in-doubt distributed transaction in the local database. Also allows the grantee to induce the failure of a distributed transaction.

TABLE C-5. *System Privileges (continued)*

System Privilege	Operations Authorized
FORCE TRANSACTION	Allows grantee to force the commit or rollback of own in-doubt distributed transactions in the local database.
GRANT ANY PRIVILEGE	Allows grantee to grant any system privilege.
GRANT ANY ROLE	Allows grantee to grant any role in the database.
INSERT ANY TABLE	Allows grantee to insert rows into tables and views in any schema.
LOCK ANY TABLE	Allows grantee to lock tables and views in any schema.
MANAGE TABLESPACE	Allows grantee to take tablespaces offline and online and begin and end tablespace backups.
RESTRICTED SESSION	Allows grantee to logon after the instance is started using the Server Manager STARTUP RESTRICT command.
SELECT ANY SEQUENCE	Allows grantee to reference sequences in any schema.
SELECT ANY TABLE	Allows grantee to query tables, views, or snapshots in any schema.
SYSDBA	Allows grantee to perform Server Manager STARTUP and SHUTDOWN commands, ALTER DATABASE OPEN/MOUNT/BACKUP, CREATE DATABASE, ARCHIVELOG and RECOVERY and inludes the RESTRICTED SESSION privilege.
SYSOPER	Allows grantee to perform Server Manager STARTUP and SHUTDOWN commands, ALTER DATABASE OPEN/MOUNT/BACKUP, ARCHIVELOG and RECOVERY and inludes the RESTRICTED SESSION privilege.
UNLIMITED TABLESPACE	Allows grantee to use an unlimited amount of any tablespace. This privilege overrides any specific quotas assigned. If you revoke this privilege from a user, the grantee's schema objects remain but further tablespace allocation is denied unless authorized by specific tablespace quotas. You cannot grant this system privilege to roles.
UPDATE ANY TABLE	Allows grantee to update rows in tables and views in any schema.

TABLE C-5. *System Privileges* (continued)

facilities that grant operating system privileges to operating system users. You can use such facilities to grant roles to Oracle users with the initialization parameter OS_ROLES. If you choose to grant roles to users through operating system facilities, you cannot also grant roles to users with the GRANT command, although you can use the GRANT command to grant system privileges to users and system privileges and roles to other roles.

For information about other authorization methods, see the *Oracle8 Server Administrator's Guide.*

GRANT (Object Privileges)

Purpose

To grant privileges for a particular object to users and roles. To grant system privileges and roles, use the GRANT command (System Privileges and Roles) described in the previous section of this chapter.

Prerequisites

You must own the object or the owner of the object granted you the object privileges with the GRANT OPTION. This rule applies to users with the DBA role.

Syntax

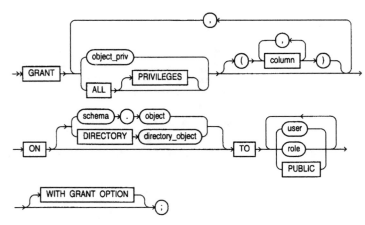

Keywords and Parameters

object_priv	is an object privilege to be granted. You can substitute any of the following values: *ALTER *EXECUTE *INDEX *INSERT *READ *REFERENCES *SELECT *UPDATE
ALL PRIVILEGES	grants all the privileges for the object that you have been granted with the GRANT OPTION. The user who owns the schema containing an object automatically has all privileges on the object with the GRANT OPTION.
column	specifies a table or view column on which privileges are granted. You can only specify columns when granting the INSERT, REFERENCES, or UPDATE privilege. If you do not list columns, the grantee has the specified privilege on all columns in the table or view.
ON	identifies the object on which the privileges are granted.
DIRECTORY *directory_object*	identifies a directory *object* on which privileges are granted by the DBA. You cannot qualify *directory_object* with a schema name.
object	identifies the schema object on which the privileges are granted. If you do not qualify object with schema, Oracle assumes the object is in your own schema. The object can be one of the following types: *table *view *sequence *procedure, function, or package *snapshots *synonym for a table, view, sequence, snapshot, procedure, function, or package *library *object types
TO	identifies users or roles to which the object privilege is granted.
PUBLIC	grants object privileges to all users.

WITH GRANT OPTION	allows the grantee to grant the object privileges to other users and roles. The grantee must be a user or PUBLIC, rather than a role.

Usage Notes

You can use this form of the GRANT statement to grant object privileges to users, roles, and PUBLIC:

If you grant a privilege to a user: Oracle adds the privilege to the user's privilege domain. The user can immediately exercise the privilege.

If you grant a privilege to a role: Oracle adds the privilege to the role's privilege domain. Users who have been granted and have enabled the role can immediately exercise the privilege. Other users who have been granted the role can enable the role and exercise the privilege.

If you grant a privilege to PUBLIC: Oracle adds the privilege to the privilege domain of each user. All users can immediately exercise the privilege.

A privilege cannot appear more than once in the list of privileges to be granted. A user or role cannot appear more than once in the TO clause.

Database Object Privileges

Each database object privilege that you grant authorizes the grantee to perform some operation on the object. Table C-6 summarizes the object privileges that you can grant on each type of object.

Object Privilege	Table	View	Sequence	Procedure Functions Packages	Snapshot	Directory	Library
ALTER	X		X				
DELETE	X	X					
EXECUTE				X			X
INDEX	X						
INSERT	X	X					
READ						X	
REFERENCES	X						
SELECT	X	X	X		X		
UPDATE	X	X					

TABLE C-6. *Object Privileges*

TABLE PRIVILEGES   The following object privileges authorize operations on a table:

ALTER	allows the grantee to change the table definition with the ALTER TABLE command.
DELETE	allows the grantee to remove rows from the table with the DELETE command.
INDEX	allows the grantee to create an index on the table with the CREATE INDEX command.
INSERT	allows the grantee to add new rows to the table with the INSERT command.
REFERENCES	allows the grantee to create a constraint that refers to the table. You cannot grant this privilege to a role.
SELECT	allows the grantee to query the table with the SELECT command.
UPDATE	allows the grantee to change data in the table with the UPDATE command.

Any one of above object privileges allows the grantee to lock the table in any lock mode with the LOCK TABLE command.

VIEW PRIVILEGES   The following object privileges authorize operations on a view:

DELETE	allows the grantee to remove rows from the view with the DELETE command.
INSERT	allows the grantee to add new rows to the view with the INSERT command.
SELECT	allows the grantee to query the view with the SELECT command.
UPDATE	allows the grantee to change data in the view with the UPDATE command.

Any one of the above object privileges allows the grantee to lock the view in any lock mode with the LOCK TABLE command.

To grant a privilege on a view, you must have that privilege with the GRANT OPTION on all of the view's base tables.

SEQUENCE PRIVILEGES   The following object privileges authorize operations on a sequence:

| ALTER | allows the grantee to change the sequence definition with the ALTER SEQUENCE command. |
| SELECT | allows the grantee to examine and increment values of the sequence with the CURRVAL and NEXTVAL pseudocolumns. |

PROCEDURE, FUNCTION, AND PACKAGE PRIVILEGES   This object privilege authorizes operations on a procedure, function, or package:

| EXECUTE | allows the grantee to execute the procedure or function or to access any program object declared in the specification of a package. |

SNAPSHOT PRIVILEGES   This object privilege authorizes operations on a snapshot:

| SELECT | allows the grantee to query the snapshot with the SELECT command. |

SYNONYM PRIVILEGES   The object privileges available for a synonym are the same as the privileges for the synonym's base object. Granting a privilege on a synonym is equivalent to granting the privilege on the base object. Similarly, granting a privilege on a base object is equivalent to granting the privilege on all synonyms for the object. If you grant a user a privilege on a synonym, the user can use either the synonym name or the base object name in the SQL statement that exercises the privilege.

DIRECTORY PRIVILEGES   The object privileges available for a directory provide secured database access to the files stored in the operating system directory to which the directory object serves as a pointer. The directory object contains the full pathname of the operating system directory where the files reside. Because the files are actually stored outside the database, Oracle8 Server processes also need to have appropriate file permissions on the filesystem server.

Granting object privileges on the directory database object to individual database users, rather than on the operating system, allows the Oracle8 Server to enforce security during file operations. This object privilege authorizes operations on a directory:

| READ | allows the grantee to read files in the directory. |

NOAUDIT (SQL Statements)

Purpose

To stop auditing chosen by the AUDIT command (SQL Statements). To stop auditing chosen by the AUDIT command (Schema Objects), use the NOAUDIT command (Schema Objects) described in the next section of this chapter.

Prerequisites

You must have AUDIT SYSTEM system privilege.

Syntax

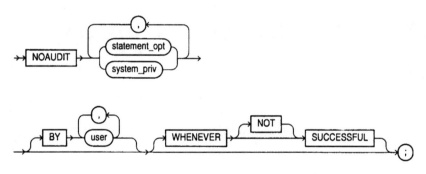

Keywords and Parameters

statement_opt	is a statement option for which auditing is stopped. For a list of the statement options and the SQL statements they audit, see Table C-1 and Table C-2.
system_priv	is a system privilege for which auditing is stopped. For a list of the system privileges and the statements they authorize, see Table C-1.
BY	stops auditing only for SQL statements issued by specified users in their subsequent sessions. If you omit this clause, Oracle stops auditing for all users' statements, except for the situation described in the section that follows.
WHENEVER SUCCESSFUL	stops auditing only for SQL statements that complete successfully.

NOT   stops auditing only for statements that result in Oracle errors. If you omit the WHENEVER clause entirely, Oracle stops auditing for all statements, regardless of success or failure.

Usage Notes

A NOAUDIT statement (SQL Statements) reverses the effect of a previous AUDIT statement (SQL Statements). Note that the NOAUDIT statement must have the same syntax as the previous AUDIT statement and that it only reverses the effects of that particular statement. Therefore, if one AUDIT statement (statement A) enables auditing for a specific user, and a second (statement B) enables auditing for all users, then a NOAUDIT statement to disable auditing for all users (statement C) reverses statement B, but leaves statement A in effect and continues to audit the user that statement A specified.

NOAUDIT (Schema Objects)

Purpose

To stop auditing chosen by the AUDIT command (Schema Objects). To stop auditing chosen by the AUDIT command (SQL Statements), use the NOAUDIT command (SQL Statements) described in the previous section of this chapter.

Prerequisites

The object on which you stop auditing must be in your own schema or you must have AUDIT ANY system privilege.

Syntax

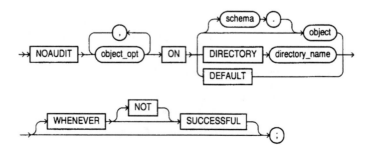

Keywords and Parameters

object_opt	stops auditing for particular operations on the object. For a list of these options, see Table C-3.
ON	identifies the object on which auditing is stopped. If you do not qualify object with schema, Oracle assumes the object is in your own schema.
object	identifies the object on which auditing is stopped. The object must be one of the following types: *table *view *sequence *stored procedure, function, or package *snapshot *library
DIRECTORY *directory_name*	identifies the name of the directory on which auditing is being stopped.
DEFAULT	removes the specified object options as default object options for subsequently created objects.
WHENEVER SUCCESSFUL	stops auditing only for SQL statements that complete successfully.
NOT	option stops auditing only for statements that result in Oracle errors. If you omit the WHENEVER clause entirely, Oracle stops auditing for all statements, regardless of success or failure.

RECOVER Clause

Purpose

To perform media recovery.

Prerequisites

The RECOVER clause must appear in an ALTER DATABASE statement. You must have the privileges necessary to issue this statement.

You must also have the OSDBA role enabled. You cannot be connected to Oracle through the multi-threaded server architecture. Your instance must have the database mounted in exclusive mode.

NOTE
It is recommended that you perform media recovery using Server Manager rather than using the ALTER DATABASE command with the RECOVER clause.

Syntax

recover_clause ::=

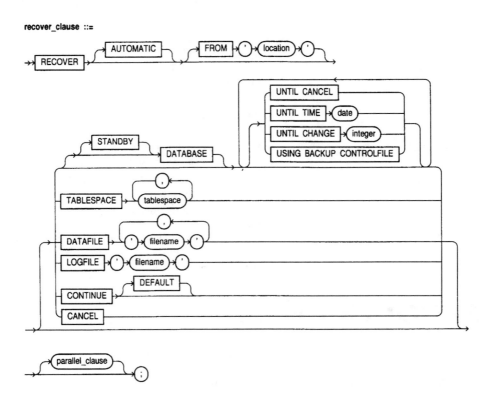

Keywords and Parameters

AUTOMATIC	automatically generates the names of the redo log files to apply during media recovery. If you omit this option, then you must specify the names of redo log files using the ALTER DATABASE ... RECOVER command with the LOGFILE clause.
FROM	specifies the location from which the archived redo log file group is read. The value of this parameter must be a fully specified file location following the conventions of your operating system. If you omit this parameter, Oracle assumes the archived redo log file group is in the location specified by the initialization parameter LOG_ARCHIVE_DEST.
STANDBY	recovers the standby database using the controlfile and archived redo log files copied over from the primary database. For more information, see the *Oracle8 Server Administrator's Guide.*
DATABASE	recovers the entire database. This is the default option. You can only use this option when the database is closed.
UNTIL CANCEL	performs cancel-based recovery. This option recovers the database until you issue the ALTER DATABASE RECOVER command with the CANCEL clause.
UNTIL TIME	performs time-based recovery. This parameter recovers the database to the time specified by the date. The date must be a character literal in the format 'YYYY-MM-DD:HH24:MI:SS'.
UNTIL CHANGE	performs change-based recovery. This parameter recovers the database to a transaction consistent state immediately before the system change number (SCN) specified by integer.
USING BACKUP CONTROLFILE	specifies that a backup controle file is being used instead of the current control file.
TABLESPACE	recovers only the specified tablespaces. You can use this option if the database is open or closed, provided the tablespaces to be recovered are offline.
DATAFILE	recovers the specified data files. You can use this option when the database is open or closed, provided the data files to be recovered are offline.
LOGFILE	continues media recovery by applying the specified redo log file.
CONTINUE	continues multi-instance recovery after it has been interrupted to disable a thread.

CONTINUE DEFAULT	continues recovery by applying the redo log file that Oracle has automatically generated.
CANCEL	terminates cancel-based recovery.
parallel_clause	specifies degree of parallelism to use when recovering.

Usage Notes

It is recommended that you use the Server Manager RECOVER command rather than the ALTER DATABASE command with the RECOVER clause to perform media recovery.

For more information on media recovery, see the *Oracle8 Server Backup and Recovery Guide* and *Oracle8 Server Administrator's Guide*.

You can use the ALTER DATABASE command with the RECOVER clause if you want to write your own specialized media recovery application using SQL.

STORAGE Clause

Purpose

To specify storage characteristics for tables, indexes, clusters, and rollback segments, and the default storage characteristics for tablespaces.

Prerequisites

The STORAGE clause can appear in commands that create or alter any of the following schema objects:

- clusters
- indexes
- rollback segments
- snapshots
- snapshot logs
- tables
- tablespaces

To change the value of a STORAGE parameter, you must have the privileges necessary to use the appropriate create or alter command.

Syntax

storage_clause ::=

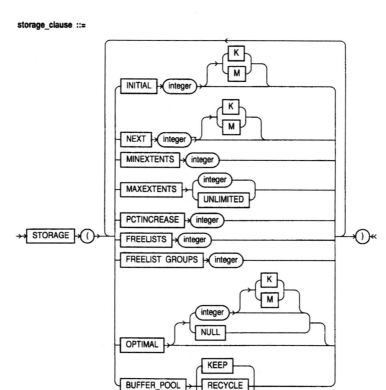

Keywords and Parameters

INITIAL   specifies the size in bytes of the object's first extent. Oracle allocates
               space for this extent when you create the schema object. You can also
               use K or M to specify this size in kilobytes or megabytes. The default
               value is the size of 5 data blocks. The minimum value is the size of 2
               data blocks. The maximum value varies depending on your operating
               system. Oracle rounds values up to the next multiple of the data block
               size for values less than 5 data blocks. Oracle rounds values up to the
               next multiple of 5 data blocks.

NEXT   specifies the size in bytes of the next extent to be allocated to the
                      object. You can also use K or M to specify the size in kilobytes or
                      megabytes. The default value is the size of 5 data blocks. The
                      minimum value is the size of 1 data block. The maximum value varies
                      depending on your operating system. Oracle rounds values up to the
                      next multiple of the data block size for values less than 5 data blocks.
                      For values greater than 5 data blocks, Oracle rounds up to a value that
                      minimizes fragmentation, as described in the "Data Blocks, Extents,
                      and Segments" chapter of *Oracle8 Server Concepts.*

PCTINCREASE   specifies the percent by which each extent after the second grows over
                      the previous extent. The default value is 50, meaning that each
                      subsequent extent is 50% larger than the preceding extent. The
                      minimum value is 0, meaning all extents after the first are the same
                      size. The maximum value varies depending on your operating system.
                      You cannot specify PCTINCREASE for rollback segments. Rollback
                      segments always have a PCTINCREASE value of 0.
                      Oracle rounds the calculated size of each new extent up to the next
                      multiple of the data block size.

MINEXTENTS   specifies the total number of extents to allocate when the object is
                      created. This parameter allows you to allocate a large amount of space
                      when you create an object, even if the space available is not
                      contiguous. The default and minimum value is 1, meaning that Oracle
                      only allocates the initial extent, except for rollback segments for which
                      the default and minimum value is 2. The maximum value varies
                      depending on your operating system.
                      If the MINEXTENTS value is greater than 1, then Oracle calculates the
                      size of subsequent extents based on the values of the INITIAL, NEXT,
                      and PCTINCREASE parameters.

MAXEXTENTS   specifies the total number of extents, including the first, that Oracle
                      can allocate for the object. The minimum value is 1. The default and
                      maximum values vary depending your data block size.

          UNLIMITED   specifies that extents should automatically be
                               allocated as needed. You should not use this
                               option for rollback segments.

FREELIST   for schema objects other than tablespace, specifies the number of
GROUPS   groups of free lists for a table, partition, cluster, or index. The default
                      and minimum value for this parameter is 1. Only use this parameter if
                      you are using Oracle with the Parallel Server option in parallel mode.

FREELISTS   for objects other than tablespace, specifies the number of groups of free lists for each of the free list groups for the table, partition, cluster, or index. The default and minimum value for this parameter is 1, meaning that each free list group contains one free list. The maximum value of this parameter depends on the data block size. If you specify a FREELISTS value that is too large, Oracle returns an error message indicating the maximum value.

You can only specify the FREELISTS parameter in CREATE TABLE, CREATE CLUSTER, and CREATE INDEX statements. You can only specify the FREELIST GROUPS parameter in CREATE TABLE and CREATE CLUSTER statements.

OPTIMAL   specifies an optimal size in bytes for a rollback segment. Not applicable to other kinds of objects. You can also use K or M to specify this size in kilobytes or megabytes. Oracle tries to maintain this size for the rollback segment by dynamically deallocating extents when their data is no longer needed for active transactions. Oracle deallocates as many extents as possible without reducing the total size of the rollback segment below the OPTIMAL value.

       NULL   specifies no optimal size for the rollback segment, meaning that Oracle never deallocates the rollback segment's extents. This is the default behavior.

       The value of this parameter cannot be less than the space initially allocated for the rollback segment specified by the MINEXTENTS, INITIAL, NEXT, and PCTINCREASE parameters. The maximum value varies depending on your operating system. Oracle rounds values to the next multiple of the data block size.

BUFFER_POOL   defines a default buffer pool for a schema object. All blocks for the object are stored in the specified cache. If a buffer pool is defined for a partitioned table or index, then the partitions inherit the buffer pool from the table or index definition, unless overridden by a partition-level definition.

NOTE

BUFFER_POOL is not a valid option for creating or altering tablespaces or rollback segments. For more information about using multiple buffer pools, see Oracle8 Server Tuning.

       KEEP   retains the schema object in memory to avoid I/O operations.

| RECYCLE | eliminates blocks from memory as soon as they are no longer needed, thus preventing an object from taking up unneccessary cache space. |
| DEFAULT | always exists for objects not assigned to KEEP or RECYCLE. |

Usage Notes

The STORAGE parameters affect both how long it takes to access data stored in the database and how efficiently space in the database is used. For a discussion of the effects of these parameters, see the "Tuning I/O" chapter of *Oracle8 Server Tuning*.

When you create a tablespace, you can specify values for the STORAGE parameters. These values serve as default STORAGE parameter values for segments allocated in the tablespace.

When you create a cluster, index, rollback segments, snapshot, snapshot log, or table, you can specify values for the STORAGE parameters for the segments allocated to these objects. If you omit any STORAGE parameter, Oracle uses the value of that parameter specified for the tablespace.

When you alter a cluster, index, rollback segment, snapshot, snapshot log, or table, you can change the values of STORAGE parameters. These new values only affect future extent allocations. For this reason, you cannot change the values of the INITIAL and MINEXTENTS parameter. If you change the value of the NEXT parameter, the next allocated extent will have the specified size, regardless of the size of the most recently allocated extent and the value of the PCTINCREASE parameter. If you change the value of the PCTINCREASE parameter, Oracle calculates the size of the next extent using this new value and the size of the most recently allocated extent.

When you alter a tablespace, you can change the values of STORAGE parameters. These new values serve as default values only to subsequently allocated segments (or subsequently created objects).

ROLLBACK SEGMENTS and MAXEXTENTS UNLIMITED

It is not good practice to create or alter a rollback segment to use MAXEXTENTS UNLIMITED. Rogue transactions containing inserts, updates, or deletes, that continue for a long time will continue to create new extents until a disk is full.

A rollback segment created without specifying the storage option has the same storage options as the tablespace that the rollback segment is created in. Thus, if the tablespace is created with MAXEXTENTS UNLIMITED, then the rollback segment would also have the same default.

TRUNCATE

Purpose

To remove all rows from a table or cluster and reset the STORAGE parameters to the values when the table or cluster was created.

Prerequisites

The table or cluster must be in your schema or you must have DELETE TABLE system privilege.

Syntax

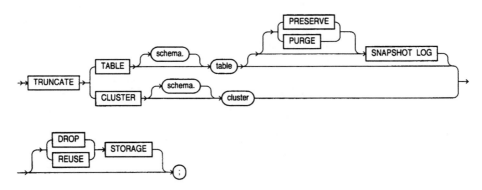

Keywords and Parameters

TABLE   specifies the schema and name of the table to be truncated. You can truncate index-only tables. If you omit schema, Oracle assumes the table is in your own schema. This table cannot be part of a cluster. When you truncate a table, Oracle also automatically deletes all data in the table's indexes.

SNAPSHOT LOG	specifies whether a snapshot log defined on the table is to be preserved or purged when the table is truncated. This clause allows snapshot master tables to be reorganized through export/import without impacting the ability of primary key snapshots defined on the master to be fast refreshed. To support continued fast refresh of primary key snapshots the snapshot log must record primary key information. For more information about snapshot logs and the TRUNCATE command, see *Oracle8 Server Replication*.

PRESERVE	specifies that any snapshot log should be preserved when the master table is truncated.
PURGE	specifies that any snapshot log should be purged when the master table is truncated.

	Oracle will preserve snapshot logs by default.
CLUSTER	specifies the schema and name of the cluster to be truncated. If you omit schema, Oracle assumes the cluster is in your own schema. You can only truncate an indexed cluster, not a hash cluster. When you truncate a cluster, Oracle also automatically deletes all data in the cluster's tables' indexes.
DROP STORAGE	deallocates the space from the deleted rows from the table or cluster. This space can subsequently be used by other objects in the tablespace.
REUSE STORAGE	leaves the space from the deleted rows allocated to the table or cluster. STORAGE values are not reset to the values when the table or cluster was created. This space can be subsequently used only by new data in the table or cluster resulting from inserts or updates. The DROP STORAGE or REUSE STORAGE option that you choose also applies to the space freed by the data deleted from associated indexes. If you omit both the REUSE STORAGE and DROP STORAGE options, Oracle uses the DROP STORAGE option by default.

Usage Notes

You can use the TRUNCATE command to quickly remove all rows from a table or cluster. Removing rows with the TRUNCATE command is faster than removing them with the DELETE command for the following reasons:

- The TRUNCATE command is a Data Definition Language command and generates no rollback information.

- Truncating a table does not fire the table's DELETE triggers.

The TRUNCATE command allows you to optionally deallocate the space freed by the deleted rows. The DROP STORAGE option deallocates all but the space specified by the table's MINEXTENTS parameter.

Deleting rows with the TRUNCATE command is also more convenient than dropping and recreating a table for the following reasons:

- Dropping and recreating invalidates the table's dependent objects, while truncating does not.

- Dropping and recreating requires you to regrant object privileges on the table, while truncating does not.

- Dropping and recreating requires you to recreate the table's indexes, integrity constraints, and triggers and respecify its STORAGE parameters, while truncating does not.

When you truncate a table, NEXT is automatically reset to the last extent deleted.

You cannot individually truncate a table that is part of a cluster. You must either truncate the cluster, delete all rows from the table, or drop and recreate the table.

You cannot truncate the parent table of an enabled referential integrity constraint. You must disable the constraint before truncating the table.

You cannot roll back a TRUNCATE statement.

INDEX

C

F

J

K

L